P9-DVF-232

JESUS CHRIST
Fundamentals of Christology

Visit our web site at
www.albahouse.org
(for orders www.stpauls.us)

or call 1-800-343-2522 (ALBA)
and request current catalog

ROCH A. KERESZTY

JESUS CHRIST
Fundamentals of Christology

REVISED AND UPDATED EDITION

Communio Book

First edition was edited by J. Stephen Maddux

ST PAULS

Library of Congress Cataloging-in-Publication Data

Kereszty, Roch A.
   Jesus Christ : fundamentals of christology / Roch A. Kereszty.— Rev. and updated ed.
      p. cm.
   "Communio book."
   Includes bibliographical references and index.
   ISBN 0-8189-0917-X (alk. paper)
   1. Jesus Christ—Person and offices.   I. Title.

   BT203 .K364 2002
   232—dc21

                                              2002018619

Produced and designed in the United States of America by the
Fathers and Brothers of the Society of St. Paul,
2187 Victory Boulevard, Staten Island, New York 10314-6603,
as part of their communications apostolate.

ISBN: 978-0-8189-0917-7
ISBN: 0-8189-0917-X

© Copyright 2002 by the Society of St. Paul / Alba House

Printing Information:

Current Printing - first digit   4   5   6   7   8   9   10

Year of Current Printing - first year shown

                  2009 2010 2011 2012 2013 2014   2015

To

My fellow Cistercians
of
Dallas and Zirc

Table of Contents

Introduction

I designed the first edition of this work ten years ago as a text for graduate students of theology. Soon, however, the comments of my critics and readers convinced me that the book has attracted a much wider audience. Not only graduate students and professors, but also priests and lay people reported that the reading of *Jesus Christ* has enriched their spiritual lives and deepened their teaching and preaching. It has also been successfully used for undergraduate courses. In order to serve better the needs of both professional theologians and the educated Christian public, I published a *Supplement* in 1997. With the first edition almost sold out this year, I decided to update and expand my work in the light of new research and new concerns for a revised, one volume edition.

Briefly put, my intention is to introduce the reader to the reality of the person and work of Jesus Christ. Had I attempted to rely only on my own research and conclusions such a goal should indeed appear presumptuous. However, I begin with the faith of the Church and seek a deeper understanding of that faith so that, at the end of the inquiry, the mystery of Christ may emerge more clearly as a divine mystery that transcends the limits of the human mind but makes our life in the universe and the universe itself intelligible.

This, then, is the major presupposition of my approach. **Theology, and in particular, Christology, is not a mere mental construct based on a number of dogmatic definitions (even less on consensus statements of biblical scholars) but intellectual reflection on the reality of the crucified and risen Christ who lives in his Church and, through the Holy Spirit, he himself guides the Church's un-**

derstanding of his mystery. In what follows I would like to spell out in greater length the details of this presupposition.

1. Written in the second half of the 1st century and in the first decades of the 2nd, the documents of the New Testament have preserved direct and indirect memories of eyewitnesses to the earthly and risen Christ. Their closeness to the originating event, their open treatment of Jesus' failure and of the disciples' cowardice and betrayal suggest *a priori* a general credibility for these sources. In the theological perspective of this book, however, the decisive reason for accepting the entire New Testament as an authentic witness to Christ is the guarantee of the Spirit of Christ himself. The Spirit has reminded these preachers and writers of all that Jesus did and taught; he introduced them "to all truth" (Jn 16:13), he guided their interpretation of the Old Testament as preparation, promise, and foreshadowing of the mystery of Christ. Accordingly, I will consider both the New and Old Testaments in all their complementary and contradictory details, as a Spirit-given, "inspired" interpretation of the Jesus event. In simple terms, only God can authentically explain the meaning of God's history.

2. However, its inspired character does not suppress the human qualities and limitations of a biblical document. We cannot lift a biblical text out of the historical context of its author's intention and culture. Inspiration guarantees that the Bible interprets authentically the history of Jesus; but it would not change the sacred authors into modern historians who are concerned about historicity according to our own standards. At the same time, their interpretation of the Jesus event is not based on their creative imagination but on historical facts, which no historian, faithful to his own method, can ignore or reject.

3. God would have been a poor communicator or rather no communicator at all, had he left the interpretation of the inspired biblical witness to his Son to the ever-changing and mutually contradictory whims of human interpreters. Working in different ways through the liturgy, the Magisterium, the theologians, and the Christian faithful, Christ himself has guided the Church through his Spirit on the often-tortuous path of understanding his own

mystery. The active presence of Christ in the Spirit throughout the Church's history explains the paramount importance of the history of Christology. Too often modern Christologies underestimate this history. They attempt a shortcut by going directly from contemporary issues and concepts to the New Testament or rather to that fragment of the New Testament that they declare to be "the authentic Jesus traditions." Inevitably, this approach leads to a distortion of the biblical data by the more or less uncritically absorbed assumptions of our own culture. The final result is an impoverished if not false image of Christ.

The history of Christology has indeed been constantly marked and marred by one-sided developments and errors. Yet, the normative apostolic witness, "the unfathomable riches of Christ" (Eph 3:8) as reflected in the writings of the New Testament can be unfolded and conceptually articulated only in a historical process. No single author, age or culture may lay claim to a full articulation of what is given in the New Testament. Its riches have been and will be brought to light only under the pressure of a never-ending questioning by new cultures, peoples and individuals.

Evidently, each new christological development must be measured against the biblical Christology that is its source and norm. This is not to say, however, that all the christological doctrines of later times should be strictly "deducible" by a logical process from the biblical sources. But, if authentic, a later Christology should cohere with the normative biblical witness. In Catholic theology, the final court of appeal of whether or not a christological development derives from a deeper understanding of the data of revelation is the Magisterium. Even though its role is decisive in the evaluative process, it is by no means exclusive. Theology itself, using its own method, has often provided a valid self-correction for its own development.

Moreover, the work of Christ's Spirit is not restricted to the visible boundaries of the Roman Catholic Church. He is present in various ways in other Christian churches and ecclesial communities as well, and, therefore, the positive contributions of their theologians must also become part of an integral Christology.

Since the Word of God enlightens all human beings who open their minds and hearts to his light (following the Fathers' interpretation of Jn 1:9), we must also discern the partial revelations of the Logos in the other religions of the world.

4. The Holy Spirit's presence is crucially important not only for the historical development of Christology but also for the individual's understanding of any faith-based christological system. Without the Spirit's presence in the reader any theological reflection, no matter how logically cogent, will appear to the latter a mere mental construct. On the other hand, the Spirit's presence convinces the reader of Christ's reality and leads him to a growing understanding of the implications of his mystery. Thus, in addition to a rigorous intellectual study, the assimilation of a Christology presupposes spiritual life in the root sense of the word, namely life in the Spirit; conversely, once assimilated, Christology should also result in a deeper and more reflective spiritual life. A better grasp of the mystery of Christ as the manifestation of divine love, a greater than which no one can conceive, will, hopefully, lead to a more intense response of love in the believer.

Corresponding to the method I have just described, the book is divided into three parts of comparable length and equipped with an Appendix and a Reader's Guide. In order to keep the reader on track for the investigation of the central christological themes, I have relegated most of the discussion of contemporary authors to the footnotes.

(I) The first part of my work deals with biblical Christology. I start with unfolding the implications of the two most firmly established facts regarding Jesus: his death on the cross, and the proclamation of his resurrection from the very beginnings of the Church. After explaining the reality and meaning of his resurrection, I outline a "theological history" of Jesus' life and death in keeping with the post-Easter perspective of the gospels. This is followed by the major christological themes of the apostolic Church, themes that interpret the Jesus-event in the light of the Old Testament. I will also point out how — starting from Old Testament notions — the

New Testament gradually formulated what was irreducibly new in the person and work of Christ.

(II) The second part is a selective history of Christology. It deals more at length with patristic thought, and then provides three samples from medieval Christology (the Christologies of St. Bernard, St. Anselm and St. Thomas). Instead of following Catholic Christology into the modern age, the book attempts to provide an adequate summary of Luther's and Calvin's Christology as well as a selective history of Protestant Christologies up to Bonhoeffer. Contemporary Catholic and Protestant Christologies are taken into account in the systematic part.

(III) The task of the systematic part is both to synthesize the results of the two previous inquiries and relate them to contemporary concerns. The comprehensive notion that should help all the elements "fall into place" is that of communion. The eternal communion of life and love which is the life of the Triune God is offered to humankind and appropriated in a twofold historical movement: The Son of God takes up complete solidarity with sinful humankind so that the latter may enter through the Son by the power of the Holy Spirit into the most intimate communion with the Father. The stages of the descending movement are the giving up of the Son by the Father, the Incarnation and the carrying of the full burden of our sins by the Son of God up to his death on the cross. The ascending movement begins with the exaltation of the Son of Man on the cross, his Resurrection and Ascension. It is consummated by the outpouring of the Holy Spirit so that in the Spirit and in the Church all peoples may come to share in the destiny and the life of the Son of Man, and thus redeemed humankind may be gathered to the eternal Kingdom of the Father.

The last two chapters of the systematic part explore the universal significance of Christ. The first studies the relationship of Christ to non-Christian religions; the second, the implications of Christian revelation regarding possible other universes and extraterrestrial intelligent beings.

(IV) Even though rarely quoted, St. Bernard's thought has

significantly influenced my work. So I include in an appendix a longer study of mine, entitled "The Relationship between Anthropology and Christology: St. Bernard, a Teacher for Our Age." (V) A "Reader's Guide" on how to use the work for different purposes, recommended literature, and study questions conclude the book.

I trust that, similarly to the readers of the first edition, not only Roman Catholics, but also Orthodox and Protestant readers will find in this revised study a credible articulation of our common christological heritage.

My hopes go even further. Beyond the Christian public I hope to reach a general audience. All those who have at least a vague intuition of, or just a sincere desire for, an Absolute that is pure love may discover the historic climax of the manifestation of Absolute Love in the mystery of Christ. Conversely, without an existential openness to the revelation of Divine Love even a massive convergence of historical evidence can easily be ignored and the most coherent systematic reflection jettisoned as futile speculation.

Above all, I am most grateful for this work to my Cistercian community whose life I share. Their faith, their lives, and an ongoing exchange of ideas among us have defined the social context in which the content and literary genre of my book has been shaped. In particular, I owe the seeds of many insights to Abbot Denis Farkasfalvy and Fr. David Balás. I am also indebted to Professor Stephen Maddux of the University of Dallas who not only edited the manuscript of the first edition, but also through his insights and persistent questioning, prompted me to strive for greater clarity and precision.

List of Abbreviations

ACWR	Ancient Christian Writers
Acta Con Oecum	Acta Conciliorum Oecumenicorum
AKG	Arbeiten zur Kirchengeschichte
CBQ	Catholic Biblical Quarterly
CF	The Christian Faith in the Doctrinal Documents of the Catholic Church, ed. J. Neuner & J. Dupuis (Staten Island, NY: Alba House)
CLF	Christology of the Later Fathers. The Library of Christian Classics, vol. III.
DBT	Dictionary of Biblical Theology, ed. X. Léon-Dufour, 2nd revised ed. (New York: Seabury Press, 1973)
DS	Enchiridion Symbolorum, ed. H. Denzinger & A. Schönmetzer (Freiburg: Herder, 1965)
GS	Gaudium et Spes. Pastoral Constitution on the Church in the Modern World of the 2nd Vatican Council
LG	Lumen Gentium. Dogmatic Constitution on the Church of the 2nd Vatican Council
MS	Mysterium Salutis. Grundriss heilsgeschichtlicher Dogmatik, ed. J. Feiner & M. Löhrer (Einsiedeln: Benziger Verlag, 1970)
NAB	The New American Bible
NRT	Nouvelle revue théologique
PG	Patrologia Graeca
SC	Sermons on the Song of Songs by St. Bernard
SDB	Supplément au Dictionnaire de la Bible
S.T.	Summa Theologiae by St. Thomas
TQ	Theologische Quartalschrift
TS	Theological Studies
TWNT	Theologisches Wörterbuch zum Neuen Testament
WA	M. Luther, Werke (Weimarer Ausgabe)

Biblical Abbreviations

OLD TESTAMENT

Genesis	Gn	Nehemiah	Ne	Baruch	Ba
Exodus	Ex	Tobit	Tb	Ezekiel	Ezk
Leviticus	Lv	Judith	Jdt	Daniel	Dn
Numbers	Nb	Esther	Est	Hosea	Ho
Deuteronomy	Dt	1 Maccabees	1 M	Joel	Jl
Joshua	Jos	2 Maccabees	2 M	Amos	Am
Judges	Jg	Job	Jb	Obadiah	Ob
Ruth	Rt	Psalms	Ps	Jonah	Jon
1 Samuel	1 S	Proverbs	Pr	Micah	Mi
2 Samuel	2 S	Ecclesiastes	Ec	Nahum	Na
1 Kings	1 K	Song of Songs	Sg	Habakkuk	Hab
2 Kings	2 K	Wisdom	Ws	Zephaniah	Zp
1 Chronicles	1 Ch	Sirach	Si	Haggai	Hg
2 Chronicles	2 Ch	Isaiah	Is	Malachi	Ml
Ezra	Ezr	Jeremiah	Jr	Zechariah	Zc
		Lamentations	Lm		

NEW TESTAMENT

Matthew	Mt	Ephesians	Eph	Hebrews	Heb
Mark	Mk	Philippians	Ph	James	Jm
Luke	Lk	Colossians	Col	1 Peter	1 P
John	Jn	1 Thessalonians	1 Th	2 Peter	2 P
Acts	Ac	2 Thessalonians	2 Th	1 John	1 Jn
Romans	Rm	1 Timothy	1 Tm	2 John	2 Jn
1 Corinthians	1 Cor	2 Timothy	2 Tm	3 John	3 Jn
2 Corinthians	2 Cor	Titus	Tt	Jude	Jude
Galatians	Gal	Philemon	Phm	Revelation	Rv

JESUS CHRIST
Fundamentals of Christology

PART I

Christology of the New Testament

CHAPTER I

The Method of Biblical Christology

If we review the history of literature on Jesus, from the Gospels to the writings of the Jesus Seminar, we will not find a single neutral account. He has become the sign of contradiction from his birth up to our own days. No one who studies his life and teaching can maintain a credibly indifferent posture: either one accepts him in faith in more or less conformity with the faith of the Church or deflates his importance and discredits his person in one way or another.[1]

Even those who claim to restrict their study of Jesus to the so-called "objective facts" seem to be guided by an implicit existential concern: they are either intent to show that nothing but these bare and neutral facts can be safely asserted about Jesus of Nazareth or, on the contrary, they attempt to build up a credible historical basis for their faith in Jesus.[2]

Thus, practically none of the claims of contemporary skeptical studies are original. For instance, the extramarital conception of Jesus has not been invented by some liberation theologians but had already been insinuated by the enemies of Jesus in the Fourth Gospel (Jn 8:41). Nor was the stealing of Jesus' body from the tomb invented by Reimarus; it had been a well-known rumor at the time

---

[1] Often the conflicting processes of debunking and elevating Jesus (according to one's personal bias) are inextricably combined. The many studies of Geza Vermes provide a recent example: Vermes rejects Christ the Son of God, but elevates him into a universal exemplar of ideal human behavior.

[2] Of course, one can only pretend to have a perfectly objective attitude when studying in depth any human person. Yet, the case of Jesus appears to be unique in provoking allegiance or rejection.

of the composition of Matthew's Gospel (Mt 28:11). It was not D.F. Strauss who first rejected the mystery of the incarnation as a myth unworthy of educated human beings. The pagan philosophers Celsus and Porphyry derided the incarnation in the 2nd and 3rd centuries as totally unworthy of a transcendent deity.

At the same time, it is naïve to suppose that the Church of the 2nd and 3rd centuries — the Church that determined the biblical canon — shared our contemporary fundamentalists' anxiety about historical accuracy. Had the Church intended to eliminate the problems that arise from the contradictory details of the four canonical Gospels, she would have never included all four in her canon. She would have chosen either only one, as the heretical Marcion did in the 2nd century, or she would have preferred one of the Gospel harmonizations in circulation in the first centuries. The biblical canon attests the Church's conviction that the four Gospels together, in their relative contradictions and essential complementarity provide the full, authentic portrait of Jesus and the full, authentic depository of his teachings. By preserving four different versions of the same story the Church expressed her belief that the truth of the "quadriform Gospel" does not depend on the historical accuracy of the contradictory details among the four documents.[3]

In the writings of the Fathers, concern for historicity was not entirely missing. When trying to make sense of the contradictory details, they either attempted harmonization or admitted that only one version of an event was literally (historically) true, while the other versions contained allegorical truth. In today's terminology we would say that the other versions further explained the meaning of the event.

---

[3]   The expression "quadriform Gospel" comes from Irenaeus (*Against Heresies* 3:11,8).

1. Critique of the "Liberal Quest," the "New Quest," and the "Third Quest" for the Historical Jesus

The above considerations are necessary for understanding what was new in the Enlightenment's approach to the Bible. It was not the discovery of the differences among the four Gospels, nor the search for historical accuracy. Begun already in the age of humanism, the Enlightenment systematically applied to the Bible the newly developed methods of literary and historical criticism.[4]

The use of the method, however, was in most instances combined with the philosophical principle of rationalism. If rationalism is true, human reason is the ultimate norm of truth. What human reason cannot comprehend could not happen and consequently did not happen. Therefore, the ecclesial and biblical portrait of Christ must be false since it contains 'irrational elements' such as miracles, the incarnation of God in human form, God's self-sacrifice, as well as angelic and demonic activities. Thus, the historian must analyze the biblical texts with critical suspicion, separating the historical kernel from conscious fabrication or subconscious mythologization. This trend, generally known today as the "Liberal Quest for the Historical Jesus," began with the publication of the *"Wolfenbüttel Fragments"* of Reimarus at the end of the 18th century. The movement spread mostly in German-speaking Protestant university circles; it produced an ever-increasing collection of studies whose avowed purpose was to recover the "real" Jesus by liberating its figure from the accumulated crust of ecclesiastical dogma. In other words, to use David F. Strauss's terminology, their goal was to isolate "the Jesus of history" from "the Christ of faith."[5]

---

[4] Literary criticism deals with the questions of authorship, literary genre, structure and style, while historical criticism investigates to what extent (if at all) a text informs us of what actually happened (*"was eigentlich geschehen"*) — to use the words of von Ranke, words that became the motto of modern historiography.

[5] The terms were coined by D.F. Strauss and their meaning has undergone various changes up to the present time. See more on this in W. Kasper, *Jesus the Christ* (New York: Paulist, 1977[2]), p. 30.

Among these scholars there were many pious Protestants who wanted to reconstruct the Jesus of history, so that they might give him their religious allegiance. However, once the unity and reliability of the biblical witness and the teaching of the Church were discarded, everyone was left with his own personal judgment to distinguish between historical and fictional elements in the traditional portrait of Jesus. Thus, each one of the historians created his own version of the "historical Jesus." The "lives of Jesus," criticizing and contradicting each other, kept proliferating for about a hundred years. The movement came to a virtual halt at the beginning of the 20th century. Kasper attributes this sudden end to three causes:[6]

The first was the impact of Albert Schweitzer's book *The Quest of the Historical Jesus.*[7]

Schweitzer showed convincingly the subjectivism of the "life of Jesus" research. Instead of reaching the historical Jesus, each epoch finds the reflection of its own ideas in him; in fact, each individual writer recreates him in his own image and likeness: the socialist makes Jesus into a social reformer, the rationalist into the admirable revealer of true virtue, the idealist into the embodiment of true humanity. Thus none of the authors could get hold of Jesus himself. According to Schweitzer, the real Jesus bypassed all the historians who tried to "grab" him and returned to his own age.[8]

The second "blow" which debilitated the "Quest" came from the representatives of form criticism. They argued that none of the Gospels (not even Mark, the favorite source of the 19th century "*Leben Jesu Forschung*") could be used as a biography of Jesus. They are the products of the faith proclamation of the Early Church. **One can reconstruct from the Gospels only what the Church proclaimed about Jesus in its missionary preaching, catechesis, and**

---

[6] Cf. *Ibid.,* pp. 31-32.

[7] A. Schweitzer, *The Quest of the Historical Jesus: A Critical Study of Its Progress from Reimarus to Wrede* (New York: Macmillan, 1948). The German original appeared in 1906: *Von Reimarus zu Wrede.*

[8] While Schweitzer has convincingly shown the subjectivism of his predecessors, his own reconstruction of the historical Jesus as the prophet of an imminent end of the world is also distorted.

liturgy, but not the real Jesus as he actually lived and acted. On the other hand, as some of these same scholars argue, the faith of his disciples is precisely the impact the real Jesus made on history. Therefore, in the words of M. Kähler, "the real Christ is the Christ of preaching."[9]

This Christ of the Church's preaching became, then, the starting point for Christology in the period between the two world wars and after the Second World War up to 1953. Even though R. Bultmann and K. Barth differ substantially in their conclusions, their starting point is similar: for Bultmann it is the apostolic kerygma, for Barth the christological dogma of the Church. They both contend that the historical reconstruction of Jesus as he actually lived and acted is historically impossible and theologically illegitimate. They argue that the attempt to justify one's faith in Christ by historical research would be as un-Christian as the effort to justify oneself by good works.

A third contributing cause to the demise of new attempts to produce the "definitive life of Jesus" was the realization that **the faith of the Church cannot be built on the constantly shifting ground of historical research.** The contradictory conclusions of historians left the faithful in confusion and bewilderment.

Yet this approach of abandoning history in favor of building Christology exclusively on the faith of the Church could not satisfy for very long.[10]

As it turned out, Bultmann's own disciples came to the conclusion that the refusal in principle to reach through the kerygma to the historical Jesus is neither historically nor theologically justifiable. Käsemann's paper on "The Problem of the Historical Jesus," given at a conference attended by former students of Bultmann in 1953, marks the beginning of a new quest for the his-

---

[9] Quoted by Kasper, *Jesus the Christ,* p. 32.

[10] For the sake of completeness one must add that many reliable biblical scholars never accepted the rationalistic prejudice of the "Liberal Quest" nor the Bultmannian skepticism regarding access to the historical Jesus and continued to make valuable contributions. Some of the most important names are C.H. Dodd, T.W. Manson, V. Taylor in England, B. Gerhardsson in Scandinavia, J. Jeremias, O. Cullmann, H.F. von Campenhausen in German-speaking countries.

torical Jesus. Käsemann points out that the form-critical method does not justify historical skepticism towards the New Testament. It is true that one cannot bypass the kerygma in order to reach directly the historical Jesus; nevertheless, the New Testament contains much authentic tradition about him. By elaborating a series of criteria, one can identify the historically true traditions and separate them from later ecclesial interpretations. Käsemann and his "allies" also showed the contradiction between Bultmann's approach and the intention of the New Testament writers. Bultmann made the Church's kerygma the ultimate object of faith beyond which one ought not to go. The New Testament itself believes ultimately not in the Church but in Jesus the Christ and knows that the earthly Jesus who was crucified for us is identical with the risen Lord who lives in the midst of the Church.

While the 19th-century "Old Quest" was exclusively a Protestant endeavor,[11] the "New Quest" is characterized by an increasing collaboration between Protestant and Catholic scholars. The proponents of the "New Quest" have been more successful than their liberal predecessors in reaching "the real Jesus as he lived and acted in history." By using various criteria they could identify with different degrees of certainty some of his authentic sayings and deeds as well as describe some events concerning his life and death and the origin of the Easter faith.

Yet **in most writings of the "New Quest" the concept of the reconstructed "Jesus of history" remains quite ambiguous if not confused.**[12]

---

[11] Under the watchful eye of the Magisterium, Catholics scrupulously distanced themselves from it even though a great biblical scholar such as Fr. Lagrange acknowledged the need for the use of the critical method but rejected its philosophical presuppositions.

[12] In this section I summarize Kasper, *Jesus the Christ,* pp. 33-36. For a penetrating analysis and history of the distinction between "historical Jesus" and "historic biblical Christ," which goes back to M. Kähler, see J.P. Meier, "The Historical Jesus: Rethinking Some Concepts," *TS* 51 (1990), pp. 3-24 and *A Marginal Jew. Rethinking the Historical Jesus,* vol. I, *The Roots of the Problem and the Person* (New York: Doubleday, 1991), pp. 21-31. For a bibliography on the "New Quest" see Kasper, *Jesus the Christ,* pp. 39-40, but for more recent works, see J.H. Charlesworth, *Jesus within Judaism. New Light from Exciting Archaeological Discoveries* (New York: Doubleday, 1988), pp. 223-243.

It has not been stated with sufficient clarity that this "Jesus of history," created and recreated in a thousand different forms by the ever-changing results of literary and historical criticism, is not identical with, but only a fragment of the "real Jesus as he actually lived and acted in history."

Another factor that diminishes the value of the Jesus portraits of the "New Quest" comes from its largely unexamined philosophical presupposition about what is historically possible and impossible. Even within the "New Quest" the Enlightenment's historiographical model prevailed to a large extent: any historical event must be understood as a particular instance of a general pattern, and therefore fully explicable by reference to analogous events and persons. This rationalistic presupposition excludes *a priori* the possibility that there may be something irreducibly new in a historical event. Categorization, of course, is a necessary tool of historical research, but, if its limits are not perceived and transcended, it misses precisely what is most important in any event.[13]

Though none of the representatives of the "New Quest" applied consistently this reductionist presupposition, neither did they critically examine it; as a result, they came under its influence to various degrees. They tended to overlook or minimize that which was truly new and unique in the Jesus event.[14]

This applies especially to the appearances of the risen Christ, a phenomenon that defies any attempt at categorization. Consequently, the "New Quest" tended to identify the reality of Jesus with that of his earthly life; the appearances of the risen Christ, if treated

---

[13] Cf. also Kasper, *Jesus the Christ*, pp. 47-48.

[14] Even such a great biblical scholar as X. Léon-Dufour enunciates this reductionist principle in his effort to reconstruct the Jesus of history: "If we want to take seriously the humanity of Jesus, we have to act *as if* Jesus were not God...Let us then approach the words of Jesus in this frame of mind: Jesus is a true human being whose original words and actions the historian wants to grasp." ("La mort rédemptrice du Christ selon le Nouveau Testament," *Mort pour nos péchés. Recherche pluridisciplinaire sur la signification rédemptrice de la mort du Christ*, Bruxelles: Facultés universitaires de Saint-Louis, 1976, pp. 31-32). If we approach the texts with the bias that Jesus was nothing more but an ordinary human being (this is the intended meaning of "homme véritable"), then we will miss precisely what is profoundly original in his humanity and in his words and actions.

at all, appeared hardly more than a legitimation of the message and the person of the historical Jesus. It was not sufficiently understood that the resurrection completed the work of the earthly Jesus and that only the appearances of the risen Christ and the presence of his Spirit in the disciples disclosed the full meaning of his earthly life and the mystery of his person.

A third factor that weakened the results of the "New Quest" was the rather unexamined acceptance of the central presupposition of the positivist school of historiography. This holds that the historian can and should isolate the facts ("what really happened") from any interpretation of these facts. They had not yet sufficiently acknowledged that — given the nature of historical knowledge — a complete separation between "facts" and interpretation is impossible, since the so-called facts are already interpreted data. Moreover, even if such a chemically pure separation were possible it is not desirable, since historical events do in fact call for an interpretation.

The "New Quest" then produced a series of "Jesus of history" figures, all of them fragmentary, stressing one or two characteristics to which the rest of the data were reduced. For example, the main characteristic of Bornkamm's Jesus is his sovereign freedom, whereas for Schillebeeckx Jesus is primarily the eschatological prophet. These traits are indeed part of the real Jesus, but what justifies the assumption that this is the reality of Jesus as he actually lived and acted in history? Can such a necessarily partial reconstruction serve as the norm against which the rest of the New Testament Christology must be measured? Can it legitimately become a canon within the canon?

While this second quest, working with a carefully articulated set of criteria, continues to produce works of valuable scholarship[15]

---

[15] One of its most important contributions concerns only indirectly, but quite decisively, the starting point of the "historical Jesus" research: J. Fitzmyer has produced convincing evidence for the traditional position that Luke was indeed a contemporary and companion to Paul. This fact re-establishes the Acts' basic historical credibility and provides evidence in support of the New Testament view of Christian origins. See J. Fitzmyer, *Luke*

(even if some of its presuppositions and conclusions call for critical review), new trends arose in the 1980's and 1990's that some designate as the "Third Quest." This common label, however, refers to three distinct groups of scholars: the first group (even though differing among each other to varying degrees) are in some way or another associated with the Jesus Seminar; the second group consists of liberation theologians both of the economic-social and feminist bent; the third group that accomplished perhaps the most lasting contributions comprises those Jewish and Christian scholars who have rediscovered the Jewishness of Jesus.

As far as the first group is concerned, their novelty consists in using some of the Nag Hammadi manuscripts, in particular the *Gospel of Thomas* as more reliable sources than the canonical writings of the New Testament. According to L.T. Johnson, another characteristic of this group is their skillful manipulation of the media. They responded well to the media's insatiable appetite for shocking news and produced one extravagant "reconstruction" of the historical Jesus after another. In order to increase their influence, they carefully planned a series of interviews for journalists before each publishing event. J.D. Crossan authored one of the most important first books of this trend, *The Historical Jesus: The Life of a Mediterranean Jewish Peasant*.[16] The novelty of this trend, however, hardly goes beyond its media consciousness and its preference for non-canonical sources of Gnostic tendency. It created a new mutant of the old virus that had infected the Liberal Quest of the 19th century: the unexamined ideological commitments of the writers have predetermined their conclusions. As a result, Jesus the cynic sage, Jesus the anti-cultural hero of the politics of compassion, all

---

the Theologian: Aspects of His Teaching (NY: Paulist, 1989), pp. 1-27. See also the monumental work of J.P. Meier, *A Marginal Jew. Rethinking the Historical Jesus*, vol. 1. *The Roots of the Problem and the Person*, vol. 2. *Mentor, Message and Miracles*, vol. 3. *Companions and Competitors* (New York: Doubleday, 1991, 1994, 2001) and R. Brown, *The Death of the Messiah*, vols. I-II (Garden City: Doubleday, 1993-94).

[16] San Francisco: HarperSF, 1991.

became the predictable projections of their authors' social agenda.[17] Just as the Liberal Quest of the 19th century, the scholars in this group all agree that their own reconstruction of the historical Jesus is the only real Jesus who is accessible to our age; therefore it must replace the Church's traditional Christ of faith. As Crossan puts it, "If you cannot believe in something produced by reconstruction, you may have nothing left to believe in."[18]

No wonder that the Jesus Seminar soon succeeded to generate a new skepticism regarding the ability of the historian *qua* historian to grasp in any way the "real Jesus." The pendulum for many seems to be swinging back again to a position similar to where it was between Schweitzer and Käsemann. This skepticism regarding historical studies spread not only among ordinary Christians but also among those biblical scholars who take seriously their Christian faith commitment. Some of them decided against venturing into any "new rethinking" of the so-called historical Jesus and chose to accept without the intermediary step of critical studies the full apostolic witness to Jesus as found in the New Testa-

---

[17] See for instance, R.W. Funk, *Five Gospels: What Did Jesus Really Say?* (San Francisco: HarperSF, 1996); R.W. Funk and Jesus Seminar Staff, *The Gospel of Jesus According to the Jesus Seminar* (Polebridge Press, 1999); R.W. Funk and Jesus Seminar Staff, *The Acts of Jesus: What Did Jesus Really Do? The Search for the Authentic Deeds of Jesus* (San Francisco: HarperSF, 1998); M.J. Borg, *Jesus: A New Vision: Spirit, Culture and the Life of Discipleship* (San Francisco: HarperSF, 1991); — *Meeting Jesus Again for the First Time: The Historical Jesus and the Heart of Contemporary Faith* (San Francisco: HarperSF, 1994); B. Mack, *The Lost Gospel: The Book of Q and Christian Origins* (San Francisco: HarperSF, 1993). All these works assume that later Church authorities suppressed or truncated the most authentic forms of the Jesus tradition while the New Testament canon is the result of their successful grab for power. Consequently, the apocryphal gospels, in particular, the *Gospel of Thomas*, the *Secret Gospel of Mark*, the *Gospel of Peter* are more reliable sources for them than the canonical Gospels. Within the canon the so-called *Q* document (hypothesized to have existed as a separate document because of the material common to Matthew and Luke versus Mark) is their preferred source (even though such a document has never been found and its existence is increasingly questioned by a growing number of scholars). While L.T. Johnson is unfairly skeptical regarding any reconstruction of the "historical Jesus," he provides a brilliant critique of the above-mentioned scholars: L.T. Johnson, *The Real Jesus. The Misguided Quest for the Historical Jesus and the Truth of the Traditional Gospels* (San Francisco: HarperSF, 1996), pp. 1-104.

[18] *The Historical Jesus*, p. 426.

ment and unfolded by the Church's tradition.[19] Others resolved to refrain from studying the historical reliability of the Gospels and to restrict themselves to a mere literary analysis that studies the Gospels as unified compositions.

Leaving for the systematic part the discussion of feminist and social liberation theologies, I will attempt to characterize here the work of the third group that focuses on the relationship of Jesus to his Jewish matrix. Even though some Jewish scholars, such as Joseph Klausner, Martin Buber, and David Flusser had produced significant works on Jesus earlier in the 20th century, Jewish-Christian studies began to proliferate and catch the interest of a larger audience only since about 1980. Surprisingly for the radical Christian critics, the Jewish authors do not share their systematic, *a priori* doubting approach. While for Käsemann and his followers the criterion of dissimilarity has been of paramount importance, for those who insist on the Jewishness of Jesus, the criterion of plausibility became decisive. According to the first criterion we are dealing with a probably authentic Jesus tradition if it is dissimilar both to Jesus' Jewish environment and to the traditions of nascent Christianity. According to the second, the authenticity of a Jesus tradition depends on how plausibly it fits into Jesus' Jewish environment. The extreme application of the first criterion would lead to the absurd assumption according to which Jesus had nothing in common with his social milieu nor with the movement that originated from him; the rigid use of the second criterion would postulate that Jesus was hardly distinguishable from the many Jewish rabbis and charismatics of the 1st century A.D. Paradoxically, in neither case could the person of Jesus account for the origin and distinguishing characteristics of Christianity. Under both presuppositions Paul is most frequently made responsible for creating the divine savior myth and for founding Christianity.

---

[19] For instance, Luke T. Johnson (*The Real Jesus*, see footnote # 17) and William M. Thompson, *The Struggle for Theology's Soul: Contesting Scripture in Christology* (New York: Crossroad, 1996). They both accept the limited usefulness of the critical method but not its mediation of the authentic teaching and deeds of Jesus.

At the same time, the search for the Jewish character of Jesus
has yielded many positive results that any future study of Jesus must
take into account. It contributed to the strengthening of the position according to which not Mark but Matthew (composed for a
Jewish audience) represents the original Gospel genre and Gospel
traditions. It has also inserted Jesus into his own concrete world
and shown how profoundly it has influenced his person, teaching
and actions. Most importantly, however, some of the Jewish scholars came closer than their hypercritical Christian colleagues to identify what is, after all, unique in the Jewish Jesus. David Flusser finds
among all the Jewish rabbis and charismatics only in Jesus a radical
love for the enemy.[20]

After asserting that "as a Jew among Jews Jesus was not
unique," Pinchas Lapide acknowledges "only in the case of Jesus
of Nazareth did his disciples experience him as the resurrected One.
Moreover, Jesus of Nazareth, and he alone became a person of vi-
tal significance for millions of believing Christians... After dis-
counting all Hellenization and foreign elements, we are left with
an irresistible residue that resists demythologizing." Like Martin
Buber, Lapide insists that "this something," "this residue" cannot
be squeezed into any usual historical category; it can only be acknowledged as "the mystery of Jesus."[21]

No historian without relying on an explicit Christian faith
could state more about Jesus than the Jewish Buber and Lapide
did.[22]

The question, then, arises with a new urgency: Is it still possible to use a critically revised critical method to reconstruct at least

---

[20] *Jesus* (New York: Herder & Herder, 1969), pp. 80-82.

[21] P. Lapide and U. Luz, "A Dialogue between a Jew and a Christian on Jesus," *Christian-
Jewish Dialogue. A Reader.* H.P. Fry, ed. (Exeter, England: University of Exeter Press,
1996), pp. 157-159.

[22] The most often quoted authors on the Jewish Jesus, however, are not Buber and Lapide,
but rather E.P. Sanders, G. Vermes and J.H. Charlesworth. I list here only some of their
most important works. E.P. Sanders, *Jesus and Judaism* (Philadelphia: Fortress, 1985);
G. Vermes, *Jesus the Jew: A Historian's Reading of the Gospels* (Philadelphia: Fortress, 1981);
The Religion of Jesus the Jew (Philadelphia: Fortress, 1993); *Jesus' Jewishness. Exploring the
Place of Jesus in Early Judaism*, ed. J.H. Charlesworth (New York: Crossroad, 1996).

a fragment of the real Jesus, and if so, how, by what criteria? How can we go from there (if at all) to the full portrait of Jesus as presented by the whole of the New Testament? While hoping to have learned something from all the three stages of the debate on the historical Jesus, I will attempt to outline an answer in the next three sections of my work.

2. Reflections on the Method of Historiography in General

1. The presupposition that a good historian is able to grasp and present the purely objective data of history without mixing with them any interpretation has turned out to be an illusion.[23]

What historians often present as objective facts are in reality the result of a long process of research in which the subjective perception, selection, description, and organization of the objective data by the historian play an essential role. Thus the historian's subjectivity is an important factor in the process of reconstructing what "really happened": his particular concerns, sensitivities, "blind spots" and limits, all determine which data he will advert to and which data he will omit, what he considers essential and not essential, how he will describe and organize the collected data. **The so-called "historical facts," then, are always a combination of what actually happened and of the historian's interpretation.** The subjective factor that necessarily enters the historian's work will not necessarily make an historical reconstruction false or distorted (provided, of course, that what happens has some decipherable meaning); but it will render any historical work limited and approximate. What "really happened" is always more than, and different from, what any single person or even a collectivity of historians could perceive, describe, and systematize.

2. Collecting, describing, and organizing historical data does not exhaust the task of the historian. In the words of Paul Ricoeur,

---

[23] Cf. P. Ricoeur, "Objectivity and Subjectivity in History": *History and Truth* (Evanston: Northwestern University Press, 1965), pp. 21-40.

"The object of human history is the human subject itself."[24]

So even if an historian succeeded in the impossible venture of noticing, collecting, describing, and organizing all the objective data of history and stopped there, he would actually falsify history by implying that the objective data are all there is to history. In reality, human history, as the history of subjects, transcends the level of objective data.[25]

Every human word and action is necessarily self-expressive, a sign of the human person who is inaccessible in himself. These signs then call for an interpretation. Whether people intend it or not, all their words, deeds, and gestures reveal in some way their inner attitudes, values, desires, and ends. Thus, human history must include this typically human dimension, the interpretation of actions, words, and gestures that express the subjectivity of persons. Without it, the historian's work would remain unfinished.

3. However, a purely "objective observer" cannot correctly interpret a person's attitudes, feelings, motives, and goals. **True interpretation requires an attitude of being tuned in to a certain person of the past, of being "congenial" to him;** one must be or become a "kindred spirit" who can decipher the meaning, the motives, and goals of this person's activity from the "raw data" of his history.

4. Moreover, if human history is the history of persons, then the assumption that every new phenomenon, every new event, can be fully understood by categorization and comparison to analogous phenomena is simply not true.[26]

A human being is capable of free acts, and a free act is not determined by external or internal causes, but it issues from the person himself. In every free act a unique person leaves his unique imprint on the world; he "creates" something new that is not fully re-

---

[24] *Ibid.*, p. 40.

[25] By purely objective data I mean those historical circumstances and events which are either completely inexpressive of human subjectivity (for instance, an earthquake or flood) or any circumstance or event which has not yet been grasped on the level of subjectivity (for instance, a marriage considered as an entry in a marriage register).

[26] Cf. Kasper, *Jesus the Christ*, pp. 47-48.

ducible to extra-personal causes, nor fully definable by some general category. A free act insofar as it is free is understandable only in reference to the acting person. The task of the historian, then, is not only to find general patterns that approximate an individual act or utterance, but also to try to understand them in their reference to that unique person who performed the act and spoke the words.[27]

5. **One can write a definitive book on a person only after he has died.** He had to complete his life, finish his words, actions, and sufferings before we can understand his goals and motives, evaluate his activity and his "contribution," positive or negative, to the rest of human history.

On the other hand, death also removes a person from the realm of communication. As we say, he takes with him to the tomb many of his secrets, which will never be known to mortal men. Thus death reveals but also hides a person.

Should, however, someone rise to a new kind of life after his death and appear in our world to historical persons, our whole understanding of his previous earthly life would require reevaluation. In encountering the risen person we would better understand the meaning of his previous life. The life of such a person could be written only from the perspective of his resurrection, just as the life of any other person must be understood from the perspective of his death.

6. A historian, however, knows that human history is not shaped only by the motives and purposes of human beings. We often wonder to what extent are we really in control of our own history. Any historical process, even if launched by a purposeful hu-

---

[27] We should not idealize human beings. While potentially free, perhaps most of us most of the time are (freely) yielding to internal and external pressures, say and do what is "expected of us," act out a "persona" rather than actualize our unique selves. Nevertheless, **there are** free human acts and a historian must be ready to grasp and describe them in their uniqueness. For instance, the sudden decision of John XXIII to call together an Ecumenical Council was prepared by many events in the life of the Church and of this pope in particular. Yet, the act is not reducible to any external or internal "force"; it was Roncalli's most personal decision, which, of course, does not exclude divine inspiration. God's transcendent act actualizes rather than impedes human freedom.

man act, may acquire a weight of its own, and develop beyond or against the expectations of those who had started it. Besides, there are many impersonal factors that derive from nature or from social forces that often work at cross-purpose with human intentions. Thus the task of the historian is not only to understand the motives and purposes of human activity, but also to investigate that which cannot be reduced to human intentions; in other words, **the proper object of the historian's investigation must include the whole web of intertwining and conflicting causes, personal and impersonal forces which have, in various ways, contributed to the historical event in question.**

7. **The attempt to understand a *whole* event in all its causes, effects, and implications, in its relationship to the *whole* of human history, inescapably posits the question of *meaning*.** For instance, when studying the history of the French Revolution, we may ask whether or not this was a positive or negative step in the history of Western civilization; did it promote or did it hinder human progress? Between these two extremes many more nuanced forms of the same basic question can be asked. Of course, this kind of question already reveals a basic "bias" (a philosophical "*Vorverständnis*") in the questioning person: his belief in the possibility of progress in history. Another historian may simply reject these questions as meaningless because he interprets the same historical data of the French Revolution not as a step forward or backward in the laborious march of humanity towards a "higher goal" (in whatever way one may interpret that goal), but as one of the many indications that the human condition is absurd, that it is going from nowhere to nowhere, without any hope of real progress.

Thus historiography, when attempting to explain an historical event by relating it to the whole of human history, cannot avoid the question of meaning. A historian may, of course, reject this question as irrelevant or impossible to answer. But in doing so he has implicitly taken a stand in this matter: he has either implied that human history is meaningless, or that there might be a meaning but not even the most searching inquiry can uncover it. **In other words, when a historian is forced to take sides, im-**

plicitly or explicitly, concerning the meaning of history, he transcends the limits of his discipline and shows the need for a philosophy or theology of history. It is then the task of the philosopher or theologian of history to investigate the question of meaning that the historian can neither avoid nor answer within the limits of his own discipline.

3. A Theological History of Jesus

If the object of history is the human subject itself, if doing history therefore requires, along with the thorough knowledge of the subject's world, a profound sympathy with his values and motives, if the new and unexpected is to be expected in the history of free persons, if the meaning of a human life can be better perceived after death, and if the intertwining of personal histories and impersonal forces challenges us to find a meaning in history, a meaning which transcends the historian's field of competence, then we have found a rationale in the very nature of historiography for going beyond mere history and attempting to inquire into the meaning of the "Jesus event." **The theological history we intend to write will interpret the events of his life from the perspective of God's plan: it affirms that God himself was acting in Jesus.** This transcending of the history of Jesus is required by the history of Jesus itself: unless we accept the perspective of faith, the Christ event presents a historical anomaly — the appearance in our world of something so disconcertingly new that it explodes all the prefabricated categories of historiography.[28]

Our main source and model in this enterprise is the New Testament itself. The documents taken into the New Testament canon

---

[28] The never-ending repetition of the attempts to reduce the phenomenon of Jesus to well-known historical analogies reveals the inadequacy of these analogies and the profound unease of the historians: none of the straitjackets designed so far really fits him and historians are forced to invent new ones again and again. Cf. J.P. Meier, "The Historical Jesus: Rethinking Some Concepts," pp. 21-22.

were those in which the Church recognized an authentic apostolic witness to Christ.[29]

She was aware that the writers of these documents were inspired by the Holy Spirit, who made them "congenial" to the Christ event, that is, capable of understanding its meaning for God's plan of salvation.

The New Testament books about Jesus, in particular the four Gospels, were written not merely after the death of their subject, but from the even more illuminating perspective of his definitive, risen state. The mystery of his person, the "secret" of his life and death, are not buried with him in the tomb, but rather revealed to the disciples through his appearances and through his abiding presence with them in the Holy Spirit.

In the light of the resurrection, the Church finally understood the mystery of the crucified and risen One: "My Lord and my God," Thomas cries out when the risen Jesus shows himself to him.

This insight into the mystery of Jesus sheds light on every event and word in his life. His history, then, is not merely human history, but the history of God himself: God has expressed himself definitively in and through the life, death, and resurrection of the man Jesus, and has reconciled the world to himself through him.

Therefore every event in the history of Jesus is filled with God's mystery, and contains inexhaustible riches. We may say, with St. Augustine, that every act of the Word is full of word, that is, full of God's self-communication to man. Likewise, every word of Jesus is a divine act in human form: it is laden with a life-giving, transforming power for all who accept his word in faith.

These considerations lead us to a better understanding of the intent of the Gospel writers: they are not interested in writing a detailed, connected biography of Jesus; they do not collect historical data for the sake of the data themselves (which is an exclusively

---

[29] Cf. W.R. Farmer and D.M. Farkasfalvy, *The Formation of the New Testament Canon* (New York: Paulist Press, 1983). On recent attempts to discredit the canonical New Testament as distorting original Christianity, see R.E. Brown and R.F. Collins, "Canonicity," *The New Jerome Biblical Commentary* (Englewood Cliffs, N.J.: Prentice Hall, 1990), 66:99-100, p.1054.

modern concern). **Their purpose is to record the events and the teachings of Jesus insofar as they have meaning for the Church to which the evangelist addresses his Gospel.** Even though she was aware of the many divergences and contradictions between the Gospels, the Church resisted all attempts at harmonization. She preferred the four-Gospel canon to Marcion's only Gospel (a truncated version of Luke), to Tatian's *Diatessaron* and other gospel harmonies. The riches and variety of the apostolic traditions were more important to her than a unified version of the deeds and teachings of Jesus. She preferred to preserve *the fullness* of the traditions as they had developed through various channels in various milieus, over against any attempt to produce a single, seemingly more consistent story of Jesus.

I accept as normative this full apostolic witness to Christ, as it is embodied in the whole of the New Testament. Following the lead of the New Testament itself, I will interpret this witness against its Old Testament background, which prepares for and anticipates the "Jesus event."

Chapters III, IV and V of the biblical part of this study may be described (using a contemporary phrase) as "narrative Christology," in the sense that it distills Christology not only from doctrinal formulas but primarily from the "story of Jesus." It is **not** narrative Christology, however, if the word "narrative" includes the bracketing of the question of historical truth. The New Testament story of Jesus is history, the history of the Word made flesh in the sense the New Testament writers intended history.[30]

Therefore, I must endeavor to show how the deeds and sufferings of Jesus, especially at the critical junctures of his death and resurrection, reveal God's action in history. In order to disclose these historical foundations, I must evaluate and use the criteria of contemporary exegesis.

---

[30] Their understanding is certainly different from ours. For more on the relationship of history and theology in the New Testament, see *Scripture and Christology. A Statement of the Biblical Commission with a Commentary*, tr. and ed. J.A. Fitzmyer (New York: Paulist Press, 1986); cf. R. Kereszty, "'The Bible and Christology' document of the Biblical Commission," *Communio* (13) 4, 1986, pp. 342-367.

4. The Historical Foundations of Faith in Jesus

As mentioned above, the New Testament documents, in particular the four Gospels, do not pretend to incorporate all the objective data about Jesus. The Gospels are not biographies but testimonies. On the basis of some selected historical facts they testify that God acted definitively in Jesus, revealing himself and reconciling the world to himself through him, and that Jesus himself is God.[31]

Their testimony is truthful because they relate sincerely what they believe to be the meaning of the events that center on Christ. The veracity of their testimony is confirmed by the martyr apostles[32] who considered their lives less important than their witness to Christ. The apostolic testimony is not only truthful; it is also true in the sense that, through the inspiration of the Holy Spirit, it perceives the true meaning of the events in God's plan of salvation.

However, neither the character of these documents as testimony, nor the inspiration of the Holy Spirit has preserved them from all historical errors. Moreover, neither the testimony character of the Gospels nor the inspiration of the Holy Spirit interfered with the freedom with which religious events were narrated at that time and in the milieu where the Gospel traditions were shaped and transmitted. The sharp and often unsuccessful distinction between fact and commentary, actual detail and literary embellishment, both added by the storyteller to illustrate the real meaning of a fact, is a relatively modern concern. The catechists and evangelists of the apostolic Church show an amazing combination of fidelity and creative freedom; fidelity to the memory of events and words pertaining to Jesus and creative freedom in shaping the Jesus traditions in order to bring out the meaning for a particular audience of what Jesus actually did and said.

---

[31] See more in detail, P. Ricoeur, "The Hermeneutics of Testimony": *Essays in Biblical Interpretation* (Philadelphia: Fortress Press, 1980), pp. 119-154.

[32] No historian doubts the martyr deaths of Peter and Paul and James, "the brother of the Lord."

Far from being troubled by the many historical uncertainties arising from this ancient literary genre, the theologian should rather see in this state of affairs a necessary consequence of the Incarnation. He will admit that many events in the history of Jesus will forever remain unknown. Many other facts can only be assessed as a matter of plausible conjecture with higher or lower degrees of historical probability. If God truly became man, he must have accepted all the consequences of the historical condition — which includes living in a particular time, place and culture. It would hardly be consistent for him to do violence to the way in which his own history was told and recorded in that culture by the people of that age. He did not arbitrarily change their way of thinking and writing by giving them a crash course on modern historiography, so that they could write a textbook about him that would satisfy the curiosity of today's historians.

Yet the same critical method which circumscribes, and calls attention to, the gray areas of uncertainty in any historical reconstruction of the life of Jesus provides also valuable tools with which we can verify historical material in the faith documents of the New Testament. Detailed discussion of these criteria belongs to New Testament scholarship and apologetics. Here I will present only some important conclusions.

The disciples who lived with Jesus for a considerable length of time were sent out by him to preach the coming of the Kingdom during his earthly life. In order to prove that the Kingdom is close at hand, they needed a collection of Jesus' sayings and parables as well as stories about Jesus' miracles. Therefore, the collection, memorization, and handing on of the sayings of Jesus and the composition of stories about him had probably already begun during his public ministry[33] rather than long after his death, as some historians have suggested. After the death and resurrection of Jesus, these "Jesus traditions" were handed on orally and then became

---

[33] H. Schürmann, "Die vorösterlichen Anfänge der Logientradition," *Der historische Jesus und der kerygmatische Christus*, ed. W. Ristow and K. Matthiae, 2nd ed. (Berlin, 1962), pp. 342-370.

gradually fixed in writing; it seems that for a while written and oral traditions were transmitted side by side. In spite of the remarkable freedom to re-interpret and actualize the teachings and acts of Jesus in different situations for different local churches, "the twelve" and other "eyewitnesses of the Word" (1 Cor 15:3-8; Lk 1:2; Ac 2:2) had an important conserving and guiding influence over the development of the Jesus traditions. They served as sources and agents of control and authentication for the whole process in which these traditions were formed and actualized as contemporary events taking place in the churches' liturgy, handed on, reflected upon, and put into writing.[34]

Those who claim that the earliest Jesus traditions developed as uncontrolled folklore that has slowly and gradually transformed the image of a wisdom teacher into the exalted Son of God ignore a twofold evidence: (1) Paul's letters that antedate the Gospels by several decades (written approximately between 49 and 64 A.D.) attest a "high Christology" the foundations of which Paul himself has received from the early communities that had existed before him. That Paul's high Christology of Jesus (as pre-existent Son of God and divine Lord) depends on previous traditions comes to light in the use of what we call pre-Pauline kerygmatic fragments in his epistles, including Rm 1:1-4, 8:15; Gal 4:6; 1 Cor 15:3-7, 11:23-26, 16:22; Ph 2:5-11. (2) Paul makes sure that his teaching agrees with that of Kephas, James and John, the "pillars" before him. He is obviously aware that he "would run in vain" if his Gospel did not agree with those who are responsible for the communities in Palestine. Thus, it is inconceivable that he would "create" a Christology of the "Son of God," and "Lord" in disagreement with the Palestinian leaders. In fact, he received very early the first expressions of this high Christology from the earliest churches in Palestine which were under the control of the three "pillars." In his Letter to the Galatians, Paul describes his visit with Peter for fifteen days and his concern to assure the handshake of fellowship with the re-

---

[34] X. Léon-Dufour, *Les évangiles et l'histoire de Jésus* (Paris: ed. du Seuil, 1963); ET: *The Gospels and the Jesus of History* (New York: Desclee, 1967), pp. 168-202.

puted pillars, James, Kephas and John (1:18-20, 2:1-10). These three figures and Paul dominate the canon of the New Testament; these four appear quite anxious to assure that there is only one gospel. The handshake of fellowship or rather communion (*koinonia*) between these four controlling figures (Gal 2:9), then, is the guarantee for the general historical reliability of the New Testament traditions.[35]

These considerations justify an open attitude towards the historical reliability of the Gospels *as a whole*. There is no reason for a systematic skepticism that would assume *a priori* that all Gospel stories and sayings are inauthentic.[36]

At the same time, of course, the above-mentioned general considerations do not guarantee the historical authenticity of an individual saying or fact. In order to establish just that, biblical historians have worked out several criteria. Here I will summarize and evaluate what appear to me the most important ones.[37]

a. The criterion of double dissimilarity

If a saying of Jesus or a story about Jesus cannot be explained as a product of the contemporary Jewish or Hellenistic milieu, nor derived from the tradition-shaping forces of the primitive Church nor the literary or theological purpose of the evangelist, while on the contrary, it fits well into the life situation of Jesus, we may assume with a reasonable degree of certainty that this saying is an authentic saying of Jesus, or that this story is based on an actual event

---

[35] On the links between Paul and the Synoptic Tradition see also G.S. Sloyan, "The Jesus in Whom the Churches of the Apostolic Age Believed," *Proceedings of the Forty-Ninth Annual Convention of the Catholic Theological Society of America*, vol. 49, ed. P. Crowley, 1994, pp. 65-79.

[36] M. Lowe rightly insists that if classics scholars followed the same method of universal doubt, we could hardly claim any knowledge of ancient history. He fails to add, however, that the reason for the contrasting situation is the philosophical prejudice of the Enlightenment that rejects *a priori* as absurd all that transcends the conventional categories of rationalist historiography. See M. Lowe, "The Critical and the Skeptical Methods in New Testament Research," *Gregorianum* 81 (2000), pp. 693-721.

[37] For a less inclusive but more detailed discussion of criteria, see Schillebeeckx, *Jesus*, pp. 88-102. For another treatment, see J.P. Meier, *A Marginal Jew*, vol. 1, pp. 167-175.

in the life of Jesus. Using this criterion, J. Dupont shows, for example, that the core of the temptation story must have come from Jesus himself, rather than having been inspired by the situation of the Early Church.[38] After the death of Jesus, political messianism held no more appeal for the Church; it was rather during his earthly life that Jesus was incessantly pressured by the crowds to assume the role of the messianic king, to liberate the nation from the yoke of Rome and set up a political Kingdom of God.

As discussed before, the exclusive application of this criterion would reduce to an unjustifiable minimum what we may know about Jesus and would place this fragment into a historical vacuum, isolating him from his Jewish milieu and from the community of his disciples.

b. The criterion of embarrassment

We can establish authenticity with an even greater certainty in case the examined saying or story is not only different from, but also clearly opposed to, the contemporary Jewish or Hellenistic milieu, and/or to the tradition-forming forces of the primitive Church so that it has caused embarrassment for the Early Church. Thus, for example, localizing the childhood, adolescence, and "private life" of Jesus in Nazareth of Galilee contradicted the messianic expectations of the age. "Can anything good come from Nazareth?" (Jn 1:46) expressed the conviction of all Jews who knew the messianic prophecies of the Bible and were proud of their racially pure origin. Galilee was despised as the home of the "half-breed," whose religious fidelity was suspect. The apostolic Church had to struggle against this prejudice by showing that Jesus was the promised Messiah in spite of his Galilean origin. We cannot suppose that the Church would have invented a fact that would make her preaching more difficult and her work less successful.

---

[38] "L'origine du récit des tentations de Jésus au désert," *Revue Biblique*, 73 (1966), pp. 30-76.

Even more embarrassing for the disciples was the fact of a crucified Messiah, rejected and condemned to death by the leaders of his own people. Jesus' failure to win over the masses and his shameful execution on the cross created a major obstacle for the preaching of the disciples. The story of the disciples' lack of faith and cowardly escape, the account of Jesus' severe reprimand of Peter, their leader, and Peter's denial of Jesus show a rarely paralleled degree of honesty and integrity that guarantee authenticity.

Regarding individual sayings, a prime example is Jesus' avowal of his own ignorance:

> As to the exact day or hour, no one knows it, neither the angels in heaven nor even the Son, but only the Father (Mt 24:36; Mk 13:32).

The Church found it very difficult to reconcile Jesus' ignorance of the date of the Parousia with her post-resurrection understanding of Jesus as the Lord who shares God's dignity and almighty power. The scandal was too great for some to endure: several manuscripts of Matthew omit the words: "not even the Son" (*oude ho huios*). The fact that, in spite of this tendency, Mark and the best manuscripts of Matthew contain the saying can most plausibly be explained by its authenticity: only because it came from Jesus himself, did the Church reluctantly preserve it.

c. The personal style of Jesus

The personal style of Jesus is recognizable in some of his sayings and in most of the parables attributed to him.[39]

---

[39] Cf. J. Jeremias, "Kennzeichen der *ipsissima verba Jesu*," *Synoptische Studien*, A. Wikenhauser... dargebracht (Munich, 1963), pp. 86-93; J.P. Meier, "Jesus," 78:22. 30-31:*The New Jerome Biblical Commentary*, pp. 1321-1323. Other exegetes add another criterion, that of "coherence," and some even prefer it to the criterion of style: All that is consistent with what has already been established as authentic about Jesus must also be regarded authentic. While it has some useful application, this criterion can easily be misused by rejecting everything that does not fit into the pre-conceived picture of the exegete. For a different opinion, see R. Latourelle, *Finding Jesus through the Gospels. History and Hermeneutics* (Staten Island, NY: Alba House, 1978), pp. 226-229.

The solemn introduction to his teaching: "Amen, I say to you," or the word "Abba" by which he calls upon God are unique formulas that characterize him alone and distinguish him from what we know about his contemporaries. Insignificant as they may first appear, these two expressions — as we will try to show later — contain implicitly the whole Christology of the apostolic Church.

The parables of Jesus possess an intense evocative power; they present the concrete details of human life and nature in such a way as to shatter our conventional ways of thinking and thus prompt us to search for the "mysteries of the Kingdom." They bear the mark of a creative religious genius. It is more plausible to assume that their author was Jesus rather than an unknown master who, for some strange reason, fell into complete oblivion.[40]

d. Multiple attestation

We have seen above how this criterion establishes a general convergence between the pre-Pauline, Pauline and Synoptic traditions. The same criterion, however, can also be applied to pinpoint the authenticity of individual Jesus traditions. **If the same story or logion is attested to with some variation in several independently developed traditions (such as the Synoptics, John and the epistolary literature, in particular the proto-Pauline corpus), the likeliest explanation is that an authentic logion of Jesus or some authentic memory of his life or works was elaborated differently in different local churches.**[41]

---

[40] Of course, one cannot deny the multiple adaptation and development of Jesus' parables in the Gospels, nor is it reasonable to assume that Jesus used each of his parables only once and all its modified versions derive from the Church.

[41] I avoid endorsing any particular hypothesis of the Synoptic question. Yet one must take notice of the fact that the "two source" hypothesis and especially the postulate of the existence of the Q document (an alleged collection of Jesus sayings without a Passion and Resurrection narrative which would have expressed the Christology of a particular community) is questioned more and more by an increasing number of New Testament scholars. Similarly, the chronological priority of Mark over Matthew is being questioned by a growing number of experts. See W.R. Farmer, "A Fresh Approach to Q." in *Christianity, Judaism and Other Greco-Roman Cults*, ed. J. Neusner. Section 12, vol. 1. *Studies in Judaism*

For example, the institution of the Eucharist is attributed to Jesus in at least three independent traditions, in Matthew-Mark on the one hand, and in Luke and 1 Corinthians on the other hand, while John presupposes its knowledge from other sources and interprets it (Jn 6:1-71; 15:1-17). Even though the literary form of the Matthew-Mark and Pauline-Lukan account may be a liturgical text, rather than a direct historical narrative, this general practice of the Eucharist at such an early date in different local churches can best be explained by assuming that the Eucharist was instituted by Jesus himself.

e. The criterion of necessary explanation

If a group of ascertained historical facts concerning Jesus defies any other intelligible explanation than the one presented in the New Testament, the latter must be accepted as historically the most probable.[42]

In the next chapter I will use this criterion to show that the facts connected with the alleged appearances of Jesus after his death resist any other explanation than the one offered by the New Testament, namely, that Jesus did indeed appear to his disciples and to Paul.

The above criteria are helpful in recovering **some** of the sayings and *some* of the facts about Jesus. **We should, however, keep**

---

in *Late Antiquity* (Leiden: E.J. Brill, 1975), pp. 39-50. C.S. Mann, *Mark. A New Translation with Introduction and Commentary*, The Anchor Bible (Garden City, NY: Doubleday, 1986), pp. 47-71; "Order in the Synoptic Gospels: Patterns of Agreement within Pericopes," a collection of papers by J. Dewey, W.O. Walker, T.R.W. Longstaff, R.H. Fuller published by *The Second Century* 6 (1987-88), pp. 65-109.

While I do not take sides in the Synoptic question, I accept with C.H. Dodd, R. Brown and Martin Hengel that at the origin of the Fourth Gospel there is a historical tradition which goes back to an eyewitness source. Cf. C.H. Dodd, *Historical Tradition in the Fourth Gospel*, (Cambridge: Cambridge Univ. Press, 1963); R. Brown, *The Gospel according to John*, vol. I. (Garden City, NY: Doubleday, 1966), pp. XLI-LI; M. Hengel, *The Johannine Question* (Philadelphia: Trinity Press International, 1989).

[42] Cf. R. Latourelle, *Finding Jesus through the Gospels. History and Hermeneutics*, pp. 229-232.

in mind that these criteria yield only a convergence of probabilities and a mere fragment of the real Jesus as he lived and taught. Nor can we use them in an exclusive sense, as if the traditions, to which they cannot be applied, were — by that very reason — inauthentic. Recent literature has demonstrated convincingly the "Jewishness" of Jesus; in many ways he did fit into his environment and must be explained in light of it.

Nevertheless, even a partial and probable reconstruction is of great value for apologetics. It can show that the New Testament faith in the crucified and risen Christ, who is acclaimed as Lord, Son of God, and God, is not opposed to any known historical fact. On the contrary, the historical facts we can recover about Jesus present us with a puzzle that resists all conventional explanations. We are unable to squeeze him into the straitjacket of the general categories of the history of religions. Jesus is not simply an itinerant rabbi, a charismatic wonder worker, or a prophet. The uniqueness of his teaching and the events that immediately followed his death call for an interpretation which history in and of itself cannot provide.[43]

As explained above, my approach will be primarily theological: I will try to determine the meaning of the earthly life of Jesus by using the perspective of Christian faith in his resurrection. While unable to present a biography of Jesus, still less the secrets of his psychological life, I will attempt to show his central place in God's plan of salvation and his role in revealing and carrying out this plan. Expanding on the happy comparison of Léon-Dufour, I view the Jesus traditions of the New Testament as a series of portraits painted under the inspiration of the Holy Spirit rather than as a series of snapshots or videotapes. A painted portrait may exaggerate and change the empirical traits of the subject and still provide a deeper insight into his reality than the most realistic snapshot could ever accomplish.

---

[43] Further reasons for the importance of this kind of Jesus research are given in J.P. Meier, "The Historical Jesus: Rethinking Some Concepts," pp. 22-24.

On the whole, the apologetic concern will be subordinate to my theological purpose: I will attempt to show that the inspired "portrait" of the New Testament is not that of a fictive character, but it illuminates the mystery of the real Jesus of Nazareth. Nevertheless, in the next chapter, which focuses on the historical and rational credentials of faith in the risen Christ, apologetics must be a central consideration.

CHAPTER II

The Death and Resurrection of Jesus

Two basic facts seem to me the "rock bottom" foundation for a theological history of Jesus: his death on the cross and the Easter kerygma of the disciples. Before Easter, there was only a small band of disciples, discouraged and scattered after the crucifixion. The proclamation of the resurrection by the disciples marks the beginning of the life of the Christian Church. Without belief in the resurrection, the disciples could have perhaps organized some sort of Jesus movement, similar to the movement begun by the disciples of John the Baptist after the death of their master. Perhaps they could even have started a religion based on the teachings of Jesus similar to original Buddhism. But it is difficult to conceive that without belief in Jesus' resurrection they would have been able to establish a rapidly expanding worldwide community whose center was not a doctrine, but the person of the crucified and risen Jesus who was believed to live and act in that community. In fact, there is no proof that there has ever been a Christian community without faith in the resurrection.[44]

This twofold starting point, then, is solidly anchored in history: what is more certain about Jesus than that he was crucified and that his disciples proclaimed him risen? The discussion of these two facts leads us also beyond the limits of historical science into Christology proper, since it raises the question of the meaning of the Jesus event. We first examine the death of Jesus.

---

[44] Of course, those scholars who believe in the existence of a *Q* document (no copy of which has ever been found) and who assume that this hypothetical document reflects adequately the Christology of an existing Christian community disagree. See the critique of their position in L. Scheffczyk, *Auferstehung, Prinzip des christlichen Glaubens* (Einsiedeln:

A. THE CRUCIFIXION OF JESUS

The crucifixion of Jesus is the most widely accepted fact about him. Here we can give only a brief review of the evidence on which this consensus is based.

The execution of Jesus is attested to by extra-biblical sources, which contain information independent of the New Testament documents. The Babylonian Talmud, for instance, in the treatise on the Sanhedrin says about Jesus: "On the eve of the Passover Jesus was hanged."[45]

Likewise, Josephus Flavius, the well-known Jewish historian, mentions the crucifixion of Jesus in his *Antiquitates Judaicae*.[46]

All the Gospel traditions and the Pauline letters report the crucifixion of Jesus. In this matter even the most skeptical critics accept their testimony. For the Early Church the execution of Jesus as a common criminal, abandoned by God and men, was the greatest scandal she had to face. She had to accept that Jesus was the Messiah **in spite** of his complete failure. There was nothing in the messianic traditions of Israel that would have made plausible the death of the Messiah as part of a divine plan. The suffering servant passages in Deutero-Isaiah had not yet been applied to the Messiah.[47]

Johannes V., 1976), pp. 129-140. Even if one accepts *Q*, one cannot conclude from it to the existence of a Christian community without belief in the resurrection, since *Q* also contains "exaltation language" (sayings about the exaltation of the Son of Man) which, at least for Paul, is complementary rather than opposed to "resurrection language" (cf. Ph 2:9-11). On the differences between exaltation and resurrection language, see P. Perkins, *Resurrection. New Testament Witness and Contemporary Reflection* (Garden City, NY: Doubleday, 1984), pp. 20-21.

[45] See B. Sanh, 43a quoted in D.R. Catchpole, *The Trial of Jesus* (Leiden: E.J. Brill, 1971), p. 4. The *Talmud* was put into writing centuries later than the time of Jesus, but it includes early oral traditions.

[46] Josephus lived from 38 to 100 A.D. On the probable Christian transformation of the text (18. 63-64) and a possible reconstruction of the original form of what is called *Testimonium Flavianum*, see J.H. Charlesworth, *Jesus within Judaism*, pp. 90-98.

[47] The only exception is a Targum of Isaiah 53 in which the Servant [*Ebed*] of Yahweh is identified with the Messiah but "by means of a curious and highly arbitrary exegesis [the author of the Targum] eliminates precisely everything which concerns the *suffering* of the *ebed*, and twists the text to mean just the opposite of what it says" (O. Cullmann, *The Christology of the New Testament* [Philadelphia: Westminster Press, 1959], pp. 58-59).

Thus, it is highly implausible that the Early Church would have invented an end for Jesus that would have made Christian preaching more difficult and missionary work less successful.[48] The same line of argumentation calls for the historicity of the datum that both the Sanhedrin and the Roman procurator, Pontius Pilate, were involved in the trial of Jesus. Even though scholars disagree over the extent to which each of them contributed to the death sentence, most agree that both were involved. That Jesus was condemned to death by the highest religious tribunal of the nation and by the highest Roman authority in Judea did not put the Church in a favorable light either among the mainstream of the Jewish people, or among the loyal Gentile citizens of the Roman Empire. The New Testament traditions preserved this fact **in spite of the embarrassment** it caused for the Church,[49] simply because it was true.

Even Soviet historians (who clung the longest to the 19th century view that Jesus was merely a myth, a symbolic projection of the messianic expectations of the masses craving for liberation) have eventually conceded that Jesus was a historical person executed under Roman law.

B. THE RESURRECTION

1. Sources

a. The earliest kerygma of the resurrection in Paul's interpretation (1 Cor 15:3-8)

It is commonly accepted that the earliest formulations of the kerygma are to be found in the letters of Paul.[50]

---

[48] Cf. M. Hengel, *Crucifixion in the Ancient World and the Message of the Cross* (Philadelphia: Fortress, 1977).

[49] Even Luke who writes for a Hellenistic audience admits that Pilate condemned Jesus to death, but emphasizes that he did so only after proclaiming three times the innocence of Jesus (Lk 23:1-25).

[50] Many scholars believe that there are summaries of the earliest kerygma also in the Acts; cf. J. Schmitt, *Jésus ressuscité dans la prédication apostolique* (Paris: Gabalda, 1949), C.H.

For our purpose the most important text with the most complete kerygma of the resurrection is 1 Cor 15:3-8:

> I handed on to you as of first importance what I also received: that Christ died for our sins in accordance with the Scriptures; that he was buried; that he was raised on the third day in accordance with the Scriptures; that he appeared to Kephas, then to the Twelve. After that he appeared to more than five hundred brothers at once, most of whom are still living, though some have fallen asleep. After that he appeared to James, then to all the apostles. Last of all, as to one born abnormally, he appeared to me.

It is commonly assumed that Paul wrote 1 Corinthians about 25-30 years after the death of Jesus. However, he certainly did not compose verses 3b-5.[51]

He refers to these verses as a tradition he had himself received and handed on to the Corinthians as the core of the kerygma, while he was with them in 50/51 A.D. The concise character and rhythmic pattern of verses 3b, 4, and 5 suggest that this passage was a stereotyped formula the Church had already created and used before Paul adopted it as the condensation of his own preaching. This formula then had to exist before 50 A.D., the time when Paul visited Corinth.[52]

Thus, far from being a secondary development in the Church, belief in the saving efficacy of the death of Christ, in his resurrection, and the tradition of his post-Easter appearances, go back to the very beginnings of the Church's existence.

Dodd, *The Apostolic Preaching and Its Developments* (New York: Harper & Row, 1964), pp. 7-35, J. Munck, W.F. Albright, and C.S. Mann, *The Acts of the Apostles*, The Anchor Bible, 31 (Garden City: Doubleday, 1967), pp. XXXVI-XLV. Despite this, we concentrate on the analysis of a text which is accepted as an ancient kerygmatic summary by everyone.

[51] Cf. J. Murphy-O'Connor, "Tradition and Redaction in 1 Cor 15:3-7," *CBQ* 43 (1981), pp. 582-589.

[52] We find such summaries of the earliest Resurrection-Exaltation kerygma in other Pauline letters too (Rm 1:3-4; Ph 2:6-11, or in a form adapted to his own statements in Gal 1:1; 1 Th 1:10). However, 1 Cor 15:3b-5 is the most complete summary of the early kerygma.

Turning now to the content of 1 Cor 15:3b-8, we notice that the death of Jesus is referred to here not as a mere fact but as part of God's plan endowed with soteriological significance: "He died for our sins according to the Scriptures." His death fulfilled God's plan that has been recorded in the Scriptures. It was neither an accident nor simply a condition for being raised to a new life, but a death that saved us.

In verse 4, the raising up of Jesus follows upon his death and burial. This contrasting sequence implies that the resurrection is an event that reverses both his death **and** burial. For Paul, as for the mainstream of Jewish thought, the body is the concrete tangible form of a person, rather than a disposable inferior element from which the soul ought to be liberated in order to reach a state of bliss. Thus a bodily resurrection that presupposes an empty tomb is implied in this ancient pre-Pauline formula of faith.

A part of Judaism at the time of Jesus expected a bodily resurrection of the dead, in particular of the just "on the last day," at the dawn of a new age. The pre-Pauline kerygma applies this well-known promise of the general eschatological resurrection to Jesus: the new age dawned on us because this one individual, Jesus of Nazareth, rose from the dead, even though the course of world history seems to go on undisturbed.[53]

As for the pre-Pauline kerygma, so also for Paul, the resurrection of Christ includes his transformed, glorified body. In the Letter to the Philippians he speaks about the risen Christ's "body of glory" (3:21). On the other hand, Paul does not conceive of the resurrection of Christ as a resuscitation into a this-worldly existence. From what Paul says about the risen body of Christians (1 Cor 15:35-54), we can infer how he views Christ's risen body, to which ours will be conformed at the end of time (Ph 3:21). The risen body is spiritual (*soma pneumatikon*), incorruptible, filled with the glory and power of God (1 Cor 15:42-44). The Holy Spirit has

---

[53] On the eschatological dimension of the early kerygma and on the fundamental identity of the kerygma in Pauline and non-Pauline churches see C.H. Dodd, *The Apostolic Preaching*, pp. 1-35.

so fully transformed it according to his own nature that Paul at one time comes close to identifying the risen Christ with the Spirit: "The Lord is the Spirit" (2 Cor 3:17).

To speak about a spiritual body sounds paradoxical, yet the expression is not a self-contradiction. Paul is attempting to describe a reality that entirely transcends our world. In his thought there is some analogy between the function of the earthly body and that of the heavenly body that justifies his usage. Just as the earthly body manifests the person to the world, and links him with the world, so the spiritual body of the Lord manifests God's glory and power and enables him to link us to himself, and to transform us into himself so that in a more than metaphorical sense we become "the body of Christ and members from his members" and manifest his suffering and the power of his resurrection to the world.[54]

The risen Christ for Paul is clearly identical with Jesus of Nazareth. The resurrection does not change his personal identity. But through the resurrection he becomes Lord, exalted above all creatures in heaven and on earth and receives the very name of Yahweh, so that he is now worshipped, obeyed, and called upon in prayer, as Yahweh alone was in the Old Testament.[55]

As the death of Christ took place according to the Scriptures, so did his resurrection (v. 4b). It was foreordained by God and foretold in the Scriptures. However, just as in v. 3b the kerygma seems to refer, not to one or two particular texts, but to Scripture in general, so v. 4b gives only a general indication that the Scriptures do speak about the resurrection of Christ. This is a first formulation of what we will see in the later texts of the New Testament: all the Old Testament Scriptures speak about the mystery of Christ.

Why does the kerygma claim that Jesus "was raised on the

---

[54] 1 Cor 12:27. Cf. 2 Cor 4:10, Ph 4:10. This identification with the risen body of Christ is so real for Paul that the fornicating Christian makes "the members of Christ members of a prostitute" (1 Cor 6:15). See in detail H. Schlier, "Ekklesiologie des Neuen Testaments," *MS* IV/1, pp. 157-161.

[55] Ph 2:11. Ph 2:6-11 is another pre-Pauline text used in the Church as a hymn prior to its insertion into the letter by Paul. Cf. J.A. Fitzmyer, "The Aramaic Background of Philippians 2:6-11," *CBQ* 50 (1988), pp. 470-483.

third day according to the Scriptures"? The only Old Testament text that mentions some sort of resurrection on the third day is Hosea 6:2: "On the third day he will raise us up, to live in his presence." The prophet is speaking here about the metaphorical raising up of Israel after Israel was rent and struck for her guilt. This text then seems an unlikely choice for describing the personal resurrection of Christ, unless the apostolic Church understood from the beginning that Jesus has embodied in himself and lived out the destiny of the eschatological Israel. The phrase "on the third day" in Hosea 6:2 seems to have directed the disciples to this prophecy. "On the third day," however, could have caught the disciples' attention only if, in their mind, it pointed to a significant circumstance of Jesus' resurrection. It either implies their knowledge of the discovery of the empty tomb on the third day or that of the first appearances of the risen Christ on the third day or, possibly, both.

How could Paul and his audience come to the conclusion that Christ was raised from the dead? Neither Paul, nor anyone else in the New Testament, claims to have witnessed the resurrection itself. Paul and the Christians know that Jesus was raised because the risen Christ appeared to a group of people including Paul himself who serve as witnesses to his glorified and risen existence.

Paul quotes an ancient list (possibly the combination of two ancient lists) of appearances. By ranking Christ's appearance to him as the last in a series, he reveals his conviction that this last appearance was of the same nature as the previous ones. Hence, by examining what Paul says about Christ's appearance to him, we can get some idea of what Paul thought about all these appearances.

"Last of all, as to one born abnormally, he appeared to me" (1 Cor 15:8). Paul carefully distinguishes this experience from the mystical visions and revelations (*ophthasiai* and *apokalupsei*) he was to experience later (2 Cor 12:2 ff.) by including this encounter with Christ in the list of the appearances to Peter, to the Twelve, to James, and to all the apostles. According to Paul, his encounter with the risen Christ, in contrast to the mystical experiences he was to have later at various points in his life, occurred once only, and at a specific point in a sequence: after the death of Jesus, and following the other post-resurrection appearances.[56]

However, in Paul's mind, though thus specified in a historical sequence, the appearance of the risen Christ to him was not an ordinary event, comparable to an everyday human encounter. In the latter, once a person is within seeing distance, we cannot avoid seeing him. He is exposed to our sight whether or not he wants it. In the former case, however, the initiative of showing himself came from the risen Christ. Paul saw him, because Christ chose to appear to him at a moment when Paul least expected it, determined as he was at the time to destroy the Church of God (Gal 1:13).[57]

Speaking about this experience, Paul characterizes it in one text as **seeing**: "Have I not *seen* Jesus our Lord?" (1 Cor 9:1); in another, as a **revelation** coming from God, "who chose to *reveal* his Son to me" (Gal 1:16). "Seeing" marks the fact that the risen Christ appeared to him in this world, in the order of sense experience; "revealing" shows that it was not an ordinary occurrence: he could see him, because God manifested the risen Christ to Paul. Both aspects are expressed in the Greek verb form *ophthe*. This form is used in the Greek Old Testament to express the appearances of God and corresponds to the Hebrew *nr'h* and Aramaic *'ythmy* (cf. Gn 18:1; 26:2,24; Ex 3:2). In the Old Testament it means that a divine reality, which is in itself invisible, becomes perceptible to some people for a short time by God's gracious initiative. In our text the divine reality that becomes visible to sense experience by God's gracious initiative is the crucified Jesus of Nazareth in his new risen state.[58]

There has been much controversy whether or not the appearances of Christ were "subjective" or "objective" visions. However,

---

[56] There is no reason to doubt that Acts 9:1-9 (and Ac 22:3-16; 26:2-18) speak about the same appearance as 1 Cor 15:8, even though Paul does not refer to any place in his concise list.

[57] According to the Acts only Paul saw him. The stories in the Acts seem remarkably consistent with the implications of Paul's own testimonies on this experience.

[58] Cf. J. Schmitt, "Résurrection de Jésus": *SDB* , fasc. 56, cols. 508-9. 543.

the Damascus experience of Paul (and the other appearances of the risen Christ listed as parallel to his) transcends the usual categories of subjective and objective.

On the one hand, Paul is convinced that the experience was not caused by himself; it was not an illusion or hallucination, but originated from the risen Christ himself. **In that sense, we may call it objective, because it was caused by a reality other than the subject.** We should even categorize the event as historical in some real sense of the word, since it had parallel events that could be confirmed by the converging testimony of many witnesses. Verse 6 is probably Paul's own addition to the kerygmatic formula. There he underlines the fact that most of the more than five hundred brothers who have seen the risen Lord are still alive. This is an implicit invitation to his readers: "You may compare notes with them so that you can see for yourself that I am speaking the truth."

On the other hand, the risen Christ was not merely an "object" facing Paul; he was both above and within the subject and transforming the subject. An ordinary human being could exist alongside of Paul, but not actually inside him. **Christ was both inside and above Paul.** He penetrated his inmost being, shattered all his resistance, caused in him a complete change of mind and heart, a true *metanoia*, so that Paul joined the Church and was baptized. He truly died to his previous self: he was no longer the zealous Pharisee who had placed all his pride and trust in the faithful observance of the Law. All this seemed to him now to be mere "rubbish," loss rather than gain. He became a new creation, a servant and apostle of Jesus Christ, living in Christ who lives in him (Ph 3:7-14; Gal 1:13-17; 2:15-21).

In spite of its power, the appearance of Christ did not force itself on Paul without the mediation of faith. Paul could recognize Christ only in the faith given to him in the encounter itself. Acts 9:1-9 correctly interprets the encounter, just as Paul himself does as "revelation." The blinding light that throws him to the ground did not make him immediately recognize Jesus. He must believe the voice speaking to him from heaven: "I am Jesus, the one you are persecuting" (Ac 9:5).[59] Paul's encounter with the risen Christ is both mediated by an incipient faith and becomes his faith's lasting foundation.

The awareness of Paul's apostolic mission and apostolic office also originates in this encounter. His awareness of being "an apostle of Jesus Christ" is based on the fact that he has seen the risen Lord (1 Cor 9:1). He still awaits Christ's coming in glory, and being in the body means for him to walk far away from the Lord: yet the Christ living in Paul (2 Cor 5:6-7; Gal 2:20) is the source of a new life for him and a source of strength for fulfilling his apostolic mission in spite of persecutions and his own weakness.

We may now summarize our findings in the following points:

1. Belief in the resurrection of Christ is not a later development in Christian consciousness, but derives from the beginnings of the Christian Church. There is no Christianity without the proclamation of the resurrection.

2. Belief in the saving value of the death of Christ, and belief that his death and resurrection fulfill God's plan of salvation as expressed in the Sacred Scriptures of the Jews, also appears at the beginnings of the Church.

3. The Church bases her faith in the resurrection of Christ on the testimony of those to whom the risen One appeared; she keeps these lists as part of her kerygma.

4. The resurrection of Jesus does not mean for Paul Jesus' return into our physical life, but rather his exaltation to the state of Lord. In this state he shares the glory, power, and dignity of Yahweh.

5. The risen Lord and Jesus of Nazareth, however, are one and the same person. Jesus rises with a spiritual body through which he reveals his glory, communicates with us, and joins us to himself.

6. In Paul's mind, the encounter with Christ, which Acts locates on the road to Damascus, was both a historical event and a

---

[59] Also Ac 22:6-11; 26:12-19 interpret the Damascus experience of Paul as mediated by faith.

personal revelation that changed his whole life and constituted him an apostle of Jesus Christ to the Gentiles.

b. The resurrection narratives in the Gospels and Acts

The Gospels and Acts expand on the kerygma of the resurrection by providing narratives of the appearances and of the empty tomb.

(1) The appearance narratives

Though we date the post-resurrection appearance narratives in their final form later than the resurrection kerygma that we can extract from the Pauline letters and from the Acts, we are not justified in concluding that the appearance narratives derive from the kerygmatic formulae by way of literary amplification. It is much more probable that the appearance narratives preserve original data from the earliest traditions. To suppose otherwise would be as unwarranted as to think that the short kerygmatic summaries on the life of Jesus in Acts served as the only source for writing up a more detailed account of his sayings and deeds in the Gospels.

The appearance narratives in the different Gospels can hardly be harmonized with regard to chronology and geography. This nearly irreducible discordance shows that the evangelists did not intend to give a connected sequential history of the appearances. Each, according to his own purpose and the needs of his audience, condensed or amplified the traditions available to him. Matthew reports one appearance of Jesus to the women in Jerusalem (28:9-10), and one "official appearance" that takes place in Galilee (28:16-20).[60]

---

[60] "Official" in the sense that only men were qualified to be public witnesses of the resurrection. Women's testimony was not accepted as valid in a court at that time in Palestine.

Luke locates all the appearances in Jerusalem or very close to Jerusalem. John's Gospel does likewise but its appendix (ch. 21) adds an appearance story in Galilee.[61]

Rather than attempting a chronological and geographical harmonization,[62] I will briefly summarize how the appearance narratives confirm, complement, or differ from the resurrection kerygma and Paul's "Damascus experience."

1. The evangelists are convinced that the encounters with the risen Christ took place in the physical order of reality. The risen Lord could be physically seen, heard, and touched. This verification of Christ's presence by sense experience is present in Matthew (28:9), but it is especially stressed in Luke and John (Lk 24:39-40; Jn 20:17; 27), presumably to emphasize the real, although spiritual, body of the risen Christ against an early Docetist tendency in the Church.

2. Even though the evangelists show the risen Christ present in our world so that the disciples can reach him with their senses, they also stress that the risen Christ is not part of this world; consequently, sense experience alone is not sufficient to recognize him. The disciples going to Emmaus recognize Jesus only after he has enkindled their faith by explaining the Scriptures to them. At the sea of Tiberias, from among the seven who are in the boat, only "the disciple Jesus loved" (Jn 21:7) immediately identifies Jesus standing on the shore. His faith makes him sharp-sighted. Furthermore, the recognition of Jesus in faith is not forced on the disciples. They remain free to believe or to doubt his presence (Mt 28:17). Thus the appearances in the Gospels are both external and internal events: the eyewitnesses need both their senses and an incipient faith to identify the risen Christ, while at the same time

---

[61] Mark's Gospel ends with the account of the empty tomb and the proclamation of the resurrection. The canonical ending (16:9-20) is a later summary of appearances that seems to be based on oral traditions and the three other Gospels.

[62] Cf. R. Brown, *The Gospel according to John, XII–XXI*, The Anchor Bible (Garden City: Doubleday, 1970), p. 972; X. Léon-Dufour, *The Resurrection and the Message of Easter*, trans. R.N. Wilson (New York: Holt, Rinehart and Winston, 1975), pp. 215-217.

the appearance confirms their faith and becomes its lasting foundation.

3. The Gospel traditions make clear that the risen Christ is not a "re-animated body" returning into our world, like Lazarus or the daughter of Jairus.[63]

Jesus does not simply take up once again the biological life that had been brought to an end on the cross. He is no longer subject to the limitations of our spatio-temporal universe. He penetrates walls or closed doors, appears or disappears at will.

4. Yet the risen Christ — in spite of his transcendent status — is the same person as the crucified Jesus of Nazareth. Luke and John especially depict him as the same familiar figure with whom the disciples lived day and night for several years. His risen body has even preserved the marks of the nails and of the lance. The disciples recognize him at the moment when the Stranger repeats a well-known gesture of the earthly Jesus: he calls Mary of Magdala by name (Jn 20:16), he breaks the bread and gives it to them (Lk 23:30-31), or sends them out for a catch of fish (Jn 21:6-7).

5. The encounter with the risen Lord is unpredictable. It does not depend on the desire of the disciples. In fact, they can hardly be convinced when he appears in front of them. His appearance depends solely on his own initiative. The perceptible presence never lasts long: a few words and gestures and he drops out of sight again.

6. The purpose of these short appearances seems to be twofold:

a) They convince the disciples not only of the reality of the resurrection, but also of Christ's new permanent presence in them and among them (Mt 28:20; Mk 16:20). In Luke and John, Jesus is going to remain present among them through the Holy Spirit (Lk 24:49; Jn 14:18-26; 15:1-8). Since the laws of the material universe no longer bind Jesus, he can be present now with a new intimacy and a transforming power in each believer and in the com-

---

[63] X. Léon-Dufour, "The Appearances of the Risen Christ and Hermeneutics," in *The Resurrection and Modern Biblical Thought*, P. de Surgy et al., tr. by C.U. Quinn (New York: Corpus Books, 1970), p. 108.

munity of the Church. His new transcendent mode of being makes a new immanence possible: as Lord and God, he can dwell in us and transform us.

b) The other purpose of the appearances is to send the disciples into mission. The appearances are seen as part of the divine act that establishes the Church. They last as long as they are needed to root the disciples firmly in faith. Hence joining the Church will mean to share in the faith and joy of those who have seen and heard and touched the Word present among them. The Church of the believers ("who did not see and still believed") will be built on the testimony of those who have seen the risen Lord and believed (Jn 20:23; 1 Jn 1:1-4).

If we compare the appearance narratives of the Gospels, Acts, the ancient kerygma, and the testimony of Paul himself, we find a fundamental agreement, within which there are many secondary differences.

The Gospels emphasize more than Paul the bodily character of the risen Christ and mention the place of the appearance as well as the physical seeing, hearing and touching of the risen Lord. Even though Paul knows about a "spiritual body" of the risen Christ and speaks about seeing the Lord, he does not describe the physical aspect of the encounter nor does he mention the possibility of "physical contact." At the same time Paul's theology of the Church as the Body of Christ presupposes a real union between his risen body and ours, and a real manifestation of his risen body in our mortal bodies. This theology of the ecclesial Body of Christ may have had its experiential basis in Paul's encounter with the risen bodily reality in Christ, further deepened and developed in his eucharistic praxis (cf. 1 Cor 10:16-17).

Acts 9:1-9 (also Ac 22:3-16; 26:2-18) interpret Paul's encounter by using apocalyptic imagery: a heavenly light blinds him; a voice incomprehensible to his companions speaks to him. Paul himself does not mention the light (Gal 1:12-16), although he interprets his experience by using apocalyptic terminology: "[God] ... chose to reveal his Son in me" (Gal 1:16).

Matthew's narrative takes up a middle position between the

eschatological splendor of the Damascus narrative in Acts and the familiar human figure of the risen Christ in Luke and John. The apocalyptic light surrounds the angel who opens the tomb, not the risen Christ. Yet the appearance on a mountain of Galilee is full of majesty: Jesus appears invested with eschatological authority and the disciples prostrate themselves before him who is surrounded by a blinding light.

The transcendent authority of Jesus appears also in John and Luke, yet the emphasis is on the identity of the risen Lord with the earthly Jesus whom the apostles had known. It is not a blinding vision or the appearance of a majestic eschatological king, but above all the recognition of a friend they had known and loved on earth.

To sum up, the use of apocalyptic literary devices on the one hand, and the presentation of the risen Christ as a friend recognized through physical contact on the other, shows the two poles of the mystery: the new eschatological world has dawned on humankind in the familiar person of the crucified Jesus of Nazareth.

(2) The empty tomb narratives

As we have seen, the empty tomb is not explicitly included in the kerygma, but merely implied. The empty tomb narratives derive from another milieu and constitute an independent tradition. The kerygma was formulated as an official witness to the crucified and risen Christ. Therefore only the testimony of male disciples, whose witness would be accepted in court, was included, while the earliest tradition linked the discovery of the empty tomb to women, whose testimony was not considered legally valid in a Jewish court.[64]

In their present form, the empty tomb stories may constitute accounts of cult etiology. If from an early time the tomb of Jesus became a place of pilgrimage, the accounts may have served to explain its origin to the pilgrims gathered around it.[65]

---

[64] Tradition has the discovery subsequently confirmed by some of the Apostles (Lk 24:12; Jn 20:3-10).

[65] J. Delorme, "The Resurrection and Jesus' Tomb: Mark 16:1-8 in the Gospel Tradition," in *The Resurrection and Modern Biblical Thought*, pp. 74-106.

All four accounts agree that certain women in the entourage of Jesus found his tomb empty on the third day after the crucifixion, which was the first day of the Jewish week.[66] The story culminates in the kerygma of the resurrection, pronounced by a young man in a white robe according to Mark (16:5); by two men in dazzling apparel in Luke (24:4), and by an angel according to Matthew (28:2).

In Matthew the women run with fear and joy to tell the disciples the good news of the resurrection.[67]

In Mark the result of the discovery of the empty tomb and of the angelic message is trembling, fear, and ecstasy;[68] the women do not dare to tell anyone what happened. In Luke the women's report is dismissed as sheer nonsense by the apostles (24:11). In John, Mary of Magdala discovers the empty tomb without receiving the angelic message of the resurrection. In despair she announces to Peter and the disciple whom Jesus loved: "The Lord has been taken away. We don't know where they have put him" (Jn 20:2).

When Peter and the beloved disciple run to the tomb, they see the burial cloths lying there; the latter, entering the tomb, "saw and believed" (20:6-8).

Thus the discovery of the empty tomb does not lead to faith by itself, except in the beloved disciple, whose deep love for Jesus made him perceptive. For the women the empty tomb becomes part of the good news only when it is explained by the angelic message of the resurrection; for the rest of the disciples, only the appearances of the risen One dissipate the doubts.

---

[66] Mary of Magdala is mentioned by name in all four stories. In Matthew and Mark "the other Mary" is probably identical with "Mary the mother of James" in Luke. Salome occurs only in Mark, Joanna only in Luke (Mt 28:1; Mk 16:1-2; Lk 24:10; Jn 20:1).

[67] And while running, they meet Jesus himself (Mt 28:9-10).

[68] See, for instance, the "Echange des Vues" after the conference of J. Jeremias, "Die älteste Schicht der Osterüberlieferungen": *Resurrexit* (Rome: Libreria Ed. Vaticana, 1974), p. 199.

2. Historical Facts Connected with the Origin of Faith in the Resurrection

After examining the literary sources dealing with the death and resurrection of Christ, I now summarize those historical facts which, in my judgment, may be established on the basis of these (and additional) sources if we apply the same criteria which are generally used in historical research:

a. Jesus was executed by crucifixion under Pontius Pilate. This manner of death was a scandal that shook the disciples' faith in Jesus.

b. Yet, soon after his death, the same disciples begin to proclaim his resurrection. They do not merely affirm that his teaching, his personal influence, or "his cause" continues in the way that a great artist or a founder of religion may live on in his disciples. Rather they announce his bodily resurrection and believe that Jesus, in a transformed spiritual body, personally lives in God, and among and within his disciples.

c. They claim that this proclamation is based on eyewitness testimony: Peter and the other disciples of the earthly Jesus, as well as Paul, a former enemy of the nascent Church, testify that they have seen Jesus alive after his crucifixion.

d. The tomb of Jesus was found empty. If the story on the empty tomb had been a later legend, it would not have been linked to the women, but to a male witness.

Moreover, even the enemies of Jesus admit the fact of the empty tomb (at least before the composition of the First Gospel in the second half of the 1st century); they merely try to explain it as part of a fraud committed by the disciples (Mt 28:11-15).

We must also conclude to the historicity of the empty tomb from the fact that the message of the resurrection was preached in Jerusalem. In the words of Althaus: "The resurrection kerygma

---

[69] The first person plural in Mary's statement reveals that also John has known about the tradition of several women's presence at the empty tomb; he simply concentrates on what happened to Mary of Magdala.

could not have been maintained in Jerusalem for a single day, for a single hour, if the emptiness of the tomb had not been established as a fact for all concerned."[70] If the opponents of the nascent Church could have pointed to the corpse of Jesus in the tomb, it would have completely discredited the message of the resurrection in Jerusalem.

e. Faith in the resurrection has radically transformed the outlook and lives of the disciples. They now understand the tragic failure of Jesus in a new light, as part of God's plan to save the world, a plan that had been foretold long ago in the Sacred Scriptures. The group, once scattered in despair, soon reassembles, and, in spite of a growing storm of persecution, announces the resurrection with courage and a serene self-confidence.

f. Many of the eyewitnesses to the risen Christ, in particular Peter, Paul, and James "the brother of the Lord," suffer martyrdom for their faith.

g. Moreover, we know from extra-biblical sources that, as a result of their preaching, millions accept the Christian faith, including faith in the resurrection of Christ. This happens in spite of the Greek world's aversion to any kind of bodily resurrection and in spite of the widespread moral corruption of the masses. The pagan crowds are ready to change their outlook and lives radically because the testimony of the eyewitnesses to the risen Christ leaves them with an inescapable certainty: these men must speak the truth, since they speak about what they have seen and heard. As a result, in less than four centuries, Christianity becomes the most powerful religion in the Roman Empire.

We need to face, then, the question: How can these facts be explained? That interpretation must be accepted which explains all the facts without denying or distorting any of them.

---

[70] P. Althaus, *Die Wahrheit des kirchlichen Osterglaubens: Einsprech gegen E. Hirsch* (Gutersloh: C. Bertelsmann, 1940), p. 25. R. Brown reasons in a similar way: "If the tomb was visited and it contained the corpse or skeleton of Jesus, it is difficult, if not impossible, to understand how the disciples could have preached that God raised Jesus from the dead, since there would have been irrefutable evidence that He had not done so." *The Virginal Conception and Bodily Resurrection of Jesus* (New York: Paulist Press, 1973), p. 126.

3. Hypotheses Denying Any Form of Resurrection

First, we will discuss three explanations that explicitly deny the resurrection. Afterwards, we will investigate those interpretations which all agree that in some sense Jesus has risen, but give various and often contradictory interpretations of what that resurrection really means.

a. The earliest "negative" explanation for what has really happened is as old as Christianity: It was all a fraud. The disciples stole the body of Jesus from the tomb. They invented the story of the resurrection to deceive the people. This story was circulating among the Jews before the Gospel of Matthew was written (Mt 28:11-15). In basically the same form it was taken up by H.S. Reimarus in the 18th century.[71]

This hypothesis, however, does not explain what motive could possibly have led the disciples to spread a lie from which all they could expect to gain was persecution, jail, and death. Their martyrdom guarantees their good faith. People may become martyrs for a false cause if they are convinced that it is true. But who would voluntarily accept dying for what he knows to be a hoax?

A variation of the above hypothesis supposes the apparent death of Jesus. According to Schonfield, Jesus did not die on the cross, but merely lost consciousness.[72]

His disciples nursed him back to life after he regained consciousness in the tomb or in the home of a trusted friend. This "miraculous" recovery served as the historical basis for the proclamation of the resurrection. In its favor one can point to the fact that Jesus died in just a few hours, while other victims of crucifixion often hung on the cross for days before expiring. Pilate himself was surprised to hear that Jesus died so soon.

---

[71] H.S. Reimarus, *The Object of Jesus and His Disciples, As Seen in the New Testament*, tr. and ed. in English by Voysey, 1879.

[72] H.J. Schonfield, *The Passover Plot: New Light on the History of Jesus* (New York: B. Geis Assoc., 1966).

The difficulties with this hypothesis, however, include not only the professional expertise of the Roman soldiers, who must have made sure that Jesus died before reporting it to Pilate, and the historical evidence that many victims died before crucifixion during the flagellation with scourges tipped with sharp bones or lead. The main problem is the same as for the first version of this hypothesis. Both assume bad faith in the disciples. They would have purposely misled people when proclaiming the resurrection. Thus neither version explains the fact of the disciples' martyrdom. Today, no professional historian holds either form of this hypothesis.

b. At first glance the hypothesis of *evolution* appears more plausible.[73]

Belief in the resurrection evolved as a *myth*, in a manner similar to the stories of dying and rising gods in Hellenistic religions (e.g., Dionysus, Mithras, Adonis) and to the apocalyptic resurrection scenarios of contemporary Judaism. Humankind invents all these myths to find an answer to the existential problem of dying.

At a closer look, however, the origin of the Christian faith in the resurrection of Jesus differs substantially from all resurrection mythologies. The comparative history of religions cannot find any parallel to it. No one has claimed the bodily resurrection of a person whom he had personally known before his death. The myths are about fictional heroes or about historical persons far removed in time. The development of myth requires a long period of time. For instance, the immediate disciples of Buddha never claimed that their master was a temporal manifestation of "the universal Buddha nature." Several hundred years had to pass before belief in the Buddha's "divinity" was established in Mahayana Buddhism.

The proclamation of Jesus' resurrection, on the contrary, goes back to the time immediately after his death and burial. Those who had known him best announce his resurrection.

---

[73] W. Bousset, H. Gressmann, *Die Religion des Judentums im späthellenistischen Zeitalter* (Tübingen: Mohr, 1926). More recently, M. Buber, *Two Types of Faith: A Study of Judaism and Christianity* (New York: Harper Torchbooks, 1961), pp. 99-100.

c. Another hypothesis attempts a *psychogenic explanation* for the origin of resurrection belief. First formulated by D.F. Strauss, this interpretation has proliferated into a variety of versions; up to this very day it remains the most popular hypothesis for those historians who exclude the possibility of any supernatural intervention in history.[74]

Common to all these variations is the conviction that the appearances of the risen Jesus were subjective visions, that is, subject-induced experiences. Simply put, Jesus was not raised up so the disciples could not see Jesus himself, they only imagined that they were seeing him.[75]

One popular form of this theory has been presented by John Hicks: the Easter experiences are analogous to either near-death experiences (in which the clinically dead person is surrounded by light that Christians afterwards identify as Jesus) or to a post-mortem vision of a lost relative or friend. After a traumatic death close relatives of a deceased person often report "seeing" the one they loved.[76]

Gerd Lüdemann's and Michael Goulder's version of the psychogenic hypothesis is "conversion-vision". People who feel locked into an impossible situation often find relief in a sudden reorientation of their whole life that brings all the emotional and subconscious forces of their psyche into play. They sometimes see visions, hear sounds and experience a great peace. In the case of Jesus, both Peter and Paul felt great guilt and their seeing of Jesus was the subconsciously induced resolution of their psychological impasse.

---

[74] D.F. Strauss, *The Life of Jesus Critically Examined*, new ed. (London, 1973).

[75] In normal speech we call such visions hallucinations, yet contemporary authors like to avoid this term because of its pejorative connotation. For instance, Lüdemann insists that his understanding of vision "can be a force within the person that leads to a complete reversal and change of one's life." *Jesus' Resurrection. Fact or Figment? A Debate between William Lane Craig and Gerd Lüdemann*, ed. P. Copan and R.K Tacelli (Downers Grove: InterVarsity Press, 2000), p. 53.

[76] See John Hick, *The Metaphor of God Incarnate* (London/Louisville: SCM/Westminster, 1993), pp. 24-26; P.F. Carnley, "Response," *The Resurrection* ed. S. Davis, D. Kendall and G. O'Collins (New York: Oxford Univ. Press, 1997), pp. 34-35.

Theirs were so-called "primary visions" to be followed soon by copy-cat, "secondary visions" in many other disciples.

The psychogenic explanation assumes that the disciples' life-long missionary activity that established a world-wide Church, as well as their final martyrdom are adequately explained by a few instances of subjective vision with no foundation other than subconscious forces in the experiencing subject. If this scenario were true, no matter how much one tries to avoid the label, they were still victims of temporary and "benign" hallucinatory episodes.

However, if we examine the effect of their preaching, the radical change in so many people from a life of corruption to a life of purity, from greed and selfishness to generosity, we can hardly conceive that victims of hallucination could inspire such a universal moral revolution in human history toward unheard-of-heights of forgiving love and unselfish service. A sick tree cannot bear healthy fruit.

Another major problem the psychogenic hypothesis must face is the conversion of Paul. He was not a disciple of the earthly Jesus, but a dangerous enemy of the Christian movement. How could his vision of Christ and the ensuing conversion be explained through a psychological process of bereavement or resolution of guilt? After all, he reports that before his conversion he was "blameless in the justice according to the law" (Ph 3:6). Moreover, an analysis of the authentic writings of Paul, who was indeed more effective than all the other apostles in gaining disciples, does not reveal any sign of a psychological disturbance. On the contrary, he possesses inexhaustible sources of energy, resilience, and courage, and he retains his serenity under the greatest pressures.

The greatest difficulty, however, for the psychogenic hypothesis is the objective fact of the empty tomb. No amount of ingenious theorizing was able to discredit the empty tomb accounts that rest on the testimony of the women disciples. Although insufficient evidence in itself, but along with the multiple attestation of the appearances of the risen One it shows the objective, bodily character of the resurrection. If the factuality of the empty tomb is accepted, one cannot relegate to apologetic concerns the bodily character and sensory perception of Jesus as a human being in the appearance narratives of the Gospels and Acts.[77]

The above hypotheses clearly deny the resurrection of Christ in any form whatsoever and attempt to explain the historical facts connected with the origin of this belief in some other way. **However, as we have seen, none of the above interpretations can account for all the facts without distorting or ignoring some of them. If we deny that Jesus has been raised, we run into an insoluble puzzle.**

Now we need to examine the most typical contemporary interpretations that in some way or another accept the claim of the New Testament about the resurrection of Jesus, but they sharply disagree on what this claim actually means.

4. Various Interpretations of the Resurrection of Jesus

a. Christian apologetics under the influence of the Enlightenment could easily point out the inadequacies of the above-mentioned hypotheses. Yet, when Christian apologetes formulated their own explanation — physical resurrection as a historically "provable" fact — they uncritically accepted the rationalistic premise of their adversaries: to distinguish it from hallucinatory visions, a **real** ap-

---

[77] Moreover, no one can prove that a near-death vision, the "seeing" of a recently deceased dear person or a conversion-vision are always mere psychogenic events. God's grace operates through the individual human psyche and may use all of its faculties, including sensory and auditory functions in order to communicate a revelation and/or effect a conversion and renewal of life. We do not experience God directly but only our own psyche as affected by God. The Christian believer knows that alleged visions or messages need to be subjected to a discernment process: Does he or she exhibit signs of mental health or illness? Most importantly, "by their fruits you will know them." If the effects of the extraordinary experiences result in an enhanced awareness of reality and unselfish love that defies common human standards, in such instances we cannot exclude the action of grace. Nevertheless, even if explained as an effect of grace, near-death experiences, bereavement or conversion visions fail to do justice to the reality of the appearances of the risen Christ. While inspiring a conversion and/or a rekindling of the faith of the disciples, the appearances communicate a more radical meaning and produce universal effects: they convince the disciples that Jesus has been raised in his glorified body, that he joins all believers to his body already here on earth, and that, enthroned as the eschatological Ruler, he sends the disciples on a universal mission.

Kant

pearance of Christ had to be an "objective" appearance so that his presence could be "verifiable" by the sense experience of everyone present at the time and place where he appeared, in the same way as one verifies the presence of any other living person.[78]

Thus the resurrection of Christ could be adequately proved as any other historical event by the consensus of reliable eyewitnesses.[79]

The biblical evidence about these appearances, as we have discussed above, does not permit such a rationalistic interpretation. The testimonies of Paul and even the more empirically descriptive narratives of the Gospels and Acts indicate the presence of a new eschatological reality: the risen Christ is present in this world but he is not of this world. In contrast to a normal historical event, his appearance is not in principle verifiable by the sense experience of anyone who could have been present. He is seen only by witnesses selected by God, whose sense perception was aided by faith and who could refuse to believe (Ac 9:7; Mt 28:17).

Many theologians and exegetes in the 20th century reacted

---

[78] A typical representative of this apologetical trend is R. Garrigou-Lagrange, who claims that the fact of the resurrection can be proved by historical science (even though he admits that the resurrection has an aspect of mystery which can be known only through faith). He also tries to show that St. Thomas agrees with his position. Cf. *De Revelatione*, vol. 2. (Rome: Libreria Ed. Religiosa, 1950⁵), pp. 314-330.

St. Thomas, however, has never made such a distinction between the resurrection as a historical fact and the resurrection as a mystery of faith. For him, the appearances of the risen Christ are signs which cannot be known by natural means ("*communi lege naturali*") but only by God's revelation through a special gift of grace ("*ex speciali munere gratiae*"): *S.T.* III, q. 55, a. 1.

Interestingly, the unwittingly semi-rationalistic understanding of the resurrection that standard Catholic apologetics had cultivated in the 19th and early 20th centuries was revived in our times by conservative Protestants. See, for instance, S. Davis, *Risen Indeed: Making Sense of the Resurrection* (Grand Rapids: Eerdmans, 1993); W.L. Craig, *Assessing the New Testament Evidence for the Historicity of the Resurrection of Jesus* (Lewiston: E. Mellen, 1989).

[79] W. Pannenberg is far from being a fundamentalist. Yet, in reacting to Bultmann's reduction of the resurrection event to a faith event in the believer Pannenberg emphasizes so much the reality of the resurrection of Jesus that he views it as a historical event, a *prolepsis*, an anticipation of the consummation of history, an event that can be proved. In this respect he comes very close to the rationalistic position of apologists like Garrigou-Lagrange. See, for example, W. Pannenberg, *Jesus: God and Man*, tr. L.L. Wilkins and D.S. Priebe (Philadelphia: Westminster, 1968), p. 99.

violently against this materialistic interpretation of the resurrection. They judged it both contrary to the real meaning of the biblical texts and incomprehensible for modern man. They all, in some sense, intended to maintain faith in the resurrection of Jesus, but they provided widely different interpretations of what actually happened. I will mention here only some of the more important persons or trends.

b. For Bultmann the resurrection is not an event distinct from that of the cross. The historical event verifiable by the historian is the crucifixion of Jesus. The resurrection is merely the meaning of his death; it is faith "in the saving efficacy of the cross." We come to believe in the saving efficacy of the cross through the kerygma of the Church in which God's word addresses us. This word calls us to die with Christ to our existence in the world (which is characterized by our clinging to earthly securities) and to rise with him into a new life here and now (which is a new existential self-understanding, a radical openness and freedom for God's future). In the words of Bultmann:

> The real Easter faith is faith in the word of preaching which brings illumination. If the event of Easter Day is in any sense an historical event additional to the event of the cross, it is nothing else than the rise of faith in the risen Lord, since it was this faith that led to the apostolic preaching.[80]

These words explain why Barth summarized Bultmann's understanding of the resurrection in the statement: "Jesus has risen into the kerygma." Bultmann was willing to concur with this Barthian summary of his own position, provided "that the kerygma itself is an eschatological event and (one) should state that Jesus is really present in the kerygma, that it is really his word which, in the kerygma, reaches the listener."[81]

---

[80] R. Bultmann, *Kerygma and Myth: A Theological Debate* (New York: Harper & Row, 1961), p. 42.

[81] R. Bultmann, *Das Verhältnis der urchristlichen Christusbotschaft zum historischen Jesus* (Heidelberg, 1960), p. 27.

From this last text it would seem that Bultmann attributes a glorified personal existence to Jesus: he speaks about "his word" and his "real presence" in the kerygma. Yet in other texts the presence of Jesus in the kerygma is reduced to, and identified with, God's word that acts in the believer. Christ does not seem to have a distinct personal existence. He cannot be talked about apart from the actual preaching of God's word.[82]

Bultmann considers it self-evident that a bodily resurrection resulting in an empty tomb and followed by appearances of the risen Christ in our world (different from "the self-attestation of the risen Lord" everywhere to every believer) did not happen because it could not happen. It could not happen because God does not miraculously suspend the necessary cause-effect processes of nature. A manifestation of God's power in nature and history interfering with the web of natural causes is nonsense for modern man. Therefore the Gospel stories about the resurrection that describe such an interference are mythology in need of a critical reinterpretation.

But even if such an event could and did happen, according to Bultmann it would be irrelevant to Christian faith: The believer accepts the word of God that authenticates itself in the very act of faith. Relying on a miraculous proof such as the empty tomb or a sense-perceived appearance of the risen Lord would destroy the purity of *sola fides*.[83]

c. The center of W. Marxsen's Christology is not the saving efficacy of the cross of Christ, but rather the activity and the mes-

---

[82] R. Bultmann, *Kerygma and Myth*, p. 41. We find a most recent re-statement of Bultmann's thesis (faith in the resurrection is nothing else but faith in the saving efficacy of the cross) in J. Macquarrie, *Jesus Christ in Modern Thought* (Philadelphia: Trinity Press International, 1990), pp. 412-414. He claims that even if nothing happened after the cross, that is, no resurrection, no ascension took place (a possibility Macquarrie neither affirms nor excludes), "the two great distinctive Christian affirmations would remain untouched — God is love, and God is revealed in Jesus Christ" (p. 412). Macquarrie forgets that, in the biblical perspective, God would not be love if he allowed his Holy One to remain in the state of corruption. God's love is revealed precisely in giving life and raising the dead to life.

[83] For a summary of Bultmann's theology, see Roch Kereszty, *God Seekers for a New Age. From Crisis Theology to "Christian Atheism"* (Dayton, Ohio: Pflaum, 1970), pp. 73-79.

sage of the earthly Jesus. He admits that after the crucifixion the disciples had some sort of experience ("*Widerfährnis*") of Jesus. They interpreted this in a twofold way. The most ancient interpretation was merely functional: the disciples are sent to continue the "cause of Jesus." As the Kingdom of God was coming in the preaching of the earthly Jesus, it is now coming in the preaching of the disciples.[84]

However, a second, later interpretation became central in traditional Christianity, which concluded that Jesus was raised from the dead. This second interpretation may have been necessary at the time of the disciples, but it is no longer possible for modern humanity. Today, we must return to the first, functional interpretation. The appearances of Christ mean that his cause continues as the eschatological event in the preaching of the Church. Thus, eventually, through a different route, Marxsen comes to a conclusion very similar to that of Bultmann: the resurrection means that Jesus is present in the kerygma of his witnesses.[85]

However, for Marxsen, the presence of Jesus in the kerygma does not mean the saving efficacy of his death for the believer but the eschatological validity of the message of the earthly Jesus.

d. H.R. Schlette and the early R. Pesch are less ambiguous than Bultmann and Marxsen in affirming the personal eternal life of Jesus in God after his death. For them, the resurrection means that Jesus himself (not only his Word or his Cause) is alive eternally in God and with God. But neither of them considers the appearances "real" in any sense of the word. The early Pesch characterizes them as mere literary devices borrowed from late-Jewish

[84] W. Marxsen, *Die Auferstehung Jesu als historisches und als theologisches Problem* (Gütersloh: Mohn, 1964), p. 20.

[85] In a later series of conferences, published as *The Resurrection of Jesus of Nazareth* (Philadelphia: Fortress, 1974), Marxsen attempts to respond to the critics of his previous book on the resurrection. He admits that even today one can affirm that "Jesus is risen" as a possible interpretation of Christian faith. Yet he hastens to qualify what it means for him: "Jesus is dead. But *his* offer has not thereby lost its validity." The offer of the same faith the historical Jesus brought to us is still valid today. He still comes today, "*he* is present today in his offer" (p. 147).

apocalyptic writings, and Schlette believes that nothing certain can be shown about the historical origin of Easter faith.[86] Both think that the disciples may have come to the conviction that Jesus is alive through mere reflection on who Jesus was for them:

> It appeared ever more unthinkable to them that this Jesus should be as dead and gone as Abraham, David and Jeremiah. When they speak of him, when they sit together and eat and drink they believe He is with them. Yahweh who had sent Him allows Him even now to be living in their midst.[87]

It is interesting to note that while R. Pesch has meanwhile abandoned the abovementioned position and now holds the visions of the risen Christ for historical events,[88] his earlier hypothesis was recently re-proposed in a somewhat new form by P. Fiedler and I. Broer.[89]

In these authors (discussed under b, c and d) I appreciate the effort to oppose a crude rationalistic understanding of the resurrection that would reduce the mystery to an historical fact capable of being proved. I also sympathize with their goal of expressing belief in the resurrection in terms understandable to contemporary men and women. It also must be admitted that, contrary to the authors treated in section 3, these theologians want to safeguard what they believe to be the message of the New Testament. However, their interpretations distort — in varying degrees — the mean-

---

[86] See R. Pesch, "Zur Entstehung des Glaubens an die Auferstehung Jesu: Ein Vorschlag zur Diskussion," *TQ*, 153 (1973), pp. 201-228; H.R. Schlette, *Kirche Unterwegs* (Olten Freiburg, 1966), p. 120. Cf. also H.R. Schlette, *Epiphanie als Geschichte* (Munich, 1966), p. 67.

[87] Schlette, pp. 70-71, quoted and translated in the article by J.J. Smith, "Resurrection Faith Today," *TS* (30), 3 Sept 1969, p. 401.

[88] See R. Pesch, "Zur Entstehung des Glaubens an die Auferstehung Jesu," *Freiburger Zeitschrift für Philosophie und Theologie*, 30 (1983), pp. 72-98. See especially p. 87.

[89] *"Der Herr ist wahrhaft auferstanden' (Lk 24,34). Biblische und systematische Beiträge zur Entstehung des Osterglaubens,"* ed. I. Broer and J. Werbick (Stuttgart: Verlag Katholisches Bibelwerk, 1988). See esp. pp. 60-61.

ing of the biblical texts. For instance, all of them ignore the evidence that the evangelists present the empty tomb as a fact and as part of the message of the resurrection. Nor does Bultmann see that, for Paul and for the rest of the New Testament, the risen, glorified body of Christ and his personal existence with God is an essential part of the kerygma rather than a mythological crust which can be discarded without destroying the true message of the New Testament.

In addition, Bultmann reduces the appearances to the same faith event that happens every time God's Word reaches a believer through the kerygma. Bultmann himself acknowledges that in 1 Cor 15:3-8 Paul evaluates the appearances of Christ differently from him. Nevertheless, he cannot accept 1 Cor 15:3-8 as kerygma because "it tries to adduce a proof for the kerygma."[90]

He considers this "line of argument fatal." At this point it becomes clear that, instead of allowing the New Testament authors to determine what they consider kerygma, Bultmann prejudges the case by introducing his own (philosophically and theologically conditioned) concept of what the kerygma ought to be.

While admitting that the appearances were some sort of experience of Christ for the disciples, Marxsen implies that in themselves these experiences were so vague and undefined that they gave rise to various subsequent interpretations. He does not see that both Paul and the Gospels present the appearances in such a way that the experience is inseparable from its content. They experienced Jesus himself as the risen One. They saw him as the Lord, endowed with a new life in God. The experience was far from being an obscure undefined feeling that would admit of alternative interpretations.

To interpret the encounters with Christ **only** in the sense that his cause continues is to reduce arbitrarily the meaning of the biblical texts to what the "modern reader" of Marxsen is prepared to accept. If the "Easter experience" of the disciples could be adequately explained by the statement that Jesus' cause goes on, then the res-

---

[90] Bultmann, *Kerygma and Myth*, p. 112.

urrection of Jesus may comfortably be reduced to what anyone without faith will readily admit about any great personality. Jesus, then, would be "alive" only in the sense in which a dead teacher, artist or poet is alive because his or her message "touches me" today.

The early Pesch, Schlette, Fiedler, and Broer ignore the intention of the New Testament writers to the extent that they reduce the kerygma and the Gospel stories of the appearances to a mere literary device. In fact, the available literary form of apocalyptic assumption-resurrection imagery was not adopted without change by the New Testament authors. They invented a new literary form by combining the appearance of the risen One as the dawn of the new age (a feature of apocalyptic narratives) with the recognition of the familiar human figure of Jesus. The invention of this new literary form indicates the disciples' awareness that the available literary devices were inadequate to express the new reality they experienced. The event the apocalyptic writings projected to the end of time has taken place within the history of Jesus of Nazareth. The New Testament authors wanted to show that the risen Lord exalted at God's right hand is the same humble man the disciples had known on earth; the risen Christ has incorporated into himself all his earthly life. Yet he is no longer of this world, but belongs to the new eschatological creation.[91]

Moving beyond hermeneutics we also need to ask a question of historical criticism: Without a radically new event, without a shocking reversal of what appeared to the disciples as the complete failure of Jesus' mission, how could they come to the conclusion that Jesus had in fact triumphed? How could they come to the conviction that Jesus was alive not only as Abraham, Moses, and the other great men of Israel's history were believed by some Jews to be alive with God and in God, but that he was present and personally active in the Church as the Lord endowed with the very glory, authority, and power of God himself?

In the face of the massive biblical evidence for the disciples'

---

[91] X. Léon-Dufour, "Appearances and Hermeneutics," pp. 107-128; W. Pannenberg, *Jesus, God and Man* (Philadelphia: Westminster, 1968), pp. 53-114.

conviction that they had truly encountered the risen Christ, I cannot help feeling suspicious about an exegesis that interprets the many biblical affirmations about the appearances as meaning something less or other than appearances. I suspect that the conclusions of such an exegesis are influenced by some — largely unexamined — philosophical presuppositions, which seem very close to those of Bultmann: the world is viewed as a closed system of cause and effect which excludes the possibility of any divine intervention. God acts only in human subjectivity. Therefore anything suggesting the contrary in the New Testament must be dismissed as not pertaining to its valid message, not even in the intention of its authors. Presuppositions of this sort determine perhaps only the theologies of Bultmann and Marxsen in their entirety, but in an attenuated form they seem also to influence the theologians mentioned under #d. The appearance of the eschatological reality, the risen Christ, in our world in such a manner that he reveals himself even to our senses seems to them highly questionable if not impossible.

What is implied in Bultmann's worldview, ultimately, is man's alienation from the material world. Human beings may conquer and use the material universe by means of technology, but ultimately they remain estranged from it.[92]

God transforms only man's consciousness, and thus the material world, including Christ's crucified body in the tomb, lies outside the realm of salvation. His body was not raised up to a new life because such a "miracle" is not only impossible, but it is also completely meaningless.

We should now sum up what we have done up to this point.

---

[92] Such a mentality — with obvious differences — seems to be very close to the Gnostic and pre-Gnostic tendencies the Early Church had to confront. The Gnostic experience begins with a basic alienation of man from the world. The material universe including man's body is hostile to man. It is the product of an evil god or principle from whose grip man's real self must be rescued. Thus for the Gnostics a true incarnation of the Son of God, his true death or his true bodily resurrection were as unimaginable as for the school of Bultmann. The Church Fathers affirm against them that Jesus truly died and rose from the dead, but already the Gospels of Luke and John seem to have in mind such tendencies when John insists that the Word was made flesh and both of them stress that the risen Jesus was not a ghost but a bodily reality even though his risen body transcends the laws of our physical universe.

Through an analysis of texts dealing with the resurrection and post-resurrection appearances of Christ, especially the kerygma of the resurrection (section 1), we established the probability of some basic historical facts (section 2). Then we analyzed the most important hypotheses that tried to explain the historical facts by eliminating any form of "resurrection." We concluded that none of them was successful because none of them could account satisfactorily for **all** the facts (section 3). Finally, we examined some influential contemporary interpretations which all claimed in some sense that Jesus had been raised from the dead. We came to the conclusion that, in varying ways, depending on their different philosophical presuppositions, they all distorted the meaning of the biblical texts: the Enlightenment-influenced apologetics that prevailed in the 19th century and the first half of the 20th reduced the mystery of the resurrection to a provable historical fact; Bultmann, Marxsen, Schlette, and others fell into the opposite extreme of questioning or denying the intention of the biblical texts to refer to any real post-resurrection appearances (section 4).

In reviewing these various interpretations we have also gained some positive insights into what the New Testament teaches about this topic[93]:

1. The death and resurrection of Jesus are inseparable. Both are moments of one eschatological saving event.

2. Yet the resurrection is not reducible to the "meaning" of the cross of Jesus; the New Testament affirms that something real happened to the crucified, dead, and buried Jesus. **He has been transformed by God's Spirit into a new man, the eschatological, final creation.** In him our history has reached its end and goal. He is the firstborn of many brothers, a radical new beginning.

---

[93] For some important interpretations which are — in varying degrees — different from mine, see especially E. Schillebeeckx, *Jesus*, pp. 320-397; 516-544, and P. Perkins, *Resurrection. New Testament Witness and Contemporary Reflection* (Garden City, N.Y.: Doubleday, 1984). For a balanced review of the former, see R.H. Fuller & P. Perkins, *Who Is This Christ? Gospel Christology and Contemporary Faith* (Philadelphia: Fortress, 1983), pp 28-38; for a credible critique of the latter, see G. O'Collins, *Interpreting the Resurrection. Examining the Major Problems in the Stories of Jesus' Resurrection* (New York: Paulist Press, 1988), pp. 11-17.

3. Through his appearances, the risen Christ, the beginning and foundation of the new eschatological creation, reveals himself in our world. He allows himself to be perceived in our history by witnesses of his own choosing. Jesus' new transcendent mode of being enables him not only to appear to his disciples but also to live within them and share his life with them. He can make himself visible to them at will. They, however, cannot see him except to the extent that he allows himself to be seen. Between his reality and the reality of our world there is a gap, "an infinite qualitative difference."

4. The empty tomb stories are part of the good news of the resurrection. They provide a necessary complement to the message of the appearances. On the one hand, the abrupt appearances and disappearances of the risen Christ reveal the discontinuity between the new eschatological creation and our world. The empty tomb, on the other hand, reveals that God has not rejected our world. It is the earthly body of Jesus, part and parcel of the old cosmos, that has been transformed by the Holy Spirit into the center of the new world to which our own risen bodies will be joined. **The empty tomb proclaims that God will not annihilate but rather transform the material world at the end of time. The pledge of this final transformation is the glorified body of Jesus.**[94]

---

[94] We could ask: If the risen Christ is the firstborn of many brothers, why do our tombs not become empty on the third day? Why do our bodies disintegrate even though we are also promised the resurrection of the body? We need to reflect on the relationship between body, sin and death in biblical revelation. Gregory of Nyssa expressed here an insight of lasting value: Our bodies must decay because they have become permanently and irreversibly distorted as the embodiment of our sins. In the resurrection we will receive a new body whose continuity with our earthly bodies will reside only in the spiritual core of the person; radically transformed, we will still be the same persons. Decay and disintegration, however, could not claim the body of Jesus because it was not the body of sin. Cf. J. Smith, "Resurrection Faith Today," *TS* 30 (1969), pp. 418-419.

5. The Resurrection in Fundamental Theology

Since this chapter seeks to lay the foundation not only for biblical Christology but also for the whole christological enterprise, I need to go beyond the questions of literary and historical criticism and inquire into what it means to encounter the risen Christ and indeed into the credibility of the resurrection for the contemporary reader.

a. The epistemological question regarding the appearances

The epistemological implications of the biblical evidence compel us to discard two extremes. 1. We cannot admit of a naïve fundamentalist realism according to which the disciples and Paul saw Jesus just as he actually was, in his glorified eschatological reality. 2. We must also reject the other extreme according to which the appearances were psychogenic visions, a figment of the disciples' imagination, or mere literary devices to express something else than the actual bodily appearances of the risen Christ.[95]

In interpreting the New Testament evidence we need to take seriously the implications of 1 Jn 3:2 regarding the appearances of the risen Christ:

> Beloved, we are God's children now; what we shall be has not yet been revealed. We do know that when he is revealed we shall be like him, for we shall see him as he is.[96]

Seeing the risen Lord "as he is" means seeing God "face-to-face," because the divine glory of the risen Christ is no longer hidden by an earthly mortal human nature. His humanity — while not disappearing — has been transformed by the Holy Spirit and be-

---

[95] That "something else" is, as we have seen, rather different according to different authors: for instance, the validity of Jesus' cause, the belief of the disciples that Jesus is personally alive.

[96] It is not clear, however, whether or not the author of First John saw these implications for the appearances of the risen One.

come completely transparent, so that his divinity shines through without any diminishment or obscuring. Such a face-to-face vision of the risen Christ has been reserved for the time of his eschatological revelation, when we will become completely conformed to him.

Our conclusions from the analysis of biblical texts are confirmed by an *a priori* systematic reflection: the appearance of the risen Christ is the appearance of **the** eschatological reality **in** our world. His true body refers him to our world; therefore, it makes sense to perceive him with our senses. In his risen, glorified state, however, he transcends our world; therefore, it makes sense that we can recognize him only through the eyes of faith.

Thus, to use St. Thomas's felicitous expression, the appearances were effective "signs" through which the risen Christ revealed himself to the disciples.[97]

They were **effective** signs because they did communicate to the seers the reality of the risen Christ. Nevertheless, they were **only signs** adapted to the sense experience, imagination, and understanding of the disciples, rather than a face-to-face vision of God the Son in his glorified humanity, a vision which is beyond the capability of any mortal man. As signs, the appearances at times revealed the glorified state of the Son; at times, the identity of Christ's risen body with his crucified body; and at other times, his entry into God's glory as it is described in the two ascension scenes in Luke-Acts and in the words of Jesus to Mary of Magdala in John (Lk 24:50-53; Ac 1:6-11; Jn 20:17-18). But to consider the vision of the ascension of Jesus as an actual "lift-off" into space with, say, a determinable speed and trajectory, would be to miss entirely the point of the account. Similarly, it would be ludicrous to ask if the piece of baked fish that Christ ate in the Lukan appearance scene (24:42-43) was actually digested by him.

---

[97] "Christus dicitur suam resurrectionem argumentis declarasse, inquantum per quaedam evidentissima signa se vere resurrexisse ostendit." "Christ is said to have demonstrated his resurrection by proofs inasmuch as he showed by most evident signs that he was truly risen" (*S. T.* III, q. 55, a. 5).

In order to understand the nature of the appearances, we need to consider also the epistemological implications of the empty tomb. The fact that it was Jesus' crucified dead body that has become his glorified risen body, excludes a Docetist understanding of the appearances, as if the risen Christ had only appeared to have a body. **To conclude, then, these appearances were true signs but only signs of various aspects of a transcendent eschatological reality that was and is not directly accessible in this world. The risen Lord is seen "just as he is," face-to-face only by those who themselves have been fully conformed to his eschatological form in heaven.**

The appearances affected the sense experience of the recipients, and thus prepared them for the act of faith in which the identity of the risen One has been recognized. For this recognition the disciples needed also God's grace that would directly touch and transform their hearts so that they might recognize the identity of the one whom they saw with their bodily eyes.[98]

As St. Thomas says, the apostles saw the risen Christ *"oculata fide,"* with eyes made perceptive through faith.[99]

In their structure, then, the appearances prepare us for the sacramental (particularly the Eucharistic) presence of Christ. There is a structural analogy (rather than identity) between these two modes of presence. Both are effective signs of Christ's active

---

[98] *S.T.* III, q. 55, a. 2. Cf. "...resurrectio Christi manifestanda fuit hominibus per modum quo eis divina revelantur." "Christ's resurrection was to be manifested to men (and women) in the way by which divine realities are revealed" (*Ibid.,* a. 4). The disciples going to Emmaus did not recognize the risen Christ because their faith was languishing. In his approach to the resurrection which considers the appearances as effective signs of encountering the risen Christ — provided that God opens the heart of the recipients to this revelation — St. Thomas follows the tradition of the Fathers. He quotes approvingly a text from Gregory the Great (*Hom. 23 in Ev.*): "His showing himself in the body [to the disciples of Emmaus] was proportionate to his indwelling in their minds; in their hearts he was still a stranger far from faith; so he pretended to continue his journey" (*Ibid.* a. 4). Cf. also Origen: "No one could reasonably object to the apostolic statements when they report that Jesus after his resurrection was not visible to all but only to those whom he knew had received eyes capable of seeing his resurrection" (*Against Celsus,* 2, 65 in *Origen, Spirit and Fire. A Thematic Anthology of His Writings* by H.U. von Balthasar, tr. R.J. Daly (Washington, DC: Catholic University of America Press, 1984), p. 139.

[99] G. O'Connor's "graced seeing" expresses the same insight; cf. "The Resurrection: the State of the Questions," *The Resurrection,* p. 9.

presence, both are received through sense experience and faith. But the appearances are signs insofar as they enable people living in this world to see the risen Christ in a manner that is possible for them,[100] while the sacrament of the Eucharist does not enable the recipient to see Christ but only the material signs that communicate Christ's active presence. The appearances served to develop the faith by which the Eucharist is fruitfully received, whereas the fruitful reception of the Eucharist presupposes the existence of this faith.

b. The credibility of the resurrection

The resurrection of Jesus was not an ordinary historical event. Its *terminus a quo*, that is, its point of departure (the death of Jesus, his dead body) and *its effects* in our world (for instance, the belief of the disciples that Jesus is risen and has appeared to them, the empty tomb, the extraordinary success of their preaching, and their martyrdom for their preaching) are historical events without further qualifications. They happened at given places and times in our world and are subject in principle to verification by everyone. Its *terminus ad quem*, the glorified risen Christ, however, has transcended our world and entered God's eternal realm. He stands beyond history but is also present in history as its transcendent consummation that draws all humankind and thereby the whole universe to himself.[101]

---

[100] St. Bernard explains that the risen Christ adjusts himself to our way of knowing through the senses, appearing in the "forma servili" so that we can perceive him. For instance, Bernard paraphrases the risen Christ's words to Mary of Magdala, "Do not touch me": "Quid tu me, ait, modo tangere quaeris, quae sensu corporis gloriam aestimas resurrectionis? ...Adhuc quidem tuis sensibus gero morem, formam ingerendo servilem, quam de consuetudine recognoscas." "Why do you seek to touch me now, you who approach the glory of the resurrection by means of corporeal sense perception? ... I am still adjusting (my way of appearance) to your way of sense perception by presenting to you the form of the servant so that, through past familiarity, you may recognize this form." (*SC* 28,9).

[101] Pannenberg, "Dogmatic Theses on the Doctrine of Revelation," *Revelation as History*, ed. W. Pannenberg (Toronto: Macmillan, 1968), pp. 139-145.

The short post-resurrection appearances are revealing signs of this permanent active presence in our history.

Thus, the appearances are historical events of a unique kind. They were not verifiable in principle by everyone, but only by "fore-ordained witnesses" (Ac 10:41) to whom the risen Christ chose to show himself. Yet we find a convergence of independent witnesses, a necessary condition for the verification of historical events in general. However, to accept these unprecedented new events in history as real, the historian must admit that in this case the usual categories of historiography break down. He cannot explain them within the limits of his own discipline. In order to understand them as indeed the appearances of the crucified and risen Jesus, the historian needs the grace of faith, just as the disciples needed faith to recognize their crucified and risen Master in the one who appeared to them. **The results of historical research, however, can prepare for faith by showing, that unless we are willing to accept the reality of the resurrection, we will be confronted with an insoluble puzzle: no this-worldly cause could satisfactorily explain all the historical facts — and here I mean the universally verifiable kind — surrounding the origins of Easter faith.**

Moreover, the philosopher and theologian can also prepare for this acceptance in faith by providing a world view in which the resurrection and the appearances of the risen One do not appear as a "*Deus ex machina*," completely unrelated to the history of the universe, but intelligible as a transcendent consummation of a "universal evolution." Here I can outline only the most important points [*Teilhard de Chardin*] of such a worldview:

The popular notion of nature as a closed, self-explanatory system is not a scientifically verifiable theory, but a philosophical presupposition incompatible with the Christian doctrine of creation. If the world is ultimately caused and sustained by a Transcendent Freedom, it remains open towards the initiatives of that Freedom. It is true, however, that God as a transcendent cause acts not by bypassing or by excluding the activity of secondary causes but by enabling them to act according to their nature or even to surpass their natural capacities.[102]

Here the process of cosmic evolution may serve as an analogy for what happens in biblical miracles and in particular the resurrection of Jesus. The "ontological leaps" in evolution, that is, the leap from non-living to living being and especially the leap from animal to man, presuppose the transcendent creative influence of God. This thesis has three presuppositions: 1. Cause and effect must be of the same order, or, to put it simply: nothing can give what it does not, in some way, already possess. 2. A living organism is on a qualitatively higher level of being than non-living matter. 3. Even more so, a human being is on a qualitatively higher level of being than an animal. If physical and chemical laws can adequately explain living things, if human nature is reducible to physical, chemical, and biological processes, our argument is invalid. But if level three is not reducible to level two, nor level two to level one, then the qualitatively more perfect being of the higher level calls for a transcendent causality. Thus God's continuous creation in this context means that he enabled non-living things to cause something higher than themselves, and enabled our hominid ancestors to engender a being (or beings) whose level of being transcended theirs. In human conception this same "miracle" happens every time a man and a woman become parents of a new human person. In the process of generation God's creative intervention enables the parents to transcend themselves. The parents by themselves are capable of providing only the biological realities of sperm and ovum, but only God can create a new spiritual soul. Yet God creates the soul in conjunction with and in dependence on the generative act of the parents and elevates it so that the parents become not only parents of their child's body but of the child itself. Thus every new human being is a "miracle," since the creation of the baby infinitely surpasses the capacity of the parents; yet the baby comes into being through the parents.

---

[102] See on this the view of B. Weissmahr discussed in Sudbrack, "Die Wunder und das Wunder," pp. 230-231; also W. Kasper, *Jesus the Christ*, pp. 95-99.

If we look at the resurrection of Jesus in the context of evolution, we may see in it a qualitatively different and infinitely greater "leap" than any of the preceding ones: When God raised the dead body of Jesus from the tomb, "the firstborn" of a definitive new creation came into being. Yet here, too, a certain continuity has been preserved. The new creation did not start from nothing, but from the human body, to begin with, crucified and laid in the tomb, and the human soul with which the Son made his supreme act of surrender on the cross. Yet these human "causes" were totally inadequate to bring about the effect, the risen Christ, who, in his spiritualized, immortal body, transcends our physical universe. It is the Father who has raised up Christ.

Once the reality of the resurrection is accepted in faith, it opens up new vistas and provides a powerful breakthrough for a new understanding of the world and human history. For instance,

(1) We understand then that the evolution of the cosmos truly leads to a climax. The qualitative leaps of evolution (from lifeless matter to living beings, to the animal kingdom and the appearance of human consciousness) do not lead to the absurdity of an ultimate disaster (which on the level of natural history seems inevitable, since our solar system will at some point necessarily disintegrate) but to a consummation in God.

(2) We see, then, that the deepest desires of the human person for the totality of truth, goodness, and life are not destined to ultimate frustration, but to be transformed and fulfilled in eternal life.

(3) Our hope for salvation will, then, appear not as an escape from our bodily condition and from the material universe. On the contrary, our bodies will be redeemed and will find a home in a new "spiritualized" material universe.

To develop the implications of the resurrection of Christ for human nature and history is the task of theological anthropology. Here I will concentrate only on the christological consequences: how we can better understand, from the perspective of the resurrection, the work and the person of Jesus of Nazareth and his preparation in the Old Testament.

CHAPTER III

The Beginning of the Gospel

1. The Virginal Conception of Jesus

The New Testament does not present the virginal conception of Jesus as a showcase miracle but rather as a hidden event. It needs God's revelation to be discovered and understood. God discloses this mystery only to a few people, just as the risen Christ is shown only to a limited number of "foreordained witnesses." We find a profound similarity and continuity between the virginal conception and resurrection: the first marks the beginning of the creation of the New Man; the second, its consummation. Both result from God's creative intervention in human history.

According to Bultmann and his school the virginal conception should not be regarded as fact but as part of the New Testament mythology in need of reinterpretation. The myth of the Virgin Birth derives from the Hellenistic religions: a god descends to earth, impregnates a beautiful virgin who bears a son, half-divine, half-human. The New Testament uses this mythological form to concretize the saving significance of the birth of Jesus as the Messiah. In Bultmann's view, to take this story for a fact is to misunderstand the purpose of mythological language and create an unnecessary problem for the modern believer, who cannot accept a god performing physical miracles.[103]

---

[103] R. Bultmann, "New Testament and Mythology," *Kerygma and Myth: A Theological Debate*, 5th ed. (New York: Harper Torchbooks, 1966), pp. 34-35.

Recently, several Catholic theologians adopted a similar position. They accept "the christological meaning" of the virginal conception: Jesus is God's gift to humankind. This they hold for a binding doctrine of faith, but they consider the fact of the virginal conception (to which they refer as a "biological fact") a doubtful *theologoumenon*.[104]

The pre-Gospel traditions that report the virginal conception display many signs of having been formed in a Palestinian Jewish-Christian milieu rather than in a Gentile-Christian community. This in itself makes unlikely the supposition that they were modeled on Hellenistic myths. Indeed, their content as well reveals far-reaching differences from pagan mythology. The gods in the mythical stories engage in sexual intercourse with the virgins; **in the case of the Holy Spirit and Mary, there is no suggestion of sexual union: the act of the Holy Spirit is an act not of generation, but rather of creation and consecration** (Lk 1:35).[105]

In the myths, the human mother gives birth to a hero who is neither entirely divine nor entirely human. Mary gives birth to a normal human being who is, nevertheless, the Son of God. In the New Testament the virginal conception results in the full humanity of Jesus and does not diminish his divine sonship, nor does his divine dignity make him less human.

The virginal conception stories of Luke and Matthew have no strict parallels in the Old Testament or extra-biblical Jewish literature either. Yet they show some affinity with the barren women stories, in particular with the stories of Sarah, of the wife of Manoah, and of Hannah. Through the power of their husbands and through their own fertility, these women cannot conceive a child. It is God alone who mercifully removes their shame, their "curse" of barrenness. The child, then, although derived from both parents, will be considered a special gift of God. He will be dedi-

---

[104] For the debate among Catholic theologians, see R. Brown, *The Virginal Conception and Bodily Resurrection of Jesus* (New York: Paulist Press, 1973), pp. 22-30.

[105] R. Brown, *The Birth of the Messiah: A Commentary on the Infancy Narratives in Matthew and Luke* (Garden City: Doubleday, 1977), p. 531.

cated to God and will have a special part in God's plan of salvation. This background helps to understand the New Testament stories of virginal conception, while it also points to their irreducible newness:

> ...Mary is a virgin who has not yet lived with her husband, there is no yearning for or human expectation of a child — it is the surprise of creation. No longer are we dealing with human request and God's generous fulfillment; this is God's initiative going beyond anything man or woman had dreamed of.[106]

In the perspective of Luke, this initiative aims at bringing forth the second Adam (cf. Lk 3:23,38), the beginning of a new creation. Mary's womb resembles the void over which the Spirit of God was hovering and bringing forth life at the dawn of the first creation (Gn 1:2): "The Holy Spirit will come upon you..." (Lk 1:35).

In the perspective of Matthew, the creative act of the Holy Spirit aims at bringing forth the Savior who will free his people from their sins (Mt 1:21).

Thus both in Matthew and Luke the virginal conception shows that human beings left alone, man and woman through their own power, cannot produce the new humanity (Luke), and cannot obtain forgiveness for their sins (Matthew). Jesus the Savior, "the holy offspring," could not be produced by human initiative but only by the creative power of God's Holy Spirit. This child is not the fruit of human love, but the fruit of God's love for humankind. He is purely and entirely a gift that could not be obtained by human efforts.[107]

In Luke, the virginal conception reveals not only the radically

---

[106] R. Brown, *The Birth of the Messiah*, p. 314.

[107] Our conclusions reveal that the Pauline doctrine of salvation through undeserved grace is very close to the meaning of the virginal conception in the Gospels. In fact, the virginal conception of Jesus is the historical manifestation of the absolutely gratuitous character of God's saving grace.

gratuitous character of God's gift in Jesus, but also his divine sonship. From Lk 1:34-35 it becomes clear that Jesus is to be called Son of God precisely because he is going to be conceived virginally by the power of the Holy Spirit. "Son of God" as used here clearly means more than Messianic sonship: Jesus is "*to gennomenon hagion*," "the holy offspring" (1:35) who is entirely the creation of the Holy Spirit. He belongs in such a radical way to God as to exclude a human fatherhood. His father is God alone. The virginal conception, then, shows that the whole being and life of Jesus — without any "remainder" — expresses his filial relationship to his heavenly Father. All that Jesus is reveals the Father in heaven. We can better understand Jesus' divine sonship if we compare our situation to his. We are children of our earthly father first, and throughout our life we are what we are to a large extent because of our relationship to him. It is only in addition to this natural relationship that we become, through grace, children of God.[108]

Therefore, all that we are and do does not and cannot "speak" about our heavenly Father. Much in us simply reflects our earthly father. Jesus, on the contrary, is the complete and unsurpassable revelation of the Father because his whole human being and life reveal him.[109]

After outlining its meaning, we will now investigate what can be established historically about the fact of the virginal conception:

1. Matthew and Luke not only suppose but also affirm this fact as part of the good news.[110]

2. A variant text of Jn 1:13 also proclaims the virginal conception, a text which seems to be the original version and was prob-

---

[108] As is well known, our divine adoption is not merely a legal change but an ontological reality; nor is it to be construed as a "superstructure," but rather as determining and elevating our whole being.

[109] One may wonder why Jesus' being the son of Mary does not diminish his role of revealing God. The virginal motherhood of Mary does not interfere with the full and direct revelation of God's fatherhood in Jesus. Moreover, being the son of Mary is the expression and guarantee of Jesus' true humanity.

[110] See Laurentin, *Structure et théologie de Luc I-II* (Paris: Gabalda, 1957), pp. 176-188.

ably changed in the 2nd century to the commonly accepted plural form in order to avoid its Gnostic misinterpretation:[111]

> ...[Jesus], who was begotten, not by blood, nor by the desire of the flesh, nor by the will of man, but by God.

However, even the commonly accepted variant in plural seems to imply an awareness of the virginal conception. In describing the spiritual birth of Christians, the Fourth Gospel intends to show the radical similarity between their birth and that of the only begotten Son; for this purpose, the author uses terminology that would apply the virginal conception ("begotten not by blood, nor by the desire of the flesh, nor by the will of man") to the spiritual birth of the believers.[112]

3. Not only do these three Gospels, written by three different authors in three different milieus, affirm this fact, but the tradition of the virginal conception can also be traced back to a pre-Gospel tradition from which all three have drawn.[113]

4. Historically, it is highly probable that Mary was known to be pregnant before she and Joseph came to live together. Both Matthew and Luke imply that her condition was already known, and Matthew explains it by reporting the angel's message to Joseph. John reports the accusation of the Jews that Jesus was born out of wedlock (Jn 8:41), which they might have based on the known fact of Mary's early pregnancy.[114]

The virginal conception itself is not a historically verifiable datum. Nor can it properly be called a "biological fact," since it transcends any biological process. It is God's creative act, similar to the raising of Jesus' dead body to a new life in the Spirit. We can ac-

---

[111] Besides the well-known translation of the *Jerusalem Bible*, a recent study also supports the singular form ("who was begotten") as the original in Jn 1:13: P. Hofrichter, *Nicht aus Blut sondern monogen aus Gott geboren: Textkritische, dogmengeschichtliche und exegetische Untersuchung zu Joh 1, 13-14* (Würzburg: Echter V., 1978).

[112] Cf. D. Farkasfalvy, *Testté vált Szó.* Elsö rész (Eisenstadt: Prugg V., 1986), p. 51; 62-63.

[113] R. Brown, *The Birth of the Messiah*, pp. 104-119; 308; 521-2.

[114] *Ibid.*, pp. 534-542.

cept it only in faith, in response to the affirmation of the evangelists and to the teaching of the ordinary magisterium of the Church.

Historical evidence, however, does not contradict this
affirmation of faith. On the contrary, in the words of R. Brown,
"it is easier to explain the NT evidence by positing historical basis
than by positing pure theological creation."[115]

The situation is similar to that of the empty tomb: both the
early pregnancy of Mary and the empty tomb are historically
verifiable data. The Church understood in both cases the transcendent cause and meaning of these events: God himself created the
New Man in Mary's womb and he raised from the tomb the dead
body of the New Man to immortal life. Those without the eyes of
faith could only misinterpret these facts: they claimed that Jesus
was born of adultery and that the disciples stole the corpse of Jesus
from the tomb.

2. "The brothers and sisters of Jesus"

From the 4th century on, the Church has unanimously taught
the perpetual virginity of Mary, before, during, and after the birth
of Jesus. The Protestant churches that came into existence in the
16th century, while continuing to believe in the virginal conception of Jesus, rejected the perpetual virginity of Mary by claiming
contradictory evidence from the New Testament. They affirmed
that the existence of the "brothers and sisters" of Jesus in the Gospels contradicts the Catholic belief of Mary's virginity after Jesus'
birth.[116]

The New Testament mentions several times the brother(s)
and once also the sisters of Jesus (Mk 3:31-35; 6:3; Jn 2:12; 7:3-9;
Gal 1:19; 1 Cor 9:5). We know the names of four brothers from
the Gospels: James and Joset (or Joses or Josef), Jude, and Simon.

Recently, the respected Catholic exegete, J.P. Meier, came

---

[115] *Ibid.*, pp. 527-528.
[116] Nevertheless, J. Wesley maintained the belief in Mary's perpetual virginity.

very close to the Protestant consensus. He stated that, prescinding from faith and later Church teaching, the most probable conclusion of the historian couldn't be anything else but that "the brothers and sisters of Jesus were true siblings."[117] Ironically, the most effective challenge to his view came from a Protestant historian, W. Bauckham.[118] While stressing his disbelief in the Catholic dogma of Mary's perpetual virginity, Bauckham, however, finds considerable new evidence in favor of the long-dismissed 4th century view of Epiphanius. According to Epiphanius the "brothers and sisters of Jesus" come from a first marriage of Joseph, and thus, Jesus is the only son of Mary. Bauckham's position is all the more noteworthy since he is convinced that after Jesus' birth Mary and Joseph had normal sexual relations. The most important arguments of Bauckham are as follows:

1. The brothers and sisters of Jesus appear older than Jesus in all Gospel traditions whereas Jesus is clearly affirmed to have been the first-born son of Mary. Younger brothers in Jewish society at that time could hardly have assumed the authority over the firstborn son that is attributed to the "brothers and sisters of Jesus" by the Gospels: they try to advise him (Jn 7:3-5); they want to stop him in his ministry (Mk 3:21, 31).

2. Second century apocryphal writings such as the *Protoevangelium of James*, the *Infancy Gospel of Thomas* and the *Gospel of Peter* (literally independent from each other) take for granted that the brothers and sisters of Jesus come from Joseph's previous marriage "as something the readers already know to be the case." Bauckham, of course, is aware that these apocryphal documents are the conflation of tradition and creative imagination. Yet, he points out that the above datum is not their creation (how could they create the same story independently from each other?), but a common tradition in (probably early) 2nd century Syrian Christianity which

---

[117] J.P. Meier, "The Brothers and Sisters of Jesus in Ecumenical Perspective," *CBQ* 54 (1992), p. 26.

[118] W. Bauckham, "The Brothers and Sisters of Jesus: An Epiphanian Response to J.P. Meier," *CBQ* 56 (1994), pp. 686-700.

evidently predates all three documents and may well go back to the oral Gospel of the church of Antioch.

3. It is a well-known fact that the Gospel of Mark never refers to Jesus as "son of Joseph," but only as "son of Mary." Up to now, no one was able to come up with an entirely plausible solution for this divergence from Jewish custom, which would normally require the identification of the son by the father's name. Bauckham thinks that "in Nazareth Jesus would have been known as 'the son of Mary' because this distinguished him from the children of Joseph by his first wife." He lists a long series of parallels for this usage from the Old Testament.[119]

Bauckham has indeed successfully demonstrated that Meier's method is quite questionable and that he has neglected some important evidence in favor of the Epiphanian view. Thus, the historical question remains much more open than Meier has suggested.

For Bauckham the whole issue is merely a question of historical method and an interesting piece of historical trivia without any theological significance. For Catholic theologians, however, it better explains why the Church was able to hold on simultaneously to the tradition of Jesus' "brothers and sisters" while, at the same time, develop the teaching on Mary's perpetual virginity.

Beginning with the 2nd century we have some explicit testimonies to the belief in Mary's perpetual virginity.[120]

A consensus on this point among the Fathers develops only after the Council of Ephesus, and gradually it becomes a Church teaching and part of the liturgical titles of Mary: she becomes the "ever-virgin Mary."[121]

Obviously, the biblical data and Early Church tradition do not constitute sufficient evidence for Mary's perpetual virginity. A Catholic accepts this teaching because the ordinary magisterium teaches it. Nevertheless, the teaching of the magisterium does not

---

[119] *Ibid.*, pp. 699-700.

[120] Cf. G. Jouassard, "Marie à travers la Patristique. Maternité divine, virginité, sainteté," *Maria. Études sur la Sainte Vierge* (Paris: Beauchesne, 1949), vol. I, pp. 76-77.

[121] See M. Schmauss, "Mariology," *Encyclopedia of Theology. A Concise Edition of Sacramentum Mundi* (New York: Seabury, 1975), p. 896.

contradict the New Testament; in fact, some biblical data are more easily explained if we accept this truth. Moreover, we cannot fully accept the mystery of the Church and the importance of virginity in the life of individual Christians, unless we understand these mysteries in the light of the perpetual virginity of Mary. Even before explicit statements were made, belief in the perpetual virginity of Mary had already been implied in the analogy and mutual inclusion that the New Testament and patristic literature has discovered between the mystery of the Church and that of Mary. The Church is called to be and remain a pure virgin, in the sense that her faith in Christ and her love for Christ should always remain pure and unstained. How could then Mary, the anticipated realization of the Church in her final perfection, not have always remained a virgin?[122]

While Gnostic Christian documents also attest Mary's perpetual virginity, they distort its meaning: Mary remained a virgin because sexual relations which produce an offspring and thereby increase matter are evil. While such anti sexual tendencies do influence to some extent the monastic movement in the Church, the patristic argument for the perpetual virginity of Mary is not based on Gnostic doctrine but on the understanding of virginity as a total consecration to God in pure faith and undivided love. They interpret Lk 1:34 as expressing the firm intention (or vow) of Mary to dedicate herself to God as a virgin; such a dedication must be total and irrevocable. They also see in the womb of Mary the New Ark of God overshadowed by the Holy Spirit, the New Temple forever sanctified by God's presence. No man may enter this sanctuary since God has made it into his own.[123]

---

[122] See H. Rahner, *Our Lady and the Church* (Chicago: Regnery, 1965), pp. 1-32.

[123] Ezk 44:1-3 often served as a basis for such an interpretation. This view is a further development of the Old Testament's perspective on cultic holiness. The High Priest who served in the sanctuary, as well as any soldier who fought in a holy war on behalf of Yahweh, had to abstain from sexual intercourse. In later Judaism, legends developed that Moses did not have sexual relations with his wife after he encountered God in the burning bush; and the 72 elders refrained from the same after they received a portion of Moses' spirit. The underlying conviction was that sexual activity is not evil but involves one in this world. One should abstain from it when facing the holy presence of God. See Laurentin, *Structure*, pp. 179-189.

Thus it was unthinkable for them that Mary, totally consecrated to God by Christ whom she conceived through faith before
she conceived him in her womb would compromise this consecration by sexual relations.

The perpetual virginity of Mary does not mean that her motherhood is restricted to that of Jesus. On the contrary, her undivided
giving of herself to God in virginity has resulted in a universal motherhood. In the patristic interpretation of Jn 19:25-27 the Church
is born on the cross through the redeeming sacrifice of Jesus. The
mother of Jesus stands at the foot of the cross: she shares in the
total self-giving of her Son. Thus through her faith and love she
cooperates in the birth of believers. By the words: "Woman, there
is your son" and "there is your mother" (19:26-27), Jesus gives Mary
over to the beloved disciple and the disciple to his mother. The beloved disciple here stands for all believers. Thus, at the foot of the
cross, Mary's motherhood is widened to embrace all the disciples
of Jesus. It becomes as universal as the Church: it extends to all
peoples and to the entire course of human history.[124]

3. The Holy Family

The virginal conception of Jesus gave rise to misunderstand-
ings among Christians about the "Holy Family." They were pictured as a make-believe couple, their marriage being a mere "cover"
to protect the reputation of Mary before those who did not know
"the real story." But part of the "real story" was — so they thought
— that Mary and Joseph lived in a certain emotional isolation from
each other in order to avoid "temptation." Joseph was regarded as
the "*pater putativus*," the make-believe father provided to insure legitimacy for the Son of God in Jewish society. Such distortions were
often made in Catholic devotional literature in order to extol the
lofty and unworldly character of the Holy Family.

---

[124] For the foundation of this view in the Gospel text itself, see A. Feuillet, "L'heure de la
femme (Jn 16,21) et l'heure de la Mère de Jésus (Jn 19,25-27)," *Biblica* 47 (1966), pp.
169-184, 361-380, 557-573.

However, the picture that emerges from the Gospels is very different. **Matthew and Luke affirm both the virginal conception of Jesus and the fact that Mary and Joseph were truly husband and wife** (Mt 1:16, 20, 24; Lk 2:5). In fact, Matthew's story emphasizes that God himself gave Mary along with her child to Joseph, a man from the house of David, as his wife and his son. Only upon the command of the angel did Joseph dare to take Mary into his home as his wife and accept her child as his own. The words of the angel, "You will call him Jesus," and the carrying out of this command: "he called him Jesus" express the taking possession of the baby by the father in Jewish society. In this way, the child was grafted into the family of David and became heir to all the promises God made to David's family.[125]

Legal paternity was taken very seriously in Jewish society. But **Matthew seems to imply more for Joseph than a mere legal arrangement. God himself bestows the child on Joseph, and God's act does more than establish a legal status. His giving is so real that the child, even though it did not biologically originate from Joseph, truly becomes his own.** We may shed some light on the reality of Joseph's fatherhood by comparing it to simple legal fatherhood. In the latter case, there is always another human being, "the real, biological father" who begot the child and through this act remains related to the child. The natural blood relationship will always interfere and often conflict with the child's relationship to his adoptive father. In the case of Jesus, however, the creative act by which Jesus the Messiah comes into being, and Jesus' transcendent relationship to his heavenly Father that results from this conception, do not interfere or conflict with the fatherhood of Joseph, but rather constitute it and fill it with meaning. Joseph becomes the instrument and the earthly image of the Father's saving and protecting love for his Son. According to Matthew, Joseph does for Jesus, the true Son of God, what Yahweh did for his "son" Israel: he saves him from destruction and brings him back from Egypt into the Promised Land.

---

[125] M. Krämer, "Die Menschwerdung Jesu Christi (Mt 1)," *Biblica*, 45 (1964), pp. 1-50.

Besides stressing that Mary and Joseph were truly husband and wife and that the son of Mary truly became the son of Joseph, the Gospels also give some hints about their relationship to one another and to Jesus. It seems likely that the reason Matthew (or at least the Aramaic tradition behind the present Greek text) gives why Joseph wanted to dismiss Mary was not a suspicion of Mary's unfaithfulness but rather the fear of getting involved with a divine mystery the presence of which Joseph sensed in his fiancée. He needed God's reassurance and command to overcome his awe. In Krämer's reconstruction, the Aramaic text underlying Mt 1:20 should be translated in this way: "Joseph, son of David, do not fear to take Mary as your wife just because the child was conceived in her by the Holy Spirit." In other words, "Do not let the fact that Mary is bearing a child conceived by the Holy Spirit frighten you from taking her as your wife."[126]

Even when Joseph took Mary into his home, this awe must have characterized Joseph's attitude towards her and the child. The phrase "the child and his mother," which occurs four times in the story of the flight (Mt 2:13, 14, 20, 21) suggests the reverential distance and awe separating Joseph from the Messiah and his mother. That the word order "the child and his mother" was purposely chosen by Matthew to describe the unique situation within the Holy Family, is suggested by the comparison of Mt 2:20-21 with Ex 4:19-20. The resemblance of the two texts is surprising, which only accentuates the difference between the sequence "his wife and his son" in Exodus, and "the child and his mother" in Matthew:

> "Go, return to Egypt, for all those who wanted to kill you are dead." So Moses took his wife and his son and ... started back for the land of Egypt (Ex 4:19-20).
>
> "Get up, take the child and his mother with you and go back to the land of Israel, for those who wanted to kill the child are dead." So Joseph got up and, taking the child and his mother with him, went back to the land of Israel (Mt 2:20-21).

---

[126] See the details and the reasons for this theory in Krämer, pp. 1-50.

In Matthew's account the child is the center of Joseph's care and concern, and Mary is Joseph's wife insofar as she is the mother of the child.

Yet it would be a mistake to suggest an emotional isolation, an existential "separation," between Mary and Joseph. The same child who causes the distance of reverence in their relationship is also the link that unites them into a family. In other human couples it is the mutual love of husband and wife expressed in their vows and consummated in sexual relations that creates their unity and brings forth the child.[127]

In the case of the Holy Family, the child himself (who is God's gift to Mary first and then along with Mary to Joseph) brings about the close intimacy between Mary and Joseph. Both Matthew and Luke show this uniting role of the child: Mary and Joseph go up together to Bethlehem, they suffer together because "there was no room for them in the place where travelers lodged" (Lk 2:7). To-gether they save the child from his persecutors (Mt 2:13-15); to-gether they present him in the Temple (Lk 2:22-38); together they search for him, and together they find him in the Temple on the third day (Lk 2:41-50). They not only feed and defend him, not only provide for his needs and educate him; his destiny and the growing consciousness of his vocation constantly challenge their faith. Their warm human love for each other may have grown and deepened precisely in this common concern, service, and love for Jesus.

The Holy Family is a unique phenomenon in the history of the world. Yet God wanted its existence for the sake of the whole world, so that it might become the model (never to be realized in such a radical way) for all Christian communities. Every Christian community is constituted, maintained, and strengthened by the common faith, love and service of Jesus rather than by the blood relationships or natural attraction among the members.

Not only do religious orders, parishes, and "basic Christian

---

[127] Here I do not consider the sacramental aspect of Christian marriage but only what natu-rally constitutes a married relationship.

communities" share in the mystery of the Holy Family, in some way every Christian family does. Through the sacrament of marriage Christ himself is present in the Christian family and transforms the flesh and blood love of the partners into an unconditional self-giving, so that, gradually, their love for each other will lead them closer to Christ himself.

4. Is Jesus "the Son of David"?

The apostolic Church emphasized the descent of Jesus from the family of David. For her, the Davidic origin of Jesus is an integral part of the evidence that Jesus is truly the Messiah in whom God's promises to the house of David have been fulfilled.[128]

Jesus' own position, however, at least as the Gospels present it, is in sharp contrast to that of the Church. He never designates himself as the son of David. On the contrary, he challenges his adversaries by the question:

> How can the scribes claim that the Messiah is the son of David? David himself, inspired by the Holy Spirit, said,
> "The Lord said to my Lord:
> 'Sit at my right hand
> until I place your enemies under your feet.'"
> David himself calls him "Lord"; so how is he his son?
> (Mk 12:35-37)

Here Jesus challenges the general belief of his audience that the Messiah is simply David's son. If he were, David could not call him his Lord.[129]

In Jewish society the son can never be placed above his father; in no sense could a father address his son as Lord. Jesus does not solve the problem he raises, but rather points to the mysteri-

---

[128] See Rm 1:3; Ac 13:23; Mt 2:5-6; Lk 3:31.

[129] Along with his contemporaries, Jesus assumes that the author of Psalm 110 was David.

ous origin of the Messiah. In the Fourth Gospel Jesus is even more reticent about his Davidic origin than in the Synoptics. He does not make the slightest effort to answer the provocation of the Jews:

> Does not Scripture say that the Messiah will be of David's family and come from Bethlehem, the village where David lived? (Jn 7:42)

This attitude of Jesus in the Gospels and the irresolvable contradictions between the Matthean and Lukan genealogies have led several exegetes to conclude that the Davidic origin of Jesus lacks historical foundation. It was created, they claimed, for a theological purpose, to prove that the Messianic promises to the house of David were fulfilled in him.

It is true that the genealogies of Matthew and Luke do not, and are not meant to give a historically reliable family tree of Jesus. But this alone does not constitute sufficient grounds for dismissing the Davidic origin as legendary. Nor is Jesus' reluctance to present himself as "son of David" equivalent to a denial. In fact, he accepts the title "son of David," when others address him in this way.

One argument in favor of historical authenticity is the fact that the Davidic origin is a common datum of the infancy narratives of Matthew and Luke, even though each developed independently from the other and contradicts the other on several issues.

But even more important is the fact that the tradition of Davidic origin can be traced back to much earlier times than the two Gospels. Paul quotes an early kerygmatic formula at the beginning of Romans about Jesus Christ who "descended from David according to the flesh" (1:3). This text derives from the very earliest days of the Church. Paul would not have accepted it had he not been convinced of its accuracy. In the words of Brown:

> ...it is cited by Paul who knew the Palestinian situation and was always sensitive to correction from Jerusalem. Would he have used it if he knew that Jesus was not really descended

from David? Would not this have left him vulnerable to the Jerusalem followers of Jesus (Gal 2:12) or to those who were questioning his apostolate precisely on the grounds that he knew little of the earthly Jesus?

Scholars who tell us that Paul may never have inquired about Jesus' ancestry forget that to a man with Paul's training as a Pharisee, the Davidic ancestry of the Messiah would be a question of paramount importance.... Paul, who twice insists on his own Benjaminite descent (Rm 11:1; Ph 3:5), would scarcely have been disinterested in the Davidic descent of Jesus.[130]

5. The twelve-year-old Jesus in the Temple

Some of the apocryphal gospels relish describing the miracles and the prodigious knowledge of the child Jesus. He astonished his playmates with his magic tricks. His clay birds would fly up into the air; he would curse his teacher who dared to hit him and the teacher would faint immediately.[131]

Questioned by a scholar of astronomy, he tells him "the number of the spheres and heavenly bodies... and other matters which surpass reason."[132]

Upon the inquiry of a physician, Jesus holds an impressive conference on the laws of physics and of living organisms. At the end, the physician "stood up, prostrated himself before the Lord Jesus and said: 'Lord, from now on, I am your disciple and servant.'"[133]

Luke's account on the twelve-year-old Jesus is markedly dif-

---

[130] R. Brown, *The Birth of the Messiah*, p. 508. Jesus himself did not refer to his Davidic ancestry because before his death and resurrection such a claim would have fueled a false expectation of political messianism.

[131] *Gospel of the Infancy according to Thomas*, 14:1-3.

[132] *The Arab Gospel of the Infancy*, ch. 51.

[133] *Ibid.*, ch. 52.

ferent from these stories. Nowhere does the narrative suggest anything but a normal, regular child; nor does Jesus perform any miracle. Jesus grows, not only in years, but also "in wisdom… and grace" (2:52). Wisdom in the Old Testament refers to the understanding of God's plan and will, and includes living according to this will. Thus Luke implies that Jesus grew in his understanding of God's will. The author of the Third Gospel sees no contradiction between the fact that Jesus is the Son of God and that he goes through the normal processes of human development. In fact, the present story seems to provide a concrete example of how this growth in wisdom took place.[134]

After three days of searching for him, his parents found Jesus "in the Temple sitting in the midst of the teachers." The narrative stresses that the teachers listening to him were astonished at his intelligent answers (v. 47), yet it depicts Jesus listening to them and asking them questions (v. 46).[135]

Listening in Luke marks the attitude of the disciple who wants to learn God's word and will.[136]

Jesus is sincerely searching the meaning of the Scriptures and, through it, a fuller understanding of his vocation.

The climax of the story is Jesus' reply to the anxious question of his mother:

> "Why were you looking for me? Did you not know that I must be in my Father's house?" (Lk 2:49).[137]

---

[134] While ending the previous pericope, Lk 2:40 also forms an inclusion with 2:52 which ends the story of the Temple episode. This device puts an emphasis on the statement that Jesus grew in wisdom.

[135] Cf. "Jesus is… depicted as a pupil, 'a genuine learner.'" J. Fitzmyer, *The Gospel according to Luke, I-IX. A New Translation with Introduction and Commentary*, The Anchor Bible, 28 (Garden City, NY: Doubleday, 1981), p. 442.

[136] Lk 6:47; 8:21; 11:28.

[137] According to Laurentin (*Jésus au Temple. Mystère de Pâques et foi de Marie en Luc 2,48-50*, Paris: Gabalda, 1966, p. 162), the literary form of this saying is *mashal*, that is, an enigmatic revelation which calls for reflection on its meaning by those who hear it.

In this twofold question Jesus declares his own identity and his vocation, to be in his Father's house.[138]

The astonished incomprehension of the parents indicates that Jesus never spoke to them beforehand in such clear terms about his relationship to the Father. Thus the Lukan narrative implies that in this incident Jesus revealed his own identity and vocation for the first time to his parents. In comparison to his vocation everything else pales in importance, even the most sacred family ties.

There is general agreement that the saying of Jesus and the kernel of the story go back to a pre-Lukan tradition. There is no agreement, however, on the thesis of several exegetes that Luke's remark at the end of story is a discreet reference to his source: "his mother kept all these things in her heart" (2:51).[139]

Nevertheless, if we take seriously the intent of the author of Luke as expressed in his prologue, we can hardly avoid the conclusion that in this story he intends to elaborate on the memory of an event from the life of the young Jesus.[140]

The "running away" of the teenager Jesus and his reply indicate a breakthrough in his self-awareness, a clearer discovery of his

---

[138] The meaning of "*dei*" ("must") in the sayings of Jesus connotes the Father's will which Jesus "must" carry out in his life and in his death. See, in detail, Laurentin, pp. 116-117.

[139] There is no reason not to take seriously the intent of Luke as expressed in his prologue, namely that, aware of what "the original eyewitnesses and ministers of the word have passed on" to his generation, he "accurately investigated everything anew" before he decided to write a connected narrative in order to provide "a solid foundation" for the teachings that Theophilus received. Cf. C.H. Dodd, *The Founder of Christianity* (New York: Macmillan, 1970), pp. 17-18. Moreover, at places Luke discreetly refers to his sources (2:19; 2:51; 23:49, 55; 24:10). The twofold reference to Mary does imply a tradition coming from the "circle of Mary" rather than a direct "oral communication" from Mary. On the historicity of the infancy narratives see the controversy between R. Laurentin and R. Brown: Laurentin, *Les évangiles de l'enfance du Christ. Vérité de Noël au-delà des mythes* (Paris: Desclée, 1982) ET: *The Truth of Christmas Beyond the Myths* (Petersham, MA: St. Bedes' Publications, 1986); — "Vérité des évangiles de l'enfance," *NRT* 105 (1983), pp. 691-710; Response by R. Brown, "More Polemical Than Instructive," *Marianum* 47 (1985), pp. 188-207.

[140] *Pace* Fitzmyer who would consider the tradition "another retrojection of christological faith, born of post-resurrection days, being pushed back to an earlier phase of Jesus' existence" (*The Gospel according to Luke, I-IX*, p. 437).

own identity. It overpowers him to the point of abandoning everything else, even his parents.[141]

Luke's account invites a comparison between the God-expe-
rience of Jesus and that of the young Samuel (1 S 2:19-26; 3:1-
18), whose story — even in its contrasting qualities — served as a
partial model for the author of the Third Gospel. The parallelism
is important for Luke, since he presents Jesus as **the** Prophet who,
at the end of time, brings to completion the work of all the prophets.

Both Samuel and Jesus are described as growing in favor before God and men (1 S 2:26, Lk 2:52); the decisive experience occurs for both of them in the sanctuary. But this parallelism only
underscores the unique character of Jesus' experience. When Samuel
is called by God, while lying in the sanctuary, he does not recognize his voice. He must learn to identify it with the help of the priest
Eli (1 S 3:9). God's mystery comes to him as strange and unknown.
Nor does he dare to obey God's command at the beginning (v. 15).
Jesus' experience in the Temple is very different. **He does not encounter God as a "Stranger" who tries to make his voice heard, but
Jesus experiences God in a clearer recognition of his own identity;
in other words, he recognizes him as his own Father with whom
he must always be.**

6. "The private life of Jesus" before his public ministry

Besides the infancy narratives, the Gospels report only the
public ministry of Jesus, his passion, and the appearances of the risen
Christ. This comprises at most three years of his life. What happened between his childhood and his baptism by John is left un-
told. We have only a few incidental remarks on his life before the

---

[141] Luke does not say that Jesus had not been aware beforehand of his true Father. All that
is suggested by the event behind the narrative is a new break-through in his self-awareness. To show the continuity and the real development of Jesus' self-awareness as Son
belongs to systematic Christology, cf. pp. 361-368 of this book.

public appearance (e.g., Mt 13:55-56; Mk 6:3; Lk 2:39-40, 51-52). However, this silence and the short references have an important message: they imply that in about 90% of Jesus' life nothing extraordinary happened which would warrant recording. He grew up, worked, and lived in the large family that the New Testament describes as his brothers and sisters. Even though at his birth and in his dying he experienced abject poverty, in his young and adult years at Nazareth he probably did not suffer any serious need. Joseph, or perhaps Jesus himself was a carpenter (Mt 13:55; Mk 6:3) and may have practiced his trade for many years. His parables reveal a familiarity with the life and the work of a carpenter who, at that time, built not only furniture but also houses and towers.[142]

In Palestine, a carpenter belonged to the "middle class" of a small town, working hard but not suffering any serious want.

He took part in the religious life of his people, going to the synagogue every Sabbath, traveling to Jerusalem once a year.[143]

His parables and sayings are shot through with allusions to the Bible and are replete with biblical imagery. All these show that Jesus must have thoroughly assimilated the world of the Bible; the implicit quotations and images became the spontaneous and original expression of his own thought. He is not like the rabbis and scribes who are anxious to repeat the tradition of previous teachers: he discovers new meanings and makes new connections that surprise and shock his audience. He must have acquired this knowledge of Scripture in his childhood and during the "hidden years" at Nazareth.

---

[142] C.H. Dodd, *The Founder of Christianity* (New York: Macmillan, 1970), pp. 120-121. According to W.F. Albright and C.S. Mann the Greek word *tekton* should be translated as "builder" rather than "carpenter." They point out that the word *tekton* "has a wide range of meanings, from a shipbuilder to a sculptor, but it generally indicates a craftsman of considerable skill... It seems clear that so far from Joseph being the simple — and poor — village carpenter making ox yokes or simple plows (which any peasant was capable of producing), he was probably a builder of some consequence, traveling over wide areas of the country" (W.F. Albright and C.S. Mann, *Matthew*, The Anchor Bible, 27 [Garden City, NY: Doubleday, 1971], pp. 172-173).

[143] Lk 1:41's information on this point is in complete conformity with what we know about the people of Galilee at that time: since the Maccabean war, they reattached themselves to the Temple worship.

The long stay at Nazareth makes him so much part of the town, that later, when he returns as a powerful prophet, he finds only resentment, incredulity, and rejection:

> "Where did this man get all this? What kind of wisdom has been given him? What mighty deeds are wrought by his hands? Is he not the carpenter, the son of Mary, and the brother of James and Joses and Judas and Simon? And are not his sisters here with us?" And they took offense at him (Mk 6:2-3; cf. Mt 13:53-58; Lk 4:23-30).

This angry reaction shows that Jesus was indeed known as a normal, "ordinary guy" among his townsfolk. And yet, in the light of faith, the ordinary character of the long "private life" of Jesus is the most powerful commentary on the realism of the Incarnation. God has truly become man: He did not come only for a period of time like the gods of pagan mythologies who would only make visits to the earth and before long return to the bliss of their heavenly abode. Jesus has gone through the whole process of becoming a man; he did not take any shortcuts, never took advantage of any divine privilege; he accepted living under the authority of parents, learning a trade, becoming part of the people at Nazareth. His consciousness and his vocation developed and unfolded gradually under the maturing influence of manifold human relationships in an ordinary Jewish environment.

CHAPTER IV

Jesus and the Kingdom

1. The baptism of Jesus by John

Since the Early Church was so concerned to show the transcendent superiority of her Lord to the disciples of the Baptist, she could not have invented the story of Jesus' baptism by John. The story implies that Jesus subjected himself to John and might even suggest that at a certain point Jesus was John's disciple. All this must have made more difficult the work of Christian apologists who were trying to prove that Jesus was above John. The fact that Jesus' baptism is attested to in all the four Gospels also points to the historicity of the event. The close connection and, at the same time, the apparent incongruity of this act of subjection with the public ministry of Jesus (who was "powerful in word and deed") calls for an investigation. In the words of Schillebeeckx, the baptism of Jesus by John may indeed be a "primary hermeneutical key" for understanding the meaning of Jesus' ministry and message.[144]

John acts and speaks as a prophet in the line of the Deuteronomic-prophetic tradition. His message does not fit in with the prevailing messianic conceptions of the age. The Jews expected either a second David to liberate Israel from the yoke of the Roman Empire or an apocalyptic divine intervention to introduce a new age and annihilate all the enemies of Israel. In both cases Is-

---

[144] E. Schillebeeckx, *Jesus*, p. 137. However, as it should become clear later, Schillebeeckx does not sufficiently exploit this "hermeneutical key."

rael is favored and the judgment of God destroys the nations. John turns the tables around: in his preaching Israel itself is the object of God's impending judgment. Luke 3:7-9 gives a summary of his message:

> He said to the crowds who came out to be baptized by him, "You brood of vipers! Who warned you to flee from the coming wrath? Produce good fruits as evidence of your repentance; and do not begin to say to yourselves, 'We have Abraham as our father,' for I tell you, God can raise up children to Abraham from these stones. Even now the ax lies at the root of the trees. Therefore every tree that does not produce good fruit will be cut down and thrown into the fire."

John is so overwhelmed by God's holiness and the gravity of Israel's sins that he cannot preach any comforting news, but only the imminent outpouring of God's wrath. The whole nation is ripe for judgment. The only way to escape from the coming doom is *metanoia*, conversion. One must change his outlook and his life, and practice the basic commands of the law: justice and love of the neighbor (cf. Lk 10-14). John baptizes people as a sign of this inward conversion and new beginning.

In John's perspective the One who is to come is not a Savior who forgives sins, but the executor of God's righteous judgment:

> His winnowing fan is in his hand to clear his threshing floor and to gather the wheat into his barn; but the chaff he will burn with unquenchable fire (Lk 3:17).

Why was Jesus so attracted to John that he underwent his influence and even his baptism?[145]

Is this not against Jesus' divine dignity? If we realize that Jesus lives out his divine sonship in and through a human existence, the problem disappears. There is a direct communication between the Father and Jesus, as we will see later. But precisely the Father's di-

---

[145] This was certainly a problem for some Christians. In the *Gospel of the Nazoreans* Jesus refuses to undergo John's baptism. See St. Jerome, *Adv. Pel.* 3.2.

rect communications to Jesus help him discover the importance of John's work and message, just as the Father inspires Jesus to discover his Father's plan in the Scriptures.

The message of Jesus seems, at first look, opposed to that of John. Jesus preaches the good news of God's forgiving love to the sinner, whereas John announces the imminent cutting down of the tree and the burning of the chaff with fire. Yet, while Jesus' message goes much beyond that of John, the good news of forgiveness presupposes the reality of guilt and judgment. Only if the servant knows that he is unable to pay back the enormous debt to his master, can he grasp the master's unlimited generosity. Only if we understand that the prodigal son does not deserve the lavish reception prepared by his father, can we appreciate the Father's love that is beyond any human imagination. Moreover, Jesus' offer of forgiveness to the sinner is the offer of an infinitely holy love that cannot be turned down without the gravest consequences. Jesus calls for decisive action because the end of times has arrived; if one fails to respond to his invitation, the good news turns for him into news of judgment. For the self-righteous, Jesus "did not come." Matthew emphasizes that for those who maintain their hypocrisy, Jesus pronounces the woe of God's judgment (23:1-36). In other words, the good news of Jesus is also *krisis* in the original sense of the word: it is a judgment that separates forgiven sinners from the self-righteous, who think that they do not need forgiveness (e.g., Mt 9:13; Lk 5:32; Mt 18:1-9; 23:1-30; 25:41; Lk 16:1-9).

Thus a more thorough comparison reveals no contradiction between the messages of John and of Jesus. On the contrary, only if we take seriously the message of John about judgment can we fully appreciate the good news of Jesus about forgiveness. All have sinned. All deserve God's condemning judgment. This is the background against which we should measure God's boundless love that acts in Jesus.[146]

---

[146] Thus Schillebeeckx is, in my opinion, somewhat one-sided in insisting that Jesus is not interested in the past of the sinner (*Jesus*, p. 146). Certainly, Jesus does not relish recalling the details of the sinner's past, but he makes very clear that he is aware of his past sins; he forgives sins rather than merely accepts human weaknesses.

His love, when accepted, does not condone but rather removes sinfulness and enables the sinner to start a new life. If we were merely unfortunate, imperfect creatures, we would only need understanding and compassion, perhaps also professional counseling, but certainly not forgiveness. Moreover, if we are only weak and wretched, we have a right to compassionate treatment on the part of God who created us so weak in the first place. Jesus' forgiveness, however, supposes more than weakness in us; it implies personal responsibility for our sins. We see now why the message of John is itself part of Jesus' good news.[147]

It guards everyone against separating Jesus' love from his holiness or viewing it as a service to which helpless humankind may register a legitimate claim.[148]

John the Baptist, then, prepares the way to Jesus for all generations.

What has been said so far still does not explain why Jesus submitted himself to John's baptism of repentance.[149]

We should start from the generally accepted fact that Jesus performed many prophetic signs. (In the light of Easter the disciples understood that all his actions were signs full of meaning.) His baptism by John was Jesus' first prophetic sign action that was meant for all the people. It approved of John's proclamation of Israel's apostasy and the urgent need for conversion.[150]

---

[147] Mark makes the ministry of John the "beginning of the good news" (1:1), and according to Luke John the Baptist himself preaches the good news (3:18).

[148] There is a real parallelism between Rm 1-2 and 3-8 on the one hand, and the ministry of John and the public ministry of Jesus on the other. Paul insists that we cannot appreciate the free gift of God's grace that justifies those who believe without first understanding the judgment we have deserved for our sins; by prefacing the ministry of Jesus through the ministry of John the Baptist, the Gospels emphasize that we cannot value the good news of God's Kingdom in Jesus' message unless we accept John's preaching about God's impending judgment that we all have deserved.

[149] If we accept with W.F. Albright and C.S. Mann that Jesus' saying in Mt 3:15 is a historically authentic logion ("It is fitting for us to fulfill all righteousness"), we learn only that Jesus undergoes John's baptism in order to fulfill God's plan that is always just and right (cf. *Matthew*, pp. 31-32). But we still wonder why this event was part of God's plan.

[150] Schillebeeckx, *Jesus*, pp. 137-138.

But it also showed Jesus' profound solidarity with his sinful people. In no tradition of the New Testament does Jesus appear in need of personal repentance or conversion. Yet here the sinless one immerses himself in the Jordan River with all the sinners. Luke expresses this aspect of solidarity in Jesus' baptism most clearly: "when all the people were baptized so was Jesus..." (3:21). Thus here, for the first time, Jesus identifies himself with sinners, more concretely, with sinful Israel, by sharing in their baptism of repentance.

The revelation Jesus receives from the Father after he emerges from the waters further explains the meaning of his baptism. In Matthew, "This is my son, the beloved, with whom I am well pleased" (3:17) is a solemn general declaration, while in Mark and Luke the Father directly addresses Jesus: "You are my son, the beloved, with you I am well pleased" (Mk 1:11; Lk 3:22). In both cases the words of the Father combine Ps 2:7 and Is 42:1, the words of enthronement of the Messiah king as God's Son with the beginning words of the first Servant Song in Deutero-Isaiah. Thus, according to the Synoptics, it is revealed to Jesus at his baptism exactly what kind of Messiah he is being called to be. He is to be very different from what the people expect, a hidden Messiah, "the Servant"; he will not cry out and shout and make his voice heard on the streets; nor will he perform any spectacular deeds (Is 42:2).[151]

He will embody the covenant of God with his people but will also become a universal light for all the nations and will establish "justice," that is, God's just order over the whole earth (Is 42:6,4). It is possible that the words of the Father to Jesus call attention also to the last Servant Song; in this case the meaning of his baptism as an act of solidarity with sinners would be further deepened. Jesus' baptism would then anticipate his taking upon himself "the sins of many" in his redemptive death (Is 53:11-12).[152]

---

[151] In the New Testament, quoting the beginning of a passage often calls attention to the whole.

[152] According to Mark and Luke, Jesus himself refers to his impending death as a "baptism" (Mk 10:38-39; Lk 12:50). Thus it is not unlikely that he himself at least at one point in his earthly life began to see his baptism as a prophetic sign of his coming death.

Jesus' death and resurrection shed more light on the baptismal scene. Just as his immersion into the water was the foreshadowing of his death, so his emerging out of the waters and the Father's words declaring Jesus to be his beloved Son anticipate his resurrection, by which Jesus will be constituted "Son of God in power."[153]

According to Matthew, the one who rises from the waters is the new Israel, the true Son of God in whom the Father is well pleased (in opposition to the old sinful Israel who has broken the covenant). According to Luke, the new Adam, the firstborn of the new human race arises out of the waters. Just as the old Adam received life from the breath or spirit of Yahweh, the Holy Spirit descends on the new Adam and will lead him during his public ministry up to the end of his life.

2. The temptations of Jesus

According to J. Dupont the likeliest "*Sitz im Leben*" of the temptation stories may be found in the life of Jesus himself.[154]

All three attempts of the devil are variations on the one great temptation Jesus faced during his public ministry: to become a Messiah who fulfills the expectations of the people. Contrariwise, while the accounts do fit into the life-setting of Jesus, they could hardly have originated in the Early Church, in which political messianism was not a problem. Moreover, a parable of Jesus by which he explains the "secret" of his successful exorcisms seems to refer to the same struggle with Satan:

> No one can enter a strong man's house to plunder his property unless he first ties up the strong man. Then he can plunder his house. (Mk 3:27)

---

[153] According to the pre-Pauline kerygma (Rm 1:4).

[154] J. Dupont, *Les tentations de Jésus au désert. Stud. Neotest.* 4 (Bruges: Desclée de Brouwer, 1968), pp. 97-108.

While the temptation stories report a genuine experience of Jesus, their language is mythological: a very high mountain from which Jesus is able to see all the kingdoms of the earth in their glory, the instantaneous and multiple transfers of Jesus from one "place" to another. The mythological language suggests that these events transcend ordinary experience.

The account in Mark does not explain what these temptations were. But the connection between Mk 1:13 and 3:27 makes clear that in Mark's perspective the fact that Jesus so easily "plunders the strong man's house," that is, liberates those whom Satan had enslaved, is due to the fact that Jesus has previously "bound" him. In other words, the victories of Jesus over Satan during his earthly ministry are the result of his first struggle with the devil and his victory over him.[155]

We can understand the meaning of the longer threefold temptation account of Matthew if we place it in its Matthean context. Jesus relives the history of Israel in his own life. His return from Egypt corresponds to Israel's leaving Egypt. His baptism corresponds to Israel's crossing the Red Sea. His forty days fast corresponds to the wandering of Israel in the desert for forty years. And so, his three temptations also correspond to the temptations of Israel in the desert and to those of her entire history.

The context of Deuteronomy 8:3 which Jesus quotes in reply to the first temptation of the devil leads us into the heart of the matter:

> You must remember all that road by which the Lord your God has led you these forty years in the wilderness to humble you, to test you and to discover whether or not it was in your heart to keep his commandments. He humbled you and made you hungry; then he fed you on manna, which neither you nor your fathers had known before, to teach you that man cannot live

---

[155] Fitzmyer ascribes "the origin of these stories to Jesus himself — in some form," but sees in them a symbolic interpretation of his struggle with his opponents during the public ministry rather than an experience before his ministry began (*Luke*, p. 510).

on bread alone but lives by every word that comes from the mouth of the Lord (Dt 8:2-3: The New English Bible).

Indeed, the "desert experience" revealed what was in the heart of the historic Israel: distrust in spite of the many signs of God's care and providence, constant rebellion against his leadership. Israel did not believe that God could and would provide for their daily need of food and drink (Ex 15-16). Jesus' "desert experience" also reveals his heart:

> It is written: "One does not live by bread alone but by every word that comes forth from the mouth of God" (Mt 4:4).

He trusts in God's providence unconditionally and is ready to endure physical hunger in obedience to him. This attitude reveals the nature of the food that ultimately sustains and energizes him: obeying every word that comes from God (cf. also Jn 4:32-34).

In the Deuteronomic tradition Moses testifies to Israel that God alone is her glory, that he has performed in her midst great and glorious deeds (Dt 10:21: Septuagint). Yet, in her wars Israel constantly tried to take advantage of God's help to prove her own greatness. This search for glory especially manifested itself in Israel's kings, who presumed on God's help when waging their own wars. Jesus, in contrast, does not use God's power to enhance his own glory. He refuses to perform a show miracle that would challenge God to prove that he is with Jesus (Mt 4:7; cf. Dt 6:16, Ex 17:1-7). Likewise, he does not throw himself off the pinnacle of the Temple, just as he will not come off the cross to demonstrate his power. His whole life will be spent seeking God's glory, not his own (Jn 7:18; 8:50).

Israel, especially in her kings, often succumbed to the temptation to pursue earthly power by abandoning Yahweh and submitting to the worship of foreign gods. Jesus, the new Israel, is offered not only the restoration of the Davidic kingdom "from sea to sea" (Ps 72:8) but also "all the kingdoms of the world" (Mt 4:8). In

Matthew's account this is the culminating point of all the offers, and it is here that their Satanic character is unveiled: Jesus would have to receive world dominion from the hand of Satan: **for him, world dominion would be tantamount to the worship of Satan.** That is why at this point he no longer tolerates Satan's presence:

> Get away Satan! It is written: "The Lord, your God, shall you worship and him alone shall you serve" (Mt 4:10).

Jesus, the New Israel, fulfills the commandment of the Law, to serve and worship God alone (cf. Dt 6:13; 10:20).

In the temptation accounts Jesus not only re-lives in a new way Israel's history; he also anticipates his own. These stories provide a key not only to understanding Israel's history from God's viewpoint, but they also illumine the meaning of the later conflicts between Jesus and his people. In the light of Jesus' "desert experience" we understand the drama of his public ministry: Jesus disappointed the expectations of the crowds who pushed him to take on the role of a political liberator Messiah. He refused to provide any "sign from heaven," that is, any spectacular apocalyptic sign to justify his mission (Mt 16:1; Mk 8:11; Lk 11:16).[156]

Jesus had to act in this way because in the enthusiastic expectations of the crowds he perceived the influence of Satan, whose intentions he had already unmasked in his "desert experience."

Of the many ways in which Luke's account differs from that of Matthew, only two should be mentioned here. In the first place, Luke inserts the temptations of Jesus into universal human history by tracing back the family tree of Jesus to Adam. Jesus, the Son of God, undergoes the temptations of the "son of Adam" (Lk 3:38). In other words, Jesus suffers **the** typical temptations of Adam's offspring, such as preferring the fulfillment of his physical needs to God's will and seeking power and glory for himself. Here we are

---

[156] According to a Jewish tradition the Messiah was to come down from heaven and appear in the Temple. Cf. J. Kremer, *Lukasevangelium. /Die neue Echter Bibel* (Würzburg: Echter Verlag, 1988), p. 52.

given a glimpse of the mystery that Jesus' whole life and death will manifest: the Son of God alone can fully realize an authentic human existence because he alone can fully accept his dependence on God and live out this dependence in trust, service, and adoration.

The second important contribution of Luke's account is found in the last sentence: "When the devil had completed all the temptations he departed from him for a while" (4:13). In Luke's presentation the temptations at the beginning of the ministry are only a prelude to the Passion, which will be the decisive struggle with Satan, "the time for the power of darkness" (Lk 22:53; cf. also 22:3, 31).

We have often misinterpreted the temptations of Christ according to a more or less Docetist model, as if they were a mere "show" for our edification rather than a real struggle. Indeed, it is hard for us to comprehend how the Son of God who was "driven out by the Spirit into the desert" (Mk 1:12) and was filled with the Holy Spirit (Lk 4:1) could really have been tempted — especially if we hold with the Catholic tradition that in Jesus there was no "concupiscence," that is, no inordinate desire or tendency toward sin. However, if we accept the mystery of the incarnation, we must also accept that God has really made our weak human nature his own, and it is in our weak human nature that he fought with Satan.[157]

Jesus was a man of his nation and culture. Just as were many Jewish boys, he may have been raised in the expectation of a glorious Messianic King and Priest who would restore the kingdom of David; he may have learned to interpret the messianic scripture passages in this sense. In this typical Jewish milieu the devil's of-

---

[157] St. Leo formulated with classic precision the mystery of the struggle between the Son of God and the devil, a struggle he saw as including Jesus' whole life: "In this struggle, fought for our sake, an admirable fairness and justice has been observed. The almighty Lord fights with this most savage enemy not in his own Majesty but in our own humble condition. He throws to him the same form and the same nature as ours, sharing in our mortality but not in our sinfulness" (*1st Sermon on the Nativity*, 1).

fers could have held a real appeal for him. Not because they were suggesting something evil, but because they promised something that he may have wished for his people with all his heart: providing food for the hungry, liberating his people from Roman oppression, establishing an earthly kingdom of God over the whole world, and providing irrefutable "heavenly signs" to convince his people of the truth of his message. These promises could not appear evil to a young Jew who was close to his people and imbued with their desires. However, when comparing these dreams with God's plan, and with his vocation as "the Servant,"[158] he may have uncovered the diabolic nature of these suggestions. At any rate, in Matthew's version, it is the offer of "all the kingdoms of the world," the temptation to accept the role of the Davidic Messiah, which prompts Jesus' definitive rejection.

The temptation accounts of Jesus serve also for the Church to unmask as false or even diabolical certain individual and collective tendencies. How often we are tempted to approach Jesus with the same demands as Satan. If you are truly the Son of God, why don't you put an end to famine, destitution, and to all suffering? Why don't you satisfy all our material needs? If you are the Son of God, why don't you perform a compelling heavenly sign to dissipate all doubts so that all people may acknowledge you? Church leaders and Church communities have often been tempted in this way and have also succumbed to the temptations of political messianism. How often the Church has been made to serve the political ambitions of rulers, their grandiose plans of extending a "Christian Empire" over the whole world by force. How often the Church has taken advantage of the "secular arm" to uproot heresies and execute heretics! From the Constantinian alliance of Church and State to the *"Action française"* to contemporary movements that reduce the Christian message to a blueprint for the transformation of society, the Church has been repeatedly lured by po-

---

[158] According to the Synoptic tradition it was revealed to him at his baptism.

litical ideologies on the left and the right, always in danger of misunderstanding and distorting her vocation.[159]

3. The outline of the public ministry of Jesus

John the Baptist's ministry began between 27-29 A.D. Jesus' first public appearances could not have taken place much later. The Fourth Gospel seems to provide a valuable corrective to the Synoptic narratives regarding the beginnings of Jesus' public ministry. According to the latter, Jesus began his public ministry in Galilee, while according to John Jesus preached and baptized (or, as John corrects himself, Jesus' disciples baptized) for a while in Judea (Jn 3:22; 4:1-2). For some time his ministry seems to have run parallel and — so some thought — in competition with that of John the Baptist (Jn 4:1). John implies that Jesus withdrew to Galilee because of the hostility of the Pharisees, who were alarmed by his success. According to Matthew and Mark, Jesus withdrew to Galilee after the arrest of the Baptist (Mt 4:12; Mk 1:14).

All four Gospels attest to a ministry of Jesus that centers on Galilee (even though John locates very few stories in that area). This period is characterized by Jesus' proclamation that the Kingdom of God is near, and by the signs he works demonstrating its nearness to those who respond with faith. The crowds hail him with enthusiasm, but the Pharisees and scribes in general follow his activities with increasing hostility, and begin to plot against him.

The feeding of the multitudes in the desert appears as a turning point in the ministry of Jesus. It marks the climax of enthusiasm for the crowds, who want to make Jesus king in a Messianic uprising; but this very attempt causes Jesus to withdraw from the crowds and brings about a crisis of loyalty among his disciples (Jn 6:66).

According to all four Gospels, Peter confesses his faith in Jesus

---

[159] Obviously, only the above mentioned reductionist kind of liberation theology can be so criticized. Struggling for "a civilization of love" is part of the Christian vocation.

as the Messiah (Mt 16:13-20; Mk 8:27-30; Lk 9:18-21; Jn 6:68-69) in the name of the remaining loyal disciples, gathered around the Twelve (Jn 6:67). After this initial confession of faith, again according to all four Gospels, there follows a first announcement of the Passion (or an allusion to it in Jn 6:70-71): Jesus "must" suffer and die (Mk 8:31-33; Mt 16:21; Lk 9:22).

According to the structure of the Synoptic Gospels, a second important phase of Jesus' ministry begins on the road to Jerusalem and unfolds in Jerusalem. Here the drama reaches its peak of tension and its dénouement: Jesus provokes the Sadducees, who control the Temple, by the prophetic sign of "cleansing the Temple" and thereby asserting his supreme authority over it. There follows a series of discussions with the leaders who want to trap him. Here Jesus' teaching no longer centers on the Kingdom but on the impending end of this age, which the future destruction of the Temple both symbolizes and anticipates. He also announces the coming of the Son of Man in power and glory to judge the world. The discussions with his enemies call attention to the mystery of his person: "By what authority are you doing these things?" — they ask him (Mt 21:23; Mk 11:28; Lk 20:2).

Unlike the Synoptics, which mention only one (last) journey of Jesus to Jerusalem, John has Jesus going to Jerusalem four times during his public ministry. The Synoptics implicitly confirm the substance of John's version, namely that Jesus spent a considerable time in Jerusalem before his last journey there. Both Matthew and Luke quote him saying:

> Jerusalem, Jerusalem, you who kill the prophets and stone those sent to you, how many times I yearned to gather your children together... (Mt 23:37; Lk 13:34).

Moreover, the enthusiastic welcome at his last entry into the city is more easily intelligible from the Johannine perspective. A prophet who had previously worked only in the despised region of Galilee could hardly have impressed the crowds in Jerusalem to the extent Jesus did.

John also refers to three Passover festivities during Jesus' ministry, while the Synoptics mention only one. Here again John seems more historically reliable than the Synoptics, so we may conjecture that Jesus' public ministry lasted two and a half or three years.

4. The message of Jesus: the reign of God is at hand

Matthew, in its editorial summaries, recapitulates the teaching of Jesus as "proclaiming the good news of the Kingdom" (*to euaggelion tes basileias*, 4:23; 9:35; cf. also 24:14), while Luke prefers the medial verb form *euaggelizesthai* to characterize the preaching activity of Jesus (4:18; 4:43; 8:1).[160]

Whether or not Jesus himself used the term "good news" (*euaggelion*) is irrelevant. The evangelists are right to use it because it manifests an important aspect of the Kingdom. In the Septuagint text of the Old Testament, the verb *euaggelizeisthai* means to announce the good news of God's victory to Jerusalem:

> O you who bring glad tidings (*ho euaggelizomenos*) to Zion, go up on the high mountain! Lift up your voice with strength you who bring glad tidings (*ho euaggelizomenos*) to Jerusalem.
>
> Lift it up; fear not. Say to the cities of Juda, "Behold your God! Behold the Lord! The Lord is coming with strength and his arm is with power" (Is 40:9-10; cf. 52:7).

What the liberation from exile only foreshadowed is happening now: through the word and works of Jesus the power of Satan is on the retreat; sickness, death, and sin are conquered. This is the beginning of a final victory over the powers that have oppressed and kept humankind captive "in the shadow of death." The time of fulfillment has come, the fulfillment that all the prophets and all the just had hoped to see but had not seen (Mt 13:17; Lk 10:24).

---

[160] Mark uses simply *euaggelion* or *euaggelion tou theou* for the same purpose (1:15; 8:35; 10:29; 13:10; 1:14).

A new age has dawned on humankind; history and the world as we have known it are fast coming to an end (Mt 11:13; Lk 16:16; Lk 7:28). Yet, unlike Jewish apocalyptic literature, which depicts the coming of the new age with signs of cosmic upheaval, in Jesus' preaching the drawing near of the Kingdom of God is not accompanied by any such apocalyptic sign.[161]

Those who do not have faith cannot perceive its hidden presence:

> The coming of the Kingdom of God cannot be observed, and no one will announce, "Look. Here it is," or, "There it is." For behold, the Kingdom of God is among you (Lk 17:20-21).

The healings and exorcisms, the raising of a few dead to life, the preaching to the poor and the conversion of a few sinners are signs that do not compel acceptance and are misinterpreted by Jesus' enemies as evidence of diabolic possession. But for those who have faith these deeds of power make the Kingdom visible.

At the time of Jesus the Jews expected the coming of the Kingdom either as a result of perfect obedience to the Law or of violent warfare.

> The Lord will be in the midst of her, and the Holy One of Israel reigning from her... for he knows that on the day when Israel is converted, the kingdom of the Enemy will be brought to an end.[162]

In Jesus' ministry the Kingdom has appeared, not as result of Israel's conversion, but as a pure gift on God's initiative. It was in no way merited; it does not presuppose but rather calls for conversion.

Among the lower classes of Jews, especially in the country-

---

[161] In the Synoptics the only sign that Jesus promises to the "evil and adulterous generation" will be the sign of Jonah, which Matthew understands in the sense of Jesus' death and resurrection (Mt 12:39-40).

[162] *Testament of Dan*, V, V:31-VI:4: quoted by C.H. Dodd, *The Parables of the Kingdom* (New York: Scribner, revised ed., 1961), p. 30.

side, periodic flare-ups of rebellion had a clear Messianic overtone. The people expected the Kingdom to come as a result of armed uprising against the Roman oppressors. As we will see, Jesus rather risked alienating the masses than accept the role of a political Messiah. The Kingdom of God cannot be brought about by violence or by any political movement.

What, then, is the Kingdom of God?[163]

In a discussion with his adversaries, Jesus points out: "If it is by the Spirit of God that I drive out demons, then the Kingdom of God has come upon you" (Mt 12:28; cf. Lk 11:20). The Kingdom of God is thus the hidden but powerful presence of God in Jesus restoring wholeness and life to all those who accept him in faith. Surprisingly, the greatest resistance to Jesus was provoked by the fact that God's power at work in him showed itself as a power of incomprehensible love. This love must have been unsettling and upsetting, not only for the religious hypocrite, but also for the average law-abiding devout Jew, who walked on the paths of righteousness and avoided the ways of the wicked. Jesus not only allowed the sinners to come to him, as John the Baptist did; he also went after them. He did not merely forgive their sins, but accepted table fellowship with them. Jesus' God pays the same amount to the worker hired in the last hour of the day (the sinner who repents now in the last hour) as to the one who endured the burden and the heat of the day (the law-abiding Pharisee or Essene) (Mt 20:1-15). God's love is like that of a foolish shepherd who leaves the 99 sheep in order to search for the one that has been lost.[164]

It is like a woman, who for the sake of one lost coin, sweeps every corner of the house and is not satisfied until she finds it. God is like the father watching the road for his son who had squandered

---

[163] The Matthean formulation "Kingdom of Heaven" is probably the term Jesus used; "Heaven" is a reverent circumlocution in Jewish usage for the ineffable divine name.

[164] Mt 18:12-14; Lk 15:4-7. Note that the *Gospel of Thomas* adds: "one of them went away; it was the largest" (Quoted by P. Perkins, *Hearing the Parables of Jesus* [Ramsey, NJ: Paulist, 1981], p. 30). This added remark destroys the original meaning which shows that God's love goes after anyone who is lost: it is both gratuitous and universal.

his share of the family inheritance; when he spots him, forgetting about his dignity, he runs to meet him, embraces and kisses him. He does not even wait until the son finishes his confession of sins but has the finest robe put on him and orders a splendid banquet to celebrate his return to life (Lk 15:1-32).

This festive banquet to which the repentant sinner and the law-abiding Pharisee (who is in worse shape than the former, since he resents the father's generosity towards his repentant brother) are both invited is the central image of the Kingdom (Mt 8:11; Lk 13:28; 14:15-24). In Jesus' message *metanoia*, a complete change of heart, and way of life, begins with accepting this invitation to God's banquet. Accepting the invitation includes the grateful acceptance of God's undeserved forgiveness of our sins and the adopting of God's forgiving attitude towards those who sinned against us. If we do not imitate God's forgiveness towards those who have offended us, God will revoke the forgiveness of our own sins (Mt 18:21-35). Thus, the love of their enemies becomes the most characteristic attitude of those who undergo *metanoia*. Only in this way can they "prove" that they have understood and accepted the love of God who "makes his sun rise on the evil and the good and causes rain to fall on the just and the unjust" (Mt 6:45).

Another aspect of *metanoia* is expressed by Jesus' call for us to become "like little children."[165]

Children are aware that they cannot earn their living and that they are dependent in everything on their parents. They trust in their parents' care regardless of what happens and are convinced that their parents are able and willing to do what is best for them. Thus an unconditionally trusting, loving, and joyful surrender to God as one's Father and a grateful acceptance of the Kingdom as pure gift characterize the disciple of Jesus.

Those who are materially poor, hungry, and grieving are called "blessed" by Jesus, because wealth, satisfactions, and pleasures do

---

[165] John shows the ontological aspect of this becoming like little children: it is a new birth from water and the Holy Spirit (Jn 3:3-8).

not blind them to their need for God's Kingdom. The poor are "at the end of their rope," or, to quote Marx's dictum, "they can lose only their chains"; in other words, they do not have a stake in their present status. They don't have an excuse for refusing the invitation. Their misery helps them to cry out to God and to trust in him since everything else has failed them. In that very moment when they do so, the Kingdom of God becomes theirs (Lk 6:20-21).[166]

Thus, "being guests at the banquet in the Kingdom of Heaven" is a celebration for those who accepted the invitation and were reborn as little children. Among them, all alienation and estrangement cease, and an intimate communion is established because, accepted by God, they also accept one another.[167]

5. The miracles of Jesus

a. The phenomenon of the miracle in the public ministry of Jesus

As we have seen, Jesus consistently refused to perform "signs" in the sense of cosmic portents that would have satisfied the apocalyptic expectations of certain Jewish circles.[168]

Thus, when describing the miracles of Jesus, the Synoptic Gospels do not use the term *terata*, the usual Greek word for won-

---

[166] I have followed here Luke's version of the beatitudes because it may be closer to the original wording by Jesus. Nevertheless, Matthew's version adds an important clarification: those who are materially poor are in a fortunate situation regarding the Kingdom. But they enter the Kingdom **only if** they take advantage of the opportunity and become also spiritually detached from wealth and develop a hunger for God's justice and holiness (Mt 5: 3-10). On the other hand, a rich man who is detached from his possessions and ready to share them with the poor also qualifies to be "poor in spirit" in Matthew's interpretation.

[167] From the immense literature on Jesus and the Kingdom, see W. Kasper, *Jesus the Christ*, pp. 72-88; B.F. Meyer, *The Aims of Jesus* (London: SCM Press, 1979), pp. 111-253.

[168] There is one sign which Jesus promises to this "evil and adulterous generation," the sign of Jonah according to Mt 12:38 and Lk 11:29-30. According to Mk, no sign will be given to this generation (8:11-12). In John sign, *semeion*, has a different meaning. It is not a synonym of *teras*, a heavenly apocalyptic sign, but refers to seven selected miracles or prophetic signs from Jesus' ministry which symbolize and anticipate the mystery of his death and resurrection.

der, portent, or miracle, especially for heavenly manifestations of divine power, but rather *dynameis*: powerful deeds.[169]

These acts of Jesus show forth the hidden but powerful presence of God's Kingdom. To the inquiry of the Baptist's messengers, "Are you the one who is to come or should we look for another?" Jesus responds by pointing to both his deeds and his preaching:

> "Go and tell John what you have seen and heard: the blind regain their sight, the lame walk, lepers are cleansed, the deaf hear, the dead are raised, the poor have the good news preached to them" (Mt 11:4-5; Lk 7:22).

These works of power show that Jesus' proclamation of the Kingdom is not just words, but actions, too. He inaugurates the new age of the Kingdom both through his preaching and through the acts of healing, exorcizing, and raising the dead. However, the bodily healings and even the raising of the dead serve only as a visible illustration for what is happening invisibly in the hearts of those who believe that God is at work in Jesus. Jesus' first words to the paralytic may sound disappointing to the sick man and to the crowds who expected a miracle: "Child, your sins are forgiven" (Mk 2:5). But Jesus goes to the root of his misery by forgiving his sins. Only afterwards does he heal him physically, in order to show that he has the power to forgive sins and to provide a tangible, visible sign of the final stage of the Kingdom when all sickness and death will be definitively overcome.

---

[169] "Signs and wonders," *"semeia kai terata"* are used in Matthew and Mark to designate the deceiving signs of the false Messiahs in the eschatological tribulation (Mk 13:22; Mt 24:24). In Acts, however, the author uses *"semeia kai terata"* to express the heavenly and cosmic wonders prophesied by Joel for the "last days," that is, the eschatological age (Ac 2: 19). By applying the same terminology to the wonders and signs wrought by Jesus and by the apostles and Stephen the first martyr, Luke probably wants to show that indeed the last days prophesied by Joel had been begun by the works of Jesus and were being continued by the apostles (Ac 2:22; 4:30; 5:12; 6:8; 14:3; 15:12). Note that already Paul applied the words *"semeia kai terata"* to the miracles accompanying his apostolic activity: Rm 15:19; 2 Cor 12:12. The use of these terms shows his conviction that his apostolic work marks the arrival of "the end of the ages" (1 Cor 10:11).

The miracle traditions in the Gospels have been re-thought, re-told and re-composed in the light of Jesus' death and resurrection, in which they receive a new meaning: they all become signs and guarantees of the new, eschatological human race, fully and eternally alive for God and with God. Thus even healings are described by the same verb as the raising up of Jesus (Mt 8:15; 9:5,7; Mk 2:12; Lk 4:39; 5:25; 17:19). The healings and the resuscitation of the dead anticipate the new, eschatological creation whose first fruits are the glorious risen body of Christ. Every miracle during the public ministry of Jesus reveals some aspect of the God who shows himself to be God by giving life. He is the God of the living, and his purpose in creation is that we may live forever for him and with him.

When, upon hearing of the death of his daughter, Jairus is about to give up hope, the words of Jesus, "do not fear, only have faith" (Mk 5:36) sum up the essence of the faith Jesus demands: facing the empirical evidence of death as the final end of human life, trust in God who brings his creation back to a new life in and through Jesus.[170]

The faith Jesus asks for is contrary to what many people take for faith in our society. How often we hear: "Believe you can do it and you can do it!" They think this is what Jesus means by declaring, "Everything is possible to one who has faith" (Mk 9:23). But Jesus does not speak about faith in one's own unlimited power. The faith Jesus calls for, the faith "the size of a mustard seed" by which we can move mountains, is very different from pushing ourselves beyond our limits. It is faith in God's almighty power and in his absolute goodness available for us in Jesus. This faith tells God: I trust that you alone are almighty and good and therefore I surrender myself to you completely: "If you want you can make me clean"

---

[170] Here we see how Romans and the Gospel of John, in their concept of faith, explicate authentically the faith Jesus demands of us in the Synoptics: For Paul, faith is to imitate Abraham's faith and thus to believe in the God "who gives life to the dead and calls into being what does not exist" (Rm 4:17). For John, faith means to believe in the word of Jesus who says: "Your son will live" (4:50, 53; 11:25-26, 40).

(Mt 8:2). By subjecting himself to God in unconditional obedience, the believer in some sense shares in God's almighty power; he can do all that God wants him to do with the strength God provides (Ph 4:13). In this sense Jesus alone is the one who has the fullness of faith; he is the archetype and leader of our faith (Heb 12:2) and we only participate in his fullness.

b. Historical foundations for the miracle accounts

Today few exegetes would subscribe to the self-confident pronouncement of Bultmann: "One cannot use electric light and radio and believe in the spirits and in the miracles of the New Testament at the same time." Gerd Teissen, a German exegete raised in the Bultmannian method of form and redaction criticism, formulates the consensus of a large number of exegetes when he declares: "Without a doubt Jesus performed miracles. He healed the sick and drove out demons."[171]

However, there is no consensus on the extent to which legendary developments amplified the miracle traditions.[172]

Most exegetes maintain that at least some miracle stories are based on historical facts. They support this positive conclusion with the following considerations:

1. All the various channels of Gospel traditions report miracles. Even the earliest layers of traditions contain them. They did not originate at a later stage, when the Church may have felt the need to counter Hellenistic stories of miracle workers.

2. One should not exaggerate the credulity and naïveté of an-

---

[171] Both texts are quoted by J. Sudbrack, "Die Wunder und das Wunder": *Internationale katholische Zeitschrift* (18) 1989, p. 237. Other studies on the miracles of Jesus include: D. Wenham and C. Blomberg (eds.), *Gospel Perspectives: The Miracles of Jesus.* Vol. 6 (Sheffield: JSOT, 1986); R. Latourelle, *The Miracles of Jesus and the Theology of Miracles* (New York: Paulist, 1988).

[172] A Catholic theologian cannot, on the basis of the doctrine of inspiration, exclude the possibility that some miracle stories are entirely legendary and that others have undergone amplifications. Human traditions do develop in this way. However, the assistance of the Holy Spirit assures that such amplifications or legendary developments correctly interpret the meaning of what Jesus truly said and did.

cient man. The Gospel traditions ascribe a greater dignity to John the Baptist than to any other prophet. Yet they attribute no miracle to him, presumably for the simple reason that he was not known to have performed miracles of any kind. The biblical authors did not feel the need to create miracle stories in order to justify John's importance in the history of salvation.

3. One of the chief charges against Jesus was that he healed on the Sabbath. Thus even his enemies admitted the fact of healing, but they attributed his healing power and his ability to drive out demons to Beelzebul, the prince of the devils.

4. Matthew and Luke preserve a saying of Jesus in which he chides Chorazin and Bethsaida for refusing to repent in spite of the mighty deeds he performed in their midst (Mt 11:20; Lk 10:13). The name of the town "Chorazin" does not occur in any of the Gospel stories. If the saying had been the creation of the Early Church, it would have probably put on the lips of Jesus other places where in the Gospel stories Jesus was known to have worked miracles. Thus the saying bears a sign of authenticity. But, if authentic, it needs to be accepted as Jesus' own witness to his having performed miracles:

> Woe to you Chorazin! Woe to you Bethsaida! For if the mighty deeds done in your midst had been done in Tyre and Sidon, they would long ago have repented in sackcloth and ashes.

Many exegetes today, while admitting the factuality of healings, tend to relegate the raising of the dead and the nature miracles to the realm of legendary developments. However, if we accept the resurrection of Christ as a reality, there can be no *a priori* objection to admitting the historicity of Jesus' raising up the dead as a prophetic sign of his own resurrection and of "the coming of the Kingdom in power." To say that the daughter of Jairus and the young man of Nain may have only appeared dead is mere speculation with no support in the texts.

The nature miracles, in particular the calming of the sea and

Jesus' walking on the water, are as much related to the coming of the Kingdom as the healings. They cannot be discarded as mere legends serving only the popular preoccupation with extraordinary and sensational events. Both stories recount prophetic signs that anticipate the final arrival of the Kingdom. In the Kingdom nature will be fully "exorcized"; in other words, it will no longer be an instrument of Satan, who seeks to destroy humankind. In the New Age nature will again serve us: peace and harmony between the human race and nature will be restored.

On the grounds of literary-historical analysis one cannot single out the nature miracles as betraying a legendary origin. I suspect that the reasons for dismissing the nature miracles are more or less consciously philosophical. On the one hand, as discussed before,[173] there is still a powerful Bultmannian tendency that restricts an "intervention of God" to human subjectivity and excludes it from the impenetrable web of necessary cause-effect relationships in nature. On the other hand, there is an inclination to explain the extraordinary healings in the Gospel stories as parapsychological or psychosomatic phenomena, an explanation the nature miracles resist.[174]

Thus, faced with a philosophical rejection of miracles, we need to examine the underlying philosophical and theological issue.

c. Theological and philosophical considerations

As discussed before, the popular notion of nature as a "closed, self-explanatory system" cannot be proved by science but is rather imposed on it by a certain philosophical world-view. We have also

---

[173] See pp. 57, 62.

[174] J.P. Meier's remark sums up this tendency with insight and precision: "The miracles were signs and partial realizations of what was about to come fully in the Kingdom. Commentators who accept all this nevertheless often seek to explain the exorcisms and cures in terms of psychological suggestion, while dismissing the more intractable nature miracles. Such a judgment is based not on historical exegesis but on a philosophical *a priori* about what God can and cannot do in this world — an *a priori* rarely if ever defended with rigorous logic. Instead, appeal is made to 'modern man,' who looks suspiciously like 18th-century Enlightenment man" (*The New Jerome Biblical Commentary*, 78:20, p. 1321).

seen that the Christian doctrine of creation is the philosophical and theological context that provides analogies for understanding the resurrection of Christ. This context applies also to the other miracles of Jesus, all anticipations and "parables in action" of that one definitive miracle.

Moreover, miracles need not be understood as God simply bypassing the activity of natural causes and directly causing the miraculous effect. Rather, God enables the natural cause to transcend its power and produce a disproportionately greater than normal effect. In all his miracles the natural actions of the man Jesus are not bypassed but enabled by the divine power to transcend their own natural results. Thus, the man Jesus commands the evil spirits and the sea, blesses and breaks the bread, touches the sick, makes mud from dust and saliva and smears it on the eyes of the blind. But these human actions are in themselves insufficient to explain the expulsion of demons, the calming of the sea, the multiplication of the loaves, and the healing of the sick. It is God's power that manifests itself through the human gestures and words of Jesus and elevates them into prophetic signs that foreshadow and guarantee the new eschatological creation.

There are indeed good reasons today to take parapsychology more seriously than was done in the past. A number of cases of telekinesis, telepathy, and medically inexplicable healings (not in a religious context) have been documented. Parapsychology does remind us of the often forgotten potential of the human spirit that, to some extent, may transcend by its own powers the physical laws of nature. The yogis are probably right in their claim that the average human being utilizes only a very small portion of his spiritual energies.

Parapsychology, then, may one day explain some otherwise inexplicable physical healings. However, the healings of Jesus achieve their real purpose only in the conversion of the heart: the rising up of the paralyzed man shows his new life with God after his sins were forgiven, the Samaritan leper is pronounced healed by Jesus only after he came back to give thanks to God. **Thus, the healings of Jesus transcend the potential of the human spirit in that**

they bring about a new life with God in the healed person. The sinner is reborn as "a little child in the Kingdom of Heaven." A parapsychological explanation could not do justice to precisely what is central in Jesus' miracles, namely their being signs of the Kingdom; they bring about "a new creation," a new relationship with God which changes also our relationship to ourselves and to our fellow men and women.

Of course, no one can accept the miracles of Jesus as signs of the Kingdom without a corresponding inner change, some form of incipient faith. The miracles may help the birth of faith, they may confirm it, but they can never impose it. The healings can always be reduced to parapsychological phenomena, or misinterpreted as diabolic acts, and the resuscitations and nature miracles can simply be denied.

On the other hand, understanding the miracles of Jesus in the context of the Kingdom opens our eyes also to seeing "miracles" in our own lives. What the healings and the raising of the dead by Jesus signify — the forgiveness of sins and the rising to a new life with God — we see continued every day in the preaching and the sacramental life of the Church.[175]

---

[175] The continuation of Jesus' mighty deeds in the Church can be better perceived in the Gospels of Matthew and John than in Mark. Léon-Dufour compares the story of the healing of Simon's mother-in-law as recorded in Mk 1:29-31 to that of Mt 8:14-15 (*The Gospels and the Jesus of History*, p. 112). Mark's account has signs of an eyewitness report. Matthew wrote an ecclesial Gospel, a Gospel for the Church, to point out that what has happened once in the life of Jesus is happening daily in the life of the Church. There are three significant changes in Matthew's account as compared to Mark's.
    1. In Mark, after being healed, Simon's mother-in-law "waited on them" — she literally did perform services for Jesus and the disciples. In Matthew, she "was raised up" and "waited on him."
    2. In Mark, Jesus goes to Simon and Andrew's house. In Matthew, he goes to the house of Peter. The name has been changed to the official name designating Peter's office as the rock of the Church. The house has already become a symbol, that of the Church.
    3. In Mark, Jesus grabs her hand and raises her up — a simple factual report. In Matthew, "she has been raised up." The action of healing is described in Matthew according to the pattern of the resurrection: she is raised to a new life by Jesus. Thus Matthew's account is a model of what is happening daily in the Church. Jesus works miracles and raises people to new life everyday by his teaching and his sacraments. Those who are raised to life in the Church serve Jesus with their whole lives.

The extraordinary manifestations of God's power and goodness in Jesus' ministry make us sensitive to the ordinary manifestations of God's power and goodness in our own lives. Gradually, we understand that nothing in our lives is pure accident. Whatever happens, good or bad, routine or unusual events, they are all signs: God speaks to us and educates us through them so that we may be made ready to live in the new creation. Even though we cannot command the wind and multiply bread, nevertheless, as St. Bernard points out, as soon as we begin to obey our Master, nature itself will recognize its Master in us and will start serving us so that everything will cooperate for our good.[176]

6. The multiplication of loaves: a turning point in the ministry of Jesus?

We have already seen that according to all the Gospels many in the ruling class opposed Jesus almost from the beginning. His eating with sinners and his healings on the Sabbath aroused the hostility of the Pharisees and scribes, even while the crowds enthusiastically flocked to him, hung on his lips, and craved for his miracles. The feeding of the multitudes, however, seems to mark a turning point in the relationship between Jesus and the crowds.[177]

This miracle is attested to in all four Gospels, with a doublet in both Matthew and Mark. After the crowds were fed, according to Mark and Matthew Jesus "compelled his disciples to get into the boat and precede him to the other side toward Bethsaida, while he dismissed the crowds" (Mk 6:45; Mt 14:22). The preceding story in Mark and Matthew does not explain why Jesus so abruptly and forcefully separated his disciples from the crowd. However, it makes perfect sense if we accept as historical the additional Johannine detail:

---

[176] *21st Serm on the Cant.*, 6.

[177] What follows in the analysis of these traditions depends to a large extent on the article of I. de la Potterie, "Die wunderbare Brotvehrmehrung. Ihr Sinn und ihre Bedeutung im Leben Jesu," *Internat. kath. Zeitschrift* (18) 1989, pp. 207-221.

When the people saw the sign he had done, they said, "This is truly the Prophet, the one who is to come into the world." Since Jesus knew that they were going to come and carry him off to make him king, he withdrew again to the mountain alone (6:14-15).

This Messianic uprising, occasioned by the feeding of the multitude, would explain why Jesus wanted to separate his disciples from the contagious enthusiasm of the crowds. It would also make understandable why the Pharisees, perturbed by the insurrection, approached Jesus to inquire about his Messianic credentials (Mt 16:1; Mk 8:11). Contemporary research has convincingly shown that in that age the Palestinian peasantry was a breeding ground for Messianic rebellions.[178]

However, if the crowds in the desert acclaimed Jesus as their Messiah king, there had to be a reason for it. I. de la Potterie rightly insists that one cannot simultaneously claim the historicity of the Messianic uprising around Jesus and reduce the historical kernel of the multiplication of the loaves story to a mere "sharing their provisions," as if Jesus had merely taken the initiative to give the crowds the five loaves and two fishes, which, in turn, would have prodded each person in the crowd to share with others his own provision. So unremarkable an expedient would hardly explain the Messianic fever that took hold of the crowd. On the other hand, a true multiplication of loaves would make it quite plausible. The Jewish belief that the Messiah would be a new Moses (Dt 18:15) was coupled with the expectation that the Messiah would renew the manna miracle of Exodus. From among several texts, I. de la Potterie mentions the *Syrian Apocalypse of Baruch*:

> And it will happen that when all that which should come to pass in these parts has been accomplished, the Anointed One will begin to be revealed... And it will happen at that time that the treasure of manna will come down again from on

---

[178] Cf. for instance, R.A. Horsley and J.S. Hanson, *Bandits, Prophets and Messiahs* (Minneapolis: Winston, 1985).

high, and they will eat of it in those years because these are the ones who will have arrived at the consummation of time.[179]

It seems, then, that the historical fact behind the multiplication of the loaves story is a prophetic sign action of Jesus, by which he intended to show the very nature of the Kingdom. The Kingdom is like a banquet to celebrate communion with God and with one other, and the source of this communion is the food that the Messiah himself provides in miraculous abundance. In the light of the Last Supper and the resurrection the evangelists understood the real nature of the Messianic banquet: the multiplication of the loaves in the desert merely prepared the Eucharistic banquet in which the food that creates communion is the very Body and Blood of the Messiah himself.

With regard to the public ministry of Jesus, however, this event has a different significance. As was said above, it represents a kind of watershed in Jesus' relationship to the crowds. It brings to light their unwillingness or inability for *metanoia*. They want Jesus to be their Messiah on their own terms, the leader of an uprising against Roman political power. Jesus rejects this role as a satanic temptation. If he were not aware of it before, this event must have made clear to him that the people of Israel refused to be converted.

---

[179] 2 Baruch 29:3, 8: *The Old Testament Pseudepigrapha,* ed. J.H. Charlesworth, vol. I. *Apocalyptic Literature and Testaments* (Garden City, NY: Doubleday, 1983), pp. 630-631. The multiple attestation of this belief in Jewish intertestamental literature makes the crowd's preoccupation about manna historically plausible in the Johannine account.

CHAPTER V

The Kingdom and the Death of Jesus

1. "Get behind me, Satan!"

We do not know when Jesus began to speak about his imminent death. However, in all four Gospels the first reference to his impending suffering comes after the multiplication of the loaves and the confession of Peter (Mt 16:21; Mk 8:31, Lk 9:22), and it is addressed to the disciples who remained faithful to him. (In John it takes the form of mentioning the chief actor in the drama of the Passion, the devil, and his instrument, Judas, who is going to betray Jesus: 6:70-71.[180])

The fact that this link is found in all four versions suggests that it antedates the Gospels themselves and that it belongs to the stage of pre-Gospel traditions and may reflect what actually happened. Moreover, the prediction of suffering is closely linked to "a new call to discipleship (Mk 8:34; par. Mt 16:24; Lk 9:23), an invitation to Jesus' disciples... to enter into the frightening mystery of his destiny."[181]

The growing rejection of Jesus is paralleled by an increased emphasis in his preaching on judgment (for instance, Lk 13:1-9;

---

[180] In John every sign is an anticipation of the mystery of Jesus' death and resurrection, thus there are several references to his death before chapter 6. But even John preserved a link between Peter's confession and a prediction of Jesus' betrayal, which seems more imminent at that point than before.

[181] B.F. Meyer, "The Expiation Motif in the Eucharistic Words: A Key to the History of Jesus?": *Gregorianum* (69) 3, 1988, p. 480.

Mk 12:1-9). This is not a sign of vindictive resentment but rather underlines the absolute seriousness of Jesus' offer of grace. As R. Pesch and B.F. Meyer note:

> Jesus' offer was free, but he did not conceive a positive response to it to be purely optional for Israel. On the contrary, the gracious proclamation was simultaneously a radical demand. On it hinged the status of Israel. Refusal would accordingly create an anomaly: the good news risked turning into a condemnation.[182]

Indeed, the more God's forgiving love is revealed in the ministry of Jesus, the more terrible the consequences of its rejection appear. The revelation of final, eternal condemnation is simply the other side of the definitive revelation of God's love in Jesus.

We need now to investigate how Jesus viewed his impending death. He did not need any divine inspiration to realize that his life was in imminent danger and that going up to Jerusalem was walking into the lion's den.[183]

He was accused of blasphemy for forgiving sins (Mk 2:7), of regularly breaking the Sabbath, and of performing magic in alliance with Beelzebul, the prince of demons (Mt 12:24); all of these charges carried the death penalty in Jewish law. John the Baptist, with whom the beginnings of Jesus' ministry have been closely linked, had been executed already. Jesus could not have been blind to what John's fate meant for his own future. In fact his reaction to John's death reflects the awareness of his imminent end (Lk 13:31).

But the question still remains, what significance did Jesus attribute to his death? Here the opinions are sharply divided.

---

[182] *Ibid.*, pp. 475-476. Meyer refers here approvingly to R. Pesch's idea in *Das Abendmahl und Jesu Todesverständnis* (Freiburg: Herder, 1978), pp. 103-105.

[183] Only those who think that Jesus was hoping and preparing for a victorious uprising in Jerusalem have reason to deny this. See S.G.F. Brandon, *Jesus and the Zealots. A Study of the Political Factor in Primitive Christianity* (New York: C. Scribner's Sons, 1967); _____ *The Trial of Jesus of Nazareth* (New York: Stein & Day, 1968); O. Cullmann, *Jesus and the Revolutionaries* (New York: Harper & Row, 1970); M. Hengel, *War Jesus Revolutionär* (Stuttgart, 1970).

Bultmann and his school claim ignorance, but, for them, Jesus' understanding of and attitude towards his death do not matter at all. Even if Jesus broke down in despair on the cross, for the believer, the kerygma of the cross retains all its saving power. Other exegetes maintain that Jesus did not see any saving significance in his death; all the Gospel texts indicating the contrary, they hold, derive from the theologizing of the Early Church. Such a skeptical approach, however, is far being from unanimous. There are exegetes for whom it is evident that Jesus must have seen and accepted his death as the way to inaugurate the Kingdom, the central concern of his life. Again others show how Jesus saw his vocation as the fulfillment of the Suffering Servant prophecies and thus his death as an expiatory sacrifice of a unique kind.[184]

Looking at the issue from a theological perspective, we must start with K. Rahner's insight: if Jesus had in no way been aware of his death as a saving event, we would not have been redeemed by a human act, conscious and free. This, however, is *a priori* unlikely since it goes against the general pattern of God's action in history. In calling and sending a prophet, God always asked for a conscious and free response. Granted that once a prophet was called, he had to be ready for ever new surprises, for having his life turned upside down and even for a violent end; yet, through his faith, he was allowed to see even the failure of his mission as part of God's plan. Could God have granted less to Jesus? Indeed, Jesus often compared his destiny to that of the prophets: rejection and violent death was their end, and he could not have expected anything else for himself.

However, in Jesus' perspective his death is unavoidable not only because Israel has always rewarded those who were sent to them by God in this way but also because it constitutes a divine "must" (*dei*): **his suffering and death is part of God's plan.** This becomes clear from his harsh rebuke to Peter: "Get behind me, Sa-

[184] Cf. especially H. Schürmann, *Jesu ureigner Tod* (Feiburg i. Br.: Herder, 1975); X. Léon-Dufour, *Face à la mort. Jésus et Paul* (Paris: Éd. du Seuil, 1979); ET: *Life and Death in the New Testament. The Teaching of Jesus and Paul* (San Franciso: Harper & Row, 1986), pp. 49-150.

tan" (Mt 16:23; Mk 8:33). He uses the same words with which he had addressed Satan in the desert (Mt 4:10). This rebuke had to be uttered by Jesus himself in order to be recorded. The churches in which the Gospels of Matthew and Mark were written held Peter, the first of the apostles, in such a great esteem that they hardly could have invented such a highly compromising reprimand. In fact Luke chose to omit it from his version of the events. However, if the rebuke of Jesus to Peter, "Get behind me, Satan," is historical, so is Peter's prior remonstrance with Jesus that provoked it. In other words, Jesus reprimands Peter because Peter wanted to prevent Jesus from suffering in Jerusalem. Jesus calls Peter Satan because, unconsciously, Peter became Satan's instrument: he tried to do what Satan had done in the desert, to block the fulfillment of God's plan by persuading Jesus to escape from his suffering.[185]

2. The Last Supper and the Kingdom

The implications of another saying generally regarded as historical shows the connection between Jesus' death and the Kingdom. At the Last Supper Jesus announces,

> Amen I say to you, I shall not drink again the fruit of the vine until the day when I drink it new in the Kingdom of God (Mk 14:25; cf. Mt 26:29; Lk 22:18).

On the eve of his death, although it has become abundantly clear that his mission to Israel was a failure, Jesus announces his unshaken trust in his imminent entrance into God's Kingdom. The words quoted above imply that only his death stands between Jesus and his full partaking in the banquet of the Kingdom. By adding: "*with you*" ("…when I drink it new with you in the Kingdom of my Father": Mt 26:29), Matthew shows that the disciples of Jesus will be

---

[185] See O. Cullmann, *Christology of the New Testament* (Philadelphia: Westminster, 1963), p. 63.

closely associated with him in the Kingdom. Luke's version makes explicit that the Last Passover meal of Jesus with his disciples was already an anticipation of the feast in the Kingdom of God: it is to be fulfilled there (Lk 22:16).

But what role does Jesus attribute to his death with regard to the Kingdom? Instead of looking at individual texts we need to consider the direction of his whole life as reflected in the Gospel traditions. If anything is certain about Jesus' attitude, it is the fact that he considered his life a service: "I am among you as one who serves" (Lk 22:27).[186]

If, on the eve of his death, aware that he was going to be betrayed and killed and aware of his failure to convert Israel, he was nevertheless so serenely certain of the imminent proximity of the Kingdom, how else could he have considered his death but as the ultimate service "for the sake of the Kingdom"?[187]

In this context, then, we can understand some of the common features of the Eucharistic texts (attested to with some variations in five places in the New Testament).[188]

The Eucharistic words and gestures symbolize and anticipate this ultimate service, the giving of his life, his body and blood "for a multitude" or "for you," that is, for the disciples. By this prophetic sign act he not only signifies what is to come but also effects it.[189]

By giving his body and blood as food and drink to his disciples, Jesus himself began entering the Kingdom and making his disciples share in it. Through the bread and wine the disciples truly share in the body-person of Jesus who offers his life for them and thereby enter into communion with each other. Giving oneself over to God through giving one's life for one's neighbor and thus achiev-

---

[186] If put into this general perspective, the parallel texts of Lk 22:27, Mt 20:28 and Mk 10:45, with their implicit references to the Suffering Servant prophecies, receive a very likely "Sitz im Leben" in the life of Jesus (cf. Kasper, *Jesus the Christ*, pp. 120-121).

[187] On this point the views of Schillebeeckx and Kasper converge with ours. See *Jesus*, pp. 303-312; *Jesus the Christ*, pp. 120-121.

[188] Mt 26:26-29; Mk 14:22-25; Lk 22:15-20; 1 Cor 11:23-25; cf. also Jn 6:51-58.

[189] See Jeremias, *The Eucharistic Words of Jesus* (New York: C. Scribner's Sons, 1966), pp. 218-262.

ing communion with God and with one's neighbor is the ultimate mystery of the Kingdom. First Jesus alone is able to accomplish it, but then he calls all disciples to follow his example and participate in what he has done.

So far, then, we have seen that, even if, as a result of critical examination, we accept at this point only a small number of Gospel texts as historical, it appears that Jesus considered his imminent death as part of God's saving plan — in fact as his ultimate service — by which he was to enter the Kingdom and make others, "the many," or "his disciples," share in it. We have seen here a double movement. Through the voluntary offering of his life, Jesus enters the Kingdom, but, at the same time, by this act of voluntary death, he makes the Kingdom present for his disciples. All this is anticipated and already realized in a hidden way at the Last Supper.[190]

3. The sacrifice of the Servant

The words of institution, in both their Markan-Matthean and Pauline-Lukan forms, contain allusions to the Suffering Servant Song of Isaiah (in particular to 53:11,12) and to the account of the covenant sacrifice at Sinai (Ex 24:8). These allusions have led several exegetes to conclude that Jesus understood his death as establishing a new covenant in his blood and as expiation for the sins of the world by carrying out the self-offering of the Servant. B.F. Meyer lucidly sums up their conclusions:

> Supposing for a moment that the Markan text approximates the original words more closely than any other, we may answer the second and third questions as follows. (How did the original words of Jesus interpret the elements? How accord-

---

[190] In John, the double action of entering the Kingdom and making the Kingdom present is expressed in other terms: Jesus goes away to the Father to prepare a place for the disciples, yet the disciples are already united with Jesus as branches to the vine: they abide in Jesus. See Jn 13-16.

ingly did they interpret the distributing to eat and drink?) A first word related the bread to the body of Jesus soon to be put to death; a second word related the wine to the blood of Jesus soon to be shed, in fulfillment of two sacrificial "types": the sacrifice that seals the covenant and the expiatory death of the Servant of God for the sins of the world. To give the disciples this bread to eat and this cup to drink was accordingly to give them a share in the eschatological covenant now defined by the imminent death of Jesus for the forgiveness of sins.[191]

If Jesus had not understood his death as fulfilling the Servant's offering of his life for the forgiveness of all sins (Is 53:10,12), we would be hard pressed to explain the origin of the earliest pre-Pauline kerygma, which goes back to the first years after Jesus' death and resurrection. How could the Early Church discover so quickly that Jesus "died for our sins in accordance with the Scriptures" (1 Cor 15:3), in an environment that knew nothing of a Messiah offering his life for the forgiveness of sins, if the disciples did not receive any directions from Jesus himself?[192]

That Jesus understood his death as expiating all sins is also confirmed by the fact that, after Easter, the disciples did not withdraw into a ghetto, as the Essenes did while expecting God's judgment over sinful Israel, but offered forgiveness to all who were baptized into the name of Jesus, including Gentiles. They were convinced that baptism in the name of Jesus forgave all sins. Where could they gain this conviction if not from what Jesus said and did before his death?[193]

Yet many exegetes refuse to attribute even the beginnings of this expiatory interpretation to Jesus himself on the grounds that the "historical Jesus" offered forgiveness freely, without implying the need for any "ransom" or "sacrifice." They see an opposition

---

[191] B.F. Meyer, "The Expiation Motif," p. 472.

[192] I owe this conclusion to an oral communication from W.R. Farmer.

[193] Cf. B.F. Meyer (agreeing with R. Pesch), "The Expiation Motif," pp. 476-477.

between what they call the Early Church's interpretation of Jesus' death as expiatory and Jesus' own free offer of forgiveness as illustrated in his parables of divine mercy. Ultimately, however, their perception of this opposition seems to rest on a narrow, cultic notion of Old Testament sacrifice. It is true that the "object sacrifices" of the Jewish liturgy are not directly related to the Eucharist by the New Testament. In other words, Jesus' blood that seals the New Covenant is not directly compared to the blood of bulls sacrificed at Mount Sinai, or to the blood of the Passover Lamb, but to the voluntary outpouring of the Servant's life.[194]

However, if — following the model of the Suffering Servant — we understand sacrifice in the existential sense of offering one's life for God in order to obtain forgiveness for humankind, the continuity between Jesus' public ministry and the Last Supper as a sacrificial meal becomes quite obvious. Jesus' free offer of forgiveness was not a condescending announcement from above, but an act of solidarity with sinners from the beginning; and acts of solidarity always require, to varying degrees and in different ways, a gift of the self to those with whom one enters into solidarity. In obeying his Father's will that prefers mercy to the external sacrifices of the Temple (Mt 9:13; 12:7), Jesus goes after the lost sheep and when he finds it he carries it back on his own shoulders (Lk 15:3-5). In other words, Jesus' life is a service for re-gaining the sinners in obedience to God's will.

While he had a relatively easy job in converting tax collectors and prostitutes, his solidarity with sinners provoked the wrath of the self-righteous leaders of society, and his preaching and miracles failed to convert the masses. Thus, it was precisely Jesus' free offer of forgiveness that revealed the intractable nature of sin, its apparently unbreakable power of resistance. Instead of converting Israel,

---

[194] Compare Is 53:10-11 with Mk 14:24. According to John Jesus is the true Passover Lamb sacrificed in the Temple only in the sense that he is the Servant who freely offers his own life as sacrifice and goes to the slaughter without opening his mouth. In this way he fulfills what the actual sacrificial lambs could have only foreshadowed (cf. Jn 1:29, 36; 19:36 with its reference to Ex 12:46; Nb 9:12).

Jesus provoked their hatred and rejection. However, rather than withdrawing from the mainstream of Jewish life and establishing his separate community as the Essenes did, Jesus gave more and more of himself for his sinful people. He went straight into the city that had murdered the prophets before him and, by announcing her imminent doom, he made a last effort to bring them to repentance. In order to fulfill his Father's will, he went right into the midst of his enemies, exposing himself to their wrath. Thus, his freely accepted death was not the first act of his gift of self to God for his people, but its consummation. Seen in this context, the notion of his death as an expiating sacrifice is not opposed to the initial announcement of loving forgiveness. From the very beginning, his life was a sacrifice in that he carried out his Father's will every day by loving his sinful people in situations that demanded an increasing gift of himself. His death on the cross merely completed the sacrifice he had begun in his life.[195]

While the Synoptics do not make explicit that Jesus suffered death out of love, the sayings of Jesus about the love of one's enemy common to Matthew and Luke provide a clue to the meaning of his death. He did practice what he preached. Instead of turning away from those who persecuted him, he turned the other cheek; he did not repay evil with evil (Mt 5:38-48) but loved his enemies even on the cross (Lk 6:27-36). Upon arriving in Jerusalem, he went into the Temple to denounce those who turned it into a "robbers' den," even though he must have foreseen that this act would provoke even more the hostility of the Sadducees. His death is, then, only the final act of this self-offering love that embraced the repentant sinner and rebuked the hardened self-righteous in order to save both from the coming doom. His solidarity with his sinful people, first dramatized by undergoing the baptism of John, now achieved its consummation when he died the sinner's death between two condemned criminals.

---

[195] The Letter to the Hebrews draws the final consequence of this view when it shows that Jesus began his sacrifice at the moment of coming into this world: 10:5-10.

4. "My God, my God, why have you forsaken me?"

Both Matthew (27:46) and Mark (15:34) report the cry of Jesus in Aramaic: "My God, my God, why have you forsaken me?" It is hardly conceivable that such a cry of despair would be the creation of the early community, which had such a hard time to reconcile the abandonment of Jesus by the Father with Jesus' divine dignity. Moreover, why would Mark create an Aramaic saying for his Gentile audience? Luke and John even omitted this cry, presumably because it seemed irreconcilable with their own high Christology. All these considerations support the authenticity of the cry.

However, if Jesus uttered these words on the cross, then he may have been praying Psalm 22, which begins with these words.[196]

It does not seem unlikely that Jesus — pious Jew that he was — prayed on the cross the Psalm that most closely corresponded to his life situation. It is a common tendency in Scripture to draw attention to an entire text by quoting only its beginning verse. This Psalm, then, while beginning with a cry of despair and an expression of abandonment, ends on a note of confidence and hope. The result of the just man's suffering will be the conversion of the gentiles and the establishment of God's universal Kingdom:

> All the ends of the earth
> shall remember and turn to the Lord;
> all the families of the nations shall bow down before him.
> For dominion is the Lord's,
> and he rules the nations (Ps 22:28-29).

5. Foretelling his resurrection?

The stylized refrain-like predictions of the handing over, suffering, death, and resurrection of the Son of Man were formulated

---

[196] Note that Jesus never addresses God as God but rather as Father, except when he quotes the Scriptures.

by the Early Church *post eventum*, after the events had taken place. Yet, as we have seen, Jesus announced his immediate partaking in the banquet of the Kingdom after his death (Mk 14:25) and implied that his death would usher in the Kingdom of God (Mt 26:64). Moreover, Jesus' belief in the resurrection of the dead is well attested to in all four Gospels (Mt 22:23-33; Mk 12:18-27; Lk 21:27-40; Jn 6:54). In this matter he agreed with the Pharisees over against the Sadducees. Why would he have made an exception for himself, especially when he was aware of the saving efficacy of his death? Thus, the prediction of his resurrection and exaltation is *a priori* very likely even if we are unable to reconstruct its exact form.[197]

The confidence of Jesus about the fact that his death signified the consummation of his service, the entrance into his reign, and the way to his resurrection need not have diminished in any way the anguish and agony (well attested to in the texts) that he experienced before his death. Jesus was truly man, truly on this side of the divide that separates our life, attached to empirical certainties, from the invisible and transcendent world of God. Jesus, of course, remained God while living a human life. **But precisely the transcendent power of his love enabled God to become so truly and really man that he fully experienced the value of our human life in this world and thus also the horror and dread of having to give up this life.** In this all four Gospels and the Letter to the Hebrews agree. According to these sources, it cost Jesus all his strength to put his human life — and through it his whole self — "with no strings attached" into the hands of the Father (Lk 23:46).

---

[197] The sign of Jonah, in its Matthaean formulation — "Just as Jonah was in the belly of the whale three days and three nights, so will the Son of Man be in the heart of the earth three days and three nights" (12:40) — could have hardly been created as a *vaticinium ex eventu* , since it contradicts the very early tradition that Jesus rose on the third day, and thus was in the earth for only one night and a half and for one full day. Thus, instead of being a creation of the Early Church or an editorial composition, the Matthean saying is more easily explained as an authentic word of Jesus. That Luke omitted the reference of the sign of Jonah to Jesus' burial may be explained as a result of his concern not to confuse his readers with such an imprecise prediction. If this is so, then Jesus predicted only that he would be dead for a short while ("three days and three nights" have this meaning in Hebrew and Aramaic style), without specifying the details (cf. O. Cullmann, *The Christology of the New Testament*, p. 63).

6. The Kingdom and the end of this world

Ever since Albert Schweitzer came upon the idea, exegesis, in one way or another, has shown a recurring tendency to attribute to Jesus the (mistaken) proclamation of an early catastrophic end of the world.[198]

The exegetes sympathizing with Schweitzer's position point to sayings of Jesus which announce that "there are some standing here who will not taste death until they see that the Kingdom of God has come with power" (Mk 9:1: par. Mt 16:28; Lk 9:27) and to the eschatological discourse in Mk, ch. 13, especially the words: "Amen I say to you, this generation will not pass away until all these things have taken place" (v. 30; cf. Mt 24:34). According to Schweitzer's followers these statements can only mean that Jesus believed in a chronologically imminent end of the world.

Here I can explore only in outline form the relationship of the Kingdom to the end of the world in the message of Jesus and in the understanding of the Early Church. It is a well-established fact that the Early Church, notably Paul in his earlier letters, expected the Parousia (the glorious coming of the Lord that would put an end to history) to occur in his own lifetime. Nevertheless, it cannot be proved that Jesus himself taught such a chronologically imminent end. Mark 9:1, which speaks of the coming of the Kingdom of God in power, and its parallels in Matthew and Luke all appear in the context of an injunction to follow Christ on his way to the cross. Moreover, the sons of Zebedee who want to sit at the right and left hand of Jesus in his Kingdom are immediately confronted with the question: "Can you drink the cup I am going to drink?" (Mt 20:20-28; cf. Mk 10:35-45). In Luke, before his death, Jesus promises a share in the banquet of the Kingdom to his disciples who stood by him in his trials (Lk 22:28-30). **Thus, at the least, there is evidence for an early and widely known tradition**

---

[198] Most recently, T. Sheehan, *The First Coming. How the Kingdom of God Became Christianity* (New York: Random House, 1986). But even O. Cullmann, who has justified a "high Christology" on the basis of the New Testament, maintains that Jesus was, on this point, mistaken.

which links the coming of the Kingdom to the death of Jesus and a share in the Kingdom to sharing in the cross of Jesus.

Furthermore, Dodd points to the interesting parallel between Mark 9:1, "the Kingdom of God come in power" and the ancient pre-Pauline kerygma preserved in Romans 1:4: "...established as Son of God in power... through resurrection from the dead." This parallelism may have resulted from the intuition of the Early Church that the Kingdom of God come in power means the risen Christ established as Son of God in power. Matthew's version makes the christological dimension of the Kingdom even more explicit.

> Amen, I say to you, there are some standing here who will not taste death until they see the Son of Man coming in his Kingdom (16:28).

In Matthew the Kingdom of the Son of Man is clearly distinguished from the Kingdom of the Father.[199]

The first is established with the resurrection when all power has been given to Christ (13:41; 16:28; 28:18-20). This Kingdom of the Son of Man is provisional and becomes visible in the community of the Church. It still contains the good and the bad and at the end it will yield to the Kingdom of the Father (13:43).[200]

What this means for Matthew becomes clear in the words with which Jesus replies to the interrogation of the high priest at his trial before the Sanhedrin. He distances himself from the claim the high priest wants to attribute to him, "Are you the Messiah, the Son of God?" He replies: "You have said so." That is, these are your words, not mine, it is your attempt to impose a claim on me, not necessarily my claim. Then he adds:

> But I tell you: From now on you will see "the Son of Man seated at the right hand of the Power" and "coming on the clouds of heaven" (Mt 26:64).

---

[199] Cf. *Matthew*, The Anchor Bible, pp. LXXXVIII-CV.
[200] Cf. the similarity with 1 Cor 15:24-28 and Col 1:13.

Thus according to Matthew Jesus is established as the heavenly Son of Man through his condemnation and crucifixion, a transcendent king, who according to Daniel 7:13-14 will share in God's power and dominion. This conception is very close to that of John, according to which Jesus will be exalted as Son of Man, the universal eschatological King, at the moment he is lifted up on the cross (12:32).

We must then conclude that the saying of Jesus underlying Mark 9:1 and Matthew 16:28 does not necessarily mean the coming of the Kingdom as the end of the world, but rather the rule of the Son of Man established through his death and resurrection.[201]

The precise time of the Last Judgment and the end of the world in the eschatological discourses of Jesus remains obscure. Mark 13:30 and Matthew 24:34 do indeed suggest that "all these things" will happen before this generation passes away. However, the words "all these things" (*tauta panta*) seem to refer in both Mark and in Matthew primarily to the destruction of Jerusalem that anticipates the catastrophic end of the world. Moreover, the saying is immediately preceded by the parable of the fig tree, which concludes: "He is near, at the gates" (Mk 13:29; Mt 24:33). This last statement restricts the meaning of "all these things" to the assertion that the Son of Man, the judge of all, is very near. The phrase "all these things" certainly includes the condemning judgment of the Son of Man over Jerusalem but not necessarily the consummation of judgment over the whole world. The destruction of Jerusalem that Jesus predicted did indeed take place in 70 A.D., before that generation passed away. Jesus described the destruction of that city as a prophet and apocalyptic visionary. In the prophetic and

---

[201] Note that Luke's parallel text to Mk 9:1 and Mt 16:28 does not apply directly to the coming of the risen Christ but rather to his transfiguration, to which it is explicitly linked in 9:28. For Luke the Church is not designated as the Kingdom of the Son of Man; the term Kingdom is reserved for what will come at the end of times, and the period following the resurrection of Jesus is the time of the Church. Yet even for Luke the Son of Man is enthroned in heaven from the moment of his condemnation (Lk 22:69) and rules his Church with sovereign power through the Spirit. In this connection, note that Stephen sees the Son of Man standing at God's right hand (Ac 7:56) at the moment of his martyrdom.

apocalyptic tradition of Israel an historic event, whether one of doom such as the collapse of the Hellenistic Empire (Dn 7:8-27) or of peace, prosperity, and religious renewal (such as the rule of the king Hezekiah described in Is 7 and 11), is seen as the anticipation and guarantee of the final doom and final Messianic Kingdom. In a similar way, according to Mark and Matthew, Jesus announces the destruction of Jerusalem as the beginning and guarantee of the end and final judgment of the world. When Jerusalem falls, the glorious coming of Jesus is indeed at the door; the spring of the new world is near. That this constantly threatening imminence did not mean a chronological nearness became clear only in the last writings of the New Testament (Jn 21:22-23; 2 P 3:3-14).

The widespread belief in the Early Church regarding an early Parousia can perhaps be explained by the popular Jewish belief that the resurrection of the dead is connected with the end of the world. Since Jesus himself is risen, the end must be near. Another reason for this expectation could have been the very obscurity of the words of Jesus who himself confessed that not even he, "the Son," knew the day and the hour of the final consummation of the world (Mk 13:32; Mt 24:36). At the same time, however, he knew and announced that his own "consummation" through death was chronologically imminent (cf., for instance, Lk 13:32).

While confessing his ignorance about the date of the end of the cosmos and final judgment, Jesus stressed that the Day of Judgment cannot be calculated; it will come absolutely unexpectedly, as a thief in the night.[202]

Therefore the only right attitude is to be constantly on the watch and live as if each moment were the last.[203]

We may summarize our findings in the following propositions.

---

[202] The saying about the thief occurs in five places in quite varied documents of the New Testament, which points to an origin in Jesus himself (Mt 24:43; Lk 12:39; 1 Th 5:2; Rv 3:3; 2 P 3:10).

[203] Bultmann's existential eschatology does indeed have a foundation in the New Testament, but the eschatology of the NT cannot be reduced to that one dimension.

1. One cannot prove that Jesus gave any chronological indication about the end of the world and the Last Judgment.
2. On the contrary, he confessed his ignorance about its date and stressed that it would come when people expected it the least.
3. Jesus reached his final "eschatological state" through his death and resurrection; he has been enthroned as the Son of Man, the eschatological King in power.
4. Insofar as the risen Lord is present and active in the world, particularly through his Church, we already anticipate the Kingdom of God in our history.
5. All those who die a death similar to his will join Jesus in his final state of glory and share in the fullness of the Kingdom.
6. The Kingdom will be established in its fullness (the "Kingdom of the Father" according to Matthew and Paul) when all suffering, death, and sin will have been destroyed, which will occur at a time only the Father knows.
7. Yet we are encouraged to pray every day for its coming and every day we are in some real sense also heard, because the more we succeed in subjecting ourselves to Christ in faith and love, the more he will rule and transform our lives.

7. The implicit Christology of Jesus

In the earlier part of the century a tension and even opposition developed between what a dogmatic or systematic theologian and what a professional exegete found in the Scriptures about Jesus. On the one hand, systematic theologians were eager to identify "explicit statements" from among the "authentic" words of Jesus himself in support of the dogmatic truth of Jesus' divinity, his equality with the Father, and his pre-existence. Many modern exegetes, on the other hand, felt compelled to acknowledge with Harnack that "the Gospel as Jesus proclaimed it, has to do with the Father only and not with the Son."[204]

---

[204] A. von Harnack, *What Is Christianity?* reprinted in 1957, p. 144.

In recent times the greatest theologians, a H. Urs von Balthasar or W. Kasper were able to resolve the dilemma and build a truly Catholic systematic Christology that is honestly and deeply biblical. Yet among many representatives of these two branches of theology the tension is still simmering. The following considerations should help to eliminate this apparent contradiction.

1. If Jesus is truly the Son, he should be expected to speak about his Father rather than about himself. A Jesus with an "explicit Christology," a Jesus who would put his own person and dignity at the center of his preaching, would appear highly suspicious, indicating a megalomaniac personality.

2. Since the mission of the Son was to become "like one of us in all things but sin," he would have defeated his mission of solidarity and self-emptying had his preaching centered on his own transcendent greatness.

3. Since Jesus viewed Jewish monotheism as the starting point for his teaching, he would not have done anything to destroy or weaken it. Thus, he had to abstain from presenting an "explicit Christology." Only at the end, when he gave up his life in obedience to the Father and rose from the dead, could his identity be understood: he is not a "second god," a rival to Yahweh, but the Son whose divine dignity and being consist precisely in receiving everything from his Father. In other words, only his disciples could develop an explicit Christology, after seeing his life and pondering his teaching in the light of his death and resurrection.

After these prolegomena, however, we need to study what is often called "the implicit Christology of Jesus"; we will ask with his contemporaries, who do you claim to be? It is clear that all the Gospels center on this question and attempt, each in its own way, to answer it. Their answer, however, is given from the perspective of the resurrection and often with the formulations that the Early Church developed after several decades of reflection on the mystery of Jesus. As explained at the beginning, in general I also approach the New Testament texts in the light of this Easter faith.

Yet, at this point, relying on the work of exegetes, I intend to isolate, with a certain degree of probability and even certainty, the sayings of the earthly Jesus from the later kerygmatic and catechetical formulations of the Church. On the basis of these sayings and events I will then try to describe the "claim" Jesus made during his earthly life. Such an investigation is necessary to show that the Easter faith of the disciples in Jesus as the Son of God and God himself is not discontinuous with, nor unrelated to, the earthly figure of Jesus of Nazareth. On the contrary, it was the itinerant rabbi from Nazareth himself who laid the foundation for their Easter faith.

Harnack exaggerates in saying that the original Gospel of Jesus is only about the Father and not the Son. Yet the important kernel of truth in his statement is that the transcendent identity and dignity of Jesus is revealed primarily in the way Jesus speaks and acts in his Father's stead and in the way he relates to his Father.

1. Thus Jesus announces: "The Kingdom of God is among you" (Lk 17:21). Those "who have ears for hearing" hear also the implication: **The Kingdom of God is among them because in the words and mighty deeds of Jesus God himself is present and active:** Jesus drives out the demons "by the Spirit of God" (Mt 12:28).

2. God's power present in Jesus is a power of merciful love that not only heals the sick but also goes after and forgives the repentant sinner. Jesus' table fellowship with sinners — as Kasper observes — implies his awareness that he has the power to proclaim God's forgiveness for their sins. The Pharisees clearly perceive the enormity of his claim: "Who but God alone can forgive sins?"[205]

By forgiving sins Jesus attributes a divine authority to him-

---

[205] Mk 2:7. By pointing to the passive voice in Jesus' words, "Child, your sins are forgiven", E.P. Sanders does not perceive anything unique or blasphemous in Jesus' claim. According to him Jesus simply claims to act as a spokesman for God, what any prophet or priest would be entitled to do. Sanders, however forgets that Jesus proclaims God's forgiveness in response to faith in him (2:5); moreover, according to Mark, the Pharisees, unlike Sanders, did perceive Jesus' claim as usurping God's authority (*Jesus and Judaism* [Philadelphia: Fortress, 1985], pp. 273-274).

self. The forgiveness he pronounces is the forgiveness of God himself.

3. When introducing his teaching on the Kingdom, Jesus' formula is most unusual. Instead of using the customary address of the prophets: "Thus says the Lord" or "Oracle of the Lord," he announces: "I (however) say to you," or "Amen, I say to you." He does not simply transmit the message of someone outside of himself as the prophets did, nor does he distinguish his own words from the word of God. His "I" speaks with an absolute divine authority that ranks above the divine Law mediated by Moses. **His words are directly God's word.** The "Amen, I say to you" is an introductory formula peculiar to Jesus and unknown elsewhere in Jewish circles, though it makes sense only in a Jewish environment.[206]

Amen is an adverb derived from the root *aman* meaning solidity, firmness, and faith. It is always used as a response, and, when as a response to God, it expresses total submission to his word (Ne 8:6); it may also serve as a liturgical acclamation by which the community makes its own the prayer and the praise of someone who prays in its name (1 Ch 16:36).[207]

Thus the "Amen" preceding an address of absolute authority: "I say to you" contains in nucleus the whole of Christology.[208]

As Grundmann remarked long ago, the Amen of Jesus has a "hidden prehistory"; it is the final act of a dialogue between the Father and Jesus.[209]

The word of Jesus is of divine authority because it comes from the Father. Yet the Father's divine word is Jesus' own, not that of an "Outsider" as in the case of a prophetic message. Here we have

---

[206] Luke in several instances translated Jesus' opening "Amen" as *alethos* or *ep'aletheian* (e.g., 9:27; 4:25) because the original would not have made sense to his Hellenistic audience. Yet the fact that the other evangelists do not translate it into Greek shows their respect for this original turn of phrase of Jesus and the importance they attribute to it. See more on this, H. Schlier, "Amen," *TWNT*, I, pp. 339-342.

[207] "Amen," *DBT*, p. 13.

[208] See Schlier, "Amen," p. 341.

[209] W. Grundmann, *Das Evangelium nach Markus* Berlin, 1959, p. 85. quoted by K. Karner, "Die Anrede in der Botschaft Jesu," *Der historische Jesus und der kerygmatische Christus*, ed. W. Ristow & K. Matthiae (Berlin: Evangelische Verlagsanstalt, 1962), p. 408.

a first hint of the mystery of Jesus' personal identity: his absolute authority is based on his absolute dependence on his Father. John's Gospel paraphrases this concise introductory formula in various ways: "My teaching is not my own but is from the one who sent me" (7:16). "I do nothing on my own, but I say only what the Father taught me" (8:28). The book of Revelation goes one step further and shows not only that Jesus' word is a response and a witness to the Father, but that Jesus himself is "Amen"; his very person is the response, the "faithful witness" to the Father (3:14).

4. The way Jesus handles his disciples is unique in comparison to the way other rabbis treated theirs. A young man who wanted to learn the Law searched out a famous rabbi and joined him, becoming part of his household until he reached a certain level of expertise. After that point the disciple left and established himself as a teacher of the Law in his own right. Not so with Jesus. He searches out and calls whom he wills, with a sovereign freedom, while others who wish to join him he sends away (Mk 1:16-20; 2:14; 5:18-19; Lk 5:1-11; Jn 1:35-51). Thus discipleship is based on Jesus' election, not on the disciple's initiative. Nor is discipleship a mere temporary relationship to Jesus. One remains a disciple of Jesus all his life and is enjoined never to aspire to the rank of teacher and rabbi (Mt 10:24-25).

> It is in the sense of this permanent difference of rank, that in Matthew's Gospel the later Church came to accept the saying of the Lord as their rule: "But you are not to be called rabbi, for you have one teacher, and you are all brethren" (Mt 23:8).[210]

Those whom Jesus calls must not only abandon all their possessions, but also prefer him to their closest family ties, in fact, to their own lives:

> If anyone comes to me without hating his father and mother,

---

[210] G. Bornkamm, *Jesus von Nazareth* ; ET: *Jesus of Nazareth* (New York: Harper & Row, 1960), p. 145. See also pp. 144-152.

wife and children, brothers and sisters, and even his own life,
he cannot be my disciple (Lk 14:26; cf. Mt 10:37).

One of the most sacred duties for a Jew was to bury his parents.
Yet the demand of discipleship takes precedence even over that
duty. Someone whom he called pleads with him:

> "(Lord), let me go first and bury my father." But he answered
> him, "Let the dead bury their dead. But you, go and proclaim
> the kingdom of God" (Lk 9:59-60).

His contemporaries must have asked themselves: "Who is this man
who dares to demand such an unconditional loyalty to his person,
an absolute allegiance that stands above the most intimate human
relationships and even the attachment to one's own life?" Yet, again,
in this area too, we encounter the paradox of Jesus' attitude: **the
absolute allegiance to his person is ultimately an allegiance to God.**
Jesus' whole life is a response to a divine "demand" (*dei*): he must
accomplish his mission in obedience, and he includes his disciples
in the same mission. **His divine authority to call to unconditional
discipleship is based on his own unconditional obedience to his
Father.**
5. The approach to Jesus' parables that had nervously declined
any allegorical interpretation as later misunderstanding and insisted
that every parable of Jesus originally must have had only one point
to make has long become obsolete. Today it is widely recognized
that in the Gospels (just as in the Old Testament and in rabbinic
literature) there is no sharp distinction between parable and allegory.[211]
In fact, Jesus' parables are meant to shake people up, make
them think and realize that they can never fully exhaust the meaning of his stories and similes. While one should not attempt to
correlate every detail of a parable with a separate significance, ev-

---

[211] For instance, the very basis of the parable of Jesus about the wicked tenants of the vineyard is Isaiah's allegory: Is 5:1-7.

ery parable has more than one point to make and is — by its very nature — applicable to a whole range of various situations. More- over, and this is our chief concern here, **many parables of Jesus, if not all of them, have an implicit Christology** the evangelists them- selves have exploited, especially the author of John, and subsequent ecclesiastical tradition followed.

The well-intentioned and biblically educated hearer of the Parable of the Lost Sheep must have asked himself: who is the shep- herd who goes after the lost sheep? He would have found that in Ezekiel it is God himself who promises to do so: "I will rescue them from every place where they were scattered when it was cloudy and dark" (34:12).

In listening to the Parable of the Prodigal Son, the audience may have realized that the father who runs to meet his lost son and prepares a great banquet for him shows forth some of the features of God the Father. If that is so, the banquets of Jesus with the re- pentant sinners make visible this merciful love of God the Father. **Thus he who sees Jesus forgiving sinners and celebrating their newly found life sees God's own merciful love in action.**

One of the shortest similes, and yet fraught with the deepest christological implications, is given by Jesus as a reply to a ques- tion about fasting:

> People came to him and objected, "Why do the disciples of John and the disciples of the Pharisees fast, but your disciples do not fast?" Jesus answered them, "Can the wedding guests fast while the bridegroom is with them? As long as they have the bridegroom with them they cannot fast." (Mk 2:18-19)

In the prophetic tradition the whole history of Israel is dramatized as a love story between Yahweh, the jealous husband, and Israel, his unfaithful wife. However, at the end of times Yahweh will bring about the conversion of his unfaithful bride and a joyous wedding feast will be celebrated (Ho 1-3; Is 62:1-5; Jr 3:1-3, Ezk 16). The audience is here confronted with the question, who is the bride- groom? Those who know the Scriptures cannot avoid the conclusion that Jesus compares himself to Yahweh, the bridegroom of his people. Could it be that in Jesus Yahweh himself is coming for the messianic wedding feast?[212]

As the storm of opposition against Jesus gathers strength and his life is increasingly endangered, he tells his enemies the Parable of the Wicked Tenants.[213]

Many parables of Jesus contain some apparently incongruous, surprising details that are meant to stir up the interest of the audience, and even more importantly, call attention to the gap that separates the behavior patterns of this world from those of God.[214]

Such shocking features serve as a clue to understanding the main thrust of the parable. In the story of the Wicked Tenants (Mk 12:1-9; Mt 21:33-40; Lk 20:9-15), the revealing incongruous feature is the reaction of the father after he learns that the servants sent to the tenants were beaten or killed. Instead of ordering the destruction of the tenants, he sends them his son, saying: "They will respect my son" (Mk 12:6 and par.). How could a father be so reckless and foolish as to act in such a manner? In the logic of the parable his decision is comprehensible only if he trusts the tenants to recognize the difference between all previous messengers, and his own son, and if he hopes that the tenants will be awed by the incomparably greater dignity of the latter. Thus the main thrust of the parable is not the prophetic prediction of judgment over Israel, but a last warning to the leaders not to murder the son, for which they would deserve the most severe judgment. The qualitative dif-

---

[212] The Early Church definitely drew these conclusions after the resurrection, which is why Matthew transformed the Parable of the Banquet into the Parable of the Wedding Feast arranged by a king for his son. He seems to have combined two original parables of Jesus, that of the Banquet and the above mentioned simile of the Bridegroom and the Wedding Guests.

[213] According to J. Charlesworth the substance of the parable in its Markan form could not have originated after the death of Jesus and is thus authentic. See *Jesus within Judaism. New Light from Exciting Archaeological Discoveries* (New York: Doubleday, 1988), pp. 145-149.

[214] For instance, the father forgetting his dignity in running to meet his lost son, a behavior totally ridiculous in an oriental head of the family; the owner of the vineyard paying the same wage of one *denarius* to those who worked all day and to those who worked for only one hour; the shepherd abandoning the 99 sheep in search of the one who got lost.

ference between the messengers (all prophets who came before Jesus) and the son (Jesus) is a given of the story; without it, the parable would not make any sense. This parable shows, then, that in trying to prevent the leaders from committing the ultimate crime, Jesus is willing to speak more about himself; he does not want to leave any doubt for the leaders of the people about his own unique dignity. Yet this self-revelation is indirect and open-ended, since it occurs in a parable. **In this way the parable-teller avoids being squeezed into any existing, prefabricated formula and rather invites his audience to think for themselves and decide about his identity.**[215]

6. The saying of Jesus common to Matthew and Luke about the men of Nineveh and the queen of the South who will arise on the Day of Judgment to condemn this generation points to the same setting: Jesus wants to stir up his unrepentant audience and make them realize that they call judgment down upon themselves because they refuse to recognize who he is:

> At the judgment the men of Nineveh will arise with this generation and condemn it, because they repented at the preaching of Jonah; and there is something greater than Jonah here. At the judgment the queen of the South will arise with this generation and condemn it, because she came from the ends of the earth to hear the wisdom of Solomon; and there is something greater than Solomon here (Mt 12:41-42; cf. Lk 11:31-32).[216]

---

[215] Jesus' question to the crowd about the identity of the Messiah ("How do the scribes claim that the Messiah is the son of David? David himself, inspired by the Holy Spirit, said: 'The Lord said to my lord, sit at my right hand until I place your enemies under your feet.' David himself calls him 'lord'; so how is he his son?": Mk 13:35-37, par.) is in the same vein as the above parable. It does not give ready-made formulas but rather shatters the customary patterns of thinking about the Messiah. Thus this question might also derive from the earthly Jesus and aim at the same purpose: to stir up further reflection about who Jesus is.

[216] Matthew also has a similar saying: "I say to you, something greater than the Temple is here" (12:6). In the previous verses Jesus compares his disciples who accompany him to those who do priestly service in the Temple on the Sabbath. His argument is: if the former are exempt from the violation of the law of rest, his disciples should *a fortiori* be even more guiltless since "something greater than the Temple is here." Thus the implication

Who, then, is this Jesus, affirmed to be greater than the prophet whose word was powerful enough to convert the Ninevites, symbol of the worst Gentile sinners? Who is the one said to be greater than Solomon, whom tradition made the wisest man and the source of the wisdom tradition in Israel? The audience itself must draw its conclusion; Jesus merely makes sure they cannot escape confronting the issue.

7. As we have seen, when encountering hostile or indifferent audiences Jesus at times pressures them to consider the question of his identity. In the presence of his disciples, however, he allows his unique relationship to the Father to become more manifest. In particular, he lets them see and hear his prayer. As J. Jeremias has rightly observed, it does not matter whether each and every instance of addressing God as "Father" ("Abba") in Jesus' prayer is historically authentic. Nor can we exclude evidence that some Jewish charismatic miracle workers may sometimes also have called God "Abba," Father. Nevertheless, no one can deny Jeremias' conclusion that Jesus uses the address "Abba," Father, in all his prayers, with the exception of the prayer on the cross in Matthew and Mark where he quotes Ps 22:2.[217]

This fact is unique in the history of Israel. Israel as a whole considered itself the son of God so some prayers were addressed to God as "Father in heaven" at the time of Jesus. Yet it never became the prevailing form of calling upon God. "King," "Ruler of the universe," "my Lord and my God" were much more frequent and more characteristic addresses for Jewish prayer in the time of Jesus.[218]

---

is clear: serving Jesus is a more sacred duty than serving in the Temple of Yahweh. Here Matthew is very close to John's view, according to which Jesus spoke about his own body as the new and definitive Temple of God (Jn 2:19-21).

[217] See J. Jeremias, *The Prayers of Jesus* (Philadelphia: Fortress Press, 1978), p. 55. For possible Jewish parallels (which Jeremias denies) see D. Flusser, *Jesus*, pp. 93-98.

[218] Cf. Jeremias, *The Prayers of Jesus*, pp. 11-29. Note that the word "Abba" expressing the unique, filial relationship of Jesus to God has been used by the earliest, pre-Pauline Christian communities to characterize the Christian's share in that relationship. When using this term in his letters (Gal 4:6, Rm 8:15), Paul assumes that his audience is already aware of its meaning and significance. See more in D. Farkasfalvy, "Jesus Reveals the Father: the Center of New Testament Theology," *Communio* 26 (1999), pp. 235-257, esp. 240-249.

The word "abba" was primarily a family word meaning "father" in the emphatic and vocative case or "my father." **In using this address in all his prayers, Jesus shows an awareness of a unique intimacy with God.** He distances himself from his disciples in this respect. He does not address God together with them as "our Father." **Yet he bestows on them a share in his own unique relationship with his Father.**[219]

For the first Christians the word "Abba" was so expressive of the unique relationship of Jesus to God in which they were all given a share in the Spirit that even the Hellenistic communities of Galatia and Rome preserved the Aramaic word in their Greek liturgy (Gal 4:6; Rm 8:15). So did the Gospel of Mark, which was meant for a Gentile Christian audience. It is remarkable that, of all possible scenes, Mark quotes the address of Jesus to his Father in the original Aramaic precisely at the moment of his agony:

> Abba, Father, all things are possible to you. Take this cup away from me, but not what I will but what you will (14:36).

Only in the agony of Gethsemane and of the cross does the full depth and strength of the relationship between Jesus and his Father come to the fore: Jesus is abandoned by everyone and is supported only by an unbounded trust in his Abba.

We have looked only at some fragmentary evidence, fragments that can be responsibly attributed to the earthly Jesus, even though I believe that all the Gospel traditions describe him authentically. However, my purpose in this section was to provide for the claim of the earthly Jesus some historical evidence based on the work of reliable exegetes; I gathered a series of converging indications, which should not be easily dismissed by an open-minded historian. Such an open-minded historian and theologian was the Jewish Martin Buber, who studied the New Testament throughout his long life and made this confession about Jesus:

---

[219] John makes it clear that we become the brothers (and sisters) of Jesus through his death and resurrection. It is then that his Father becomes our Father (Jn 20:17).

My own fraternally open relationship to him has grown ever stronger and clearer, and today I see him more strongly and clearly than ever before.

I am more than ever certain that a great place belongs to him in Israel's history of faith and that this place cannot be described by any of the usual categories.[220]

Buber's words come very close to my own conclusion in this section. **Without the perspective of the resurrection all one can say is that the words and works of the earthly Jesus do not fit any preconceived human category:** he appears greater than a rabbi, a charismatic miracle worker, or a prophet; he seems closer to God than any other human being, but he is also more humiliated and a more abysmal failure than any so-called "great historical personality" as he hangs on the cross abandoned by even his closest disciples. **Yet this very inability to squeeze him into the straitjacket of familiar human roles and identities spurs us on to ask the question again and again, "Who is this man?"** This urgency applies, not only to those who are searching and have not yet found him, but also to the believers who can never feel satisfied with their own grasp of his mystery.

We then return to pursue the understanding of the mystery of Jesus in the light of his resurrection by following the lead of the Apostolic Church.

---

[220] *Two Types of Faith. A Study of the Interpenetration of Judaism and Christianity* (New York: Harper Torchbooks, 1961), pp. 12-13.

CHAPTER VI

The Understanding of the Mystery of Christ in the Apostolic Church

The shameful death of Jesus on the cross appeared, even to his followers, a scandal, a stumbling block, which suggested that his claim was false and his mission a failure. The Jews took seriously Dt 21:23: he who was executed by being hanged on a tree is rejected by God; he cannot be the Messiah: instead of God's favor, it is his curse that rests on him.[221]

Only the appearances of the risen One could have convinced the disciples that the crucifixion had to be the way to the resurrection and exaltation of their Master. Then, by receiving the Spirit of Christ and Christ himself in the Spirit, they began to understand the Scriptures. They discovered that his death and resurrection took place "according to the Scriptures."

Already the earliest kerygma declares that the whole of the Old Testament, not merely a collection of "proof texts" (even though such "*testimonia*" may have been collected), announces Jesus as the Messiah. They see that what happened **had to** happen in this way, because this fulfilled God's plan. They begin to identify the patterns or, to use a technical term, the "types" of Jesus and of his saving work in the major figures and events of the Old Testament. What would otherwise have remained an incomprehensible scandal, the "cursed death" of a false Messiah, appears now in the light of its Old Testament types as the event that has saved the world. All the promises God has made in the Old Testament find their fulfillment in Jesus of Nazareth. But an even more startling dis-

---

[221] See more on this in M. Hengel, *Crucifixion* (Philadelphia: Fortress, 1977), pp. 84-85.

covery is made: Jesus the Messiah is Lord in the same sense as Yahweh is the Lord of his people and of the entire universe. While there is only one God, the man Jesus himself is God. However, if Jesus himself is God and nevertheless Jesus has a personal relationship to God, there must be a distinction in the one God: Jesus cannot simply be identical with the God of the Old Testament; he is the Son of God who, after his death and resurrection, sends the Holy Spirit from his Father upon all the believers. As the eternal Word, and Wisdom of God, the Son has been already at work from the beginning of history: he is the one in whom the universe has been created, and he is Yahweh himself in whom Israel encountered God in many forms and ways throughout her history. These mysteries, however — including even what is irreducibly new in the New Testament revelation — could only be expressed by re-thinking and re-applying the terms of the Old Testament.

According to M. Hengel the essential part of the process of this "apotheosis of the crucified Jesus" took place in less than two decades:

> The discrepancy between the shameful death of a Jewish state criminal and the confession that depicts this executed man as a pre-existent divine figure who becomes man and humbles himself to a slave's death (Ph 2:6-8) is, as far as I can see, without analogy in the ancient world. It also illuminates the riddle of the origin of the Christology of the Early Church. Paul founded the community in Philippi in about the year A.D. 49, and in the letter which he wrote to the believers there about six or seven years later he will have presented the same Christ as in the preaching which brought the community into being. This means that the "apotheosis of the crucified Jesus" must already have taken place in the forties....[222]

We need to investigate some of these issues in more detail.

---

[222] *The Son of God. The Origin of Christology and the History of Jewish-Hellenistic Religion* (Philadelphia: Fortress Press, 1976), pp. 1-2.

A. "ACCORDING TO THE SCRIPTURES"

1. "In all the Scriptures" (Lk 24:27)

As we have seen above, the death and resurrection of Christ took place "in accordance with the Scriptures" already in one of the earliest pre-Pauline kerygmatic formulas of the Church (1 Cor 15:3-4). In his Letter to the Romans, when summarizing the kerygma of the Early Church, Paul says even more: God has already "promised" or "announced beforehand through his prophets in the Holy Scriptures" the good news, the *euaggelion* about his Son (1:2). While in other places Paul sums up the whole Old Testament as "Law and Prophets" (Rm 3:21), he sees also in the books of Moses a prophetic anticipation of Christ (cf. 1 Cor 10:1-11). Thus it is likely that in Rm 1:2 the "Holy Scriptures" stand for all the sacred books of the Jewish people.[223]

The whole of the Old Testament, then, appears as a promise or "pre-Gospel" whose object is Jesus Christ.[224]

We find the clearest theological synthesis on the christological interpretation of the whole Old Testament in 1 P 1:10-12:

> Concerning this salvation, prophets who prophesied about the grace that was to be yours searched and investigated it, investigating the time and circumstances that the Spirit of Christ within them indicated when it testified in advance to the sufferings destined for Christ and the glories to follow them. It was revealed to them that they were serving not themselves but you with regard to the things that have now been announced to you by those who preached the good news to you (through) the Holy Spirit sent from heaven.

---

[223] See D. Farkasfalvy, *A római levél* (Eisenstadt: Prugg Verlag, 1983), p. 2.

[224] Cf. also Lk 24:27, 44-45. The enumeration of "the law of Moses," "the prophets" and "the psalms" was a standard way of summing up all the sacred Jewish books at that time. Again, these terms show that according to Luke all the Sacred Scriptures of Israel refer to Jesus.

What assures the unity of the prophetic and apostolic proclamation is that the object and subject of the two proclamations are ultimately one and the same. The object of the prophetic proclamation and of the preachers of the good news is "the sufferings destined for Christ and the glories to follow them." The subject is the Spirit of Christ who "testified in advance" through the prophets and now inspires the evangelists.

While the New Testament insists that all the Scriptures refer to Christ, one can discover only a limited group of texts that had already been used in the earliest kerygma of the Church and a further group added by the individual writers of the New Testament documents. C.H. Dodd has convincingly shown the existence of the former and identified the texts (which he calls *testimonia*). He divides these apparently disparate texts into four classes. Here I list and explain — with some modifications — only those testimonies which Dodd considers of primary importance:

I.   Jl 2-3; Zc 9-14; Dn 7.
II. Ho 6:1-3; Is 6:1-9:7; 11:1-10; 28:16; 40:1-11; 61:1-2;
     Jr 31:10-34.
III. Is 42:1-44:5; 49:1-13; 50:4-11; 52:13-53:12; Ps 69; 22;
     31; 38; 88; 34; 118; 41; 42; 43; 80.
IV. Ps 8; 110:2; Gn 12:3; 22:18; Dt 18:15, 19.

The first group consists of eschatological-apocalyptic texts which speak about the end of history and the tribulations, final victory, and exaltation of the purified remnant of Israel, which is symbolized in Daniel 7:14 as one individual, the Son of Man. This eschatological Israel will become the center of a renewed humanity upon whom the Spirit of the Lord will be poured out. The second group contains prophetic texts that announce God's condemnation of sinful Israel and, after the destruction, the raising of Israel to a new life by God as well as the coming Kingdom of God himself. The third group consists of the Servant passages in Deutero-Isaiah and some Psalms, all of which describe the suffering of the innocent whom God rescues from certain death. The fourth group contains a variety of texts without a common theme.[225]

Dodd sees in the Servant passages of Deutero-Isaiah, and particularly in 52:13-53:12 (every verse of this song is quoted in the New Testament) the key by which the New Testament writers discovered a "single plot" in all these different texts that, at first sight, do not seem to fit together at all.[226]

I would rather propose that both the Suffering Servant and the Son of Man texts provide the key for the christological reference of many Old Testament themes.[227]

The Suffering Servant without sin takes upon himself the sins of Israel, in fact, the sins of all humankind, and thereby undergoes the condemning judgment God inflicts upon sinners. By suffering vicariously for the sins of a multitude, he is exalted as the Son of Man. The Son of Man in glory represents and embodies the eschatological Israel restored to life and glory with God. Thus, according to the New Testament it is through the Suffering Servant exalted as the glorious Son of Man that God himself establishes his Kingdom.[228]

This selection and conflation of texts results in a creative new understanding of Israel's history and of world history, an understanding that both respects and extends the original historical meaning of the texts. Moreover, it enables the individual theologians of the New Testament, in particular Paul and John, but also later ex-

---

[225] C.H. Dodd, *According to the Scriptures. The Sub-Structure of New Testament Theology* (Collins, Fontana Books, 1965), pp. 107-108.

[226] Recently, R. Schwager has also selected the Servant Songs of Deutero-Isaiah as the climax of the Old Testament. But he thinks that this text is irreconcilably opposed to many other Old Testament passages which do not contain any revelation of the true God but rather project human violence into his image. Dodd, on the contrary, shows this text as a key to a synthesis through which the whole Old Testament coalesces into a whole and finds its meaning. See R. Schwager, *Must There Be Scapegoats? Violence and Redemption in the Bible* (San Francisco: Harper & Row, 1987), pp. 1-135.

[227] Here I follow the insight of O. Cullmann who sees the combination of these two titles by Jesus as the key to understand his mission. See, *The Christology of the New Testament*, p. 161.

[228] Cf. Dodd, *According to the Scriptures*, pp. 102-103.

egesis, to enlarge the selection of texts and ultimately to center the whole Old Testament around this one single "plot," God's plan of salvation culminating in Jesus Christ.[229]

Here I will only outline some of the most important christological themes that emerge from the Old Testament through the mediation of the Servant and Son of Man texts.

2. The Suffering Servant of Yahweh

There are four "Servant of the Lord" songs inserted into Deutero-Isaiah: 42:1-9; 49:1-6; 50:4-11; 52:12-53:12. The Servant appears to be primarily an individual, occasionally identified with Israel (49:3). But, as an individual, he accepts full solidarity with his people. Jesus never designates himself explicitly as the "Servant." His characteristic self-designation is "Son of Man." However, according to Jesus, the Son of Man, in order to be glorified, must fulfill the destiny of the Suffering Servant. As we have seen, the words of Jesus allude to the Fourth Servant Song while the Apostolic Church relates all four songs to the figure of Jesus. Thus, it may be helpful to summarize the contents of all four, taken as a unit.

The Servant was chosen by God; God's favor rested on him. God formed him in the womb; he gave him a name from his mother's womb and put his spirit on him. His vocation was not just to return a remnant of Israel to the Lord but also to be a light to the nations, so that God's salvation might reach to the ends of the earth (42:1-6; 49:1-6). He was to open the eyes of the blind, to bring out prisoners from confinement and darkness, and to establish God's justice over all the earth (42:4, 7). God would give a covenant to his people in the person of his Servant (42:1, 6).

The Servant had the tongue of a disciple (50:4). God opened

---

[229] *Ibid.*, pp. 102-103. Like Cullmann, Dodd does not hesitate to attribute the origins of this highly creative interpretation of the Old Testament to Jesus, since the other creative geniuses of apostolic Christianity, Paul, the author of John, and the author of the Letter to the Hebrews all presuppose rather than create it. *Ibid.*, pp. 109-110.

his ear morning after morning so that he might hear God's Word (50:5). Thus the Servant was like a sharp-edged sword, an arrow in God's quiver (49:2).

He fulfilled his vocation without any great publicity or ostentation (42:2). He was merciful: "A bruised reed he shall not break and a smoldering wick he shall not quench" (42:3). Yet his work called forth opposition, hatred, and torture. But he continued to obey God's call and perform his work. He did not return violence for violence. He gave his back to those who beat him and his cheeks to those who plucked his beard and did not turn away from buffets and spitting (50:5-6). Even though his life and work seemed to be a complete failure, he never lost trust in God (50:9-10).

He was disfigured beyond human appearance: people spurned and avoided him because they thought his suffering and humiliation were due to God's just punishment (52:14; 53:3). But in reality he was innocent (53:9), and, as a lamb led to slaughter, he remained silent before his accusers and voluntarily submitted to the punishments we ourselves deserved for our sins (53:7-8). "The Lord put upon him the guilt of us all" (53:6). He was condemned (by a court) and put to death, and it seemed that his fate would be forgotten (53:8). A grave was assigned to him among evildoers (53:9). Yet, since he gave his life as a sacrifice for sin and interceded for sinners, the saving will of God was to be accomplished through him (53:10). Because of his voluntary sacrifice the Servant was to take away the sins of many, including those of the Gentiles.[230]

He would be exalted by God to the heights, would see the light and his descendants in a long life (52:13; 53:10-11).

When reflecting on these details of the four songs, one cannot help recalling the outline of Jesus' public ministry and the account of his passion in all four Gospels. The Songs of the Servant helped the Apostolic Church to understand the meaning of Jesus' life and passion, but, in turn, these texts also shaped and formed the way the story of Jesus was told.

---

[230] Note that the "many" in 53:12 and 52:14-15 are parallel and therefore the "many" in 53:12 includes also the Gentiles. Cf. B.F. Meyer, "The Expiation Motif," pp. 477-478.

3. The Son of Man

Jesus does not call himself Messiah or Son of God in the Gospels; his usual self-designation is "Son of Man," "*bar enasha*" in Aramaic.[231]

The expression has various meanings in various contexts. It simply refers to Jesus as "any man"; it designates him as the Servant who has to be delivered unto death and rise again; it characterizes him as a witness before God at the eschatological judgment; and it can also mean Jesus himself as the eschatological judge.[232]

There are analogies in the Old Testament, in intertestamental literature and later Jewish writings for the eschatological use of "Son of Man."[233]

However, we find three unique features in Jesus' usage of "Son of Man" for which no parallels have been found: First, the generic meaning "any man" used as a circumlocution for "I." Second, the conjunction of the role of the Servant in Deutero-Isaiah with that of the Son of Man in Daniel 7:14. Finally, the conjunction of the

---

[231] The expression makes sense only in Aramaic or Hebrew, in Greek it becomes awkward and ambiguous.

[232] An enormously vast literature exists on the subject and it has been inconclusively debated whether Jesus used this expression at all; and if so, what occurrences of the phrase should be attributed to him; moreover, did he refer to himself or to a future figure and what are the meanings of the phrase? See W.O. Walker, Jr., "The Son of Man: Some Recent Developments," *CBQ* 45 (1983), pp. 584-607; M. Müller, *Der Ausdruck "Menschensohn" in den Evangelien. Voraussetzungen und Bedeutung* (Leiden: Brill, 1984); J.R. Donahue, "Recent Studies on the Origin of 'Son of Man' in the Gospels," *CBQ* 48 (1986) pp. 484-498.

[233] Ezk, passim, Dn 7:14, Talmud, the Ethiopic version of the *Similitudes of Enoch*. Donahue agrees with J. Fitzmyer and G. Vermes that "the Son of Man is not a *messianic title* in any of its pre-Christian stages" (487), while J.H. Charlesworth on the contrary believes the opposite. In interpreting I En 48:1-10 and 53:6 (which, according to Charlesworth, "originated in Judea and was in use at Qumran before the beginning of the Christian period": *The Old Testament Pseudepigrapha*, ed. J.H. Charlesworth [Garden City, NY: Doubleday, 1983], vol. I, p. 8), he argues in this way: "Are not 'that Son of Man,' 'the Chosen (or Elect) One,' 'the Righteous One' (53:6), and 'the Messiah' different titles or descriptions for the same person?" Charlesworth is also persuaded that Jesus "knew and was influenced by Daniel and 1 Enoch 37-71, even if it was via the traditions that flowed to, or through, or from these apocalypses" (*Jesus within Judaism* [New York: Doubleday, 1988], pp. 41-42).

Son of Man in Daniel 7:14 with the "Lord" sitting at God's right hand in Ps 110:2.[234]

In Daniel, the vision of "one like the Son of Man" follows the vision of the four beasts representing four earthly kingdoms. The Son of Man is a mysterious heavenly figure: he comes "on the clouds of heaven," which shows he belongs to God's sphere of mystery, and reaches the Ancient One, from whom he receives dominion, glory and kingship. A mysterious heavenly being, he is the symbol of eschatological Israel: he stands for "the holy ones" or the "holy people of the Most High" (7:22, 25, 27). Before their glorification, the "holy ones" will be oppressed by the fourth beast (representing the kingdom of Antiochus IV), but in the book of Daniel their suffering is not considered redemptive.

As Jesus' self-designation in the Gospels, the title "Son of Man" identifies Jesus with every human being, especially those in extreme need; but the title refers also to one individual, the Servant of God, who is handed over into the hands of sinners in order to redeem us from our sins. It is through his redemptive suffering that the lowly Son of Man assumes the role of the heavenly, glorious Son of Man in Daniel who comes in judgment. He will not only approach the throne of the Ancient One but will sit as Lord at his right hand (Ps 110:2). Thus, combined with the role of the Servant of Yahweh and with that of the "Lord" sitting at God's right hand, the title "Son of Man" embraces a depth, breadth, and height unprecedented in its previous or contemporary usage. In the words of Cullmann, "'Son of Man' represents the highest conceivable declaration of exaltation in Judaism; *ebed Yahweh* is the expression of the deepest humiliation."[235]

We may add that the "Son of Man" meaning "any man" expresses the universality of Jesus' identification with all human be-

---

[234] See Mk 10:45; Mt 12:40; Mt 17:9; Mk 9:12; Mt 17:22; Lk 9:31; 9:44; Mt 20:18; Mk 10:33; Lk 18:31; Mt 26:2; 26:4; Lk 24:7; Mk 8:31; Mt 20:28; Mt 26:62; Mk 13:26; Lk 21:27.

[235] O. Cullmann, *The Christology of the New Testament*, p. 161. Note that *Ebed Yahweh* is the Hebrew term for "Servant of Yahweh."

ings, while its combination with the "Lord" sitting at God's right hand of Psalm 110 further emphasizes Jesus' transcendent dignity. The enormous range of meaning the title "Son of Man" thus takes on, stretching from any man at one end to the glorious divine judge on the other, helps us understand what is to be the criterion of the last judgment: The Son of Man in his glory reveals that he was the human being in need, any man and every man, whom we encountered as the hungry, the thirsty, the naked, the sick, or the prisoner on the roads of our earthly journey.[236]

This synthesis helps us understand the christological meaning of the whole history of the Old Testament, of its priesthood and sacrifices, of its Davidic messianism, and of its connection in Adam with universal human history.[237]

4. Jesus the new eschatological Israel

If Jesus is the Suffering Servant become glorious Son of Man, then he is "the inclusive representative" of his people; he is not merely one of the Israelites, he is in fact the new, eschatological Israel. Hence we can understand from a new perspective that, in being called back from Egypt (Ho 11:1 as interpreted by Mt 2:15), in his temptations, and also in his public ministry that the temptations anticipate, he appropriates and re-lives the history of Israel. In his death he, the sinless one, accepts solidarity with sinful Israel and takes upon himself the judgment that Israel has deserved and thereby allows a new, purified, and glorious Israel to be raised to life.

---

[236] Cf. *Ibid.*, pp. 158-159.

[237] Dodd, Cullmann, Charlesworth, and others attribute the origins of this creative synthesis (not each "Son of Man" saying) to Jesus. Those who refuse to do this, find the origin of the title "intractable," as J.R. Donahue candidly admits: "One of the most intractable problems with the Son of Man is that it appears as a self-designation for Jesus only in the Gospels. If the phrase was important to either the original Palestinian community, to early Hellenists, or to pre-Pauline communities, why is it not attested? If it is so significant in the Gospels, why is it not attested in the later NT literature?" ("Recent Studies," p. 498).

In this perspective, far from being contrived, the application of Ho 6:1-3 to the resurrection of Jesus on the third day sheds light on the mysterious link between the destiny of Israel and that of Jesus:

> It is this far-reaching identification of Christ, as Son of Man, as Servant, as the righteous Sufferer, with the people of God in all its vicissitudes that justifies the apparent employment by the Early Church of Hosea 6:1-3 as a prophecy of the resurrection of Christ; for the resurrection of Christ *is* the resurrection of Israel of which the prophet spoke.[238]

This embodiment in Jesus of the eschatological people of God in the ancient kerygma corresponds to the image of head and body by which Paul expresses the union between Jesus and his Church and to the image of vine and branches, which expresses the same relationship in Jn 15.

5. Jesus as High Priest and Perfect Sacrifice

Without the mediation of the theme of the Suffering Servant we cannot understand how Jesus fulfills the role of the high priest and all the sacrifices of the Old Testament.

Sacrifice, a tangible gift offered to the god or gods, constituted an essential feature of every primitive religion. The motives for offering a sacrifice varied from assuring the favor of a god, expressing thanks, atoning for sins, and celebrating the communion reestablished between God and man.[239]

In Israel, all the above-mentioned features of sacrifice were present, but the unique relationship between Yahweh and the people resulting from their Covenant gave a special character to

---

[238] Dodd, *According to the Scriptures*, p. 103.

[239] Nevertheless, these features are constantly distorted in primitive religions and often turn into the opposite of true sacrifice: instead of expressing man's dependence on the Sacred, they want to assure man's control over the sacred forces.

magic

their sacrifices: the Israelites gave thanks for the blessings of the Covenant, celebrated the communion established by the Covenant, and atoned for the offenses committed against it. The attitude they call for is the faith of Abraham by which he was ready to give to God what was dearest to him, his beloved and only son, the carrier of God's promises (Gn 22).[240]

This inner attitude of complete surrender and obedience to God was to be symbolized in the offering of material gifts. Similarly, the sacrifices for the forgiveness of sins were rejected as of no value unless they expressed the inner attitude of a humble and contrite spirit (Ps 51:19, 21).

In practice, however, sacrifice in Israel became reduced to a daily routine, an abuse the prophets did not cease to condemn:

> Hear the word of the Lord,
> princes of Sodom!
> Listen to the instruction of our God,
> people of Gomorrah!
> What care I for the number of your sacrifices?
> says the Lord.
> I have had enough of whole-burnt rams
> and fat of fatlings;
> In the blood of calves, lambs and goats
> I find no pleasure...
> Your hands are full of blood!
> Wash yourselves clean!
> Put away your misdeeds from before my eyes;
> cease doing evil; learn to do good...
> If you are willing, and obey,
> you shall eat the good things of the land (Is 1:11, 16, 17a, 19).

The perversion of sacrificial practice denounced in such passages lay in replacing conversion of heart and obedience to God's will with a material gift to God. Instead of using the ritual gift as an expression of the obedience of faith, the Israelites trusted in the

---

[240] Cf. "Sacrifice," in *DBT*, p. 513.

magic efficacy of the ritual sacrifice: If they performed the prescribed rite and made the obligatory offering, **God had to save them.** A commercial transaction was made; a bargain was struck, so they could safely continue their crimes.

Jesus makes his own this prophetic criticism of the sacrificial system and the Temple when he reminds his hearers: "Go and learn the meaning of the words: 'I desire mercy, not sacrifice'" (Mt 9:13 quoting Ho 6:6; cf. Mt 12:7; Mk 12:33). From this perspective we can also understand his cleansing of the Temple. In the Synoptics Jesus complains with the words of Jeremiah that God's house has been turned "into a den of thieves" (Jr 7:11); in John he echoes Zc 17:21 in denouncing the Jews for turning his Father's house into a market place (Jn 2:16; Mk 11:17 and par.).

In view of Jesus' emphasis on the importance of inward attitude we can understand why no text of the New Testament presents the death of Jesus simply as the fulfillment of the ritual sacrifices of the Old Law. The direct foreshadowing of Jesus' sacrifice is the self-offering of the Servant. Thus, for example, the meaning of the Passover sacrifice had first to be reinterpreted through the voluntary self-oblation of the innocent Servant in the Christian tradition before St. Paul could declare that "Christ, our paschal lamb, has been sacrificed" (1 Cor 5:7). Paul and his audience were aware that this true paschal lamb was not an animal but a living human being, the Servant, who allowed himself to be led to the slaughter silently (Is 53:7; cf. also 1 P 1:19).

In John Jesus is even more explicitly identified both with the Servant and the paschal lamb in the declaration of John the Baptist: "Behold the Lamb of God who takes away the sins of the world" (1:29, 36). This declaration prepares us to understand his death as that of the true paschal lamb whose bones were not broken and whose blood flowed out immediately (19:33-34).[241]

---

[241] *Talja* in Aramaic can mean both lamb, child, and servant. The phrase "lamb of God" is nowhere applied to the paschal lamb, while, on the contrary, the Servant of God is compared in Is 53:7 to a lamb who takes away the sins of many (53:12). Thus it is likely that John purposely joins together the two figures. See O. Cullmann, *The Christology of the New Testament*, pp. 71-72.

In the Letter to the Hebrews the description of the ritual sacrifices as unceasingly offered by the high priest underscores their uselessness for obtaining the forgiveness of sins. Jesus, the high priest according to the order of Melchizedek, is described as having some similarities with the ritual priesthood of the Old Testament (cf. Lv 16). Yet some of the features that makes his priesthood unique, such as offering his own life rather than the blood of goats and bulls, his sympathy for, and solidarity with sinners come not from the priestly figure in Leviticus, but from the last Suffering Servant Song. Isaiah 53 is present in the form of implicit quotes throughout Hebrews.[242]

The exegetes who try to downplay the importance of the sacrificial interpretation of Jesus' work in the New Testament are often led to do so by the fear of giving too much weight to cult and ritual at the expense of Jesus' personal self-giving.[243]

In the light of the *Ebed Yahweh* Songs that form its immediate background, however, it is clear that the sacrificial interpretation of Christ's death in the New Testament brings forth precisely this personal and existential aspect of his ultimate act of obedience.

6. Jesus the Messiah

The combination of "Son of Man" and "Suffering Servant" sheds light on a favorite title of the early catechesis. It may seem surprising that Jesus never attributed to himself the title "Messiah," "*Christos*," which was to gain such popularity in the Apostolic

---

[242] For instance, Is 53:4 in Heb 2:10; 53:12 in Heb 7:25; 9:28; 53:10 in Heb 9:25; 10:12; 53:4 in Heb 13:13. On the theology of sacrifice in the New Testament see in more detail A. Feuillet, *The Priesthood of Christ and His Ministers* (Garden City, NY: Doubleday, 1975).

[243] This was, at least, my impression in reading X. Léon-Dufour, *Life and Death in the New Testament* (San Francisco: Harper & Row: 1986), pp. 85-89.

Church that it was soon added to his personal name. Jesus became known as Jesus Messiah, *Iesous Christos,* Jesus Christ.[244] When others called him "son of David," which is a form of address equivalent to that of Messiah, Jesus tolerated it. But when in the name of the Twelve Peter confessed him to be the Messiah, according to the Synoptics Jesus immediately imposed silence on the disciples. He even corrected, or at least deepened their understanding of the title "Messiah" by adding that the Son of Man must suffer and be raised from the dead (Mk 8:30-31; Mt 16:20-21; Lk 9:21-22). In other words, according to the Jesus of the Synoptics, the true meaning of Jesus' Messianic Kingship was to be revealed only in his death and resurrection, when the Son of Man — through the path of suffering — would have been exalted.

John sees the death, resurrection, and exaltation of Jesus as one event. Pilate had the cause for his crucifixion hung above Jesus' head in three languages, Aramaic, Greek, and Latin: "Jesus of Nazareth the King of the Jews" and stubbornly defended it against the protest of the Jewish leaders. In doing so, he acted out of mockery. But in John's perspective this is a case of supreme irony; unknowingly, Pilate became an instrument in God's plan and proclaimed to the world what really happened in the crucifixion: Jesus was enthroned on the cross as the king of the universe (Jn 18:28-19:22).

The kings from David's dynasty, the types of the Messianic king, failed to live up to their calling; even the greatest one, David himself, committed sins. Their vocation was to represent Yahweh to his people, to be instruments by whom Yahweh would carry out his rule. Yet they could not resist the temptation to disobey the true king of Israel and attribute God's role to themselves (cf. 2 S 24:1-25). It is most remarkable that, when the Son of God himself be-

---

[244] The use of the title *Christos* in the Gospels is another indication that the Gospels deserve more credit regarding historical facts than extreme critics are willing to admit. If the evangelists simply put on the lips of Jesus the titles created by the Early Church without any regard for historical tradition, why did they do it precisely with the "Son of Man" which is not used in the early kerygma or catechesis and why did they not use *Christos* as a self-designation of Christ, a title most common in early kerygma and catechesis?

comes man, he does not claim kingship here on earth before he suffers. According to the Letter to the Hebrews, it was appropriate that the leader to salvation be perfected through suffering (2:10) and that, even though he was Son, he learn obedience from what he suffered (5:8). **Jesus becomes the perfect instrument of God's universal rule and the perfect revealer through his humanity of God's glory only after he has completed the giving over to God of his entire human existence by the last act of obedience on the cross.**

7. Jesus as son of Adam and the last Adam

As already mentioned, the phrase "Son of Man" also has a meaning quite opposed to that of the heavenly King and the glorified Israel: it simply identifies a member of the human race, a son of Adam. In this sense it often brings out the fragile, small, and mortal condition of man in contrast to God:

> When Ezekiel, a man of mute adoration prostrates before the glory of God, is called by Yahweh "son of man" (Ezk 2:1.3, etc.), the term marks the distance, and reminds the prophet of his condition as a mortal.[245]

In several "Son of Man" sayings of Jesus this humble and universal human condition appears in the foreground, while his transcendent dignity remains hidden (Mt 8:20 and par.; Mt 11:19; 12:32, and par.). This meaning provides a basis for Luke and Paul to stress the universal dimension of the person and work of Jesus. For Luke, Jesus is not only Abraham's son, but also the son of Adam. Just as Adam had no other father but God, so does Jesus (Lk 1:35; 2:49). As Adam is the beginning of sinful humanity, so is Jesus the inaugurator of a new, re-created humanity (Lk 3:38).[246]

The first Adam was expelled from Paradise; the new Adam

---

[245] "Son of Man," *DBT*, p. 563.

reenters Paradise as he enters upon his reign on the cross and takes with him the forgiven sinners exemplified in the "good thief" (Lk 23:42-43). In the theology of Paul the parallelism and the contrast between the two Adams is even more explicit. Through the disobedience of the first Adam, death, physical and spiritual, began to reign over humankind. However, the gift of grace that came through Jesus Christ was more powerful than the avalanche of sin the first Adam had started. Through Jesus' obedience everyone is offered the grace of a new life with God (Rm 5:12-21).

The first Adam fell and brought death upon humankind because he wanted to grab equality with God for himself. The second Adam became the source of new life for all humankind by not clinging to his status of equality with God but emptying himself, taking the form of a slave, and becoming obedient even to death on a cross (Ph 2:6-8).

In his resurrection and exaltation, the second Adam became "a life-giving spirit" for all humankind. Those who believe in him and share in his sufferings will be gradually transformed into his likeness; at the resurrection they will all share in his glory (1 Cor 15:45-49; 2 Cor 3:17-18; Rm 8:29; Ph 3:21).

Thus this transcendent heavenly man, the last, the eschatological Adam, has shown us the way to become truly human in a direction exactly opposite to what human wisdom would suggest, not by achieving independence, power, and greatness, but by the way of humility, obedience, and embracing one's cross.

8. Jesus as the final and complete theophany of God

The Apostolic Church not only characterizes Jesus by the historical and ideal figures of the Old Testament (the Servant of God, the Son of Man, the new Israel, the new David, the true high priest and sacrifice, the new Adam)[247]; at a somewhat later stage of

---

[246] Cf. *Bible de Jérusalem* (Paris: Cerf, 1974), p. 1487, n. c.

reflection (in Matthew, Colossians, and John), it discovers that **the various revelations of God in history beginning with the creation of the world, and the saving events of Israel's own history, are all gradual manifestations of the Son, the personal Wisdom and Word of God.** According to Colossians, Christ has been already at work in the creation of heaven and earth — obviously as Divine Wisdom, although this is not made explicit here — "all things were created through him and for him... and in him all things hold together" (Col 1:16-17; cf. also Heb 1:2).

Matthew implies that Jesus is Wisdom incarnate. After chastising the lack of response in the people, Jesus refers to himself by declaring: "but wisdom is justified by her children" (Mt 11:19). Jesus as Wisdom invites everyone to take upon himself his yoke (Mt 11:28-30).

While in Matthew the Old Testament activity of Wisdom, her seeking a home and coming to dwell in Israel, is only alluded to,[248] John makes the pre-incarnation history of the Word-Wisdom explicit. The Prologue of the Fourth Gospel presents the outlines of a universal salvation history. All that God has done, beginning with the creation of the universe, he has done through his pre-existent personal Word or Wisdom who is the same subject as Jesus Christ. The whole of history, of both Israel and the world, is to be viewed as a progressive coming of the Word who at length becomes flesh as Jesus Christ. He is the light who has illumined every member of the human race. He was present in the Meeting Tent of the desert and in the Temple. Isaiah saw his glory when he saw the glory of Yahweh in the Temple (12:41). His presence among the Israelites in the desert and in the Temple, his indwell-

---

[247] We could have also added, the new Moses, in the sense of the eschatological prophet (cf. Dt 18:15, 19). This title of "prophet" appears in some of the sayings of Jesus (Mk 6:4 and par.), in the reactions of the people (e.g., Lk 7:16) and in the kerygma recorded by Ac 3:22-23; 7:37. However, the title "prophet" was soon abandoned by the Apostolic Church as inadequate.

[248] The allusion consists in the fact that Jesus' activity parallels the activity of Wisdom in the Old Testament.

ing as Wisdom in the hearts of the just are mere preludes to that definitive "pitching of his tent" among us which is the incarnation.[249] John goes farther than any New Testament document in penetrating the transcendent identity of Jesus. He reflects on the scene of Jesus' walking on the stormy sea (a scene described also by Matthew 14:22-33 and Mark 6:45-52) and on the meaning of the encouraging words Jesus gives to the frightened disciples: "Courage! It is I. Do not be afraid." In the reassuring words of Jesus, "It is I" or literally, "I am," John perceives a reference to the divine name, Yahweh, and he understands the scene as a theophany, the revelation of Jesus' divine identity (6:20).[250]

The person who walks on the raging sea and reveals himself as Master over the chaotic forces of nature is the same one who revealed himself to Moses in the burning bush, and freed Israel from the devouring waves of the Red Sea.[251]

The veiled references to Jesus' divine name, Yahweh, constitute an unfolding theme in the Fourth Gospel (8:24, 28, 58; 13:19; 18:5-6, 8). These absolute "I am" (*ego eimi*) statements without a predicate noun or predicate adjective express the absolute mode of divine being that transcends time. Jesus assures the cynical crowd: "Amen, amen I say to you, before Abraham came to be, I AM" (8:58).[252]

Besides describing Jesus' divine nature, however, the "I AM" formula seems to refer to the subject in Jesus. **If the name "Yahweh" describes primarily the personal identity of Israel's God, rather than his divine being, then, applied to Jesus, it must also describe the personal identity of Jesus himself.** In other words, ac-

---

[249] See more on this in D. Farkasfalvy, *Testté vált Szó. I. rész* (Eisenstatt: Prugg Verlag, 1986), pp. 44-64.

[250] Other Synoptic texts which may imply a reference to the divine name are: Mk 13:6 / Lk 21:8; Mk 14:62 / Lk 22:70.

[251] God reveals his name to Moses to provide them assurance, but keeps the mystery of his being intact: "God replied, 'I am who am.' Then he added, 'This is what you shall tell the Israelites: I AM sent me to you'" (Ex 3:14).

[252] See more on this in R. Brown, *The Gospel according to John, I-XII*, The Anchor Bible 29 (Garden City, NY: Doubleday, 1966), pp. 533-538.

cording to John, the name "Yahweh" seems to designate directly the Son. John declares that no one, not even Moses, has ever been able to see God. This has always been the privilege of the Son who alone reveals him (1:18). Thus, in John's perspective, it is the Son whom Moses has encountered, and it is the Son who identified himself as Yahweh for Moses in Ex 3:14, and whom Israel has worshiped as her own God throughout her history. However, just as Jesus, the incarnate Son, always spoke not about himself but about his Father, similarly, the Son in his pre-existent state as Word, Wisdom, and Yahweh, had always pointed beyond himself, to the invisible God (1:18). This interpretation fits in well with the general understanding of the Fourth Gospel (further developed by patristic theology): the incarnation was the definitive arrival of the same One who was speaking to Israel from the beginning and who was gradually drawing near throughout Israel's history.

In this perspective the full meaning of Jesus' prophecy becomes manifest:

> When you lift up the Son of Man, then you will realize that I AM, and that I do nothing on my own, but I say only what the Father taught me (Jn 8:28).

The final and complete theophany of history will take place in the drama of the crucifixion. Only when his own people crucify Jesus, will they realize that they crucified their own Lord and God, Yahweh himself.[253]

But the act of crucifying him will also be the providential means of Jesus' exaltation and of universal redemption:

> And when I am lifted up from the earth, I will draw everyone to myself (Jn 12:32).

---

[253] The pre-Pauline hymn of Ph 2:6-11 reveals an understanding very similar to that of John. Through his obedience unto death on the cross Jesus is exalted and the "name above every other name," that can only be the divine name "Yahweh," is bestowed upon him.

9. The unexpected newness of the New Testament

This last theme shows most clearly that the understanding of the mystery of Christ through the Old Testament transcends all that the Old Testament itself had expected. Even if we consider the Old Testament books in themselves rather than from a Christian perspective, we cannot help perceiving a messianic dynamism and expectation as its most powerful driving force. The growing number of defeats Israel had to endure, the subsequent destruction of the Northern and the Southern Kingdoms, especially the destruction of the holy city of Jerusalem in 586, shook the Jewish spirit, but did not break the hope of a messianic restoration. The Israelites accepted the calamities as well-deserved punishments for their sins, yet their hope in Yahweh's mercy and for a glorious future only grew bolder. Neither the sobering effect of a less than glorious restoration nor the later oppression by Hellenistic kings could make them abandon their messianic hopes. In the apocalyptic literature, however, their hope was transferred from this world to the next, from the realm of history into the new world that God was going to create for his people and for all those who would join his people in the worship of the true God.

Yet, as Daniélou has observed, there ran two parallel lines of messianic expectations all along the Old Testament: on the one hand, a new and greater Moses, a new and greater David, a returning Elijah and a renewed Israel symbolized by the Son of Man, in sum, great men of God or a renewed people of God were awaited who would be patterned upon, but would surpass the men of God and the people of God in the past. On the other hand, the prophets and the apocalyptic visionaries promised the coming of God himself in his reign. These two lines of expectation remained parallel and did not meet in the Old Testament itself. In other words, the incarnation of God in a human being was never promised nor explicitly expected. **The unexpected newness of the New Testament is that God himself becomes the new David, the new prophet, the new Israel, and that God as man takes upon himself** the condemning judgment Israel and mankind have deserved for their sins. However, the New Testament expresses even the irreducible newness of what happened in Jesus Christ primarily by transforming the meaning of the titles and notions taken from the Old Testament. On the following pages I will examine the transformed meaning of the most important titles that have been applied to Jesus.

B. JESUS AS "LORD," "SON OF GOD," AND "GOD"

1. Jesus is Lord

At the time of Jesus the unspeakable divine name "Yahweh" was often substituted for, especially in liturgical prayers, by *Adon* in Hebrew, *Kyrios* in Greek, meaning Lord. In addition to standing for the divine name, in other texts of the Old Testament *Adon - Kyrios* expresses the sovereign dominion of God over the whole universe and, in particular, over his people. Israel belongs to him and owes absolute allegiance only to him, while the Lord God exercises his lordship for the benefit of his people. As long as they obey him, justice prevails and peace flourishes in Israel.

The Gospels attest that the disciples and others called Jesus by the Aramaic title *mari*, analogous to "my lord" or even "sir" in his earthly life, a title appropriate for a highly respected rabbi. This usage was still far from the "absolute sense" of a divine name.

The study of the earliest fragments of Christian kerygma and liturgy has concluded that only in encountering the risen Christ did the disciples understand his transcendent "lordship": Jesus is "Lord" in the absolute sense of possessing divine power and majesty as well as the right to the unconditional allegiance of every human being. One of the earliest texts on the lordship of Jesus is a liturgical hymn (Ph 2:6-11) that Paul incorporated into his Letter to the Philippians, a hymn written within the first three decades of the Church's existence. After it describes the pre-existent Jesus' self-emptying, the hymn also declares his exaltation:

> Because of this, God greatly exalted him
> and bestowed on him the name
> that is above every name,
> that at the name of Jesus every knee should bend,
> of those in heaven and on earth and under the earth (Is 45:23),
> and every tongue confess that
> Jesus Christ is Lord,
> to the glory of God the Father (2:9-11).

Here, as Hengel has pointed out,[254] we have in a concise and conceptually undeveloped form the full christological confession of the Church. The bestowal of the "name above every name" upon the risen Christ clearly means the bestowal of the unspeakable divine name "Yahweh" expressed by the term "Lord" — just as the Jewish liturgy addressed Yahweh by this title. The Isaian text (45:23) that had originally referred to the universal dominion of Yahweh and to his right to the worship of all humankind is enlarged and applied to the exalted Christ. He rules the whole cosmos (the angelic world, the human race and those in the netherworld) and all owe him worship.

Fragments of the kerygma in other Pauline letters and in Acts also contain the very early, pre-Pauline formula: "Lord Jesus" and show its origin in the encounter with the risen Christ (Ac 2:36; Rm 10:9; 1 Cor 12:3). The summary of Peter's first sermon in Acts expresses in archaic language the earliest kerygma of the Church: "God has made him Lord and Messiah, this Jesus whom you crucified" (2:36). Jesus enters upon his reign and receives universal dominion from God at the moment when God raised him from the dead.[255]

In Romans 10:9 the outward confession of faith that "Jesus is Lord" ought to be connected with faith in the heart that "God raised him from the dead." This is the summary of "saving faith" for Paul. But to believe in the resurrection and make this confession of faith

---

[254] See p. 149, footnote #222.

[255] Rm 1:4 speaks about the same reality expressed in synonymous terms. See below, p. 178.

is possible only "by the inspiration of the Holy Spirit" (1 Cor 12:3).[256]

The place where the lordship of the risen Christ is most clearly manifested is the Eucharistic celebration, the "Lord's Supper" (2 Cor 11:20). It is there that his personal presence as the Lord of his Church who rules and transforms our lives is most keenly experienced. The fervent prayer for his coming at the Eucharistic meal, is expressed in the Aramaic acclamation, *Marana-tha,* "Come, Lord" preserved in its original form by Paul at the end of 1 Cor 16:22.[257]

His present coming in the Eucharist is perceived also as a pledge and anticipation of his final advent.[258]

While the risen Christ is Lord over his Church in a special way, his lordship extends over heaven and earth and the netherworld. The power of Satan is broken: he fell from heaven (Lk 10:18; Rv 12:9). The world is still under his influence (1 Jn 5:19), yet he is "bound," and serves the purposes of God (Rv 20:2). The Christian has conquered him in Christ and, when tempted, in faith he can resist him (1 Jn 2:13; 1 P 5:8-9). The difference between the two forms of lordship (the one over the Church, the other over the world) is expressed in various ways. According to Paul, Christ is not only Lord but also the spouse of his Church;

---

[256] Paul describes his "Damascus experience" in a twofold way: he speaks about God revealing his Son to him (see below, p. 179) and seeing "our Lord" (1 Cor 9:1). Luke probably quotes a piece of ancient kerygma when he puts on the lips of the apostles the exclamation: "The Lord has truly been raised and appeared to Simon" (Lk 24:34; cf. 1 Cor 15: 4-5).

[257] Cullmann shows that *Marana-tha* ("Come, Lord") as a liturgical acclamation is a more likely meaning than *Maran-atha,* "the Lord comes," as a confessional formula. Moreover, the fact that Paul preserved the text in Aramaic shows that he considered it a sacred tradition which links the Hellenistic churches to the Palestinian mother church. Those who, following Bousset and Bultmann, assume that Jesus was called 'Lord' in the absolute sense of the word only in Hellenistic communities cannot explain the presence of this Aramaic liturgical acclamation in a Pauline letter addressed to a predominantly Gentile church. See more on these matters in O. Cullmann, *The Christology of the New Testament,* pp. 203-218.

[258] The liturgical acclamation *Marana-tha* is part of the Eucharistic celebration in the *Didache,* x. 6. Cf. on this also L. Sabourin, *The Names and Titles of Jesus* (New York: Macmillan, 1967), p. 254.

thus he not only rules his Church but also unites her to himself in love.[259]

Moreover, in the Spirit the Church is nourished by the Body of Christ and thus becomes herself the Body of Christ. Thus the Church is filled with Christ and manifests Christ to the world. According to John the Christians are "branches" attached to the "vine" who is Christ. Thus the lordship of Christ in the Church is interiorized, it becomes the result of a loving union with him in the Spirit.

Paul also emphasizes that Christ's lordship determines the whole existence of the Christian. The Christian belongs to the Lord. He who eats meat eats it for the Lord, he who abstains from it also does it for the Lord:

> None of us lives for oneself, and no one dies for oneself. For
> if we live, we live for the Lord, and if we die, we die for the
> Lord; so then, whether we live or die, we are the Lord's. For
> this is why Christ died and came to life, that he might be Lord
> of both the dead and the living (Rm 14:7-9).

Accepting the unconditional lordship of Christ as his servant or slave makes the Christian free from the dominion of the law since the Spirit enables him to do God's will freely rather than being constrained by an external prohibition. He is also made free from the tyranny of sin while still struggling daily so that sin may not rule his body; in the power of the same Holy Spirit he is now able to overcome the sinful inclinations of the flesh (Rm 6-8).

Being under the lordship of Christ relativizes every other relationship. The Christian ought to obey the secular authorities even if they are pagan not merely for fear of their punishments but because of his conscience, since all authority is from God for the safeguarding of the common good (Rm 13:1-7). Yet belonging to the Lord liberates us from any kind of slavish attitude towards man. In the absolute sense we have only one Lord and we are only his slaves (1 Cor 7:23; 8:5). From this understanding of freedom and

---

[259] For example: 2 Cor 11:2; Eph 5:25-27; 1 Cor 10:16-17; 12:12-27; Eph 1:23; Col 1:18.

authority Paul draws conclusions about slavery that have scandalized many modern Christians. They fault him for not declaring slavery to be against the God-given dignity of all human beings. Paul indeed does not make such a declaration, and even less does he incite the Christian slaves to escape from or rebel against their masters. He does encourage Philemon to liberate his slave Onesimus (Ph 7-20) and does perhaps suggest that if a slave can become free, he should take such an opportunity (1 Cor 7:21)[260]; yet ultimately one's social standing does not matter, for in the new creation that Christ has brought about "there is neither Jew nor Greek, there is neither slave nor free person, there is not male and female; for you are all one in Christ Jesus" (Gal 3:28).

In this radical unity with each other in Christ and under the lordship of Christ the external social structures remain intact, but they no longer count. In the Christian community the free person should consider himself a slave of Christ while the slave should consider himself a freedman of the Lord. **The new relationship to Christ abolishes all barriers among classes, shows the ground of a radical unity, and provides an integrated Christian community structure.** His relationship to Christ gives such a sense of dignity and inner freedom to the Christian slave that he can endure even an inhuman master in patience and love, while a Christian master ought to be aware of his total dependence on Christ so that he can respect his slave as a man freed by Christ (1 Cor 7:21-23).[261]

In the Gospel of Mark the title *Kyrios* is used primarily of God (Mk 5:19; 13:20).[262]

---

[260] This interpretation, however, is not certain and recommends itself only in the context of the Letter to Philemon. See a different translation for 1 Cor 7:21 in *NAB*.

[261] In the long run, such inner attitudes, once spread throughout the Roman Empire, contributed substantially to the abolition of slavery. Today we rightly emphasize the hard won insight that slavery is indeed against the dignity of human nature and we must work to abolish unjust social structures. Nevertheless, the teaching of Paul has great importance for us even today. Paul knows that those suffering under inhuman oppression, as long as they keep their faith, remain inwardly free; no torture, no human or diabolic power can deprive them of the core of their human dignity which is based on their relationship with Christ. This point has been neglected by certain types of liberation theologies.

[262] Except Mk 11:3 where it applies to Jesus but the meaning is rather that of a Messianic king.

Yet its use in the story of the curing of the Gerasene demoniac has a subtle christological message. After he has cured him, Jesus dismisses the man with these words:

> "Go home to your family and announce to them all that the Lord in his pity has done for you." Then the man went off and began to proclaim in the Decapolis what Jesus had done for him; and all were amazed (Mk 5:19-20).

The words of Jesus reflect his consistently theocentric attitude. For him God the Father is the only Lord. Each Gospel in its own way reveals this all-pervading attitude of worship, praise, and thanksgiving in Jesus who always gives all glory to God. In Mark he tells the young rich man, "Why do you call me good? God alone is good" (Mk 10:18), and he points out the chief commandment: "The Lord our God is the only Lord" (Mk 12:29).

Yet, while Jesus commands the man to announce what the Lord has done for him, the man begins to proclaim (*keryssein* is a technical term for the proclamation of Christian faith) what Jesus has done for him. Thus, the same action of curing that Jesus attributed to the Lord, God of Israel, is attributed by the man (who represents here the Christian evangelists) to Jesus himself. This narrative then hints at the theological rationale on the basis of which the other evangelists began to apply the title *Kyrios* in a transcendent sense to the earthly Jesus (while retaining their fundamental conviction that "the Lord our God is the only Lord"). **The one Lord God acts through Jesus; God's divine lordship is exercised through this man so that, when Jesus performs a divine deed, God himself performs it.**

On this basis Matthew and Luke have people address the earthly Jesus as *Kyrie* in a sense that implies a transcendent dignity. For example, according to Matthew, the disciples threatened by drowning in the storm cry out to Jesus: "Lord, save us, we are perishing" (8:25; cf. 14:30). The use of this form of address reveals the evangelist's conviction that the earthly Jesus is Lord because he acts with the power of God, who alone can save from the powers of chaos and death (cf. Lk 5:8; 7:13).

John adds a unique nuance to the meaning of *Kyrios.* On the one hand, the risen Christ is always called "Lord" by the disciples in John (20:18,25; 21:7,12), and the title is clearly synonymous with "God" (20:28). On the other hand, Jesus, their Lord and God, remains an intimately known human figure who shows the disciples the wounds in his hands and in his side, and prepares a breakfast for them (20:20,27; 21:12). **The identity between Jesus, Lord and God, and the crucified Jesus of Nazareth receives a special emphasis in John. His divine presence is at the same time a familiar human presence that revives and perpetuates the personal ties he forged with the disciples during his earthly life.** This Johannine perspective appears, to some extent, also in Lk 24:3; 24:34.

In a Hellenistic environment where the emperors received divine worship under the title *Kyrios Kaisar,* the Christian confession of *Kyrios Iesous* acquires a very special meaning. In his letter to Trajan, Pliny relates the procedure he used to make Christians recant: they had to acknowledge that "the emperor is Lord," make a sacrifice before the image of the emperor, and curse the name of Christ. Polycarp, a few decades later, would rather be burnt at the stake than say, "Caesar is Lord."[263]

Thus, in the milieu of emperor worship, the confession "Jesus is Lord" expressed the Christian's refusal to recognize any human being other than Christ as divine, any human power over himself as absolute. Under the lordship of Christ he becomes free from enslavement to the state or political rulers while, at the same time, he accepts the order of society in which he lives and its authorities as receiving their power from God.

Especially this aspect of the meaning of the title "Lord Jesus" has retained all its relevance for our age; not only in a dictatorship in which the ruler attempts to usurp absolute control over the individual but also in democratic societies in which people are lured

---

[263] *Martyrdom of Polycarp* VIII, 2.

into embracing political causes or "worship" charismatic leaders with a religious enthusiasm. Jesus remains the only absolute Lord, "the Lord of lords and King of kings" (Rv 17:14) throughout the duration of history. Nevertheless, his rule in this "interim" period remains hidden and he is still struggling in his members against the power of the Evil One. Therefore, the Church and the individual Christian, inspired by the Spirit, do not cease to await the "day of the Lord," the revelation of his presence (1 Cor 1:7). The New Testament ends with the Greek translation of the ancient Aramaic acclamation, "Come Lord Jesus!" (Rv 22:20).

In summary, according to the ancient kerygma the title "Lord" which stands for the unspeakable divine name is bestowed on Jesus at the moment of his resurrection (even though the title has its roots in the reverential address *mari* by the disciples during the earthly life of Jesus). Moreover, the title expresses the divine sovereignty and divine activity, and the universal rule of the risen Christ that demands absolute allegiance on the part of every creature. In the light of the resurrection the Gospels are able to perceive the signs of Christ's divine lordship even during his earthly ministry. Although unknown to the rest of humankind, Christ's dominion extends over the whole world including Satan. His transforming presence in the Eucharistic gathering is a constantly renewed guarantee of his manifest coming at the end of time for which the Church prays unceasingly.

2. Jesus is the Son of God

The title "Lord" expresses the Church's faith that the risen Christ is equal in power, and majesty with God and that God exercises his dominion over the Church and cosmos through him. However, since both the God of the Old Testament and Christ are called "Lord," the term does not elucidate the relationship between God and Jesus. The Apostolic Church attributed several titles to Jesus, such as "the Servant of God," "the Prophet," "the Holy and Just One," "the Messiah," "Lord" and "Son of God." The first three did not survive for a long time. "Messiah" in the form *Christos* became part of the personal name of Jesus, "Lord" continued to be used in the liturgy, but the title, "Son of God," gained decisive importance in kerygma and catechesis. "Son of God" proved to be more theologically expressive than the other titles since it explained the relationship between the God of the Old Testament and Jesus. This title, too, has some important Old Testament roots, and in some instances the Old Testament meaning does appear in the foreground. Israel is considered in the Old Testament the firstborn son of Yahweh (Ex 4:22), the Davidic king is declared son to God in 2 Samuel 7:12-14, and at his enthronement the Davidic king is described as being begotten by God (Ps 2:7). Thus, in some texts of the New Testament Jesus is named Son of God in the sense of being the new eschatological Israel who relives in a new, salvific way his people's history (Mt 2:15); in other texts he is called Son of God in a predominantly Messianic sense (Jn 1:49). Yet in the light of the resurrection the Church realizes that Jesus is Son of God in the two former senses because he is **the** Son of God in an absolute or transcendent sense. It is very significant that in the Synoptic Gospels Jesus does not call himself directly "Son of God," just as he never calls himself "God."[264]

The disciples had to witness his public life, his prayers to his "Abba," and his obedience to him up to the agony of the Garden and up to his last cry on the cross in order to grasp what it means for Jesus to be the Son of God. Any mere verbal self-revelation by Jesus before the crucifixion would have been misunderstood.

In interpreting the appearances of the risen Christ, the Early Church coined a kerygmatic formula, which Paul quotes at the beginning of the Letter to the Romans:

---

[264] In the Synoptics there are only two instances in which Jesus refers to himself somewhat cryptically as "the Son": Mt 11:27 and Lk 10:22; Mt 24:36 and Mk 13:32. Critics are divided whether these sayings are *ipsissima verba*. For our purpose the discussion is of no great importance. The filial relationship of Jesus to God was revealed to the disciples in many ways, but understood only in the light of the resurrection. Yet, as pointed out above (p. 27), Mk 13:32 can hardly be a creation of the Church. Moreover, "Son" in Mt 11:27 has the same transcendent meaning as in Mk 13:32.

> Descended from David according to the flesh,
> established Son of God in power according to the
>   spirit of holiness
> through resurrection from the dead,
> Jesus Christ our Lord (Rm 1:3-5).[265]

This formula presupposes the appearances of the risen Christ in which the disciples understood that their Master lives in the manner of God and is one with God. In the light of this experience they begin to understand the mystery of his earthly life. They know now that since the risen Christ is the same person as the crucified Jesus of Nazareth, Jesus was all along the Son of God in his earthly life. Reflecting back on his prayers, and on his relationship to God during his earthly life they now perceive his prayer and his obedience to be the expression of the Son's relationship to his Father.

In particular, through the literary device of inclusion, by using it to frame his account of Jesus' ministry, Mark makes the title "Son of God" the key to understanding the mystery of Jesus. At one end, we have the statement by the author Mark: "The beginning of the Gospel of Jesus Christ the Son of God" (1:1). At the other end, the climax of Mark's Gospel is reached in the confession of the Roman centurion:

> When the centurion who stood facing him saw how he breathed his last he said, "Truly this man was the Son of God" (15:39).

Only on the cross, while crying out to the world his abandonment by God, does the ultimate depth of the relationship between Father and Son come to light; only here is his obedience to his "Abba"

---

[265] See more on it in M. Hengel, *The Son of God* (Philadelphia: Fortress Press, 1976), pp. 59-60. Our tentative reconstruction of the kerygmatic formula is somewhat different from that of Hengel who follows the work of H. Schlier.

consummated and does it become clear that he has always been the obedient Son of God.[266]

In interpreting his Damascus experience, Paul testifies that God "was pleased to reveal his Son to me" (Gal 1:16). In the appearance of the risen Christ to him Paul must have understood the transcendent, absolute sense in which Jesus is the Son of God. Paul became also aware that the earthly Jesus who descended from David was already Son (Rm 1:3), even though he was established Son of God in power only by his resurrection. In fact, Paul has also understood the pre-existence of the Son. In his theology, to the sending of the Son by the Father there corresponds a voluntary act on the part of the Son prior to his incarnation: the one who was in the form of God and equal to God, empties himself (Ph 2:6-7), the one who was rich becomes poor for our sake (2 Cor 8:9).[267]

Nevertheless, it is in John that we find the most developed understanding of Jesus' eternal sonship. The Son who has always been in the bosom of the Father (1:18), who had his glory with the Father before the creation of the world (17:5), becomes flesh so that he might extend this perfect communion to all who accept him in faith (17:20-26; 1 Jn 1:3). There exists a total and eternal communion of mutual knowledge, love, and life between Father and Son: "everything of mine is yours and everything of yours is mine" (17:10). This communion is so perfect that Jesus declares: "I and the Father are one" (10:30). Yet, even more than the Synoptics, the high Christology of John stresses the obedience of the Son. The Son says only what he hears from his Father (8:26) and does only what the Father tells him to do (5:19-20. 30; 8:28-29). His whole

---

[266] Cullmann rightly points out against the followers of Bousset and Bultmann that Jesus' sonship manifested in his obedience is totally opposed to the Hellenistic stories of "sons of god" or "divine men" (*theioi andres*). *Christology of the New Testament*, pp. 271-278; cf. also other reasons in M. Hengel, *The Son of God*, pp. 21-56. On the title in Mark, cf. L. Sabourin, *Christology: Basic Texts in Focus* (Staten Island, NY: Alba House, 1984), pp. 31-52.

[267] J.D.G. Dunn (*Christology in the Making. A New Testament Inquiry into the Origins of the Doctrine of the Incarnation*, London, 1980) admits pre-existence only in the Gospel of John. L. Sabourin takes issue with this position in *Christology*, pp. 53-69.

life and death express his conscious and willing dependence on the Father.

In both Paul and John the sonship of Jesus is not a jealously guarded privilege he intends to keep for himself — as is the case with the Greek gods. According to Paul God sent his own Son as expiation for our sins (Rm 3:25; 5:6-10; 8:3-4). What the Son of God did to Paul applies to everyone: he "has loved me and given himself up for me" (Gal 2:20). The purpose of Christ's expiatory sacrifice was our adoption as sons of God (Gal 4:5).[268]

This is to be understood not as a mere legal act of adoption: God sent into our hearts the Spirit of his Son in whom we share in the very same relationship the firstborn Son (Rm 8:29) enjoys with his Father, and thus we are able to pray in the same way as Jesus did when we cry out in the Spirit of Jesus, "Abba," Father (Gal 4:6; Rm 8:15).

In John the Son comes to take away the sin of the world (1:29) by giving his flesh for the life of the world (6:51). Those who accept him in faith he gives the power to become in reality children of God (1:12). The Son extends to them the same unity, love, glory and joy that he has had with the Father from the beginning (17:20-26). He goes away in dying so that he may return to them and dwell in them through the Spirit in a new and permanent way and thereby take them to the Father (14:1-30). We become not only his brothers (20:17), but also branches of Jesus, the true vine, so that we may share in his very life (15:1-17). Thus the washing of his disciples' feet sums up symbolically the whole mission of Jesus that culminates in his death (13:1-20). **Jesus' unique sonship, majesty and glory are revealed precisely in the voluntary humiliation by which he puts his whole self at our service.**[269]

---

[268] Paul uses non-inclusive language yet it is obvious that he includes also women in the adoptive "sonship" of God. John's language is here preferable who consistently speaks about "children of God."

[269] Cf. D. Farkasfalvy and R. Kereszty, *The Basics of Catholic Faith* (Irving, TX: Cistercian Preparatory School, 1985), p. 60.

3. Jesus is God

As we have seen, the awareness that the risen Christ shares in God's sovereignty and power, and that he has existed in a condition equal with God before his human birth, was already formulated in the first decades of the Church's existence. The belief itself originated most probably in the appearances of the risen Christ and was prepared for by what Jesus did, said and suffered in his earthly life. Nevertheless, it took a long process of reflection, hesitation and even reluctance on the part of the nascent Church before some of the latest writings of the New Testament dared to apply the term "God" to Jesus.

Two reasons make this long hesitation understandable. The Apostolic Church remained faithful to the teaching of Jesus in reserving the title "God" to the God of the Old Testament, "the Father of our Lord Jesus Christ." In other words, for the Early Church God meant the Father. In calling Jesus God, Jesus' personal relationship to his Father would have become obscured. For instance, if the Father is God and Jesus is God, did Jesus pray to himself?

The other reason that called for extreme caution was the polytheistic environment in which the Christian Church had to proclaim the Gospel. The Christian missionaries fully adopted the monotheism of the Old Testament and wanted to avoid any confusion on the part of a Jewish and Hellenistic audience, which could have easily misunderstood Jesus as a "second god," a rival to the one God of Israel.

The fact that the Fourth Gospel makes the proclamation of Jesus' divinity its most solemn and central teaching, already indicates the awareness of some initial conceptual distinction between divine nature and divine persons.

The Prologue alludes to the eternal communion of God the Father and the Word or only Son who is also God:

> In the beginning was the Word,
> and the Word was with God,

> and the Word was God...
> No one has ever seen God.
> The only Son, God,
> who is at the Father's side,
> has revealed him (Jn 1:1, 18).

The climactic scene of the Gospel is the appearance of the risen Lord to the "doubting Thomas" whom he addresses in these words:

> "Put your finger here and see my hands, and bring your hand and put it into my side, and do not be unbelieving, but believe." Thomas answered and said to him, "My Lord and my God!" (Jn 20:27-28).

Thus the familiar figure of the man Jesus still carrying the wounds of the crucifixion in his hands and side is confessed to be the God who is eternally at the Father's side. Here then, we have a clear understanding that the eternal Son who is God is the same person as the risen Lord and the risen Lord is identical with the earthly, crucified Jesus. Moreover, if the Son is God, he must transcend time[270]; thus both his eternal pre-existence and his birth in time become part of the Christian faith.[271]

Once the divinity of Jesus is expressed conceptually, the drama of our redemption also appears in a new light. Now we can understand the ultimate depth of God's love for humankind. God the Father gave up something not less than himself; he gave God the Son for us. The Father gave all that he has and all that he is in the Son.

Moreover, the real nature of every sin also comes to light: it is an attempt to dispose of God and take his place. The implication of the Parable of the Wicked Tenants becomes clear: the ten-

---

[270] Cf. for instance, "Amen, amen I say to you, before Abraham came to be, I AM" (Jn 8:58).

[271] This belief does not have anything to do with the adoption of a Hellenistic myth; see M. Hengel, *The Son of God*, pp. 21-56. Other texts of the New Testament in which Jesus is called God are: Rm 9:25 (its application to Jesus is questionable); Tt 2:13; 1 Jn 5:20; Heb 1:8-9; 2 P 1:1.

ants wanted to kill the Son precisely because he was the heir. Jesus' murderers (and Satan himself who influenced them) were ultimately intent on eliminating God and taking his place. We also begin to see why in fact no one had a greater love than Jesus, who died not only for his friends but also for his enemies. In the death Jesus freely accepted, the love of God has become manifest in a form the greater than which no one can conceive.

We also begin to see that in the man Jesus God himself carries the full burden of our sins, that God himself is the price of ransom by which we are freed from the slavery of sin (1 Cor 6:20; 1 P 1:19; 2:24).[272]

Finally, if Jesus is truly God, and is given to us, then, once redeemed, we share in God's own divine nature (2 P 1:4).

4. The value of the Old Testament for the contemporary Christian

Most Christians see the value of the Old Testament for the first converts who came from a Jewish background as a preparation for understanding the Gospel. But many of our contemporaries cannot comprehend its importance for themselves; a vast number of clergymen find it hard to integrate the Old Testament readings of the new Lectionary into their homilies. On the other end of the spectrum are those biblical scholars who, engaged in a dialogue with their Jewish colleagues, find the term "Old Testament" ecumenically offensive and theologically inaccurate, and substitute for it the term "Hebrew Scriptures." They point to the documents of Vatican II and to recent papal statements to support their view that the so-called "Old Covenant" with the Jewish people is not obsolete, so that the two parts of Sacred Scriptures ought to be considered of equal value.

---

[272] For more on redemption as ransom, see A. Schökel, "La rédemption, oeuvre de solidarité," *NRT*, 93 (1971), pp. 449-472.

I hope this present chapter has shown that not only Jews but also everyone coming to Christianity can understand the Gospel only if he works his way to it through the Old Testament. The human mind can grasp something new only by means of a "pre-understanding" (*"Vorverständnis"*). This preliminary understanding is then modified, denied, corrected and/or amplified in the light of the new knowledge. Therefore, it is imperative that we try to grasp the Christ event through the "pre-understanding" God himself has provided for us in the Old Testament. To dismiss the Old Testament would be similar to the approach of a student who decided to understand the concluding lecture of a series while ignoring all the preceding ones. The student would then understand (or rather distort) the conclusions of the professor according to his own preconceived ideas. Thus, if we discard God's own "preparatory course," we will necessarily distort "the conclusions," namely the meaning of the work and words of his Son. Liberal Protestantism for all practical purposes tried to do just that, and we have seen the results.

I can give here only a few positive examples to illustrate my point. We can appreciate God's mercy in taking upon himself our punishment if first we understand that through our sins we have truly deserved God's judgment. We can be grateful for God's unspeakable closeness to us in Christ if first we have a glimpse from the Old Testament of the holiness of God whom no mortal can see and live. Each of us, in his own way, first must try to keep the Law, that is, to love God with one's whole mind, soul and heart and one's neighbor as himself and so arrive "at the end of the rope"; in other words, we must acknowledge that we cannot fulfill the Law, that we are sinners and lost if left to our own resources. Only after this experience, the experience of all the saints in the Church beginning with St. Paul up to St. Thérèse of Lisieux, can we appreciate that we have been saved not by our own works but by the cross of Jesus Christ. As these examples show, the "preparatory course" of the Old Testament is not just a communication of abstract knowledge, but rather the process of going through an experience of what the people of Israel went through in order to be ready to encounter God himself in the flesh and to value his redemption. Thus the Old Testament leads us to the New. But once we accept the New Testament we have to go back again to the Old in order to grasp better what we have received in Christ. In Jesus we are given the fullness of God, "condensed" as it were in one human being. In his work we see the fullness of redemption. The great men and women of God in the Old Testament, all its theophanies, all the partial and various ways in which God revealed himself previously, as well as the various anticipations of the final redemption, provide the details, the "individual features" that appear in a uniquely concentrated form in Christ. To use an image, the blinding white light of the New Testament revelation must be refracted through the prism of the Old Testament so that we can better appreciate its components, all the colors that make up the unique beam of the light in Christ. Just to mention a few examples, Moses interceding for his sinful people, Elijah, the only true prophet of Yahweh left in Israel, Ezekiel lying on his side to expiate the sins of his people, Jeremiah betrayed by his own kinsfolk, and, above all, the innocent Servant's offering of his own life: all these figures provide valuable insights that enrich our understanding of the person and work of Jesus Christ.

Moreover, wherever the Old Testament describes an experience of God's forgiving mercy and union with him through faith, it anticipates what will historically be realized in the life, death and resurrection of Christ. The gift of grace, justification and sanctification through faith in the God who does not want the sinner to die but that he should turn again and live shows the presence of the New Testament within the Old. Abraham is the type of the Christian believing in the God who has raised up Jesus from the dead; but it is equally true that Abraham is the father, the perfect model of all Christian believers. By believing in the resurrection of Christ we all imitate the faith of Abraham, who believed that God is able to bring forth life from his "dead" body and from the "dead" womb of Sarah (Rm 4:17-25).

Thus the two Testaments mutually enlighten each other; the Old prepares the acceptance of the New, while we can fully appreciate the New only if we discover the presence of its components within the Old. Yet, on the level of history, one cannot deny that the New does fulfill the Old. The terminology itself of "Old" and "New" is founded on a prophetic text of Jeremiah (31:31), the Pauline-Lukan version of the institution of the Eucharist, (1 Cor 11:25; Lk 22:29) and on a commmentary on Jeremiah 31:31-34 in the Letter to the Hebrews (8:6-13). It does not imply that the Old Covenant with Israel has been canceled. The Pontifical Biblical Commission suggested an alternative way of referring to the two parts of the Bible: "The First and Second Testament." This formulation better expresses the belief that the First Covenant was not revoked; on the other hand, it obscures the aspect of fulfillment in Christ. "Hebrew Scriptures," however, seems quite inappropriate on various grounds: first, not all Old Testament books were written in Hebrew; second, it restricts the significance of the Old Testament to the Jewish people and ignores its universal message.

These observations lead us to one last point concerning the contemporary value of the Old Testament. The Old Testament traditions and books developed over a period of more than two thousand years of constant interaction with the religions of surrounding peoples. Thus the religious notions and institutions of the Old Testament provide a link to the religious notions and institutions of the history of humanity in general. For instance, the notion of the heavenly god, the institutions of theocratic kingship, priesthood, sacrifices, as well as the phenomenon of prophecies and theophanies find their analogies in the religious history of that geographic area but also in the general history of religions. Thus seeing how these general categories have been changed and developed in Israel and finally seeing how Christ and his Church evaluated them provide a criterion for discerning and selecting what is true and "Christic" (patterned on Christ) in the history of other religions. To this point we need to return in the second and third parts of our study.

PART II

Historical Christology

Patristic Christology

1. The character and significance of patristic Christology

The Christology of the Fathers is a profoundly biblical Christology: for them Christ is the ultimate meaning of all the Scriptures. They know that every text of the Bible reflects and expresses a moment or aspect of the one plan of salvation in which the Old Testament prepares and anticipates Christ and the New Testament attests to him. Thus, every biblical text, both in the Old and in the *really?* New Testament, sheds light on some aspect of the one mystery of Christ. Once the literal meaning of an Old Testament text is established, the Fathers explore how this text expresses some aspect of the mystery of Christ (the allegorical meaning), how Christians can live this aspect of the mystery in their own lives (moral meaning), and how the mystery referred to in the text is to be fulfilled eschatologically (anagogical meaning). Thus, the center of the whole Bible is Christ; but also, conversely, all Christology is biblical exegesis. Even when the Fathers create new philosophical concepts to articulate more precisely the christological mystery, they do so with the conviction that, by means of these new concepts, they express more precisely, vis-à-vis certain errors, the biblical revelation of Christ.

Their theological method includes not only a rigorous intellectual inquiry but also prayer and the praxis of Christian living. They know that their intellect needs the light of the Holy Spirit who alone can reveal to them the mystery of Christ; they are also aware that the practice of the love of Christ will help their understanding: only by being conformed to Christ through imitating him can they hope to progress in knowing his mystery. They are also convinced that the Holy Spirit and the love of Christ are available only within the community of the Church; therefore no Christology is possible if one cuts himself off from that communion. Hence their Christology is **ecclesial:** it explores the Scriptures in the light of the faith of the Church.

For all these reasons, patristic Christology is not a system of intellectual abstractions, but is intimately linked to the faith experience of the Christian in the Church and gives an intelligible foundation for that experience. The Fathers faced a bewildering pluralism of religions and religious philosophies while, at the same time, their own Christian religion lacked the credentials of cultural respectability: they had the difficult task of showing **the universal significance** of an itinerant Jewish teacher from Galilee who was executed as a common criminal under the orders of the Roman procurator of Judea. Even though Paul, Luke, and the Gospel of John have already faced this question, it becomes the challenge of patristic Christology to work out the relationship between Christian faith and non-Christian religions and religious philosophies.

Confronted with philosophical questions and distortions regarding the Christian notions of Trinity, incarnation, and redemption, the Fathers were prompted to work out the philosophical implications of the Christian message. **In this way, they created a dialogue between contemporary philosophy and Christianity:** under the impact of the Christian mystery they were led to create new philosophical notions better suited than any they found in the pagan culture to articulate the mystery of Christ. Far from surrendering the Christian Gospel to Hellenistic philosophies, they transformed these philosophies so that they could express the metaphysical implications of the Christian message. **Thus the paradox arose: the Fathers were compelled to use new, non-biblical, philosophical language in order to safeguard the truths of biblical Christology in a new cultural context.**

All this shows the importance of patristic Christology for us.

Contemporary Christology also faces the task of expressing the full dimensions of the mystery of Christ in a new cultural context. Like patristic Christology, it intends to build an intellectual synthesis that can enrich spiritual life. The Christian of our day is even more impressed than the Fathers by the plurality of world religions. He hopes to reconcile the universal claim of Christianity with the enduring presence of other major religions. Like the Fathers, he also faces a plurality of philosophies and is anxious to build a bridge between his faith and modern ways and systems of thought. In order to avoid repeating ancient errors, contemporary Christology needs to integrate into itself the accumulated insights of patristic thought.

2. The relationship between Christianity and non-Christian religions

For the Fathers Christianity is not merely one religion among many, not even as the best or highest; in the words of de Lubac, the word "religion" cannot univocally be applied to Christianity and other religions. Christianity is religion in a qualitatively different sense from any other religion; it is the absolute religion. The Fathers ground the unique dignity of Christianity on three considerations.

1. Other religions are the result of human effort to find God, an endeavor often distorted by error and even by satanic influence (for instance, in the case of polytheistic idolatry). **Christian teaching is not a human invention but rather comes from God himself.** It is revealed and taught by God.[1] In the words of the *Letter to Diognetus*:

> It was not an earthly invention, as I have said, that was committed to their keeping; it was not a product of mortal brain

---

[1] Cf. Athenagoras, *Legatio* 7:1, in *Legatio & De Resurrectione*, Oxford Early Christian Texts, ed. & tr. by W.R. Schoedel (Oxford: Clarendon Press, 1972), p. 14.

that they consider worth safeguarding so anxiously; nor have they been entrusted with the dispensing of merely human mysteries. Quite the contrary! It was really the Lord of all, the Creator of all, the invisible God himself, who, of his own free will, from heaven, lodged among men the truth and the holy incomprehensible Word, and firmly established it in their hearts.[2]

2. The absolute claim of Christianity is based not only on the fact that it presents God's teachings. Already in the Old Testament, even though through messengers and go-betweens, God himself was teaching and educating humankind. **But in Christ God himself has become personally present to us and he himself teaches us without any intermediary.** As the same *Letter to Diognetus* continues to explain, God sent to us not a subordinate, created spirit, but "the Designer and Architect of the universe in person."[3]

After he has shown that all the teachings of Christ can be gleaned from the pages of the Old Testament, Irenaeus asks the question, "What, then, did the Lord bring to the world by his coming that was new?" "He brought all the newness," — Irenaeus answers — "by bringing himself."[4] Since the man Christ is the Logos, we possess in him not only the seeds of the Logos, but its fullness.[5]

3. Christianity is the absolute religion because all men are ordained to find their fulfillment in Christ. Every human being has been created in the image of God — according to many Fathers, in the image of the Logos who himself is the perfect image of the Father. Sin could distort but not eliminate this ontological resemblance and ordination to the Logos. Thus, when the Logos became man, he became a center of universal attraction. In the words of Gregory of Nazianzus, he "became leaven for the dough of all hu-

[2]   7:1-2: ACW, n. 6, 140.
[3]   *Ibid.*, 7, 2: 141.
[4]   *Against Heresies*, 4:34:1.
[5]   Cf. Justin, *Second Apol.*, 8, 10.

manity."[6] Christianity is then universally valid, since the leaven of the Word is destined to raise the dough of all humankind.

In spite of their emphasis on the universal and absolute claims of Christianity, **the Fathers see in other religions and religious philosophies more value than either neo-orthodox or fundamentalist Protestantism, or than modern Catholic theology did until the dawn of Vatican II.** Unlike pre-conciliar Catholic theology, the Fathers recognize properly religious values in some non-Christian philosophies. They do so because they know about the universal revealing activity of the Logos. "The Word of God has never ceased to be present to the human race," says Irenaeus.[7] "The rays of the Word are ready to shine wherever the windows of the soul are opened," comments St. Hilary on Jn 1:9.

The Fathers see the revelatory effect of the Word especially in Platonic philosophy. According to St. Justin, long before his final and full revelation, God had sown his *logos spermatikos*, the seed of his Word, his partial revelation in the souls of philosophers like Heraclitus and Socrates. Against the pagan accusation that, in the Christian view, all human beings born before Christ were of no moral value, he responds that everyone, whether he lived before or after Christ, is a Christian if he lived "with the Word," that is, in accord with and by the revelation of the Word:

> We have been taught that Christ is the firstborn of God and we have declared him above to be the Word in whom the whole human race has participated. And those who lived with the Word are Christians even if they were held to be atheists like Socrates, Heraclitus and such as these among the Greeks.[8]

Clement of Alexandria concurs by comparing the function of Greek philosophy to the Law of Moses. Just as the Law was a

---

[6] *Theol. Or.*, 5:21.

[7] *Against Heresies*, 3:16:1.

[8] *First Apol.*, 46.

schoolmaster, a *paidagogos*, for the Hebrews to lead them to Christ, so was philosophy for the Hellenic mind. "Philosophy... was a preparation, paving the way for him who is perfected in Christ."[9]

Yet the Fathers also see the other side of non-Christian religions and religious philosophies. St. Justin, so appreciative of Heraclitus and Socrates, does not hesitate to denounce the ignorance and moral corruption in the myths of the polytheistic Greco-Roman religion. He points out the superficial similarity between the mythological stories and the Christian mysteries (for instance the stories about gods impregnating young virgins on earth versus the mystery of the virginal conception of Jesus) but also the errors and the moral depravity in the pagan myths. He attributes this strange mixture of similarity and fundamental difference to the maleficent influence of demons who, by imitating the mysteries of Christ, intended to deceive people into taking the true story of Christ for a mythological story.[10] Indeed, according to the Fathers, even in the works of the philosophers "wisdom is mixed with filth." According to Origen and St. Augustine, the philosophers often discover partial truths, but in their pride they begin to worship the work of their own intellect. Thus, in their own way, they also become idolaters.[11]

The above considerations show the twofold relationship of Christianity to other religions and religious philosophies. At one and the same time Christianity criticizes and respects them, exposes their errors but upholds and integrates their truths.

The position of the Fathers is thus characterized by both an openness and a critical attitude. They would reject a certain contemporary view according to which all major religions are anonymous Christianity, whose true identity needs only to be made explicit. They would insist that these religions need to be purified of all errors and distortions and, even if purified, possess only a par-

---

[9]   *Strom.* 1:5: ANF, p. 305.
[10]   *First Apol.*, 54.
[11]   Cf. *Hom. on Lev.* 7:6; *Hom. in Jesu Nave* 7:1; *City of God*: 8:11.

tial revelation of Christ. However, as we have seen, St. Justin would have no difficulty in accepting the contemporary assumption that there were and are anonymous Christians outside the visible boundaries of the Church.

The source of the Fathers' openness to non-Christian religions and of their claim for the uniqueness and universality of the Christian religion is the person of Jesus Christ: as pre-existent Logos, he enlightens the soul of every human being who opens himself to his light, but in the fullness of time this same Divine Word has become flesh in the man Jesus.[12]

---

[12] In the above section I followed closely the essay of H. de Lubac, "The Pagan Religions and the Fathers of the Church," *The Church: Paradox and Mystery* (Staten Island, NY: Alba House, 1969), pp. 68-95.

CHAPTER I

The Soteriology of the Fathers

Most contemporary Christologies, if they include patristic thought at all, emphasize the Christology of the Fathers, and, from among the christological texts, give pride of place to the dogmatic definitions of the christological councils. Without a doubt, these dogmatic definitions are important milestones in the history of Christology, yet their true meaning can easily be lost apart from their soteriological context. The Fathers never ceased to repeat in one way or another that Christ could not have saved us had he not been in one person true God and true man. The saving work of Christ is the center of their interest, even when they pursue a metaphysical analysis of the natures and person of Christ. Following, then, the thrust of patristic thought itself, I will first study the soteriology of the Fathers, and only afterwards their Christology.

Keeping in mind the scope of this study, I will not present individual differences among the authors in much detail. I will outline here only their basic ideas, which will, hopefully, serve as a foundation and stimulus for a contemporary soteriological synthesis.[13]

---

[13] On patristic Soteriology, see B.E. Daley, B. Studer, *Soteriologie. In der Schrift und Patristik. Handbuch der Dogmengeschichte* III/2 (Freiburg: Herder & Herder, 1978); J.P. Jossua, *Le salut, incarnation ou mystère pascale, chez les pères de l'Église de saint Irénée à saint Léon le Grand* (Paris: Cerf, 1968); R. Schwager, *Der wunderbare Tausch. Zur Geschichte und Deutung der Erlösungslehre* (Munich: Kösel, 1986), pp. 1-160; M. Slusser, "Primitive Christian Soteriological Themes," *TS* 44 (1983), pp. 555-569; B. Studer, *Gott und unsere Erlösung im Glauben der Kirche* (Düsseldorf: Patmo, 1985); H.E.W. Turner, *The Patristic Doctrine of Redemption* (London: Mowbray, 1952).

1. Sin

Sin, as distinct from a fateful mistake, ignorance, or moral fault, is a specifically Jewish-Christian concept. Even though the Fathers understand it in the context of Hellenistic philosophies, by transforming Hellenistic notions they preserve and develop the biblical notion of sin.

According to St. Augustine, when rebelling against God, the first man caused a rebellion in himself: his passions turned against his reason.[14] This disordered state has been passed on through the sexual act of generation to every human being. Thus the natural inclination of the human will in every human being, prior to any free decision on the part of the individual, has become disordered: it has a natural gravitation towards sin.

The Eastern Fathers also teach that the sin of Adam and Eve caused a moral deterioration for all humankind, but, instead of concupiscence (the disordered inclination of the will in St. Augustine), they emphasize the corruptibility that has befallen the human race.[15] Because of sin, humanity lost God's gift of immortality, and, by refusing to contemplate God who is life, it has separated itself from life and has been destined to corruption. The physical corruption in death is only the sign and consequence of the moral corruption that began with the first human couple, whose sin has since been ratified by every individual sin.

In whatever concrete way it is manifested, every sin is a freely committed disobedience against God. According to St. Augustine, the sinner attributes to himself what belongs to God; he wants to possess himself in a false way, as if he did not depend on God; he wants to be his own norm of action. Thus he offends God, and gets into a conflict with his own self, created in the image of God, and destined to be fulfilled in knowing and loving God. Not being at peace with himself, he turns frantically to created goods in a fu-

---

[14] Cf. M. Huftier, "Le péché actuel," *Théologie du péché* (Paris: Desclée, 1960), pp. 294-322.

[15] Cf. R. Schwager, *Der wunderbare Tausch*, p. 64.

tile attempt to satisfy himself. The more he becomes attached to the goods of this world, the less fulfilled he feels and the more he keeps dissipating himself in a multiplicity of goods. In this way he is skidding downhill from higher goods to lower ones and thereby intensifying his self-alienation and his alienation from his fellow men and women.

For the Fathers the fall is a cosmic drama in which the human race plays a central but not exclusive role. We are not the only intelligent creatures in the cosmos; we were created to replace the fallen spirits, Satan and his angels. It is Satan or the devil who tempted and led into sin the first human couple, and henceforth, as a result of sin, exercises dominion over humankind. Being under the power of the devil means that sinful men and women become the instrument of the devil's projects; the evil effects of their deeds far exceed human comprehension and intention.

In God's plan, humanity as "microcosmos" (the miniature recapitulation of the whole cosmos, both material and spiritual), was to serve as the natural "link" ("*syndesmos*") between the whole of creation and God. However, because of the fall, we failed in this vocation; as a result, the state of the whole cosmos has deteriorated.

2. Redemption

According to the Fathers the purpose of the incarnation and redemption is not only to undo the consequences of sin, but also to assume humankind into God's own Trinitarian life. Yet the concrete form of this assumption is determined by our fallen state. Therefore, by discussing the various aspects of sin, we have already anticipated the various aspects of redemption. If, through sin, human nature itself has been affected by corruptibility and has been pushed to the brink of nothingness, we need a redeemer who recreates our human nature and restores it to health. If we have been estranged from God, from ourselves, and from each other, we need to be reconciled and united with God and thereby recognize and accept our true selves and the selves of our fellow human beings as creatures and images of God. If, unwilling to know God, we have turned to the world of matter, our "sight" needs healing so that we may see again God's light. If our will has become incapable of breaking out of its self-induced imprisonment, we need to be restored to true freedom. If our sins earned death for us, we need someone who did not have to die so that by dying freely out of love for us, he may save us from death. If we have come under the dominion of the devil, we need to be rescued. If we could not give ourselves over to God as a gift in sacrifice, someone else has to help us. If, left to ourselves, we could not fulfill our vocation of uniting the cosmos with God; we need someone else who can help us to accomplish this task. These dimensions of redemption emerge when the Fathers look at the needs of fallen humanity. Yet, in presenting the full depth of the mystery of redemption, they point to God's love whose gift has infinitely surpassed our needs and expectations.

None of the Fathers created a systematic treatise on redemption; rather, each of them developed a group of overlapping and interweaving themes that explain the mystery from various angles. In the words of St. Athanasius:

> ...do not be surprised if we frequently repeat the same words on the same subject. For since we are speaking of the counsel of God, therefore we expound the same sense in more than one form, lest we should seem to be leaving anything out, and incur the charge of inadequate treatment.[16]

However, through the variety of themes and images, and beyond the individual differences of the authors, there emerges a basically coherent patristic soteriology. By analyzing its various themes, we hope to bring this coherent theology to light.

---

[16] *On the Incarnation*, 20: *CLF*, p. 75.

a. The metaphysical foundation of redemption

This is often called the "physico-mystical aspect" of the patristic notion of redemption.[17] The terminology, however, is misleading. Instead of physical reality in the modern sense, "physico" in this context refers to the metaphysical concept of nature: the eternal Son, the Logos, has made our human nature (*physis*) his own. "Mystical" does not refer here to mystical experience, but rather to a mysterious relationship of solidarity and even identity between the incarnate Son of God and all humanity, a relationship that has resulted from the assumption by the Son of our human nature. Contrary to widespread misinterpretations, this physico-mystical aspect of redemption is never held up by the Fathers as a self-sufficient theory that could explain the whole process of redemption. The following text of Gregory of Nazianzus shows a typical way in which the Fathers explain this metaphysical foundation in conjunction with the many other aspects of redemption:

> So he is called man, not only that through his body he may be apprehended by embodied creatures, whereas otherwise this would be impossible because of his incomprehensible nature; but also that by himself he may sanctify humanity, and be as it were a leaven to the whole lump; and, by uniting to himself that which was condemned, may release it from all condemnation, becoming for all men all things that we are, except sin — body, soul, mind, and all through which death reaches — and thus he became man, who is the combination of all these.[18]

Following a Platonic heritage, Gregory, as did all the Fathers, assumes the unity of human nature: the same human nature exists in every human being. Therefore, when God the Son became man,

---

[17] Cf. *Word and Redeemer. Christology in the Fathers,* ed. with Introduction and Commentary by J.M. Carmody and T.E. Clark (Glen Rock, NJ: Paulist, 1966), pp. 7-8.

[18] *Theol. Or.,* IV,21: *CLF,* p. 192.

he united human nature to himself and thereby fulfilled the meta-physical condition for redemption. Becoming man does not merely mean that the invisible God, who in himself cannot be grasped by embodied creatures, has now become knowable. It also includes the fact that, by assuming human nature, God, the Word, has sanctified directly, by himself, all humanity. Yet the incarnation is only the first step. The metaphysical identification of the incarnate Son with all human beings is not sufficient for salvation. Gregory suggests that the purpose of the incarnation is for the Word to become all things for all men and women: all that he assumed, body, soul and mind, he assumed for our sake and for the sake of giving them to us. It is through his whole existence, including his death and res-urrection, that he accomplishes our sanctification, and that the leaven of God the Word raises the lump of all humanity. The physico-mystical concept, however, is present, implicitly or explic-itly, in virtually every theme of redemption the Fathers discuss.

b. Christ as mediator

Before Arianism, the early Fathers presented the eternal Logos as the universal mediator — even prior to the incarnation — between God the Father and his creation. Beginning with cre-ation, throughout the whole of Salvation History the Father has always acted through his Logos. The divine ideas or "blueprints" according to which every creature was to be made, have always been present in the eternal Wisdom and Word of the Father; however, by creating the world, the Father "brought forth" his wisdom, his Son, by manifesting his wisdom in creation. For this reason, the apologists, for instance, Justin and Athenagoras, do not clearly dis-tinguish the creation of the world from the generation of the Son by the Father.[19] Later, post-Arian theology will make this distinc-tion clear. Yet this undeveloped conception has some lasting value

---

[19] They understand it according to the Stoic schema of the *logos endiathetos* and the *logos prosphorikos*. See Justin, *Dialogue*, 61.2; 138.2; *Second Apol.*, II 6.3; Athenagoras, *Legatio* 11.3.

precisely in showing the intrinsic link between the creation of the world and the eternal generation of the Son: the universe expresses and reflects the wisdom that, in a transcendent way, has always existed in the Son.

The Father is invisible and inaccessible in himself. The Son alone, as the perfect image and the perfect representation of the Father, can reveal him. He reveals the Father through the created world, but in a more intimate way through Salvation History. Whenever God has communicated with the human race, beginning in Eden before the Fall and continuing up through the arrival of Jesus, this communication has always taken place through the Son. Thus the universal mediation of the Son did not begin but has only been consummated in the incarnation and in the life, death, and resurrection of Jesus Christ.

While they tend to subordinate the Logos to God the Father, the pre-Nicene Fathers emphasize that the Logos belongs to uncreated, divine reality. He is not an intermediate being between God and his creation. For the Fathers, Christ is our **mediator**, but not in the Arian sense of a being who is below God but above humanity. The Arian conception of Christ as neither truly God nor truly man but an ontological in-between is a false Hellenization of Christianity. Platonism, in its various forms, postulated the existence of such a mediator because it could not accept a direct contact or union between the Transcendent Divine Reality and Creation. For the Fathers, the Arian conception distorts the mediation of Christ. How can Christ join together God and humanity if he is in himself neither fully divine nor fully human? In their view, the true humanity and the transcendent divinity of Christ, joined together, are the metaphysical basis for his mediation. In the Fathers' view Christ's humanity becomes the way through which we reach his divinity.

The mediation of Christ, however, includes not only the ontological assumption of a human nature by God the Son; it also comprises his whole work of redemption. St. Gregory the Great expresses the theme of mediation in a beautiful synthesis:

The Word himself helped man by becoming man. Man left to his own resources could not return to God. Only the God-man could open up the road to return. We, mortal and sinful, were far away from the Immortal and Just One. However, between the Immortal Just One and the mortal evil ones there appeared the mediator of God and men. He is mortal but just; he shared death with man and justice with God. Since we were far away from the heights because of our lowliness, he joined together in himself the highest with the lowest; and by uniting our lowliness with his highness, the road for returning to God was opened for us.[20]

c. "He who descended is the very one who ascended"

The theme of the descent and ascent of Christ, closely related to the theme of mediation, was worked out in detail especially by St. Augustine. The basis for his comments is the Letter to the Ephesians, in particular 4:10. This theme shows that the whole process of humankind's redemption may be validly described by the personal history of Jesus Christ, his self-emptying in descending from heaven to earth, the cross and hell, and his glorification in rising from the dead and ascending into heaven. Just as no one else could die for us and thereby liberate us, so no one else could ascend to the Father but Jesus Christ. On the one hand, all that Christ becomes, does and suffers, takes place for our sake, and causes our salvation. On the other hand, no one but Christ the Son can share in the Father's life and love. Thus, we are saved only insofar as we are united to Christ as members to the head. This union with Christ does not abolish but rather perfects our human identity, since it is a union through grace that unfolds in mutual love. One of Augustine's classic texts on this theme is as follows:

Thus Christ is many members, but one body. He descended from heaven through mercy, nor did anyone else but he him-

---

[20] *Moralia*, 22,13.

self ascend since we are also in him through grace. In this way
only Christ alone descended and only Christ alone ascended;
not that we should confuse the dignity of the head with that
of the members, but that the unity of the body be not separated from the head....

He who descended from heaven does not jealously keep
heaven from us, but rather shouts at us, as it were: "Be my
members, if you want to ascend into heaven."[21]

d. "Admirabile commercium"

From among the many interwoven soteriological themes and
images, the "*admirabile commercium*" (marvelous exchange) is one
of the most often used and has an uncommon potential to synthesize the soteriological thought of the Fathers.[22] Although related
to the theme of mediation, it expresses communion more directly
than unity. The Son not only joins us to God by his divine and
human nature and by his redemptive work; he also brings about a
complete exchange between himself and humanity, an exchange
both ontological and existential. The nucleus of this theme is already found in St. Paul: "He who was rich became poor for our sake
so that we might become rich through his poverty" (2 Cor 8:9).
Irenaeus expresses all its aspects in these words: "the Word of God,
Jesus Christ our Lord.... because of his overflowing love, became
what we are so that he may make us what he himself is."[23]

The ontological aspect of this exchange is expressed in the
well-known patristic dictum: God the Word became man so that
we might be made god.[24] The divinization of the human race
through the incarnation of the Word is part of the common pa-

---

[21] "Hom. on the Ascension": *Sermons: Collection Mai 98*.

[22] Cf. H.U. von Balthasar, *Theodramatik* III *Handlung* (Einsiedeln: Johannes V., 1980), pp.
224-234.

[23] *Against Heresies*, V, Preface.

[24] Of course, not by nature, but by sheer grace.

tristic heritage. But, as far as I know, only Gregory of Nazianzus establishes a strict parallelism between Christ's incarnation and our deification. The incarnation took place, he asserts, so that "I too might become God to the extent that he became man."[25] There can be no doubt that, according to Gregory, by ourselves and in ourselves we are creatures, not God. But, being united to the one Son by the incarnation and by the sanctifying Spirit, in and through the one Son we become God. Gregory emphasizes **the reality of our deification** because he also stresses **the reality of our being included in the incarnate Son.**[26] For the Fathers there is no contradiction between our divinization and our reaching perfection as human beings. Since we are created in the image of God, the more we are given a share in the divine nature, the more perfect human beings we become.

Here is one of Gregory' s most insightful formulations of "exchange":

> ...in the form of a slave, he (the Word) descends to his fellow slaves, nay, to his slaves, and takes upon himself an alien form, bearing all me and all mine in himself, so that in himself he may consume the bad, as the fire consumes the wax, or as the sun the mists of the earth; and that I may partake of his nature by the blending. Thus he honors obedience by his action and experiences it through his passion... He probes our obedience and, through his inventive love, he measures everything by his own sufferings. Thus he can learn from his experience what we experience, how much is demanded from us and how much we are excused. He weighs our weakness according to what he suffered.[27]

"Bearing all me and all mine in himself" expresses not only the metaphysical taking up of human nature but also the existential taking into himself of every human person and of every human life.

---

[25] *Theol. Or.*, III, 19.

[26] Cf. *Ibid.*, IV, 6.

[27] *Ibid.*

The eternal Son becomes the subject of a full human experience; in particular, his own human experience of hard obedience is the medium through which he lives our destiny, probes and measures the difficulties and sufferings that we have to undergo. Without committing any sin, Christ nevertheless in some real sense makes also our follies and transgressions his own, and thereby also our abandonment by God. As a result of Christ's "carrying me and all mine in himself" throughout his life but especially on the cross, all evil is purged from me and I, united to him as member to Head, become God by partaking of his divine nature.[28]

St. Ambrose, and later St. Augustine, develops the same theme by showing why the Son has made his own our human emotions. Here is Ambrose's commentary on Christ's agony in Gethsemane:

> "Father, if possible, take away this cup from me." Many cling to this text in order to use the sadness of the Savior as proof that he had weakness from the beginning rather than taking it on for a time. In this way they distort the natural meaning of the sentence. I, however, consider it not only as something that does not need to be excused, but nowhere else do I admire more his tender love and majesty. He would have given me less, had he not taken on my emotions. Thus he suffered affliction for me, he who did not have anything to suffer for himself. Setting aside the enjoyment of his divinity, he is afflicted with the annoyance of my weakness. He took on my sadness so that he might bestow on me his joy. He descended into the anguish of death by following in our footsteps so that he might call us back to life by following in his footsteps. I do not hesitate to speak of sadness since I am preaching the cross; he took on not the appearance but the reality of the incarnation. Thus, instead of avoiding it, he had to take on the pain in order to overcome sadness.[29]

---

[28] Cf. *Ibid.*, IV, 5.
[29] *Commentary on Luke*, 10:56.

The subject who takes on our sadness is God the Son. St. Ambrose does not see in the acceptance of our emotional pain a weakness to be excused, but rather the most amazing manifestation of his divine majesty and tender love. St. Ambrose is imbued with the Stoic ideal of courage, which sees only weakness in sadness, but he also tries to do justice to the Gospel texts, which do attribute sadness to Jesus. He avoids the difficulty by explaining that Christ feels **our** sadness, not his. Later in the commentary, he presents the sleeping of the Apostles in the Garden of Olives as the symbol of what is truly happening in the Passion of the Savior. Christ feels the pain the sleepers cannot feel. Quoting Is 53:4-5, Ambrose points out that Christ carries **our** sins and suffers the pain **for us** not for himself. He exclaims: "You suffer the pain, O Lord not of your wounds, but of my wounds, not of your death but of my weakness."[30]

The purpose of taking on our sadness is expressed again in terms of exchange: "He took on my sadness so that he might bestow on me his joy."[31]

Before we dismiss Ambrose's explanation as emaciating both the meaning of the Gospel texts and the reality of the emotional life of Jesus the man, two observations are in order. First, according to Ambrose, Christ really and truly feels our emotions and our sadness, just as his incarnation is real and true. It is not a make-believe compassion of a condescending king who does not suffer the privations of his subjects. The divine transcendence of God the Son enables him to feel truly and suffer truly what we feel and suffer. In fact, in comparison with him we are all numb and asleep: he alone feels our sins and our wounds.

Second, we can find faint but real analogies in the experience of other sufferers for Ambrose's understanding of Jesus' suffering. The effect of terrible suffering on some individuals is that they begin to feel compassion for all suffering people. Aware that what they are feeling is, in some sense, the human condition, they feel

---

[30] *Ibid.,* 10:57.
[31] *Ibid.,* 10: 56.

united with all who suffer. Furthermore, many parents feel that they suffer more from the moral or physical evil that affects their children than the children themselves.

St. Augustine treats at length the passages in which the Gospel of John states that Jesus was deeply moved.[32] He explains this fact by the love and sovereign freedom of the One who took up as his own our entire humanity. However, when Jesus is moved or distressed, he is not simply reacting passively to events; it is rather that he himself stirred his emotions because he judged it to be necessary. Even though his emotional life is set in motion by his divine love and freedom, he has true human feelings, so that we can all recognize our weakness in his weakness, our voice in his voice. We ourselves, with our fears and anxieties, are all taken up into Christ our head:

> ...He has transferred us into himself, taken us into himself, our head has taken on the emotions of its members. Therefore he was not moved by anyone else, but as it is said about him when he raised up Lazarus: "He moved himself."[33]

Thus Jesus' deep emotional suffering gives hope to all the weak members of his Church lest despair swallow them:

> What great good we are to expect and hope from participating in his divinity, when even his distress calms us and his weakness strengthens us.[34]

In contemporary theology we would stress more the autonomy of Christ's human emotions than St. Augustine. Nevertheless, Augustine and Ambrose provide for us a valid way to appreciate Christ's human emotions. The divine love of Christ and the almighty power of his divine will enable him to be universally human in his emotions and to embrace even the *ima*, the pit of emo-

---

[32] *Commentary on John*, 40:1-5.
[33] Jn 11:33: *Ibid.*, 52:1.
[34] *Ibid.*, 60:5.

tional distress. The Fathers are not so far from what Bonhoeffer believed, that Christ's divinity manifests itself in his existing entirely for us, in his being the "man for others."

This patristic discussion of the Son's emotional identification with all humankind illuminates an important aspect of the "marvelous exchange": it is not God in his divinity alone who has achieved our redemption: we are given a share in the divine joy of Christ **because** his human soul endured our anguish and has carried the wounds of our sins.

e. *Redemption as victory and deliverance*

The New Testament often describes the redemptive work of Christ as victory over sin, death, and Satan, as well as a deliverance from their power (cf. Rm 5-7; Lk 10:18; Jn 12:31, 16:11; Rv 12:9).[35] Irenaeus further elaborated this theme, and his basic insights influenced subsequent patristic thought:

> He fought and conquered. On the one hand, he was man who struggled for his fathers and through his obedience cancelled their disobedience. On the other hand, he bound the strong one and freed the weak and bestowed salvation on his handiwork by abolishing sin. For he is our compassionate and merciful Lord who loves the human race... Had not man conquered man's adversary, the enemy would not have been conquered justly. Again, had it not been God who bestowed salvation we would not possess it securely.[36]

Even though we have not ceased to be God's possession, the devil obtained dominion over us since we have disobeyed God. The loss of our freedom and the tyranny of sin, death, and Satan over us is for Irenaeus as well as for the New Testament a necessary and just punishment for sin. Hence, only God had the power to liberate us

---

[35] Cf. G. Aulén, *Christus Victor. An Historical Study of the Three Main Types of the Idea of Atonement* (London: SPCK, 1953), pp. 17-99.

[36] *Against Heresies*, III, 18,6-7.

from such slavery. Moreover, it was in keeping with justice that the disobedience of one human being was cancelled by the obedience of another. It was also appropriate that Christ's obedience did not automatically free all human beings. It only created a situation in which individuals could, by accepting the persuasion of the Word, liberate themselves through their free decision.[37]

Gregory of Nyssa explains that, by freely committing sin, the human race sold itself to the devil, and thus justly became subjected to the devil's power. The devil's dominion over us derives from the order of reality, which God himself has established. However, one cannot argue, as many commentators do, that, according to Gregory, Satan had a right to dominate humankind, a right that God could not have justly taken away from him without compensation. In fact, "the due recompense" owed to the devil was nothing other than a deception "by which the deceiver himself" was deceived. The devil who had tricked man into sinning by offering him the bait of pleasure was to be lured "by the camouflage" of Christ's flesh hiding his divinity. Like a greedy fish, the devil swallowed Christ's divinity along with the bait, our human nature. In this way, life came to dwell in death and light in darkness, and life overcame death, and the light dissipated the darkness.[38] One cannot accuse Gregory of inconsistency in attributing deception to a holy and just God. The deception was not a personal act on God's part, but was brought about by the order of reality that a wise, just and merciful God had created. By deceiving man, the devil himself sowed the seeds "with his own free will," the seeds whose harvest he had to reap when he in turn was deceived by the humanity of the incarnate Son. The devil, deprived of God's light by his own choice, cannot recognize God in the human nature of the Son.[39]

---

[37] *Ibid.*, V, 1,1.

[38] Gregory believes that gradually even the devil will be converted by the close contact with Life and Light.

[39] *Address on Religious Instruction*, 24-26: *CLF*, pp. 300-303. Following Origen, Gregory also believes that, in the end, the proximity of God to the devil that came about through the death of Christ would eventually benefit the devil himself and destroy the darkness he had caused for himself.

heresy

Since Christ has overcome sin, death, and the devil as a human being, we are also enabled by him to share in his victory. Those who believe in him and follow him anticipate victory over these powers already here on earth. This is true in a special way of the martyrs:

> In ancient times before the divine sojourn of the Savior took place, even to the saints death was terrible; all wept for the dead as though they perished. But now that the Savior has raised his body, death is no longer terrible; for all who believe in Christ trample on it as it were nothing and choose rather to die than deny their faith in Christ. And that devil that once maliciously exulted in death, now that its pains were loosed, remained the only one truly dead.[40]

The importance of the theme of victory and deliverance lies in two insights that are often forgotten in our culture:

1. Sin has necessary consequences. It alienates us from our own nature, deprives us of the freedom to change the direction of our lives, results in death, subjects us to the dominion of Satan. Because by its very nature sin implies a diminishing of freedom, we cannot free ourselves from it. Without God's initiative, mere moral self-improvement is doomed to failure. But, in his plan of redemption, God respects the order of the reality he has created. If he is to act justly and wisely, he will not ignore the situation our sin has caused and will not, by a sovereign act, abolish the consequences of sin.

2. When speaking about slavery to sin and the devil, the Fathers mean the slavery of **all humankind**. The human race as a whole fell prey to the tyranny of sin and the devil because of the first sin of the first man. We are all influenced by that first sin and our individual sins re-enact and ratify that first disobedience. But just as we have solidarity in sin, so we have solidarity in redemption. This fundamental doctrine of the New Testament receives from the

---

[40] St. Athanasius, *On the Incarnation*, 27: *CLF*, p. 81.

Fathers an ontological justification: The obedience of Christ was able to cancel the disobedience of Adam because Christ made his own our human nature, and thereby his obedience became in some sense our obedience and made it possible for us to follow freely his example.

f. Redemption as sacrifice

Among the Fathers, St. Augustine has developed the most detailed and consistent doctrine of sacrifice.[41] He points out that sacrifice has exclusive reference to the divine: No one has ever thought of offering sacrifice to human beings as such but only to someone "whom one knew, or supposed or imagined to be God."[42] Augustine does not give an explicit answer to why this has always been the case, but his train of thought implies two reasons: First, sacrifice is the expression of *latreia*, an honor which befits God or the gods exclusively. Second, as its name indicates, the *sacrificium*, even though it is offered by human beings, belongs to the sphere of divine reality.[43]

Augustine defines sacrifice in these terms:

> ...true sacrifice is every act done for the purpose of adhering to God in a holy fellowship, every act directed to that final Good which makes possible our true happiness.[44]

Born in a discussion with Neo-Platonists and using Neo-Platonist terminology, this definition is nevertheless capable of synthesizing the prophetic and the priestly traditions of the Old Testament, the

---

[41] On the history of the idea of sacrifice in the Judeo-Christian tradition, see R.J. Daly, *Christian Sacrifice. The Judeo-Christian Background before Origen* (Washington, DC: Cath. Univ. of America, 1978); _____ *The Origins of the Christian Doctrine of Sacrifice* (Philadelphia: Fortress, 1978); Y. Congar, *Jalons pour une théologie du laicat* (Paris, Cerf, 1953), pp. 159-169.

[42] *City of God*, 10:4.

[43] *Ibid.*, 10: 1; 6.

[44] *Ibid.*, 10:6.

anti-cultic statement of Jesus (Mt 12:7) as well as the sacrificial doctrine of Paul and the Letter to the Hebrews. God speaks out against the sacrifices of the Old Law because he does not want them in themselves, as if they provided something useful or enjoyable to him. God ordained these sacrifices as a sign of a true invisible sacrifice, the contrite and humble heart by which we return to God and cling to him.[45] The true sacrifice, then, which these external animal sacrifices were meant to express, is repentance, conversion, and love for God.

Augustine includes also the love of neighbor in the notion of true sacrifice, provided that the mercy shown others is for the sake of God. The purpose of loving people and showing them mercy is to free them from their misery by helping them to be united with God. The right use of the body, the conformation of the soul to God so that by the beauty received from God the soul may please him more and more, all these are true sacrifice. In fact one can say that "man himself, consecrated in the name of God and dedicated to God, insofar as he dies to the world so that he may live to God, is sacrifice."[46] Thus all individual Christians are meant to become sacrifice, if their whole being, soul and body is given over to God and conformed to God; but this can happen only if the individual is in the Body of Christ, which is the Church. Thus

> the whole redeemed community, that is to say, the congregation and fellowship of the saints, is offered to God as a universal sacrifice through the great high priest who offered himself for us in his suffering so that we might be the body of so great a head — "in the form of a servant" (Ph 2:7).[47]

The sacrifice of Christians can then be defined simply as "the many making up one body in Christ." The Church's self-offering does not stand on its own, nor is it an act accomplished once and for all.

---

[45] *Ibid.*, 10:5.

[46] *Ibid.*, 10:6.

[47] *Ibid.*

She is in the process of learning to offer herself every day in the Eucharist, the sign through which the sacrifice of Christ is made visible in the Church.[48] The sacrifice of Christ is then the source from which the value of the Church's self-offering derives. This is "the one and most real sacrifice."[49]

Augustine does not explicitly say why the sacrifice of Christ is "the one and most real sacrifice," but an implicit answer may be found in two of his reflections. If the essence of sacrifice lies in joining us to God as one body, then the sacrifice of Christ is the one and most real sacrifice, since it unites us most effectively to God and to each other. Christ is "the one and true mediator reconciling us to God" who remained "one with him to whom he offered, and made one in him those for whom he offered the sacrifice."[50] The other reason may be found in the context of the expression: "the one and most real sacrifice." For Augustine, as for all the Fathers, biological death is the punishment we all have incurred for sin. All human beings, therefore, must die. Jesus alone had the freedom not to die, since he alone did not sin. His freedom, then, in accepting suffering and death has made the sacrifice of Christ unique, and for this reason his death liberates all humankind from death and causes our resurrection.

g. Christ as Teacher and Example

The above title does not do full justice to this theme. For the Fathers, Christ is not only teacher but also light that enters and transforms the soul. Nor is he merely an example to follow: we can only follow him to the extent that he gives himself as our food and drink, that is to say, insofar as we receive him as a gift to be participated in. According to Origen, Christ is goodness and justice itself, and any true virtue in us is a share in his virtues. However,

---

[48] *Ibid.*, 10:20.

[49] *On the Trinity*, 4:13:17.

[50] *Ibid.*, 4:14:19.

we could not be enlightened by Christ nor participate in his virtues had we not been redeemed by the cross of Christ. Thus, the
theme of Christ as Teacher and Example in the Christology of the
Fathers is very different from a similar theme in the rationalist
Christologies of the 19th century, which reduce the work of Christ
to these external functions while eliminating the mystery of the cross
and of grace.

As we have seen above, according to many Fathers the eternal Logos has shone for all since the beginning of creation, but the
fallen human race could appropriate only fragments or "seeds" of
his revelation. St. Athanasius explains the need for the incarnation
in these terms:

> For, once men's minds have fallen to things of sense, the Word
> lowered himself to appearing in a body so that he might, as
> man, transfer men to himself, and center their senses on him-
> self, and that from now on, by the works he performs, he may
> persuade those who see him as man that he is not only man
> but also God and the Word and Wisdom of the true God.[51]

The incarnate Christ reveals himself only gradually to the
human race. The beginners in spiritual life, the "fleshly" Christians,
know Christ only according to the flesh. They learn about his birth,
his childhood, his public ministry, miracles, and suffering on the
cross. They know directly only the man Jesus. To the extent that
they try to follow his teachings, and especially carry his cross and
share in his sufferings, they begin to participate in Christ, share in
his virtues and become conformed to him. Then they will know
Christ according to the spirit, the risen Christ whose humanity no
longer hides but rather fully reveals his divine glory. Yet no matter
how far we have progressed in the spiritual life, we must always return to meditate on the mysteries of the earthly life of Christ and
will thereby gain further understanding. For instance, from know-

---

[51] *On the Incarnation*, 16.

ing the divine glory of Christ we will better understand his humility in the incarnation and the greatness of his divine love revealed
in the mystery of the cross.

The knowledge of the "perfect Christian" can be expressed
only by paradoxes: he sees and touches God the Word by a sight
and a touch that is beyond the touch and the sight of the senses;
he experiences him by transcending any experience through faith.
Mary of Magdala, says St. Leo the Great, represented the Church
when she tried to touch the risen Christ. But Jesus enjoined on her
not to touch him by physical hands. He calls her to touch him in
his divine splendor, spiritually:

> "Do not touch me, since I have not yet ascended to my Fa-
> ther." This means, "Do not approach me with your body, do
> not wish to know me by your senses. I have higher things in
> store for you; I prepare you for greater things. After I have
> ascended to my Father you will touch me more perfectly and
> more really: you will grasp what you do not touch, believe what
> you do not see."[52]

According to the Fathers, the object of this experiential
knowledge in faith, Jesus Christ, is truly and really present in the
believer. This knowledge is based on the connaturality of the soul
with the Word. The more the soul created in the image of God
(or of the Word) regains its similarity to God by following Christ
on the way of virtues and by embracing his cross, the deeper and
stronger this union will become. Of course, this knowledge includes
love; in fact, as Gregory the Great has put it with classic precision,
"*amor ipse notitia est*": the love of Christ is itself knowledge, since
this knowledge derives from a loving union with him and, in turn,
deepens that union.

---

[52] *Sermon on Ascension*, 2:4.

h. Redemption as uniting all creation to God

According to Gnostic ideas that nurtured a powerful religious and philosophic current in the ancient world, both the human body and the material universe are forces hostile to the divine element in the human being, keeping captive what is divine in us. Redemption consists in liberation from the body and from the material universe. The Fathers, in contrast, regard the body and the material world as God's creation and the object of God's redemption. Just as human sin has caused the corruption of the human body and the disruption of the order and unity of the universe, it will be the task of the New Human Being, the incarnate Son, to save the human body and restore the unity of all creation.

According to St. Maximus Confessor (who echoes and synthesizes the thought of the Fathers before him), the human race was created last because it was destined to become the natural link between the opposite extremes of all creation.[53] God gave it the vocation to unite in itself these extremes and "the all" of creation with God. According to Maximus, there are five pairs of opposites the human race was destined to unite: male and female, paradise and earth, earth and heaven, that is to say, earthly and angelic beings, sensible and intellectual realities, and finally, creation and God. Humankind was to unite the whole of creation with God so that it might enter completely into God and become god by participation.

However, instead of uniting these things in an upward movement towards God, humanity moved downward toward that which was below and properly subordinate to it. It abused its power to unite by disrupting the existing unity of the universe. Thus God himself became man in order to carry out the original vocation of the human race. He united in himself all the five pairs of opposites and thus

---

[53] On the cosmic aspect of redemption in Maximus, see E. von Ivánka, *Maximos der Bekenner. All-eins in Christus* (Einsiedeln: Johannes V., 1961).

...He fulfilled the great design of the Father in that he gathered and united as head all that is in heaven and on earth in himself, in whom everything had been created.[54]

St. John of Damascus sums up the same thought of cosmic redemption in a famous text:

The gracious will of the Father has worked out in his only-begotten Son the salvation of the whole universe. His gracious will has joined together all things in his only-begotten Son. For, if man is indeed a small universe (*microkosmos*) who bears in himself the link (*syndesmos*) for all visible and invisible substances, being actually both (visible and invisible), well did the Lord, the Creator and Governor of all things decide that the conjunction of divinity and humanity, and of the whole creation through humanity, might take place in his only-begotten consubstantial Son so that God might be all in all.[55]

The assumption of the material world into union with Christ depends on the redemption of the human body. The human body must disintegrate before the glorified spiritual body can rise to eternal life. Yet there is a mysterious continuity between the earthly bodies of believers and their risen bodies, so much so that, according to the Fathers the Eucharist nourishes their bodies for eternal life. The material universe will end in a cosmic cataclysm; yet, like the link between the earthly body and the glorified body, there exists a mysterious connection between our world and the new heaven and new earth that we expect at the end of times. Just as our bodies anticipate final redemption, so does our material universe. Every event in the redemptive history of Christ involves nature. His incarnation was celebrated by the ass and ox and announced by the star. When John immersed Jesus in the Jordan, Jesus sanctified all the waters of the world, so that, henceforth, they might sanctify

---

[54] *Ambigua: PG* 91 (1304D-1313B).
[55] *Hom. on Transfiguration*, 18.

every person baptized in the Holy Spirit. As Jesus rose from the waters, he raised up with himself the whole created world.[56] As he walked on the water and multiplied the loaves, the elements recognized their Maker and promptly obeyed him (St. Augustine). The whole creation took part in the passion of Jesus:

> As the Creator hung on the cross, the whole creation groaned and every element felt with him the nails of the cross. Nothing withdrew itself from suffering… The world had to testify to his Creator, all things as it were, wanted to stop existing.[57]

As it shares in his passion, so does the universe share in his resurrection: "The world rose in him, the heaven rose in him, the earth rose in him, for there will be a new heaven and the new earth," writes St. Ambrose.

The Fathers' naive descriptions of how nature feels with and responds to the gradual unfolding of the mystery of Christ are poetic hyperbole containing a deep theological and existential truth: nature's present and future existence is intimately bound up with humanity and both humanity and nature share a common dependence on God. How opposed this attitude is to that of the Gnostic philosopher, and, we might add, to that of the modern unbeliever! Both of them profoundly distrust nature, while the Christian feels at home in the universe.

Only at the end of history is the promise of the new heaven and new earth to be fulfilled, only then will the material universe fully share, in its own way, humankind's complete union with God. But even now, to the extent that we subject ourselves to God, and our passions to God's will, we begin to regain our royal rule over the universe. The material world still prepares a cross for us, but the sufferings caused by the cross serve Christians in their journey towards God.

---

[56] Gregory of Nazianzus, *Oration on the Holy Lights.*
[57] Leo the Great, *Hom. on the Passion*, VI, 4.

3. Conclusion

Can we detect a unifying notion in these different themes that would make them more intelligible? If we abstract from details, we can arrange most of the soteriological themes and images around the central notion of **communion**. Sin has destroyed an original communion by alienating us from God, from ourselves, and from our fellow men and women and by destroying the harmony of the universe. Out of an undeserved love the Father has decided to restore this communion in an all-surpassing way through his Son. The Son enters into communion with humankind by becoming man; without sinning personally, he agrees to take upon himself all our sins by enduring the results of sin, suffering and death. It is through this kind of complete identification with sinful humankind that he gains victory over sin, death, and Satan, and completes a most pleasing sacrifice to God. Through his resurrection and ascension he returns to the Father and makes it possible for all humankind to enter into complete communion with the Father on condition that they accept to follow Christ and be united with his death and resurrection. Through Christ and through the human race renewed in him, the cosmos is also restored to harmony and to union with its Creator. The communion between every renewed individual and Christ and between the whole of renewed humankind and Christ is so intimate that we are not only one in him but also one with each other in him.

The process of achieving communion between the Son and humankind has both a **metaphysical** and a **historical-existential** aspect. The incarnation of the Son implies the metaphysical union of the divine and human natures. This is the necessary condition for the history of Christ and for his complete existential identification with the fallen human race. Yet, the metaphysical union does not, in itself, suffice. It is through the mysteries of the life of Christ, through his words, deeds, and sufferings as well as through his resurrection that our redemption is accomplished.

It will clarify matters if we apply here the later distinction between **objective and subjective redemption.** Objective redemption is the gift of communion offered to us, and subjective redemption is our personal acceptance of this communion through faith and the sacraments. In every theme we outlined above, these aspects can be distinguished: On the one hand, Christ the Mediator, Christ descending to assume the form of a slave and leading his humanity back to God through the cross and resurrection, Christ assuming our emotions, sins and sufferings, Christ overcoming the powers of sin, death and Satan, Christ offering himself to the Father as a most pleasing sacrifice, Christ as teacher and model, Christ achieving the union of the cosmos through his humanity; all these themes unfold the objective aspect of redemption. Briefly, we may summarize objective redemption as Christ himself in his life on earth consummated through the mystery of the cross and resurrection. Subjective redemption, on the other hand, is our gradual participation in Christ, variously designated as passing through his humanity to his divinity, ascending with him and in him to the Father, sharing in his divinity and joy, learning to make his sacrifice and his victory our own, knowing him and imitating him, and entering into a union of love with him so that at the end of time, as St. Augustine liked to repeat, the one Christ will love and praise the Father, the one Christ, however, who is both head and members. To the words of the Father of Western theology correspond the words of Origen that point out the direction of Eastern theology: "Then those who have reached God through the Word will have only one activity, that of knowing God, so that, by being transformed through the knowledge of the Father, they all may become perfectly one Son, just as now only the Son knows the Father."[58]

---

[58] *Comm. on John*, 1:92.

CHAPTER II

The Christology of the Fathers

Every soteriological theme in the Fathers, as we have seen, presupposes a correct, if sometimes implicit, Christology. Briefly, Jesus Christ could redeem us because he was truly God and truly man in one being. We will now sketch out the most important stages and most typical errors in the development of this Christology. No one can attempt to build a contemporary Christology without retracing its development in patristic thought. The Fathers, in the long run, succeeded in expressing the reality of Jesus Christ by using and transforming the thought patterns of Hellenistic culture. By investigating their efforts, we can learn much for our own task of using and transforming contemporary thought patterns for the same purpose. Moreover, the christological errors the Fathers had to confront have been, by and large, typical distortions of the human mind, which, in a new form and with new nuances, recur in every age.[59]

The end of the development of patristic Christology, customarily identified with the Christology of the Third Council of Constantinople, does not constitute a departure from the Christology of the New Testament. It is rather a conceptual articulation of the basic intuition present already in the New Testament: The one and the same Jesus is truly and fully God and truly and fully man. Yet the conceptual formulation has gone through tortuous paths, fierce struggles and confrontations, and taken almost seven centuries to

---

[59] I am greatly indebted in this chapter to the most detailed and reliable history of Christology, A. Grillmeier, *Christ in Christian Tradition*. Vol. I. *From the Apostolic Age to Chalcedon (451)*, (Atlanta: John Knox Press, 1975²); cf. also L. Liébart, *Das christologische Dogma bis zum Konzil von Chalcedon (451)*. *Handbuch der Dogmengeschichte* III/1 (Freiburg: Herder & Herder, 1978).

achieve a high degree of precision. Of course, even these carefully elaborated dogmatic definitions of the patristic age — though always true in the sense they were intended — remain imperfect and constantly call for a new grasp of the mystery in the context of changing languages and cultures.

With some simplifications, we may sketch out the stages of christological development in the following way: (a) First, what it means that Jesus Christ is truly and fully man (against Docetism, Gnosticism, and Apollinarianism), as well as truly and fully God (against Adoptionism and Arianism) was clarified. This phase is roughly completed around the end of the 4th century. (b) Next, the relationship between the humanity and divinity of Christ is debated. Clarification is achieved in two steps: First, against the Nestorians, the Council of Ephesus defended the ontological unity of Jesus Christ by affirming in Christ one ontological subject, that of the eternal Word made man. Then, against the Monophysites, the Council of Chalcedon, in a more balanced formulation, professed two integral natures, divine and human, in the one person of Jesus Christ. (c) As an epilogue to this development, the Third Council of Constantinople asserted against Monotheletism that the one Christ has two active wills, divine and human. We will now investigate this development in greater detail.

1. Docetism and Gnosticism

According to Docetism, Christ was not truly man but merely appeared to be man (*dokein* means "appear"); his human life, suffering, death, and resurrection were apparent rather than real. Docetism is rooted in the perennial human suspicion that the human body, and material reality in general, are impure, unworthy of direct contact with divinity. The transcendent Divine Spirit would soil himself by becoming enfleshed in a human body.

Preparing to meet a martyr's death in Rome at the beginning of the 2nd century, St. Ignatius of Antioch understands the fatal consequences of Docetism for Christian faith and existence. If

Christ did not truly suffer and die for us, we are not truly redeemed. Nor is the Christian martyr's death of any value. Ignatius suffers in vain if he thereby does not participate in the sufferings of Christ:

> Stop your ears, therefore, when anyone speaks to you that stands apart from Jesus Christ, from David's scion and Mary's Son, who was really born and ate and drank, really persecuted by Pontius Pilate, really crucified and died while heaven and earth and the underworld looked on; who also really rose from the dead, since his Father raised him up — his Father, who will likewise raise us also who believe in him through Jesus Christ, apart from whom we have no real life.

> But if, as some atheists, that is, unbelievers, say, his suffering was but a make-believe — when, in reality, they themselves are make-believes — then why am I in chains? Why do I even pray that I might fight wild beasts? In vain, then, do I die? My testimony is, after all, but a lie about the Lord![60]

Docetism, in its crude form, no longer exists in the Church. Yet, in the pre-Vatican II Church, one often heard statements like this one: "When our Lord still walked on earth disguised as a man...." Catholics often did not quite understand that the humanity of our Lord was not a convenient disguise or appearance — a cryptodocetic belief — but it was and is still part of his true identity. He was truly human, a true physical, material being like each one of us.

In the post-Vatican II Church, Docetism has asserted itself in a new form. Some theologians propose Krishna and Rama, the chief human forms of divine reality in Hinduism, as having the same religious value as the man Jesus Christ. Krishna and Rama, however, are not historical, flesh and blood human beings, but rather the human appearances of the divine in the Hindu religious imagination. If the mere human appearance of a divine figure is seen as identical in truth and importance with the historical reality of Jesus

---

[60] *Trall.*, 9-10.

Christ, believed to be God made man, then, indeed, Docetism is part of the contemporary theological climate.

Closely to Docetism in the ancient Church were the various forms of Gnosticism. In the anxiety-laden atmosphere of the expanding Roman Empire, whose military might shattered the safety of small city communities in the ancient world, millions of estranged and uprooted people turned inward in their search for happiness. The Gnostics assured them that in some people, whom they called spiritual (*pneumatikoi*) a portion of immortal divine reality was encapsulated. Redemption consisted in *gnosis*, the knowledge of one's true divine identity. This knowledge liberated one from the oppressive fetters of the body that kept the divine spark imprisoned.

We find various groups of Christian Gnostics, too, opposing and accepting in varying degrees the teachings of the Catholic Church. Here I summarize only the form rejected as clearly heretical by the Fathers. In this view, Christ is the spiritual being fully aware of his divine identity, whose ministry consists in revealing to his followers the secret of their own divine identity. Christ thereby liberates them from the prison of their bodies and from the narrow confines of an evil, material world. The resurrection, consequently, takes place here and now, and does not have anything to do with the resurrection of a material body: it is merely the appropriation of true knowledge, *gnosis*, of the divine superiority of the spirit over the body and the material world. Just as in any other spiritual person spirit and matter are two beings, so also Jesus Christ consists of two beings: Jesus and the Christ. The divine element, named Christ, is joined to, or dwells in the material being Jesus. Their union is only temporary, and Christ leaves Jesus before the beginning of the latter's suffering. A divine being cannot be soiled by identifying itself with a material body; much less can it endure suffering and death. We find here the same repugnance towards the incarnation as in Docetism.

Already the Gospel of John and the First Letter of John struggle against a proto-Gnostic tendency. They stress that "the Word became flesh" and that Jesus Christ has come in the flesh;

he came not only in water, but "in water and blood" (Jn 1:14; 1 Jn 4:2; 5:6), that is, he truly died for us.

Irenaeus repeats again and again that Jesus the man and God the Word is "one and the same" rather than two realities, or two subjects. It is through his blood and through his flesh that the Lord rescued us.[61] The Eucharist, the flesh of the Lord, nourishes our flesh to eternal life. In fact, through the Eucharist we sanctify and return to God in thanksgiving his material creation.[62] Tertullian expresses a basic principle in the anti-Gnostic theology of the Fathers by coining this lapidary phrase: *caro salutis cardo* : "the flesh is the hinge of salvation."

Yet the Fathers, especially Clement of Alexandria and Origen, adopt and transform a basic insight of Gnosticism into a Christian principle: it is by knowing oneself that one can know God. However, this happens not because our true human self is God but because we have been created in the image of God. Moreover, self-knowledge is not a simple realization of identity but a recognition of sinfulness, an asking for pardon, and a starting out on the way of moral purification by receiving the light of Christ and by participating in his virtues. Thus, as the purity of the image is gradually restored, God is mirrored more and more clearly in the soul, and the soul, by knowing itself, knows God more and more perfectly.

2. Adoptionism

Another way of avoiding the stumbling block of the incarnation is Adoptionism. Jesus is only a man whom God has adopted as his Son and endowed with a special grace. Jewish monotheism is a possible influence for some form of Adoptionism, while the Hellenistic concern for God's absolute transcendence is another.

---

[61] Cf., for instance, *Against Heresies*, V:1:1; V:14:1-4.
[62] *Ibid.*, IV:18:4-5.

Paul of Samosata is the most important representative of the Hellenistic form of Adoptionism. According to him,

> Jesus Christ and the Word are other and other (*allos kai allos*) … The Word is… from above; Jesus Christ the man is from below. Mary… gave birth to a man equal to us, but better in every respect because (she gave birth) from the Holy Spirit.[63]

Thus the eternal Word and the son of Mary are two "he"s, two ontological subjects, two beings rather than one. The Logos dwells in the man Jesus Christ but is not one and the same as Jesus Christ. Moreover, the Logos is not a distinct Son from the Father, but rather his Word and Wisdom, another mode of God's existence. The Church condemned the teachings of Paul of Samosata at the Synod of Antioch in 268.

Adoptionist Christology has not lost its appeal today. It remains attractive to those who are trying to explain the relationship of the divine and human in Jesus in a way more accessible to the human mind than the incarnation. Those who say that the divine sonship of Jesus means no more than that God is present in the man Jesus with a unique intensity are close to a form of Adoptionism. The Fathers would say that, in such a Christology, God cannot truly take our sins and death upon himself, since he is not Jesus but only dwelling in him, much as he dwelt in one of the prophets or saints. In an Adoptionist perspective there is only a difference of degree between God's indwelling in other people and his presence in Jesus.

3. Arianism

In some sense Arianism is diametrically opposed to the view of Paul of Samosata. The Logos and Jesus are not two beings but one since the Logos has indeed become flesh (*sarx*). However, the

---

[63] Quoted in Carmody and Clark, eds., *Word and Redeemer*, pp. 39-40.

Logos and the flesh unite directly in such a way as to exclude a human soul in Jesus. Thus the Logos himself not only is the subject of all the actions of Christ, but also constitutes one nature with the flesh of Christ. Therefore — conclude the Arians — the Logos cannot truly be God: "If he (the Logos) were very God of very God, how could he become man?"[64] They cannot attribute change and suffering to God himself. Thus, they affirm that the Logos or the pre-existent Son is not God in the proper sense of the word, but a creature, albeit the first and highest creature, and mediator between God and the rest of his creation.

As is well known, the Council of Nicea solemnly rejected Arianism in 325. It distinguished between generation and creation, and defined that the Son has been "generated" (not "created") from the being (*ousia*) of the Father, rather than made from nothing (*ex ouk onton*). He is of one being (*homoousios*) with the Father, rather than merely similar (*homoiousios*) to the Father.[65]

Arianism is a prime example of a false Hellenization of Christianity. In Middle Platonism there are intermediate beings (the *nous* and the world soul) between the absolutely transcendent *monas* and the world because immediate contact between the transcendent divinity and the world is inconceivable. In Arianism the *nous* is identified with the Logos or the pre-existent Son, the world soul with the Holy Spirit. Accordingly, a true incarnation of God is ruled out as absurd.[66] In response, the Church at Nicea defined the absolute transcendent divinity of the pre-existent Son, and defined the same about the Holy Spirit at the First Council of Constantinople in 381. Again, the metaphysical clarification had important consequences for soteriology: the transcendent God himself has become man, suffered for our salvation, and united our nature with his own divine nature. In the words of Athanasius, the great defender of orthodoxy against Arianism:

---

[64] Quoted by Athanasius, *Against the Arians*, III, 27.

[65] See *DS*, 126.

[66] See A. Grillmeier, "Moderne Hermeneutik und altkirchliche Christologie," *Mit ihm und in ihm. Christologische Forschungen und Perspektiven* (Freiburg: Herder, 1975), pp. 532-538.

Our nature could be united with the divine nature because the Son is truly God. No creature would have been able to bring about this conjunction. Likewise, man would not have reached the presence of the Father, had not the true connatural Word of the Father taken on himself our nature ... For the purpose of our Lord's incarnation was to join what, by nature, is human to him who, by nature, is God... Thus he would have been as unsuitable for the work of salvation... had not his nature been identical with that of the Father as if he had not taken on a true and real body.[67]

4. Apollinarianism

Apollinaris, the bishop of Laodicea uses the same Logos-*sarx* formula as the Arians, but, in opposition to them, he affirms clearly the transcendent divinity of Christ. Just like the Arians, however, he denies the existence of a rational human soul in Christ because he believes that the Logos, directly united to his human flesh, takes over the function of the rational human soul. He can conceive of the Logos and Jesus as truly one being only according to the analogy of the soul and body uniting in one human nature. He is convinced that otherwise one cannot avoid the two beings Christology of Paul of Samosata.

The Fathers, especially Gregory of Nyssa and Gregory of Nazianzus, oppose his Christology vehemently and point out that if the Son of God did not take on a human mind, he has not really become man. Moreover, "what has not been assumed has not been healed, while what is united to God is saved."[68] In fact, the mind is the noblest part of a human being and it is also the part in which sin took its origin. How is it conceivable that God would not heal the mind? Taking up the insight of Origen, Gregory of Nazianzus explains that the Logos cannot be united directly to the flesh, but

---

[67] *Second Oration against the Arians*, 69-70.
[68] Gregory of Nazianzus, *Letter 101, First to Cledonius*, 32.

only through the mind, the human rational soul: "mind is mingled with mind, as nearer and more closely related, and through the mind with flesh, the mind mediating between divinity and materiality."[69] Apollinarianism was condemned by Pope Damasus and by the First Council of Constantinople.[70]

Towards the end of the 4th century, confronted with various errors, the Church clarified the full humanity (true body, true human suffering, rational soul or mind) and full divinity of Christ (identical in nature with the Father rather than an intermediate being between God and the rest of creation). She also made it clear that our Savior is not two beings; it is the one and the same Jesus Christ who is truly God and truly man. We have also seen that the conceiving of the union of divinity and humanity according to the analogy of soul and body, the only available analogy for explaining the mystery, led to two impasses, that of Arianism and that of Apollinarianism. In the anti-Apollinarian polemics, one more step of clarification occurred; Origen's insight was recovered and re-asserted: it is through the human rational soul, related to the transcendent God and ordained to union with the body, that the union between the Logos and the flesh is accomplished. However, the conceptual formulation was still lacking that would explain the relationship of the humanity and divinity in Christ, or, to put it in other words, it has not yet been clearly stated, what is one and what is twofold in Christ. Without using any technical terms, Gregory of Nazianzus came the closest to formulating accurately the insight of faith:

> If I am to speak concisely, the Savior is of this and that (*allo kai allo*) since the invisible is not the same as the visible, nor is the timeless identical with what is subject to time, but he is not this one and that one (*allos kai allos*). God forbid. For both (things) become one by the combination, God being made man and man being made God or however one should ex-

---

[69] *Ibid.*,1°, 11.
[70] *DS*, 149, 151.

press it. I say, this (thing) and that (thing) (*allo kai allo*) because it is the reverse of what is the case in the Trinity. For in
the Trinity there is this one and that one (*allos kai allos*) so as
not to confound the persons (*hypostaseis*), rather than this
(thing) or that (thing) (*allo kai allo*) because the three are one
and the same in divinity.[71]

In English the precise difference between the masculine and neu-
ter form *allos* and *allo* cannot be literally expressed. *Allos kai allos*
could be paraphrased as "this person and that person" and *allo kai
allo* as "this thing" or "that thing." However, such a paraphrase
would use a conceptual clarification that will occur only in the 5th
century. Yet Gregory intuitively anticipates this development by
affirming one "personal subject" in the incarnate Son but two
"things" or "elements," while in the Trinity he speaks about three
"personal subjects" but one "thing" or "element."

We should also remark that the clarification of Trinitarian terminology preceded that of Christology. The Cappadocians speak
of three *hypostaseis* in God and one *ousia*, at the time when their
christological terminology along with that of the whole Oriental
Church, remains fluid and undecided.

Further development in Christology will come from the interaction of Alexandrian and Antiochene Christology and from the
Christology of the West (where a more adequate christological terminology had been worked out earlier), mediated to the East
through the dogmatic letter of Pope Leo the Great, known generally as the Tome to Flavian. Before treating this last development,
however, we will review the prior christological development in the
West.

---

[71] *Letter 101, First to Cledonius,* 20-21.

5. Christological development in the West

Tertullian's christological terminology should be understood in the context of his polemics against the Monarchian heresy. In Tertullian's account the Monarchians rejected the Trinity in God himself. According to them God in himself is the Father, whereas the Son is, strictly speaking, only the human being united to God. Thus, the Monarchians considered Christ a composite being: insofar as he is God, he is identical with the Father; insofar as he is flesh or human, he is Son. In other words, in Jesus Christ, Christ is the name for God the Father, Jesus the man, who is called Son. Against this doctrine, Tertullian shows that there is a real Trinity of persons (*personae*)[72] in God. At the same time he avoids the opposite error of polytheism by explaining that there is only one substance (*substantia*) in the Father, the Son, and the Spirit. The Father has the fullness of divine substance; the Son is an effluence (*derivatio*) of this substance; both the Son and the Spirit have a share (*portio*) in it.[73] Thus there is some gradation or subordination between Father, Son, and Spirit, yet the Son and the Spirit are not separated from the unity of one divine reality.[74]

While, for Praxeas, the leader of the Monarchians, only the flesh — that is, the man Jesus — stands in a personal vis-à-vis with the Father, in Tertullian, it is the Word (*Sermo*), or Spirit (*Spiritus*), a divine subject, who does so. In the incarnation, the Word and the flesh do not become transformed into a third substance; the Word only clothes himself with flesh (flesh for Tertullian meaning all that is human, including a soul). His classic formula paves the way to the future:

---

[72] Note that *persona* is only one possible term for distinguishing what is three in God, though it is a term that marks the way of the future. But Tertullian also uses other explanatory terms, such as *nomen, species, forma, gradus*. For explaining the unity in God, *deitas, virtus, potestas, status* and *res* are also used in addition to *substantia* (cf. *Against Praxeas*, 12:6; 2:4).

[73] *Portio* here does not mean a limited portion but rather a share or participation.

[74] *Against Praxeas*, 9.

> We see a twofold reality, not fused but joined in one person, God and the man Jesus — I defer what I have to say concerning Christ — and the property of each substance is so preserved, that the Spirit did in him what was its own, that is to say, deeds of power, works, and signs, and the flesh showed its passions, was hungry when tempted by the devil, was thirsty when meeting the Samaritan woman, cried over Lazarus, was in anguish up to death and finally also died.[75]

When we inquire further into the term *persona* in the theology of Tertullian, we find that it has a twofold background. One is the Stoic understanding of both *substantia* and *persona*, which, fortunately, he does not consistently apply to Christology.[76] The other is the meaning of *persona* as theatrical mask and hence speaker in a drama. This meaning was adopted by Christian exegesis when they attributed some words of Scripture to the Father, some to the Son, and yet others to the Spirit. Tertullian, then, argues that there is a distinction of persons in God because there are three who speak, and they speak to each other and about each other:

> ...in these few quotations the distinction of persons in the Trinity is clearly indicated. For there is the Spirit himself who speaks, and the Father to whom he speaks, and the Son of whom he speaks.[77]

This characterization based on Scripture of the Trinity as actors and speakers in the drama of salvation history helps Tertullian toward understanding the *persona* as a subject who acts and speaks. Without providing full speculative underpinnings for the meaning of personal distinction in God, Tertullian does move toward a dialogical understanding of personhood, the theological implications of which have not yet been completely developed even now.

Besides the fact that he provided an impetus towards the dialogical understanding of person in theology, the great merit of

---

[75] *Ibid.*, 27.

[76] See Grillmeier, *Christ in Christian Tradition*, pp. 123-131.

[77] *Against Praxeas*, 11.

Tertullian lies in the fact that he developed for the first time a consistent terminology in both Trinitarian and christological discourse, a terminology that paved the way for further development. In the Trinity there are three persons and one substance, while in Christ two substances or *status* are united in one person.

Augustine uses the Trinitarian and christological terminology that originated with Tertullian. In the early Augustine, *persona* may mean the appearance or manifestation of someone.[78] Later, *persona* means more clearly the pre-existent subject of the eternal Son, who takes up human nature into the unity of his person so that this one subject is both God and man, "not because of the fusion of nature(s) but because of the unity of the person."[79] Even though the one person does not result from the combination of two natures, nonetheless Augustine uses not only the expression "the one person in both natures," but also the phrase "the one person consisting of two substances."[80]

The natural analogy for the union of the Word and man in Christ is the union of soul and body in man. Augustine would consider the soul-body union even more incredible than the incarnation, if the former were not a regular feature of the world. According to Augustine's Neo-Platonic background, it is harder to accept that the body unites to the soul than that the soul unites to God. After all, the intellectual soul on the one hand, and the mind of the Father, the Word, on the other, have an internal kinship, and the Word unites himself to the body only through the mediation of the human soul of Christ.[81]

Augustine's formulations express with striking poignancy the mystery of the perfect unity of God and man in the pre-existent personal subject of the Word. Christ has only one identity, wholly divine and wholly human at the same time. Commenting on the sanctification of the Son of Man, he explains:

---

[78] Cf. for instance, *Comm. on Gal.*, 27.

[79] *Sermon*, 186,1,1.

[80] *Sermon* 294:9; *Comm. on John* 99:1.

[81] *City of God*, 10:29. Cf. Grillmeier, *Christ in the Christian Tradition*, pp. 411-412.

In (God the Word) the Son of Man himself was sanctified from the beginning of his creation, when the Word became man, for the Word and man became one person. So he then sanctified himself in himself, that is, himself the man, in himself the Word; for the Word and man are the one Christ, sanctifying the man in the Word.[82]

6. The School of Alexandria

The Alexandrian school had its deviations, such as the Arianism and Apollinarianism we have already considered, but it produced great Catholic theologians as well — St. Athanasius, the champion of orthodoxy against the Arians and St. Cyril of Alexandria, the influential leader at the Council of Ephesus. The orthodox Alexandrians use the same Logos-*sarx*, Word-flesh terminology as the Arians and Apollinarians, but avoid their conclusions. Their Christology is predominantly Johannine, their view of the incarnation is based on Jn 1:14: "the Word has become flesh" or "has been enfleshed." The subject of every act of the man Jesus, and even the source of power for every act of Jesus, is the eternal Word: he is born of the Virgin Mary, and he suffers on the cross; he divinizes his flesh while retaining its humanity, and thereby his flesh becomes life-giving food that nourishes us for eternal life. Athanasius does not deny the existence of a rational soul in Christ, but, apart from one controversial text, he never mentions it. Cyril of Alexandria, likewise, acknowledges that Christ has a rational human soul, but, just as the Alexandrian school in general, does not give the humanity of Christ an active role. It is merely the *organon*, the instrument, through which we come to know the Word, which the immortal Word offers for us in sacrifice and through which the divine power of the Word transforms us and makes us share in his own divine life.

---

[82] *In quo et ipse filius hominis sanctificatus est ab initio creationis suae, quando Verbum factum est caro; quia una persona facta est Verbum et homo. Tunc ergo sanctificavit se in se, hoc est, hominem se in Verbo se; quia unus Christus Verbum et homo, sanctificans hominem in Verbo* (*Comm. on John*, 108:5).

Thus, the great value of Alexandrian Christology is the emphasis it puts on the ontological unity of Jesus Christ and its consistent affirmation that the eternal Word is the one ontological subject of all the actions and sufferings of Christ. However, the Alexandrians do not fully understand that the transcendent power of God does not diminish, let alone replace, the activity of the creature. Thus, they do not emphasize the fullness and the active autonomy of the humanity of Christ. The frequent expression of Cyril, "the one incarnate *'physis'* of the Word of God," is ambiguous. Whether he understands "*physis*" in an undifferentiated way as either "being," or subject, the Antiochenes rightly object that this formula does not express the full humanity of Christ and gives the impression that God and humanity are fused into one.

7. The School of Antioch

The main concern of the Antiochene theologians is to safeguard the full humanity of Christ against the Apollinarians and the absolute transcendence of God the Word against the Arians. Hence, they are wary of the Logos-*sarx* terminology; their characteristic terms are: Logos-*anthropos*, Word-man. The most characteristic representatives of this school are: Theodore, bishop of Mopsuestia; John, bishop of Antioch; and Nestorius, bishop of Constantinople.

Instead of starting with the Logos becoming man, these writers begin with the full human reality of Jesus. The eternal Word assumes this man and unites him to himself. The assumed man shares in the honor and the titles of the assuming Word; thus he is Son, God, and Lord. God dwells in the assumed man in a way different from his dwelling in the saints, because he dwells in this man as in his Son.[83]

The Antiochenes also teach that, just as sin and death came through man, so also the resurrection will happen through a man.

---

[83] Cf. Theodore of Mopsuestia, *On the Incarnation*, 7.

Our redemption is not only God's doing, but requires as well the human activity of the man assumed by the Logos:

> As death was by man, so also the resurrection from the dead (will be) by man... Therefore it was necessary that he should assume not only the body, but also the immortal and rational soul; and not only the death of the body had to cease, but also that of the soul, which is sin. Since, according to the sentence of the blessed (Paul), sin entered the world through man, and death entered through sin, it was necessary that sin, which was the cause of death, should have first been abolished, and then the abolition of death would have followed by itself.[84]

The Antiochenes are anxious to stress the unity of the assumed man and the assuming Logos, while, at the same time, excluding any Apollinarian fusion of divinity and flesh into one nature. In their view, *physis*, that is, essence or nature, cannot exist unless it has individual characteristics (*idioteteis*), which for them implies that the *physis* must have its own *hypostasis*. Thus for them *hypostasis* is an undifferentiated term: it can mean either an individual nature or an existing individual. According to their view, then, there must be two *physeis* and two *hypostaseis* in Christ, a human and a divine of each kind, and therefore the unity of Christ must be sought on another level. Each *physis* manifests itself in a *prosopon* (self-manifestation) and since in Christ the two *physeis* are combined by a *synapheia* (conjunction), they manifest themselves in one common *prosopon*, a *prosopon* of union. Christ shows himself in the world as one. The unity of Christ, then, is explained on the phenomenological level, that which appears and manifests itself in the world, rather than on the level of being.[85] Given this terminology, the Antiochenes could not but misunderstand the Christology of Cyril of Alexandria. Cyril's insistence on the one *physis* and one *hypostasis* of the Word made flesh seemed to them a denial of the human

---

[84] *Cat. Homilies* 5: *Word and Redeemer*, p. 85.

[85] For more details on the school of Antioch and the events around Ephesus, see Grillmeier, *Christ in the Christian Tradition*, pp. 417-487.

reality of Christ. For his part, Cyril found some Antiochene positions, such as that of Nestorius clearly heretical, as will be explained below.

The forte of the Antiochenes was their insistence on the full humanity of Christ and the active role of the man Jesus in our redemption. They also avoided any improper fusion between humanity and divinity. The weakness of their thought, on the other hand, derived from their inability to express with sufficient clarity the ontological unity of Christ and to show that this unity is based on the one ontological subject of God the Word. Nevertheless, we find Antiochene texts that come close to the later definition of Chalcedon. For instance, "And for our salvation he took upon himself to become man and to manifest himself to all. And he took to himself all that (belongs) to the nature of man...."[86] It is clear here that for Theodore the "Logos assuming man" means the same as the "Logos becoming man." Nevertheless, these two theological trends, the Alexandrian and Antiochene, developed into two rival factions in the Church which clashed and produced mutual anathemas at Ephesus. In dealing with the condemnation of the Nestorian heresy at Ephesus, I want to abstract from the political intrigues and even from the strictly historical question of whether Nestorius himself was a Nestorian. My wish is rather to concentrate on the christological issue that was, to some extent, clarified at Ephesus and on the christological error that was rejected.

What Cyril called the *skandalon oikoumenikon*, a universal scandal in the Church, arose because Nestorius denied that Mary was *theotokos* — God-bearer. This title was part of the kerygmatic and liturgical life of the Church and its denial brought to surface an even more fundamental problem: the Nestorians did not want to acknowledge that God himself suffered in the flesh. Both denials raised an uproar in the Church because it was instinctively felt that the Nestorian party endangered the very truth of the incarnation and redemption.

---

[86] Theodore of Mopsuestia, *Cat. Homilies*, 5:5.

To put it in technical terms, the Nestorians could not accept the *communicatio idiomatum* — the mutual predication of properties in christological statements. Beginning with the New Testament, the kerygma, liturgy, and theology of the Church developed a form of christological discourse in which one should predicate the properties (*idiomata:* qualities, actions or sufferings) of both the human and the divine natures about the one christological subject, designated according to his human or divine nature. Thus, one rightly says that God himself suffered and died in the flesh; God the Word was a small child; but one should also admit that this man from Nazareth is God's own Son, or this prophet from Galilee is God himself. We may speak in this way because one and the same subject is wholly divine and wholly human, possessing the properties of both natures. According to the same rule of discourse, one should also say that the eternal Son of God has Mary for his mother, or that Mary is the mother of God. This statement does not make Mary the source and origin of the divinity of the Son but it affirms that the Son is born of Mary according to his humanity. A mother is always the mother of a "subject," the child who is born of her, not of a "human nature." Thus, if the child Jesus and God the Son is one and the same subject, then Mary is the mother of God the Son. In this way the acknowledgment of the divine motherhood of Mary becomes the litmus test of christological orthodoxy: if we profess Mary as mother of God, we thereby also confess the ontological unity of the divine and the human in Jesus: Jesus is the Son of God made man. The two beliefs imply each other.

Nestorius later reluctantly agreed to the legitimacy of the use of *theotokos*, but only in the sense that "Mary is the mother of the inseparable temple of God the Word," that is to say, she is the mother of the man Jesus who is inseparably united to God the Word as the Word's living temple. Such a formulation, then, although intending to stress the inseparable conjunction of the Word and the man Jesus, cannot avoid implying that there are actually two subjects in Christ.

8. The Councils of Ephesus and Chalcedon (431, 451)

The Council of Ephesus, called together to settle the Nestorian controversy, was dominated by Cyril and his party. Cyril's second letter to Nestorius was read at the Council and solemnly approved as being in accord with the profession of faith of Nicea. By accepting this letter, the Council affirmed that the union between the Word and the man Jesus is not merely "according to the will or to good pleasure,"[87] nor does it consist in the assumption of a *prosopon* (self-manifestation) only. It takes place by the initiative of the Word "who, having united to himself *kath' hypostasin* (in reality) flesh animated by a rational soul, became man in an ineffable and incomprehensible manner and was called Son of Man." The other important statement in the letter of Cyril, which the Council approved, is about the title "Mother of God":

> It was not that an ordinary man was born first of the holy Virgin on whom afterwards the Word descended; what we say is that, being united with the flesh from the womb, (the Word) has undergone birth in the flesh, making the birth in the flesh His own... Thus (the holy Fathers) unhesitatingly called the holy Virgin "Mother of God" (*theotokos*).[88]

The Antiochene bishops separated themselves from the Cyrillians and met in special sessions. Mutual excommunications followed and, as a result of the Council, the Church became even more divided. The "Orientals" (as the Antiochenes were called) simply would not accept Cyril's formulations. Yet, in 433, Cyril and John of Antioch were able to agree on a compromise formula that did justice to the concerns of both parties. They confessed that one and the same Jesus Christ is "perfect God and perfect man composed of rational soul and body... consubstantial to the Father as to his divinity and consubstantial to us as to his humanity." They acknowl-

---

[87] That is, the Word finding his good pleasure in Jesus whose will is totally united to his.

[88] *CF*, 604-605.

edged two *physeis* in Christ but also the union of the two *physeis*. However, they still did not succeed in formulating the principle of union in Christ.

The peace did not last long. Eutyches, the superior of a monastery in Constantinople, stirred up controversy through a hardened interpretation of Cyril's christological formulas. He insisted that Christ was of two *physeis* before the union (of the incarnation) but one *physis* after the union. He was also reluctant to accept that Christ's humanity was consubstantial with us.[89] When condemned by a synod in Constantinople, he appealed to other bishops. With the leadership of Dioscorus, Cyril's successor in Alexandria, and the participation of a large number of monks, an aggressive movement was organized to vindicate Eutyches. This party became known in history as the Monophysite movement, since they acknowledged only one *physis* in Christ. They clarified the ambiguous formulas of Cyril in the wrong direction. In their usage, or at least as the bishop of Constantinople, Flavian and the bishop of Rome, Leo the Great, understood their usage, the one *physis* of Christ meant simply one nature. This would imply such a fusion between the humanity and divinity as to compromise both the transcendence of Christ's godhead and the integrity of his human nature. Since the very mystery of the incarnation was in danger, Leo felt obligated to expound the Catholic doctrine in a long dogmatic letter to Flavian, which became known as the Tome to Flavian. Using the best insights of Western theology, this letter affirmed the one *persona* and two *naturae* in Christ, excluding both Nestorianism and Monophysitism. In a masterfully balanced formulation, Leo explained both the preservation of the character of both natures and the paradoxical union of human and divine qualities, actions, and sufferings in the same subject:

> The character proper to each of the two natures, which come together in one person, being therefore preserved, lowliness was taken on by majesty, weakness by strength, and mortal-

---

[89] Cf. *Acta Conc. Oecum.*, ed. E. Schwartz (Berlin, 1914 ff.) 2.11, pp. 142-144.

ity by eternity. And, in order to pay the debt of our fallen state, the inviolable nature was united to another (nature) subject to suffering so that, as was fitting to heal our wounds, one and the same "mediator between God and the human race, Christ Jesus, himself human" (1 Tm 2:5), could die in one nature and not in the other. The true God, therefore, was born with the complete and perfect nature of a true human being; He is complete in His nature and complete in ours....[90]

For a while the party of Eutyches prevailed. His main opponents were deposed at a gathering in Ephesus (449 A.D.), which Pope Leo called a robbers' synod (*latrocinium*, rather than *concilium*) and whose decrees were condemned by a Synod in Rome. After the death of the emperor Theodosius II, however, the new emperor convoked a new Council at Chalcedon. The letter of Leo was read in assembly, and the 520 bishops exclaimed: "Peter has spoken through Leo." They recognized the apostolic faith of Peter in Leo's teaching, which served as a guideline and source for the document they were about to compose. New research has made it clear that the dogmatic definition of Chalcedon was not intended as a confession of faith to stand by itself. The Council Fathers preceded their own document with the creeds of Nicea and Constantinople, which they acknowledged as sufficient for the full knowledge of the faith. The reason for composing a new document was not to replace the existing creeds with a better one but, in view of new heresies, to clarify the meaning of one article in the Nicene-Constantinopolitan creed: "He became flesh... and was made man." Thus, the definition of Chalcedon is a commentary on one statement of the creed and receives its full meaning only within the latter's historical, Trinitarian, and soteriological perspective.[91] One should not then fault it for its "static, ontic language," as many interpreters have done recently, since it was meant to be integrated into the whole of the Church's confession of faith. Because of its importance we quote the text here in full:

---

[90] *CF*, 611.

Following therefore the holy Fathers, we unanimously teach to confess one and the same Son, our Lord Jesus Christ, the same perfect in divinity and perfect in humanity, the same truly God and truly man composed of rational soul and body, the same one in being (*homoousios*) with the Father as to the divinity and one in being with us as to the humanity, like unto us in all things but sin (cf. Heb 4:5). The same was begotten from the Father before the ages as to the divinity and in the latter days for us and our salvation was born as to his humanity from Mary the Virgin Mother of God (*theotokos*).

We confess that one and the same Lord Jesus Christ, the only begotten Son, must be acknowledged in two natures (*physis*), without confusion or change, without division or separation. Their union never abolished the distinction between the natures but rather the character proper to each of the two natures was preserved as they came together in one person (*prosopon*) and one *hypostasis*. He is not split or divided into two persons, but He is one and the same only-begotten, God the Word, the Lord Jesus Christ, as formerly the prophets and later Jesus Christ Himself have taught us about Him and as has been handed down to us by the Symbol of the Fathers.[92]

If we investigate the content and the wording of the Chalcedonian definition, we do not find a single new idea or expression. It is a synthesis of the best elements in the Cyrillian and Antiochene tradition, while it is also influenced by the Western theology of the Tome to Flavian. This "ecumenical" provenance, however, only adds to its importance, which may be summarized in the following points.[93]

    1. For the first time in history, an Ecumenical Council rep-

---

[91] Cf. W. Kasper, "*Einer aus der Trinität…*" *Zur Neubegründung einer spirituellen Christologie in trinitätstheologischer Perspektive: Theologie und Kirche* (Mainz: Grünewald, 1987), esp. pp. 217-227. Kasper also provides an informative bibliography of recent works on the issue.

[92] *CF*, 614-615.

[93] Concerning the reactions to the Council of Chalcedon and its gradual universal acceptance, see A. Grillmeier, *Christ in Christian Tradition*, Vol. II. *From Chalcedon to Justinian I* (Atlanta: John Knox, 1987).

resenting both the East and the West was able to express in clear language both the unity and the diversity in Christ. It took over the Antiochene terminology of *physis* to designate what is twofold in Christ, but deepened the Antiochene conception of what is one in him by adding to the Antiochene *prosopon* the Cyrillian *hypostasis*: "the two *physeis*... came together in one *prosopon* and one *hypostasis*." The Council did not invent these terms as a result of philosophical inquiry, nor did it define them, but recognized intuitively that, in their present situation, these terms safeguarded best the mystery of the incarnation, united various factions in the Church, and excluded definite errors. It was left to later theologians to define the exact meaning of these terms. Yet it is evident that, by explaining *prosopon* as *hypostasis*, the Council Fathers wanted to affirm that the unity of Christ was not merely phenomenological, one in appearance only, but a unity of being. Thus, the Council document no longer understands *hypostasis* in the usual Stoic sense of the Antiochenes as individual nature (since in that case one should attribute two *hypostaseis* to Christ), but rather in a sense that comes very close to that of *persona* in the Tome to Flavian, designating an ontological subject to whom the human and divine natures, human and divine qualities, should be attributed. In this way under the "weight" of the Christian mystery, a new concept is born, that of the person, which had hitherto been unknown in pagan Hellenistic culture,[94] but from now on will prove crucially important for the

---

[94] Historians of dogma wonder about the strange fact that in the West a unified Trinitarian and christological terminology had already been developed by the end of the 2nd century: in God there are three *personae* and one *substantia* or *natura*, in Christ there are two *substantiae*, or *naturae*, but only one *persona*; whereas, in the East, the Trinitarian terminology became clarified relatively early, in the 4th century (three *hypostaseis* in God, but one *ousia*), yet the same terminology was not applied to Christ till a century later. Why did the christological clarification in the East take so much more time and effort? Perhaps the clue lies in the different background to the key terms, *hypostasis* and *persona*. If *hypostasis* means individual nature, that is, *ousia* and *idiotes*, essence and individual property, then, with some transformation, it can easily be applied to the Trinity. The one *ousia* in God exists only in three *hypostaseis*, that is, as individualized by the properties of opposing relationships, fatherhood and sonship, etc. Yet the same schema does not fit Christology so easily: the human *ousia* of Christ must have individual characteristics, but then it becomes a human *hypostasis* parallel to the *hypostasis* of the Word. Thus, *hyposta-*

growing understanding of the mystery of the Trinity, of Christ and of the human person.[95]

2. Rather than being the consummate Hellenization of Christianity as many historians have tried to present it, the Chalcedonian dogma fends off a new effort of Hellenization. Taking up Hellenistic terms, the Church transforms them gradually until they adopt a new meaning more apt to express the Christian mystery of faith. Interestingly, it is Monophysitism that represents an uncritical acceptance of Hellenistic principles: The fusion of the Logos and humanity into one nature in Monophysitism corresponds to the Hellenistic thought pattern we have also seen in Arianism in a crasser and more overt form. Both Arianism and Monophysitism conceive of Christ as the intermediary being between the transcendent God and humanity. If Christ is not of the same essence (*homoousios*) with us, then he is not truly human; he is above us. On the other hand, if the human nature of Christ is absorbed into his divinity, then he cannot truly be a transcendent God either, since the Logos and humanity have been fused into one nature. In the words of Kasper,

> The mingling of divinity and humanity, as conceived of by Eutyches, corresponded entirely to the Hellenistic mentality and stood in sharp contradiction to the Christian mentality, which emphasizes the qualitative transcendence between God and man. For the Bible it is of fundamental importance that man is not God (Ezk 28:1.9) and that God is not man (Nb 23:19; 1 S 15:29; Hos 11:9). Any kind of divine-human mixture or intermediary is inconceivable on Christian grounds. Thus Chalcedon, just as Nicea, says in Hellenistic terms

---

sis, in order to be applied to Christ in the sense of personal subject, had to undergo a radical change of meaning. In the West, the key term, *persona*, had a twofold background meaning, and the Stoic concept corresponding to that of *hypostasis* is only one of them. As we have seen in the usage of Tertullian, *persona* also means an actor in a drama, an interlocutor in a dialogue. This meaning lends itself more easily to the theological notion of "personal subject": he who acts and speaks, and ultimately, he who is.

[95] See A. Grillmeier, "Moderne Hermeneutik und altkirchliche Christologie," *Mit ihm und in ihm. Christologische Forschungen und Perspektiven* (Freiburg: Herder, 1975), pp. 549-554.

something that is quite un-Hellenistic, in fact, anti-Hellenistic.[96]

3. The above struggle around words may seem to the casual reader much ado about nothing, a hairsplitting exercise without existential relevance. However, if correctly understood, the Chalcedonian definition appears as a necessary explication of the metaphysical foundations for our redemption. If the Nestorians are right and God the Word is joined to the man Jesus only by a common appearance, then God did not take upon himself our sins, our sufferings; then God himself did not die for us in his human nature. This would rob Christianity of its very center. If the Monophysites are right, again, the incarnation is deprived of its reality. God did not truly become one of us in everything but sin. Moreover, if this is so, human beings cannot be saved **as humans**, because in order to conform to Christ we must lose our full humanity.

Monophysitism, while officially repudiated as a heresy, has survived up to recent times as a mentality among Catholics. Many of us have a hard time accepting the limited and simple humanity of Christ as it appears in the Gospels. For instance, we tried to circumvent for a long time the fact that Jesus displayed real ignorance and asked true questions.

Yet, as happens with every dogmatic definition, the precision of, and the emphasis on, certain truths has the side-effect of causing other truths to be neglected, and in particular the larger whole of which the defined dogmatic truth is only a part.

1. Thus, in the course of history, the Chalcedonian decree was interpreted in increasing isolation from its context in the creed of the Church. Instead of being an explanation of one aspect of Christology, it became the foundation for the whole christological treatise.

2. The Monophysites hardened into a Hellenistic thought form a genuine Christian truth, and this truth, as a result of Chalcedon, became more and more forgotten until modern times. Even

---

[96] Kasper, *Einer aus der Trinität*, pp. 224-225.

though St. Paul calls the earthly Jesus Son, he still affirms that Christ Jesus "was constituted Son of God in power according to the spirit of holiness by his resurrection from the dead" (Rm 1:3-4). He who was in the form of God took on the form of the slave, but through his obedience unto death on the cross, he was exalted and given the divine name (Ph 2:5-11). According to the ancient kerygma preserved in the Acts, Peter announces that, through the resurrection, "God has made both Lord and Messiah this Jesus whom you crucified" (2:36). Melito of Sardis proclaims about Christ: "Buried as man, he rose from the dead as God, being by nature both God and man."[97] Origen, while maintaining that Jesus remains a human being forever, also affirms his deification after the resurrection.[98] Thus, continuing a biblical theme, a patristic tradition maintained the deification of the man Jesus through his resurrection. However, the deification did not eliminate but rather perfected his humanity, so that, entirely transformed by the Holy Spirit, it fully shares in God's splendor and power. His flesh no longer screens and dims the divine light but rather becomes a transparent medium that communicates the fullness of divine glory.

With the later general acceptance of the Chalcedonian decree, attention became fixed on the moment of the incarnation, and the relationship of the human and the divine in Christ was considered from a static, metaphysical perspective. Thus, a gain in understanding was accompanied by a gradual loss: the dynamic perspective of salvation history according to which there were two distinct stages in the history of Christ, his earthly and his risen existence, was increasingly neglected in the theological mainstream. Moreover, the link between Christology and anthropology weakened: our personal history of salvation was no longer seen in a causal and participatory relationship with the history of Christ.[99]

3. It was important to stress that the divine and human na-

---

[97] *Paschal Hom.*, 8.

[98] For instance, in *Hom. on Luke*, 29.

[99] This tradition survived in the monastic theology of the Middle Ages, in particular in the theology of St. Bernard. See pp. 251-256.

tures in Christ remain "without confusion or change, without division or separation." In the context of the Council this formula means that the humanity of Christ finds its own full reality through union with the divine nature.[100] Yet, in later "popular" theology, this carefully balanced understanding degenerated into a simplified conception which considered the two natures as being almost on the same level, running parallel yet unconfused "like water and oil," according to an unfortunate comparison of J.A.T. Robinson.[101]

We must admit that Chalcedon did not treat the dynamic relationship of the two natures. Nothing was said about how they are related to each other in their respective activities. In this matter Leo's Tome says more and points toward the future: "Each of the two natures performs the functions proper to it in communion with the other: the Word does what pertains to the Word and the flesh what pertains to the flesh."[102]

9. The Second and Third Councils of Constantinople (553, 680-681)

In spite of incorporating the best insights of Antioch and Alexandria, Chalcedon did not bring the desired unity and peace to the Church. The Monophysite tendency continued, and won over the support of the emperor. Moreover, those of a Nestorian inclination interpreted the Chalcedonian definition of the one *hypostasis* of Christ as resulting from the coming together of the divine and human natures.

The Second Council of Constantinople clearly affirmed what was already implicit in the Chalcedonian definition,[103] namely, that the one person and the one *hypostasis* of Christ did not result from

---

[100] Cf. Kasper, *Einer aus der Trinität*, pp. 225-226.

[101] See *Honest to God* (London: SCM Press, 1963), pp. 63-70.

[102] *CF*, 612.

[103] According to Chalcedon, one and the same subject who has been born from the Father before all ages was born in the last days for our salvation according to his humanity. Clearly then, the subject has pre-existed to, rather than was constituted by his humanity.

the coming together of two natures, but rather the eternal Son, "one of the Holy Trinity" took on a full human nature, and was crucified in the flesh.[104]

Another, even more important, clarification occurred at the Third Council of Constantinople. A Monophysite group accepted a human nature in Christ but denied his human will; others, while admitting the existence of a human will, denied that his human will had any activity. Their concern was to avoid any division in Christ, and for them the affirmation of two wills in Christ would necessarily divide him. Following the teaching of Pope Agatho in his letter to the emperor, and including the insights of Maximus the Confessor, the Council felt obliged to state explicitly the existence of a human will and also the activity of that will in Christ:

> We likewise proclaim in (Christ), according to the teaching of the holy Fathers, two natural volitions or wills and two natural actions, without division, without change, without separation, without confusion. The two natural wills are not — by any means — opposed to each other, as the impious heretics assert; but His human will is compliant, it does not resist or oppose but rather submits to His divine and almighty will. For, as the wise Athanasius says, it was necessary that the will of the flesh move itself, but also that it should be submissive to the divine will; because, just as His flesh is said to be and is the flesh of God the Word, so too the natural will of his flesh is said to be and is God the Word's very own, as He Himself declares: "I have come down from heaven, not to do my own will but the will of Him who sent me" (Jn 6:38). He calls the will of His flesh His own will, because the flesh also has become His own.[105]

---

[104] Cf. especially *CF*, 620 canons 4-10. The Second Council of Constantinople started its deliberation in rebellion to Pope Vigilius. Vigilius opposed the Emperor who wanted him to condemn the writings of the best representatives of the school of Antioch, the so-called *Tria capitula*, the Three Chapters. The Pope confirmed the decrees of the Council only later and reluctantly. Thus the dogmatic weight of these decrees should not be exaggerated; however, their teaching clearly continues Chalcedon and prepares the Third Council of Constantinople whose dogmatic definitions cannot be called into question.

[105] *CF*, 635.

The same four adjectives ("without division, without change, without separation, without confusion"), that characterize the relationship of the two natures in the decree of Chalcedon, were applied here to describe the relationship of the divine and human wills. But the result of this affirmation is not a "split Christ." Not only is the moral submission of the human will to the divine emphasized, but also the metaphysical truth that the human will is God the Word's very own. The belonging of the human will to the one divine subject excludes any dichotomy in Christ.

With this teaching, the Council explicated what is most essential in the humanity of Jesus for contemporary man and woman, our human freedom. Without human freedom, he would have lacked what makes us most human, the struggle to choose freely what is right, and the gradual self-realization of the person by a series of free decisions.

Moreover, by expounding the free human will of Christ, the Council provided the metaphysical foundation for the soteriological teaching that, even though our salvation is God's undeserved gift, the human race has been saved by a human being, and more precisely, by the free acts of the man Jesus of Nazareth.

With the decree of the Third Council of Constantinople, the most important christological truths have received a classic formulation and become the common heritage of the Catholic Church. They are not to be regarded as an unsurpassable peak that a developing Christology could never transcend, but rather guideposts to warn against dead-end trails and to mark the right direction for further deepening and articulating the Church's understanding of the mystery of Christ.

CHAPTER III

Medieval Christology

I will provide only three examples from the diverse and rich Christologies of the Middle Ages: St. Bernard, whose thought continues that of the Fathers in a new age, with a new sensibility; St. Anselm, who stands between the patristic and scholastic ideal of theology, and St. Thomas, who represents the highest achievement of scholasticism.[106]

1. St. Bernard of Clairvaux

In the monasteries the heritage, method, and ideal of patristic theology survived and flourished throughout the Middle Ages. However, the center of attention shifted from the mystery of Christ to its personal appropriation in the spiritual life of the monk — in technical terms, from "objective" to "subjective redemption."

St. Bernard has often been called the "last of the Fathers," since his thought provides a synthesis (though highly original) of patristic theology. In his Christology — more consistently perhaps than any of the Fathers — he works out the correspondence and the causal relationship between the stages of the history of Christ and the stages of the soul's spiritual development.[107] Just as Christ himself has been given to us, so all his mysteries are "for us" and

---

[106] This order of treatment is based on the development of ideas rather than chronology. Anselm died before St. Bernard's literary activity began.

[107] For a detailed treatment of St. Bernard's Christology and further bibliography, see the appendix of this work: "Relationship between Anthropology and Christology. St. Bernard, a Teacher for Our Age."

"are effective for us."[108] In other words, all that Jesus did and suffered, from his birth through his public ministry and suffering on the cross up to the ascension and the sending of the Holy Spirit, serves the various needs of our souls. In following Christ, the soul can participate in his mysteries only gradually.

For St. Bernard, original sin consisted in trying to rise to the greatness of God by acquiring knowledge; ever since, Adam's posterity has been engaged in the same attempt: in seeking knowledge, man seeks a divine exaltation opposed to his creaturely status. Thus our sin is primarily and pre-eminently the sin of the human spirit: an attempt at false self-possession, denying the very truth of oneself. The consequences of sin then follow from the very nature of sin itself: the false self-possession distorts the spiritual nature of man, who has been created in the image of the Son, himself the perfect image of the Father. Thus the human spirit who wanted to rise through knowledge to the height of the absolute spirit falls away through this very attempt from his own spiritual nature and becomes flesh: the freedom of his spirit is lost, his corruptible body weighs him down, he gets involved in the sins of the flesh; he can now know, value, and desire only what belongs to the realm of the flesh. Yet, even though sin has distorted the image of God in him, it could not fully destroy it.

This is the background against which the process and goal of redemption can be understood. The goal is expressed in various complementary ways. Individual Christians realize in themselves the vocation of the Church, the one pure Spouse of Christ, and in mutual love become one spirit with Christ. The goal is also described as the union of the members with their Head, Christ, and as a complete conformation of the soul to Christ who dwells within her. While union with Christ is spiritual, it will be perfected only when we receive back our risen glorified bodies at the end of times.

The process of redemption is presented in many different concepts. I will outline here only two aspects. The first is primarily an

---

[108] *Hom. on Ascension*, 4:1.

anthropological schema with christological implications; the other is predominantly a schema of the history of Christ but it is presented in its anthropological significance. Every stage in the history of the Word incarnate effects a certain stage in our redemption.

1. Afraid to face their distorted selves, sinners avoid looking at their soul; they dissipate themselves in worldly pleasures. Conversion begins when, shaken up by God's call, we return to our heart, face ourselves, and acknowledge the misery we see there. St. Bernard calls this state knowing the Truth in ourselves. Truth in this context means Christ himself. How can we know Christ the Truth by knowing our own sinful state and by judging ourselves? We can judge ourselves in the light of Truth if we somehow already know the Truth; we can condemn the present state of our soul only if we have some knowledge of what our soul, as the pure image and mirror of God the Son, should have been. Thus, the judging of oneself with a realistic self-knowledge presupposes and reinforces the knowledge of Christ in whose image our soul has been created.

Once the sinner acknowledges his own misery, he knows that only mercy and grace can save him. Thus by realizing his own need for mercy he develops mercy and compassion for his neighbors. Through the experience of his own misery, the sinner feels the misery of his neighbors as his own and accepts solidarity with them:

> Just as pure truth is seen only with a pure heart, the misery of a brother is more truly felt with a miserable heart. But in order to feel misery in your heart because of another's misery, you must first recognize your own so that you may find your neighbor's mind in your own and learn from yourself how to help him, according to the example of our Savior, who willed his passion in order to learn compassion.[109]

Instead of looking down on his neighbors, like the Pharisee who rejoices that he is not a sinner like the rest of humankind, the con-

---

[109] *The Steps of Humility*, III:6.

254 JESUS CHRIST: FUNDAMENTALS OF CHRISTOLOGY

verting sinner embraces all human beings as his brothers and sisters in need of the same mercy as he himself is. In this way, by practicing mercy and love, he discovers the Truth, Christ, in his neighbors in a new way. At this point he can now appreciate and appropriate the love and mercy of Christ, who was not a sinner and thus had no misery, but out of love for us wanted to share in our misery. In this way, the divine image in the soul is gradually purified from distortions and begins to reflect the Divine Word more clearly. The soul becomes ready now, through her own purified self, to know God more directly. She is ready for the "wedding," in which she will become, through perfect mutual love (a love which is simultaneously knowledge), "one spirit" with the Lord.

2. The second schema coordinates the stages of the Word's descent in the incarnation and passion and his ascent in the resurrection and ascension with the stages of the sinner's journey towards full union with Christ. Since the sinner is imprisoned in the realm of the flesh, the Son of God himself becomes flesh, taking upon himself all the misery of the sinner. His birth, his existence in the flesh, and his death on the cross hide his divine glory and power. However, he could not have revealed more perfectly his divine goodness and love than through his life and death in the flesh. The revelation of the Father's love reaches its perfection on the cross, when Jesus' heart is pierced with the lance and there, through Jesus' side wound, the invisible love of the Father's own heart becomes visible. Since fleshly man can know and love only what is flesh, the Son of God, showing his divine love in and through his life and death in the flesh, attracts and focuses our love on his flesh; thereby, fleshly man is first introduced to the love of God.

If the sinner (the fleshly man) has faithfully meditated on the mysteries of the earthly Christ, obeyed his teachings, especially that of loving and serving one's neighbor, and carried his cross faithfully, then, gradually, he will become ready to know and love the risen Lord. He will need less and less the lantern or the screen of Christ's flesh to dim the blinding light of his divinity: he will know and love Christ the Word, in other words, he will gradually become capable of knowing and appreciating the glory of God shining through the risen Christ. But this cannot happen unless Christ first ascends to heaven, that is, unless his presence accessible to sense experience is withdrawn from us. Everyone intent on spiritual growth has to go through this phase. It is better for us that Christ goes away. Only then will we be able to receive the Holy Spirit and thereby appreciate his invisible spiritual presence in us as Word, Truth, and Wisdom. Christ the Wisdom of God will then transform the soul so thoroughly that he himself becomes the soul's own wisdom. At that stage one will know what is good by a certain spiritual "taste" (*sapere* means both "to taste" and "to have wisdom") and will do what is right, not just because of an intellectual conviction and by a sheer effort of the will, but because it "tastes" good to do good. There will be a deep connaturality between the soul transformed by Christ, the Wisdom of God, and all that is morally right and true, because Christ to whom the soul is united is Justice and Truth itself.

Thus, at the end of the spiritual journey, the soul is granted in a different way what she had been seeking for in her sin: a superior knowledge. This knowledge, however, does not puff up; it is not only knowledge but love, knowledge through love the source of which is Christ, Wisdom in person, who dwells in the soul and transforms her.

The following text illustrates many aspects of the Wisdom theme in Bernard and shows the climax of spiritual life, the conformation of the soul to the indwelling Wisdom who is Christ:

> "Write about wisdom in leisure" — says the wise man. Thus Wisdom's leisures are work; the more leisurely wisdom is, the more it is exercised in its own way. On the other hand, well-exercised virtue shines more brightly, and the more duties it performs, the more tested it becomes. If one defines wisdom as the love of virtue, in my opinion, he does not deviate from the truth. For where love is, there is no labor but only savor. Perhaps wisdom is named after savor which, accruing to virtue as a seasoning, makes savory what had been experienced by itself as somewhat saltless and rough. Nor would I find it wrong if someone defined wisdom as the savor of goodness.

We lost this savor almost at the very beginning of our race. As soon as the venom of the ancient serpent infected the palate of the heart, with the experience of the flesh prevailing, goodness no longer tasted to the soul but rather a harmful savor entered it. The emotions and thoughts of man, then, are prone to evil since his youth, that is, since the folly of the first woman. Thus the folly of the woman expelled the savor of goodness because the malice of the snake circumvented the folly of the woman. But through the same means by which Evil appeared to have conquered for a while, Evil is now painfully aware to have been conquered forever. For, look, Wisdom filled again the heart and body of a woman, so that we, who have been deformed into folly by a woman, might be conformed to Wisdom by a woman. Now Wisdom conquers Evil unceasingly in the minds it entered, expelling the savor of Evil, which the woman introduced, by a much better savor. When Wisdom enters the soul, it deprives the experience of the flesh of its taste, purifies the intellect, heals and repairs the palate of the heart. Goodness is now tasty to the healthy palate, in fact, Wisdom itself tastes better than which nothing exists among good things.[110]

2. St. Anselm of Canterbury

St. Anselm's inquiry into why God has become man and why he died for us takes place within the perspective of faith.[111] He intends to provide understanding and joy for those who contemplate what they believe and show non-Christians, Jews, and Moslems, on the grounds of what they themselves believe (the existence of a

[110] *Sermons on the Canticle of Canticles*, 85:8.

[111] For details and further bibliography, see Ansélme de Cantorbery, *Pourquoi Dieu s'est fait homme*. Introduction, bilingual text and notes by R. Roques, *Sources chrétiennes*, 91 (Paris: Cerf, 1963). Many contemporary theologians, such as Rahner, Schillebeeckx, and Küng, dismiss Anselm's theory. In contrast, R. Haubst (*Vom Sinne der Menschwerdung. 'Cur Deus homo,'* Munich, 1969), W. Kasper (*Jesus the Christ*, pp. 219-221), H.U. von Balthasar (*Theodramatik*. III. *Handlung*, pp. 235-241) find it most valuable.

just and merciful God and of human sinfulness), the necessity of the incarnation.[112]

Anselm first criticizes and discards a patristic theory for the necessity of the death of Christ, according to which the devil held humanity justly in his power, because we had gone over to him of our own free will. Therefore, the devil could be justly deprived of possessing the human race only by being led to commit an excess of his own. This he does by killing the God-man, who did not deserve death.[113]

Anselm asserts to the contrary that the death of Christ was necessary, not for the just treatment of the devil, but for preserving the just order of the universe. According to this just order, the will of the rational creature ought to be wholly subject to God:

> This is all the honor and the only honor which we owe to God and which he requires of us.... He who does not render this due honor to God, takes away from God what is God's and dishonors God; and in this sin consists.[114]

Whenever we steal someone's property or honor, we owe restitution. Not only must we give back what we have unjustly taken, we must also make some compensation pleasing to the offended person and in proportion to the pain our offense inflicted. This is called satisfaction.

By freely yielding to the temptation of the devil, our ancestors have violated the honor due to God. Of course, if God's honor is considered in itself, nothing can increase or decrease it. The sinner has dishonored God only in himself and thereby disturbed the order and the beauty of the universe.[115] For this he must either suffer punishment involuntarily or provide a voluntary satisfaction. Even though God is so merciful that no greater mercy can be conceived

---

[112] *Why God Became Man*, I:1.
[113] I:7.
[114] I:11.
[115] I:15.

of, he does not forgive us without satisfaction; mercy without justice would not be fitting for God, since it would allow disorder to enter into God's kingdom. Moreover, if the unjust acts of humankind were forgiven by mercy alone, without due satisfaction, "injustice would operate more freely than justice"; in fact, injustice would become "like God," the supreme power in the universe, since it would not be subjected to any law whatsoever. As it is, God is inseparably both supreme mercy and supreme justice.[116]

What would due satisfaction for sin be? Since sin offends against the infinite majesty of God, every sin is in some sense an infinitely grave offense. Accordingly, the sinner owes God something greater than everything that has been created or can be created; in other words, the satisfaction would have to surpass everything that is not God.

If this is so, only God is capable of satisfaction, because only God can give something greater than everything that is not God. However, only the human being owes satisfaction, not God. Therefore, it is necessary that the God-man, he who is fully divine and fully human in one person, should do it.[117]

But what can Jesus Christ, the God-man, offer as satisfaction to the Father? As a creature, he owes obedience in every act to God throughout his life. This, then, cannot constitute a satisfaction. However, having committed no sin whatsoever, Jesus does not "owe" death. Nor may the Father impose on Jesus the obligation to die since this would be most unjust. Jesus freely chose to die in order to serve justice with courage.[118] He "gave his precious life, in fact himself, I mean, such a unique person with such a unique act of will."[119]

It was most appropriate for the God-man to give his life for us as satisfaction. Human sin was the easiest conceivable victory

---

[116] *Ibid.*

[117] II:6-9.

[118] I:9.

[119] "...*tam pretiosam vitam, immo se ipsum, tantam scilicet personam tanta voluntate dedit*" (II:18).

for the devil. Now in satisfying, man must conquer the devil in the hardest way conceivable, that is, by dying. By sinning, man has removed himself from God so much that he could not have removed himself more; in satisfying, he gives himself to God so that he could not give himself more. Thus the life of Christ freely given in death is more deserving of love than all the sins committed are deserving of hate; it can provide infinitely more than is sufficient to satisfy for all sins.[120]

In this way, then, the Father is in debt to the Son for what the Son has done; however, the Son does not need any remuneration. What is then more appropriate than that the Son should yield the fruits of his death to his parents and brothers for whose sake he became man?[121]

We could not think of a greater or more just mercy than what has become manifest in our redemption through the death of the God-man:

> Can a more merciful way of acting be conceived than when God the Father tells the sinner who is condemned to eternal torments and deprived of what could redeem him, "Take my only Son and give him for yourself," and the Son himself saying, "take me and redeem yourself"?

This gift, then, is more precious than any debt, and God forgives all debts if we offer this gift to God with the right disposition.[122]

Even though the expression "satisfaction" occurs in Augustine and Hilary, Anselm created an original synthesis that has exerted an enormous influence on both Catholic and Protestant soteriology. Today, some reject it as a time-conditioned theory that is totally opposed to the merciful God in Jesus' message, while others believe that it does formulate, in the categories of Anselm's own feudal society, a valid aspect of New Testament soteriology. I share

---

[120] II:14.

[121] II:19.

[122] II:20.

the latter view. The expression "honor of God" intends to bring close to Anselm's reader God's infinite holiness. The sinner, insofar as his own existence is concerned, violates this holiness and, left to his own human resources, cannot extricate himself from the consequences of his infinitely grave offense.

In addition to being based on the Bible (by whose authority he hopes to confirm his arguments from reason), St. Anselm's treatise answers the perennially valid existential question about the power of evil in this world. If, without becoming the occasion for a greater good, the evil acts of the human race are simply forgiven by a transcendent God, then indeed evil overpowers good within this world. If, on the other hand, Anselm's view is true, then evil is conquered in this world because it becomes the occasion for an infinitely greater good, the giving of himself of the God-man in death. Moreover, this infinitely precious gift is mediated to us by the human decision of the God-man who freely gives himself for us by his human will.

3. St. Thomas

The developing universities of the 12th and 13th centuries constituted the sociological context for scholastic theology. After some initial rationalistic exaggerations, scholastic theology in its mature form worked out a harmonious relationship between reason and revealed truths. Its goal was to construct a system in which each theological truth rests on ultimate principles derived from divine revelation and is inserted into a logically consistent whole. The *Summa Theologiae* in general is the most ambitious literary form of the scholastic theological enterprise; its immediate goal is knowledge, a limited and analogous knowledge of the divine mysteries by human reason aided by faith. In this it is opposed to the patristic and monastic ideal of theologizing. For the latter even the immediate goal was not simply knowledge but the enrichment and formation of spiritual life through knowledge.

In the thought of St. Thomas, scholastic theology achieved a unique synthesis incorporating the heritage of the Latin Fathers and (through translations) the thoughts of some of the Eastern Fathers as well. Christology is treated in the third part of his *Summa Theologiae* (*quaestiones* 1-59), after St. Thomas has already dealt with the mystery of God in himself and with the creation, fall and return to God of the human race through grace and with the practice of divine and human virtues.[123]

The basic principle supporting the whole edifice of his Christology is the hypostatic union. In Thomas's thought, the person is the subject (*suppositum*) of an intellectual nature existing as one in himself and distinct from anything and anyone else (I, q. 29, a. 1-2). In the incarnation, the eternal divine person of the Word has united to himself a human nature in such a way that the human individual does not exist in himself but in the person of the Word. The union between this man and the Word is so intimate that the eternal person of the Word exists not only as the subject of the divine but also as the subject of the human nature (III, q. 2, a. 1-3).[124] Looked upon from the viewpoint of personhood, the man Jesus is closer to the (eternal) Son than the Son is to the Father, since Jesus is the same person as the Son while the Son is not the same person as the Father (q. 2, a. 9). The purpose of the hypostatic union is soteriological. God has become man so that fallen humankind may return through the incarnate Word to the happiness of divine life.

The characteristics and the perfections of Christ's humanity are deduced from the nature of the hypostatic union. Because of the ineffably close union between Christ's humanity and God, it is most appropriate for this humanity to be endowed with all perfections. Accordingly, the man Jesus possesses the fullness of grace both for himself and for all humankind. He enjoys the beatific vi-

---

[123] On St. Thomas's Christology, see F. Ruello, *La christologie de saint Thomas d'Aquin*, Théologie historique 76 (Paris: Beauchesne, 1987); on his Soteriology, see H.U. von Balthasar, *Theodramatik*. III. *Handlung*, pp. 241-245.

[124] Cf. "...in Christo... humana natura est assumpta ad hoc quod sit personae Filii Dei." *S.T.* III, q. 2, a. 10; "Verbum caro factum est' id est homo; quasi ipsum Verbum personaliter est homo." *Disputed Questions, V. On the Union of the Incarnate Word*, 1.

sion from the first moment of his conception, but also the infused knowledge of the angels. Moreover, he has also the fullness of typical human knowledge that he has acquired through the senses. Jesus the man knows all that the human race can know by knowledge through sense experience. Only with regard to this latter type of knowledge is there any growth or development in Jesus. Even though Jesus often asks questions in the Gospels, this is a mere pedagogical device rather than a sign of genuine ignorance and a desire to learn. It would be inappropriate for anyone to teach the Teacher of all humankind (III, q. 7-12).

The Son of God took upon himself the human nature of Adam's offspring in order to redeem them. Thus the only deficiencies of his human nature are those that constitute the punishment of Adam's sin for all his offspring, namely, the passibility and mortality of the body. Christ's soul, in substantial union with the body, partook in his suffering which was both physical and psychic. Jesus' soul suffered sadness and fear, and trembled in his agony. He suffered more intensely than any other human being for various reasons, among which the two most important are: he took upon himself the sins of everyone, and, through his wisdom and love, he understood and suffered more the evil of these sins than those who committed them. Thus the pain of "contrition" in Christ exceeded that of any other human being. Moreover, his physical life without any sin, in union with his divinity, and full of moral goodness, was of incomparable value. It was harder for him to give up voluntarily his most precious life than for us to give up our life which has been affected by sins (III, q. 46, a. 6).

The human nature of the Son was exempt not only from original sin, but also from the concupiscence resulting from it. Thus every faculty of his human nature performed its proper function without being overwhelmed by another. His most intense fear of death did not diminish the dedication of his will to do God's will, nor did the terrible suffering of his body and soul prevent him from enjoying the beatific vision at a certain point in his soul even when he was tortured on the cross (III, q. 14-15).

It follows from the hypostatic union that the earthly life of

Jesus, his suffering, death, resurrection, and ascension, all have a theological significance (III, q. 27-59). Whatever Jesus did and suffered, God himself did and suffered through the full cooperation of his humanity, which St. Thomas calls — after the Alexandrian Fathers — "an instrument conjoined to the divinity" (*instrumentum coniunctum divinitatis*).

His soteriology synthesizes the major patristic themes of redemption.

Even though St. Thomas maintains that the whole sacred history of the Word made flesh, including his resurrection and ascension, have a saving efficacy for us (III, q. 48, a. 6), he attributes a central role to his passion. The passion of Christ brought about our salvation by way of merit, satisfaction, sacrifice, redemption, and efficient causality (III, q. 48, a. 1-6).

First, as regards merit, there is a certain identity between Christ as Head and all humankind as his members. Thus, just as Christ has received grace not only for himself, but for all men and women, through his passion he has merited salvation for all. St. Thomas admits that, with regard to the subject (Christ), every act of Christ is infinitely meritorious for us, since it is the act of the God-man. Thus, in some sense, he has merited our salvation already at the beginning of his human life. Yet, with regard to the object, namely, what he did or suffered, the passion was most suited to merit our salvation.

Second, Christ's passion has also gained our salvation by way of satisfaction.[125] In this matter Thomas recapitulates the theory of Anselm, with two important modifications. Contrary to Anselm's thought, God could have forgiven humankind without due satisfaction, yet it was most fitting for him to demand complete satisfaction (III, q. 46, a. 2). Moreover, what is only implied by Anselm is made explicit in the *Summa:* the superabundant value of Christ's satisfaction derives not only from the (infinite) dignity of the life

---

[125] For a personalistic interpretation of St. Thomas's theory of satisfaction, see R. Cessario, *Christian Satisfaction in Aquinas: Towards a Personalistic Understanding* (Washington: Univ. Press of America, 1982).

of the God-man, but more directly from the greatness of his love. The love of Christ, which more than balanced the wickedness of his executioners and which ultimately explains why his suffering was greater than any other human suffering, is the direct principle of satisfaction in St. Thomas.[126]

Third, the passion of Christ brought about our salvation by way of sacrifice. Though he quotes St. Augustine, Thomas defines sacrifice more narrowly than his source: "sacrifice, properly speaking, designates what men do in token of the special honor due to God in order to reconcile him." He views Jesus' sacrifice from this aspect alone, as an atoning sacrifice for sin. Since Christ offered his own life freely, "motivated by the greatest love," his was a true sacrifice most acceptable to God (III, q. 48, a. 3).

Fourth, Christ's passion could also be viewed as redemption, in the etymological sense of the word, as a ransom of sinful humankind from their slavery to the devil who kept us in sin and administered the punishment for sin. The devil acted unjustly in deceiving us into sin, but in punishing us he carries out God's just judgment. Therefore, the devil had no claim for a just treatment; the ransom was not to be paid to the devil but to God. The ransom required by God's justice consisted in the satisfaction Christ "paid" by shedding his most precious blood, that is, by giving up his life for us (III, q. 48, a. 4-5).

Finally, we have seen in patristic Christology the correspondence and causal relationship between the sacred history of the Incarnate Word and the spiritual history of every Christian in the Church. St. Thomas reformulates this teaching by the analogous use of the Aristotelian categories of efficient and exemplary causality. On the one hand, since his humanity was hypostatically

---

[126] The ultimate principle for the *magnitudo caritatis* in Christ is, of course, the hypostatic union. It is interesting to compare how St. Anselm and St. Thomas differ in treating the case of Christ's enemies who crucified him. For Anselm their sin could be atoned for by Christ because they acted out of ignorance: they did not know that they crucified God himself. Thomas does not mention their ignorance. For him it is the love of Christ expressing itself in his suffering which satisfies for all sins. This love more than offsets the offence of his executioners (Cf. *Why God Became Man*, II:15; *S.T.* III q. 48, a. 2).

united to God the Son, all that Jesus did and suffered at any moment in time, in its effects transcends all times. Through the infinite power of the divinity which uses his humanity as an instrument, Jesus' actions and sufferings extend to all subsequent history and cause the salvation of every human being in whom they can unfold their power "by way of a spiritual contact... through faith and through the sacraments of faith" (III, q. 48, a. 6).[127] On the other hand, receiving salvation through Christ involves a process of transformation of which Christ is the exemplary cause. We are gradually conformed to Christ in the two main stages of his history, in his suffering and death as well as in his resurrection and exaltation. As an illustration of what has just been explained, let me quote St. Thomas himself on the efficient and exemplary causality of Christ's resurrection:

> The resurrection of Christ is not, strictly speaking, the meritorious cause of our resurrection. It is the efficient and exemplary cause. The efficient causality is through the humanity of Christ in which the resurrection took place and which is like an instrument acting in the power of divinity. Therefore, just as all other things which Christ in his humanity accomplished or suffered for us are saving acts through the power of his divinity, so too is his resurrection the efficient cause of ours through the same divine power whose proper effect is to raise the dead to life. This power is extended by being present in all times and places, and this contact of power is sufficient to fulfill the definition of efficient causality (III q. 56, a. 1).

Since Christ's body is personally united to the Word, the resurrection of this same body will be first not only in time but also in dignity and perfection. "Less perfect beings imitate in their own fashion whatever is at the summit of perfection." Thus Christ's resur-

---

[127] The life-giving power of the sacred history of Jesus reaches, in a different way, all history before his coming. It offers salvation to those before Christ, for whom he is the object of faith foreshadowed in the prophecies and institutions of the Old Testament (*S. T.* III, q. 8, a. 3; q. 68, a. 1).

rection is the model for our own. We must rise from the dead with our resurrection patterned on the resurrection of Christ "who will transfigure these wretched bodies of ours into copies of his glorious body" (Ph 3:21: *Ibid.*).

St. Thomas built a consistent christological system from elements of the patristic and medieval tradition. He deduced his Christology from one basic principle accepted in faith, that of the hypostatic union. His system shows convincingly the intrinsic unity between Christology proper and soteriology. He maintains a theological interest in the history of the Incarnate Word, rather than restricting soteriology to a treatise on his death as happened in later times. However, his speculative, metaphysical emphasis results in various deficiencies of both structure and content. Structurally, Christology is misplaced in the *Summa*. The final goal of human life, the grace offered to fallen humankind, and our moral life, all receive their concrete shape and form through Christ. As a consequence, Christology should have preceded the treatise on grace and morality. Moreover, his one-sided deductive method does not do justice to the portrait of Jesus as it emerges from the Synoptic Gospels. Thomas does not admit ignorance or even limitations in the knowledge of the earthly Jesus, nor does he see any real development in him. According to Thomas, there is no real difference between the earthly and risen Jesus except for the glorification of his body.

CHAPTER IV

Christology of the Reformation

1. Luther

Even though Luther accepts the christological teaching of the first Ecumenical Councils, Nicea, Ephesus and Chalcedon, his interest does not focus on the metaphysical questions but rather on what the person of Christ means for us. Rejecting scholasticism, which cultivated speculation for its own sake, and strongly influenced by the prevailing nominalism of his age, Luther returns to the Scriptures and to the patristic tradition, in particular to Augustinian theology. His Christology is thoroughly biblical, uniting inseparably the person and the work of Christ. In late medieval Christology the mysteries of the life of Christ, so important for the Fathers, monastic theology, and St. Thomas, were no longer deemed worthy of theological reflection and became exclusively the object of popular sentimental devotion. Luther rediscovers their theological significance in that the humanity of Christ and the mysteries of his life reveal who God is for us. However, before and beyond everything else, Luther's theology is a *theologia crucis*. Spurred on by a passionate search for a merciful God, he selects and combines various elements of patristic soteriology and St. Bernard's thought in a highly personal way. Yet, in spite of his lasting contribution to soteriology, Luther's bold presentation of the drama of redemption distorts some of the essential truths of the christological tradition of the Church. Each of these points warrants some explanation.

Commenting on the christological Councils of the patristic

age, Luther insists that they do not teach anything new, but rather defend the biblical doctrine of Christ, and, for this reason, their definitions are true: in Jesus Christ there is a divine and human nature and Jesus Christ is one person. Since Jesus Christ is one person, Mary is indeed the mother of God.[128] However, when Luther explains the meaning of the *communicatio idiomatum* — the mutual predication of the properties of both natures — it becomes clear that he misunderstands the doctrine of the Councils. He does not see any difference between a statement that attributes the *idiomata* (properties) of both natures to the one person and a statement that attributes the *idiomata* of one nature to the other nature. For him both types of predication mean the same thing, while the tradition of the Church insists on the first type of predication and excludes the other.[129] Luther misunderstands the *communicatio idiomatum* because he stresses a fusion of divine and human characteristics in Christ to the point of speaking not only about the suffering and dying of God in Christ but also about a "dead God," to indicate that, on the cross, death has, in some form, affected divinity itself.[130] That God died in his human nature on the cross belongs to the core of Christian faith. That death affected divinity itself has always been denied before Luther by the Christian tradition. Yet the denial of the second statement would imply for Luther also the denial of the first, and thus Luther would have to conclude that God himself did not suffer and therefore the cross of Jesus did not redeem us.

Luther's unbearable experience of sin and the punishment he

---

[128] *On the Councils and the Church: Selected Writings of Martin Luther*, ed. T.G. Tappert (Philadelphia: Fortress, 1967), pp. 289-313.

[129] For instance, Luther blames Nestorius because the latter "does not want to give the *idiomata* of humanity to the divinity of Christ" and he also blames Eutyches (misunderstanding his doctrine) because "Eutyches... does not want to give the *idiomata* of divinity to the humanity." On the same page, however, Luther defines the *communicatio idiomatum* in the traditional terms: "...whoever confesses the two natures in Christ, God and man, must also ascribe the *idiomata* of both to the person." *Ibid.*, p. 301.

[130] Cf. *Ibid.*, pp. 295-296; "Luther holds that the deity of Christ, because of the incarnation and of its personal unity with the humanity, enters into the uttermost depths of its suffering" (P. Althaus, *The Theology of Martin Luther* [Philadelphia: Fortress, 1966], p. 197).

deserved for his sins is the existential starting point of his theology. As he said once about the experience of guilt,

> At such a time God seems terribly angry, and with him the whole creation. At such a time there is no flight, no comfort, within or without, but all things accuse. At such a time as that the Psalmist mourns, "I am cut off from thy sight" (Cf. Ps 31:22).... In this moment (strange to say) the soul cannot believe that it can ever be redeemed other than that the punishment is not yet completely felt.... All that remains is the stark-naked desire for help and a terrible groaning, but it does not know where to turn for help.[131]

Luther's anguish is unbearable because he is convinced that his sins have not only disturbed the order of creation, but they reached and offended God himself. They have challenged God as God and thereby provoked his wrath. Against this background, we can understand Luther's appreciation for the incarnation, the earthly history and the cross of Christ. He rejects the late medieval piety that contemplated and loved the humanity of Christ for its own sake. He runs from the God hidden in his majesty who threatens him with condemnation to the God hidden under and in the man Christ, because this man reveals to him the mercy of the Father. It is in the humanity of Jesus, in his life and suffering, that God's heart, his love, and his forgiveness are revealed to the despairing sinner:

> "This is my beloved Son with whom I am well pleased." With these words God gives a joyous and happy heart to the entire world and fills all creation with divine sweetness and comfort. How so? Well, if I know and am certain that the man Christ is God's Son and pleases Him — as I must be certain because the divine majesty from heaven itself says this and it cannot lie — then I am also certain that everything the man says and does is the word and the work of that dear Son which

---

[131] *Explanations of the Ninety-five Theses*: Luther's Works, ed. J. Pelikan, H.S. Oswald and H.T. Lehmann (Philadelphia: Fortress Press, 1957), vol. 31, p. 129.

must please God best of all.... Now how could God pour out
more of himself and offer himself in a more loving or sweeter
way than by saying that his heart is pleased because his Son
Christ speaks so friendly with me, is so heartily concerned
about me, and suffers, dies, and does everything with such
great love for me? Do you not think that a human heart,
should it actually feel that God is so well pleased with Christ
when He serves us in this way, must shatter into a hundred
thousand pieces because its joy is so great? For then it would
peer into the depths of the fatherly heart, yes, into the inexhaustible goodness and eternal love of God, which He feels
and has felt toward us from eternity.[132]

Yet this inexhaustible goodness and eternal love of God remains in tension with his righteousness and wrath, which our sins
have aroused. His holiness requires that he judge and condemn the
sinner. However, out of his unspeakable goodness, he takes upon
himself the judgment that we have deserved. In his only Son on
the cross, God the judge becomes himself the judged one. This deep
awareness of both God's holiness and his mercy explains Luther's
bold dramatization of the exchange between Christ and the sinner. As we had shown, the theme of exchange is central to the Fathers: the Son takes upon himself all that is ours, our human nature and existence including our sins, as well as our sufferings and
death which we deserved for our sins, and he bestows on us all that
is his, his justice, his joy, but also his divine nature and divine life.
However, Luther develops the theme of exchange one-sidedly in
the direction of sin and justice and presents it at the same time as a
dramatic struggle. The Son of God was charged both juridically
and existentially with all the sins of the world, in such a realistic
way that he alone appeared as **the** Sinner before God:

All the prophets foresaw that Christ would be the greatest
bandit of all, the greatest murderer and thief, the greatest per-

---

[132] *Sermon on the Baptism of Jesus,* quoted by P. Althaus, *The Theology of Martin Luther,* p.
187.

petrator of sacrilege and blasphemy etc., a greater than which has never existed in the world.[133]

In obedience to his Father, Christ took upon himself all sins, so that there was no sin but in him, and as totally as if he himself had committed them. More than just taking into himself their sins, Christ became the "person" of all the sinners. His Father told him:

> Be Peter, the one who denies, be Paul, the violent and blasphemous persecutor, be David the adulterer, be the sinner who ate the apple in Paradise, be the bandit on the cross. In summary, be the person of all men, the one who committed the sins of all men.[134]

As a result of this total identification with all sins and all sinners, Christ also suffered anxiety, guilt, and abandonment by God. For Anselm, satisfying for the sin of someone else is not the same as suffering the punishment for that sin. However, Luther identifies Christ's satisfaction with his enduring the punishment for sin. He suffered the total punishment for all sins, which means that he offered not only his physical life for us, but endured the punishment of hell temporarily, beginning on the cross, and continuing after his death through his descent into hell. He felt God's eternal wrath and considered himself cursed and rejected forever. Yet Christ did not suffer hell as we sinners would. Even on the cross he was not only the greatest sinner but simultaneously the most righteous, the greatest liar but also the greatest truth-teller, the most blessed and the most condemned, at the same time.[135] Christ, then, suffered all that we who are under the Law have deserved to suffer, but in a

---

[133] *WA*, vol. 40, part 1, p. 433. The idea that we find the loving heart of the Father in the human love of Jesus is very close to the Bernardine theme: "The One who has come forth from the Father's heart has revealed the feelings of that heart towards us" (2 Epi 4: IV, 304).

[134] *Ibid.*

[135] Cf. *WA*, vol. 5, pp. 602-603. See also R. Schwager *Der wunderbare Tausch. Zur Geschichte der Erlösungslehre* (Munich: Kösel, 1985), p. 199.

new and terrible way. The evil of our sins is mostly hidden to us, but, in his troubled conscience, the absolutely pure Christ experienced the horror of the evil of sin in its totality.[136] On the cross, then, the dialectic of God's revelation appears in the sharpest possible form. His love is hidden under its very opposite, wrath, and his forgiveness under condemnation. Christ's attitude on the cross is also characterized by this paradox. His *noluntas*, his lack of willingness to endure the punishment for our sins and his complaining to God ("My God, my God, why have you forsaken me?") hide the most glowing will to love God.[137] And it is through this love hidden under the cry of despair and under the terror of his troubled conscience that he overcomes sin, death, and hell:

> His (Christ's) human nature behaved not differently than a human being who must remain damned forever in hell. Because of his love for God, God has soon woke him up from death and from hell and thus he has swallowed up hell.[138]

Thus the victory over Satan, death, and hell has been won through the love of Christ. For a Catholic reader it would appear from the context that it is the human love of Jesus that wins the victory.[139] Yet in other texts Luther enunciates a basic principle of his theology: "the divinity alone effects everything without the cooperation of the humanity."[140] On the cross the divinity alone destroyed sin and overcame hell and the devil.

Moreover, in Luther's system the human nature of Christ possesses the *idiomata* of the divine nature, since for Luther, the union

[136] *Ibid.*, vol. 5, pp. 603-604.

[137] *WA*, vol. 56, p. 447.

[138] *WA*, vol. 56, p. 392.

[139] This is also the way a Catholic theologian, R. Schwager, interprets it (*Der wunderbare Tausch*, p. 213).

[140] *WA*, vol. 40, part 1, p. 417. In this text the human nature is symbolized by the bait, the divinity by the hook which the devil swallowed along with the bait. Thus the divinity was the only active agent in destroying the devil. The humanity cooperated, but only in a passive manner, as the bait inducing the devil to kill Christ.

in one person is synonymous with union in one substance. He contrasts the works of Christ with the good works of Christians:

> Luther wants to have good works (for Christians), but they should not bear the glorious divine *idiomata* such as atoning for sin, reconciling God's wrath, and justifying sinners for such *idiomata* belong to another whose name is "the Lamb of God, who takes away the sin of the world." Truly such *idiomata* must be left to the blood and death of Christ....[141]

On the basis of such texts Congar believes that Luther would suspect as Nestorian any effort to attribute an active role to the human will of Christ in our redemption.[142] While Luther insists that Christ has a human will, he does not attribute any act of will to Christ "which would not be a divine act of will.... For in the *Deus-homo, homo* means something else than what we are: simple human beings. There is nothing in Christ that would not be divine."[143] Thus, according to Congar, there is a mono-energistic tendency in Luther, even though Luther insists that Christ's human nature retains an activity proper to it. In spite of this insistence, in Luther's Christology, according to Congar, God alone works out our salvation in Christ.

I must distance myself to some extent from Congar's evaluation. Luther's position is certainly far removed from that of St. Thomas, according to whom the humanity of Christ, joined to the Word as a free instrument, is an efficient instrumental cause of our salvation. However, the texts quoted above on Christ's humanity revealing the Father's good pleasure for us, suggest a more positive

---

[141] *On the Councils and the Church: Selected Writings of Martin Luther* (Philadelphia: Fortress, 1967), vol. 4, pp. 296 and 303.

[142] Y. Congar, "*Lutherana*: Théologie et Eucharistie chez Luther," *Revue des Sciences Phil. et Théol.* 66 (1982), pp. 190-194. See the whole article, pp. 169-244.

[143] Congar refers here to *WA*, vol 39, part 2, p. 107 in "*Lutherana*: Théologie et Eucharistie chez Luther," p. 193. According to Congar, it is not an accident that Luther never treats of the Third Council of Constantinople, which speaks about Christ's human will and the human activity of that will; cf. *Ibid.*, pp. 193-194.

role for this humanity.[144] The humanity of God is essential for our redemption, not only because God himself could suffer, and die through a "mixture" or "fusion" of divinity with humanity, but also because the Father's tender love for us is revealed through it. We see "God's entire heart in Christ, in all his words and works."[145] In explaining the earthly humanity of Christ, his words and deeds as revealing to us God's love, Luther continues a long patristic tradition that had reached a unique depth in St. Bernard's Christology.[146]

After seeing one pole of the exchange, Christ, we now turn to the other, the sinner. While the individual dimension of the exchange is present also in the Fathers, their emphasis is on humankind and the Church as renewed humanity; for the Fathers and for monastic theology, individuals participate in the exchange only insofar as they are members of the Church, or rather, insofar as they embody the Church in themselves. For Luther, the emphasis is on the individual sinner who becomes exposed to the proclamation of the Gospel. It is through faith in Christ that the exchange takes place for a particular sinner. Faith is the "wedding ring" that joins together in one body Christ and the soul:

> The... incomparable benefit of faith is that it unites the soul with Christ as a bride is united with her bridegroom. By this mystery, as the Apostle teaches, Christ and the soul become one flesh (Eph 5:31-32).[147] And if they are one flesh and there

---

[144] See footnote #132. I agree with Althaus's position in this matter, *The Theology of Martin Luther*, pp. 180-190.

[145] *WA*, vol. 20, p. 229.

[146] Althaus shares a popular misconception about St. Bernard's Christology in viewing his devotion to the humanity of Christ as a paradigm of late medieval piety in which "Luther's primary concern, to meet the Father in the man Jesus, receded far into the background" (*op. cit.*, pp. 182-183). In reality, the humanity of Christ has significance for St. Bernard only insofar as it reveals the tender mercy and humility of God himself. Cf. for instance these texts in St. Bernard: "The secret of the heart lies open through the holes of the body; there lies open that great mystery of love, there lie open the entrails of the mercy of our God, in which the sun rising from on high has visited us" (*SC* 61:4); "the heart of the Bridegroom is the heart of his Father" (*Ibid.*, 62:5). It would be worthwhile to investigate to what extent Luther's Christology depends on that of St. Bernard.

[147] It is remarkable how, unconsciously, Luther changes the marriage partner in the text: in Eph 5:31-32 the bride is the Church; for Luther it becomes the individual soul.

is between them a true marriage — indeed the most perfect
of all marriages, since human marriages are but poor examples
of this one true marriage — it follows that everything they
have they hold in common, the good as well as the evil. Accordingly, the believing soul can boast of and glory in whatever Christ has as though it were its own, and whatever the
soul has Christ claims as his own. Let us compare these and
we shall see inestimable benefits. Christ is full of grace, life
and salvation. The soul is full of sins, death, and damnation.
Now let faith come between them and sins, death, and damnation will be Christ's, while grace, life, and salvation will be
the soul's.... Thus the believing soul by means of the pledge
of its faith is free in Christ, its bridegroom, free from all sins,
secure against death and hell, and is endowed with the eternal righteousness, life, and salvation of Christ its bridegroom.[148]

Thus "the eternal righteousness" which covers my sins, and makes
me just before God, is the righteousness of Christ himself. The faith
in which this righteousness becomes mine is both an unconditional
acceptance of God's judgment over my sins and an acceptance of
God's promise, which forgives my sins.[149] The first aspect of faith
destroys my self-righteousness; the second brings about an exchange
between Christ and myself. I "give" all my sins to Christ, and he
himself becomes mine and bestows on me his righteousness. The
righteousness which makes me just before God is, then, an "alien"
righteousness, since it is Christ's, not mine, and it is "imputed,"
since God imputes it to me just as he imputes my sins to Christ
and on that basis condemns Christ and acquits me. Yet this juridi-

---

[148] *The Freedom of a Christian: Selected Writings of Martin Luther*, vol. 2, pp. 27-28.

[149] For the exchange to take place for me I must believe in God's promise of forgiveness for
me, namely that for the sake of Christ God forgives my sins and saves me. Thus the certainty of being saved seems to be an essential ingredient of authentic faith, even though
this certainty is constantly exposed to temptation. This, again, shows the individual character of faith. The Fathers believed with the certainty of faith only in the salvation of the
Church and for the individual only to the extent that he remains a living member of the
Church. When speaking about his own salvation, Saint Bernard never stops repeating
the saying of Job that one cannot be sure whether one deserves God's hatred or love.

cal concept of exchange presents only one dimension of Luther's thought. Just as Christ becomes **the** sinner in a much deeper than juridical sense, in that Christ bears and feels the horror of the evil of sin in its totality, so the righteousness of Christ in the sinner is more than a merely juridical imputation: Christ himself is present in the sinner, and the Holy Spirit begins to create a new man, "the inner man," who struggles against sin which still dwells in his flesh. Thus, through the gift of the Holy Spirit, the Christian becomes transformed inwardly and conformed gradually to Christ by following him in his way of life and in his suffering and death. In this way, genuine faith results in good works, but these good works — while pleasing to God — must never be regarded as meritorious of salvation. That quality applies only to the works of Christ. One can never boast of the new life unfolding in him, or of any good works, because they do not belong to him, but to Christ and to the Holy Spirit. This process of sanctification lasts as long as one is alive; sin is never completely uprooted as long as one lives in the flesh. Thus one remains *simul justus et peccator*, both righteous and sinful in this life.[150]

In summary, the judgment of those Luther scholars who claim that Luther's Christology constitutes an important new step in the understanding of Christ's redemption seems justified to me.[151] Yet this judgment needs some nuancing. Luther's new portrait of Christ is not entirely new in that it continues a line of patristic soteriology, and in what is new it shows one-sidedness and distortions. In spite of these reservations, I see two important contributions to soteriology in Luther's works:

1. There is a new emphasis on the horror and gravity of sin, which not only disturbs the order of creation but also offends God himself. Consequently, the drama of redemption, as it unfolds in

---

[150] See P. Althaus, *The Theology of Martin Luther*, pp. 224-250; R. Schwager, *Der wunderbare Tausch*, pp. 201-208.

[151] Cf., for instance, R. Schwager, *Der wunderbare Tausch*, p. 201, quoting approvingly E. Vogelsang: "Das Bild des so angefochtenen Christus hat Luther als erster in der Geschichte der Christenheit in diesem Ernst geschaut" (*Der angefochtene Christus bei Luther* /AKG 21/, Berlin 1932, p. 22).

history, deeply involves God himself. The drama is ultimately played out between God's justice, holiness, and wrath on the one hand, and his tender mercy and fatherly love on the other.[152] However, in Luther's thought God's involvement in our sin is stretched to the breaking point. In declaring the Son "guilty" and "sinner" because of our sins, and in presenting the Father as condemning his own Son to hell temporarily, Luther risks suggesting the opposite of what he intends. Instead of appearing infinitely holy, Luther's God may seem arbitrary and unjust. In liberal Protestant theology, the image of Luther's God, who makes the innocent Christ guilty and punishes him while he absolves the truly guilty, will be declared absurd and untenable.[153] The Fathers remain faithful to the whole of the New Testament soteriology when they refuse to say that the Son is guilty because of our sins and suffers damnation for our sins. They do affirm, however, that, by accepting suffering and death as the consequence of our sins in this life, the innocent Son does carry the burden of all sins.[154]

2. In presenting the exchange between Christ and the sinner, Luther describes in a new, powerful way, how Christ carries the anguish of the sinful conscience and, precisely because of his innocence, suffers in a new and unique way the horror of evil in its totality. This voluntary existential identification of God with all sinners and with all their sins out of love is based on the Scriptures and on the Fathers, yet it is new in its emphasis and dramatic presentation. Moreover, Luther integrates the theme of the miraculous exchange with that of victorious struggle by showing what reality lay behind the mythical images that the Fathers (and Luther himself) used in describing the struggle between Christ and the

---

[152] Cf. G. Aulén, *Christus Victor* (New York: Macmillan, 1931), p. 131.

[153] If one also adds Luther's theory on the human will as slave rather than free with regard to God, so that the devil and the sinner sin necessarily while those destined to eternal life accept faith through God's grace necessarily, then, logically, the struggle between good and evil is introduced into God's own being and is played out there with an inner necessity. However, Luther never draws these consequences and the Lutheran confessional documents reject his view on the *servum arbitrium*. Cf. Schwager, *op. cit.*, pp. 214-220.

[154] Cf. for instance, Ambrose and Augustine, pp. 206-209.

devil: Christ conquered sin, death, and the devil not in some mythical combat, but by taking upon himself the guilty conscience of the sinner and by loving the Father in the sinner's stead with a glowing love. Thus, Luther's notion of the miraculous exchange is a step forward in understanding the meaning of redemption. But it needs to be disentangled from the theory of a juridical imputation of sins to Christ by the Father, and of penal substitution; moreover, the exchange, according to the tradition, takes place between Christ and the Church rather than Christ and the individual. The individual participates in the exchange to the extent that he lives the life of the Church. Furthermore, the active cooperation of Christ's free human will needs to be re-emphasized. Briefly, in Luther's notion of the "admirable exchange," the exchange is not quite complete: on the side of Christ, his free human will does not take an active part in the work of God; on our side, Christ's divine life does not quite become ours since our good works — even though they derive from the gift of the Holy Spirit — cannot share in the merits of Christ himself.[155]

2. John Calvin

Calvin also accepts the traditional doctrine of the Church about the divine and human natures of Christ united in one person. However, while Luther's main concern is to show the involvement of the divinity in our redemption, to the point of attributing divine properties to the human nature of Christ, Calvin emphasizes the transcendence of God even over against Christ's human nature. The *idiomata* of the two natures are not mixed or fused in the same way as in Luther's works. According to Calvin, Scripture attributes the sufferings and death of the human nature "improperly but not without cause" to the divine nature.[156] Attributing in

---

[155] Cf. Althaus, *The Theology of Martin Luther*, pp. 245-250.
[156] J. Calvin, *Institutes of the Christian Religion*, tr. H. Beveridge (Grand Rapids, MI: Eerdmans, 1945), II,14: vol. I, p. 417.

the strict sense of the word the properties of one nature to the other would offend against God's transcendence.

In Calvin's thought Christ the man does have an active role in the redemptive work and does merit our salvation. Of course, if Christ the man "were opposed simply, and by himself, to the justice of God, there could be no room for merit, because there cannot be found in man a worth which could make God a debtor." However, Christ was able to merit our salvation because, through God's pure mercy, the man Christ, without any merit of his own, was assumed into personal union with the eternal Word. Thus the ultimate source of Christ's meritorious works is God's free mercy.[157]

Calvin builds his Christology on the notion of Christ as Mediator. Because of their sins, human beings experience the holy God as their enemy and try to escape from him. For this reason, they need a mediator who can show them the mercy of God the Father and reconcile them to God. Relying on biblical and patristic tradition, Calvin systematizes the mediating work of Christ under the threefold office of Prophet, King, and Priest. His mediation is coextensive with the whole of salvation history. Even before his coming God taught and ruled his people through Christ, and all the sacrifices of the Law had value insofar as they pointed to Christ. Thus the elect in the Old Testament who saw the legal sacrifices as the foreshadowing of the promised perfect sacrifice were saved by faith in Christ.[158]

The goal of the incarnation and the glorification of Christ is to carry out the work of mediation foreshadowed and promised in the Old Testament. He begins this work on earth but perfects it in heaven:

> The purpose of... prophetical dignity in Christ is to teach us, that in the doctrine which He delivered is substantially included a wisdom which is perfect in all its parts.[159]

---

[157] *Ibid.*, II,17: I, pp. 453-454. Note that here as in many other areas, Calvin follows Augustine's thought.

[158] *Ibid.*, II,6: I, p. 293.

[159] *Ibid.*, II,15: I, p. 427.

Christ completes his work as the prophet after his ascension, by sending his Holy Spirit into our hearts. He then teaches us not only outwardly, through the preaching of his Word in the Church, but also inwardly, by enkindling our hearts through his Holy Spirit.[160] His kingly rule is closely connected with his prophetic office: he rules where his Word is accepted and obeyed in faith. His rule prepares us for eternal life and endows us with all the gifts of the Holy Spirit, so that we will be victorious against the devil, the world, and everything that could prevent us from reaching eternal life. Paradoxically, in this world the proof that one is ruled by Christ is suffering and persecution:

> Not being earthly or carnal and so subject to corruption, but spiritual, it (the Kingdom of Christ) raises us even to eternal life, so that we can patiently live at present under toil, hunger, cold, contempt, disgrace, and other annoyances; contented with this, that our King will never abandon us, but will supply our necessities until our warfare is ended, and we are called to triumph: such being the nature of his Kingdom, that he communicates to us whatever he received of his Father. Since then he arms and equips us by his power, adorns us with splendor and magnificence, enriches us with wealth, we here find most abundant cause of glorying, and also are inspired with boldness, so that we can contend intrepidly with the devil, sin, and death.[161]

Christ rules not only over those who are his own through faith, but also over the realm of Satan.

Christ's priesthood is also linked to his prophetic office. The revealing of God's saving will is already the beginning of the priestly work of reconciliation. As priest, "by the sacrifice of his death, he wiped away our guilt, and made satisfaction for sin."[162] This Calvin

---

[160] Cf. B. Willems, *Soteriologie. Von der Reformation bis zur Gegenwart: Handbuch der Dogmengeschichte*, Vol. III/2c (Freiburg: Herder, 1972), p. 29.

[161] Calvin, *Institutes*, II,15: I, p. 429.

[162] *Ibid.*, p. 431.

explains similarly to Luther as a juridical substitution: God imputes our sins, our guilt, and our punishment to Christ and imputes his righteousness and purity to us. The punishment Christ endures is not only physical death:

> Nothing had been done if Christ had only endured corporeal death. In order to interpose between us and God's anger, and satisfy his righteous judgment, it was necessary that He should feel the weight of divine vengeance. Whence also it was necessary that He should engage, as it were, at close quarters with the powers of hell and the horrors of eternal death.

By descending into hell, Christ endured the death "which is inflicted on the wicked by an angry God... He bore in his soul the tortures of condemned and ruined man."[163] Yet Christ could expiate God for our sins only because he himself was sinless.[164] While Calvin follows Luther in affirming a juridical imputation of our sins to Christ, he is much less dramatic than Luther in describing Christ's existential identification with the sinner. Nor does he claim that God was ever truly angry or hostile with his Son in whom he was well pleased and whose intercession he accepted.

Calvin follows faithfully the teaching of the Letter to the Hebrews. The priestly work of Christ is only begun on earth; it is consummated in heaven where he constantly intercedes for us. Christ, however, is not satisfied to

> render the Father favorable and propitious to us, but also admits us into this most honorable alliance. For we, though in ourselves polluted, in Him being priests (Rv 1:6), offer ourselves and our all to God, and freely enter the heavenly sanctuary, so that the sacrifices of prayer and praise which we present are grateful and of sweet odor before Him.[165]

---

[163] *Ibid.*, II,16: I, p. 443.

[164] B. Willems, *Soteriologie. Von der Reformation bis zur Gegenwart*, p. 27. For more on Calvin's doctrine of reconciliation, see P. van Buren, *Christ in Our Place. The Substitutionary Character of Calvin's Doctrine of Reconciliation* (Grand Rapids, MI: Eerdmans, 1957).

[165] Calvin, *Institutes*, II, 15: I, p. 432.

The mediation of Christ comes to an end with the consummation of history and the last judgment. Then, as 1 Cor 15:24-28 states, "Christ will deliver the Kingdom to the Father so that God may be all in all." Christ's mediation ends because he has fulfilled its purpose by bringing the elect to full communion with the Father. "Christ's humanity will no longer be interposed to keep us back from a closer view of God." He "continues to wear our humanity, but in such a way that we see Him in the full glory and majesty of Godhead."[166]

As already indicated, Calvin, faithful to the Scriptures and to the Fathers, points out a correspondence and causal relationship between the various phases of the mystery of Christ and our redemption. By the death of Christ sin was abolished and death annihilated, but by his resurrection "righteousness was restored and life revived." His resurrection is the effective cause of new life in us. While the terminology of righteousness indicates only imputed external righteousness, the terminology of sanctification in the Holy Spirit refers to a real inner transformation of our being. In the Holy Spirit the believer is regenerated, lives outside of himself in Christ, and is effectively united to him. This union is a "true and substantial communion" with Christ.[167]

Moreover, the object of sanctification is not the believer as an individual (as is often the case in Luther), but the Church united to Christ as the body to its head. The individual is to participate in the mystery of Christ insofar as he is the member of Christ's Body the Church. The Church participates already on earth not only in the suffering and death, but also in the resurrection and ascension of her Head. The ascension plays a particularly important role in Calvin's Christology.

By the ascension of her Head, the Church has not only a hope

---

[166] T.F. Torrance, *Kingdom and Church. A Study in the Theology of the Reformation* (Fair Lawn, NJ: Essential Books, 1956), p. 138. Cf. also Calvin, *Institutes*, II,14: I, p. 418; II: 15: I, p. 430.

[167] *Corpus Reformatorum* 78, p. 199 (In Gal 2:20). Cf. also *Institutes of the Christian Religion*, II, 16: I, pp. 436-452; B. Willems, *Soteriologie. Von der Reformation bis zur Gegenwart*, pp. 29-31.

of heaven, but, being united to Christ as the body to its head, she already possesses heaven in her Head. Christ occupies his exalted seat at the right hand of the Father, so that

> thence transferring his virtue unto us, He may quicken us to spiritual life, sanctify us by his Spirit, and adorn his Church with various graces, by his protection preserve it safe from all harm, and by the strength of his hand curb the enemies raging against his cross and our salvation; in fine, that He may possess all power in heaven and earth, until He have utterly routed all his foes, who are also ours, and completed the structure of his Church. Such is the true nature of the Kingdom, such the power that the Father has conferred upon Him, until He arrive to complete the last act by judging the quick and the dead.[168]

With the ascension of Christ, his flesh is present only in heaven while his divinity is present everywhere. Calvin sharply rejects the ubiquity of Christ's flesh, which Luther, because he believed in a fusion of divine and human properties in Christ, strongly affirms. Christ's flesh cannot "lurk" under the Eucharistic bread and wine as the Lutherans assert. Yet the believers do eat the flesh of Christ and drink his blood in a real, yet spiritual way. In the celebration of the Lord's Supper, the believer, when eating the Eucharistic bread and drinking the Eucharistic wine (which do remain bread and wine), is raised by the power of the Holy Spirit to heaven where he truly communes with the flesh and blood of Christ. Calvin here refers to the Alexandrian Fathers in explaining that, through the Holy Spirit, the flesh of Christ is truly vivifying.[169] Accordingly, in Calvin's understanding every Eucharistic celebration is a real anticipation of the eschatological communion.[170]

---

[168] Calvin, *Institutes*, II, 16: I, p. 450.

[169] *Ibid.*, IV, 17: II, pp. 585-587; *The Clear Explanation of Sound Doctrine Concerning the True Partaking of the Flesh and Blood of Christ in the Holy Supper*: Calvin, *Theological Treatises*, tr. and ed. J.K.S. Reid, The Library of Christian Classics, vol. 22 (Philadelphia: Westminster), pp. 311-317.

[170] Cf. Torrance, *Kingdom and Church*, pp. 145-146.

While Calvin does not present the drama of redemption with the power and depth of Luther, he has built a consistent christological system based on a perceptive reading of the Scriptures and the patristic tradition.[171] In my opinion, its greatest values are the doctrine on the threefold office of Christ, the close link between Christology, pneumatology, and ecclesiology, and the conception of Christian life as a real, gradual participation in Christ. His doctrine had a lasting effect on Protestant thought and, in our century, also on Catholic theology. The systematic presentation of the threefold office of Christ in the Catholic theology of our century has certainly undergone the influence of Calvin. Through the mediation of Catholic theologians such as Congar, some of Calvin's thought found its way also into the official teaching of the Catholic Church in the conciliar document *Lumen Gentium* of the Second Vatican Council.

3. Liberal Protestant Christology

The period after the great reformers is the age of Protestant scholasticism. Textbook theologians simplified, systematized, and often impoverished the thought of the Reformers. For instance, the many aspects of the redemptive work of Christ in Luther and Calvin were neglected and only the theory of penal substitution, Christ suffering the full penalty for our sins, was emphasized. This theory, which implies a manifest injustice in God, proved to be an easy target when the Enlightenment came to attack Protestant orthodoxy.

For the ideology of the Enlightenment, human reason is the supreme norm of truth.[172] After the long and bitter controversies on points of dogma, after the long and bitter wars of religion in

---

[171] Calvin's doctrine of predestination further hardens that of Augustine and, if pursued to its logical conclusions, leads to the image of an arbitrary and cruel God. However, it is rather well isolated from his Christology.

[172] On the background to the theology of the Enlightenment, see J. Dillenberger and C. Welch, *Protestant Christianity Interpreted through Its Development* (New York: Macmillan, 1988²), pp. 136-143, 161-163.

which great multitudes were killed and tortured in the name of opposing religious views, a growing intellectual elite began advocating tolerance in the name of enlightened reason. All in Christianity that, in their eyes, contradicted human reason had to be discarded, if humankind was ever to emerge from the Dark Ages of religious persecution and irrational superstitions. The same standards of enlightened reason were applied to the nascent science of historiography. Thus, whatever historical criticism found contrary to reason in the biblical image and doctrine of Christ had to be discarded as legend or myth, or at least re-interpreted in a way not opposed to reason. The ideal of the Enlightenment was the autonomous free man who rejects the shackles of political dictatorship and religious dogma and believes in the unlimited capacity of the human mind and the unlimited moral perfectibility of human freedom as well as in the alliance of both to guarantee unlimited human progress. Protestant thinkers who accepted this perspective and still wanted to remain Christians were forced to transform their understanding of Christianity, and of Christ in particular. Since I am unable to treat all the major representatives of liberal Protestantism, I selected only three, Kant, Hegel and Schleiermacher, whose christological views influenced many lesser thinkers. In fact, not even crisis theology and neo-orthodoxy could suppress their influence, and many of their ideas have survived up to our own times either in a popularized form or as part of new christological hypotheses.

a. Kant

In his philosophical works, I. Kant drastically restricted the competence of human reason and acknowledged the propensity of the human race to evil, yet his religious thinking and his "Christology" in particular was profoundly shaped by the rationalism of the Enlightenment.[173] His goal was to discover and expound the reli-

---

[173] I put the word in quotation marks because Kant never spoke about Christology.

gion that is rationally justifiable, "the religion within the limits of reason alone" into which the ecclesiastical faith of Christianity was to be transformed. Since, according to Kant, only "practical reason" (the reason which investigates moral obligation) postulates the existence of God, religion (and, of course, Christology) must be restricted to the realm of morality. Of Christianity, only that which is a necessary presupposition or implication of moral obligation is rationally justifiable. The rest of the Christian message, such as the historical figure of Christ and the dogmas of the Church, he re-interprets as symbolic expressions of this pure rational faith. These symbols are important for the uneducated crowds until they reach the level of rational faith, which, for Kant, means the arrival of the Kingdom of God. I will summarize here only the re-interpretation he gives of the major christological dogmas of Christianity.

"What alone can make a world into the object of a divine decree and into the goal of creation is humanity (the rational worldly being as such) in its total moral perfection."[174] This idea and ideal of a morally perfect humanity has existed from all eternity in God and derives from the very essence of God. In this sense, then, the primordial idea of a humanity pleasing to God and existing within God is not a created thing, but "his only-begotten Son." Everything else exists only in relation to this idea and for the sake of the realization of this idea, namely, for the sake of a morally perfect humanity. It is in this sense that Kant believes he has given a rationally acceptable meaning to the Gospel of John: this idea is "the Word (the *Fiat*) through which all other things are and without which nothing exists that is made." It is in "Him" that God loved the world and it is "only in Him and only by making our own his disposition that we can hope to become children of God."[175]

Kant cannot explain how this ideal or archetype, which the human mind did not cause, could have come into our minds since

[174] *Religion within the Limits of Reason Alone*, tr. and ed. T.M. Greene and H.H. Hudson (New York: Harper & Brothers: 1960), p. 54. Note that I modified the translations of some of the quoted passages.

[175] *Ibid.*, p. 54.

even the ability of human nature to receive it is incomprehensible. For this reason Kant thinks it is appropriate to say that "this archetype came down to us from heaven and that it has assumed humanity." This coming down to us from heaven means for Kant that every human being has in his mind the archetype of the morally perfect humanity as a source of moral power and a goal to motivate him. Jesus is only one significant individual in whom this ideal has been imperfectly realized. The human mind naturally tends toward the representation of the moral ideal in a concrete human being, who not only lives according to the ideal but does it in the midst of opposition and suffering. Hence the life of Christ as an example to follow is very useful for the masses. Kant insinuates, however, that we can never be fully certain of the example of Christ or of any outward example as an embodiment of the moral ideal since "the outer experience does not disclose the inner disposition." Therefore, in the purely rational religion "we need no empirical example to make the idea of a person morally well-pleasing to God into our ideal; this idea as an ideal is already present in our mind."[176]

It follows from Kant's understanding of moral obligation and sin that no human being can be redeemed by someone else. He rejects any form of satisfaction or penal substitution for the guilty by the innocent:

> This debt (of moral evil a person has freely committed) can never be discharged by another person, so far as we can judge according to the justice of our human reason. For this is no transmissible liability which can be made over to another like a financial indebtedness (where it is all one to the creditor whether the debtor himself pays the debt or whether someone else pays it for him); rather is it *the most personal of all debts*, namely a debt of sins, which only the culprit can bear and which no innocent person can assume even though he be magnanimous enough to wish to take it upon himself for the sake of another.[177]

---

[176] *Ibid.*, pp. 56-57.
[177] *Ibid.*, p. 66.

Thus Kant reduces the doctrine of satisfaction to a symbolic description of the moral conversion of the individual. The new man (different from the old not physically, but morally), whose inner disposition became good in that he now intends to fulfill his duty for the sake of duty itself, must endure a most difficult struggle with the old sinful man. Only through suffering can the new man gradually realize in outward actions of obedience his new inner disposition. This suffering or "dying" is something that the old sinful man deserves, but it is the new man who actually undergoes it, and in this sense the new man (symbolically speaking, "the Son of God" who takes flesh in man) performs a satisfaction because the new man suffers for and in the place of the old man (who is morally but not physically different from him).

Kant reduced consistently the whole of Christology to anthropology, and further reduced religious anthropology to a philosophy of ethics. Even though few followed him with the same consistency and clarity, this twofold reduction became a lasting influence on certain trends of christological thought. The divinity of Christ understood as the perfect realization of man,[178] all "theoretical" dogmas discarded as irrelevant since religion is nothing but the art of living "a good moral life," has become popular "wisdom" in many circles up to our own times.

Kant's method, however, had an even wider influence and triggered a further positive development in Catholic theology in particular. Just as in philosophy transcendental Thomism came about instigated by, and in response to Kant's transcendental method, in theology, a transcendental theology developed in response to Kant's method. As Kant investigated and formulated the necessary presuppositions of any empirical knowledge and the necessary postulates of moral obligation, so the transcendental theology (and Christology) of Rahner has investigated and formulated the necessary presuppositions of the concrete facts of revelation, both in God and in human nature.

---

[178] In the second half of the 20th century even some Catholic theologians attempted to understand the divinity of Christ as the realization of human perfection.

b. Hegel

Hegel opposes the rationalistic theology of the Enlightenment and the reduction of Christianity to morality. Ultimately, his whole philosophy is centered on the Trinity and on Christ, and his intention is to provide a rational, speculative understanding of the basic Christian claim, "God is love." Nevertheless, he considers his philosophical explication of Christianity superior to Christian faith itself since it explains conceptually its naive representations such as "Father," "Son," and "Holy Spirit," and thereby replaces the mysteries by understanding.

By conceiving of God as the Supreme Being, Hegel contends, the theology of the Enlightenment "made Him hollow, empty, and poor." However, for the thinking reason God is not emptiness but Spirit and the nature of the Spirit unfolds itself for rational thought as the Triune God.

> Thus God is conceived as making himself an object to himself, and further, the object remains in this distinction in identity with God; in it God loves himself.[179]

This self-movement of the Spirit is its very nature, yet absolutely free. The absolute Idea is absolutely free in making itself an object to itself and thus positing a differentiation in itself and in overcoming this difference in love. Its freedom means that nothing other but itself causes this process:

> It is only the absolute Idea which determines itself, and which, in determining itself, is inwardly certain that it is absolutely free in itself; and in thus determining itself it implies that what is thus determined is allowed to exist as something which is free, as something independent, as an independent object.[180]

---

[179] G.W.F. Hegel, *Lectures on the Philosophy of Religion, Together with A Work on the Proofs of the Existence of God*, tr. E.B. Speirs and J.B. Sanderson (New York: Humanities Press, 1962), vol. I, p. 30.

[180] *Ibid.*, vol. III, p. 36.

There is much ambiguity in Hegel's thought as to whether or not this self-thinking Absolute Idea is God independently from the world process. There are texts that speak of "Eternal Being, in and for itself" and the Eternal Being differentiating itself and returning to itself eternally.

> This act of differentiation is merely a movement, a playing of love with itself, in which it does not get to be otherness or Other-Being in any serious sense, nor actually reach a condition of separation and division.[181]

Thus there is in Hegel a self-movement of the Absolute Idea, "a playing of love with itself," in contradistinction to creation, a self-movement that seems to describe what traditional Christian theology calls the life of the immanent Trinity. However, if the movement of the Absolute Idea remained on this level, it would be nothing more than an abstraction; it would be only abstract universal truth, rather than the identity of truth and reality. For the Absolute Idea to become Absolute Spirit, the fullness of reality and truth, which is both universal and concrete, infinite and definite, it must evolve dialectically through the historical process of creation and history. This process is described by Hegel as both necessary and free, a threefold movement, thesis, antithesis, and synthesis, on various levels. The Absolute Idea (thesis) must negate itself by passing over into its own opposite, or "Other-Being," that is, the world of nature (antithesis). The world of nature is characterized by particularity, concreteness and finitude, the negation of the abstract and universal. Then in humankind this process reaches fulfillment by a way of synthesis: our destiny is to negate the negation of the Absolute Idea, that is, the world of nature, yet preserving and integrating in a higher synthesis whatever is valuable in it. Thus in us the abstract and universal, the Absolute Idea, comes fully to itself by becoming conscious in humanity of itself as the concrete universal, as definite infinity, as Absolute Spirit. In other words, God

---

[181] *Ibid.*, p. 35.

comes to self-knowledge (or self-consciousness) through human-kind. Looking at the end stage of the process from another aspect, it is not only God knowing himself through humanity, but also humanity knowing itself in God.[182] These aspects ultimately coincide since in the self-differentiating Absolute the Object of the Absolute Idea is "original Man."[183] For Hegel there is a "substantial unity" between the human and divine natures.

This substantial unity of the two natures had to be manifested to all people, not only to those who are capable of philosophical thinking. Thus the manifestation had to be on the level of sense perception. This requirement explains for Hegel the historical particularity of the "incarnation":

> This unity must... show itself to consciousness in a purely temporal, absolutely ordinary manifestation of reality, in one particular man, in a definite individual who is at the same time known to be the Divine Idea, not merely a Being of a higher kind in general, but rather the highest, the absolute Idea, the Son of God.[184]

Although for Hegel every human being is the potential unity of human and divine natures, since there is only one Son in the Absolute (the one Object of the Self-Thinking Absolute Idea), it had to manifest itself in one individual alone.[185] Moreover, the Absolute Idea coming to itself in self-consciousness constitutes one consciousness, one subjectivity. This one subjectivity, then, had to become manifest in one subject. In Hegel's words,

---

[182] G.W.F. Hegel, *Enzyklopädie der philosophischen Wissenschaften im Grundrisse*, Ed F. Nicolin and O. Pöggeler (F. Meiner: Hamburg, 1959), Par. 564, "Gott ist nur Gott, insofern er sich selber weiss; sein Sich-wissen ist ferner ein Selbstbewusstsein im Menschen und das Wissen des Menschen *von* Gott, das fortgeht zum Sich-Wissen des Menschen *in* Gott" (p. 447).

[183] *Lectures on the Philosophy of Religion*, p. 31.

[184] *Ibid.*, p. 73.

[185] *Ibid.*, p. 75.

> God as Spirit (as the Absolute Idea returning to itself through
> the consciousness of man)... contains in himself the moment
> of subjectivity, of singleness; his manifestation, accordingly,
> can only be a single one, can take place only once.[186]

In Christ, however, the divine exists in the form of finitude, and
natural (bodily) life, in a state of self-alienation. This contradiction comes to a climax in his death:

> This death is... at once finitude in its most extreme form, and
> at the same time the abolition and absorption of natural
> finitude, of immediate existence and estrangement, the can-
> celing of limits.[187]

His death, then, ends in resurrection, because his death is the can-
celing of the limits of natural physical existence, the overcoming
of the state of self-alienation through love and the "reconciliation
of the Spirit with itself." The existence of Christ as Spirit, however, does not mean for Hegel the putting off of his human nature.
The Spirit is precisely Spirit in that it preserves its own negation
in itself.

> When, accordingly, the Son of Man sits on the right hand of
> the Father, we see that in this exaltation of human nature its
> glory consists, and its identity with the divine nature appears
> to the spiritual eye in the highest possible way.[188]

Here, however, the distance of Hegel's position from orthodox
Christology becomes most obvious. In Christ the "identity (of hu-
man nature) with the divine nature appears... in the highest pos-
sible way." As we have seen above, this identity consists in that the
Object of the Absolute Idea is simultaneously the "Son" or the
"Logos," and "the original Man."[189] All human individuals are

---

[186] *Ibid.*, p. 76.
[187] *Ibid.*, p. 93.
[188] *Ibid.*, p. 91.
[189] *Ibid.*, p. 31.

fulfilled when they actualize this implicit identity of human nature with the divine. For all those who contemplate the death of Christ and follow his teaching, this identity becomes a reality. As Christ, they also must deny their natural reality, which is finitude, separateness, independence, and selfishness.[190] When they realize their *one* identity[191] with their own notion, that of "original Man" (which is *and* the Object of the Absolute Idea), they move away from selfishness *the* and realize that the multiplicity of human subjects is only an illu- *many* sion. By achieving identity with the universal notion of man in themselves through "self-knowledge in God," they become one with each other and love reigns in them. This is the "Spiritual community," the community of what the Church ought to be and "this love is Spirit as such, the Holy Spirit."[192]

Christian religion is thus the most perfect, "the absolute religion" in which the end of the divine cosmic process, the Spirit, is present, real and accessible to "the ordinary uncultured consciousness."[193] Yet there is an even higher stage, the philosophy of Hegel, in which the naive representations of religious images and terms, such as Father, Son, and Holy Spirit, are explained. It is in Hegel's philosophical system that the self-movement of the Absolute Idea coming to itself through its own negation and through the negation of its negation comes to an end. It is there that the level of pictorial representation is overcome, when, in Hegel's philosophy, "Spirit has grasped its own Notion."[194]

Hegel's philosophy became a challenge to modern theology similar to what Gnosticism was for the ancient Church. In both cases God is reduced to the human spirit, knowledge of God to

---

[190] *Ibid.,* p. 49.

[191] The realization of this identity is both a noetic and a metaphysical process; more precisely, it is metaphysical in so far as it is noetical. By coming to know their identity with the notion of "human being," the individual subjects achieve a unity of being, they become one subjectivity.

[192] *Ibid.,* pp. 106-7.

[193] *Ibid.,* p. 108.

[194] *Sämtliche Werke.* Jubiläeumsausgabe in 20 Bänden, ed. H. Glockner (Stuttgart: Frommann, 1927-1930; reprinted 1959), vol. 2, p. 525. Cf. also *The Phenomenology of the Mind,* tr. R. Kroner (New York: Harper Torchbooks, 1961), p. 694.

self-knowledge, and salvation to the understanding that self-knowledge is the knowledge of God. However, there is a significant difference. For Gnosticism salvation consists in leaving behind the world of matter utterly and unambiguously; for Hegel, existence in the world of nature has a value to be preserved even when the Absolute returns to Itself through negating the world of nature. In fact, it is by going through the phase of nature that the Absolute becomes truly and fully real.

In Hegel's achievement a supreme irony reveals itself. Instead of putting his philosophy at the service of revelation, he attempted to master the latter by attempting an understanding of the central Christian mysteries, an understanding he claimed to be superior to the "naive representations" of revealed religion. But, in the end, what he grasped was not God but only Man, whose notion he dialectically identified with God. Instead of unveiling the mystery of God, he merely reduced it to ideal humanity that is to be realized in the course of history. From Hegel there is only one step to Feuerbach's explicit claim that all theology is in reality a self-alienated anthropology.

Yet, Hegel's system can be transformed in such a way as to provide a better understanding of the Christian mysteries, while safeguarding their absolute transcendence. That God is eternal self-movement in love, a self-movement in which freedom and necessity coincide, is a deep insight that has not yet been sufficiently explored and explicated. That the whole process of creation and history is centered on Christ and can only be understood from a Trinitarian perspective is also a truth whose implications we have begun to understand only in our own times. That the material world and human life in this world have a value to be integrated into God's own life is a true counterbalance to a one-sided traditional understanding of finite created being as containing no value whatsoever in comparison to Infinite Uncreated Being.

However, while it is true that, within God, necessity and freedom coincide, creation, in contrast, is not necessary at all, but an entirely free act of God. It is not a necessary finite moment in God's own self-movement; otherwise creation would be (dialectically) identical with God, and both God's transcendence and the reality of created being and of human freedom (other than divine) would be lost. Only if creation is understood to be really (ontologically, not just dialectically[195]) other than God, is the full mystery of creation and redemption preserved. God creates beings truly other than himself and truly valuable, even though he is the fullness of Being and Value in himself, prior to and without his creation. He freely gives being and value to that which does not have being and value. Only in this perspective does sin appear as a free act of self-alienation from God, rather than the necessary consequence of the Absolute moving into its own opposite. Only then can we perceive the incarnation and redemption as pure unexacted favor, as the manifestation of God's *agape* in the full biblical sense of the word.[196]

c. Schleiermacher

In his childhood, as a member of a devout Protestant community, F. Schleiermacher lived in a pietistic environment in which religious emotion and religious experience played a pivotal role.[197] After studying Kant and Hegel, he clearly distanced himself both from Kant, who reduced religion to the implications of morality, and from Hegel, who attempted to "sublate" ("*aufheben*") religion into philosophical thinking. Influenced by the warm religious ex-

---

[195] In Hegels' system the world is dialectically other than God, but nevertheless only a moment in God's own self-movement, from which It (the Absolute Idea) necessarily returns to Itself. In the Christian view, while creation is caused by God, it is not another form of God but irreducibly other, created, as it is said, *ex nihilo*. Thus, while the world depends on God for its being and value, yet, precisely as a result of this ontological dependence on God, creation has being and value in itself.

[196] For a similar evaluation of Hegel see W. Kasper, *Jesus the Christ*, tr. V. Green (New York: Paulist, 1976), pp. 182-185; _____ *The God of Jesus Christ*, tr. M.J. O'Connell (Crossroad: New York, 1984), pp. 265-267. For other, more favorable evaluations of Hegel from a Christian viewpoint, see, among others, J.N. Findlay, *Hegel: A Re-examination*, (New York: Doubleday, 1966); H. Küng, *Menschwerdung Gottes. Eine Einführung in Hegels theologisches Denken als Prolegomena zu einer künftigen Christologie* (Freiburg: Herder, 1970).

[197] For a more detailed exposition of Schleiermacher's thought, see J. Dillenberger and C. Welch, *Protestant Christianity Interpreted through Its Development* (New York: Macmillan, 1988²), pp. 163-169.

periences of the Moravian community of his childhood, as well as by the anti-rationalism of romanticism, he attempted to show that, primarily, religion is neither ethics nor metaphysics. It is rooted in an experience that is *sui generis*, "a kind of primal and immediate awareness which is really more basic than either ordinary knowing or acting." In his first major work, the religious experience is "a sense and taste for the Infinite."[198] "The contemplation of the pious is the immediate consciousness of the universal existence of all finite things, in and through the Infinite."[199] All creeds and doctrinal formulations, all institutions, even though unavoidable, are secondary manifestations of the religious feeling. Thus the attacks of the rationalists are misguided. When they attack the creeds and doctrines of Christianity they miss what is primary, the religious experience, which does not need any justification by reason or by moral principles; the truth of religious experience is self-authenticating.

In his later work, *The Christian Faith*, Schleiermacher reformulates religious experience as the immediate awareness or feeling of absolute dependence on God: "It is the awareness that the whole of our spontaneous activity (both our acts of receptivity and our free interventions in the outside world) comes from a source outside of ourselves."[200] On the basis of religious experience, which he also terms "God-consciousness," he attempts to re-build the whole Christian faith. According to his methodology, only that which pertains to the history of God-consciousness and its recovery through Jesus Christ can be conceptually articulated as a valid Christian teaching.[201]

The person of Jesus Christ occupies a central place in Schleiermacher's reconstruction. Jesus is not the incarnation of a pre-existent divine person, but the man whose God-consciousness (the

---

[198] *Ibid.*, p. 165.

[199] F. Schleiermacher, *Speeches on Religion to Its Cultured Despisers* (K. Paul, Trench, Trübner: London, 1893), p. 36.

[200] #4,3: English translation of 2nd German edition, ed. H.R. Mackintosh and J.S. Stewart, vol. I. (New York: Harper & Row, 1963), pp. 15-16.

[201] *Ibid.*, #29,3, vol. I, pp. 124-125.

awareness of absolute dependence on God) is perfect and normative for all people. He "is like all men because of the same human
nature, but different from all because of the enduring power of his
God-consciousness, which was a being of God in him in the proper
sense of the word."[202]

Jesus' work ought not to be limited to teaching and giving a
good example in moral living, as the theologians of the Enlightenment claimed. Schleiermacher recognizes a universal state of sinfulness that, according to him, consists in the state of a universal
weakening of God-consciousness. We are forgetful of God and
unable to recover God-consciousness on our own. The redemptive
work of Jesus consists in letting the estranged sinners share through
faith in his own strong God-consciousness. The Church is the community made up by those who participate in Jesus' God-consciousness and thereby constitute an intimate communion of life with him
and with each other.

While avoiding a reduction of Christianity to a rationalistic
religion or morality, Schleiermacher created his own form of reductionism by trying to derive all that matters in Christianity from
religious experience. One cannot deduce the whole of Christology
and soteriology from the experience of absolute dependence on God
without truncating the Christian message. For instance, in his system, the doctrines of the resurrection and ascension of Jesus become irrelevant, since they do not matter with regard to the history of religious experience.[203] Nevertheless, Schleiermacher has also
made some lasting contributions to Christian thought and to Christology in particular. He rightly called attention to the unique and
irreducible character of religious experience. The analysis of Christian experience, richly developed in the Fathers and in medieval
monastic theology, will continue in the 20th century. We also agree
with Schleiermacher's thesis that Jesus had a uniquely powerful experience of absolute dependence on God. But this vague statement
should have been made more concrete and biblical by pointing to

---

[202] *Ibid.*, #94, thesis: vol. II, p. 385.

[203] *Ibid.*, #99, 1-2: vol. II, pp. 417-421.

Jesus' obedience in which he lived out his absolute dependence on God. Moreover, in the Christian tradition, the divine sonship of Jesus may not be reduced to the unique power of his human experience of God, but rather the former grounds the latter. Yet there is a kernel of truth, I believe, in Schleiermacher's insight. Only Jesus, the eternal Son, consubstantial with the Father, could live out our total creaturely dependence on God; the Son alone in his humanity could become the perfect worshipper of the Father.

CHAPTER V

Protestant Christologies in the Twentieth Century

1. Crisis Theology

The first decades of the 20th century signaled the end of liberal Protestant theology. Its various forms were radically opposed to the beliefs of the rank and file church members and confused rather than enlightened the Christian faith of those studying for the ministry. Moreover, the barbaric sufferings the civilized nations of Europe inflicted upon each other in World War I had suddenly brought to light the human capacity for evil. The naive faith of the Enlightenment in unlimited moral progress through mere human efforts, a faith that had deeply influenced liberal Protestantism, was suddenly shaken to its foundations. The Jesus of liberal Protestantism who was ultimately only a human being and provided only an example of moral living, but did not redeem us from our fallen human condition, proved suddenly irrelevant.

Karl Barth, a young Swiss pastor who was himself raised in the liberal tradition, soon realized that his academic training did not prepare him for the job of preaching God's Word to his congregation. In order to help himself and other pastors in a similar position, he published a commentary on the Letter to the Romans in 1918. He was surprised by both the tumultuous welcome and the controversy that ensued. When later reflecting on what happened, Barth compared himself to a man who, climbing up a church steeple in the middle of the night, and reaching out for support, accidentally seized the bell rope and woke up the whole city.[204] Barth was not alone in his endeavor to return to the Word of God in the Bible and to the insights of the great reformers, Luther and Calvin. Rudolph Bultmann, Emil Brunner, Paul Tillich, to mention only the greatest names, shared his concern. For some years, they together constituted a recognizable new trend, that of "crisis theology."

"Crisis" in this context means God's judgment upon the human being. God is experienced as the Holy One, and because of his holiness, he appears as the wholly Other to sinful humanity. God's Word for us cannot be anything but judgment, a condemning no to all that is human. The distance and opposition between God and unredeemed humanity is perceived to be absolute. Such a view excludes the possibility of the incarnation. For crisis theology the divine dignity of Christ does not imply an ontological truth. It only means that God's definitive, eschatological Word comes to us through Christ, and it is through this Word that we are both condemned and saved.

Each of the "crisis" theologians developed later in his own personal direction, even distancing himself (to one degree or another) from the initial program. I will here outline only the Christologies of Bultmann, Barth, and Bonhoeffer, who is perhaps Barth's most original disciple.

2. Rudolph Bultmann

Bultmann's fundamental goal is to present to his age the authentic Christian message purified from its liberal distortions. Yet in his philosophical presuppositions and in his method he is strongly determined by the liberal heritage. On the one hand, in reaction against Schleiermacher, Bultmann emphasizes that the transcendent Word of God cannot be reduced to a datum of religious consciousness. On the other hand, accepting the conclusions of the

---

[204] Cf. J. Dillenberger and C. Welch, *Protestant Christianity*, pp. 234-235.

school of the history of religions (W. Bousset and W. Heitmüller), he sees the world view and the language of the New Testament as entirely mythological: The pre-existent Son of God was born of a Virgin by a miraculous divine intervention. He sacrificed himself on the cross, thereby placating God's wrath by shedding his own blood for the sins of a fallen humanity. Rising from the dead, he conquered the demonic powers and death, ascended into heaven and is soon to come, to judge the world in an apocalyptic catastrophe. Then the redeemed human being will be transferred into a celestial realm and endowed with a spiritual body.[205] According to Bultmann, all the major elements of this story were borrowed from Jewish apocalyptic and Gnostic redemption myths, and in this mythological form they remain completely incredible to the modern reader.[206]

Bultmann does not explain very carefully what he understands by myth. It is only in one of the footnotes of his famous essay, "New Testament and Mythology," that he gives a rather loose definition:

> Mythology is the use of imagery to express the otherworldly in terms of this world and the divine in terms of human life, the other side in terms of this side. For instance, divine transcendence is expressed as spatial distance.[207]

In spite of the far-reaching structural identities he sees between the New Testament story and other ancient religious mythologies, Bultmann emphasizes two important differences. First, there is a historical core behind the mythical story of the incarnate, crucified, and risen God, namely, the historical figure of Jesus of Nazareth. Second, in and through the mythical language of the New Testament the early Church proclaims her faith that in Jesus of Nazareth God's redemptive act has taken place for all humankind. How-

---

[205] R. Bultmann, "New Testament and Mythology," *Kerygma and Myth, A Theological Debate*, ed. by H.W. Bartsch (New York: Harper & Row, 1966⁵), pp. 1-8. This essay, delivered by Bultmann in 1943, started the debate on demythologization.

[206] *Ibid.*, p. 15.

[207] *Ibid.*, p. 10, n. 2.

ever, according to Bultmann,[208] the history of Jesus, as he lived and died, remains inaccessible for us. Only this proclamation of faith, the kerygma of the early Church about the crucified and risen Christ, is available for our age. But this is all we need, since it is in the kerygma that God's saving Word encounters us.

Nevertheless, the mythological crust prevents the people of our scientific age from hearing God's Word in the kerygma. It creates an unnecessary obstacle to faith. In our times no educated person is capable of believing in a spatially divided three-storied universe (heaven above, earth in the middle, and hell below), in the existence of angels and devils, in actual miracles, and in a physical resurrection. For modern man, whose thinking is "shaped for good or ill by modern science," mythological language is "not only irrational but utterly meaningless."[209] Thus "demythologization," the "restatement of the event of Jesus Christ in non-mythological terms," becomes a necessary task for theology; it is not a discarding but rather an interpreting of the myth of the New Testament. Its purpose is not to destroy faith, but rather to eliminate an unnecessary stumbling block to faith for us and to facilitate our encounter with the Word of God.

But how should one interpret the New Testament non-mythologically, without distorting its meaning? Bultmann believes that a philosophical study of myth in general provides an initial clue for the right method of interpretation. "The real purpose of the myth is not to present an objective picture of the world as it is, but to express man's understanding of himself in the world in which he lives."[210] Thus the myth itself, in order to be properly understood in its original intention, calls for an existential interpretation. The same applies to the New Testament. In fact, the theologian has only to continue what the New Testament itself has already begun, namely an existential re-interpretation of the mythical event

---

[208] Cf. pp. 6-7 of this book.
[209] Bultmann, "New Testament and Mythology," p. 8.
[210] *Ibid.*, p. 10.

of the saving death and resurrection of Jesus Christ. For instance, St. Paul understands the death and resurrection of Jesus primarily as an existential event for and in the believer. Bultmann's goal is, then, to bring to completion the process of the existential re-interpretation of the New Testament with the help of the existential philosophy of the early Heidegger.

Everything in this re-interpretation centers on dying to the old life, and rising to a new life; that is, going over from the old self-understanding, which is called "life according to the flesh," a life of slavery under the power of sin, death, and the devil in biblical terminology, to a new self-understanding, which is called "life according to the spirit" or "life in faith" in the New Testament. The first is inauthentic life, the second authentic. In the first, we cling to the securities, rewards, and achievements that this visible and tangible world provides, but in the process one "becomes the slave of that very sphere which he had hoped to master, and which he hoped would give him security."[211] In the second, the authentic life, we abandon all "self-contrived security." If we possess the attitude that the New Testament calls "faith," "the unseen, intangible reality actually confronts us as love, opening up our future and signifying not death but life." We let all our earthly attachments go, surrender all our self-confidence and resolve to trust in God alone and accept our future from him in unconditional obedience.[212]

Facing his critics' challenge on why the historical event of Jesus Christ was still important for this existential analysis, Bultmann insisted that the Heideggerian categories serve only as a means to understand the New Testament kerygma. No philosophical analysis can bring about this new self-understanding in any human being; only God's saving Word can, and the believer encounters this Word exclusively in the kerygma of the cross of Jesus Christ. It is the Word of Christ in the kerygma that judges one and condemns one's inauthentic existence and gives one the power to rise to a new life. In

---

[211] *Ibid.*, p. 18.
[212] *Ibid.*, p. 19.

this regard Bultmann remains an orthodox Lutheran who believes in the fall of humanity and in our inability to rise from the state of sin by our own power of will and understanding.[213]

Bultmann's influence can hardly be overstated. His thoughts and the opposition to his thoughts shaped a whole generation of Protestant scholars. After Vatican II, when Bultmann's influence was already waning among Protestants, Catholics were just beginning to wake up to the challenge of his program of demythologization.

Bultmann's program is seductive, because it speaks to a real need and offers a simple solution. It is true that God's Word does indeed come to us in and through the time-conditioned language and world view of a past age, and thus we do need to distinguish what God's Word intends to reveal from the time-conditioned medium in which revelation takes place. The Bible needs to be re-interpreted in every age. However, in the process the whole of God's revelation needs to be preserved and "re-translated" rather than deformed or discarded. Bultmann, in spite of his own intention, could not avoid the latter.

He is led by his Kantian epistemology to the position that the Word of God does not reveal anything, provides no deeper knowledge of God; it has no object, no content. It is merely an act that transforms one's self-understanding.[214]

Furthermore, Bultmann's definition of myth is so broad as to include the mystery of the incarnation. If myth is the expression of the otherworldly in terms of this world, then indeed the figure of the man Jesus as God in human form is a myth and needs to be discarded. It would only obscure the true message of the New Testament to call this man God or Son of God in the traditional sense of the term. Jesus is God or Son of God only in the sense that he is the carrier of God's decisive Word addressed to man. Thus Bultmann ends up not merely re-interpreting but eliminating the Christian message.

---

[213] *Ibid.*, pp. 27-33.

[214] "The Concept of Revelation in the New Testament," *Existence and Faith*, translated and introduced by S.M. Ogden (New York: Meridian, 1960), pp. 87-88.

Bultmann's program needs to be criticized not only from the theological viewpoint of the New Testament itself, but also from the viewpoint of his so-called "modern man" with a scientific world view. The educated person of today expects much less from science than Bultmann's hypothetical "modern man" did regarding a valid explanation of objective reality in general. Today we are more aware of the inherent limitations of science and more ready to admit the existence of mysterious powers beyond what is empirically detectable.

Some of Bultmann's disciples could not live with the inconsistencies of his system. They moved away from his "heritage" in different directions. As we have seen, Käsemann became convinced that Bultmann's *a priori* injunction not to go beyond the kerygma to investigate the historical events concerning Jesus of Nazareth is historically unwarranted and theologically false. He and his group started a new quest for the historical Jesus.[215] Others thought that Bultmann was not radical enough in demythologizing Christianity. After all, he still clung to a transcendent act of God that reaches us in the preaching of the kerygma of Jesus Christ. Speaking about an act of God is as mythological — these writers claimed — as the rest of the New Testament language. Thus, they kept the existential analysis, but dismissed the need for the intervention of a transcendent God.[216] Still others accepted the need for God's grace in order to arrive at a new self-understanding, but questioned that God's grace was necessarily connected to the kerygma of Jesus Christ.[217] God's gift of love — they said — is available everywhere in human existence, not only in the kerygma.[218]

---

[215] See pp. 7, 56-57, 59-60 of this book.

[216] See. P.M. van Buren, *The Secular Meaning of the Gospel* (New York: Macmillan, 1963), pp. 63-74.

[217] See S.M. Ogden, *Christ without Myth* (New York: Harper, 1961).

[218] For a balanced evaluation of Bultmann, see R. Marlé, *Bultmann et l'interprétation du Nouveau Testament*[2] (Aubier: Éd. Montaigne, 1966). On the connection between Bultmann and the theology of Christian atheism, see R. Kereszty, *God Seekers for a New Age. From Crisis Theology to "Christian Atheism"* (Dayton, Ohio: Pflaum, 1970), pp. 73-79.

3. Karl Barth

The early Barth was the most radical among the "crisis theologians." He could not stress enough the infinite distance between sinful humanity and the holy God who confronts the sinner as the wholly Other. In losing this perspective on God, liberal Protestantism has lost, according to Barth, the very substance of faith. It reduced faith "to the highest possibility of human reason, revelation to the highest peak of human history, the God-consciousness of Jesus to the highest possibility of human religiosity." Briefly, God came to be seen as an amplification to the infinite degree of mere human perfections. This God — Barth thought — was nothing but our own projection, and Feuerbach was right in pointing that out.[219]

In contrast to liberal Protestantism, the early Barth advocates such an absolute opposition between God and humanity that, in his vision, there is no potential in us to know or to receive God. The most we can do is become an "empty room," a "bombshell crater" into which God's word falls.[220] Our sinfulness does not derive from the abuse of our freedom, but is identical with our actualization of freedom. In this perspective one cannot accept the incarnation as God becoming man and living with man. For the early Barth, the incarnation can only mean the playing out of the conflict between God and man in history as the murder of God by sinful man and the judgment of sinful man by God, a judgment which, in the strange process of a divine dialectic, turns into acquittal and salvation for all humankind.[221]

---

[219] Kereszty, *God Seekers for a New Age*, pp. 92-93. Perhaps the best presentation and evaluation of Barth's theology from a Catholic viewpoint is by H.U. von Balthasar, *The Theology of Karl Barth*, tr. by J. Drury (New York: Holt, Rinehart & Winston, 1971).

[220] K. Barth, *The Epistle to the Romans*, tr. E.C. Hoskyns (London: Oxford University Press, 1953), pp. 35-42; 102-103; 296-297.

[221] There is still too much Hegelian dialectic in the first stage of Barthian theology, the world going from original oneness with God through the Fall, which is identical with creation, into a new oneness with God through Christ's redemption, a necessary process of self-estrangement and return. Cf. H.U. von Balthasar, *op. cit.*, pp. 48-72.

One cannot endure for long such a one-sided version of divine transcendence. It is no accident that the theologians who invented the "Christian atheism" of the sixties were all disciples of the early Barth. Psychologically, it is very easy to flip from an affirmation of divine transcendence that negates humanity (and the whole of creation) to its exact opposite, an affirmation of humanity that necessitates the "death of God."[222]

Barth himself grew out of this stage and developed a christological synthesis that proved to be of lasting value for both Protestant and Catholic Christologies. The center of this new vision is no longer God's otherness, but Jesus Christ, who alone makes known to us God, ourselves, and the whole of creation. In the light of Christ, Barth sees God's transcendence in a new perspective. God's divinity is revealed to us in his freedom to humble himself as man and die for us as man. "The *forma Dei* consists in the grace in which God Himself assumes and makes His own the *forma servi.*" God's glory is the freedom of his love by which he takes up the cause of man.

> His omnipotence is that of a divine plenitude of power in the fact that (as opposed to any abstract omnipotence) it can assume the form of weakness and impotence and do so as omnipotence, triumphing in this form... His wisdom does not deny itself, but proclaims itself in what necessarily appears as folly to the world; his righteousness in ranging himself with the unrighteous as one who is accused with them, as the first, and properly the only one to come under accusation; his holiness in having mercy on man, in taking his misery to heart, in willing to share it with him in order to take it away from him.[223]

Barth rediscovered the faith and language of the Fathers and of St. Bernard, the faith and language that centers on the reality of the

---

[222] Cf. R. Kereszty, *God Seekers for a New Age*, pp. 92-99.

[223] K. Barth, *Church Dogmatics*, IV/1, ed. G.W. Bromiley and T.F. Torrance (Edinburgh: T. & T. Clark, 1956), pp. 187-188.

incarnation. God is no longer the enemy or the absorber of humanity. The later Barth perceives a humanity, a "human side" (*Menschlichkeit*) in God himself, and this humanity of God is mirrored in and through the humanity of Jesus Christ.[224]

Barth accepts the teaching of the great Ecumenical Councils on the two natures and the one person in Christ. But he refuses to see the hypostatic union as distinct from soteriology. Influenced by existentialist thinking, he states that the being of Christ is his action. For him the doctrine of the human and divine natures of Christ and of the unity of the person of Christ is identical with the "three forms of the doctrine of reconciliation."[225]

The divinity of Jesus Christ is revealed in the first aspect of the work of atonement: God humbling himself; God, in his almighty freedom, becoming our servant, and taking our place, the place of the sinner. In the first part of the Gospel accounts Jesus appears as the divine Judge who comes to judge the world. In the passion accounts, from the scene in Gethsemane on, he becomes the very object of judgment. The Judge accepts to be judged and to be punished by the verdict we have deserved:

> We now return to our question: Why did the Son of God become man, one of us, our brother, our fellow in the human situation? The answer is: In order to judge the world. But in the light of what God has actually done we must add at once: In order to judge it in the exercise of his kingly freedom to show his grace in the execution of his judgment, to pronounce us free in passing sentence, to free us by imprisoning us, to ground our life on our death, to redeem and save us by our destruction… That was the eternal will of God and its fulfillment in time — the execution of this strange judgment. If this strange judgment had not taken place, there would be only a lost world and lost men.[226]

---

[224] *The Humanity of God* (Richmond, VA: John Knox Press, 1960), p. 51.

[225] *Church Dogmatics*, IV/1, pp. 128-156.

[226] *Ibid.*, p. 222.

Barth understands the mystery of the Judge being judged in our place in the same radical sense as Luther did. Christ made our sin his very own, so that he became the sinner "greater than which there never was in the world." In him clashed the greatest and only sin with the greatest and only justice so that in him "all sin is overcome, killed and buried, and in Him victorious and reigning justice remains forever."[227] Since the Son of God took upon himself all sins, he alone suffered the appropriate punishment for sin, hell itself. This is shown, according to Barth, in the statement of the Apostles' Creed, "He descended into hell":

> The Creed tells us that the execution of this verdict is carried out by God in this way: that He, God himself, in Jesus Christ his Son, at once true God and true man, takes the place of condemned man. God's judgment is executed, God's law takes its course, but in such a way that what man had to suffer is suffered by this One, who as God's Son stands for all others. Such is the lordship of Jesus Christ, who stands for us before God, by taking upon himself what belongs to us. In Him God makes himself liable, at the point at which we are accursed and guilty and lost. He it is in his Son, who in the person of this crucified man, bears on Golgotha all that ought to be laid on us. And in this way He makes an end of the curse. It is not God's will that man should perish; it is not God's will that man should pay what he was bound to pay; in other words, God extirpates the sin. And God does this, not in spite of his righteousness, but it is God's very righteousness that He, the holy One, steps in for us the unholy, that He wills to save and does save us.[228]

This enduring of hell in our place and for our sake marks the lowest point in God's descent as our Servant where, paradoxically, his divine justice, holiness and transcendence are most clearly revealed.

---

[227] *Ibid.*, p. 238.

[228] *Dogmatics in Outline*, tr. G.T. Thomson (New York: Harper & Row, 1959), pp. 118-119.

Just as Barth discusses Christ's divinity not metaphysically, but as the descending movement of God's self-abasement, so he considers his humanity not "statically," or metaphysically, but as an ascending movement of man's exaltation. This is the second aspect of the work of atonement. Since the Lord has become a servant, the servant has also become the Lord. The humiliation of the Son of God resulted in the exaltation of the Son of Man. This means that God has assumed our *humanitas*, our human nature (not only our nature as created by God but also in its state of being fallen away from God) and "set it in motion" "from the far country" (the state of alienation from God or from the earth, created good by God but darkened by man) toward heaven, that is, toward peace and an intimate partnership with God.[229]

The exaltation of the man Jesus does not simply mark a second stage that follows upon the humiliation of God; although caused by it, the exaltation runs parallel to the humiliation. Revealed in the resurrection, it was "shown retrospectively by the evangelists to be the secret of his whole life and death."[230] Barth interprets the Son of Man sayings of the New Testament as referring to the exalted man, to the "new and royal man" who is Jesus Christ. Even though God is called Lord in both the Old and New Testaments, the New Testament reveals that God is Lord and King "in the form and person of this man."[231]

> He was among his fellow-men as the Lord, the royal man. To be sure, He was a man as they were. He did not exercise divine sovereignty or authority or omnipotence. But all the same He was its full and direct witness. And as such He was unmistakably marked off from other men. He was a free man. Neither on earth nor in heaven (apart from his Father) was there anyone or anything over Him… He was wholly free to

---

[229] *Church Dogmatics*, IV/2, pp. 20-29.

[230] *Ibid.*, IV/1, p 135.

[231] *Ibid.*, IV/2, p. 155. The phrase "in the person of this man" is not intended by Barth in the metaphysical sense of a human hypostasis in Jesus. He often explains that this man is God himself.

> do the will of His Father.... Subject to this one imperative,
> and therefore not arbitrarily, not under any outward compul-
> sion or constraint, He came and went with absolute superi-
> ority, disposing and controlling, speaking or keeping silence,
> always exercising lordship. This was no less true when He
> entered and trod to the end the way of his death and passion.
> Indeed to those who looked back, it was even more plainly
> true on this way. The presence of the man of Nazareth meant
> the presence of a Kingdom — the Kingdom of God or the
> Kingdom of Heaven the tradition calls it. This is what made
> Him absolutely unique and unforgettable.... As Origen puts
> it, He is the *autobasileia*.[232]

The lordship of the royal man means that his presence in the community of the disciples is irrevocable. The Gospels were written after
the life and death of Jesus. Yet what they look back to is not "past"
but rather "perfect." They are monuments to the memory of this
man "who still is what He was" and who sees to it that he is not
forgotten.[233]

The royal man is the "new man" created "after God" (*kata
theon:* Eph 4:24). This means that "He exists analogously to the
mode of existence of God." All that he thinks, wills, and does, all
his attitudes mirror on the creaturely level the plan, the purpose,
the work, and the attitude of God. Thus Jesus shares in God's destiny in the world: He is ignored, forgotten, despised and discounted
by us. He has nothing that the world counts as authority, honor,
or success.

He, in turn, ignores — almost to the point of prejudice —
those who are high, powerful, and wealthy in favor of those who
are weak, meek, and lowly. He accepts solidarity with those who
are poor, not only economically but also morally and spiritually. He
is known as a friend of sinners and tax collectors.[234]

---

[232] *Ibid.*, pp. 161, 163.
[233] *Ibid.*, p. 163.
[234] *Ibid.*, pp. 166-170.

Even though Jesus does not represent, defend, or champion any program, whether political, economic, moral, or religious, conservative or progressive, he is suspected and disliked by the representatives of all such programs. His royal freedom with regard to the established values and orders of society unsettles and puts in question all these values and orders.

Thus, Jesus the royal man represents God as "the Judge of our world; the One whose will is that the world be totally changed and renewed." But, at the same time, Jesus as the royal man "is not merely one man with others but the man for them"; he is the man who is the work of God's mercy, Gospel and atonement; as man, he echoes the divine Yes to man.[235]

The royalty of this man is revealed primarily in his "life-act," in the unity of his words and deeds. In both his words and deeds, "an alien will and unknown power invaded the general course of things in what the majority of men accepted as its self-evident and inflexible normality.... The Sermon on the Mount... was no less a miraculous Word, the irruption and occurrence of something incomprehensible to man, than the raising of the young man at Nain."[236] The miracles of Jesus are signs of the Kingdom and they anticipate "the glory and peace of the final revelation of the will and Kingdom of God."[237]

As Jesus acts in his commission and power, it is clear that God does not will that which troubles and torments and disturbs and destroys man. He does not will the entanglement and humiliation and distress and shame that the being of man in the cosmos and as a cosmic being means for man. He does not will the destruction of man but his salvation... The shame that comes on man is primarily a violation of (God's) own glory.... God cannot tolerate that man perish.[238]

---

[235] *Ibid.*, pp. 171-181.
[236] *Ibid.*, p. 211.
[237] *Ibid.*, p. 246.
[238] *Ibid.*, pp. 225-226.

Jesus is the free royal man also in facing death. In all the Gospels this is the final outcome towards which his whole life has been directed. In going toward and in accepting his passion Jesus freely accepts a divine "must" (*dei*). In the whole of the New Testament Jesus is the Crucified One. The whole of the New Testament sees him "in the light of his death as it shines forth in his resurrection."[239] His death is his coronation:

> In (Christ's) passion the name of the God active and revealed in Him is conclusively sanctified; (God's) will is done on earth as it is done in heaven; his Kingdom comes, in a form and with a power to which as a man He can only give a terrified but determined assent. And in the passion He exists conclusively as the One He is — the Son of God who is also the Son of Man. In the deepest darkness of Golgotha He enters supremely into the glory of the unity of the Son with the Father. In that abandonment by God He is the One who is directly loved by God. This is the secret that we have to see and understand. And it is not a new and specific secret. It is the secret of the whole. Nor is it a closed secret. It is a secret that has been revealed in the resurrection of Jesus.[240]

Barth treats the Church within this second aspect of reconciliation, since it derives from the exaltation of humanity in Jesus Christ. In some sense the sanctification of all humankind and all human life has taken place in Christ, because the human nature sanctified and exalted in him is our human nature. Through his Spirit Christ brings forth a people, the community of the Church, which is his Body, the earthly-historical form of his existence. Even though they are still sinners, they may be called a communion of his saints, because they render him obedience and thanksgiving. In all this, however, they are only a provisional representation of the sanctification of all humanity.[241]

---

239 *Ibid.*, p. 250.
240 *Ibid.*, p. 252.
241 *Ibid.*, pp. 264-840.

The third form or aspect of the doctrine of reconciliation concerns the unity of Jesus Christ: "Jesus Christ himself is one. He is the 'God-man,' that is, the Son of God who as such is this man, this man who as such is the Son of God."[242] As the one Mediator in his own person between God and man, Jesus Christ is the guarantor that our reconciliation with God did indeed take place.[243] Thus, all that has been said so far about soteriology, about God becoming our servant and the servant becoming the royal and free man, presupposes the unity of Jesus Christ.

Barth believes that his threefold treatment of reconciliation brings out the full meaning of the traditional threefold office of Christ: priest, king, and prophet. The humiliation of God and his taking our place in judgment is the fulfillment of Christ's priestly work, while the exaltation of the man Jesus corresponds to his royal office. The unity of Jesus Christ reveals both the faithfulness of God to man and man's faithfulness to God (as the result of God's victory over man's sin), and thus it is the summary and the guarantee of Christian witness. The prophetic office of Jesus Christ consists, then, in revealing himself as the one who, in his own person, is the actualization of the Covenant, the indestructible union "between God and each of us men."[244]

In Barth's theology every truth of faith centers on Christ and on the reconciliation achieved by him. Creation is the external basis of the Covenant in Jesus Christ; our justification is achieved by God who endured in Christ the verdict we have deserved by our sins; our sanctification, in other words, our inner transformation by receiving new being in union with Christ, is the result of humanity's exaltation in the history of Jesus Christ. The ministry of the Church consists in bearing witness to the one Jesus Christ, the one who achieved and who guarantees our reconciliation with God. The whole of Christian life as anchored in faith, love, and hope corresponds to these three aspects of reconciliation. At the

---

[242] *Ibid.*, IV/1, p. 135.
[243] *Ibid.*, pp. 136-137.
[244] *Ibid.*, IV/3, p. 41.

end of times, the Parousia of Christ, which has already begun through the appearances of the risen One and continued through the gifts of the Holy Spirit throughout history, will become manifest to the whole world.

However, for Barth the condemning judgment has taken place already on the cross, where God the Son has been judged and condemned in our place. Therefore, out of sheer grace all humankind will be saved. We should, then, await the Last Judgment with confidence and joy:

> In the biblical world of thought the judge is not primarily the one who rewards some and punishes the others; he is the man who creates order and restores what has been destroyed. We may go to meet this judge, this restoration, or better, the revelation of this restoration with unconditioned confidence, because *He* is the judge... To the seriousness of the thought of judgment no injury will be done, for there it will be manifest that God's grace and God's right are the measure by which the whole of humanity and each man will be measured. *Venturus judicare*: God knows everything that exists and happens. Then we may well be terrified, and to that extent those visions of the Last Judgment are not simply meaningless. That which is not of God's grace and right cannot exist. Infinitely much human as well as Christian "greatness" perhaps plunges there into the outermost darkness. That there is such a divine No is indeed included in this *judicare*. But the moment we grant this we must revert to the truth that the Judge who puts some on the left and the others on the right, is in fact He who has yielded himself to the judgment of God *for me* and has taken away all malediction from me.[245]

Barth's view of universal salvation as the necessary consequence of Christ's condemnation results more from the logic of his own system of dialectics than from a careful exegesis of Scripture. Nevertheless, apart from this and some other minor points, he built

---

[245] *Dogmatics in Outline*, pp. 135-136.

up a most impressive synthesis of biblical, patristic, and reformation Christology, in which he showed the inner coherence of the mysteries of faith; his theology has deeply influenced subsequent Protestant and Catholic thought[246] and needs to be taken seriously in every new christological reconstruction.[247]

4. Dietrich Bonhoeffer

The starting point of Bonhoeffer's theological activity, just as that of K. Barth, is a passionate rejection of the liberal heritage. He criticizes as un-Christian any theological effort that deduces the idea of God from human religious needs. At this point in his development, Bonhoeffer sees an absolute opposition between the human Logos and God's Logos. God's Logos is an "anti-Logos" to ours. He sees more than a dialectical opposition between the two. He rejects Hegel's dialectic as a subtle attempt to assimilate the "anti-Logos" into human reason, for in this dialectic, precisely by negating itself, human reason re-asserts its own supremacy. For Bonhoeffer the opposition is irreconcilable: the Logos of God is death to the human Logos, while the human Logos attempts to kill the former:

> Because the human Logos does not want to die, the Logos of God, who would be the death of it, must die so that the human Logos can live on with its unanswered questions of existence and transcendence. The Logos of God incarnate must be crucified by man's Logos.[248]

---

[246] H.U. von Balthasar, one of the greatest Catholic theologians of the 20th century, was deeply influenced by Barth's thought, especially in his understanding of the death of Christ and his descent to hell.

[247] This evaluation deals only with Barth's Christology rather than with his treatment of nature and grace, faith and philosophical reason. On these and other questions, see H.U. von Balthasar, *The Theology of Karl Barth*, pp. 197-298.

[248] D. Bonhoeffer, *Christ the Center*, intr. E.H. Robertson and tr. J. Bowden (New York: Harper & Row, 1966), p. 34.

Accordingly, the history of theology continues the passion story of Christ in history. Christ goes through the ages, questioned anew, missed anew, killed anew. However, just as Jesus rose from the dead in history, the divine Logos whom theology tries to kill in various ways confronts his executioners again and again as the risen One.[249] Because of this irreconcilable opposition between the divine Logos and human reason, the only appropriate question we should ask when encountering the crucified and risen Christ remains, "Who are you?" If we asked, "*how* is it possible that Christ is both God and man?" we would yield to the attempt of the human Logos to put ourselves above God's Logos and reduce it to our own categories. We can hope to hear the answer to the question, "Who are you?" only in the Church, where Christ reveals himself every day even before our question is asked. Moreover, only in faith can this question be rightly asked. In other words, only the ones who know that they have already been addressed by Christ and that they have already been questioned to the very depth of their being by Christ, can ask the question, "Who are you?"[250]

Bonhoeffer unfolds the answer to this question in several steps. "Jesus is the Christ present as the crucified and risen One." This confession of faith is not to be reduced to the assertion that his influence or that his image as an ideal for human living is present in history. Because of the resurrection, Christ himself is present as a living person. It is in the light of this personal presence in all times and places that we should interpret the meaning of his humanity and divinity:

> Only because Jesus Christ is man is He present in time and space. Only because Jesus Christ is God is He eternally present everywhere. The presence of Christ necessitates the statement "Jesus is fully man" — and it necessitates the statement, "Jesus is fully God." The contemporaneity and presence of Jesus

---

[249] *Ibid.*, p. 34.
[250] *Ibid.*, p. 36.

Christ in the Church are predicates of the one whole person, of the God-man.[251]

The personal presence of Christ *pro me* (for me) is not something added to the already existing person; rather, it is identical with the "essence," with "the being of the person himself."[252] The *pro me* of this presence means that he is a pioneer, the head and the firstborn of many brothers who follow him. It includes also Christ's standing in the place of his brothers by going to the cross and by bearing sin and dying. "Mankind is crucified, dies and is judged in Him." Finally, his presence *pro me* means that our new humanity exists in him. Thus, "because our new humanity is in Him, God is gracious towards it in Him."[253]

The presence of Christ occurs in the Church, and has a threefold form, the Word, the sacraments, and the community.

It would not suffice to say that Christ is present in the Church's word of preaching. He is also present as the spoken word of preaching: "Christ's presence is his existence as preaching.... The Word of God has really entered into the humiliation of the word of man."[254] Yet, with a hardly consistent twist of reasoning, Bonhoeffer continues to re-affirm his introductory theme that the Logos of God remains not only distinct but also divorced from the human Logos. The human Logos is word in the form of an idea, whereas the Word of God is a word addressed to us. Its contents are not abstract ideas but a word of forgiveness and command spoken to the human person.[255]

Christ is also present as sacrament. Fallen creation is in itself not a sacrament since it does not reveal Christ. Only when addressed by name, and hallowed by God's Word, do water, bread, and wine become sacraments. The sacraments are not a second incarnation

[251] *Ibid.*, p. 45.
[252] *Ibid.*, p. 47.
[253] *Ibid.*, pp. 48-49.
[254] *Ibid.*, p. 52.
[255] *Ibid.*, pp. 50-51; 53.

of a bodiless Word, but rather Christ the God-man is concealed in the sacraments. "The word of preaching is the form in which the Logos reaches the human Logos. The sacrament is the form in which the Logos reaches man in his nature."[256]

> In the sacrament He (Christ) is the penetration of fallen creation at a particular point. He is the new creature. He is the restored creation of our spiritual and bodily existence.
>
> He is the Word of God made bread and wine. As new creature He is in the bread and in the wine. So bread and wine are the new creation. They are real nourishment for the new being.[257]

The Logos is not only the weak human word of preaching; he is also the powerful Word of creation: he speaks, and by speaking "He creates the form of community." Thus, the community does not merely receive the Word of revelation; "it is itself revelation and Word of God." It not only *represents* the body of Christ; it *is* the body of Christ.

In all these three forms it is the one Word of God, the one God-man who exists. "His being as community, like his being as Word and sacrament, has the form of a stumbling block," since he remains hidden and becomes manifest only to those to whom he wants to reveal himself.[258]

Bonhoeffer is not indifferent to Jesus as he lived in history. He registers with satisfaction the collapse of the liberal quest for the so-called historical Jesus and accepts M. Kähler's twofold conclusion, namely, (1) that the quest for the historical Jesus took a false course when it tried to separate the historical Jesus from the Christ of the Christian community, and (2) that the historical Jesus is identical with the Christ of preaching. But he acknowledges the problem inherent in the historical method itself. Dogmatics needs

---

[256] *Ibid.*, p. 54.
[257] *Ibid.*, p. 59.
[258] *Ibid.*, pp. 60-61.

an absolute certainty about the identity of the historical Jesus with the Christ of the Christian community, whereas historical science, by its very nature, can never provide this absolute certainty. "Historical science never reckons with an individual fact as the absolute."[259] But the historically contingent fact of the life and death of Christ is of absolute significance for the Church. Therefore, historical investigation and its method must here be transcended even though they are not contradicted, since no historical research can ever absolutely deny the existence of Jesus Christ (just as it can never absolutely affirm it). The absolute ground of faith does not lie in history, but in the witness of the risen One who is present in the believer and

> bears witness to himself as the One who was historical then...
> The risen One himself creates belief and so points the way to himself as the historical One. From here faith needs no confirmation from history. The confirmation of historical investigation is irrelevant before the self-attestation of Christ in the present.[260]

Even though Nazism had come to power in Germany, Bonhoeffer decided to return to his country after a journey to America. His theological convictions led him logically to a certain way of life. He opposed the Nazi-sympathizer German Church and became active in the underground Confessing Church. He lived an intense life of prayer and Christian brotherhood in a semi-monastic community. Finally, he decided to take part in the conspiracy against Hitler. He was discovered and imprisoned; after two years of captivity, a few days before the liberating Allied troops arrived, he was executed. In his life and in his end we can detect an inner consistency that translated into practice his theological vision. The foundation of this vision is already present in his Christology and in the close link between Christology and ecclesiology that we have

---

[259] *Ibid.*, p. 74.
[260] *Ibid.*, p. 75.

just reviewed. He believed already in 1933 (when he delivered his lectures on Christology and on the Church) that Christ is the one whose very being is to be present for us by taking our place and by suffering the cross for us; and the Church must conform to, and participate in, Christ's *pro nobis* existence. As a consequence, Bonhoeffer wanted to leave the world in order to be conformed to Christ in the Church. This desire explains his life in the "monastic" community of the Confessing Church. Yet it was not intended to be an escape from the world. On the contrary, being conformed to Christ led him to exist for others. He accepted living, suffering, and dying for his countrymen as the concrete form of participating in Christ's sufferings. Thus, his Christology determined the shape and final outcome of his life; but also, conversely, his involvement in politics, his developing friendships with unbelievers, and especially his two years in prison further shaped and determined his Christology. He did not have time to work out a mature new synthesis. Only outlines, questions, and scattered insights remain in the letters, poems, and notes he wrote from prison.[261] We can only summarize here the most important ideas of this last stage of Bonhoeffer's development.

The transcendence of the true God is explained in the same way as in his previous works: it is Christ existing solely and entirely for others, a state of existence lived up to his death on the cross. This existence for others is the ground of Christ's omnipotence, omniscience, and omnipresence. Any concept of transcendence that begins with the infinite greatness and power of God is spurious: it is merely the projection and amplification of human qualities to an infinite degree. However, in his last writings, there is a change in the object of the preposition "for." Instead of explaining Christ as "the one who is present for me" or "for us," meaning, "for us in the Church," Christ is now defined as the "man for others," meaning "for all human beings."[262] Bonhoeffer's horizon has widened; he

---

[261] Published posthumously as *Letters and Papers from Prison*, ed. E. Bethge, tr. R. Fuller (New York: Macmillan, 1967).

[262] *Ibid.*, p. 202.

understands now that Christ's suffering is for the whole world, including the unbelievers. Christ is Lord not only of the Church but also of the whole world.[263]

Most surprisingly, in the constant anguish of prison life Bonhoeffer develops a new appreciation and love for the world. The world becomes so central to his thinking that he calls for a "worldly" re-interpretation of the whole of Christianity. His development is similar to that of Barth, but Bonhoeffer seems more radical in saying yes to the world. In his early years, just like Barth, Bonhoeffer viewed any free human act as an actualization of sin, and the world as an object of divine judgment. But his growing awareness of the universal dominion of Christ and his discovery of many honest and courageous unbelievers in prison gradually changed his view. He understands now that, since such a man as Jesus lived on earth, everything, the earth and people, every moment of one's life becomes valuable, and worth living:

> In Jesus God has said Yes and Amen to it all, and that Yes and Amen is the firm ground on which we stand. In these turbulent times we repeatedly lose sight of what really makes life worth living. We think that, because this or that person is living, it makes sense for us to live too. But the truth is that if this earth was good enough for the man Jesus Christ, if such a man as Jesus lived, then, and only then, has life a meaning for us. If Jesus had not lived, then our life would be meaningless, in spite of all the other people whom we know and honor and love.[264]

He draws a parallel between Chalcedonian Christology, polyphony, and Christian life. Just as the human and divine natures in Christ are undivided and yet distinct, so there is a *cantus firmus* in polyphony whose strength allows the full development of a musical counterpoint. Similarly, in Christian life we should love God with

---

[263] *Ibid.*, pp. 140-142.
[264] *Ibid.*, p. 207.

our whole heart but not in such a way "as to injure or weaken our earthly love." If the *cantus firmus* of love for God is strong and secure, it calls for the counterpoint of pure and passionate earthly love.[265]

Bonhoeffer never gives up his belief in eschatology. When he is taken to be executed, his last words to his fellow-prisoners express his faith: "This is the end — for me the beginning of life."[266] But he believes that participating in the existence of the crucified and risen Christ on earth means to live and die for the world just as Jesus did. This is the heart of Bonhoeffer's "non-religious," "worldly" interpretation of Christianity. It means not to concentrate on oneself, one's own needs, problems, and anxieties, not to expect God's intervention when everything else fails, but rather to participate in God's own suffering for the world.[267] I find in the following passage the most beautiful summary of Bonhoeffer's "wordly" spirituality, which is entirely based on the experience of participation in Christ:

> By this-worldliness I mean living unreservedly in life's duties, problems, successes and failures, experiences and perplexities. In so doing we throw ourselves completely into the arms of God, taking seriously, not our own sufferings, but those of God in the world — watching with Christ in Gethsemane. That I think is faith, that is *metanoia*; and that is how one becomes a man and a Christian (cf. Jr 45). How can success make us arrogant, or failure lead us astray, when we share in God's sufferings through a life of this kind?[268]

Bonhoeffer's Christology is certainly one-sided and incomplete. The relationship of Christ to the Father is hardly ever mentioned. He does not show us that Christ can become "the man for others" only because he exists entirely for the Father. This lack of

---

[265] *Ibid.*, pp. 150-151.
[266] *Ibid.*, p. 225.
[267] *Ibid.*, pp. 188-192.
[268] *Ibid.*, pp. 193-194.

theocentrism combined with his radical opposition of religion to faith occasioned in the United States a short-lived secularist and even atheist interpretation of the last stage of his work and life.[269] However, his intimate union with Christ, lived and consummated in a non-religious, secular environment, his love and commitment to the world whose fundamental goodness he could affirm only because of his faith in Christ, do remain a constant source of inspiration. Today, in particular, liberation theology could find a completion and deepening by reflecting on Bonhoeffer's understanding of participation in the cross of Christ.[270]

* * *

I have provided some representative samples of Protestant Christologies from the beginnings of the Reform up to the middle of the 20th century, because no contemporary Catholic synthesis would deserve to be called Catholic that did not attempt a critical assimilation of Protestant thought. I have not included contemporary Protestant or Catholic trends in this section, because it is not yet possible to place them in historical perspective.[271] Nevertheless, as it will appear from the footnotes, the final, systematic part of this study owes much to the insights of contemporary theologians.

---

[269] Cf. R. Kereszty, *God Seekers for a New Age*, pp. 100-122.

[270] For a thorough analysis of Bonhoeffer's life and thought see the work of his close friend, E. Bethge, *Dietrich Bonhoeffer: Eine Biographie* (Munich: Kaiser V., 1967); ET: *Dietrich Bonhoeffer: A Biography*, ed. Victoria J. Barnett (Minneapolis: Fortress Press, 1999). Cf. also J. Moltmann and J. Weissbach, *Two Studies in the Theology of Bonhoeffer* (New York: Scribner, 1967).

[271] For information on contempory Christologies see D. Edwards, *What Are They Saying about Salvation?* (New York: Paulist, 1986); G. O'Collins, *What Are They Saying about Jesus?* (New York: Paulist, 1983²); J. Macquarrie, *Jesus Christ in Modern Thought*, (Harrisburg, PA: Trinity Press International, 1991), pp. 293-335. Though his own christological reconstruction does not do justice either to biblical Christology or to the Catholic tradition, Macquarrie presents the major trends of contemporary Christology with acumen and objectivity. W.M. Thompson, *The Jesus Debate. A Survey and Synthesis* (New York: Paulist, 1985) is informative and comprehensive.

Part III

Systematic Christology

The Unity of the Mystery of Christ

The brief survey of historical Christology has brought to light a vast range of approaches to the one mystery of Christ. None of these efforts was truly comprehensive. Each of them selected some aspects of the mystery and tried to build a system on that basis. Such a selective and limited approach is all but inevitable for our human way of knowing. Nevertheless, not all attempts should be deemed equally successful. Those Christologies remained within the limits of orthodoxy that, in one way or another, managed to preserve at least implicitly the whole mystery rather than denied or distorted some of its essential aspects. The orthodox Christologies can be further evaluated according to a set of criteria. Of the various criteria according to which one could measure the relative success of a christological synthesis, I would propose two: one objective, the other subjective.

The objective criterion is derived from God's revelation. A christological system should start from what is central to revelation itself. Thus, approaches centering on the hypostatic union, the psychological consciousness of Christ, or Christ the liberator from social injustice may produce good monographs, but cannot provide an adequate christological synthesis. For the latter, one needs a perspective which — although it cannot treat all the christological problems — is still able to synthesize the major elements of revealed mystery.

The subjective criterion is determined by the needs and questions of the contemporary believer and unbeliever. No matter how comprehensive and true a christological synthesis is, if it does not speak to the questions of a contemporary audience, it fails to achieve its purpose. Tillich's insight, that a good theological system is built on the correlation of the questions philosophy poses and the answers theology provides, needs to be further refined. It is true that theologians do not work in a vacuum, but answer the questions of thinking people in a given age; and they do that by making intelligible for their age the meaning of "what Jesus did and taught." However, just as Jesus challenged the questions and expectations of his audience and led them to discover their deepest needs, so should theologians attempt to challenge, transform, and deepen the questions and expectations of their audience.

In proposing an outline for a christological synthesis, I have selected a theme central to both the New Testament and the Fathers: that of communion. The Father created humankind for communion with the Son (and with each other through the Son) in the Holy Spirit. Likewise, he created the material universe to reveal his beauty and wisdom and, thus, to become united with him through humankind. Having refused this call to communion, the members of the human race have become estranged from God, and thereby from themselves and each other; at the same time, the harmony and unity between human beings and the universe have been disrupted. Human sinfulness could not destroy yet could not fully enjoy the revelatory function of the universe; the latter has weighed down upon the human race through our own corruptible and suffering bodies; it has become a source of affliction for us and a stumbling block on our way to God.

However, the fall of the human race was not an unforeseen accident, for which God tried to compensate with a secondary "contingency plan." His eternal plan to assume humankind into his own Trinitarian life has been so designed as take into account the Fall. He allowed sin to triumph for a time, in order to reveal his love that turns all evil into a means of developing a greater love in those who are open to his prompting. After the Fall, God himself took on increasing solidarity with us, by choosing Israel as his own people and, in the fullness of time by becoming a true human being that represents Israel and all humankind through Israel. Expressing an infinite, divine love while living and dying in a mortal body, under the conditions of estrangement caused by sin, Jesus, the Son of God made human, obtained forgiveness for us from his Father, gave us a model in himself to imitate, and communicated to us his Spirit. In the power of the Spirit we may now turn our estrangement, physical pain and dying into the means and expression of a new and deeper communion with God.

Thus, in this perspective, the mystery of human sinfulness, of the hypostatic union and the mystery of the cross receive intelligibility from the one central mystery of the love of the Triune God. This love reaches its all-surpassing expression in Jesus Christ under the conditions of evil on the cross.[1]

Since humans are historical beings, both their estrangement and their reconciliation with God have taken place in a historical process, in a particular time and place: Jesus Christ suffered under Pontius Pilate in Jerusalem rather than under Adolf Hitler in Berlin. Nevertheless, since God's saving will is universal, by virtue of the historical life, death, and resurrection of this one man, Jesus Christ, salvation, the turning of human estrangement into the way of regaining divine and human communion, has become a universal possibility for all humankind. It is in the Holy Spirit that the salvation achieved by Christ can be longed for and appropriated in various ways and to various degrees by all men and women wherever and whenever they lived, live or will live in this world.[2]

In our age the human condition of estrangement from self and society, and the longing to overcome it, are experienced with particular intensity. We are torn between the desire to achieve personal self-fulfillment regardless of the needs of others and the equally powerful yearning to belong to others in order to alleviate our unbearable loneliness. The apparent conflict between a desire for self-affirmation and a desire for communing is the initial ques-

---

[1] Insofar as I present salvation in Christ as the revelation of divine love the greater than which one cannot conceive, I am inspired by the Christology of Balthasar. See especially H.U. von Balthasar, *Love Alone* (New York: Herder & Herder, 1969).

[2] See more on the dialectic of universality and historical concretion in the history of salvation in K. Rahner, *Foundations of Christian Faith* (New York: Seabury, 1978), especially pp. 138-175.

tion that Christology takes up, transforms, and answers from the perspective of the Triune God, who loves each person as if this one alone existed and fulfills him or her in a communion both human and divine.

On the basis of the above reflections, the structure of the systematic part of this study should become intelligible. First we will analyze the state of sin as multiple alienation (chapter I); then we will study the process by which God accepts full solidarity with our alienated condition and raises human nature in Jesus to himself. This entails a preparation in the Old Testament, reaches its decisive phase in the incarnation and is consummated through the cross and resurrection of Jesus (chapter II). After dealing with various aspects of the humanity of the Son (chapter III), we will describe the reconciling work of the Triune God: the role of the Father, the Son and the Holy Spirit. Then the final goal of redemption, including the transformation of the material world, will be outlined (chapter IV). The systematic part ends with examining the relationship of Christ to non-Christian religions (chapter V) and to possible intelligent beings on other planets of the universe (chapter VI).

CHAPTER I

Sin as a Threefold Alienation

1. Sin

In order to understand the way of redemption we need to examine the state of sin from which we have been redeemed. According to Christian faith, man and woman committed sin at the very beginning of human history.[3]

In this first sin man and woman chose to realize their human existence (an option made possible by their nature as a finite created freedom) in conscious independence from and opposition to God. As a result of this first sin, all human beings are born without God's grace and with the inclination to ratify the same option for themselves. The propensity in humankind for a false autonomy from God has been reinforced by the accumulation of personal sins that has created a universal sinful environment. Nevertheless, in virtue of the redemption accomplished by Jesus Christ, and even before the historical realization of that redemption, all human beings have always been offered the grace of Christ, so that they may resist the "gravitational pull" of sin or at least repent of their sins and yearn for communion with God.[4]

However, in this first chapter, the omnipresent influence of

---

[3] In a christological work it would be superfluous to enter into the contemporary discussion of a monogenistic or polygenistic explanation of the first sin. On this, see especially the encyclical *Humani Generis* (*DS*, 3897), which does not exclude outright the possibility of a polygenistic interpretation of human origins.

[4] Regarding the concrete forms this offer of grace may take to pagans or atheists before Christ and after Christ, see pp. 440-441.

God's grace in human history will not be treated but only the state of universal sinfulness from which God wants to save us.[5] Every time I consciously and freely oppose an imperative of my conscience, I go against my "better self." I knew before the act what was the "right thing to do," yet I overruled my own judgment and set my own sinful will above the awareness of my duty to do what I recognized as right. Thus, through the act of sinning, a split or estrangement is introduced into the very core of my subjectivity, into my judgment and will. My sinful will — seeking the support of a rationalizing judgment — is set against my right judgment and will to do what is right. If I persevere in my sin, then my sinful judgment and will are going to overpower and, to a greater or lesser extent, "silence" my "moral self," the self who appreciates and obeys moral values. My sinful self affirms himself as absolute, higher than the recognized moral order I had previously acknowledged through my conscience. The result is self-estrangement: I find myself in conflict with my own "truth," with my own real self whom I chose to ignore. I act as if I were an "Absolute Being" who can simply decree what is right and wrong for myself. Yet, while in my acts this false "absolute" self dominates the true "moral self," at the core of my being I know that my self-affirmation as an Absolute is false since, at least at the beginning of this process, I acted consciously against my own better judgment.

When I overrule the judgment of my conscience, I always do so for the sake of some limited good I decide for myself to be superior to the values my conscience proposes. For instance, a married man may decide that for him here and now an extramarital affair is more important than his obligations to his family; the satisfaction and pleasure he finds in the relationship with "the other woman" becomes more important for him than his family. In fact,

---

[5]   Note that a new-born child in the state of original sin is in some sense truly innocent, since original sin simply means the fact of being born without God's grace. It is not the result of a personal sinful act in the child. Yet the child's state of being without grace is opposed to God's call to communion with himself; moreover, without the grace coming from Christ's redemption, each child would realize its human existence in a false autonomy from God.

for the sake of this affair he may be ready to risk everything that he had cherished before. In other cases the limited good the sinner idolizes may be wealth, power, or fame.

Yet in every choice against one's own conscience it is ultimately not an external object that becomes the idol; rather, through choosing any created good as an absolute, the sinner idolizes himself or herself. In setting up arbitrarily one's own values, for instance, the pleasures of an extramarital relationship, against the order of reality itself as it has become known to us through our conscience, the sinner acted as a "god" by deciding arbitrarily what was right or wrong. That in every "idol" the sinner actually idolizes himself or herself, becomes very clear when the idol is no longer satisfying. A man's ecstatic love will immediately turn into hatred if the idolized woman no longer fulfills the role he assigned to her. If the people a dictator idolizes turns against him, he will try ruthlessly to suppress or destroy them.

Thus, if I understand myself as in some sense the "Absolute," the highest and the only true value, I will get into a conflict not only with my own true self, but also with my fellow human beings. I cannot accept my neighbors as my equals, since that would require me to dethrone myself. As long as I hold myself to be the center of the universe, others cannot be accepted for their own sake, but only as a means to further my own interests or else as potential rivals to be overcome. Depending on the kind of society I live in, my methods will be covert or overt, crass or subtle, but my goal will always remain the same: I will attempt to suppress, manipulate, and exploit the freedom of others.

I will also use the material world to enhance my own interests, without regard to the interest of others, and in the process I may contribute to destroying the environment for future generations.

The conflict with one's conscience and one's neighbor necessarily implies a conflict with God. Through the awareness of the absolute obligation to do what is right, believer, agnostic and atheist alike encounter the true Absolute, God himself. Moreover, we know from God's revelation that the voice of conscience calls one not only to respect the order of reality established by the Creator, but, ultimately, to accept the love of God the Father who wants to transform us into his children.[6]

Thus the one who sins mortally not only opposes the will of God the Creator, but also God's will to be our Father. Hence sin — to varying degrees and in various ways — is always a personal offense against God the Father.

In committing a sin, I also necessarily distort my understanding of God. If I was an unbeliever (even innocently) before sinning, the sin will confirm me in the received notion that "God" is an arbitrary and tyrannical power from which I must be set free. If I was a believer before my sin, in rationalizing my sin I may gradually come to believe that it is not God who actually forbids this or that sinful act, but only a Church teaching or other human tradition. In another scenario, I may continue to think what I did was sinful, but begin to resent God as the cause of my guilt, a tyrant and vindictive judge. I might even repress my instinctive knowledge of God and come to the conclusion that God does not exist. My resentment or cynicism will then be directed against "life" or "reality" in general. In any case, by sinning, we distort or repress our knowledge of God and no longer know the holy and loving One who has created us out of love and whose will is our life and fulfillment.

While sin is always committed by the will, a spiritual faculty, it expresses itself, and influences others, through the body. Through the body sin becomes "contagious"; it creates a milieu that affects everyone to varying degrees, and increases its power by enticing or pressuring other freedoms to commit the same sin or to oppose it with other sins. Thus violence begets counter-violence, promiscuity provokes self-righteous indignation, arrogance begets hatred, and infidelity in one spouse tempts the other to become unfaithful.

---

[6] Of the many hidden but real ways in which this offer of God's love takes place in daily life, the short stories of Flannery O'Connor provide powerful examples. See especially, "A Good Man Is Hard to Find," *The Complete Stories* (New York: Farrar, Straus & Giroux, 1985), pp. 117-133.

Moreover, by replacing the true Absolute with an idol, with some limited created good made into a false absolute, I oppose my own spiritual nature, which is naturally drawn towards the infinite spiritual Absolute. By embracing a creature as my ultimate value, I lose my ability to know and love spiritual realities. All that interests me now is the goods of this world, pleasure, possessions, power, and self-aggrandizement. Scripture and patristic tradition are describing this change when they say (speaking existentially rather than metaphysically) that every sinner becomes flesh: in conflict with their spiritual nature, they are captivated by the things of this passing world rather than by the things of God.

The contaminating influence of sin spreads not only through the body but is also further extended and reinforced through the structures of society; the economic, political, and cultural institutions are — to varying degrees and in various ways — all deformed by sin. While a sinful environment does not eliminate all individual freedom to be good and to do good, it curtails its range of action and makes some semi-conscious or unconscious appropriation and imitation of the sins of others inevitable. Thus hypocritical parents may produce hypocritical attitudes in their children, even before the children are able to recognize hypocrisy as evil. Promiscuous parents may produce promiscuous offspring. Parents alienated from their true selves (through their own or through others' fault) may influence their children to develop a "persona," a mask, which covers up their true selves even before the children are able to recognize that such an attitude is wrong. Institutionalized economic exploitation and political oppression create a climate in which individuals become unconscious or half-conscious instruments of injustice.[7]

---

[7] The fact that the individual is born into a sinful world that affects him through his genetic heritage and environment is not only a burden; it also limits or eliminates the individual's subjective sinfulness insofar as his moral awareness and freedom is diminished or sometimes non-existent.

2. The punishment of sin

The punishment I receive for my sin is not something extrinsic to sin itself. It is not like the application of a penal code whose penalties have only a legal connection with the sin committed. God respects our human dignity to shape freely our own being. If by sinning I freely distort my own reality and thereby my relationship to my neighbor and to God, God allows this freely chosen distortion to take effect. **The punishment of sin, then, is its necessary, "natural" consequence.** Thus, while sin is the freely chosen opposition to one's true self, to God and to one's neighbor, the punishment is the suffering that results from this threefold estrangement. Yet, as long as the sinful choice is not finalized in death, the suffering that comes from the estrangement remains a powerful incentive for sinners to seek a reversal of their state. We need to investigate this in more detail. For simplicity's sake we examine only that kind of alienation for which the person himself or herself is responsible. In real life, however, responsibilities always intertwine, and we carry in our own alienation — prior to our own decisions — the alienation caused by everybody else's sins.

In refusing to obey my conscience, I negate my own true being and live in a state of falsehood and self-deception. Hence the experience of self-alienation. It manifests itself in diminished self-worth and in a diminution of my own sense of identity. Often, I will try to compensate for it by inflating my ego and by exaggerating my self-importance. I need to convince myself more than anyone else of my own worth against the nagging suspicion of worthlessness.[8]

In refusing to accept myself as a gift from God and to accept God's own self offered to me in love, I am trying to be independent from God, and attempting to become what I am not, an ab-

---

[8] Obviously, as explained above, not every feeling of diminished self-worth is the result of personal sin. If a child does not receive unconditional love from those around him, especially in the first years of his life, he will develop a feeling of worthlessness or at least some serious doubts about whether he is lovable. Thus the child becomes the victim of others' sin.

solute in myself. By cutting myself off from Being Itself, I necessarily experience the fragility of my own being, which borders on nothingness and is threatened by nothingness. The result is a heightened sense of anxiety, a dread before the inevitability of my own death. Heidegger's "Angst" is the anxiety of sinful humankind. There is a connection between living as if "I were my own god" and experiencing my existence as a sliding towards death, a "Sein zum Tod."

In refusing to accept my neighbor with equal rights and a claim for personal relationships, I isolate myself from everyone. I end up with nothing but alliances and enmities based on self-interest; I become incapable of personal relationships, which demand mutual respect and acceptance of the other for the other's own sake. In either case, using everyone around me as a means for my ends or looking on him or her as a rival to be overpowered, I will be treated by others in exactly the same way.

While serving the true Absolute results in growing freedom and harmony, if I set myself up as an "absolute" by choosing limited goods like pleasure, wealth, glory, or power as ultimate values, I end up in slavery and must endure the disintegration of my freedom. I become "addicted" to my "idol," as the idol begins to exert more and more power over me, so that even when I want to shake free from it I can no longer do so. The object of my desire shapes and transforms my being to the likeness of the desired object. If I desire as my ultimate value things of this world, they will restrict my horizon and sensitivity to their level. Moreover, the instincts and drives these values give free rein to, the sex drive, the drive to possess things and dominate people, and the hunger for fame and greatness gradually weaken the freedom of my will, my personal, spiritual center that is the cause of my free acts. Now, even if I wanted to reverse the trend, I might not be able to assert myself against the internal forces that have taken control of my life. I am no longer free, because it is no longer my personal self that determines myself; one or several of these internal forces, of which each and all are less than my person, dictate my decisions. Yet I remain responsible for my actions, because I freely surrendered my freedom to these internal forces, and my will remains attached to them. **Thus the sinners who began by asserting themselves as "absolutes" end up as slaves to the goods of this world and to their passions.** All these forms of alienation, the self-estrangement, the estrangement from others, the slavery to the goods of this world, and the disintegration of the person as a free agent cause not only emotional and physical pain but also a feeling of numbness, of not really being alive.

Just as sin expresses itself and acquires power and influence through the body, so does the punishment for sin: the suffering, which results from my threefold alienation and from my conflict with the material universe, affects me through my body. It is in the death of the human body that the process of alienation and the suffering caused by alienation comes to a climax. This makes intelligible why physical death is viewed by Scripture as the natural punishment for sin and — but for Christ's death — also the image and anticipation of eternal death, that is, eternal damnation.

The human soul and human body constitute one being, one person. Thus, when I die, directly only my body dies, but since I am my body, I experience the disintegration of my body as something not external to myself; rather I experience **myself** dying (even though my soul, the very "core" of my person is immortal). This explains why the anticipation of the separation of our body and soul is so threatening and so painful for us: it is experienced as the disintegration and annihilation of the person who had originally been created for eternal life.

If the dying persons are believers but find themselves in the state of sin, they experience their dying as the foretaste of that final separation from the living God who is now perceived as absolutely distant from them. If unbelieving sinners are in the process of dying, their alienation from God will be felt as a cruel, impersonal fate indifferent to their personal concerns and aspirations. Either way, the sinners who attempted to be their own "absolute," their own god, must come to the realization that they are the exact opposite of an absolute; they are dependent, contingent beings whose annihilation is not only not impossible, but appears to be the most natural outcome of the process of dying.

In dying I also become more and more separated from my fellow men and women. If I considered them beforehand merely as means to further my interests, they are now slipping out of my control. I cannot force them to undergo the experience of dying in my place. Nevertheless, if some vestiges of humanity still remain in me, I will now long for the companionship and personal closeness of some human beings, whom I had not even noticed as persons before.

The conflict between the sinner and the material world also comes to a tragic climax at the moment of death. The material goods I used and abused in my lifetime refuse to serve me. They are no longer attractive but often become a source of pain. In general, the material universe appears as totally indifferent and even hurtful to the dying person.

3. The need for redemption

1. As long as sinners are alive, they have not entirely immobilized themselves in the state of this threefold alienation. Thus the misery that results from their state, especially when they are facing death, may serve as a powerful "therapy" to bring them back to reality. Yet, while we were free to distort ourselves and our relationships with God and with our fellow men and women, we are no longer free to reverse the process. Sin has affected our nature so deeply that only the author of nature, God, can create us anew.

2. If we consider sin as the free rejection of God's love, we find another reason why we cannot rescue ourselves from the state of sin on our own. We cannot earn back God's love. Even at the outset we could not have earned the absolutely free initiative by which God offers himself to us; much less can we gain it back now by our own resources. The analogy of human friendship may shed light on this truth of faith. Even a human friendship is a freely

bestowed gift, and if, by an act of disloyalty, I become unworthy of my friend's trust, I lose all "rights" to his or her friendship. I may repent and may try to repair the broken relationship, but I cannot restore it on my own. I am completely dependent on my friend's forgiveness and mercy. If this is the case with a human friendship, how much more is it true of the lost friendship of God. The initiative to restore us to God's friendship must come from God himself. Left to our own resources, we cannot rescue ourselves.[9]

But the question still remains: Why did God redeem humankind by the way of the incarnation and death of his Son? Why could he not simply offer his grace for repentance and declare the repentant sinner forgiven?

4. Why redemption through the death of God's Incarnate Son?

1. As a result of our sins we have distorted God into either a cruel tyrant or a permissive, non-demanding force of love or simply into the non-existent sanction of an oppressive morality — to mention just a few of the many possibilities. In rescuing us, God responded to our needs. He took into consideration our distortions of his divine reality, our suspicions, mistrust, and aggressiveness towards the Divine. In the state of sinfulness we needed more than just a moral exhortation and a divine offer of grace to convert us. God's grace had to provide us with convincing and tangible evidence for the reality of his infinite compassion and of his holiness; if it was to respect our rational nature, this evidence had to be both external and internal: historical facts and inner persuasion of grace; it had to be of such power as to shake our fiercely defended idols and dislodge our chained will from slavery and move it towards the right relationship with the living God. In this context the incarnation and the cross appear indeed as the most appropriate way for our rescue. God himself became a human being, and made his own

---

[9]   Cf. K. Rahner, "Salvation," *Encyclopedia of Theology. The Concise Sacramentum Mundi* (New York: Seabury Press, 1975), p. 1519.

— not the guilt of humankind, a metaphysical absurdity — but the consequences of human sinfulness, that burden of threefold alienation that reaches its climax in death. In this way God showed us in a most convincing manner his own true nature that is pure love and mercy.

The public ministry of Jesus itself shows that even the teaching, the powerful deeds of the incarnate God were not enough to change the hearts of his audience. All that Jesus could achieve through his life was to unmask and provoke the power of evil in both the leaders and the crowds of his people so that they crucified him in the name of religion and the defense of public order. But precisely through his death on the cross, through his side pierced by a lance did God reveal his compassionate love in its fullness, a love by which God himself took upon himself the burden of each human being's sins. Only then could the Holy Spirit be breathed upon us, only then could God's grace working inside our will win over our free cooperation, so that by the power of grace we might change our hearts and begin a new life.

2. Another consideration is a simple re-working of St. Anselm's argument. Sin is in fact an offense against God himself, not in the sense of threatening or diminishing God's divinity, dignity, or glory, but in the sense of affecting God himself since God takes seriously the human being whom he has created in his own image and likeness. If then sin is an offense against God himself, then it is, in some real sense, of infinite gravity. If, consequently, God decides to treat sinful humankind as adults so that the sinners must face the consequences of their actions and obtain forgiveness by making up for their "infinite" offense, they cannot do this on their own. Only if God becomes a human being, if God takes upon himself the death of the sinner and turns the process of estrangement ending in death into the human expression of infinite divine love, only then can the sinners "make satisfaction" for their sins, because only then can they unite themselves through faith with the life and death of the incarnate Son of God. To put it briefly, if God had not satisfied as a human being for the sins of humankind, humankind could not make its own this satisfaction. If the incar-

nate Son of God had not offered an infinite love through his living and dying to the Father, we could not have united ourselves to Christ's death, and could not have obtained forgiveness.

3. If our sins offended God in his fatherly love by refusing the grace of being a child of God, then it appears very appropriate that the only Son of God should become incarnate and as a human being offer to God that unique filial love which God the Holy Father deserves; only then can we, through faith, unite ourselves to the only Son and offer "through him, with him, and in him" the love and honor the Father deserves to receive from us.

Instead of asking for a hypothetical answer, whether or not God would have become incarnate if man and woman had not sinned, we have investigated the actual situation of human sinfulness. It is in response to this actual situation that we can understand and appreciate the mystery of Christ, which contains inseparably both incarnation and redemption on the cross.

CHAPTER II

The Mystery of the Incarnation

If we isolate the metaphysical truth of the incarnation — in technical terms, the hypostatic union — from the context of God's plan of salvation (as has often happened since late scholasticism), it appears as a subtle exercise in metaphysical speculation, and even an impediment to faith, rather than one of its essential truths.

This chapter intends to show the essential connection between incarnation and salvation history. **The truth of the hypostatic union becomes intelligible as the necessary metaphysical presupposition for God's acceptance of ultimate solidarity with sinful humankind.**

1. The Old Testament: God entering into solidarity with humankind through Israel

That God has begun to accept solidarity with us appears already in the history of Israel. At a certain point in Israel's history revelation became clear and unambiguous: Yahweh is not like the gods of other tribes, a god from whom the tribe physically descends, so that a natural kinship and mutuality of interests exist between the tribe and its god. Yahweh enters into a Covenant with Abraham on his own sovereign initiative and chooses Israel as "his firstborn son" out of love rather than in hope of any personal gain he might derive from this Covenant. He becomes "their God" and Israel becomes "his people." Yahweh also agrees to become the "goel"[10] of Israel, which, in a broad sense, means that he accepts responsibility for his people. He liberates them from the slavery of the Egyptians and leads them to the Promised Land. He descends to dwell among his people, is not ashamed to be called "the Holy One of Israel" and entrusts his word to his chosen messengers, the prophets. In this way God "enters" history, because in the history of Israel he chooses to act and speak through human intermediaries. Accepting solidarity with Israel also includes becoming vulnerable to their actions. He exposes himself to a series of infidelities, to constant provocations of his jealous love for Israel. Yet he does not disengage himself from his people. He responds to disloyalty with loyalty, to the repeated breakings of the Covenant with punishment, but also with the promise of a New Covenant for a purified remnant. Thus the mystery of Israel's history consists in God's growing solidarity with Israel in spite of the repeated infidelities of the people as a whole. Yet, in the Old Testament, the infinite gap between Israel and God, and thus between humankind and God, still remains unbridged. Israel is God's people, and his just ones are men and women of God; yet the ultimate step of solidarity has not yet been taken. Israel is only God's adopted son; Israel is not God and God is not Israel.

2. A new stage in solidarity with humankind: God has become a human being

A qualitatively new stage has begun in God's growing solidarity with humankind when in Jesus the Word becomes flesh. Jesus of Nazareth is not simply a man of God, nor is God just present in him. In a Nestorian type Christology there is no qualitative difference between the prophets, the holy men and women of the Old

---

[10] In ancient Hebrew law, "the goel is the near relative upon whom falls the duty of defending the family interests when there is a question of maintaining the patrimony, freeing a 'brother' fallen into slavery, protecting a widow, or avenging an assassinated kinsman." *DBT*, p. 309.

Testament or the saints of the New Testament and Jesus. What distinguishes Jesus from anyone else in a Nestorian system is simply a very strong presence of God. But, if we press the issue, it turns out that there are two subjects in Jesus, God and Jesus the human being. However, if God is only present in Jesus but is not this Jesus nor is Jesus God, then in Jesus God did not take upon himself full solidarity with humankind. It is not God himself who became the subject of a full human experience including our purest joys and greatest burdens, our suffering and our death. God did not die for us in Jesus; only Jesus the human being died who was joined to God by God's unique presence in him. If Jesus and God are two subjects, then in the Eucharist we consume only the flesh of the man Jesus; it is not God who directly and unreservedly gives himself to us through the flesh and blood of the man Jesus.[11]

Thus the very logic of complete solidarity, the nature of a complete exchange between God and humankind requires as a necessary presupposition that there be only one subject in Jesus who is truly and fully God and truly and fully human. God would not be in full solidarity with humankind if he had not assumed all that we have and are. On the other hand, if Jesus were not truly and fully God, we would not receive the fullness of God in the self-giving of the man Jesus to us.

Here we have arrived at a simple formulation of the hypostatic union without any recourse to philosophical speculation. We have used only as much metaphysics as was absolutely necessary to show that the hypostatic union is the necessary condition of redemption. Without this union God would not have accepted full solidarity with us nor could a complete exchange between God and humankind have occurred.

This soteriological notion of complete exchange can also serve as a clarifying criterion for a number of contemporary Christologies

---

[11] Here and elsewhere I use the expression "the man Jesus" when I intend to emphasize Jesus' concrete human nature including his maleness. The stress is on his human nature, yet the transcendent sonship of the Second Divine Person is expressed in Jesus' maleness.

that reject or relativize the Chalcedonian doctrine. H. Küng, J. Macquarrie, E. Schillebeeckx (in the first part of *Jesus*[12]), and more recently R. Haight all agree, in one way or another that, in the man Jesus, God accepted full solidarity with humankind and that Jesus is God's perfect self-communication to us.[13]

However, anyone who accepts this twofold truth with full seriousness, rather than as a rhetorical exaggeration, would thereby be logically led to affirm its necessary ontological presupposition. God can assume full solidarity with humankind only if the crucified Jesus is God himself. No one but God can communicate God to humankind in his fullness. Thus, Jesus must be God, but at the same time a true human being.[14]

---

12   The last part of Schillebeeckx's study (pp. 636-674) comes close to an explicit endorsement of the Chalcedonian teaching, but it does not become clear how this doctrine follows from the conclusions of the biblical part.

13   Cf. the statement by H. Küng that Jesus is "the visage or face of God." *On Being a Christian* (Garden City: Doubleday, 1976), p. 444; J. Macquarrie calls Jesus the "focus of Being" because "He sums up and makes clear a presence that is obscurely communicated throughout the cosmos." *Jesus Christ in Modern Thought*, p. 381.

14   R. Haight in his *Jesus, the Symbol of God* (Maryknoll: Orbis, 1999) rejects such a forthright statement; nevertheless, he admits that "Jesus is both truly human and divine" (p. 462) and that "Jesus is the reality of God" (p. 455). All this, however does not mean more for Haight than that God as Spirit is ontologically present and active in Jesus (pp. 458-466). Haight refuses to say that Jesus is God or that God is this man Jesus, because he wants to safeguard Jesus' true human existence. The basis for Haight's refusal seems to be his misunderstanding of the hypostatic union as if that admitted only a human nature or essence in Jesus, but no human existence. Haight believes that in the usual Chalcedonian interpretation Jesus cannot be called a human being who is truly consubstantial with us since his humanity subsists in the person of the Logos. In all fairness to Haight, we must admit that such a misinterpretation of Chalcedon did exist in some neo-thomistic circles. However, as Lonergan has pointed out, St. Thomas does posit in Christ a created "esse secundarium" which results from the assumption of Christ's humanity by the eternal Son (*Disputed Questions*, *V. On the Union of the Incarnate Word*, 4). Lonergan presents several analogies to show the appropriateness of the mystery that God, by his own infinite act of being, assumes Jesus **as an actual human being** into personal union with him (*De Constitutione Christi ontologica et psychologica. Supplementum* [Rome: Gregorian University Press, 1964[4]], pp. 77-82).

Returning now to Haight's justified insistence on the fact that we encounter God in Jesus, the question remains unavoidable: Does not the immediacy (and thereby the fullness) of our encounter with God in Jesus call for a twofold affirmation whose compatibility can only be grasped in faith? 1. When encountering Jesus, we encounter our brother, a true human being who is like us in all things but sin. 2. When encountering Jesus, we encounter God himself who speaks to us and acts in us so that we must cry out to Jesus: "My Lord and my God!" If God is only present in Jesus, if Jesus is not God himself, we are still in the Old Testament since God has not yet taken up full solidarity with his people.

All those who are ready to admit this much agree with the intended meaning of the Chalcedonian dogma, even if, for various reasons, they distance themselves from the Chalcedonian formulation.

3. The immanent Trinity as the metaphysical condition for divine freedom in the incarnation

The formulation that "there is one subject in Jesus who is truly and fully God and truly and fully human" is still incomplete. The crucial question of the controversy today concerns the pre-existence of the Son. Recently Monika Hellwig has formulated in a poignant way the difficulty for many contemporary theologians: "personal models for the pre-existence of Jesus as divine are liable to be taken literally in a way that makes the Christian claim absurd, because two persons cannot be one person."[15]

According to these theologians, if the Son were a person prior to his incarnation, then becoming a human being would result in two persons or two subjects in Jesus, a conclusion Christian faith must obviously avoid. Thus the tendency to affirm a non-personal pre-existence of God's Wisdom or Spirit who would then become a subject, a person, or a hypostasis precisely in and through the incarnation. The problem with such hypotheses is that they contradict the doctrine of the immanent Trinity, and change the whole meaning of redemption and the nature of divine love for humankind.[16]

---

[15] "Re-emergence of the Human, Critical, Public Jesus," *TS* (50) 3, 1989, p. 480. For an earlier, more detailed explanation of M. Helwig's position, see P. Schoonenberg, *The Christ. A Study of the God-Man Relationship in the Whole of Creation and in Jesus Christ* (New York: Herder & Herder, 1971). For a critique of Schoonenberg's position, see R. Kereszty, "The Pre-existence and Oneness of Christ," *Am. Eccl. Review* 167 (1973), pp. 630-642.

[16] For a detailed treatment and criticism of process theologies and for further bibliography, see W.J. Hill, *The Three-Personed God. The Trinity As a Mystery of Salvation* (Washington, DC: Catholic Univ. of America Press, 1982), pp. 185-216. For a positive evaluation of process theism by a Catholic theologian, see J. Bracken, "The Two Process Theologies: A Reappraisal," *TS* 46 (1985), pp. 115-128.

The doctrine of the immanent Trinity, namely, that God exists from all eternity, and prior to creation and incarnation, as the perfect communion of Father and Son in the Holy Spirit is, in its essential outline, a datum of faith, implicit in the New Testament; its explicit formulation was a long-fought-for achievement of the first two Ecumenical Councils and has been re-asserted several times since then. As Grillmeier and Kasper among others have demonstrated, rather than being a discardable theologoumenon of Hellenistic origin, the doctrine of the eternal Trinity was formulated in conscious opposition to a Hellenization of Christianity.[17]

If God is not Trinity in itself, prior to creation and incarnation, then redemption does not mean the assumption of humankind into an already existing eternal personal communion of love. Rather, God, one person in himself, would become a communion of persons only by creating humankind and becoming incarnate among them. Thus, in the ultimate analysis, God would not be loving, consequently not perfect (since love is the greatest perfection) and therefore not truly God prior to creation and incarnation. In such a system humankind becomes a necessary partner for God, without whom God would not be wholly God because he would not be loving. This conclusion, which implies a temporal process of growth in God, would change the very heart of the biblical message, which insists that creation, and even more so, the incarnation are pure gifts of God's unselfish love. God has created the world and humankind not for personal gain but for our good. He became incarnate and died for us not to perfect himself but to save us and assure us a share in his own fullness.

Hence, eliminating the doctrine of the immanent Trinity would be to eliminate a foundation of Christian faith and to change the meaning of the basic Christian realities. If, on the contrary, there is an eternal Trinity of Divine Persons in a total communion of love with each other, then the incarnation must be explained as the Son's becoming man in such a way that Divine Reality does not change

---

[17] Cf. A. Grillmeier, "Moderne Hermeneutik und altkirchliche Christologie," pp. 528-538; W. Kasper, *The God of Jesus Christ* (New York: Crossroad, 1984), pp. 233-263.

into human reality, nor does a duality of subjects result from it. This conclusion, however, leads us back to the problem M. Hellwig has posed. The question must be asked: is the notion of person necessarily synonymous with individual human being, free will, and consciousness? If it is, then indeed we cannot avoid the absurd consequences M. Hellwig has outlined. I will argue, however, that — as the historical part of our study has suggested — Christian revelation has led to the discovery of a new notion of person which does not imply a manifest absurdity but rather expresses more adequately the mystery of God and the incarnation.

4. The feminist critique of the Christian mysteries

However, before we address the above question, which will inevitably lead us to discuss the person of the "Father" and that of the "Son," we must first face the feminist critique of traditional theological language.[18]

This critique charges that the exclusive or preponderant use of masculine images and characteristics in God-language is a remnant of a patriarchal culture that kept women oppressed as second-class human beings. The prolonged use of such a language is offensive to women and, willy-nilly, *de facto* conspires with male-chauvinist forces that refuse to acknowledge the equal human dignity of women. In a more strictly theological vein, feminist critics also charge that the use of exclusively or preponderantly masculine images of God easily leads to the sin of idolatry, since it assumes that

---

[18] "Motherhood: Experience, Institution, Theology," ed. A. Carre and E. Schüssler Fiorenza, *Concilium* 206 (1989) contains a collection of essays that present various aspects of feminist critique including the critique of traditional God-language; For a sharp, but somewhat superficial critique of feminist theology, see W. Oddie, *What Will Happen to God? Feminism and the Reconstruction of Christian Belief* (San Francisco: Ignatius Press, 1988). L. Bouyer, *The Seat of Wisdom* (Chicago: Regnery, 1965) analyzes the role of woman in salvation history and the feminine aspect of God from the perspective of the Bible and patristic tradition. It remains even today a classic. I am greatly indebted to this book in my treatment of the topic. Cf. his more recent book, *Woman in the Church* (San Francisco: Ignatius Press, 1979).

these masculine images portray God adequately. According to them, this language creates a male idol, instead of speaking about the transcendent and incomprehensible God.

a. Historical considerations

The prophets waged an unrelenting battle in Israel against the worship of the male and female deities of the surrounding pagan cultures. These deities represented biological and sexual forces in which humans tried to participate by means of sacred prostitution.[19]

In Israel, the creation of plant life is not the result of a sacred intercourse (hierogamy) between a male and a female deity. Sexuality and gender differentiation belong to the created world, not to the transcendent God of Israel. It is only against this background of God's absolute transcendence of any sexual and gender differences that we can appreciate the complementary character of masculine and female images that describe God in the Old Testament. If human beings are created in the image of God in the complementarity of male and female (Gn 1:27), then such complementarity of male and female images of God is to be expected. While the masculine images, such as lord, king, warrior, and bridegroom, prevail, Yahweh is also likened to a mother "pregnant with a child in her womb, crying out in labor, giving birth, nursing, carrying and cradling her child, comforting and having

---

[19] If those historians are right who draw conclusions from the religions of the most primitive tribes in our age concerning the most primitive stage of general religious development, then the first stage of religious history was characterized by belief in the heavenly gods. These almighty creator gods, whose infinity was symbolized by the infinite dimensions of the sky, were so transcendent as to be above sexual differences. The sexual differentiation into a male storm or rain god and into mother earth (the sacred intercourse between these two gave rise to all life and is imitated by human intercourse) seems to be a later development connected with the development of agriculture. Thus the pantheon of male gods and female goddesses represents a "fall" in the history of human religiosity, a fall from belief in a transcendent God to belief in complementary male and female deities who personify the awesome powers of biological vitality and sexuality. Cf. M. Eliade, *The Sacred and the Profane, The Nature of Religion* (New York: Harcourt, Brace & World Inc., 1959), pp. 116-128.

womb love (tender mercy and compassion) for her child."[20]

Moreover, the Spirit of Yahweh and his Wisdom, both personifications of the one God and both of feminine gender in Hebrew, show God as a life-giving, "nurturing," and thus, in some sense, feminine presence in the midst of Israel. This complementarity is all the more significant and indicative of God's revelation because it occurred in a heavily patriarchal society in which women were held in an inferior position.

In The New Testament God's transcendent spiritual nature is even more emphasized than in the Old. The male Jesus is named primarily by masculine titles, Son of God, Son of Man, and Lord; nevertheless, like Yahweh in the Old Testament, Jesus expressed his desire to gather the children of Israel as a mother bird gathers her little ones (Mt 23:37; Lk 13:34). It is also implied in Matthew, in the Fourth Gospel, and in the Letter to the Hebrews that he is the incarnation of Divine Wisdom, expressed with a feminine noun both in Hebrew and Greek and endowed with some feminine characteristics in the Old Testament.

The Fathers further emphasize God's spiritual, genderless nature over against the deities of the popular Greco-Roman religion, the mystery cults, and Gnosticism, most of which speak of sexually differentiated deities or female and male divine principles.

Following the usage of the New Testament, the Fathers call the First Person of the Trinity "Father," the Second Person "Son, Word, or Wisdom." Yet their theology makes it abundantly clear that these names are applied to the Holy Trinity in a transcendent spiritual sense rather than univocally. Because of this transcendent meaning, they do not hesitate to use maternal images of the Father. For instance, in Latin Christianity the official translation of the Nicene Creed affirms that the Son has been born eternally from the Father ("*ex Patre natum*"). This spiritual birth obviously transcends the conditions of human procreation, the father begetting

---

[20] E. Johnson, "The Incomprehensibility of God and the Image of God Male and Female," *TS* (45) 3 Sept 1984, p. 447.

and the mother giving birth. St. Bernard speaks about the "Son of the Father's womb" and attributes the Vulgate text of Ps 109:3 to the eternal birth of the Son from the Father: "'from the womb before the daystar I have given you birth' — says the Father."[21] In the spiritual union between Christ and the Church, the former is usually called bridegroom, the latter virgin, spouse and mother. Obviously, the Church, and the individual Christian (male or female) within the Church, is united to Christ by the Holy Spirit rather than by a sexual union. The more the union between Christ and the soul becomes perfect, the more the love of the Christian is spiritualized in the sense of being filled with the Holy Spirit.

In the patristic and medieval spiritual tradition there is a complementary term that qualifies the *Sponsus - Sponsa* (Bridegroom and Bride) imagery: Christ, the bridegroom, is also described as wisdom — *sophia - sapientia*, feminine words in both Greek and Latin. The spiritual union between Christ and the soul is then allegorized as the union between the soul and Woman Wisdom who — according to St. Bernard, for example — embraces the soul in her arms.[22]

The complementarity of the images "bridegroom" and "wisdom" make it quite clear that the relationship between Christ and the soul transcends not only sexual, but all human categories.

The transcendence of our relationship to Christ is also expressed by a Johannine image that permeates the whole patristic and medieval tradition: as the Son leaning on his Father's breast draws from him all the treasures of knowledge and love, so does the beloved disciple (representing all believers) draw the waters of divine life from the breast of Jesus (Jn 1:18; 13:23-25). The mixture of male and female imagery (Father-Son, yet drinking from

---

[21] *Sermon on the Feast of Circumcision*, III,3 and *Sermon on the Birthday of Mary*, 1. This transcendent meaning of God's fatherhood has been kept alive throughout the whole tradition of the Church. For instance, Congar quotes Bérulle, according to whom, in the generation of the Word, God "performed the functions of father and mother, begetting Him in himself and bearing Him in his womb." Bérulle, *Les grandeurs de Jésus*, X, 2, ed. J. P. Migne (Paris, 1856), col. 355.

[22] *Sermon on the Song of Songs*, 32,2: I, 227.

the breast of the Father and from the Son) manifests the non-sexual, ineffable character of mystical experience.

Nevertheless, while complementary feminine images pervade the whole tradition, there is no doubt that the First Person of the Trinity is presented primarily as Father, and the Second as Son. Moreover, in the tradition the Woman par excellence (Virgin, Bride, and Mother) is primarily Mary and the Church, a connection that extends the role of Mary throughout the ages. The Church is Virgin and Bride because of her loving surrender to her Bridegroom Christ, and she is also Mother, because together with the Father she has an active role in bringing forth the life of Christ in the believers. The individual Christian, both male and female, is also virgin, bride, and mother to the extent that he or she participates in the Church. The Church as one universal supra-personal subject, endowed with the presence and the gifts of the Holy Spirit, is a loving partner to Christ, the object of his passionate love, and a dependent yet active co-principle with the Father in bringing forth the life of Christ in her members. Since the Church is Church because she is filled and transformed by the Holy Spirit, a less pervasive trend among the Fathers identifies the Woman as both the Church and the Spirit. Just as the first Eve was not begotten but came forth from Adam's side, so does the Church originate not by way of generation, but by coming forth from the side of the second Adam, Christ. It is from his pierced side that the waters of the Spirit have flown forth.[23]

b. Systematic considerations

The theological issues of feminism are discussed with too much passion at this point in history, since they are conceived of as part of an emerging universal struggle of women to reach full equality. Thus the present situation is not yet ripe for attempting

---

[23] See Y. Congar, *I Believe in the Holy Spirit*, vol. III. (New York: Seabury, 1983), pp. 155-164; E. Johnson, "The Incomprehensibility of God and the Image of God Male and Female," pp. 457-460.

any kind of definitive evaluation. Nevertheless, there are some points that can and must be clarified even today, while other questions can be answered only very tentatively. Many feminist theologians rightly emphasize that there are no "two halves to human nature," but rather a male and female way of being human. Indeed metaphysically, there is only one human nature actualized in two complementary ways, masculine and feminine. If we started defining the difference between the masculine and feminine way of being human by qualifying, *a priori*, certain human qualities, such as tenderness and intuitiveness as feminine, other characteristics, such as detached logic and aggressivity as masculine, it would be a dangerous enterprise. It would risk absolutizing differences that are in reality only relative. Although certain psychological characteristics prevail among males, and other traits among females, such a differentiation is not exclusive. In fact, a mature individual who realized his or her humanity to the fullest possible degree does not fit easily into gender stereotypes. The mature man has some of the tenderness, compassion, and sensitivity of a woman, all the while he is strong, objective, rational, and task-oriented. The mature woman has some of the objectivity, strength, and rationality of a man, yet she is a true woman, tender, affectionate and nurturing.[24]

Moreover, we all have seen women who had more strength and objective logic than most men we know and men who had a more tender and compassionate heart than most of our female acquaintances. Yet these individuals are not abnormal and may have a happy married life. Thus it is impossible to define some characteristics as exclusively masculine or feminine.

In searching for the difference between the male and female way of being human, the biological, sexual differences provide a less debatable and more fruitful starting point. Even our society, which

---

[24] According to Jung, psychological maturity depends on the extent that the male actualizes not only his "animus" (male archetype) but also his "anima" (female archetype) which is — to a lesser extent — present in every male. The opposite applies to the woman's process of achieving maturity.

emphasizes so much the equality and even uniformity of the sexes, cannot deny the sexual differences between males and females. However, if the human being is a unity of body and soul, then the different sexual organs and the correspondingly different roles in procreation do result not only in physical, but also in some metaphysical differences between males and females. The male initiates the process of procreation by penetrating the woman's body and depositing his seed in her, while the woman receives his seed and provides not only her ovum but also her own body for the sheltering and developing of the fetus. This difference in biological roles results in a difference of relationship to each other and to their child. The relative difference between masculine and feminine psychological characteristics depends on these different relationships. The woman is not fertile without the man's seed. After the act of fecundation, however, the man may withdraw from her: his biological activity is no longer needed. Man's role in procreation corresponds to the typical male attitude of objectivity and detachment, his ability to be absorbed in tasks beyond the family more easily than the woman. On the other hand, the woman's body becomes the shelter and the source for the growth of the new life. Through her body, her whole being is involved in nurturing her baby. Living with her baby in a unique symbiosis for nine months may develop in her a sensitivity, a tenderness, an ability to empathize with others and make decisions based more on intuition than abstract reasoning. This aptitude, of course, exists also in women who have no children.

To sum up, man and woman represent different complementary ways of being human that is determined primarily by their different role in the sexual relationship and by their different relationship to their offspring. The relative difference between masculine and feminine characteristics originates from these different relationships. The male is not more perfect than the female nor is the opposite true. Each of them may realize human perfection in his or her own mutually complementary way.

When we think about applying feminine characteristics to God we need then to keep in mind the following principles:

1. Genesis 1:27 makes it clear that man and woman are images of God in their complementarity. Thus **both** masculine and feminine ways of being human, their different relationships and their (relatively) different psychological characteristics, reveal something real about God.

2. Insofar as masculine and feminine traits are ways of being human, the law of analogy applies here: all that is good and perfect in the masculine and feminine ways of being human must be equally predicated about God, in such a way that the dissimilarity between the divine and human way of perfection appears greater than their similarity. For instance, we should say that God is infinitely more tender and compassionate than the best human mother, infinitely more just and "objective" than the best human father.

In applying both male and female characteristics to the nature of God in an analogous sense, we do indeed obviate the danger of idolatry that is an ever-present danger of the human spirit. The feminists are right in calling attention to the fact that a one-sided male representation of God — the protestations of analogical usage notwithstanding — may reduce God to human dimensions, to an idol that justifies male superiority in society. The complementary use of feminine and masculine images and characteristics does help us to express the transcendent reality of God.

Nevertheless, the law of analogy warns us that the human image (or human masculine or feminine characteristics) is only a starting point that needs to be dialectically negated and transcended: God is neither masculine nor feminine, but has that which is perfect in masculine and feminine qualities in a supereminent way, the precise mode of which we cannot comprehend. If we did not take seriously the requirements of analogical affirmations about God, instead of a male idol, we would simply create another human projection, that of the androgynous personality.

3. **Insofar as masculine and feminine traits refer to qualities of being, both sets of characteristics, male and female, should be applied equally but analogously to divine nature in general, not to one or another Divine Person.** Thus, for example, tenderness and strength, justice and compassion in God's love need to be equally

applied to all three Persons, for they characterize the one divine nature. Contrary to the suggestions of several theologians, it would be wrong to select the person of the Holy Spirit as the carrier of feminine traits, while the Father and Son would be the subject of masculine qualities. This would logically result in tritheism, because it would divide the one nature and essence of God.[25]

4. Insofar as masculine and feminine names and images refer primarily to different relationships, such as father and son, mother and daughter, we cannot apply them indiscriminately to the Divine Persons. Our investigation has shown that the biblical and traditional use of the terms Father and Son regarding the first two persons of the Holy Trinity is not based on male prejudice but on the very mystery of Trinitarian relationships. Only the First Divine Person can and must be called Father, because he is the unoriginate origin of the whole Trinity. The motherly image of the Father's womb and of birth from the Father serve only to underscore the absolutely transcendent character of the divine fatherhood. The Second Person should be called Son rather than daughter of the Father since he represents the Father for the world; he initiates the divine life of the Church as the seed of a father initiates the conception of new life. The womanly image of the Son as Wisdom underscores only the supra-sexual, transcendent character of his sonship. Moreover, the unique divine character of God's fatherhood manifests itself also in the fact that the Father gives his whole divine being to the Son; thus, his being Father is identical with his personhood. The Son's relationship to his Father is, likewise, dif-

---

[25] Orthodox Catholic theologians, such as Congar, avoid the consequence of tritheism by asserting the feminine traits of the Holy Spirit in the sense of "attribution." On the basis of their special role within the Trinitarian relationships, scholastic theology "attributes" certain qualities only to one of the Divine Persons, qualities that in principle must be attributed to all the three. This way of speaking is certainly justified but does not do full justice to the feminine dimension in God.

Up to this point, then, I agree with the conclusions of E. Johnson, namely that feminine traits ought to be predicated about God not merely as a secondary complement to male images, nor as a "female dimension" manifest in the Spirit, but in complete mutuality. I disagree with her on a point she does not seem to consider, the relational use of the terms Father and Son (cf. "The Incomprehensibility of God and the Image of God Male and Female," pp. 454-465).

ferent from any human son-father relationship. The Son's person-hood is identical with his being Son, that is, with receiving his whole being from the Father by way of spiritual generation or birth and with returning it to the Father in thanksgiving. The Holy Spirit, however, while receiving the fullness of divinity from the Father and the Son (or from the Father through the Son), is pure recep-tivity, pure gift within the immanent Trinity itself. As the one Son is revealed in the one man Jesus Christ, the Spirit in whom Father and Son are united is revealed in the Church in which the many are made one. **Insofar as this one Church becomes, by the pres-ence of the Holy Spirit, a virginal Bride of Christ in self-surren-dering love and a dependent yet active partner with the Father in bringing forth divine life in the members of the human family, the Church is called Woman (virgin, bride, and mother) in the tradi-tion.** We will discuss the image of the Woman in more detail when we speak about the final goal of redemption. Since the Holy Spirit as a Person dwelling in the Church constitutes the Church as a womanly partner to the Son, a virginal mother who gives birth to the one Christ in many different individuals, it becomes under-standable why a segment of the Church's tradition called also the Spirit Woman.

5. The ontological aspect of the hypostatic union

If the human person is created in God's image, it is under-standable that the revelation of God's own personal life, the mys-tery of the Trinity revolutionized our self-understanding. This revo-lution included a new understanding of "person" in the Christian tradition. When "person" was analogously applied to God, it could not be considered synonymous with divine nature. If it had been a "content of being" or "part of being" added to nature, it would have introduced inequality of being into the different Persons of the Trinity. When it was clarified that the Second Divine Person has become a human being by assuming an individual human nature, "person," obviously, could not be thought synonymous with an individual human nature. If so, lacking a human person, the human nature of Jesus would not have been complete. Omitting the description of the differences among various schools of theology, I propose here a definition of person based on elements of thomistic and scotist theology. **"Person," analogously applicable to both God and a human being, may be defined as the mode of being of a spiritual nature: a subject who is and who relates himself or herself (either actually or potentially) to other beings. Therefore person is not simply identical with an individual nature.** Regarding God, Christian faith imposed the elaboration of a real distinction between Father, Son and Holy Spirit while maintaining that there is only one divine nature, one Divine Being, one God. This was expressed conceptually by asserting three Divine Persons (*hypostasis, persona*) in God who all simultaneously "possess" the one divine being, essence or nature. The Divine Persons are distinguished and thereby constituted as persons by their opposing relationships: the Father is Father because he generates or gives birth to the Son and thereby gives his whole divine being or essence to him. The Son is Son insofar as he receives by way of generation or birth his whole divine being or essence from the Father. The Holy Spirit is constituted as a distinct person by receiving the fullness of divine being or essence from both Father and Son (or equivalently, from the Father through the Son). Thus there are three subjects or Persons in God, each of whom is identical with the whole divine nature and being, but each of them is distinguished in his unique personhood from the other two through his relationship to them. In God, then, the Persons are "subsisting relationships."

In the Incarnation, the Second Divine Person, the Son, has assumed as his own a human nature so that he began to exist as man in time and history. Thus Jesus has a full human nature; however, this human nature does not subsist[26] in itself, but in the eternal Son.

---

[26] The word "subsists" may be paraphrased as "exists as a distinct subject."

Therefore Jesus' human nature lacks a corresponding ontological human personhood.[27]

Nevertheless, the incarnation does not entail a diminution of the full human reality of Jesus of Nazareth, since "person" in a metaphysical sense does not mean any "part" of human nature but the mode of existence of a full human nature. It is the Divine Person of the Son in whom the human nature of Jesus subsists as the Son's very own, and this Divine Person, in virtue of the assumed human nature, truly becomes a human being.[28]

In the lapidary formulation of St. Thomas: *"quasi ipsum Verbum personaliter fit homo*: the Word himself, as it were, becomes a human being by way of his personhood."[29]

When God the Word takes up as his own the human reality of Jesus, in the act of creating it as his own, he does not diminish but rather actualizes the full humanity of Jesus. As we will discuss later, the more closely a created reality depends on God and participates in God, the more the created reality comes into its own. **In other words, precisely the hypostatic union, the ineffably close union of Jesus' human nature with the Son, assures Jesus' full human identity.**

If we understand the hypostatic union in this way, we avoid

---

[27] By personhood is meant here a metaphysical personhood or metaphysical subject as defined above: the one who has a spiritual nature and who is and acts as distinct from anyone and anything else. It follows from this understanding of metaphysical personhood that, apart from Christ, every concrete human nature subsists in itself and by itself; consequently there is no real distinction between person and nature in us. We are persons metaphysically insofar as our human nature exists in itself and in (at least) potential relationship with other human beings. Christ's human nature is not a metaphysical person, because it does not exist in and by itself but in and by the Divine Person of the Son. In this regard our definition of personhood comes close to that of Duns Scotus. Cf. H. Mühlen, *Sein und Person nach Johannes Duns Scotus. Beiträge zur Metaphysik der Person,* Werl, 1954.

[28] Another problem (see footnote # 14 in this section for Haight's misinterpretation of Jesus' human existence) that may have led Haight to reject the hypostatic union seems to be his misunderstanding of metaphysical personhood. "Ontological Personhood" for Haight seems to imply a "Seinsinhalt" (content or part of being). Therefore in his view, if Jesus is not (metaphysically) a human person, he cannot be fully human (See *Jesus, Symbol of God,* p. 289).

[29] *Disputed Quest. V. On the Union of the Incarnate Word,* 1.

the above objection of assuming a duality of subjects in Christ. Moreover, a union of this sort cannot be shown to be impossible on the part of God. **How could we *a priori* exclude the possibility that through his transcendent power, the Person of the Logos may fulfill in an infinitely more perfect way the function of the human personhood in Christ, so that the Son of God, without losing his divinity, becomes Jesus of Nazareth, a true human being?** Nor can the incarnation be proved to be impossible as regards the human nature of Jesus, since every creaturely reality has a "*potentia obedientialis*," an unlimited openness or "pliability" towards its Creator who can raise it up to an existence that transcends its natural mode of being. Thus, according to St. Thomas, from the perspective of God's transcendent power and the "*potentia obedientialis*" of the creature, one cannot *a priori* exclude the possibility that God would become incarnate in an irrational creature.[30]

St. Thomas's formulation, however, ignores the essential difference between infrahuman and human nature. It seems that only the potential infinity of a spiritual nature (manifested in the human drive for unlimited truth and goodness) is sufficient ground for its elevation as God's own created nature.

6. The psychological aspect of the hypostatic union

As we have seen, the patristic and medieval tradition, under the guidance of Christian revelation, developed the notion of person, meaning an ontological subject in distinction to nature. In the modern age, when person came to mean human consciousness and freedom, new problems arose. Those who accepted the new definition, like the theologians mentioned above by M. Hellwig, did not see how person in this sense could be applied — even analogously — to the Trinity and the incarnation. It would result — they

---

[30] However, St. Thomas explains that only the assumption of human nature was appropriate. *S. T.* III, q. 4, a. 1.

claimed — in three consciousnesses and three freedoms in God and two consciousnesses and two freedoms in Christ.[31] Thus, the consequence would be tritheism instead of Trinity, and two persons in Christ instead of the hypostatic union. However, to anticipate the conclusions of this section — if we define person as **subject of consciousness and freedom,** the above difficulties disappear. In point of fact, a real continuity exists between the notion of person in Christian metaphysics and this contemporary understanding of person as psychological subject. Moreover, the person understood as subject of consciousness and freedom leads to the metaphysical notion of person as its necessary presupposition; it will also provide analogies that increase the intelligibility of the mystery of the Trinity and the hypostatic union.

Consciousness in terms of self-reflection and freedom was already implicit in the thomistic definition of person, according to which person is the one who exists as a whole and distinct from anyone or anything else "*in rationali natura,*" in spiritual nature.[32]

His specific mode of existence is self-possession through self-reflection (defined as the "*redire completum in seipsum*" of the spiritual subject) and through freedom (defined as being the cause of his own acts rather than the passive object of outside forces).[33]

For this reason personhood is the highest form of perfection for St. Thomas.[34]

In the modern age, however, the notion of person has changed and begun to mean simply an individual consciousness and freedom. Thus, in contemporary culture we need to re-examine the mystery of the Trinity and incarnation in the terms of psychological subject and consciousness. Here I will concentrate on the incarnation, but within the context of the Trinitarian mystery.

When inquiring into the consciousness of Christ, our starting point — in accord with the general method of this work — is

---

[31] Or in one consciousness and one freedom, the divine suppressing the human.

[32] See on this in more detail F. Bourassa, "Personne et conscience en théologie trinitaire I; II." *Gregorianum* (55) 3, 4: 1974, pp. 471-493; 677-720.

[33] *S.T.* I, q. 29, a. 1.

[34] *Ibid.*

the fully developed christological dogma of the Church. Yet our conclusions must ultimately be founded on the New Testament witness to Jesus and will hopefully bring to light some of its implications.

In my attempt to understand human consciousness in general, I am very much indebted to the reflections of B. Lonergan.[35] His insight, so self-evident after it has been grasped, yet overlooked by most everybody else who wrote on the consciousness of Christ, is of capital importance: Consciousness is a quality of the person or subject, rather than of nature or faculty. Neither a human faculty, such as intellect or will, nor human nature can be conscious. Only the acting person or subject is conscious. Consciousness is subjective in the fundamental sense that it is always a subject's consciousness. In fact, consciousness means precisely that the subject, the person, is in some way actively involved. Through consciousness, even such impersonal, non-spiritual processes or states as breathing, having a cold, and so forth are appropriated by us as we become aware of them. (Of course, there are some bodily functions of which we remain, as a rule, unconscious, such as metabolism).

When I am thinking, willing, or feeling, I am aware of thinking, willing, or feeling, and I am also aware of myself as thinking, willing, or feeling. **This direct awareness of acting and of the self as acting is a primordial phenomenon of personal life.** It cannot be reduced to some more basic category; we can only explain it by describing it **as a presence of the subject to himself**, his being with himself, his "being lit through."[36]

---

[35] *De constitutione Christi ontologica et psychologica,* pp. 83-148; _____ *Insight. A Study of Human Understanding* (New York: Longmans, 1958) 2nd ed., pp. 320-328. Cf. also H.U. von Balthasar, *Die Personen in Christus/Theodramatik,* II/2 (Einsiedeln: Johannes V., 1978), pp. 137-167; K. Rahner, "Dogmatic Reflections on the Knowledge and Self-Consciousness of Christ," *Theological Investigations,* Vol. V (Baltimore: Helicon, 1966), pp. 193-215 with further bibliography; R. Kereszty, "Psychological Subject and Consciousness in Christ," *Communio* 11 (1984), pp. 258-277.

[36] This is, according to Rahner, "Das innere Gelichtet-sein" of the spiritual being. "Probleme der Christologie von heute," *Schriften zur Theologie,* I (Einsiedeln: Benziger, 1958), 3rd ed., p. 178.

Consciousness or self-awareness is prior to and different from self-knowledge. The latter results from the reflexive operations of the subject: the conscious subject reflects on his consciousness, treats it as an object to be analyzed and understood by means of concepts and judgments. He tries to understand what he is being aware of and who he is who is being aware of himself.

My consciousness constantly changes, because my being changes; I am involved in a never-ceasing interaction with a changing world. Yet amidst a wide variety of actions and reactions on many different levels, within the incessant flow of changing states of consciousness, I always experience myself as the one who initiates or undergoes these changes. While always changing, I remain identical with myself. We call this unifying permanent center of the flow of consciousness, the one who acts and reacts in this process, the psychological subject.

In being conscious of myself, I intuitively experience myself as qualitatively unique: I am irreplaceable, unconfusable with any other psychological subject. However, when I attempt to conceptualize my uniqueness, I can do so only inadequately, by accumulating a certain amount of accidental characteristics (the color of my eyes and hair, the circumstances of my birth, my ancestors, my intelligence, my life history, and so forth), which in principle could characterize another individual just as well.[37]

There is an essential correlation between psychological and metaphysical subject or personhood. The metaphysical subject or person is the necessary presupposition of the psychological subject or person: **I can be aware of myself as a unique self** (unconfusable with any of the other selves with whom I am interacting), **only because I am a unique self. The psychological subject, through his consciousness, becomes aware of himself as a metaphysical subject. To put it simply: awareness of one's unique self presupposes that this unique self exists.** However, this reasoning cannot be reversed: that someone is a metaphysical person or subject does not imply

---

[37] Cf. H.U. von Balthasar, *Die Personen in Christus,* pp. 187-191.

that he must be aware of himself as such (for example, someone in a coma, or an acute schizophrenic, is incapable of such an experience).

Since consciousness is a basic quality of spiritual existence, it must be analogously applied to the eternal immanent Trinity. Since consciousness belongs to the subject rather than to nature, we must also affirm that the Father is conscious of himself as Father, the Son as Son and the Holy Spirit as Holy Spirit. Meanwhile, of course, all three Persons are equally conscious of being God, having the same divine nature, the same knowledge and will.[38]

The dogma of the incarnation implies that the metaphysical subject of Jesus is the eternal Son himself. If, in the case of ordinary human beings, the psychological subject implies the metaphysical subject as his necessary presupposition, we must also affirm that **just as there is one metaphysical subject in Christ, there is equally one psychological subject.** If, however, the one metaphysical subject has a full divine and human nature, we must also maintain, with Lonergan, that the incarnate Son of God has both a divine and human consciousness. Yet the relationship of these two consciousnesses cannot be abstractly and statically stated as if it were the same for the earthly Jesus and the risen Christ — as Lonergan seems to imply. The metaphysical subject of the eternal Son did not cease to exist in his divine nature when — by assuming a human nature — he began to exist as a human being. On the other hand, he did not allow his divine nature to penetrate and transform his human nature in his earthly life; on the contrary, he "emptied himself" in order to exist in the form of a slave, "a man like us in all things but sin." Correspondingly, we should also affirm that the psychological subject of the eternal Son did not cease to have a divine consciousness when he became a human being. Becoming incarnate, he also acquired a full human consciousness. But just as he lived and expressed his divine sonship in his earthly existence in dependence on his Father, so was the enlightenment of his human

---

[38] B. Lonergan, *De Deo trino*, II (Rome: Gregorian Univ., 1964), pp. 196-208.

consciousness by divine consciousness limited by the Father's will. Thus, through his self-awareness as a limited, mortal human being, the Son "emptied himself" psychologically as well. **We affirm then that the incarnate Son is conscious of himself through a human consciousness.** This seems to be the correct way of formulating the mystery, rather than claiming that the human nature or the human soul of Jesus is aware of itself as the Son.[39] As we have seen, it is always the subject who is conscious of himself. In Jesus' case, it is the Son who, through his human consciousness, is aware of himself as the Son made man.[40]

How this is possible remains the very mystery of the incarnation considered from the viewpoint of its psychology. Yet our conclusion is hardly avoidable if we reflect on the ontological structure of Christ as it is formulated in the Chalcedonian definition. We have done nothing more than spell out on the psychological level the central truth of the Christian faith: God himself has become a human being. **God would not have truly become incarnate**

---

[39] Rahner's position is somewhat different from the one I outlined above. He starts with affirming the full human consciousness of Christ as a consequence of his full human nature. But, because of the hypostatic union, Jesus' human consciousness had to be taken away from itself ("Sich-Enthobenheit") and substantially appropriated ("substantiell übereignet") by the Logos. Yet, this appropriation by God does not alienate the human consciousness of Jesus but rather enables this consciousness to be with himself ("bei sich sein") and thus be a full human subject. Since for Rahner the Divine Persons should more precisely be called in contemporary theology "modes of subsistence - *Subsistenzweisen*" rather than subjects, it remains ambiguous in his discourse whether or not it is the eternal divine subject of the Son who has become the psychological subject of Jesus. See "Current Problems in Christology," *Theol. Invest.*, Vol. I (Baltimore: Helicon, 1961), pp. 68-174; "Dogmatic Reflections on the Knowledge and Self-Consciousness of Christ," *Theol. Invest.*, Vol. V (Baltimore: Helicon, 1966), pp. 193-215; *Foundations of Christian Faith. An Introduction to Christianity* (New York: Crossroad, 1978), pp. 249; 302-305. In this issue, then, *pace* L. Renwart (see his review of the first edition of my book in *NRT* 115 [1993], pp. 90-91), Rahner's view differs from that of Lonergan.

[40] Note that this conclusion is not a dogma of faith, nor even a directly taught doctrine of the ordinary magisterium. In my judgment, it is merely a true and important theological conclusion. The Encyclical *Sempiternus Rex*, written for the 1500th anniversary of Chalcedon by Pius XII, left this question purposely open in the final, official edition of the text. See *DS* 3905.

if he had not experienced himself as a human being, if he himself had not consciously gone through the experience of a full human life, death, and resurrection.

Christ had to be aware of his being the Son from the very beginning of his life. If he had discovered his real identity at a later point in life, for example, at his baptism or at his resurrection, and if he had had no awareness whatsoever before that event of his being the Son, then Christ could not have been the same psychological subject or person before and after that discovery. Such a discovery would have caused a split, a radical breakdown in the awareness of his own identity. The identity of the psychological subject of Christ and the fundamental continuity of his consciousness does not exclude, but — being a human consciousness — rather demands a continuing growth calling for ever new and clearer realizations of his own identity.

Closely related to the development of Christ's consciousness is the growth of his self-knowledge. Through self-knowledge the Son made man objectifies his self-awareness by means of concepts and judgments and expresses this self-understanding to himself and to others. In simple terms, he gives an account to himself and to others about who he thinks he is.

This self-knowledge of Jesus is completely and genuinely human, expressing in human images and concepts the human self-awareness of God the Son. We can only conjecture about its content from what we know of the sayings of the earthly Jesus in the New Testament. He understands himself to be a genuine human being whose whole life is dedicated to the worship and service of God. At the same time, however, he speaks and acts as the beloved Son of God his Father whose mission is absolutely unique: he is sent to bring about the Kingdom of God on earth. He knows that God's almighty love is at work in his person, in his words and in his acts of forgiving, healing, and reconciling the world to the Father. The awareness of being charged with this mission seems to be the center of his self-knowledge. This mission determines his whole existence, and through this mission he knows who he is; according to Balthasar, because of this mission Jesus alone, of all human beings, can adequately express his uniqueness.[41]

7. The intelligibility of the incarnation as a mystery of Trinitarian love

In the first half of the 20th century the philosophy of dialogical personalism shed much light on the dialogical nature of the human person and on the structure of personal encounter.[42]

So today it is almost a philosophical commonplace to point out that the self-possession of the person through self-consciousness and self-determination is actualized only through interpersonal relationships. To discover my unique self, my "I" in its irreplaceably unique worth, it is not enough that I come to know other objects of knowledge; I need to know a "thou," another self whose unique worth I discover and who reciprocates by discovering and accepting my own unique self. We become mirrors for each other, each reflecting (and shaping through reflecting) the other's unique face for the other.

What the Fathers described by the metaphor of "marvelous exchange" can deepen our understanding of the modern notion of "personal encounter." We discern in personal encounters, in varying intensity and completeness, a twofold movement. **In the first movement I compare the other person to myself and, along with some affinities and common features, I also discover the abyss of difference that separates us.** Then, if love prevails, I try to bridge

---

[41] H.U. von Balthasar defines "person" (in contrast to a spiritual subject) as someone who is fully aware of his unique existence through being aware of his unique mission. In this case, of course, only Jesus is a person in the full sense of the word and we, ordinary humans, only by participating in him and receiving a unique mission from him. See *Die Personen in Christus*, pp. 191-209.

[42] See esp. M. Buber, *I and Thou* (New York: Scribner, 1958[2]). This philosophy, through the mediation of Hegel and through its conscious reaction to Hegel was indirectly influenced by the Christian notion of Trinitarian personhood. Cf. W. Kasper, *Jesus the Christ*, pp. 245-246.

the gap of difference by trying to empathize with the thoughts, feelings, values, goals, as well as the external and internal situation of this person, in order to receive into myself what he or she has and is. While retaining my personal identity, values, and goals, I try to live myself into his or her existential situation. **I try to experience in and through myself what it means for the other to be himself or herself.** Without this first movement of the vicarious experience of the other as other in and through myself, my love would not be sincere, because I could not really empathize with the other person's being, existence and world. It is important to realize that empathy has a rational component of forming concepts and judgments and drawing conclusions and an emotional component as well, but both are only means to achieve the goal of empathy, which is more than the sum of both; **it is in some imperfect way the acceptance of the being of the other into my own being.**

The second movement consists in affirming the value of the other self, wanting him or her to flourish, to develop his or her best self, and pledging my whole being, all that I have and all that I am to assist this person in the process. Thus my existence is at his or her service to further that person's full flowering. And, paradoxically, only in this exchange do I personally come to full flourishing in my own unique selfhood.[43]

If this psychological exchange "works" among human beings, who are not "subsisting relationships," how much more must this be the case with the Triune God, in whose image and likeness we were created. Applying the metaphor analogically to God, we must say that each Divine Person receives the Other fully and totally into himself, affirms the Other in his otherness while giving to him (each in his own way) the fullness of divinity that he has. Thus in the Trinitarian mystery the sameness of one being and essence is the result of total love and total exchange.

---

[43] In a human encounter, neither the first nor the second movement of the exchange is possible without grace. Without grace I might destroy myself by giving up my own personal identity and by cherishing the sins of the other in the first movement. In the second, I might destroy the other person by imposing on him or her my own limited self, along with my sins.

This same metaphor can shed some light on the mystery of the incarnation as well. In a human encounter, the empathic lover, the husband, the wife, or the friend quickly discovers the limits of the exchange he or she is capable of. The more intimate the relationship the person is striving for, the more he or she realizes the impossibility of eliminating the abyss that separates two human beings. I cannot really receive into myself the beloved in order to share fully what my beloved is, has, enjoys, or endures. Nor can I really give my life to my beloved so that this person would truly live and flourish by my life. The reason is not only human sinfulness, but also and more importantly the metaphysical finiteness of the human person.

However, God the Son is infinite spirit and infinite, transcendent love. Why should it be impossible for this love to bridge the gap in reality between God and humankind? Why should God not be able in full reality (metaphysically) to become a human being (while remaining God)? Why should he be limited to trying to "identify" with us only through feeling and imagination as we human beings do? Moreover, if he wants to share his own life with us, why would that be impossible for him? **In simple words, the dogma of the hypostatic union says that what human beings can achieve only imperfectly, on the level of empathy, God has achieved perfectly, on the level of reality. The infinite creative freedom of God's love makes the mystery of the hypostatic union intelligible.** It is also important to notice that the object of God's creative, empathic love is not the man Jesus, but all humankind. By becoming the man Jesus, the Son makes a concrete human nature and a human existence his own, so that he may bridge the gap between himself and **all** humankind and may communicate his own divine fullness to all of us.

The application of the analogy of empathic love to God suggests that the incarnation is not impossible on the part of God. We can also show the same with regard to human nature. Regarding human nature, it is not only a general *potentia obedientialis* of the creature towards its Creator that accounts for the possibility of the incarnation, but the specific potentiality of our spiritual nature.[44] We come to fulfillment precisely in interpersonal encounter, and ultimately in encountering God. In the incarnation, our "natural" capacity to know God and to give ourselves over to God in love, as well as to receive God himself through knowledge and love, is fulfilled in a manner infinitely beyond what our nature can achieve by itself. Yet, this fulfillment is in the same direction that our natural desire tends. In the incarnation, the human nature of Jesus is created to become the human expression of God's eternal Son; thus, Jesus is enabled to give himself over to God and receive God through his life, death, and resurrection in such a perfect way that no human being could ever have imagined it. Such a unique fulfillment, however, does not "stretch" Jesus' human nature to the breaking point. **Since human nature is created in the image of the Son, it does not appear impossible for the image (human nature) to express its transcendent archetype (the eternal Son).** For, in spite of the infinite distance between God and humankind, there is also an analogical correspondence between God the Son and us. As the Son receives his whole being from the Father by way of generation, so we receive our being from God by way of creation. As the Son returns his divine being to the Father in thanksgiving and transmits the love of the Father for all humankind, so are all human beings called to return their being to God in thanksgiving and to share in their Creator's love for all humankind. In other words, the vocation of both the Son and humankind is to receive their being as gift and become a gift for God and for their fellow men and women. **Thus, in Christ human nature achieves a fulfillment infinitely beyond its own power but in the direction of its natural dynamism. Jesus becomes a human being in a real and yet transcendent way; he alone is in the full sense of the word the "human being for others" because he alone exists fully for God. He alone may become in his whole being a perfect gift for others because he**

---

[44] Cf. K. Rahner, "Current Problems in Christology," *Theol. Invest.*, Vol. I (Baltimore: Helicon, 1963), pp. 181-185.

alone has become, consciously and freely, a perfect gift for his Father. We need to look at this process in more detail.

8. The incarnation as an existential process

Simply to describe the incarnation from the perspective of the hypostatic union (under its ontological and psychological aspects) would not do justice to the biblical and patristic doctrine. Before the metaphysical truth of the incarnation (and much before the psychological constitution of Christ) was formulated, the New Testament and some of the Fathers looked upon the mystery of Christ from another perspective, that of the two or three stage Christology, as it is known today. They distinguished first the stage of the self-emptying of the eternal Son when he crossed over from eternity into history, then the stage of the earthly Jesus, culminating in the crucifixion, and finally the stage of the risen Christ in his glorified eschatological reality. This perspective was lost in late scholastic Christology, but it has received a new formulation and emphasis in Barth's synthesis. Here, relying on the data of tradition, on Barth's thought, and on the achievements of existentialist and personalist philosophies, I will attempt to provide an existential reformulation of this aspect of traditional Christology.

Becoming a human being is a process. The fetus developing in the womb, the newborn baby, the adolescent, the middle-aged, the dying, and the risen ones in their glorified bodies are all human beings, yet each of them is at a different stage in the process of developing human nature. From revelation we know that we become human beings in the full sense of the word only at the end when we rise in our immortal spiritual bodies, because only then have we reached the final perfection God has planned for us from all eternity.[45]

If becoming a human being is a process, then the incarnation — God becoming a human being — must also occur in an analo-

---

[45] Cf. Eph 4:13; Ignatius of Antioch, *Rm* 6.

gous process. The incarnation, however, initiates a twofold movement, in which the second movement is coextensive with, but opposite in direction to, the first. God becoming a human being in Christ causes the opposite process: the human being Jesus becoming God. Of course, this twofold movement is possible because the ontological "event" of the incarnation has been accomplished at one point in history, at the conception of Jesus in Mary's womb. From that moment on, in a fundamental sense God has already become a human being and Jesus the human being is God. Yet it is this once and for all metaphysical reality that enables the twofold movement to take place: the one downwards from above (God becoming a human being), and its consequence, the one upwards from below (the assumption of Jesus' human nature into God's own life).

a. The Word becoming a human being

We may look at this process from two perspectives, that of human experience and that of free human decisions.

The Word has known human existence and the fullness of human experience from all eternity through his divine knowledge. But in the process of the incarnation, he empties himself of his divine "status," renounces — it seems — the direct use of his divine consciousness and knowledge, and becomes aware of himself as a human being and as such learns gradually about God, himself, people and the world.[46]

He consummates his human experience in all these dimensions only in dying and rising to a new, definitive form of human existence.

This process takes place not only on the level of human experience, but — closely joined to this — on the level of human decisions. The Word becomes a perfect human being in the full exis-

---

[46] I say "direct use" because it is impossible simply to separate psychological subject and consciousness. Just as the qualities of the Son's divine nature, his divine love and humility, are gradually translated into the "language" of human love and humility, so may we assume a similar process of mediation on the level of consciousness and knowledge.

tential sense of the term by realizing the eternal decision of the Trinity to reconcile the world to the Father through a series of human decisions. As he learns step by step, through the events of his life and through the inspiration of the Holy Spirit, how to carry out his mission, he lives out his divine Sonship in the changing situations of his human existence.[47]

We might say that he "translates" his divine Sonship into the language of human words, attitudes, actions, and relationships, as he constantly listens to his Father and says and does nothing other than what he hears from his Father. He gradually actualizes those human relationships by which the eternal Son relates as a human being to his Father, to Mary and Joseph, to his relatives, to his disciples, to the crowds, and to his enemies, ultimately to the whole world.

The human realization[48] of his eternal Sonship reaches its consummation only on the cross, because only on the cross does he live out and express the full depth of the Son's love for the Father, with the finality that only a freely accepted death can give to love in human life.

After his resurrection, Jesus does not cease to be human.[49]

On the contrary, it is through the resurrection that Jesus reaches his final definitive state as the perfect human being, the goal, model, and unifying center of the new human race that he has brought into existence. From the resurrection on, through all eternity, the Son knows, loves and praises the Father as the human being who incorporates all those united to him through faith and love as "members of his body." The incarnate Son, perfected through the whole of his human history, has become forever the firstborn brother of all human beings. In him humankind has reached the climax of its natural and supernatural evolution.

---

[47] Cf. H.U. von Balthasar, *Die Personen in Christus*, pp. 181-183.

[48] "Realization" is meant here in an existential sense of "living out" his eternal Sonship on the level of human existence.

[49] The Church has resisted the attempt to ascribe an end to the human existence and kingship of the risen Christ. Cf. *DS* 150, 152 (15).

b. Jesus the human being "becoming God"

The Son assumed his human nature at the very moment of his conception. The creation and assumption of his human nature are not two subsequent acts, but two aspects of one and the same divine operation. The human nature of Jesus has come into being as the Son's human nature.[50]

Yet the humanity of Jesus is a "normal," ordinary humanity, in spite of its ineffable closeness to the Son during his earthly life. He is passible and mortal, limited by time and space, and part of a definite social and cultural milieu; his general knowledge and culture are on the level of his contemporaries in Galilee.

Just as through Jesus' human decisions and through the Father's response to them, the Son becomes the perfect human being in the resurrection, so through the same human decisions of obedience, trust, and love Jesus gives over, step by step (according to the laws of human existential "giving"), his human existence to the Father and receives from him a divine mode of existence at the resurrection. As we have said, this divine mode of existence perfects rather than abolishes his humanity.

The healing, forgiving, and life-giving activity of the earthly Jesus receives new meaning if viewed from this perspective: his saving activity is not the "automatic result" of the hypostatic union, but derives from a dialogue of prayer with his Father. He never acts alone, as if he were self-sufficient in himself. He listens to the Father and freely carries out his will. His human words and gestures are healing, saving, and life-giving, because Jesus never does anything alone by himself, but in obedience to the Father. The Father's saving power shines through and works in him because, instead of blocking it out, Jesus always yields to his Father in trust and love.

The dogma of the hypostatic union does not exclude, but rather postulates, such a Christology of obedience: Jesus can hand

---

[50] Following Augustine, Leo the Great expressed this mystery with admirable precision: "ipsa adsumptione crearetur" (*DS* 298).

over his human existence to the Father so perfectly only because he is the incarnate Son.

As a result of the structure of fallen human existence, the self-surrender of Jesus becomes definitive only on the cross.[51]

Not that, beforehand, any of his free acts of self-giving would have been morally imperfect. But human beings can give definitively their whole selves only in freely accepting death. In dying freely, out of love, we give not only a limited service, a part of our time and energy; we give not only our body, but — because of the essential unity of soul and body — our whole humanity. Only in dying out of love can we finalize the direction of our existence. Now we can no longer take back by a new act what we have previously vowed. We gather up, as it were, the time-and-space-fragmented pieces of our existence and give the whole irrevocably to God. In dying out of love for God and for all men and women, Jesus indeed becomes gift in the full sense of the word: gift for God and gift for us. Moreover, since in Jesus humanity does not exist in itself, but it is the Son who exists as a human being through his human nature, Jesus gives back his whole divine self to the Father on the cross in and through his humanity.

This stage of total gift that Jesus has reached on the cross is eternalized in the resurrection. To put it simply, the Father has raised up the crucified Christ. In the resurrection the crucified humanity of Jesus is completely "spiritualized"; not only in the sense that his body becomes a pliable instrument and perfect expression of his soul, but more than that: both his human body and soul are transformed by the Holy Spirit. As a result, the risen Jesus himself can be called "Spirit," and he breathes forth the Holy Spirit upon all those who are ready to receive him (2 Cor 3:17). He is no longer passible and mortal, no longer subject to the limitations of our spatio-temporal universe. He is not merely present to some of his disciples, but present in all of those who love him.

---

[51] On death as the potential moment of definitive self-giving, see K. Rahner, *On the Theology of Death* (New York: Herder & Herder, 1961).

His humanity has become so translucent that those who see him now in his risen state see God himself face to face, without any intermediary to screen out the blinding light of Christ's divinity.

In the above sense, then, we must affirm, with Scripture and the Fathers, the gradual divinization of Jesus. He is constituted "Son of God in power" (Rm 1:4) and becomes "life-giving spirit" (1 Cor 15:45) only as a result of his life-long obedience, culminating in his death on the cross, to which the Father responds by raising him up and glorifying him. But rather than ceasing to be human, Jesus fully divinized is the perfect eschatological human being, the final goal of God's creation.

CHAPTER III

The Humanity of the Son

1. What does it mean for all of us that the Son has taken on human nature as his own?

In order to better understand this question, we must clarify what human nature is and what happens when the Son assumes it as his own. Human nature is not a mere mental construct, a result of comparing different objects on the basis of some accidental similarity (as, for instance, we establish the concept of a table or chair). The concept of human nature expresses the essential reality of every human being: the one specifically same human nature is actualized in every human individual. We find many signs or indications within human experience that point to this specific identity. A few examples should suffice: I can make the thoughts of other human beings my own and I can empathize with other people by "reproducing" in myself feelings that are analogous to theirs. The possibility of enjoying a drama, a poem, or a work of art that is created by others and expresses the life, the values and the world of other human beings, points to a real commonness in our basic human experience. Moreover, whatever happens to any other human being on this planet (or anywhere else in the universe) in some real sense happens to me. This fact was brought home to us in a dramatic way by the first landing of two men on the moon. When the two Americans stepped out of their landing module on lunar soil, millions all over the world watching them were aware that this event affected them all: it was indeed a big step for all humankind. Individuals could not experience something that actually happens to others as — in some real sense — happening to them unless humankind were, in some real sense, truly one. The ground for this unity is our common human nature, basically, or (to use technical language) specifically identical in every human individual.[52]

God becoming incarnate in Jesus Christ was an infinitely great step for all humankind; although in different ways, it has affected all human beings of past, present and future. In Christ human nature has reached its highest, freely bestowed actualization as the human nature of the eternal Son. This has radically changed not only the situation but also the concrete nature of every human being. **Because of the incarnation, to be a man or woman means to be a brother or sister of God the Son and to have a right to be loved by him as his own brother or sister; moreover, for each one of us to relate to and to love another human being means to relate to and to love a brother or sister of God the Son.**

2. Why human nature?

The most obvious answer is that the Son has assumed human nature because men and women (unlike the fallen angels) sinned in such a way that they would still be able to change their will and convert. If we accept the theological opinion that angels are pure spirits,[53] we can understand that, once they have sinned, they are unable to repent because of the simplicity of their spiritual nature. The decisions of pure spirits are all final: upon choosing evil or good they have freely but fully determined their nature in one direction or another, without leaving any potentiality in their will for a change of direction. They have definitively made themselves into what they intended to become. We humans, however, have a composite na-

---

[52] Not all human beings actualize their common nature to the same extent. Yet, paradoxically — as S. Weil have pointed out — we actualize our individuality to the extent that we existentially appropriate what is universally human. Cf. S. Weil, "Human Personality," *The Simone Weil Reader*, pp. 313-339.

[53] Note that, contrary to a wide-spread belief, the doctrine that angels have no body at all is not of faith. The Fathers and many medieval theologians, including St. Bernard of Clairvaux, thought that angels are endowed with some form of a subtle body.

ture, body and soul, and thus, instead of being simple and whole, we are ontologically "fragmented." We cannot definitively determine ourselves by one act.[54] We need many successive decisions to do so. In fact, we really need our whole earthly life (including our death) to become definitively what we have intended to become. The analysis of a concrete human decision can lead us to a better understanding of our fragmented state. When I decide to commit a grave sin, especially for the first time, even while carrying out the sinful act, and even more after its completion, something inside me does not agree with my act; there is at least a weak impotent desire in me to go in the other direction. This is also true, however, when I make a difficult good decision: I often remain divided; I must work against a "gravitational force" in me lest I reverse the good deed. Thus, as long as we are in this world, we cannot fully identify ourselves with our good or evil acts. For this reason, then, we still may convert during our earthly life. Only in death do we irreversibly become identified with our actions.

Reflection on the goal of God's plan may shed some more light on the issue. God has created the universe so that, according to its own mode of being, every creature (raised above its own created nature by grace) may share in the very life of God himself. Given this purpose of creation, we can better understand why God has become precisely a human being. Ever since patristic theology human beings have been viewed in the Christian tradition as the natural link between the spiritual and material worlds. In the unity of our body and soul, we are meant to effect and represent the unity of both realms. Consequently, if God assumes us into his own life, then in and through us he assumes the whole cosmos.

---

[54] A longer analysis would, of course, reveal that the above statement oversimplifies the issue. Even human freedom implies that human agents freely determine their being and the direction of their life. Even one single act may be sufficiently free and important to do exactly that. Otherwise, the Church's tradition could not speak about mortal sin. But this self-determination is not necessarily irreversible unless death follows. Moreover, the Christian spiritual tradition speaks about "confirmation in good" as well as "the hardening of heart in evil," both of which make an actual reversal of one's basic orientation extremely difficult if not impossible.

The organic unity of the universe has become even clearer today with the extension of the theory of evolution to the history of the whole cosmos. We may no longer consider the incarnation as the culmination of human history alone. Viewing the whole creation as an evolutionary process, we must say with Teilhard de Chardin that the glorious Christ is not only the endpoint of human history, but also the climax, the "Omega Point" of cosmic evolution.

The Omega Point of Teilhard de Chardin, the union of all creation with God through Christ at the end of time, is indeed the "entelecheia," the goal present and operative in every stage of the cosmic evolution. Christ is the centripetal force that draws the whole cosmos towards himself. He is both the transcendent cause that directs the evolutionary process from less complex to more complex forms, towards more and more "interiority," and its transcendent consummation. Every new step in evolution is in organic continuity with the previous step, yet in each step something new appears that is not quite reducible to what preceded it. At certain points, qualitatively higher levels of complexity appear, "leaps" as it were in the process: the appearance of life, the appearance of the human race, and finally the incarnation. Each of these "leaps" leads to a qualitatively more perfect level than the previous one, until in Christ God himself takes to himself the whole of creation so that at the end of history all be united under one head, Christ.[55]

Even though the cosmos has been directed towards it from the very beginning, the Omega Point cannot be verified by scientific methods. Only through faith do we know about the incarnation and the second coming of Christ. Only through faith do we know that the history of the cosmos is not destined to end up in ultimate disaster. Humankind may render planet earth uninhabitable, the whole universe may come to an end in its present form, but Chris-

---

[55] Cf. pp. 69-71. See also C.F. Mooney, *Teilhard de Chardin and the Mystery of Christ* (New York: Harper & Row, 1960); K. Rahner, "Christology Within an Evolutionary View of the World," *Theol. Invest.*, Vol. V (Baltimore: Helicon, 1966), pp. 157-192.

tians expect a renewed, spiritualized universe which will provide a home for all of redeemed and renewed humankind.

To sum up then, God assumed a human nature, because human beings are the "key" to the unity of the cosmos. By uniting humankind to the one Christ, God unites to himself the material universe as well.[56]

3. Why only one incarnation?

Why did God become only one human being, at one point in time and space? This question is often raised today. The more we become aware of the dimensions of human history, the plurality of cultures and the number of people who have not had a chance to know Christ, the more problematic it appears to affirm only one incarnation. It seems arbitrary and incompatible with God's universal saving will that he should have become incarnate only once, in a small province of the Roman Empire two thousand years ago. Had he become incarnate in several human beings, at least once in every major culture, we would not have this apparently unjust situation in which only a handful of men and women had direct contact with the incarnate God.

One cannot deny the theoretical possibility of several incarnations on earth, since God's power is almighty and human nature in every individual has the potential to transcend itself through God's intervention.[57]

We must also admit the possibility of other incarnations on other planets of our universe. However, as we have seen above, **Christian revelation insists that there has been only one incarnation for humankind:** Jesus alone is the perfect image of God and the one mediator between God and the human race. Once we accept this fact from revelation, we can find good reasons for it.

---

[56] At this point we omit the question of possible other "worlds" and incarnations and speak about the cosmos as we know it today.

[57] Cf. St. Thomas, *S.T.* III, q. 3, a. 7.

How could the one Son with one divine "identity" be identified with several human individuals? If every human individual is unique and not interchangeable with anyone else, how could many human individuals equally reveal the unique Son? Not merely some aspect or trait of his, but his own uninterchangeable personal center? **Several incarnations would obscure rather than reveal the unique Person of the Son.**[58]

An indirect confirmation for our thesis comes from the study of the idea of divinity in Hinduism and Mahayana Buddhism. On the one hand, Brahman or the universal Buddha nature can manifest itself in every human being, in fact, in any phenomenon of this world; on the other hand, Brahman, or the universal Buddha nature is not understood to be a personal reality after the fashion of the Son or Logos of Christian faith. Absolute Reality in the Upanishads and in Mahayana Buddhism is ultimately impersonal. These two aspects of Hindu and Buddhist doctrines are very likely interconnected: to have an infinite variety of faces is to have no face at all.

Another reason that makes appropriate the once and for all character of the incarnation is based on human nature. Human beings are both spiritual and physical, more exactly, the essential unity of soul and body. If, then, there were many incarnations, the unity of humankind would be established only on a spiritual level. True, all men and women would be united to the one Logos spiritually, but at the same time they would belong to an irreducible plurality of religious centers based on the plurality of incarnations. To stretch the imagination a little further, there would be as many different Eucharists as there are incarnations: say, some would share in the body of Jesus, others in the body of Siddharta Gautama, and so forth.

As it is, however, in the present order of salvation, humankind has only one spiritual and physical center of unity, Jesus of Nazareth. All men and women are called not only to participate in

---

[58] Cf. *S.T.* III, q. 4, a. 5.

the divinity of the Logos but also to do so through the flesh and blood of Jesus of Nazareth. Not the invisible Logos alone, but this rabbi from Nazareth, with all his historical contingencies and limitations, with his Hebrew Scriptures and Aramaic mother tongue, with his band of uneducated disciples and with his typically Jewish dream of the imminent reign of God, this man who was executed under Pontius Pilate, is the concrete center of universal history. Here we confront the very scandal of the incarnation: God makes his absolute fullness reside in one limited human being at one point in the space and time of human history. Yet, as history progresses, the appropriateness of such an arrangement for the future becomes clearer and clearer. Whether the religious leaders of today agree with it or not, our rapidly growing interdependence is not limited to the spiritual sphere: the world is becoming economically, socially, politically, and culturally one interrelated system; as they say, "a global village" or indeed a spaceship: "the spaceship Earth." Looking, then, at the direction of recent history, it seems providential that the cornerstone of humankind's religious history should be both visible and invisible, physical and spiritual[59]; concrete enough for all men and women to relate to one man by learning his words and finding a home in his heart, yet comprehensive enough (due to its divinely transcendent character) to promote rather than suppress the riches of their individuality.

The one incarnation of the Son and the one Redeemer for all humankind, however, does not mean that we encounter the Son of God only in Jesus. Through the incarnation the Son has united himself to every human being. Thus, in loving truly any man or woman, one already loves Christ. One can also know Christ more closely by knowing those human beings who, consciously or unconsciously, realize in themselves some traits of Christ — for instance, his readiness to suffer for others, his confidence in God when confronting total failure, his courage, simplicity, and truthfulness. Such a Christ-like figure does not necessarily have to be a Chris-

---

[59] Cf. St. Ignatius of Antioch, *Eph* 7.

tian. The Church presents the non-Jewish Job to Christians for imitation, as a paradigm of those saints who, before Christ and outside of Israel, realized in themselves the pattern of Christ. To know these Christ-like saints, Christian and non-Christian, is important even for the one who knows Jesus himself. The white light contains all the colors of the rainbow, yet its components can be known only if refracted by a prism. In a similar way, the infinite riches hidden in the one Son of God, Jesus of Nazareth, can be fully known only when reflected in the unique personality of every human being who accepts being united to the Son. In this sense, I believe, Paul Knitter's poignant formula is right: "the totality of Jesus is the Christ… but the totality of the Christ is not Jesus."[60]

The totality of Christ is both Jesus the Head **and** the members of his Body. This totality is gradually formed in history and will be fully accomplished only at the end of time, when we all "form that perfect man who is Christ come to full stature" (Eph 4:13).

4. Why has the Son assumed our fallen nature?

The Church has taught, from the beginning, that the Son of God did not assume human nature as it was before the Fall, or an ideal form of human nature, but the human nature of Adam's offspring, subject to the consequences of original sin. Thus the human nature of Jesus is mortal and capable of suffering.

Yet the question must be faced: How was Jesus fully human without original and personal sin? The Gospels do not report any conversion experience about him. He never had to break with his past. For us, human beings cannot be honest, sincere, and genuine unless they admit their faults. The attempt to appear perfect is the best way to appear false. Jesus, however, gives the impression of complete sincerity and truthfulness with no awareness of guilt or need for conversion. According to the Gospel of John, he confronts

---

[60] "Christianity As Religion: True and Absolute? A Roman Catholic Perspective," *Concilium* 136 (New York: Seabury, 1980), p. 18.

his enemies with the simple question, "Who among you can convict me of sin?" (Jn 8:46).

Many people today cannot comprehend how Jesus could fully identify with us if he were completely sinless. One of the most difficult, though uplifting, human experiences is to admit our sinfulness, to struggle against it, and finally to overcome it. If Jesus did not go through this process, how can we feel close to him? Briefly, how can Jesus show us the way out of sin if he himself did not fight his way out of it?

We can gain a better understanding of this problem by reflecting on the identity of Jesus and on the nature of sin and sinlessness. If Jesus is truly the incarnate Son of God, then the ultimate subject of all his acts is God the Son, and so it is metaphysically impossible for Jesus to commit any sin, since God cannot sin. He is holiness itself. But even supposing that Jesus had sinned, his sins would not have brought him closer to us. Every sin is some form of self-centeredness: In sinning, we affirm ourselves at the expense of others. Consequently, if Jesus had sinned, to that extent he would have been self-centered and separated from us as we are separated from others to the extent that we are sinful. Once we recognize our sin, and repent, we again discover our neighbors. Now, if Jesus had repented at age 30, when he was baptized by John, for those first 30 years he would not have been in full and complete communion with us.

Moreover, only the one who is sinless understands truly the Father's holy love for every human being, and only this person can fully appreciate the evil of sin by which we reject the God who loves us. Thus only the sinless one may empathize perfectly with the misery of the sinner, since the sinless one alone feels the full burden of the sinner's sins. In the words of Simone Weil:

> The innocent victim who suffers knows the truth about his executioner; the executioner does not know it. The evil which the innocent victim feels in himself is in his executioner, but the executioner does not feel it. The innocent victim can only know the evil in the shape of suffering....

It is the innocent victim who can feel hell.[61]

This happens in the most radical form to Christ who manifests in a human way God's innocence and holiness. The sins that caused him to suffer unmasked the intention hidden in every sin, which is to destroy God himself. Thus, the sinless Lamb of God alone understands and suffers the full burden of our sins.

We can also approach Christ's sinlessness from another perspective. To quote Simone Weil again:

> We experience evil only by refusing to allow ourselves to do it... When we do evil we do not know it, because evil flies from the light.[62]

Sinners necessarily embellish their evil deeds in order to alleviate their guilt. Only the innocent one who refused to engage in evil by unmasking its evil character sees its real ugliness. **Thus, rather than an obstacle, Christ's sinlessness was a necessary condition for him to be in full solidarity with sinful humankind throughout the whole duration of his earthly life.**

Although he assumed our fallen human nature, according to the teaching of the Church Jesus was not only sinless, but also without concupiscence (*DS* 434). Concupiscence in the theological sense designates a disorderly state of our inner life in which reason and will, instincts and emotions intrude into each other's domain, weaken and overpower each other, while the lack of concupiscence means, in the words of S. Weil, "each (human) faculty freely playing its role without intruding upon the other, all starting from one single principle."[63]

The lack of concupiscence in Jesus, then, means that his instincts and emotions could never diminish the union of his will with God. During his agony on the night he was betrayed the evange-

---

[61] "Evil," *The Simone Weil Reader,* ed. G.A. Panichas (D. McKay Company: New York, 1977), p. 383.

[62] *Ibid.*

[63] *Ibid.,* p. 365. I modified the translation according to the original text.

lists portray a terrible struggle in Jesus, a painful opposition between his will and reason on the one hand, and his emotions and instincts on the other. Jesus' emotions and instincts rebelled "within their own sphere" and did not diminish or overpower the dedication of his will to God.[64]

He felt with all intensity the horror of his own death, and his emotions vehemently protested against it, but without weakening his obedience to the Father. Because our adverse emotions most often reduce our inclination to do God's will, we find Jesus' case difficult to understand. Saints who managed to restore some order in their inner lives provide an analogy for it. Some martyrs underwent great suffering, against which their emotions vehemently protested, yet they embraced their fate with an undivided will. **Thus, in the last analysis, the lack of concupiscence in Jesus expresses more precisely the meaning of his sinlessness: his will to do good was never diminished by temptation. In simple words, Jesus never did his Father's will in a half-hearted way.**

Concupiscence includes another disorder in us. In making a difficult decision, or feeling too much pain our will often suppresses or blocks the undesired emotions so that our decision may become easier and our situation more endurable. Simply put, instead of acknowledging the pain honestly, we tend to deny it. Yet this half-conscious or unconscious manipulation can happen only at the expense of our humanness. If we repress or deny our painful emotions we may feel less discomfort, but we become numb and less "alive." This shows that Jesus' lack of concupiscence has not diminished but may have actually increased his emotional suffering. While struggling to accomplish God's will, he acknowledged his mortal anguish openly (Mt 26:38; Mk 14:34). What is more human, for someone facing death: to repress anxiety, or to admit it?

---

[64] See *S. T.* III, q. 46, a. 6; K. Rahner, "The Theological Concept of Concupiscentia," *Theol. Invest.*, Vol. I (Baltimore: Helicon, 1963), pp. 347-382.

5. The human knowledge of Jesus

The divine knowledge of the Son is completely identical with that of the Father and the Holy Spirit. In Christology, however, we are not dealing with this eternal divine knowledge, nor with the Son's eternal divine consciousness, but rather with the nature and the different forms of his human knowledge as they are connected with his human consciousness. Thus, a review and expansion of what has already been outlined regarding the psychological aspect of the hypostatic union will become unavoidable.[65]

As we have seen before, the purpose of the Son's incarnation is complete solidarity with humankind. This purpose could not have been achieved had he not known himself, people, the world, and God in a human way.

a. The common human knowledge of Jesus

No theologian today questions that Jesus had the same kind of experiential knowledge as all human beings.[66] Yet, just as his humanity serves to make the eternal Son humanly available for us, his common human knowledge also serves this purpose of mediation. Whatever Jesus learns about this world becomes for him a parable or symbol of God's world. Nonetheless, the transcendent reference of Jesus' experiential knowledge does not make it less human. His parables reveal him as a keen observer of nature and people, both of which he describes with vivid detail, humor, and sympathy. The budding seed of grain first produces the blade, the blade the ear, and the ear is filled with grain: Jesus depicts this process so graphically that, once heard, it engraves itself on the hearer's memory (Mk 4:28). He observes not only the processes of nature but also the life of people: the business venture of the merchant who risks all his

---

[65] See pp. 67-68.

[66] While Jesus had the same *kind* of common human knowledge as we do, its concrete reality was transformed by its close link with Jesus' unique vision of the Father and the Father's inspiring and guiding activity.

wealth for one single precious pearl, the crafty dealings of the recently sacked manager, and the anxious waiting of the father who refuses to give up on his lost son, are portrayed with the realism and imagination of an unusually sensitive observer. As it happens to all human beings, the common human knowledge of Jesus was limited yet constantly growing. We have no reason to assume that Jesus knew more in the realm of natural sciences, history, or mathematics than any of his contemporaries who had been raised in the same cultural milieu. Even in questions of religious history, which were of no consequence for his divine mission, Jesus shared the views of his fellow-Jews. For instance, Jesus spoke of the Davidic authorship of Psalm 110 (Mk 12:36), not because out of modesty he concealed his superior knowledge of literary criticism, but because he sincerely but mistakenly believed that the Psalm was indeed the work of David.

b. Jesus' knowledge of God

Both the Synoptics and the Fourth Gospel affirm a unique knowledge or vision of God in Jesus.[67] According to Mt 11:25-27 and Lk 10:21-22, the mutual knowledge of Father and Son is of comparable breadth and depth, and consequently the Son's knowledge of his Father is unique and surpasses that of all creatures. Mk 13:32 also implies the Son's transcendent knowledge of the Father, while excluding the knowledge of the time of the Parousia.[68]

We can also deduce Jesus' transcendent knowledge or vision of God from the hypostatic union: the human nature of Jesus is the Son's own human nature; consequently, it is appropriate for this

---

[67] Cf. for instance, Mt 11:25-27; Lk 10:21-22; Mk 13:32; Jn 1:18, 5:20, 10:15, 14:7.

[68] "But of that day or hour, no one knows, neither the angels in heaven, nor the Son, but only the Father." The order "angels," "Son," "Father" is an ascending one, going from the lower to the higher. This implies that the Son is above the highest creatures, the angels in heaven. Moreover, the statement about the Son's ignorance of the time of the Parousia makes sense only if the disciples would otherwise have assumed that the Son knew this date. In other words, the Son's ignorance of this particular fact is presented by the Gospel traditions as an exception to the assumed general sharing of knowledge between Father and Son. Cf. O. Cullmann, *The Christology of the New Testament*, pp. 286-288.

human nature to share in a human way the divine knowledge of the eternal Son.

Jesus knew not only God himself with a unique intimacy but also revealed God's plan of salvation with an unparalleled authority. He taught not as the other rabbis, by interpreting the teaching of the rabbis before him, but in his own name, with a power and certainty that astounded his audience. His teaching is directly God's teaching (Mt 16:19; 18:18; Jn 8:26; 28-29).

At the same time, Jesus was growing in wisdom (Lk 2:52); his questions were not mere rhetorical devices, but showed the limits of his knowledge. He even publicly acknowledged his ignorance about the exact date of the end of times (Mk 13:32).

Scholastic theology explained Jesus' knowledge of God as a special case of the beatific vision: in his earthly life Jesus was simultaneously *viator et comprehensor* (pilgrim on his way to God, yet possessing the beatifying vision of God). He saw directly the essence of God on the higher plane of his soul and found supreme delight in it. Yet, this face-to-face vision and joy in the highest "part" of his soul did not prevent Jesus from suffering more than anyone else in the rest of his soul and in his body.[69] Regarding his knowledge of God's plan of salvation, St. Thomas taught that Jesus knew by direct divine inspiration or by infused knowledge (*scientia infusa*) what he had to reveal.[70] Scholastic Christology, however, does not treat the issue of Jesus' human consciousness.

It seems, however, more consistent with the scriptural data if, instead of explaining Jesus' unique knowledge of God in terms of the beatific vision, we derive it from his human self-awareness.[71]

---

[69] See St. Thomas, *S.T.* III, q. 46, a. 8.

[70] Congar interprets *S.T.* III, q. 11, a. 1 in this way. Cf. Y.M. Congar, *Jesus Christ* (New York: Herder & Herder, 1966), pp. 51-65.

[71] Here I have changed my opinion from the one I presented in the first edition of this work. There, following Lonergan (*De constitutione Christi ontologica et psychologica*, pp. 135-137), in addition to Jesus' self-awareness as the Son I also assumed a direct (objective) vision of the Father in the earthly Jesus. But more reflection on Jesus' human self-awareness as always implying a direct awareness of his Father made me realize that the assumption of an immediate objective vision would be an unnecessary hypothesis, which might not be compatible with the state of the earthly Jesus.

Through his human consciousness, it is the eternal Son who experiences himself in a human way, therefore his human consciousness must also include the awareness of his relationship to the Father since his self as Son is constituted precisely by his being born from the Father. Thus, the self-awareness of the Son includes the awareness of his Father. This reasoning brings to light the unique character of Jesus' knowledge of God: He does not simply know or even see God the Son and God the Father as quasi objects distinct from himself (as the doctrine of the *visio beatifica* would require) but rather his immediate self-awareness includes his awareness of being the Son of the Father. At the same time, the above hypothesis accounts for the constant growth of Jesus' reflexive knowledge of himself and of the Father, since it does not presuppose a distinct objective vision of God's essence in which Jesus would have had a comprehensive knowledge of God and of his plan of salvation from the beginning of his human existence. Human self-awareness is always immediate, intuitive, global and luminous, but in need of clarification and a gradual, conceptual articulation that will result in growing reflexive self-knowledge. In Jesus' case his growing reflexive self-knowledge depends on the Father's constant revealing, guiding and inspiring activity. The Father and Jesus communicate in the Holy Spirit and Jesus reveals only what he hears from his Father in the Spirit.[72] We can better explain in this way why Jesus in his earthly life did not know the date of the end of human history: it was not part of the revelation the Son has received from his Father.[73]

The important role Jesus' common human knowledge plays in his mission appears clearly in this context. Neither his self-awareness as Son nor the Father's inspiring and guiding action through the Spirit dispense him from engaging his mind to the fullest as he contemplates in the Scriptures, in the events of his life, and in the reactions of people, the unfolding of his Father's plan and his own

---

[72] Cf. Lk 3:22; 10:21; Jn 3:22, 8:26, 8:40, 15:15.

[73] St. Bonaventure has already explained Jesus' vision of God along similar lines. See *In Sent* III, D 14, a. 2, qq. 1-3.

role in that plan. Through God's inspiration Jesus discovers and lives God's will from moment to moment, from one day to the next. The Father's inspiration ensures also that Jesus correctly understands himself, his Father, and his own task in the Father's plan, and that he can express these divine realities in human words with infallible certainty. Thus the close cooperation of these three kinds of knowledge (his awareness of God as his Father, his knowledge of God and God's plan through the Father's revealing and inspiring activity, and his common experiential knowledge of this world) is necessary for the completion of Jesus' mission and explains in particular the power and depth of his parables. Through his direct awareness of the Father and through the Father's revealing and inspiring activity every phenomenon of the world appears to him as pointing beyond itself: every created reality becomes an image or symbol of God's own life and of his plan of salvation. What he learns of God's world he communicates to us through the images and stories he learned in a human way about our world. Through the Father's inspiration he is able to express infallibly through the words, images, symbols, and stories of this world the invisible realities of God's life and plan of salvation.[74]

6. The human will of the Son

1. From revelation we know that Jesus had a free human will, and that his life was a series of free decisions by his human will.

---

[74] Cf. Congar, *Jesus Christ*, pp. 63-65. At this point it might be useful to compare my hypothesis with that of Thomas. Instead of supposing a *visio beatifica* in the earthly Jesus, I assume that Jesus was aware of his divine identity and his own Father through his human consciousness. What Thomas called the *scientia infusa* of Jesus I see as a constant dialogue between Jesus and the Father in the Holy Spirit, a dialogue that guided and inspired every step of Jesus' life. In order to accomplish his saving mission, Jesus needed the close cooperation of his human self-awareness, the Father's revelation and inspiration in the Spirit, and his common human knowledge acquired from experience. I differ from Lonergan's position in that I do not see the need to affirm the beatific vision in Jesus in addition to his direct self-awareness as the Father's Son. In this regard my present hypothesis is closer to that of Rahner. Cf. K. Rahner, "Dogmatic Reflections on the Knowledge and Self-Consciousness of Christ," *Theol. Invest.*, Vol. V (Baltimore: Helicon, 1966), pp. 193-215.

2. However, it is also revealed that Jesus' human will is the human will of the eternal Son. Through his human will Jesus lived out gradually in his earthly life the Son's eternal union with the will of his Father.

3. Since the eternal Son is the subject of Jesus' human will, we must conclude that Jesus not only did not sin but could not sin. The mutual compatibility of these truths needs some justification.

If the earthly Jesus had no active human will he would not have been a true human being. Without the exercise of his human will, his life would have been merely a show, a stage production. Moreover, the Son needed to assume human freedom in order to redeem it.

In spite of his free human will, however, we cannot attribute the possibility of sin to the Son of God, who is the ultimate subject of Jesus' acts. Yet, how can we claim true human freedom for Jesus and still assert his impeccability?

As a starting point, we must establish something about the proper functioning of both the human intellect and the human will. The intellect is ordained towards knowing the truth, and becomes perfected by possessing the truth. Error is a result not of the proper functioning of the intellect, but of its imperfection. An intellect that does not err is not a less but rather a more perfect intellect than the one that errs.

We need to apply the same principle to the will. The object of free will is what is truly good. That person has perfect freedom of the will who freely determines himself — rather than is compelled by external and internal forces — to choose always what is truly good. The fact that the human will often chooses what is only apparently good (sin), does not derive from the perfection of the will, but is the sign of its imperfection. This notion of human freedom differs from the one that is commonly accepted today. People think they are free if they "can do whatever they want." However, this view ignores the fact that the human will is a value-oriented faculty — it is oriented to goodness (just as the intellect is oriented to the truth). The more my free will is able to choose freely what is truly good, the more my freedom is perfect. If I freely choose sin, it is only a sign that my freedom is defective. It follows, then, that the impeccability of Jesus does not limit his freedom, but rather shows its perfection.

If impeccability belongs to the perfection of the free will, the question is not yet solved: how can a free will so perfect as to be impeccable still remain human? It seems that the free human will is, by its very nature, finite, therefore imperfect, and capable of sin. Thus we need to consider a further distinction. **If we view the free human will of Jesus in itself, then, as any finite, created will, it includes in itself the possibility of sin. But this finite created human will of Jesus is united hypostatically to the Logos; it is the Logos's free human will. And it is only because of this ineffably close union with the Logos that the free human will of Jesus is incapable of sinning.**

How the human will of Jesus remains human, and yet, as part of his human nature, becomes the free will of the Logos, we cannot comprehend. This is the very mystery of the incarnation from the perspective of human freedom. While we cannot comprehend it, we can at least grasp that our assertion does not necessarily imply a contradiction. We can even go one step further, and show that there is an intrinsic intelligibility to the fact that the human freedom of Jesus is not destroyed but rather enhanced by its becoming the human freedom of God himself. We can show this intelligibility if we consider the relationship between God and the human will on a general scale.[75]

According to many of the Fathers, the image of God lies precisely in our free will. We are the created image of uncreated freedom. To the extent that our act is free, we are not determined by any created cause — external or internal force — but by ourselves alone and therefore we are truly independent, exist and act by ourselves and shape our own existence. But precisely to the extent that

---

[75] Cf. K. Rahner, "Current Problems in Christology," *Theol. Invest.*, Vol. I (Baltimore: Helicon, 1963), pp. 162-165.

human beings resemble God in being a cause of their own acts and of their own existence, they participate in a qualitatively new and more perfect way in God than the rest of creation, which has no free will and intellect. This new participation extends to each and every free act. One cannot make any free act without participating in God's freedom. **Thus a higher level of independence does not contradict but presupposes a higher level of dependence on God.** Among human beings, the saints have a special relationship to God. A saint depends even more on God, because he or she wants to be united with God in everything. And precisely because of this more intimate union with God, saints experience a blossoming of their freedom; they are freer than the rest of us. No longer under the pressure of their instincts, passions, and emotions, and even less dominated by the threats and lures of their environment, they do what is truly good, freely, out of their own personal center. Saints have a new level of dependence on God and a new level of independence in themselves.

Because of the hypostatic union, we must attribute to the will of Christ a qualitatively higher form of dependence on God than even to the will of the greatest saints. His human will depends in such a radical way on God that it should be called the human will of the Son himself. For this reason Jesus the man is supremely free. He chooses some people with sovereign freedom to follow him while others he sends away. His reactions to people are totally unpredictable, without appearing in any way capricious. He is in command of every situation, even when he is led as a helpless defendant before the highest court of his nation and before the Roman procurator. He silences his accusers, confounds those who want to trap him. At the end no one dares to contradict him. The sovereign human freedom of the man Jesus is not destroyed by God, but rather makes the divine will present with a powerful immediacy.[76]

---

[76] G. Bornkamm thinks that this unparalleled sovereign freedom is one of the unique characteristics of the historical Jesus. See *Jesus of Nazareth* (New York: Harper & Row, 1956), pp. 58-61.

CHAPTER IV

Redemption as Assumption of Humankind into Trinitarian Communion

After discussing the hypostatic union from various points of view, as the condition for the perfect communion God has intended to establish with the human race, we need now to examine **how** this communion has been achieved. In other words, we will attempt to understand the meaning of what is traditionally called the doctrine of redemption, or soteriology.

We have already seen that, once the first man and woman have rejected personal communion with God, the initiative to restore the broken relationship with God and to re-create distorted human nature had to come from God himself.[77]

Yet, since we possess the dignity of free will, the ability and right of self-determination, it was most appropriate — as beginning with Irenaeus the Fathers have repeatedly emphasized — that, through God's free initiative, a human being should redeem the human race. This explains the structure of the present chapter: we examine the roles of the Divine Persons in our redemption, as well as the role of the man Jesus, and we will end this treatise with an outline of the eschatological fullness of salvation.

1. The role of the Father

Redemption has two inseparable aspects: the transformation of our being and faculties, and the assumption of the sinner into

---

[77] See pp. 339-340.

Trinitarian communion. Regarding the first, God, the efficient cause (*causa efficiens*) acts as one. Regarding the second, each Divine Person has a distinct role to perform, since our entering into personal communion with the Trinity results for us in a different relationship with each of the Divine Persons. The Father gives his Son to humankind (Jn 3:16; Rm 8:32; 1 Jn 4:10). The hymn of praise to the Easter Candle sums up wonderfully the mystery of what the Father has done:

> Father, how wonderful your care for us! How boundless your merciful love! To ransom a slave you gave away your Son.

With the Son's full acceptance, the Father sends the Son as man to us as his gift, so that the Son may become truly and definitively ours in his full divine-human reality. The Father's act of giving his Son to us must not be explained away as a "mere metaphor," the metaphorical language being an exaggeration of what really happened. The truth is exactly the opposite. **The human image of a father giving up his only son to rescue a slave is only a weak analogy of the true and perfect giving that only God the Father can accomplish.** When a man gives his only son, he does not give all that he has and all that he is; much less can he do it with pure and infinite love. Also, the "value gap" between son and servant in human society is incomparably narrower than the infinite abyss separating a sinful creature and God. **God the Father giving his Son gives away all that he is, the fullness of his divinity; he gives him out of pure, infinite love and gives him to his sinful creatures who, apart from God's creative and redeeming love, are absolutely nothing.**

Today it has become fashionable to speak about the suffering of the Father in giving up his Son. Whether or not such a way of speaking is correct depends on what we understand by suffering. If by suffering we mean that the Father's being is diminished, destroyed or even threatened by diminishment or annihilation, then the Father does not suffer. We will see later, however, that the Son truly suffered in his humanity.

It is less ambiguous to speak with the Bible and with patristic and medieval tradition about the compassion of the Father.[78] Through his transcendent, infinite love, the Father does make another's experience of suffering his own: first, that of sinful humankind, then that of his own Son, who has in some sense concentrated upon himself the suffering of all men and women. The reality of the Father's compassion can be further shown if we ask the question: Could the Father remain indifferent to the suffering of his Son? Could what is sinful insensitivity on the part of a human father be construed as transcendent perfection in God the Father? How could "giving his only Son" not imply an infinite divine compassion in God the Father? The intensity of compassion is proportionate to the existential closeness of the sympathizer to the sufferer, to the love of the sympathizer for the sufferer, and to the intensity of the suffering in the sufferer. Thus the intensity of the Father's compassion must be commensurate to his being totally in and with his Son, to his infinite love for the Son, and to the intensity of the Son's suffering. And since, according to the Father's plan, the Son endures in his human nature the sufferings of all human beings, the Father embraces with the same compassion (which he has for his Son) all men and women whose sufferings the Son has taken upon himself.

Compassion does not contradict God's transcendent perfection. No power outside or inside God has been imposed on the Father to force him to give his Son. **To claim that the Father is affected as Father by his Son's life and death does not diminish the perfection of God but rather shows the Father's infinite sensitivity. Moreover, only God's transcendent love can make it possible that the Father truly gives in the Son all that he has and all that he**

---

[78] On the question of God's suffering there exists today an ever-proliferating amount of literature. For instance, J. Galot, *Dieu souffre-t-il?* (Paris: Lethielleux, 1976); J. Moltmann, *The Trinity and the Kingdom* (San Francisco: Harper, 1981); H. Mühlen, *Die Veränderlichkeit Gottes als Horizont einer zukünftigen Christologie* (Münster: Aschendorff, 1969); J. Young Lee, *God Suffers for Us: A Systematic Inquiry into the Concept of Divine Passibility* (The Hague: M. Nijhoff, 1974); F. Varillon, *La souffrance de Dieu* (Paris, Ed. du Centurion, 1975); ET: *The Humility and Suffering of God* (Staten Island, NY: Alba House, 1983).

400 JESUS CHRIST: FUNDAMENTALS OF CHRISTOLOGY

is, and does it so effectively that the Son truly becomes ours and we truly participate in him.

Since God is absolute, simple perfection, the Father's compassion for his incarnate Son and for us is not a finite accidental quality, but identical with the Father's giving eternal birth to the Son. Thus our reflection merely applies to compassion what St. Thomas teaches about the Son's mission by the Father: the Son's mission to humankind is identical in God with the eternal generation of the Son by the Father. What is new in the mission is the creation of a reality distinct from God, yet assumed by God the Son as his own reality: the humanity of Jesus. The Father's act of generating the Son has such infinite perfection that speaking about an increase to that perfection through the mission of the Son would be nonsensical.[79]

The same principle applies to the Father's compassion. It is not a new accident added to the Father's eternal act of giving birth to the Son. **The Father is involved with infinite intensity in the personal fate of his Son and of humankind through the infinite perfection of his eternal divine fatherhood.**

As salvation history originates in the Father's eternal decision to give or send his Son to us, so it will end in our full communion with the Father: once our conformation to the only Son and our union with his glorified body is consummated, our participation in the one Son's relationship to the Father will be brought to completion. Thus the Father's love, the absolute origin of creation and redemption, brings about — through the Son and in the Spirit — an innumerable multitude of sons and daughters, all one with the Son and in filial communion with the Father.

---

[79] Cf. *S.T.* I, q. 43, esp. a. 1, 2.

2. The role of the incarnate Son

a. *The unique character of the suffering of Jesus*

The Son agrees from all eternity with the Father's decision to save us. He makes the Father's love for fallen humankind completely his own and thus accepts being sent; he takes up full solidarity with us by accepting not only to become man, but also "to become flesh," that is, to endure the consequences of sin, the state of threefold alienation, up to its last logical stage in this world which is physical death experienced as the anticipation of eternal spiritual death.

He accepts alienation from his Divine Self. By emptying himself, he freely renounces "enjoying" the infinite glory and power of his Father which is also by right his own. He accepts not letting his divine consciousness permeate his human consciousness, and he experiences in himself the infinite distance that separates the sinner from God.

Thus, here on earth, while remaining aware of being the Son, Jesus exists in a state of distance or "alienation" from his own Father as well. But paradoxically, he endures the distance and "alienation" from his Father in order to express his perfect love for him.

Finally, fully human and experiencing all that is human in himself, he suffers a complete alienation from almost all human beings. We have already seen how, at the end, not only the leaders oppose him, but also his own people reject him, his chosen disciples abandon him in fear and disappointment.

It is on the cross that the threefold alienation of the incarnate Son reaches its utmost intensity, but so does also his love. **His divine love for God and for us obtains its most perfect human expression in this state of greatest alienation; therefore it is through his death that Christ overcomes for himself and for us all forms of alienation, and enters into full communion with his Father, and with us forever.**

As Simone Weil remarked, it is only the innocent victim who understands the evil of his torturer's sin.[80] The torturer may rationalize his crime by all sorts of excuses, but the victim, in feeling the pain, cannot avoid feeling the evil done to him. Thus Jesus, in becoming the victim of typical human sins, experiences the evil of all sins. As Ambrose explained, Jesus suffers under the weight of what the sinners themselves do not (or only very dimly) understand, the horrendous evil of their own sins.[81]

According to the Gospel of John Jesus alone understands the true nature of the crime committed against him, the crime in which the Satanic intent of all sins surfaces. He knows that — using human beings as his instruments — Satan, who was "a murderer from the beginning" (Jn 8:44), intends to do away with God himself in his person. He counters this sin and all sins by expressing his love for the Father in the name of all men and women, for whose sins he freely accepts death on the cross.

Since he carries our sins out of love, one cannot say that Jesus endured hell, which only those suffer who lack all love. But, as pointed out before, Jesus alone carries the full burden of our sins in the sense that, through his divine compassion and holiness, he alone experiences the evil of our sins in their full gravity. **Identical with the holy God and making his own the misery of the sinner on the brink of damnation (a misery the sinner cannot fully experience), Jesus suffers in a way that no other human being can comprehend.**

Two more questions arise regarding the death of Jesus: How does God himself suffer death in the death of Jesus? And how does Jesus' death turn our threefold alienation into the means of regaining our own integrity and communion with God and with our fellow men and women?

---

[80] Cf. pp. 386-387 of this book.
[81] Cf. pp. 206-207.

b. In Jesus God himself died for us

As discussed above,[82] a human being is the substantial unity of soul and body; consequently, our body is part of our self-identity. Thus we experience the dying of our body as our own dying, rather than the shedding of a "cocoon" which is somehow extraneous to us. Even though our soul is immortal, it is the whole person who goes through the experience of dying. **In fact, if we had no immortal soul, we could not experience the horror of death; it is our spiritual soul that dreads death as totally opposed to its own immortal nature.** The eternal Son is not substantially but hypostatically united to his human nature, which results, from one viewpoint, in an even closer union than the union of soul and body in us. The soul of a human being is **not** his body, while the Son of God **is** this man Jesus. Thus, when speaking about the death of the eternal Son in his human nature, we may apply here the analogy of the "dying" of the human soul. **As the human soul does not cease to exist yet experiences dying, so the Son of God does not cease to exist yet experiences dying.** Since God is infinitely closer to the man Jesus than our soul is to our bodies and since death is incomparably more opposed to the divine nature than to the nature of the human soul, the Son had to suffer incomparably more in his humanity than we do when we are confronted with our own dying.

The self-emptying of the Son (just as the love and compassion of the Father for his incarnate and crucified Son) does not contradict divine perfection. It is only the human distortion of divine transcendence, such as we find in non-Christian religions (and even in the thought of some Christian thinkers), which denies the possibility of God's incarnation and God's dying for the human race. The sinner is inclined to imagine divine transcendence only as aloofness and distance, majesty and threat. As a result, outside of the realm of Christian revelation, people left to their own resources,

---

[82] Cf. pp. 338-339.

cannot conceive of the idea of the one transcendent God becoming one of them and dying for them.[83]

In the incarnation and redemption, however, God has shown that his transcendent perfection is the perfection of transcendent love. For the sake of his beloved (humankind in the grip of sin), the eternal Son — while remaining Son and precisely through his almighty power as Son — did truly identify himself with us in dying where we are most God-forsaken. **Thus it is God's almighty freedom of love that enabled the eternal Son to "taste death" for us all in his humanity.**

c. The self-giving of Jesus to God on the cross as the reversal of our alienation

As we have seen, the process of physical death is the most potent "reality therapy" for the sinner.[84]

It is in dying that we may be shaken out of our self-deception and forced to acknowledge that we are not an absolute, but came "from dust and unto dust we shall return." Yet left to ourselves, we are unable to use our dying as "medication." Some rebel against the absurdity of their dying in the name of human dignity; others deny their own spiritual nature and welcome death as the absolute end, rather than accept moral responsibility before a transcendent judge.

Jesus' death, however, which he has undergone for our sake enables us to use our death as the most powerful cure for our sinfulness. While abandoned by God on the cross, Jesus cries out to God in anguish and loneliness, but does not cease to trust him (Mt 27:46). Facing his own annihilation (in the sense described above), he does not cling to his life but puts himself unconditionally into his Father's hands (Lk 23:45). In this most difficult moment of dis-

---

[83] The "incarnate" and suffering gods of pagan mythologies are "second-rate" gods, intermediaries between a transcendent divinity and man.

[84] Cf. pp. 338-339 of this book; "Evil," *The Simone Weil Reader*, p. 383.

tance from God (how can one be more distant from the living God than when facing the end of his own life?), his divine love of and trust in his Father reach their most perfect and irrevocable human expression. In his final act of loving surrender, he gives us the perfect model of how we should renounce our "imagined divinity,"[85] that is, our imagining ourselves to be absolute, and accept our creaturely condition. Paradoxically, of all human beings it is God the Son alone[86] who lives out his creaturely relationship to God up to the very end on the cross with full authenticity and without any distortion. Moreover, in handing over his human life to the Father on the cross, the eternal Son has completed the "translation" into the finite acts of an alienated human existence the eternal act of returning his divine being to the Father in the Holy Spirit. Thus, according to the Fourth Gospel, in the act of breathing his last, Jesus hands over to the Father and to us the *pneuma*, the Holy Spirit.

The Father responds to the perfect self-giving of his Son by raising him from the dead. He transforms his humanity, body and soul, by the Holy Spirit and thereby makes Jesus the man the sender of the Holy Spirit. The risen Christ has not abandoned us; on the contrary, in the Holy Spirit, whom he now pours out upon humankind through his glorified body, he becomes not only a model but also a source of life and strength for his extended body, the Church. Through the Spirit he enables us to share in his own acts of love and trust on earth and to turn our threefold alienation and especially our death into a way of threefold union, unity in ourselves, union with God and with our fellow men and women.

After this brief summary I will examine in more detail certain aspects of redemption, the self-giving of Jesus to his Father, which, in keeping with biblical and patristic terminology, I call the sacrifice of Jesus. *wheres the blood?*

---

[85] This is a favorite idea of S. Weil. See, for instance, "Decreation," *The Simone Weil Reader*, p. 352.

[86] According to Catholic faith, Mary also has realized a perfect creaturely relationship to God; but she does so not by herself but in complete dependence on the Son as the model and anticipation of eschatological mankind.

d. The sacrifice of Jesus

Offering sacrifice is an archetypal human gesture, as old as the human race itself.[87] Analogous to it and shedding light on it is another primordial human act, the offering of a gift in various forms: by one person to another, by one person to a community, by a community to one person, or an exchange of gifts between communities. The motives for a gift are also quite varied: thanking for a service, an attempt to win the good will of a person or community, making up for a willful or inadvertent offense, or establishing a closer relationship. The material gift is the external, tangible sign of these inner motives. The same motives are also present in an act of sacrifice, except that no one has ever offered sacrifice to someone believed to be a "mere human being." (The sacrifices offered to kings and emperors always implied their divine status.)

What, then, is, the distinctive feature of sacrifice? In giving God (or a god) a material object as thanksgiving-sacrifice, a gratitude is implied in the gift that we are never justified to express for another human being: a gratitude for **all** that we have and are — we owe our very being to God.[88]

---

[87] This section owes much to O. Semmelroth, "Sacrifice," *Encyclopedia of Theology. The Concise Sacramentum Mundi* (New York: Seabury Press, 1975), pp. 1488-1491. For other approaches regarding sacrifice in human history, see M. Eliade, *The Sacred and the Profane* (New York: Harcourt, Brace & World, 1959), pp. 99-104; R. Schwager, *Must There Be Scapegoats? Violence and Redemption in the Bible* (San Francisco: Harper & Row, 1987). A further study could, I believe, synthesize the notion of sacrifice in the works of Eliade and Schwager, and point to its archetypal form at a certain stage of religious history, this form being the ritual re-enactment of the murder or self-sacrifice of a divine figure. All the blessings of renewed life flow from the murder or self-offering of the god. However, this form of sacrifice cannot be traced back beyond the beginning of agricultural societies to the most primitive stage of religious history, characterized by belief in a transcendent sky-god. My analysis of sacrifice attempts to reconstruct the most primitive form which corresponds to the religion of the sky-gods.

[88] This phenomenological analysis applies primarily to sacrifice in monotheistic religions. Nevertheless, even in a polytheistic religion, the god one worships takes on some features of the Absolute and thus some features of the sacrifice may also be realized in the worship of that particular god. However, the distortions of sacrifice, the "bribing" of a god or attempting to control a god by magic, can more easily happen in a polytheistic religion.

When asking for a favor through sacrifice, we are ultimately asking for life, a favor only God can bestow. When "making up for an offense" in a sacrifice of atonement or expiation, we acknowledge that through our sin we have forfeited our right to live: we deserve to die, and through the sacrifice we are asking God to forgive us and restore us to life. In communion-sacrifice, we are yearning for a communion with God (and through God with our fellows) that cannot be achieved through mere human mediation. **Underlying all these particular forms of sacrifice is the motive of adoration: sacrifice is a tangible external way of acknowledging God as God, as the absolute source and lord of one's life.** To him I owe everything, to him I want freely to return myself as a gift. Only God has the right to this total self-giving, since he alone gives to us all that we are and he alone is absolute goodness and holiness.

Of all creatures on earth, only the human being is capable of offering sacrifice, since men and women alone have reason and free will. As rational beings, we humans alone truly "possess ourselves," and by our free decisions we alone can give shape and direction to our existence. By freely choosing to surrender in love to God's will, we can in some real sense give ourselves to God. On the other hand, by freely choosing to disobey him, we can refuse the gift of self to God (although even our refusal would not be possible without God's permission, who would allow it for a greater good in his plan).

Through our body, we are part of the material universe. Through our activity, we are called to carry out God's design in the universe by studying and using it as well as preserving and perfecting it. **In this way we are to offer a "cosmic sacrifice" to God, in that we carry out God's will concerning not only our own person and our community but also the universe.**

However, our concrete situation disqualifies us from offering God an acceptable sacrifice. Because of original sin, we are inclined to prefer ourselves to God; As a result of concupiscence, our lower faculties often oppose, weaken and enslave the decisions of the will. We are not whole; thus, even if we wanted to, on our own we could not wholly give ourselves to God.

Moreover, without Christ's grace, all men and women would

have separated themselves from God through their personal sins, and thereby become incapable of offering him an acceptable sacrifice.

But even if we had not sinned, being only creatures, we could not have offered God a perfect sacrifice, because we cannot fully know God's holiness and goodness, nor can we love, praise, and give thanks to God as God deserves to be loved, praised, and thanked. **To put it briefly, being a finite creature, the human being cannot give God a gift worthy of God himself.**

Only against this background can we appreciate the significance of Christ's sacrifice. **Fully integrated in himself because sin has not infected him, Jesus subjects himself to God with an undivided heart. His love for God is not weakened by any disorder in his personality. His giving of self extends to every moment of his life and is consummated on the cross, where it becomes complete and irrevocable.** The sign in which this sacrificial attitude is expressed is not an object distinct from himself (such as an animal or the first fruits of the crops), but his own body. An "object-sacrifice," even though it may symbolize the giving of the self, has only a tenuous, extrinsic relationship to the self. Jesus gave his physical life, his body, which is not just linked to his self, but is its concrete tangible expression. By freely giving up his body, he gives his whole humanity, and by giving his humanity — because of the hypostatic union — he gives his whole divine self in a human way to God. This is, then, the other reason why Jesus gave God **the** one perfect sacrifice. **Through the man Jesus, through his human freedom, love, and obedience, the eternal Son himself loves, obeys, and worships the Father.** The human race has finally realized what it has striven for through the unending flow of the blood of its sacrifices; in the God-man we have the one sacrifice that alone is worthy of God: God the Son made man offering himself to God the Father in such a way that all humankind may unite itself along with the material universe to this one, perfect, once-for-all sacrifice.

e. *The sacrifice of Christ as satisfaction*

Beginning with the Middle Ages, sacrifice and satisfaction have become separate themes in soteriology. Then, beginning with the Age of the Enlightenment, liberal Protestant theology attacked both the concept of sacrifice and the concept of satisfaction as remnants of the "Dark Ages" and incompatible with the idea of a humane and loving God.[89]

In recent times the satisfaction theory has become less and less popular even in Catholic circles because its conceptual framework was considered to have been closely tied to the feudalistic structure of medieval society. In this section I attempt to show that the core insight of the satisfaction theory goes much deeper than its time-conditioned language in which it is couched and that it expresses an essential aspect of the mystery of redemption. The true meaning of satisfaction needs to be integrated into that of sacrifice in the following way. **The satisfaction Jesus offers his Father for the sins of the world is his sacrifice.** My analysis will start by examining the meaning of satisfaction on the human level and apply it analogously to satisfaction regarding God, and then see how the sacrifice of Jesus embodies this satisfaction.

Satisfaction even on a human level should not be regarded solely from the viewpoint of justice (after the analogy of paying a sum equivalent to the damage caused), but primarily from the perspective of the sacred dignity of the person. If a good belonging to a person is taken away or damaged (for instance, if his property has been stolen, his personal freedom unduly restricted), justice demands a restitution of what had been taken and a compensation for the damages caused. However, to the extent that the offense was directed against the person himself (an expression of indifference or hatred regarding that person), no amount of material com-

---

[89] Liberal Protestant theology attacked directly not the Anselmian-Thomistic understanding of satisfaction, but its Protestant version according to which God imposed the punishment we deserved upon his Son. Yet, its individualistic mentality was opposed to the Catholic notion of satisfaction as well.

pensation could ever satisfy. The value of a human person cannot be measured by material means. Having been created in God's image, every human person participates in God's sacred dignity. Thus an offense committed against a person demands a **personal** act for satisfaction. It must reverse the slighting, the indifference, or the hatred expressed in the offense by showing sorrow and appreciation for the person offended. In this case the purpose of the external acts is to manifest the sincerity of the inner change. And it is appropriate that the offenders should express their sorrow and love by acts contrary in nature to the offense committed.

The need for a personal satisfaction is strongly experienced by children who feel close to their parents, and by friends who are anxious to restore a broken relationship. The more sensitive a child's conscience is, the more clearly he realizes that he cannot make up for the offense against his father just by "doing some chores" for him; rather he must show sorrow and love by accepting these chores. Children know instinctively that what matters is not the external work, but the sincerity of their change of heart. In a similar way, repentant friends will be intent first of all on showing their sorrow and renewed love for the offended friend through some external sign.

Such personal satisfaction does not operate automatically, as if straightening out a balance of payments. It cannot be anything else than an appeal for forgiveness. Those who intend to offer satisfaction put themselves to some extent into the hands of the offended person, hoping that the latter will perceive the sincerity of their sorrow and love and, by a free act, restore the broken relationship. **In this putting oneself into the hands of another person, in acknowledging a certain dependence on him/her by the offering of a compensating gift, even among humans satisfaction is similar to sacrifice.**

To sum up, what truly satisfies for the offense against persons (not merely for the injustice against some of their rights, but for the indifference or hatred expressed in the offensive act against the persons themselves) is the repentance and greater love for the offended coming from the heart of the offender. **It seems appropriate that this love should be greater than that which the offender had before the offense and ought to embody itself in external deeds that attempt to reverse the results of the offensive act.** For our sense of justice and faith in the order of the universe are satisfied only when we see that an evil act was the occasion for a greater good, for a greater love.

The satisfaction to be given (the intensity and nature of this greater love expressing itself in appropriate deeds) must be commensurate with the gravity of the offense. This gravity depends on several factors.

1. It depends on how closely linked to the person is the good against which the offense was directed (one's property is much less intimately bound up with the person than one's health, physical life, or honor), and to what extent the offense was motivated by hatred or indifference and how intense was the hatred, how willful the indifference.

2. The gravity of the offense depends also on the personal worth or dignity of the offended person. Every human individual is sacred. Yet, depending on the extent of one's participation in God's goodness and holiness, there are various degrees of personal worth.[90]

3. Finally, the gravity of the offense depends on the nature of the relationship between the offender and the offended. The closer the tie, the greater the gratitude and love the offender owed to the offended, and the greater the offense.

---

[90] Everyone would consider it a greater crime to murder an innocent child than a dangerous criminal. St. Thomas explains this gradation through examples from the social status of individuals within a hierarchically organized society: the higher one stands in this sacred order, the greater the offense committed against him. For us, such consideration is less convincing. We would rather think in terms of personal categories: the more virtuous a person is, the greater the offense against him. Yet, for Thomas, the hierarchical rank of a man in the sacred order of society comes from God. Thus for Thomas as well, even though from a different perspective, the gravity of an offense depends on the extent to which the offended person participates in God's sacred dignity. Cf. *S.T.* Suppl. q. 13, a. 1.

We will now apply these anthropological notions — analogously — to sin against God and to satisfaction for sin. First we
must face the often-raised question: how can sin be an offense
against God? It seems more respectful of God's transcendence to
define sin as a moral defect in a human being, a deliberate failure
to achieve one's own moral goodness. It is true that most sins are
not explicitly directed against God, but rather violate the sinners'
own human dignity and that of their fellows. Yet, by violating the
order of creation willed by God, all sinners — to the extent that
they truly sin — implicitly wish to eliminate the person of God
himself. By choosing to live and act independently from their Creator, they wish that God had not set up this order and ultimately
that God had not existed.

Moreover, every sin rejects not only the Creator but also the
grace of sonship God the Father keeps offering to every human being. The sinner does not want to be and to act as God's child.

But can this rejection of God by the sinner truly reach God?
Are not God's holiness and dignity so transcendent as to be completely "invulnerable" to any human offense? Truly, God's holiness
and dignity cannot be destroyed or threatened by our sin. We must
exclude any ontological "vulnerability" in God. Yet revelation com-
pels us to speak about a personal vulnerability that is commensurate with God's infinite love. God has allowed himself to become
vulnerable to us by creating us free and calling us to become his
children through the only Son. **By becoming not only our Creator,
but intending to be also our Father, God the Father has made himself "vulnerable" to us in his most intimate personal quality, his fatherhood.** If a good human father is hurt by the rejection of his
children, how much more — infinitely more — is God the Father
affected by the fact that we refuse to treat him as our Father? The
Gospel parables could not be more explicit on this point. Nor should
one object on the grounds of an *a priori* philosophical concept of
divine love that cannot do justice to the data of revelation. **Such
vulnerability does not contradict God's transcendence, since God
freely made himself accessible to our rejection. It is precisely the**

transcendent perfection of God's love that allows him to become infinitely vulnerable to us.

Thus, whenever we reject the infinitely holy God as our Creator and Father, we commit an infinitely grave offense. If God's holiness is infinite, the gravity of the offense against his holiness must exceed any human, finite measure.

In his mercy, God could have simply forgiven our offenses without demanding a commensurate satisfaction (supposing, of course, that in response to and with the help of God's grace, we would have repented of our sins). The holiness and dignity of God would not have been "injured" or "diminished" in this case, but we would have been treated as a "minor" deemed incapable of living up to the demands of God's holiness, or of facing up to, and doing something about, the disaster our sins have wrought on him and on the social order. In fact, however, God has demanded full satisfaction from us for our sins. This was not a vengeful act on God's part. **Rather than eliminating the necessary consequences of sin in us, God has upheld the order of reality he created. By acting in this way, he has shown respect for our human dignity, for our freedom that makes us responsible for our acts and its consequences.** He appealed to our ability to appreciate the impact of our sins: distorting our own nature and offending against the infinite holiness of God (this holiness gradually revealing itself as a transcendent, "wholly other" love greater than which cannot be conceived). By requiring us to satisfy for or undo these offenses, God has treated his creatures as "adults."

While we have to realize our obligation to satisfy, we must also see that, left to our own resources, we are unable to do so. We had the freedom to offend God with an infinitely grave offense, but we cannot offer any commensurate satisfaction for it. We had the power to distort our nature and fall into the trap of death, but by ourselves we cannot transform our actions and dying into an expression of love-filled satisfaction that is worthy of God himself. Only a Divine Person of infinite worth and holiness could love God with an infinitely holy love that would satisfy for our infinitely grave offenses. And only the Son could satisfy for our rejection of the grace of sonship. Yet a Divine Person, in his transcendent distance from us, could not satisfy in our place. The eternal Son had to become one of us, a fellow human being, ontologically and psychologically identifying himself with us in order to satisfy as a human being for all of humankind. Moreover, only a human being can die. Thus only God made man could transform the process of dying from an expression of sin into the expression of a self-giving love that provides an abundant satisfaction for all sins.

As we have seen,[91] only the Son of God made man appreciates the full weight of man's sin. Since he alone knows God's infinite goodness, he alone knows how evil our rejection of this goodness is. At the same time Jesus fully identifies himself with the sinner. As one of us, in our place and for our benefit, he wants to love and serve the offended Father as the Father deserves to be loved, and served. **It is, then, the Son's infinite love, manifested in his human love for the sinners and for his Father that is the heart and center of Christ's satisfaction. The most appropriate expression of this satisfying love is Jesus' death. On the one hand, it is in freely dying for us that Jesus identifies himself most radically with us, who must die for our sins; on the other hand, it is in dying that he contradicts most radically our sinful attitudes.** By sinning, we had denied our existence as gift, our dependence on the love of God as Creator and Father. We wanted to possess our being independently from God. In dying, we can see that our attempt to live as a god has failed. We could not make ourselves into what we are not. The falsification of our existence has in fact led to self-destruction. If even in dying we persevere in our resistance to submitting to God, our self-destruction will become irreversible.

Being totally innocent, Jesus did not have to die. Yet he freely accepts dying and commends his life into the hands of God. Thus, he makes the radical gift of himself in the most adverse situation, when everything tempts him to give up hope and love. **In this way,**

---

[91] Cf. pp. 401-402 of this book.

Jesus' death becomes a total renunciation of our claim to exist as a god and a radical confession of trust in God's goodness. The satisfaction of Jesus, then, is not the repellent vengeance of a bloodthirsty God, who demands the death of the innocent for the sins of the guilty. It is rather a restoring of the order of the universe that sinful humankind has violated, by transforming the necessary consequence of sin, physical death, into a gift of infinite love, through which we now may effectively give ourselves back to God.

Finally, another legal distortion of the idea of satisfaction needs to be addressed: Jesus' satisfaction ought not to be reduced to a mere balancing of payments. His giving himself out of infinite love in dying was a perfect satisfaction insofar as it was a perfect sacrifice, the opposite in other words of a *quid pro quo* legal transaction. He placed himself unconditionally, with "no strings attached," into the Father's hands and left the response entirely up to the Father. Jesus could not have become a perfect gift if he had prescribed for the recipient what to do with the gift. In perfect trust, he left the acceptance of the satisfaction and the new life resulting from it up to the initiative of his Father.

The satisfaction of Jesus, however, does not save us without our cooperation. In no way does it make our satisfaction superfluous. On the contrary, it enables all of us to unite ourselves, our life, sufferings, and death, to the one superabundant satisfaction of Christ. Through this union effected by the Holy Spirit, Christians truly participate in the being, love, and activity of Christ, so that when they offer their lives, sufferings, and dying as satisfaction for their own sins and for the sins of the world, Jesus himself perfects their satisfaction; in fact, he himself satisfies through them.

3. The role of the Holy Spirit in redemption

In order to appreciate the role of the Holy Spirit in our redemption, we must briefly recall his role within the Trinity and in the mystery of Christ.

Within the immanent Trinity, Father and Son transcend their personal distinction and give themselves totally to one another and dwell in one another through the Holy Spirit.[92] Because the Holy Spirit is wholly in the Father and wholly in the Son, Father and Son communicate so perfectly that they are one. If the communion of Father and Son takes place in the Holy Spirit, so must the assumption of humankind into that communion be mediated by the same Spirit. We need to consider the different stages of this assumption.

In effecting the incarnation, the Father sent the Holy Spirit so that the Holy Spirit might sanctify the humanity of Jesus by making it into the humanity of the Son.[93] Thus, in the Spirit, the eternal relationship of the Father and the Son has been extended to the man Jesus. Throughout his earthly life, Jesus acted out his vocation and communicated with his Father in the Holy Spirit. The Holy Spirit, as it were, brought the eternal common plan of the Father and Son to the human consciousness of Jesus. He inspired and guided him so that every action and suffering in his life might become the effective realization of the plan of salvation upon which Father and Son had decided in the Holy Spirit from all eternity.[94]

Even though the Holy Spirit dwelt in the earthly Jesus, and acted through him, he had not yet transformed his body. As we have seen above, the psychological and physical life of the earthly

---

[92] In what follows, I am much indebted to H. Mühlen, *Der heilige Geist als Person. In der Trinität, bei der Inkarnation und im Gnadenbund: Ich-Du-Wir* (Münster,[2] 1966). Cf. also, Y. Congar, *I Believe in the Holy Spirit*, Vol. II, *"He Is Lord and Giver of Life"* (New York: Seabury, 1983), pp. 5-64.

[93] In whatever pertains to effective causality, such as the creation of Christ's humanity, the Holy Trinity acts as one. However, whatever will result in different relationships to each Divine Person, is caused (through a quasi-formal causality) by one of the Divine Persons. Thus only the Son becomes incarnate, only the Spirit makes the humanity of Christ the Son's own humanity, and only the Father sends the Son and sends the Holy Spirit through his Son. Cf. K. Rahner, "Some Implications of the Scholastic Concept of Uncreated Grace," *Theol. Invest.*, Vol. I (Baltimore: Helicon, 1961), pp. 319-346.

[94] Cf. H.U. von Balthasar, *Theodramatik, II/2 Die Personen in Christus* (Einsiedeln: Johannes V., 1978), pp. 181-183.

Jesus enabled him to concentrate and endure in himself all suffering, the consequences of all the sins of the human race. As a helpless child, as the victim of typical human sins, hanging on the cross with his heart opened by a lance, Jesus expressed in the most perfect way the compassionate love of God for us, but at the same time hid from us God's glory and splendor.

At the moment of the resurrection, the Holy Spirit transformed Jesus' body into a spiritual body that can no longer suffer and die. His risen body has become fully transparent to his divine glory, so that to see the risen Christ as he really is means to see God face to face; this vision is possible only for those who are fully conformed to the risen Lord by a similar resurrection from the dead.

With his last breath on the cross Jesus returns the Holy Spirit to the Father and pours him out upon humankind (Jn 19:30; 34). What the crucified Jesus has made himself into through his freely accepted death receives eternal actuality in his state of glory. Thus the risen Lord continues forever this twofold act through his glorified humanity: returning in love the Holy Spirit (and himself in the Spirit) to the Father, and becoming the source and sender of the Holy Spirit for all believers (cf. Jn 20:19-23). The Spirit has so thoroughly penetrated and transformed Jesus that St. Paul can state plainly: "The Lord is the Spirit" (2 Cor 3:17) and "the last Adam became a life-giving spirit" (1 Cor 15:45). Through the Spirit the risen Christ transcends the limits of space and time, offers himself to all men and women, dwells and acts within all the believers. Yet the Gospel of John and the Fathers of Alexandria alike emphasize that it is Jesus' risen body, his flesh, that is the source of the life-giving Spirit. While the Spirit of Jesus works even outside the visible boundaries of the Church, nevertheless it is in the preaching, the sacraments, and the community of his Church that the body of the risen Christ takes "form and shape"; his active presence becomes "visible" for the believer in the signs whose efficacy he himself has guaranteed. This is especially true of the Church's Eucharist. In the Eucharist the risen Christ is present as our perfect gift to the Father, intent on including us by the Spirit into his sacrificed and risen Body, so that united to Christ in the Spirit we may become the perfect spiritual sacrifice, a "living sacrifice of praise." **Briefly, the risen body of Christ communicates the Holy Spirit, but the goal of the Spirit's activity is to build up the Body of Christ, which is the Church.** To elucidate in detail the role of the Holy Spirit in building up the Church would not be appropriate here; only the central mystery needs to be formulated. As the Spirit transcends the personal distinction between Father and Son and joins both together, so does he transcend the distinction between himself and our spirits and joins us to the Son and through the Son to the Father. By uniting himself to us, his transcendent power raises us above ourselves, while actualizing rather than suppressing the unique personality of each one of us. By his presence, the risen Christ becomes ours and we become Christ's, so that Christ himself loves the Father and his fellow men and women through us and — through our incorporation into Christ — we become sons and daughters of the Father. The Church is then not only the means of communicating the Holy Spirit, but also the community in which, through the Spirit's presence, Christ himself continues to be incarnate, active, and visible to those who have faith.

To the extent that the risen Christ lives in the Church, and that our bodies, lives, and the visible structures of the Church express and communicate his love, the Church also becomes an effective sign of freedom, where the personalities of the members and, in particular, their potential to love can freely unfold. **In fact, to the extent that the members of a church community live by the love of Christ, they will not shut themselves up in a protective ghetto. They will share in the joys and anxieties of people living around them and will attempt to put into action the love they have received from Christ. Their love and activity will affect not only individuals but also the economic, political and cultural structures of society. In cooperation with other persons of good will, they will attempt to transform society so that, instead of suppressing true freedom, its structures may foster the full growth of the human person.**

Thus, a certain theology of liberation is a necessary part of soteriology. The Spirit, wherever he blows, transforms not only individuals but also human relationships and builds up a community. Again and again, he inspires a transformation of the visible structures of the Church and moves Christians and non-Christians to improve the order of society as well.

However, love and enthusiasm, even if they come from the Holy Spirit, do not substitute for economic and political expertise. The knowledge and application of economic "laws" (subject to moral laws, yet possessing a real autonomy) are indispensable for a flourishing economy and just society. Pointing to the goal of a civilization of love, denouncing personal and systemic injustices, as well as inspiring her members to work for a more just society, is the task of the Church as an institution. But finding the best concrete economic and political means for achieving this goal lies beyond her competence. It belongs to the Church's qualified lay members in cooperation with everyone else who can and are willing to work on such projects. Any Constantinian symbiosis of Church and State, of either the rightist or leftist variety, will inevitably lead — as history has repeatedly shown — to the idolization of the State and the corruption of the Church. Moreover, even a utopian society where the rights of everyone are respected and everyone cooperates for the common good is still **not** the Kingdom. Liberation theologians admit this distinction, but in practice the messianic zeal of bringing about radical social change **in a certain way** blurs for some of them the radical difference between human political action and God's transcendent gift of the Kingdom.[95]

---

[95] Of course the Kingdom of God is already present as seed and as a veiled mystery among us (cf. *Lumen Gentium*, 5). Wherever the Eucharistic Body of Christ is present, wherever people are united to Christ in pure love, whether through explicit or implicit faith, we may speak about a real foretaste and anticipation of the Kingdom. Moreover, as *Gaudium et Spes* pointed out, the values of human dignity, brotherhood and freedom, wherever realized, foreshadow in some way the final reality of the Kingdom (39). Yet, our belief that the Kingdom in its full reality will be an undeserved gift rather than the result of our work, must also influence the way we consider earthly affairs. If we think that our particular economic and political program brings about the Kingdom, we will easily idolize this platform as the only good one and the position of our political opponents as morally evil.

For instance, according to Sobrino, christological reflection in Latin America "seeks to show how the truth of Christ is capable of transforming a sinful world into the Kingdom of God."[96] A statement like this may be easily misunderstood as if the fullness of the Kingdom could result from our human activity.

4. The final goal of our redemption

Revelation does not satisfy our curiosity about the details of the eschatological state. Yet Scripture makes some general statements whose implications we can clarify. Moreover, the eschatological age has already begun with the redemptive work of Christ. Thus, the hidden, anticipated forms of the Kingdom provide us with some insight into its full realization.

The New Testament and the patristic tradition present the goal of redemption in a threefold perspective.

1. According to the Pauline tradition, the goal of God' plan is the *Christus totus,* the whole Christ, head and members, the incarnate Son extending his life into all members of redeemed humanity. We are "to form that perfect man who is Christ come to full stature" (Eph 4:13); God will bring "all things in the heavens and on earth into one under Christ's headship" (Eph 1:10).

2. Yet this centering on the role of Christ serves only to underline the absolute primacy of the Father. We should "attain to the fullness of God himself" (Eph 3:19). In the end, "God will be all in all" (1 Cor 15:28).

3. In a complementary perspective, the goal of creation is the

---

[96] J. Sobrino, *Christology at Crossroads* (New York: Orbis Books, 1978), p. 349. Cf. also L. Boff, *Jesus Christ Liberator. A Critical Christology for Our Time* (New York: Orbis Books, 1979). The first document of the Magisterium on liberation theology was predominantly critical: "Instruction on Certain Aspects of the 'Theology of Liberation,'" by the Congregation for the Doctrine of the Faith, *Origins* 14 (1984), pp. 193-204; the second instruction, however, outlined the principles for building an orthodox theology of liberation: "Instruction on Christian Freedom and Liberation," *Origins* 15 (1986), pp. 713-728. See also John Paul II's vision for the Church's role in modern society: "Sollicitudo Rei Socialis," *Origins* 17 (1988), pp. 641-660.

Woman (virgin, bride, and mother), the image of redeemed humanity, shining with the glory of the Holy Spirit and united to Christ by the same Spirit. These three perspectives complement rather than contradict each other.

In the present age, between the Resurrection and the Parousia, the presence of Christ in the Church, in humankind, and in the universe is a hidden, inchoate presence. It is so hidden that the eschatological manifestation of his presence (2 Th 2:8; 1 Tm 6:14; 2 Tm 4:8) may also be called a return (Ac 1:11). Christ himself is already in the eschatological state; his body is fully transformed by the Holy Spirit. Our bodies, however, are still mortal and sinful. There is, therefore, a "gap," a disproportion between our state and his, so that even if he dwells in us and acts in us, we can perceive him only through faith. Thus, instead of imagining his coming in glory as a kind of space travel, the reversal of what happened at the Ascension, we rather understand it as our transformation. The change will take place in us, not in him. The disproportion between our state and his will disappear, when the Spirit transforms this lowly body of ours into the likeness of his glorified body (Ph 3:21). Then we will become his members in the full sense of the word, the extension of his glorified personal body. As a result, we will then see Christ as he is in his glory, dwelling in him and he in us; and through Christ, with Christ, and in Christ, we will see the Father face to face and will recognize him as our Father.

Thus the final state of redemption does not mean that the Eternal Word will be present in humanity in the form of many individual "temples,"[97] but rather all of redeemed humanity will be transformed into the one Temple of God, the body of the crucified and risen Lord. He will express himself, live and act in all those whose bodies have become the extension of his own glorified body. Paul's statement will then fully apply to each of the redeemed and to the whole glorified Church: "I am living now, yet not I, but rather Christ is living in me" (Gal 2:20). **In the heavenly Church, then,**

---

[97] This would be the logical conclusion of a disincarnate Logos Christology. Cf. S.J. Beggiani, "A Case for Logocentric Theology," *TS* 32 (1971), pp. 371-406.

each of the redeemed and the whole of the redeemed community will receive as its own the filial consciousness of Jesus and share in his activity. We will see the Father face to face as the Son does, love the Father and all the redeemed as the Son loves them, worship the Father with the same dedication and reverence as the Son. We will be given as our own the very heart, mind, and body of Christ. In the words of St. Cyril of Alexandria, all that Christ has and is will be truly offered to us as our gift and we will participate in him to varying degrees, according to the potential we have developed in our earthly life.

The *totus Christus*, the suprapersonal mystical Person living and manifesting himself in the whole Body, should not be understood in a pantheistic way. Just as with the beginning of the Mystical Body here on earth, the full appropriation of Christ in the Parousia will take place in the Holy Spirit. As we have seen, the special characteristic of the Holy Spirit is that **he unites persons as persons** rather than fusing them into some sort of an impersonal amalgam. He does this within the Triune God and also in the Church. As the Spirit unites the Father and the Son in their unique personhood, so does he join every member of the Church and the whole Church to Christ while preserving the personal identity of each.

So far from abolishing the personal distinctions in the *totus Christus*, the Holy Spirit actualizes our unique personalities by transforming us into Christ, the transcendent archetype of every human being. Instead of becoming carbon copies, the more we participate in Christ, the more we become ourselves.

Just as the redeemed individual develops his identity through a loving union with Christ, so the whole Church uniting herself to Christ is not absorbed by him, but rather develops her own communal identity distinct from that of Christ. The mysterious union of Christ and the Church is expressed by the metaphor of the Church as Body of Christ, but this metaphor must be counterbalanced by the metaphor of the **Church as Woman** (virgin, bride, and mother), to show that the union of the Church and Christ is not the result of an impersonal fusion, but springs from the intimacy of personal love.

In the figure of the eschatological Woman, fully realized in Mary, glorified in soul and body, and — to a lesser degree — in the saints in heaven, "the eternal feminine" obtains its full theological significance both in its relational meaning and also in its reference to feminine qualities. The creation of this Woman is the final goal of all of God's works. This final perfection of creation, however, exceeds creation's own capabilities. It is achieved through the Holy Spirit, through whom humankind, uniting to itself the whole cosmos, becomes the beautiful, highly desirable and beloved partner of the Son. More than that, in this Woman the creature is in some sense raised by God's free mercy above God himself, because in Mary, and analogously in the whole Church, the Woman becomes the mother of God, she brings forth the Son of God in the flesh and in the hearts of all redeemed men and women. **The eschatological Woman, then, reveals what is most divine in God, his infinite humility and gratuitous love. Through this love and humility, God elevates creation out of nothing to the status of a worthy partner for himself (as bride) and even above himself (as mother). The Woman remains a creature, but she is endowed by God's grace with such beauty that God himself finds in her his joy and delight.**

This is, then, the final goal of our redemption, expressed in three complementary ways, the glorification of God the Father, the perfection of the Body of Christ which is the Church and the shining beauty of the Church as Woman, the virginal spouse and mother of the Son. The personal Christ will forever remain the one born of the Woman and will unite to himself his Bride in an eternally faithful and admiring love. The one Christ then will love and worship the Father in and with his Body, which is the redeemed human race. **As a result of this worship, the great ambition of the Son is to be fulfilled: God the Father will be all in all of creation.**

Having reflected on their relationship with the Persons of the Holy Trinity, I shall now venture into some speculation about the humanity of the eschatological man and woman. As we have seen, the ideal, even from the perspective of personal growth in this life, is the integrated human being. The male can actualize his full humanity only if he liberates in himself the feminine dimension, and the woman only by actualizing in herself a masculine dimension, while either becomes in the process a more mature man or woman. This seems to be only a prefiguration of what happens in the eschatological transformation. If we are to perfect rather than lose our humanity, as God's revelation assures us, everyone should preserve his or her personal identity as man or woman. Nevertheless, both man and woman will become united with, and transformed, by the risen body of the man Christ. Yet at the same time, both men and women will also embody in themselves the eschatological Woman, the Bride and Mother of Christ. Likewise, regardless of their different genders, they will share in the attitude of the Son, loving and worshipping his Father by "breathing back" the Holy Spirit to him and breathing him forth into all the redeemed. But they will also share in the attitude of the Woman (Mary and the Church) in that they surrender themselves to Christ their Bridegroom in pure love and become nurturing "mothers" for all the redeemed, who cherish the continued growth of divine life in them.[98]

Here an excursus seems warranted on what we may call *eschatological humanism*. By this we mean that only eschatological salvation achieves our perfection as human beings. Our full potential is realized not only through our union with Christ, but through Christ, with every member of redeemed humankind. Separated individuals cannot unfold in themselves all the perfections of human nature. The "idea of humanity" in its full richness, as conceived by God from all eternity and realized gradually in history, can be actualized in each individual only in a limited and one-sided fashion. For instance, it is hardly possible to develop simultaneously such diverse gifts as poetic creativity and mathematical talent, let

---

[98] Cf. L. Bouyer, *The Seat of Wisdom* (Chicago: Regnery, 1965); H.U. von Balthasar, *Theodramatik, II/2 Die Personen in Christus* (Einsiedeln: Johannes V., 1978), pp. 260-330.

alone to combine the self-giving love of a mother with the single-hearted devotion of a virgin. Every individual is only one variation of the potentially limitless ways of being human. Thus the individual will become perfect as a human being only if, in some way, he or she can appropriate all human values. No individual man or woman can do this except by entering into communion with all men and women, past, present, and future who have developed their humanity. Thus, the only one through whom we can reach all men and women of all ages is the one in whom they are alive and who keeps them united: the risen Christ present in them through the Holy Spirit. Through the Spirit of Christ we will participate not only in everyone else's supernatural gifts but also in their human perfections. Of course, such mutual possession of one another's perfections will not lead to the extinction of the unique beauty of each individual. The poet will still be very different from the mathematician, the mother with a large family will still be easily distinguishable from the twelve-year-old St. Agnes, virgin and martyr. Yet by loving the special beauty of the other and by loving it as belonging to the other, each will in some real way share in the perfections of all. Thus will the love uniting all the redeemed in Christ result in the enrichment of each individual by the riches of all. A radical humanism, the full actualization of the human potential, is possible only in the eschatological Christ.

5. The "redemption" of the material world

Revelation does not say much about the shape and role of the material world in the final age.[99]

We find only a few texts that refer to this issue: "What we await are new heavens and a new earth where, according to his

---

[99] Cf. S. Lyonnet, "The Redemption of the Universe," *Contemporary New Testament Studies*, ed. M.R. Ryan (Collegeville: Liturgical Press, 1966), pp. 423-436; P. Teilhard de Chardin, *Hymn of the Universe* (New York: Harper & Row, 1965).

promise, the justice of God will reside" (2 P 3:13; cf. also Is 66:22; Ac 3:21; Rm 8:19ff; and Rv 21:1). The image "new heavens and a new earth" does not designate primarily the material world but symbolizes the Kingdom of God realized in its fullness, to which the new shape of the material universe serves only as a "cosmic background." The New Testament, following the prophetic tradition, cannot envision the final state without a new material creation. We are to rise in a new spiritualized body, which is nonetheless a true body and therefore needs a corresponding material environment: "The former heavens and the former earth had passed away" (Rv 21:1). This statement underlines the difference between the old and new creation. Yet the discontinuity cannot mean a complete destruction of our world and a "creatio ex nihilo," the emergence out of nothing of a new universe. The risen body of Christ guarantees that the material elements of our universe will be assumed into the new world. Christ's risen body transformed from his earthly body is the foundation and the pattern of the new creation to be completed at the end of times.

Beyond this, there is very little evidence in Scripture about the shape and function of the new material world. However, by reflecting on the available data in the light of the whole Christian mystery, we can hope to gain some further insights.

Humankind is the climax of the evolution of the material world: in our spiritual reality we transcend the whole of matter, but through our body we belong to the world of matter as an integral part of it. Our redemption cannot be complete without the redemption of our body, and our body requires a corresponding material environment. But what could "redemption" mean for matter?

As a consequence of human sin, a conflict arose between the human race and nature: instead of developing the full potential of the material world, we abused it for our sinful purposes (Rm 8:19ff). Beginning with the first stone hurled at an innocent victim and continuing to the destruction of Hiroshima and Nagasaki by nuclear bombs and the present destruction of the environment, human beings have regularly harnessed nature's powers to harmful ends. The progress of civilization (that has also accomplished many worthwhile goals) became inextricably linked with the increasing abuse of nature. However, as the material world became a tool for our sins, so did it also become an instrument of punishment for our sins. Ever since the Fall, nature has not simply served us; we have been laboring to subdue nature through constant struggle; and nature has repeatedly threatened our happiness and our very existence.[100]

The Fall has also affected our view of nature as revelation. Instead of serving as a sign through which God shows us his power, wisdom, and glory, the universe has become a trap for us sinners. We became overwhelmed by its power and charm; we worshipped the sun, the moon, the stars, and mother earth, and later, at a more sophisticated stage we endowed nature as a whole with the attributes of divinity. Pantheism and nature worship in various forms seem as widespread today as they were in ancient times.

In the eschatological state, we expect that, just as the Spirit of Christ will transform our mortal bodies into the likeness of Christ's glorified body, so will he change our material world into a "worthy habitat" for risen humankind. We will no longer abuse nature for sinful purposes, nor will it threaten our life and happiness. Peace between the human race and nature, as it existed in Paradise, will be restored. The material world will serve humankind, and through humankind it will be integrated into Christ.

Nor will nature, through its beauty and mystery, impede our vision of the Creator. Instead, it will become fully transparent to the Son through whom it has been created, and the Father, who is its primordial source and final goal. Two analogies will shed some further light on this role of the new cosmos.

The first we take from the union of body and soul in us. Already in our earthly life, the body is the expression of our soul. Yet its substantial unity with the soul does not abolish its material re-

---

[100] Without sin we would still have had earthquakes, droughts and other natural disasters. But their impact on human existence would not have led to tragedy and loss of happiness.

ality; on the contrary, matter reaches its highest form of organization and complexity precisely as the expression of the human spirit.
If the finite human spirit can raise matter to a higher level of being
without suppressing its material nature, how much more will God's
Spirit be able to unite the material world to Christ through humankind in such a manner as to actualize it in its highest possible
perfection?

The sacraments provide an even closer analogy, since they
foreshadow the function of material elements in the eschatological
state. In the sacraments, material elements (water, oil, bread, and
wine) become part of a symbolic act and, as such, they communicate and manifest (to those who have faith) the sanctifying and
worshipping activity of Christ. This happens most radically in the
Eucharist. The bread and wine in the Eucharist become not merely
the carriers of Christ's action (as, for instance, water is in baptism),
but are changed into the Body and Blood of Christ. In this transformation the material world reaches its highest perfection: the
material reality of Eucharistic bread and wine are not annihilated
by the consecration in order to be replaced by the presence of Christ,
but their material reality **is transformed into** the effective sign of
Christ's real personal presence. We must speak about a substantial
transformation of the Eucharistic elements because their whole
material reality is exhausted in becoming effective signs of Christ,
in pointing to Christ, and in communicating him to us as sacrificial
food. For this reason, the Eucharist is indeed the best analogy for
the world to come, because it is its initial realization. The new universe in which Christ will be all in all (Col 3:11: to transpose Paul's
statement from the present situation to eschatology, where it will
be fully realized) may be conceived of — with Teilhard de Chardin — as the cosmic extension of an unveiled Eucharistic presence.
At the present stage of salvation history, "the species" of the consecrated bread and wine point to, but also veil the presence of Christ.
At the end of times, when the whole material universe will be transformed by Christ as an (attenuated) extension of his glorified body,
it will no longer hide from us his glory. We will see his presence

manifested in the whole cosmos, which will radiate him to humankind. In this act of manifesting and communicating Christ, and through Christ God himself, the material world will transcend itself and reach the final perfection God has intended for it from eternity. Then, indeed, not only the heavens but also the earth (not only the world of angels but also the material universe) will be filled with God's glory.

CHAPTER V

The Universal Significance of Christ in the Context of Other Religions

In encountering the unexpected wealth and diversity of non-Christian religions,[101] many Christian theologians feel the urgent need to inquire into the universal significance of Christ: in comparing Christ to the other great religious figures of humankind, can we still claim that Christ is the fullness of God's revelation and mediator of salvation for all?[102]

To answer this question in the affirmative seems to limit God's revelatory activity. At first sight such a universal claim seems to derive from the limited perspective of historic Christianity, rather than from the demands of Christian revelation. The New Testament certainly claims that the fullness of God dwells in Jesus and that he is the savior of all. But should we interpret these statements as doc-

---

[101] In this article we treat only those religions which have developed outside the sphere of influence of the Judeo-Christian tradition; Judaism and Islam are therefore omitted.

[102] A relatively full bibliography on the question can be found in L. Richard, *What are They Saying about Christ and World Religions?* (New York: Paulist Press, 1981). P. Knitter, "Christianity as Religion: True and Absolute? A Roman Catholic Perspective," *Concilium*, 136 (New York: Seabury Press, 1980), pp. 12-21; H. de Lubac, "The Pagan Religions and the Fathers of the Church," *The Church: Paradox and Mystery* (Staten Island, NY: Alba House, 1969), pp. 68-95; D. O'Hanlon, "Hans Urs von Balthasar on Non-Christian Religions and Meditation," *Communio* 5 (1978), pp. 60-68; R. Panikkar, *The Unknown Christ of Hinduism* (New York: Orbis, 1981, revised ed.); *The Trinity and the Religious Experience of Man* (New York: Orbis, 1973); *The Intra-religious Dialogue* (New York: Paulist Press, 1978); K. Rahner, "Christianity and the Non-Christian Religions," *Theol. Invest.*, Vol. V (Baltimore: Helicon, 1966), pp. 115-134; "Anonymous Christians," *Theol. Invest.*, Vol. XVI (Baltimore: Helicon, 1969), pp. 390-398; "Anonymous Christianity and the Missionary Task of the Church," *Theol. Invest.*, Vol. XII (New York: Seabury, 1974), pp. 161-180; "The One Christ and the Universality of Salvation," *Theol. Invest.*, Vol. XVI (New York: Seabury, 1979), pp. 199-224; L. Swidler, ed., *Toward a Universal Theology of Religion* (New York: Orbis, 1987).

trinal language? Some theologians qualify them as "caressing language," the language game of love,[103] which expresses the subjective reaction of the lover to the beauty of his beloved. As long as the lover is in love, his beloved is indeed unique and "the greatest" of all. According to these theologians, we should interpret the New Testament claim in a similar way: Christ is unique and mediator of salvation for Christians: through our religious experience we have found in him the fullness of life and light; for us he is indeed the definitive, full revelation of God. The New Testament, however, does not preclude the possibility that for other people another person or constellation of religious symbols could and perhaps have become God's definitive revelation and salvation.

The question merits a more thorough investigation than I am able to present in these pages. I can only offer some reflections toward constructing an answer consistent with both the self-understanding of the Christian faith and the phenomena of non-Christian religions.

1. What can the history of religions tell us about the significance of Christian revelation?

Even though Jesus Christ and Christianity are historical phenomena, a mere historical investigation comparing them to other great religious figures and religions of humankind cannot provide the decisive criteria on their uniqueness and universal significance.[104]

It can compare the claims, beliefs, moral rules, and institutions of the various religions, identify similar patterns, and pinpoint unique characteristics in one religion or in another. But within its own realm historical research lacks the criteria for a value judgment:

---

[103] This expression was often quoted with both approval and disapproval at the *CTSA* Christology seminar in Washington, D.C., 1984.

[104] Richard's statement: "...the actual final court of appeal for determining what is the best way, the historical realm, has no grounds for exclusivity and absoluteness" (*op. cit.*, p. 73) is misleading. Indeed, historical science is incompetent to judge the absoluteness of a religion. But it is in the realm of history that the Absolute reveals himself, and faith is able to discern his presence in history.

it cannot decide which one, if any, of the many religions claims rightly to be the full, final self-revelation of Absolute Reality. If it could, the human mind would be the judge of God's revelation, which would imply the human being's superiority over God. Only God can give us the light of faith to appreciate God's "values" and thus recognize his own "language," his revelation. Consequently, only in the light of God's grace can we discern who Jesus really is, and whether or not Jesus is the fullness of God's self-expression and universal savior.

Yet historical studies are not irrelevant in this search. They can prepare the answer of faith by situating Christianity in the context of other religions. Thus, on the basis of recent historical studies one can confidently state with a high level of probability that, while conforming to some general patterns found in almost all religions, the basic beliefs of Christianity present unique features in the history of religions. Here I offer only three concrete examples and some reflections on the general dynamics of the history of religions.

1. There have been many myths of dying and rising gods in the history of religions. But there is no parallel to the appearance list of First Corinthians or of the appearance and empty tomb stories of the Gospels. No historical person was claimed by his contemporaries, by his disciples and by one of his enemies to have been raised back to immortal, divine life in such a way that his appearances changed the outlook of the disciples and gave rise to a worldwide missionary movement. Moreover, these same disciples gave their lives for their belief in the resurrection of this crucified, alleged criminal.

2. No other historical human being spoke and acted in such a way that, soon after his death, his own contemporaries proclaimed him to be equal to the one transcendent God.[105]

---

[105] The title "God" was applied to Jesus only in the later writings of the New Testament, around the end of the 1st century and the beginning of the 2nd. But equivalent formulas had been used even before Paul, as we have seen in the fragments of the early kerygma. The divine power and dignity of the risen Lord has been expressed in the liturgical acclamation of the earliest Aramaic-speaking communities (*Marana-tha:* 1 Cor 16:22).

Of course, the first Roman emperors were proclaimed gods after their death and later ones even during their reign. Greek and Roman religion as well as other mythologies have produced the figure of the divine hero, an intermediate being between humans and the higher gods. Also, in a pantheistic context, both in the East and the West, one can routinely call god any human being who in some way actualizes his own divine nature. But three features make the Christian affirmation, "Jesus is God," unparalleled: the historicity of the man Jesus, the cultural context in which the affirmation is made and the combination of Jesus' absolute claim with humble service. All those who called Jesus God for the first time did so on the basis of the strict monotheism of the Old Testament, which stresses the infinite abyss between Creator and creature, the holy God and sinful humanity. The history of Buddhism puts into sharper relief the unique genesis of the Christian belief in the divinity of Jesus. His own contemporaries acclaimed Jesus Lord in a transcendent, divine sense soon after his death. It took several hundred years for the historical figure of Siddharta Gautama to be transformed into some sort of a "divine being," or into a manifestation of the universal Buddha nature, by the adherents of Mahayana Buddhism.[106]

The divine heroes in other religions emphasize their power and majesty. While presented in the Gospels as laying claim to absolute authority, Jesus is at the same time the Servant of all who lives and gives away his life in constant obedience to his Father.

3. Another example of the uniqueness of Christian beliefs is the mystery of the cross. The feeling of a need for expiation surfaces in many different ways in many religions. It is also widely believed or at least instinctively felt that the suffering of the innocent can help the guilty. There are savior figures in a number of religions; expiatory sacrifices abound in different forms, throughout the religious history of humankind. But Christianity alone claims that, out of undeserved freely given love, the one almighty

---

[106] Cf. *The Teachings of the Compassionate Buddha*, ed. with commentary by E.A. Burtt (New York: The New American Library, 1955), pp. 123-127.

God has become man so as to suffer with us where we are most God-forsaken, in the process of dying in order to liberate us from the consequences of our sins.[107]

Clearly, these examples do not prove the truth of Christian beliefs, or that they are the highest form of religious phenomena in history. They merely illustrate that in its basic beliefs Christianity has so far been unparalleled in the religious history of humankind.

The uniqueness of the Christian phenomenon emerges even more clearly if we situate it in the context of the general patterns that prevail in all religions. Again, I can present here only one example.

At the heart of the evolution of religions we find a dramatic struggle to reconcile immanence and transcendence in the idea of god.[108]

As the study of the most primitive peoples in Africa, America, the islands of the Pacific Ocean, India, and China has shown, at the earliest stage of religious history there is an almost universal belief in an almighty, all-good creator god (with or without belief in lesser gods and spirits) who manifests himself primarily in the infinite dimensions of the sky. However, this heavenly god is judged too remote, too good, and too majestic for the needs of man, who often feels unworthy of the personal attention of such a great god. As a result, the heavenly god is not often called upon in prayer and is not the center of sacrificial cult. His transcendence is experienced as aloofness and irrelevance. As history goes on, the heavenly god either "retires," and becomes a *deus otiosus*, "an idle god," who does not fill any religious need, to be eventually replaced by lesser gods; or he is transformed into a more immanent anthropomorphic god: he may change into a storm god, enter into a "hierogamy" with

---

[107] Cf. D. Farkasfalvy and R. Kereszty, *Basics of Catholic Faith* (published for the private use of their students, 1982), pp. 36-37.

[108] I owe this insight to the unpublished lectures of D. Farkasfalvy at the University of Texas in Arlington, 1967.

Mother Earth, and father many lesser gods. These transformed sky-gods and the lesser gods who take the place of the heavenly god, are responsive to human needs. They are immanent, within human reach, manipulable by sacred rites, and guilty of human sins. But they have lost the transcendence of the heavenly god, they are no longer almighty and all good: their power is limited by that of other gods; their goodness, by human faults and crimes.[109]

Against this background, the God of the Old Testament emerges as a very special heavenly god. He is a transcendent, almighty Creator, holy and good. But he does not "retire" and does not yield his place to other gods. Even though his people are constantly tempted to abandon him for the sake of the controllable, "relevant" fertility gods of Canaan, he remains present and active among them. As history continues, Yahweh draws nearer and nearer to his people in spite of their infidelities, until he becomes Emmanuel, "God With Us," in the incarnation. In Christianity, then (and to a lesser extent in Judaism and Islam), God's transcendence appears not as aloofness, remoteness or irrelevance, but as the almighty power of divine love that bridges the chasm between Creator and creature, God and humankind, without confusing their distinct identities.

When the development of a religion reaches the stage of philosophical speculation, the same struggle to reconcile divine immanence and transcendence re-appears on a more abstract level. The thinkers of the Upanishads, and of Mahayana and Zen Buddhism are aware that Absolute Reality or Divine Reality must be so transcendent that it is totally beyond speech, imagination, and comprehension. According to the Upanishads, Brahman is "neither this, nor that," absolutely other than the world. So is the universal Buddha nature of the Mahayana tradition. In Zen Buddhism, the divinity cannot even be designated by a name. Only a deep si-

---

[109] Cf. M. Eliade, *Patterns in Comparative Religion* (New York: Sheed and Ward, 1958), pp. 38-56.

lent bow can express the experience of what concepts and words would only distort and falsify.[110]

But in removing divinity completely from the realm of speech, imagination, and comprehension, one has also removed it from the realm of meaningful reality. Religious people become frustrated: how can one communicate with "sacred nothingness"? Hence, in all these religions we observe a movement which is contrary to the one mentioned above. The ineffable and incomprehensible Brahman flows out of itself into this visible, tangible, finite universe; our universe does not have any reality of its own, but, according to a major trend of Hindu thought, it is the external form of Brahman. The one Brahman is also identified with each and every one of the 33 million gods of the Hindu pantheon and with the avatars of these gods, especially with Krishna and Rama. In Mahayana Buddhism, the universal Buddha nature is potentially identical not only with every human being but with everything in this world.[111]

The Zen Buddhist, when he decides to speak about the unspeakable experience of satori, will describe it as a state of consciousness in which meditators are awakened to their own True Self that is one and the same in all phenomena.[112]

In this identification of the Divine with the whole or with a part of finite reality, both the Divine loses its transcendence and the finite world its own distinct reality and value. Thus the same dilemma emerges on the level of philosophical speculation as was observed in primitive religions: while struggling to reconcile both, religions and religious philosophies lose either the transcendence or the immanence of the Divine.

Against this background of the history of religions the Christian dogma of the incarnation reveals its full force: the Son of God

---

[110] Cf. D.F.K. Steindl-Rast, *A Deep Bow. Gratitude As the Root of a Common Religious Language* (a printed lecture without bibliographical data).

[111] Cf. M. Eliade, *A History of Religious Ideas.* Vol. 2, *From Gautama Buddha to the Triumph of Christianity* (Chicago: University of Chicago Press, 1982), p. 223.

[112] Cf. Z. Shibayama, *Zen Comments on the Mumonkan* (New York: The New American Library, 1974), p. 180.

becomes man not by abolishing the metaphysical distinction between divine and human natures, but by uniting a human nature to himself. While becoming true man he remains true God, and his human reality develops in full perfection precisely through its union with God. Thus Christianity maintains God's divinity and the distinct reality and value of creation — of man in particular — while announcing that at the consummation of history the Son will unite to himself all redeemed humankind and all creation through his humanity (Eph 1:3-14).

I have outlined the above patterns to illustrate how the comparison of Christianity with the history of religions can make the Christian claim of uniqueness intelligible. Although we can prove this claim only from Christian revelation itself, once we accept it in faith, the history of religions discloses for us "a Christology in search,"[113] the yearning of humankind for a totally transcendent and totally immanent God, for which desire Christianity presents God's answer.

2. What does Christian revelation say about its own place among other religions?

The statement that our age is the first in human history to be marked by a "pluralistic attitude of mind that questions the claims to universality and absoluteness of every form of religious belief, not only from outside the religious belief but also from within" reveals an astonishing ignorance of late antiquity's religious history.[114]

---

[113] This is Rahner's term. See "The One Christ and the Universality of Salvation," *op. cit.*, p. 220.

[114] Richard, *op. cit.*, p. 1. How differently from Richard does J. Pelikan evaluate the first centuries of Christian history! He admits "the unprecedented threat" to the Christian claim of finality by today's "heightened sense of world history." Yet he affirms: "... Christian thought has been concerning itself with the dilemma of finality *versus* universality since the first century. Christianity became Catholic by successfully resolving the apparent contradiction between universality and identity. This it did in its faith and in its life, in its structure and in its strategy." *The Finality of Jesus Christ in an Age of Universal History* (Richmond: John Knox Press, 1966), p. 5.

The period in which the New Testament was composed was a time of religious ferment and syncretism: the absolute religious certainties of small city religions were shaken up in the religious potpourri of the Roman world empire. Mythologies and philosophical speculations coming from every part of the Empire met, interbred and formed new amalgams of beliefs, rites, and speculations. The situation in the first and second centuries A.D. seems very similar to ours in this respect, except that then the religious ferment limited itself more or less to the cultures within the Roman Empire, while today it includes the whole world. The New Testament authors, especially the authors of the Pauline epistles, Acts, the Johannine literature, and Hebrews, had to be aware of this dazzling religious pluralism and syncretism; not only because this was part of their general culture but also because their writings display an awareness of popular religions, of Stoic, Platonic and pre-Gnostic influences. When they proclaim Jesus as the final eschatological revealer and the universal Savior through whom God has reconciled the world to himself and in whom the absolute fullness of God has been communicated to us, they do it in a conscious confrontation with the many revealer and savior figures of their own times. What they use is not the "caressing language" of love experience, but that of doctrinal statements that aim at universal validity.

As we have already seen, the Fathers of the first centuries took up the challenge of religious pluralism even more explicitly than the New Testament had and situated Christianity in the context of a universal history of religion. Their task was quite similar to our own today. The Gnostics, the adherents of various philosophies, and the initiates of the mystery religions, all claimed a superior wisdom, which allowed them to despise Christianity as provincial and even barbarous. To claim that the religion of a crucified Jew condemned under a legitimate Roman tribunal was the absolute and universal religion for all humankind seemed as absurd an undertaking for sophisticated intellects at that time as it seems today. Undeterred, the Fathers explained that Christianity is not merely a better or more perfect religion than the others; it cannot even be compared to them, since it is on a different plane: it has been given to us by God, while all other religions are man's efforts to reach God. Yet, since the same Logos who was made flesh in Jesus has been shining for all human beings from the beginning of the human race, we find the reflection of his revelation — even though mixed with errors — in pagan religious philosophies.[115]

Besides the teaching of the Fathers, there is another, even more fundamental way in which the Church has revealed her mind with regard to non-Christian religions. In forming and closing the canon of the Bible, the Church was guided by the conviction that the center of all revelation is Jesus Christ: she accepted those books of Israel in which she recognized some prophecy or foreshadowing of Christ and selected those Christian books in which she recognized an authentic apostolic witness to Christ.[116]

By closing the canon of inspired books definitively, she made it clear that God has revealed himself fully and definitively through his Son and through the prophetic and apostolic witness to his Son. After the Christ event, no new revelation is to follow.[117]

This conviction must not be understood in the sense that God has stopped communicating with humankind. God the Father speaks always and everywhere to all through the Holy Spirit. But he speaks nothing else and nothing more than his Word, who was made flesh in Jesus of Nazareth.[118]

3. How can we accept Christ as the fullness of God's revelation and universal Savior?

So far we have briefly investigated belief in Jesus against the background of the history of religions and outlined the universal claim of Christianity. However, historical or philosophical research

---

[115] See pp. 191-195.

[116] Cf. W.R. Farmer and D. Farkasfalvy, *The Formation of the New Testament Canon* (New York: Paulist Press, 1983).

[117] Cf. "The Dogmatic Constitution on Revelation," I:4: *The Documents of Vatican II*, edited by W.M. Abbott (New York: Guild Press, 1966), p. 113.

[118] Cf. K. Rahner, "The Development of Dogma," in *Theol. Invest.*, Vol. I, pp. 48-49.

alone cannot decide us in favor of this claim. For this last step, we need the light of grace. Only if God's grace transforms our value system and inspires our will, can we come to believe that the Ultimate Reality is unselfish compassionate love; a congeniality with this love will provide us the criterion for evaluating the various religions: we will be searching in them for the historical manifestations of Absolute, Pure Love. While we will find many such manifestations in a number of religions, the Christ event will appear for us in its full splendor and universal significance as the unsurpassable fullness of Absolute Love's self-communication.

However, the fullness of revelation and the salvation of all in and through the one man Jesus Christ must be seen together with the universal saving activity of God throughout history (as is presented by both the Scriptures and the Fathers). While the Son made man is the concrete center and universal archetype to whom all human beings are to be conformed, the Holy Spirit is offered to all in order to lead them to Christ and to chisel out the image of Christ in them. Just as the two Divine Persons are inseparable, so is their mission. It is the Holy Spirit that makes the concrete Christ event, the *mysterium paschale,* universally available to all; not only to those who are exposed to the explicit proclamation of the Gospel, but even to those who have lived before Christ or have not yet encountered him in his Church, the Spirit has revealed the Logos — in varying degrees and in varying ways — but clearly enough to provoke acceptance or rejection. Those who accepted the grace of the Spirit, a grace always obtained by the saving mystery of Christ, were saved by this grace and developed in themselves at least some features of what we may call the pattern of Christ's life and death.

In this universal self-communication of God through the Son in the Holy Spirit that has reached all humankind, the teachings and practices of non-Christian religions have played an important role. Yet these teachings and practices have not only communicated Christ's revelation but also distorted it. I would like to illustrate this double role of non-Christian religions by means of the life and teachings of M. Gandhi. A Christian may be quite surprised to see how much his life displays the pattern of the life and death of Christ and how strikingly his teaching echoes that of Christ. Gandhi served his people with unselfish dedication. He urged love of truth and love of the enemy in his struggle for India's independence. He died convinced that the work of his life was a failure: he could not prevent war between Muslims and Hindus and was killed by a fellow Hindu for betraying the Hindu cause. Gandhi became a "saint" by using the traditions of his own Hindu religion. But it seems that he was inspired by God's grace to develop insights beyond and even against his own religion. For instance, Gandhi opposed a fundamental practice of Hinduism, the religious segregation of the untouchables. Scorn for these pariahs, placed below even the lowest caste of society, was based on the doctrine of *karma* and reincarnation that is at the heart of Hindu religion. Yet Gandhi loved and respected them in a way similar to how Jesus loved the outcasts of his own society.

Thus the fact that Christ's grace works outside the visible boundaries of the Church to produce pagan saints does not contradict but rather confirms the centrality and finality of the Christ-event, source of all truth and grace, made available to all through the universal activity of the Holy Spirit.[119]

---

[119] In his carefully articulated monograph *Toward a Christian Theology of Religious Pluralism* (Maryknoll: Orbis, 1997), J. Dupuis emphasizes so much the positive role of other religions that, instead of evangelization, he proposes only a dialogue of mutual enrichment. He sees only the positive aspect of religious pluralism that "in principle rests on the immensity of a God who is love." However, if — as Dupuis admits (p. 387) — Jesus of Nazareth is "'constitutive' of salvation for the whole of humankind" ought we not to do our utmost to offer an explicit encounter with Christ to all human beings? Dialogue with other religions should indeed enrich also Christianity, but not in the sense of acquiring additional truths from the outside, but rather by discovering ever new dimensions of that fullness which resides in Christ (cf. John Paul II, *Redemptoris Missio*, n. 56). See the "Notification" on Dupuis's book by the Congregation for the Doctrine of the Faith, Rome, January 24, 2001. The same Congregation issued earlier a "Declaration 'Dominus Jesus' On the Unicity and Salvific Universality of Jesus Christ and the Church" (August 6, 2000) which rejects a pluralistic approach to religions. See conflicting reactions to it in *"Dominus Jesus." Anstössige Wahrheit oder anstössige Kirche?*, ed. M.J. Rainer (Münster: Lit Verlag, 2001).

CHAPTER VI

Christ and Possible Other Universes and Extraterrestrial Intelligent Beings

This is not the place to discuss the degree of probability of universes besides our own.[120] Opinions are diverse and constantly shifting; they are partly scientific, partly philosophical in nature, and entirely speculative. Nor can we enter into the debate on the probability of intelligent life in other parts of our universe or in another universe. Only the theological question needs to be confronted here: if there are extraterrestrial intelligent beings, either in our universe or in another, what can Christian revelation say (if anything) regarding their relationship to Christ? It is important for a Christology to explore this issue not only so that we will have something to say to a generation raised on science fiction, but also because such questioning may help us understand more deeply the universal significance of Christ himself. I treat here only in outline form a question that deserves a monograph.[121]

---

[120] By a possible other universe we mean one which is in no causal connection with ours.

[121] See a very informative article on this subject, T.F. O'Meara, "Christian Theology and Extraterrestrial Intelligent Life," *TS* 60 (1999), pp. 3-30. Read also the theological science fiction trilogy of C.S. Lewis, *Out of the Silent Planet, Perelandra, That Hideous Strength* (New York: Macmillan, 1965).

1. Biblical-historical considerations

a. Concerning other universes

According to the Old Testament, God created everything through his word and wisdom. While only man and woman are created in God's image and likeness, the whole creation reflects the beauty and order of God's wisdom. In the New Testament it becomes clear that God's word and wisdom is a Divine Person, the Son, distinct from, but equal, with God the Father. The Father has created everything through the Son, his Word and Wisdom. The Son "holds together" the whole of creation and he is also its final goal. All was created through him and for him (Col 1:16; Jn 1:3,10; Heb 1:3). Later theological reflection (Origen above all) explained that the Son as the uncreated Wisdom and Logos of God has contained in himself from all eternity the divine ideas or the divine "blueprint" according to which everything was created.[122]

Moreover, as we have discussed before, the whole of creation will reach its perfection in the eschatological state, when renewed humankind, and through humankind the whole cosmos, is united to Christ, and Christ leads back all creation to union with God the Father.[123]

b. Concerning intelligent extraterrestrial beings

According to the revelation we have received, the final stage of cosmic and human evolution is Christ come to full stature who unites to himself humankind and through humankind the whole of material creation. Christ's goal, on the other hand, is the manifestation of the Father's glory in all creation and the mediation of

---

[122] See, for instance, Origen, *Commentary on John* XIII, 280-283; XIX, 147; XXXIV, 243-244.

[123] See especially the Christologies of Maximus the Confessor and John of Damascus, pp. 217-219.

the universe's praise and thanksgiving to the Father. Thus the transcendent entelechy (the universal moving force) of history is Christ and its final goal is God the Father. Nevertheless, according to the same revelation humankind is the center of God's loving concern and actions: the Father wants to adopt us as his children. The Son became a human being for our sake, died for our sake and has sent us the Holy Spirit.

In spite of being the special object of God's overabundant mercy, we should not neglect (as most Christians have done in modern times) the important role of the angels in God's plan of salvation. Granted, the Bible presents the angels in the service of human salvation: they are God's agents and messengers for us. They watch with awe and longing the unfolding of the work of human salvation (1 P 1:12). "Surely (God) did not help angels but rather the descendants of Abraham" (Heb 2:16). Yet, the angels appear as higher beings than humans; they form the court and household of God and are "the sons of God."[124] They always see the face of God and praise God night and day (Mt 18:10; Rv *passim*). In the Gospel of Matthew the address, "Father in heaven," does not merely express God's transcendent fatherhood, but also points out the Father's heavenly court of angels. We pray that his will be obeyed on earth as it has already been among the angels of the heavenly court (Mt 6:10). The peacemakers will be called children of God in the sense that they will be counted among the angels (Mt 5:9). The just will be "like the angels in heaven" (Mt 22:30; cf. Mk 12:5; Lk 20:36). Thus, God's Kingdom did not originate here on earth: Jesus came to extend to the earth the Kingdom that has already been realized among the angels.[125]

Patristic theology and the Magisterium follow and unfold this view of Scripture. The Fathers also concentrate on the creation and redemption of humankind, yet their theology is far from being anthropocentric. For instance, the Nicene-Constantinopolitan Creed

---

[124] God created all angels good and even the fallen ones, Satan and his angels, serve against their will God's good purpose.

[125] See D. Farkasfalvy, *Commentary on Matthew* in the making.

further specifies "the heaven and earth" of the Apostles' Creed: God is the creator of all visible and invisible creatures, our universe and that of the angels. According to several ancient theologians, men and women were created to replace the fallen angels. Thus, in their view humankind is not the crown of creation but a replacement for one missing chorus of the angelic world.

The above considerations have, of course, only an indirect relevance to our question. We may conclude, however, that the authors of the Bible and especially the Fathers would have had no difficulty in integrating the existence of intelligent non-human beings into their world view. In fact, the Fathers and even early medieval authors conceived of angelic beings not as pure spirits but as endowed with a refined spiritual body. This patristic conception is not far removed from the way people imagine today the bodies of extraterrestrial intelligent beings.

In the modern age, however, in order to preserve its importance, theology's central task became more and more the justification of human dignity. The doctrine on the angels first was organized by scholastic theologians into a separate treatise dominated by subtle metaphysical distinctions; then, in our lifetime it became the object of "benign neglect" on the part of the "cutting edge" theologians. It is most ironic that philosophy and theology turned anthropocentric exactly at the time when the natural sciences rejected the image of an anthropocentric universe and began to discover the unimaginably vast and complex dimensions of a fast expanding universe.[126]

---

[126] In some sense, of course, theological anthropology should remain central for us: without discovering the fundamental orientation of human nature toward infinite goodness, truth and being, the revelation of the mystery of God will leave us indifferent. Moreover, without belief in the Trinitarian God of gratuitous love the foundations of human dignity are bound to collapse. Some scientists also postulate an "anthropic principle" at work in the evolution of the universe: the cosmic laws seem to favor the development of intelligent life like ours (cf. P. Davies, *The Mind of God. The Scientific Basis for a Rational World* [New York: Simon & Schuster, 1992], pp. 200-222). However, the omission of the angels' role in salvation history leads to the distortion of this history and makes it more difficult for theologians to create space for the role of possible extra-terrestrial intelligent beings in God's universal plan.

2. Systematic considerations

Theology is not competent to judge the probability of "other universes" in a scientific sense.[127]

Yet it can point out that all universes would have a common transcendent cause in God and a common transcendent end in him. Even if these universes lacked intelligent life, the angels and human beings seeing God face to face would know and admire these universes as well in God. In God the Father all these "other universes" would find one common origin and one final end, as well as acknowledgment and appreciation by intelligent creatures. Thus, in a theological sense all possible universes would converge in an ultimate unity, because there is only one God, the alpha and the omega of all created worlds. In God, then, at the point of their eschatological fulfillment, men and women would not face any being that would be completely "alien," or completely different from them. **All universes would find a common home in God, and through God men and women would find their extended home in all the universes.**

However, here we are primarily concerned with the christological question. What would the relationship of an "other universe" be, not to Jesus the man whose earthly life was limited to our planet, but to the eternal Son of God? It seems reasonable to understand Col 1:16, Jn 1:3, and Heb 1:3 in the sense that the Son or Wisdom of God had a universal role in all of creation, rather than just in that part of creation which was known to the author:

> For in him were created all things in heaven and on earth, the visible and the invisible, whether thrones or dominions or principalities or powers; all things were created through him and for him (Col 1:16).

---

[127] The philosopher, however, may point out that it is also beyond the competence of any scientist to prove even the probability of a philosophically "other universe." If the other universe has no causal connection with ours, then, by definition, there is no effect, no trace of it in our universe from which we could conclude to its probable or certain existence. Thus if a scientist could prove the existence of another universe it would not be completely other; it would stand in some causal connection with ours.

The authors of Colossians and of the Prologue of the Fourth Gospel (1:3) both emphasize that **all** was created in the Son, the Wisdom and Word of God; one would need to find a special reason to exclude from this universal statement a possible different universe.

If we now consider the implications of the truth that creation is God's self-expression, we could shed further light on the role of the Son regarding other possible universes. If in creating any universe God can be compared, analogously, to an artist, we must also say that any creation is, in some way, a self-expression of God. **In creation God expresses himself precisely in what is other than God, in the finite, small, and contingent.** But if any creation is, in some way, a self-expression or self-revelation of God, then any creation reveals, to some extent, God as he really is, that is, in his Trinitarian structure. **The uncreated self-expression of God, his Son as uncreated Wisdom, is the divine archetype, model, or (to use a scholastic term) exemplary cause — in varying ways and degrees — for the whole of creation.** From this principle we should not conclude that the hypothetical "other universes" must have intelligent beings endowed with intellect and free will, because there is no compelling reason why God must provide for every universe his highest created self-expression. Even a human artist has a wide range of choices for expressing himself in an artwork.

Nevertheless, if on another planet of our universe or in another universe there are beings endowed with an intelligence and free will, we must assume that in one way or another they have all been created in the image of the Son of God. We make this assertion on the basis of the patristic tradition according to which human beings are images of the Son precisely because they are endowed with intellect and freedom. However, we cannot determine *a priori* just how these beings would be related to the Son. We could conceive of a number of possibilities. At the one end of the spectrum there could be another "incarnation" uniting these creatures to the only Son in such a way that they all become by participation what the Son is in his fullness, similarly to redeemed humankind. This incarnation could exist with or without redemption depending on whether or not these intelligent creatures had sinned. At the other end we could conceive of intelligent beings who did not sin and were not called to that intimate participation in the Son as humankind and the angels. Nevertheless, since they, too, are spiritual beings, they, too, can find fulfillment and happiness only in some form of personal communion with God through his Son. To be a spiritual being means precisely to possess a "capacity for God," a desire to be in communion with the One who is fullness of Being, Truth, Goodness and Beauty.[128]

Thus, we should conclude that any conceivable spiritual being is called to some form of personal communion with God through the Son.[129]

There is no compelling reason to postulate that, if God created other spiritual beings, he had to call them to the same intimate communion with himself as he called the angels and humankind. He remains sovereignly free in his gifts. **Yet, considering the consistency and unity of what we already know about God's plan of salvation, a plan which calls both humankind and all angels who stood their trial into a most perfect participation in God's life through the Son in the Holy Spirit, we may assume with some probability the same supernatural goal for all other possible spiritual beings.**

Regardless of the various possibilities, if all intelligent beings are created by God through the Son and in view of some form of communion with God the Father through the Son, then, **if we should encounter an "alien" from another planet, he would not**

---

[128] A spiritual being knows every particular being against the horizon of Being Itself, and a particular truth only against the horizon of Absolute Truth; he can desire a particular good because that particular good helps him most under the circumstances to come closer to Absolute Goodness. (Even in sin this striving prevails, except that a particular good is consciously and willfully endowed with the status of Absolute Goodness.)

[129] We know that the animal world has various forms and degrees of intelligence. In this context we speak about only that type of intelligence which is combined with free will and thus indicates a spiritual nature. We could also conceive of various forms and degrees of union or link between these spiritual natures and matter. But for our purpose these differences are of no consequence.

actually be totally "alien" for us. Christian faith would encourage us to welcome him as a more or less close "relative" because of our common origin and goal and because of our common resemblance to the one Son.[130]

This last conclusion has perhaps the most important implications for our lives. A Christian shares the curiosity, excitement, and fear of the present generation concerning extraterrestrial beings, but he ought not to be paralyzed by this fear, since in the one Father, the one Son, and the one Holy Spirit he has a true kinship to all intelligent beings.

Finally, we must emphasize again that the existence of other universes or extraterrestrial intelligent beings is theologically possible but not more probable than their non-existence. God the Father expresses his infinite wisdom, goodness, and beauty in his Son and finds complete fulfillment in the intra-Trinitarian communion with his Son in the Holy Spirit. One or two or even an infinite number of created universes (if infinite number of created universes were logically possible) would not add anything to the fullness of his perfection. When God creates, he creates out of love for the creature; his purpose is that the intelligent creature should share in some way or other in his own joy. Even when God the Son makes his creation a desirable partner for himself and finds joy and delight in it, the source of this elevation and desirability is always God's freely bestowed gift of grace. **Thus the last word about this topic must be a word of respect before God's absolute freedom to create one universe, many universes, or none at all.**

---

[130] Even if we encountered intelligent beings who have made themselves definitively incapable of receiving God's love by sin, we should not be intimidated by them: they still remain God's creatures and carry out his plan of salvation even against their will. If, with the grace of Christ, we can overcome the attacks and ruses of Satan, we could also overcome theirs.

Conclusion

We began the **biblical part** of this study with an analysis of the historically most certain facts, namely the ancient kerygma of the death and resurrection of Jesus. This way of proceeding had some significant consequences. Beyond establishing the credibility of Christ's resurrection from both a historical and philosophical perspective, we have been able to understand the Gospels themselves from the very perspective in which they were composed, the perspective of the cross and resurrection of Jesus. It is only his death and resurrection that has clarified the meaning of what Jesus said and did during his earthly life; in particular, it has shed light on the center of his teaching and actions, the Kingdom of God. Jesus has been enthroned through his death and resurrection as King of the universe and Head of his Church. The visible appearances of the risen Christ in our world to fore-ordained witnesses are the sign and guarantee of his permanent, invisible yet active, presence in all who believe in him, lasting until his glorious manifestation at the end of times.

However, the Kingdom of God, present in a hidden way among us, is not simply God's rule through Christ; Christ's lordship is experienced in the Church as a communion of love, which is the fruit of Christ's redemption: if the crucified Jesus is God the Son, then in Jesus God himself carried the burden of our sins and bestowed his own life on us in the Spirit.

In the **historical part** we have seen the unfolding of the above theme. The various soteriological themes that developed from the biblical doctrine of redemption found a unifying center in the notion of perfect and complete exchange between God the Son and sinful humankind. The resulting communion between God and the human race would not have been possible without the hypostatic

452 JESUS CHRIST: FUNDAMENTALS OF CHRISTOLOGY

union. Thus the biblical and patristic notion of redemption presupposes as its necessary ontological condition the truth of the Chalcedonian dogma.

From Protestant Christologies, the existential (not the juridical) aspect of the *"admirabile commercium"* of Luther's Christology, Barth's treatment of the incarnation and redemption as a twofold existential process (God becoming servant and man becoming Lord), and Bonhoeffer's insight that the divinity of Jesus manifests itself in his being the man for others, have all become important building blocks for the systematic Christology I have proposed.

The **systematic part** emphasizes that the Absolute is not a solitary being in need of a partner who alone would make God loving and thereby perfect (which is the supposition of process theology), but the Absolute is Love Itself, the perfect communion of Father and Son in the Holy Spirit. Against this background the creation of the universe appears not as the result of any necessity, but as a free manifestation of divine creativity. God calls into being creatures that did not exist before, beings that are truly new and real, and truly other than God. Yet with the creation of humankind it becomes evident that the goal of creation is not merely the production of a divine artwork, an expression of divine power, wisdom, and beauty. Rather, God has intended from the beginning to unite the universe in humankind and join humankind to himself in a personal communion of divine life and love.

The full dimension of this plan of God becomes manifest only with the Fall of the human race into sin and their redemption through Christ. The "moral structure" of the universe is not a sum of abstract principles concerning rewards and punishments, but on the contrary is identical with its ontological structure. Sin necessarily causes self-alienation, alienation from God and from one's fellow human beings. The Fall of humankind, and the resulting threefold alienation, was the occasion for God to show the ultimate depth of his Trinitarian love. Given over to us by the Father, the Son has freely taken upon himself the full burden of our alienation. He alone could fully experience this burden, the result of our sins: as the holy Son of God, he alone must have fully understood and suffered, beyond the scope of our imagination, the evil of our sins. However, he redeemed us precisely by counterbalancing and overbalancing this evil with his infinite love. By carrying in himself our alienation to its climax on the cross, he has turned it into the most powerful expression of love that atones, praises and worships the Father in our place and for our sake. The love of the Son, reaching its full human expression on the cross, has become the source of our redemption and provides the key to understanding the meaning of the various traditional soteriological themes: by means of this love, Christ offered himself as a perfect sacrifice and a perfect satisfaction for our sins. By this love he has overcome the power of Satan and freed us for a new life in which we are empowered by his Spirit to share in his sacrifice, satisfaction, victory, and freedom.

Precisely by enduring the conditions of this threefold alienation with Christ and in Christ, already here on earth we are given the grace to reverse it gradually: we begin to know and accept ourselves in the truth, enter into communion with the Father, and reach out for communion with all humankind. The more we are conformed to Christ, and the more we are united to each other through Christ, the more we all, male and female, are being formed into that one "Woman," virgin, bride, and mother, who, throughout the tribulations of world history, is being readied for the eternal wedding feast with her Bridegroom, the crucified and risen Son of God. This Woman shining with the glory of the Holy Spirit is united to Christ as his own Body and along with Christ and through Christ loves and praises the Father.

Relationship Between Anthropology and Christology

St. Bernard, A Teacher For Our Age

For our age Bernard's thought is particularly intriguing and relevant: on the one hand, he has thoroughly appropriated and synthesized the theological and spiritual heritage of the Fathers, on the other, he anticipates in himself our modern sensitivity. In full command of the Church's patristic heritage, he stands at the threshold of modernity. Thus he is uniquely qualified to help modern theology and spirituality in its twofold task of recovering the riches of tradition and "translating it" into the language of our age.

Bernard's central concern is personal and spiritual: how can the sinner return to God and be united with him? Although this intensely religious quest dominates his works, it does not restrict his vision of reality nor does it limit the genre of his writings to what we call today devotional literature. The student of his works can hardly avoid the conclusion that Bernard has thought through the ultimate theological foundations and philosophical implications of humankind's return to God. However, he has not written any single work that would systematize all of his doctrine. Moreover, while trying to capture the many aspects and individual nuances of our spiritual journey, up to the very end of his life he keeps changing his paradigms and the description of the different stages of our ascent to God. Nevertheless, behind the shifting images and concepts we can uncover an integral and consistent vision of all reality complete with a metaphysic, anthropology, epistemology and experiential psychology.[131] A fruit of continuous meditation on the Scriptures and the works of the Fathers, a result of interaction with the Platonic heritage and with such contemporary theologians as William of St. Thierry and Hugh of St. Victor, this unified vision appears already in the *De Gradibus Humilitatis*, and, with some minor changes, remains constant throughout Bernard's career.[132]

Bernard's two overriding interests are God and his own personal self; but it is in Christ that he finds the key to understand both God and himself in the wider horizon of God's relationship to all humankind. Christology, then, in its twofold relationship to anthropology and theology, is the focal point of the Bernardine

---

[131] I quote the works of Bernard according to the accepted abbreviations of the critical edition and use my own translation except for the epistles. The Roman number refers to the volume, the Arab number to the pages of the critical edition: *Sancti Bernardi Opera* Vol. I-VIII. Ed. J. Leclercq, C.H. Talbot and H.M. Rochais (Rome: Editiones Cistercienses, 1957-1977). Here follow the Latin titles of the works used in this article: Adv: *Sermones in Adventu Domini*; Ann: *Sermones in Annuntiatione*; Asc: *Sermones in Ascensione Domini*; Asspt: *Sermones in Assumptione*; Circ: *Sermones in Circumcisione Domini*; Conv: *Sermo de conversione ad clericos*; Csi: *De consideratione*; Ded: *Sermones in dedicatione Ecclesiae*; Dil: *De diligendo Deo*; Div: *Sermones de diversis*; Ep: *Epistola*; Epi: *Sermones in Epiphania Domini*; Gra: *De gratia et libero arbitrio*; Hum: *De gradibus humilitatis*; Mil: *Ad milites Templi*; Miss:*Homiliae super Missus est*; Nat: *Sermones in Nativitate Domini*; Nat V:*Sermo in Nativitate B. Mariae Virginis*; OS: *Sermones in festo Omnium Sanctorum*; Pasc: *Sermones in die sancta Paschae*; Pent: *Sermones in festo Pentecostes*; Pur: *Sermones in festo Purificationis B. Mariae Virginis*; SC:*Sermones super Cantica Cantocorum*; Sent: *Sententiae*; IV HM: *Sermo in feria quarta Hebdomadae Sanctae*; XC: *Sermones in Ps. 90 "Qui habitat."* Some valuable older English translations of Bernard's works include: *On the Love of God*, transl. T.L. Connolly (New York: Spiritual Books Associates, 1937); *Of Conversion*, transl. W. Williams (London: Burns Oates & Washbourne, 1938); *The Steps of Humility*, transl. G.B. Burch (Notre Dame: Univ. of Notre Dame, 1963). More recently, Cistercians Studies Publications (W.M.U. Station, Kalamazoo, Michigan) has undertaken the publication of the most important works of Bernard in English. See especially *CF 1, 13,19 Treatises I, II, III*; *CF 1A Apologia*; *CF 4, 7, 31, 40 On the Song of Songs*; *CF 13A Steps of Humility and Pride*; *CF13B On Loving God*; *CF 19A On Grace and Free Choice*; *CF 19B In Praise of the New Knighthood*; *CF 25 Sermons on Conversion*; *CF 37 Five Books on Consideration*; *CF 53 Sermons for the Summer Season*. The excellent translation of his letters is out of print: *The Letters of St. Bernard of Clairvaux*, transl. B.S. James (Chicago: Regnery, 1953).

[132] Other aspects and paradigms of spiritual ascent are presented in *De conversione ad clericos, De Diligendo Deo, De Libero Arbitrio*, in the *Sermones Super Cantica*, and in his last major work, *De consideratione*. The results we obtain from studying these major works need to be complemented by the investigation of his sermons, whose genre ranges from highly elaborate literary masterpieces through mere outlines to actual sermons that have preserved the informal style of oral delivery to a living audience.

synthesis. On the one hand, the historical stages of Christ's redemptive work are structured according to the needs of fallen humanity; on the other, Christ gradually reveals and communicates God to the human race through the stages of redemption. We will, then, study Bernard's Christology in this twofold relationship to humankind and to God in order to better understand its significance for our contemporary theological and spiritual concerns.[133]

I. The Universality of Salvation and the Structure of Salvation History

With the Augustinian tradition St. Bernard stresses the consequences of our relationship to Adam: through generation we all share in Adam's sin, which we also imitate by our personal sins, and thus all experience concupiscence in our flesh and deserve to die. Nevertheless, our relationship to Christ transcends in importance our relationship to Adam: our election in Christ has taken

---

[133] While the Christology and anthropology of Bernard have been extensively studied, I know of no work which would have focused on their mutual correspondence. Some of the major studies on Bernard's Christology: C. Bodard, *"Christus-Spiritus*, Incarnation et Résurrection dans la théologie de saint Bernard," *Sint Bernardus van Clairvaux, Gedenkboek* (Achel, 1953), pp. 89-104; J.M. Déchanet, "La christologie de saint Bernard," *Saint Bernard Théologien. Actes du Congrès du Dijon 15-19 Sept. 1953: Anal. S.O.Cist.* 9 (1953), pp. 78-91; A. van den Bosch, "Christologie bernardine," *Cîteaux* 9 (1958), pp. 5-17; "Présupposés à la christologie bernardine," *Ibid.*, pp. 85-105; "Le mystère de l'Incarnation chez saint Bernard," *Ibid.*, 10 (1959), pp. 85-92; 165-177; 245-267. "Dieu rendu acessible dans le Christ d'après saint Bernard," *Coll. Ord. Cist. Ref.* 21 (1959), pp. 185-205; "Dieu devenu connaissable dans le Christ d'après saint Bernard," *Ibid.*, 22 (1960), pp. 11-20; "Le Christ Dieu devenu imitable d'après saint Bernard," *Ibid.*, pp. 341-355; "Le Christ, Dieu devenu aimable d'après saint Bernard," *Ibid.*, 23 (1961), pp. 42-57; "Christ and the Christian Faith according to Saint Bernard," *Cîteaux* 12 (1961), pp. 105-119; R. Kereszty, "Die Weisheit in der mystischen Erfahrung beim hl. Bernhard von Clairvaux," *Cîteaux* (1963), pp. 6-24; 105-134; 185-201. A. Altermatt, *"Christus pro nobis.* Die Christologie Bernhards von Clairvaux in den *Sermones per annum,"Anal. Cist.* 33 (1977), pp. 3-176. For Bernard's anthropology, see W. Hiss, *Die Anthropologie Bernhards von Clairvaux*, (Berlin, 1964). It would, however, be unfair to omit the fact that in the above mentioned works the mutual relationship of Christology and anthropology in Bernard's thought is affirmed and sometimes emphasized. Cf. A. Altermatt, *"Christus pro nobis",* p. 155.

place before the Fall in God's eternity; our birth from God over-comes the consequences of our fleshly descendance from Adam (Mil 23-25: III, 232-234).

While no one may be sure of his or her own election and sal-vation, the Father's mercy embraces all humankind. He does not want the death of the sinner but his conversion and life. When the Father shows his mercy he derives his cause and origin from his own nature; when he judges and condemns us, "in some way we force him to do so" (5 Nat 3: IV, 268. Cf. also Ep 77, 1.11: VII: 185.193). Christ, responding to the mercy of his Father, and me-diating this mercy, has redeemed all human beings through his death.[134] His blood freed also those who died before his coming.[135] Thus, not only baptized Christians but also the Jews and even the pagans had a chance to be saved through faith (Ep 190 18: VIII, 33). For the Jews this faith certainly meant a faith in the coming redeemer even though they may have had only a vague notion of him (Ep 77: 14: VII, 195). Lazarus in the Lukan parable symbol-izes all the elect before the coming of Christ, and Lazarus is saved by his faith in the coming redeemer (Ep 190:18: VIII, 33). More-over, Letter 77 defines faith in general as faith in God's promise to send a redeemer (Ep 77 15:VII, 196). Therefore, Bernard prob-ably holds that also the pagans are saved by some implicit faith in a redeemer:

> We believe that whoever were found believers among the na-tions, the adults were reconciled to God by faith and sacrifices while their children were helped only by the faith of the par-ents which, however, sufficed for them (Ep 77:4: VII, 187).

As shown above, in Bernard's vision **Salvation History is uni-versal and God's mercy extends to all humankind in all stages of**

---

[134] See, for instance, 28 SC 2: I, 193; 41 SC 6: II, 32; 1 Pur 2:IV, 335, 3 Sent 35: VIB 87, etc.

[135] But with the Fathers, St. Bernard holds that those just men who died before the death of Christ were held in the netherworld until Christ descended there to liberate them (cf. Adv 3:VIA, 11; 4 OS 1: V, 354-355).

this history. He cannot conceive of a God who would save only a few people before the coming of his Son. At the same time, however, Bernard maintains the privileged character of the time of the Savior's coming: this time alone is the time of grace. Those who preceded the Savior received a blessing but its fullness was reserved for those who came after him (Ep 190, 18: VIII, 33). Bernard opposes the view according to which all the just of the Old Testament who were to be saved knew about "the time, manner and order of redemption" (Ep 77:14: VII, 195). The knowledge of the mystery of salvation grew in the holy fathers as the time of the Savior's coming drew nearer. Yet even John the Baptist, greater than all the prophets, the friend of the bridegroom, still harbored doubts about the identity of the one who was to come (*Ibid.*, 13:194).

The coming of Christ fulfilled the desire of all the just of the Old Testament. He was the kiss (the pressing together of the two lips, God and man into one) for whom all the just were longing (2 SC 3: I, 10).[136] When Christ began to teach, God opened his own mouth, the same God who used to open the mouths of the prophets in the Old Covenant (1 OS 7: V, 331). Through his blood, Christ redeemed all who were before him, and who came after him.

Bernard, then, concentrates on this privileged period of salvation history, the mystery of the incarnation, death and resurrection of the God-man, and shows how every phase of this one mystery serves the needs of the fallen human race. Thus, in order to understand the mystery of Christ we need first to get acquainted with these needs.

II. The Misery of Fallen Man: The Threefold Alienation

Human beings have been created *sui iuris*, that is, with the ability to possess themselves or determine themselves in freedom (Gra 36: III, 191). The ability of self-determination is the image

---

[136] Cf. the Vulgate text of the Song of Songs 1:1, "May he kiss me with the kiss of his mouth."

of God in us, for God himself is absolute self-possession and self-determination. As the imprint in our soul of God's eternal being, this image is indestructible, and remains even in the state of sin, including eternal damnation (Gra 28; 31: III, 185-186; 187-188). In the first sin, which has determined the human condition and which every individual sin personally appropriates, man and woman attempted to become gods on their own by determining through their own will what is right and wrong; thereby they usurped what belongs to the Word and Wisdom of God who alone determines by his peaceful will (*placida voluntate*) the order of the universe including the order of morality (Gra 33: III, 189; 3 Sent 94: VIB, 150).

The misery that has resulted from sin is not an arbitrary punishment inflicted upon the creature by a vengeful God, but is, rather, derived from the sinner's willful distortion of his own nature. We attempted to transcend ourselves by trying to acquire the wisdom of the Son through our own power. As a result, we fell below ourselves; we became flesh, that is, we are no longer capable of possessing ourselves in the truth, and even less capable of giving ourselves over to God and to our fellow human beings in love. The sinner's moral conscience (his *ratio* insofar it represents the Word and Wisdom of God) condemns his false self-consciousness. Therefore, he does not want to face himself, runs away from self-knowledge and loses himself in sensing, knowing and craving the manifold material things of this world. If we had freely subjected ourselves to the order of God's Wisdom, we would have shared in God's Wisdom by God's gift. Since we wanted to become our own wisdom, we became a foolish beast. Instead of becoming like God, our senses and instincts dominate and enslave us, and our bodies drag us down. Thus the sinner who has opposed God finds himself necessarily in a multiple conflict with himself. He who does not want to be ruled by God cannot rule his own body but is rather tyrannized by it. Moreover, the soul who loses God's life loses her ability to give life to her own body: spiritual death will necessarily result in physical death. So the unity between the soul and body of the sinner has been broken, and has resulted in conflict and ulti-mate separation.

Not only did the harmony and unity of body and soul become shattered, but the very identity of the soul with herself was com-promised by sin. The original simplicity, immortality and freedom of the soul could not be eliminated but it was covered up and dis-torted by opposite qualities. Her simplicity became obscured and contradicted by the many rationalizations through which reason tried to cover up the truth and escape from the inescapable judg-ment of her own conscience. Since she cut herself off from God's life, her immortality turned into a living death; her existence has become an unending process of dying, a *mors immortalis*. Her free will, the image of the Word in the soul, remains even in the state of sin insofar as her will clings voluntarily to what is evil. Yet she cannot will now what is truly good, because she has made herself her own prisoner: the will has freely imposed necessity on herself.[137]

In this state the sinner cannot know God because he ignores himself, the self-distorted but real image of God. Unable to face up to the truth of his situation, he rationalizes his sin by imagining a god who is either without holiness or without mercy (1 OS 13: V, 339; 38 SC 2: II, 15).[138] Thus, instead of knowing the true God whose very nature is love and mercy, the sinner fabricates an idol for himself.

The sinner is alienated not only from himself and God but also from his neighbor. Blind to his own sins, he acts as the Phari-see in condemning the tax collector because he believes himself to be better than everybody else (Hum 17: III, 29). Whatever knowl-edge he has he abuses it to inflate his own ego. He cannot love

---

[137] Hum 28-30: III, 38-40; Gra 39-40: III, 194-195; Dil 36: III, 150; Mil 19: III, 230; 4 Asc 3-5: V, 140-142; 1 Adv 3-4: IV, 163-164; 3 Sent 94: VIB, 150; 81 SC 7-10: 288-291; 82 SC 1-7: II, 292-297.

[138] Cf. D. Farkasfalvy, "La conoscenza di Dio nel pensiero di San Bernardo," *Studi su San Bernardo di Chiaravalle nell'ottavo centenario della canonizzazione. Convegno internazionale Certosa di Firenze (6-9 Nov. 1974)* (Rome, 1975), p. 208.

anything but his own flesh, only what satisfies the needs of his body, flatters his vanity, increases his possessions and makes him appear greater in his own eyes (Dil 23: III, 138-139).

If we died in this state, the threefold alienation would become irreversible and eternal. Yet precisely this extreme danger of ours prompted the Son of God to become man and rescue us from this state of living death.

III. The Descent of God and the First Phase of Man's Redemption

We can summarize the whole of salvation history by paraphrasing the words of Bernard: In creation God gave ourselves to us, in the work of redemption he gave us himself, and, by giving himself, he restored us to our real selves; in other words, he reversed our threefold alienation (Dil 15: III, 132).[139] This total gift of God to us in Christ (and giving us in Christ the whole of creation) calls forth a reciprocal gift of our whole selves to God.

The Word's gift of himself takes place in history, and in various stages. Every stage of the Word's history effects in some way our salvation, and our spiritual development results in a gradual conformation to the incarnate, crucified and glorified Word. Bernard makes his own the Origenian principle: what happened once in salvation history unfolds its effects everyday in individual souls. "The whole (mystery of the Son) is given to me, the whole is used up for my benefit" exclaims Bernard (3 Circ 4: IV, 284). Elsewhere he points out the saving function of every stage in Jesus' history by putting these words into his mouth:

> I give you not only my conception but also my life; and I give you all this step by step through the stages of being a baby, a child, an adolescent and a young man; I add to it also my death, resurrection, ascension, and the sending of the Holy

---

[139] "In primo opere me mihi dedit, in secundo se; et ubi se dedit, me mihi reddidit."

Spirit. This will happen so that my conception may cleanse your conception, my life may instruct your life, my death may destroy your death, my resurrection may precede your resurrection, my ascension may prepare your ascension, and the Spirit may strengthen your weakness (2 Pent 5: V, 168).

There are two phases in the Word's history: The first is his descent, his self-emptying, which begins with the incarnation and is consummated in Christ's death on the cross. The second phase is his ascent, which begins with the resurrection and is completed with the ascension and Pentecost. Characteristically Bernardine in the description of the first phase is the close link between incarnation and the cross: he can hardly speak about the mystery of the Son's birth without linking his birth to his death on the cross.[140] The birth marks the beginning of the Word's self-humiliation and self-emptying, the death its consummation. In the second phase the mystery of the ascension dominates Bernard's attention because Christ's ascension to God causes the crucial transition in spiritual life, the transfer of the gravitational center of our affections from the realm of the flesh to that of the spirit.

From Bernard's perspective the saving power of the incarnation is particularly important in what it does to the sinner's distorted relationship to himself, to his neighbor and to God. This threefold relationship constitutes a whole, both their distortion and healing takes place as a whole, but for the sake of clarity we need to analyze the three aspects both individually and in their interdependence.

As we have seen, man and woman have committed the first sin (from which every personal sin derives and which it imitates) in order to share in the knowledge of the Son. Created in the image of God the Son, they envied the Son's status and tried to become God by snatching away the type of knowledge and, in ultimate analysis, the level of being which did not belong to them but to God alone. God did not fault the innate human drive for greatness, eternity and for sharing in God's life and glory (4 Asc 3: V,

---

[140] Cf. for instance, 1 Nat 8: IV, 251; 2 Nat 5: IV, 255; 3 Nat 4: IV, 261.

139-140). However, he opposed the way by which man and woman attempted to assure this greatness for themselves, the boasting in their own power (4 Asc 6: V, 142-143). In the incarnation the Son offered a saving alternative to our false way of striving for divine status. He presented himself to humankind in such a form that would bring salvation to all those who try to imitate him. By becoming a human being the Son became small and lowly, and thereby he showed how mistaken we were when we tried to imitate God by the way of pride (1 Adv 4: IV, 164). The incarnation has revealed God's humility. The Word himself became the Word who cannot speak, the *"verbum infans,"* poor, lowly and obedient to Mary and Joseph (1 Nat V 1: IV, 198; 3 Nat 2: IV, 259). Encountering God as this little child, we who had aspired to greatness are called to convert and become like this little child, small, lowly and obedient.[141] Thus through the incarnation the way toward a true self-understanding and true greatness is opened up for sinful man. Precisely because we aspire to be like God, we should imitate God in his humility.

God's humility goes beyond just becoming a small helpless child. It also includes God's free acceptance of the misery that we deserved for our sins. The Son has immersed himself into the universal misery of all humankind (IV Hebd S. 10: V, 63): He has taken upon himself not only a human shape but also the shape of a sinner; when circumcised, he was branded with the mark of an evildoer (3 Circ 3: IV, 283). He has taken upon himself not only the shape of a servant but also that of an evil servant who deserves to be flogged. In fact the one who is completely innocent made himself into sin (SC 25: 9: I, 168; SC 71:11: II 22; IV Hebd S. 10: V, 61).[142] This "making himself into sin" means for Bernard that the

---

[141] From the many texts which apply the *parvulus iste* of Mt 18:4 to Christ, see 1 Miss 5: IV, 17; 3 Miss 14: IV, 45; 4 Nat V 9: IV, 226; 2 Quad 1: IV, 359; P 1 1: VIA, 28. See more on this topic in D. Farkasfalvy, "The First Step in Spiritual Life: Conversion," *Analecta Cisterciensia* 46 (1990), pp. 65-84.

[142] Note that Bernard's version of 2 Cor 5:21 is different from that of the Vulgate: It is not God the Father who made Christ sin, but Christ "made himself sin" (*seipsum fecit peccatum*).

Son of God has freely taken upon himself the necessary consequences of our sins, which consisted in undergoing physical death and enduring the suffering that our sins inflicted upon him. Even though the Son of God in his divine state had compassion for us without experiencing our wretchedness, he wanted to become wretched so that he might also experience it in himself. This experience was not necessary for himself but for us who needed to be convinced of his mercy (Hum 12: III 25). If, then, the Son of God has freely taken into himself our misery, how much more should we face up to our own misery and sinfulness, and accept them rather than try to escape from them by dissipating ourselves in finding pleasures through sense experience (Hum 13.28: III, 26.38)!

Moreover, as the Son of God made our misery his own out of love in order to learn compassion for us we should also learn compassion for our neighbors. We suffer misery as a punishment for our sins. For us, then, the way to compassion for our neighbors is to feel their misery through our own and to find their mind in our own mind. In this way we identify with them to the point that we feel what is good or bad for them as if it were good or bad for us (Hum 6: III, 20-21). This compassion is the beginning of love for our neighbor and opposed to the attitude of the Pharisee who rejoices because he believes himself to be superior to his neighbor.

The incarnation leads not only to restore the right relationship to ourselves and to our neighbor, it also begins to restore our relationship to God. By learning to know ourselves in the truth we learn to know the Truth in ourselves, the Truth who is Christ. Since we have been created in the image of the Image of God, the Word, we cannot know ourselves in the truth unless we compare our wretched state to what we ought to have remained, the image of the Son. Then, by developing compassion for our fellowmen and women who share in the same dignity of being created in the image of the Son and suffer the same misery and have the same need of forgiveness and healing as we do, we begin to discover the Truth who is Christ not only in ourselves but also in our neighbors; this is already the beginning of knowing God (Hum 14-18: III, 26-30). The final step will be to know the Truth not only in ourselves and in our neighbor but *in sui natura*, in his own nature (Hum 6: III, 20-21).[143] This final step is only anticipated here on earth for short moments of ecstasy and reserved in its fullness for the eschatological state.

The above mentioned process moves from the sinner's flight from himself to self-knowledge in the truth and to the knowledge of, and acceptance of one's neighbor by means of contemplating, participating and imitating the humble Son of God made man. However, St. Bernard also develops another aspect of the restoration of our relationship to God: in *De diligendo Deo* and in various sermons the starting point is the fleshly love of the sinner who can love only himself and anyone else only because of himself, while the end point of the process is the spiritual love of those who love God for God's sake and themselves only for the sake of God. In the transformation of this love the Word made flesh plays a crucial role. God wants to save all human beings but he does not want to save them against their will. As long as we can experience only the threat of God and fear his punishment, we do not really know God in his own nature, which is love and mercy; nor can we be saved by fear alone. Fear is the beginning of salvation, not salvation itself. Terror and force can move animals but cannot convert a human being:

> Intending to regain his noble creature God said: "If I force him against his will, I will not have a human being but an ass who did not come freely or gladly so that he might say: 'I will offer a voluntary sacrifice to you.' Should I give my Kingdom to asses?" (Div 29: VI/1, 211)

> So God tried another "experiment": He attempted to stir up humanity's desire for eternal life. But not even this appeal to our coveteous nature moved our heart. Aware that love exerts the most powerful attraction for a human being, God then used a last approach. He began to attract, educate and transform our capacity to love.

---

[143] Since for Bernard "Truth" is the very person of Christ, I translated *in sui natura* by "in his nature" rather than "in its nature."

Seeing that all human beings became entirely entangled in the flesh, God revealed to them such a great sweetness in the flesh that they had to have a completely hardened heart if they did not love him with all their hearts. [...] So he came in the flesh and made himself so lovable that he gave us a love the greater of which no one has, namely, he gave his life for us. Whoever then refuses to convert will he not rightly hear: "What else should I have done to you and did not do it?" In fact nowhere else does God commend us his love so effectively as in the mystery of his incarnation and passion (Div 29, 2.3: VI/1, 211; 212).

God's power, strength and wisdom were all covered up in the incarnation and passion, but "his goodness could not have been more abundantly revealed, more profusely expressed and more clearly presented to us" (*Ibid.*, p. 212; cf. 1 Epi 2: IV, 293; 1 Nat 2: IV, 245). Already for beginners the contemplation of the birth, life and suffering of the Man God (*Homo Deus*) is such an overwhelming sweetness that it draws them to focus all their love on him, and thus, in loving Jesus in the flesh, they already love God himself in the flesh. If beginners persevere in this contemplation, they will gradually see and savor in Christ's human love the divine love of God the Father himself. Already the infant Jesus shows us the heart of the Father: "such is the heart of God the Father for us as it has been disclosed by the one who came from the Father's heart" (2 Epi 4: IV, 304; cf. also 2 Pent 3: V, 167). Nevertheless, it is on the cross that through the wounds of Christ the ultimate depth of God's love is shown to those who are able to perceive it. Bernard's approach to the heart of Jesus differs somewhat from the modern devotion to the Sacred Heart. For him the pierced heart reveals ultimately not the human love of Jesus, but the "bowels of God's mercy":

The secret of his heart lies open through the holes of his body; that great mystery of love lies open, there lie open the bowels of God's mercy in which the Rising Sun from on high has visited us (61 SC 4: II, 150-151).

In other texts Bernard explains also the Trinitarian dimension of God's love: "*Cor Sponsi cor Patris sui*" (SC 62: II, 158, 158)[144]: the heart of the Church's bridegroom opens up for us the heart of his Father.

Once we begin to appreciate the love of the crucified Christ, we want to be crucified with him, which, according to Bernard, would draw us to a Cistercian monastery.[145] The sweetness that comes from contemplating the passion of the Son of God in the flesh makes it possible for the monk to remain on the cross and be conformed to the suffering of Christ until the very end of his life.[146]

IV. The Mystery of Redemption: Liberation, Satisfaction, Sacrifice, Buying Man Back at a Precious Price

However, if the passion and death of Christ were nothing more than the mere revelation of God's love for us, we could not be conformed to his suffering, and consequently, we could not be saved. Although Bernard treats with preference the passion and death of Christ as the ultimate expression of God's love for us, he is fully aware that our redemption consisted in more than a mere revelation of God's love. Christ's love for us results from his love for the Father for whom he has intended to save humankind (1 Adv 4: IV, 164) and whom he has reconciled to us by the outpouring of his blood. His blood has become a most pleasing sacrifice to the Father; it has satisfied for our sins and thereby obtained for us forgiveness from the Father and liberated us from the power of the devil. This redemptive work of the Son made man, described interchangeably as liberation, satisfaction, sacrifice, or "buying back" (the original meaning of *redemptio*), insofar as it constitutes an impenetrable mystery is called by Bernard *sacramentum redemptionis*.

---

[144] Cf also "Profecto enim tale est cor Dei Patris erga nos, quale nobis expressit qui de corde eius processit" (2 Epi 4: IV, 304).

[145] 21 SC 2: I, 123; 3 Sent 1: VIB, 59-60; 3 Sent 119: VIB 216.

[146] 1 And 3: V, 428-429; 1 Pasc 8: V, 83-84.

Bernard always presupposes its truth but does not speak about it at length in his major works. However, when he feels that this *sacramentum* is belittled or denied, he comes out in full strength to defend it. We see Bernard's passionate defense of the traditional doctrine of redemption in the letter he addressed to Innocent II against the errors of Abelard (Ep 190).[147]

Abelard's critique of redemption, which Bernard quotes in his letter to Innocent II, sounds surprisingly contemporary:

> To whom does it not appear cruel and wicked that anyone should require the blood of an innocent person as some kind of a price, or that anyone in any way should be pleased by the murder of an innocent person? How, then, could God find the death of his Son so acceptable as to be reconciled by it with the whole world? (Ep 190, 22: VIII, 36)[148]

In his reply Bernard explains that God did not thirst for the blood of his Son but for our salvation, which was in the blood; nor did he require the blood of his Son but accepted it when it was offered to him. In Bernard's theology, Christ's will to satisfy for our sins comes from the Son's initiative rather than as an act of obedience by the Son to the Father. The sin of humankind has led, necessarily, according to the order of reality, to both physical and spiritual death. The Son, out of love for his Father and for us sinners, decided to

---

[147] See especially Ep 190, 24-25: VIII, 37. It is a well-known fact that not only Abelard but also Anselm rejected the patristic notion of redemption from the devil's rightful dominion through the death of Christ. According to the patristic theory, we have been justly held under the devil's power since we had freely subjected ourselves to his dominion. Thus it was appropriate for God to free us from the devil's power in a just way, i.e. by the death of the innocent Jesus whom the devil unjustly tried to subjugate by putting him to death. Anselm replaces this interpretation with his theory of satisfaction. Bernard, however, retains the essentials of both the traditional theory and that of Anselm, but re-thinks both of them, as it most clearly appears in his controversy with Abelard. He explains the underlying truth in the patristic speculation about the alleged "rights of the devil over sinful humankind": the devil's dominion over the sinner is just but not his will by which he wickedly acquired dominion over him. Ultimately, the justice belongs to God who allowed sin to result in its necessary consequence, the sinner's subjection under the devil (Ep 190, 14: VIII, 29).

[148] Bernard quotes Abelard's *Commentary on Romans II*, ed. Buytaert, vol. I, pp. 117-118.

become man and die in the sinner's place and for the sinner's sake. Being innocent, he died freely and undeservedly. Being the Son of God made man, he has united himself to all of humankind as head to his members, and so he could satisfy for all of us an could free us all from both physical and spiritual death.[149] Thus, in the Son's mission the requirements of both justice and mercy were fulfilled (1 Ann 9-14: IV, 22-29; 3 Sent 23: VIB, 81-82).

St. Bernard also speaks at times about the redemptive work of Christ as sacrifice, but he does not restrict Christ's sacrifice to the crucifixion. He most often combines the birth of Jesus with his suffering on the cross. According to III Pur 2-3, Jesus offered himself to the Father as the most precious morning sacrifice when, as an infant, he was presented in the Temple. His self-offering on the cross, the evening sacrifice, has only completed the first offering in the Temple.

The above themes of redemption as liberation, satisfaction, and sacrifice receive inner coherence and intelligibility if we understand them with St. Bernard as the victory of divine love over evil. Just as the dying flies cannot eliminate the sweet ointment, the blasphemies and insults of those who killed the Son of God could not stop the flow of the sweet ointment from the side wound of Christ. On the contrary, the Jews were stones who hit a softer stone from which the sounds of love echoed forth and the ointment of love poured out in abundance (IV HM 8-9: V, 62-63). In other words, the murder of the Son of God which made the whole world turn pale and tremble and almost made everything turn back to the state of primordial chaos, this worst sin of all, became the means of redemption:

> He who made himself into sin endured this death in himself, so that he might condemn sin by sin. For in this way all sins, both original and personal, were deleted and this particular sin was eliminated by itself (*Ibid.*, 7: V, 61).

---

[149] We still have to undergo physical death but our physical dying will become for us the way to everlasting life (Ep 190,15: VIII, 29-30; 1 Adv 4-5: IV, 163-165; Mil 23-28: III, 232-236).

This could happen because the insults Christ endured called forth in him not only a patient but a generous, overabundant love in which he asked his Father to forgive his executioners. His divine word did bring about that for which it had been sent, the Father's forgiveness. Thus Christ was not merely not conquered by evil, but he in fact conquered the evil with good (*Ibid.*, 8-9: V, 61-63). Salvation is then in the blood of Christ not by way of some magic force but because the outpouring of his blood is the expression of a love the greater than which no one can have. It obtains forgiveness from the Father and transforms the hearts of his executioners.

It is here that Abelard and Bernard part company. A superficial reading of their respective texts makes the reader wonder why, in spite of the same emphasis, Bernard is so vehemently opposed to Abelard. After all, both emphasize the life, suffering and death of Jesus as the manifestation of divine love for us and as an example to imitate. However, Abelard is ambiguous on the saving effect of Christ's cross: he does not clearly affirm that Christ's death saved us from the power of the devil and, to my knowledge, never mentions the satisfactory value of Christ's death for us. In his own individualistic frame of mind Abelard cannot understand how the death of the innocent Son of God may obtain forgiveness for us sinners from the Father. For Bernard, however, who sees Christ in a mysterious unity with all humankind (as the head of his Body, the human race), such satisfaction for others is intelligible and belongs to the very heart of the Christian faith. If Christ's death had not satisfied for our sins, if it had not obtained forgiveness from the Father and liberated us from the power of the devil, we could not participate in the love of God, and, consequently, we could not imitate Christ.[150] From this perspective those texts of Bernard which speak about God's efforts to call forth a response of love in us receive a new depth: they should not be interpreted

---

[150] For Bernard the redemption of Christ works a true ontological transformation in us prior to any response of love. Therefore an infant is saved by the "sacrament of redemption" even though he is still unable to express his love. Infant baptism thus becomes the "litmus test" which brings to the fore the real disagreement between Bernard and Abelard (cf. Ep 190, 24: VIII, 37).

simply according to the paradigm of a human call for love, a call that remains outside the person who is called. Since Christ died for us, God works in the heart of the sinners an inner transformation, a new birth. He re-creates us by sending his Spirit into our hearts so that we may return God's love in and through his Spirit (cf. Ep 107:6: VII, 273 & XC 9, 3: IV, 437).[151]

Bernard does indeed agree with Abelard that Jesus came to show us an example of humility and love. But without the sacrament of redemption (the work of satisfaction to the Father, liberation from the power of the devil and the inner transformation of the sinner by the Holy Spirit) the former would be of no value for us. If we are not forgiven and liberated from the power of the devil and death, if we do not receive a share in the humility and love of Christ, how can we imitate them?

> So he taught justice but did not communicate it to us; he showed us love but did not pour it into us; and then he just returned to his own? (Ep 190:17: VIII, 31)

Thus, according to St. Bernard the humility, the virtues and especially the love of Christ can only be imitated if they are first participated; and they can be participated only as a result of Christ's death on the cross, which obtained the forgiveness of our sins. The following passage summarizes clearly both the affinity and the difference between Bernard's position and that of Abelard:

> I perceive three important aspects in the work of our salvation: the form of humility by which God emptied himself; the measure of love which he extended up to death, even to death on the cross; and the sacrament of redemption in which he took away death by enduring it. The first two without the last may be compared to trying to paint upon nothing. Great and necessary is indeed the example of humility, great and most

---

[151] We must admit that — contrary to Bernard's accusation — Abelard does speak about our love for God as the work of the Holy Spirit in us. However, I have not found any Abelardian text which would explain that the outpouring of the Holy Spirit into our hearts is the result of the saving death of Christ.

worthy to accept the example of his love. However, if there is
no redemption, the first two remain without foundation and
therefore, they cannot stand. I want to follow the humble Jesus
with all my efforts; I want to embrace the one who loved me
and gave himself over to me with the arms of a reciprocating
love. But I need to eat the Passover lamb. For unless I eat his
flesh and drink his blood, I will not have life in myself. (*Ibid.*,
25:38).

Eating his flesh and drinking his blood means for Bernard not only
Eucharistic communion but also our manifold participation in the
true Passover Lamb on whose sacrifice our participation in the life
and love of Christ depends.[152]

V. The Ascension of Christ and Man's Ascension

The death of Jesus is, then, the focal point of the mystery of
our redemption. Our gradual conformation to Christ — which be-

---

[152] The limits of this section prevent me from a detailed discussion of Abelard's views on
redemption. I believe that Bernard rightly perceived and rejected a rationalistic tendency
in Abelard's soteriology (the reduction of the mystery of redemption to a mere example
of divine love for us) without noticing or acknowledging that Abelard himself did not
follow up consistently on his own reductionism and that in some texts he maintained the
traditional views. See on this A.V. Murray, *Abelard and St. Bernard. A Study in Twelfth
Century 'Modernism'* (Manchester: Manchester Univ. Press, 1967), 117-130. In the same
book, however, Murray misrepresents Bernard's position by reducing it to a misleading
statement: "In short, Bernard looks on the work of Christ as a transaction (between God,
Christ and the devil) and Abelard does not" (p. 117). Murray does not perceive the most
important insight in Bernard's understanding of redemption: The death of the Son effects our redemption not as a juridical transaction, not even because of the infinite dignity of the person of the Redeemer (as in Anselm's theory) but because the Son's dying
expressed his almighty love for the Father. For a somewhat different evaluation of the
positions of Bernard and Abelard on redemption see F. Gastaldelli's comments in *Lettere
1-210, Opere di San Bernardo*, Vol. VI/1 translated by E. Paratore, commentary by F.
Gastaldelli (Milan, 1986), pp. 808-812, with further bibliography on p. 812. Gastaldelli,
however, seriously misrepresents western soteriology by stating that it was exclusively
preoccupied at this time with redemption as a juridical transaction with the devil (cf. pp.
808-809). What about redemption as "admirabile commercium," as sacrifice, what about
the saving efficacy of all the mysteries of the earthly life of Christ? All these soteriological
themes have been the common patrimony of western patristic thought and remained alive
up to the high middle ages.

gins by becoming like the child Jesus and continues through our ascension with Jesus — is seen by Bernard as a real participation in his mysteries, and this participation was made possible by Christ's redemptive death.

As we have seen above, through the incarnation, earthly life, and especially through the passion of Christ, we reach God himself; everything in the history of the Word incarnate, the infant Jesus, the preaching, the miracles but especially the pierced side of Christ reveal and communicate God to us. Yet until we have experienced the ascension of Christ, God's humility, goodness and love as mediated to us through the life of the earthly Jesus will call forth in us only an emotional love (*amor cordis*) which, in some way, is only an *amor carnalis*, a "fleshly love." This should normally develop into an *amor rationalis*, a love ordered according to the right judgment of reason.[153] Even though the *amor carnalis et rationalis* reaches God himself through the man Jesus, it is still fleshly, because it is moved only by the memories of the Word's history in the flesh. It is through the *dulcedo*, the attraction of the flesh of the incarnate Word that the soul has her first taste of God's attractiveness. This love is so emotional that it is prone to exaggerations; it is somewhat blind and can easily fall prey to heresies or at least to an extreme asceticism, and, therefore, it needs the tempering, ordering, sobering activity of a reason enlightened by faith.[154]

However, the risen Christ as he is in himself cannot be reached by the *amor carnalis et rationalis*, just as he can no longer be perceived by our senses in the state in which he actually is. He is no longer in the form of the slave, which could have been the object of sense experience. He exists now in the glory of the resurrection and is sitting with his Father on the throne of glory. In the state of glory Jesus has not divested himself of his humanity nor even of his flesh; but this flesh is of a different kind, a heavenly flesh that is no longer susceptible to suffering and death (28 SC 10: I, 198). It is no longer a lantern that screens the blinding light of the divin-

---

[153] Div 29,1: VIA, 210-211; 20 SC 4-9: I, 116-121.
[154] 20 SC 9: I, 120-121; 50 SC 4: II, 80; Div 29:1-4: VIA 210-213.

ity, but has become completely transparent so that it reveals the divine beauty, the infinite dimensions, the length, the width, the height, and the depth of the Son's divinity.[155] Thus, when he appears to Mary of Magdala, he cannot show himself as he is now in his divine glory but rather adjusts himself to her sense experience, by presenting himself in the form of the slave so as to comfort her weak faith.[156]

In Bernard's theology the resurrection of Christ receives much less emphasis than his ascension.[157] The latter is crucial for Bernard because he attributes to it a decisive influence on the spiritual ascent of the soul to God. Bernard knows that God's way of transforming us by his grace corresponds to the sinner's psychological condition. For Elisha to receive the spirit of Elijah it was essential that he actually saw Elijah to be taken up to heaven. The psychological experience of this vision made him ready to enter a new stage in his spiritual life so that he could receive a double portion of Elijah's spirit. Thus, for the disciples it was essential to see the Lord ascending in the flesh so that all their affection — which had long been centered on the Lord's flesh — might be taken up with him into heaven and be purified of the limitations of fleshly love. They had to be deprived even from the presence of the pure flesh of Jesus in order to be ready to receive the fullness of the Spirit who changed their *amor carnalis et rationalis* into *amor spiritualis*.[158] From that point on they were able to "taste" not only the sweetness of God's love as manifested in the flesh, but also Wisdom's sweetness which

---

[155] 3 Asc 3: V, 132; 6 Asc 11: V, 156; 3 Sent 93: VIB 150.

[156] Bernard gives these words into the mouth of the risen Christ: "Adhuc quidem tuis sensibus gero morem, formam ingerendo servilem, quam de consuetudine recognoscas" (*SC* 28:9: I, 198).

[157] In the critical edition there are four sermons *De Resurrectione*, and six *De Ascensione*. However, the third and fourth sermon *De Resurrectione* do not treat the theme of the resurrection. See on this theme, J. Leclercq, "Le Mystère de l'Ascension dans les sermons de Saint Bernard," *Collectanea Cisterciensia* 15 (1953), 81-88.

[158] We say fullness of the Spirit because no one can love the flesh of Christ, more precisely, no one can love the Man-God in the flesh without some participation in the Spirit of Christ (20 SC 7: I, 119).

is the "taste" of truth, justice and goodness (20 SC 8, I, 120). All believers have to go the same route. Only if we "see" Christ ascend into heaven can our love be purified and changed into spiritual love. The ascension changes not only our love but also our faith. An incipient faith which clings to the memory of Christ's presence in the flesh, a faith weighed down by sense experience, is to be transformed into a faith which transcends the limits of the senses, embraces the infinite dimensions of Christ's divinity, and touches with its fingers the one who is transformed into divine beauty and endowed with God's majesty and glory (28 SC 9: 9-10: I, 198-199).

Nevertheless, the perfect soul who has ascended with Christ to the realm of the spirit, does not abandon the *memoria* of the mysteries of the Word made flesh. On the contrary, she discovers ever more the divine love opened up for us in the wounds of the crucified Jesus. Her prayer life is stretched out between the two poles of *memoria* and *praesentia*: she recalls the mysteries of the earthly life of Jesus in order to enkindle her desire for the presence of the glorified Lord (Dil 7-12: III, 124-129).[159]

The soul who, in an incipient way, begins to know the Christ of glory already here on earth, no longer fears to be rebuked and crushed by divine glory since she no longer tries to grab God's wisdom and glory by her own power; she has learned to share in the humility and love of the incarnate and crucified Son who himself did not cling to his divine glory and divine state of being but emptied himself for our sake (62 SC 4: II, 157-158).

The "deification" of the man Jesus does not mean a loss of his human nature or even flesh, but rather a deification of his affections (Asspt 1: V, 262). Both his body and his affections have been glorified. This means that he can suffer neither in the body nor in his soul. Yet he does not neglect those who are still struggling and suffering on earth. He loves those who suffer without himself suffering or being disturbed. This mystery of divine affec-

---

[159] Cf. D. Farkasfalvy, "La conoscenza di Dio," pp. 212-213.

tion is far above our experience; it means mercy without experiencing misery, compassion without passion (SC 26:5: I, 173). The glorified Christ can only rejoice, yet his love for us who still suffer on earth is unspeakably greater and more effective than the compassion of the apostle Paul on earth who rejoiced with those who rejoiced and wept with those who wept (Div 34:5: VI/1, 232).

A superficial reading of St. Bernard's works may suggest that the flesh of Christ has a function only for the beginners in spiritual life; for those who are truly "spiritual" the flesh of Christ is of no use; they contemplate only Christ the Truth, Justice and Wisdom. In reality, however, St. Bernard sees an important role for the glorified flesh of Christ. The angels in heaven had thirsted for the presence of Christ in the flesh and their desire has been fulfilled in the ascension. Bernard, to my knowledge, never provides a direct explanation for this desire of the angels; yet we can surmise the reason for it from what Bernard likes to present as the goal of God's love, to unite perfectly and definitively the highest with the lowest: *summa imaque consocians* (Csi 2,18: III, 426. Cf. also 2 Nat 4: IV, 254). With the ascension of Christ and Pentecost, then, a most faithful and most gratifying exchange and union between heaven and earth has been consummated: "the Spirit is on earth, the flesh is in the heavens and from now on all share all things in common for ever" (3 Pent 2: V, 172).

By contemplating the ascension of Christ and receiving the fullness of the Holy Spirit at Pentecost, we anticipate already here on earth our ascension into heaven. To the extent that we love the glorified Christ for his own sake (rather than for a reward other than love itself), we become the "spouse" of the Word, or rather we realize in ourselves the love of the one unique Spouse, the Church.[160] To the extent that we pass into God and become one spirit with God, we come into our own perfection and beauty, and the Word Bridegroom will find in us his desired and unique spouse. What the Word desires in his spouse is not her good will, knowl-

---

[160] 74 SC 10: II, 239; 83 SC 5: II, 301; 20 Epi 2: IV, 320.

edge, virtue or wisdom, but her beauty; this beauty comes from the soul's regaining her similarity with the Word. Just as the Word is the shining splendor and form of God's substance (*splendor et figura substantiae Dei*) insofar as he is Truth and Wisdom, so the beauty of the soul consists in her conscious conformity to the Word as Truth and Wisdom. "The Truth shines in her mind and the mind sees herself in the Truth."[161] This beauty may also be called the *honestum*: the serene self-possession of a purified conscience who is not aware of any guilt and attributes all her wisdom and beauty to God.[162] The beauty of the spouse that the Word desires is this shining light (and there is nothing more bright than this light) of the soul's self-awareness. She sees herself as modest, shy, and fearful while firm in her resolve not to commit anything that might spoil the glory of her conscience (85 SC 10: II, 314). Here we have arrived at the counterpoint of the first stage in spiritual life: at the beginning of conversion the sinful soul must face the truth in herself and face herself in the truth, the result of which is intense suffering, shame and confusion. At the end of the spiritual ascent, however, the threefold alienation has ceased: when facing the truth in herself, the soul is filled with the humble self-awareness of her beauty and dignity; she is at peace with herself, with her neighbor and with God.

We see here the twofold paradox of what we may call the eschatological humanism of Bernard. The spouse becomes fully beautiful in herself when she has been fully conformed to the Word. She flourishes when she does not keep anything to herself but shares all of herself with her Bridegroom (7 SC 2: I, 31-32). She remains beautiful as long as she acknowledges that all her beauty comes from God. The peace and joy of her human consciousness is the result of God's Wisdom that fills and transforms her. Moreover, the individual soul comes into her own full perfection and beauty to the extent that she realizes in herself the features of the one Spouse,

---

[161] "Veritas in mente fulget, et mens in veritate se videt" (85 SC 10: II, 314). See also 3 Asc 3- 5: V, 132-134; 6 Asc 12: V, 157; 6 Asc 14-15: V, 159.

the unique dove, who is the Church of Christ. Thus the individual soul must lose herself in a twofold way, both in Christ and in the Church in order to develop her very own beauty. Here on earth, however, this state of becoming the fully purified spouse is never completely and permanently attained. Up to the end of his life St. Bernard remains acutely aware of himself as a sinner. In his last letter he begs his friend to pray for him:

> Pray our Savior, who wills not the death of a sinner, that He will not put off my timely departure, but that He may watch over me in my passing. Support, I beg you, with your prayers a poor wretch destitute of all virtue, so that the enemy who lies in wait for me may find no place where he can grip me with his teeth and wound me. (Ep 469)[163]

To the extent that the soul conforms to Christ, the whole creation conforms to her in that the whole of creation cooperates for the good of those who love God. Thus the brothers of Christ possess not only the goods of heaven but also all the goods of the earth. The less they desire the things of the earth the more they are the masters of all the earth:

> The faithful man possesses the whole world as his own wealth; he possesses the whole world because both adversity and prosperity, in fact everything equally serves him and cooperates for his good (21 SC 7: I, 126).

---

[162] One should write a monograph on the beauty in St. Bernard's theology. The *decor* of the soul has many related meanings to the one that is explained in detail in 85 SC 10-11. It is also called by Bernard a combination of innocence and humility, or purity and humility, the purity of intention which intends the truth for the sake of loving the truth (45 SC 2-3: II, 50-51; 62 SC 13: II, 160; 74 SC 10: II, 245. Cf. also Ep 113:4-5: VII, 289-290 in which Bernard lays down a philosophical foundation for the theology and morality of beauty in human beings).

[163] The translation of Letter 469 is taken from B. James's translation, *The Letters of St. Bernard of Clairvaux*, (Chicago: 1953), p. 521. On its authenticity, see D. Farkasfalvy, "The authenticity of Saint Bernard's 'Letter from His Deathbed,'" *Analecta Cisterciensia* 36 (1980), pp. 263-268.

Our eschatological consummation is analogous to that of Christ and is caused by Christ. It includes the glorification of our bodies and the deification of our affections (Dil 28: III, 143; 3 OS 3: V, 351). Even if fully purified, the soul is not yet completely free after the death of the body to be totally united with God. The soul's need for her body still keeps her from being absorbed in God. Thus, while the first coming of the Son in the incarnation intended the redemption of our souls, the goal of his final, glorious coming is the resurrection and glorification of our bodies. Only after receiving our own resurrected and glorified bodies will we become "complete" in ourselves so that nothing that belongs to us will be lacking. Only then can all our affections be fully directed to God.[164]

Until the end of history, there remains another obstacle for the full happiness of the saints: they await the consummation of their number. The transformation of their affections into some kind of divine affection[165] only extends and intensifies their compassion for us who are still struggling here on earth. The saints in heaven cannot feel pain but they feel what we feel when we suffer by taking us into themselves. In all this they act together with their Head, the glorified Christ, whose compassion embraces all those who suffer or are in the grip of sin on earth. But at the end of history, with the final separation of the saved and damned and with the glorification of our bodies, there will be no more need for compassion.[166]

We will then also completely forget about ourselves and unite our whole selves with the will of God. In this act of becoming one with God's will the whole human being loves God and this love transcends everything human: nothing human remains in the human being so that God may be all in all. In particular, our human affection must "melt away from itself and be poured over into God's will." Our delight will not center on the fulfillment of our needs

---

[164] Dil 29-33: III, 143-147; 2 OS 4-8: V, 345-348.

[165] "...in divinum quendam totus mutatur affectum" (SC 26:5: I, 173).

[166] Dil 40: III, 153-154; 3 OS 1: V, 349-350; 5 OS 11: V, 369-370; XC 11: IV, 433; 26 SC 5: I, 173.

nor even on our own happiness, but on the fact that God's will is fulfilled in us and by us. Then we will love even ourselves for God's sake and everyone and everything else as he loves (Dil 28: III, 143).

> In fact he who adheres to God is one spirit with him and the whole person changes into a somewhat divine affection; being filled with God, he cannot feel or taste anything but God and what God feels and tastes (26 SC 5: I, 173).

It is in this act of loving with our whole selves (*ex tota se*) that we return God's gift of his whole self. It is also in this act of total self-transcendence,[167] that all glorified human beings will perfectly become that one and unique Spouse in whom the Word Bridegroom finds all his delight.

Conclusions: The Importance of St. Bernard's Christology for Our Age

I hope that this essay provided some evidence to show that Bernard's thought does contain the seeds of a new synthesis between Christology and anthropology for our age.

1. Bernard agrees with our modern sensitivity that sees the human being as a free, self-determining individual. In fact, he points out that free self-determination is the very essence of human nature, and the image of God the Son in us. But Bernard is no individualist. He shows that individuals can develop themselves only in a twofold process of self-transcendence: by becoming one spirit with Christ and by realizing in themselves the features of the unique Spouse, the Church of Christ.

2. To our contemporaries who prefer to speak about the various forms of self-estrangement rather than sin Bernard shows that self-alienation and alienation from other people is the result of alienation from God; the latter comes about when we attempt to

---

[167] "Alioquin quomodo omnia in omnibus erit Deus, si in homine de homine quidquam supererit?" (Dil 28: III, 143).

become what we cannot be: absolute self-possession, our own gods. 3. Bernard views salvation history as God's work of overcoming this threefold alienation by appealing to the most powerful faculty in us, our ability to love. This divine plan to re-orient and develop our capacity to love God, neighbor and the self, and to appreciate everything according to its true value takes into account our fallen nature and designs a strategy to appeal to our freedom. However, this appeal through the events of Jesus' life, death and resurrection does not remain as it were "outside of us." Through his Spirit, God inspires us within to freely respond to him. However, we may receive God's enabling love only because the Son of God made man has obtained forgiveness for us on the cross from his Father. Thus the way is opened for humankind to full communion with God: the Son offers all of himself (and the whole creation along with himself) to us while asking for a full gift of ourselves to him in love.

Just as the fall of the human race is seen as a threefold alienation, eschatological salvation is celebrated as the overcoming of this alienation in our full unity with God, with ourselves and with our neighbors.

4. Bernard views human misery with a modern sensitivity in that he feels and describes graphically the emotional disorder of fallen humanity. The gradual participation in salvation brings about "a healing of emotions" and at the end a deification of our emotions. This healing takes place to the extent that we participate in the various stages of the self-emptying and the glorification of the Son.

5. Bernard succeeds in laying down the foundations for a universal and Christocentric vision of all history. I don't hesitate to say that Rahner's theory of the anonymous Christian would have found both a sympathetic hearing and a necessary Christological clarification in an exchange with Bernard. According to Bernard, everyone is offered salvation including even the children of the pagans. But salvation is encountered in the life of the pagans not in the form of accepting or rejecting the fullness of one's human existence but in the form of an implicit faith in Christ the redeemer.

6. In emphasizing the incarnation as the manifestation of

God's humility, Bernard provides the theological context in which the lasting results of the modern "search for the historical Jesus" can find their theological meaning. A truly human Jesus with all the limitations of being a helpless child and a normal human being is for Bernard the most awe-inspiring manifestation of God's self-emptying humility. Bernard shows us that the "low Christology" of modern historical research makes theological sense only as the concrete description of the voluntary humbling himself of the eternal Son of God for our salvation.

7. Bernard's understanding of the appearances of the risen Christ as an adaptation of a transcendent eschatological reality to our sense experience (*"morem gerit nostris sensibus"*) points out the way to escape from the impasse of contemporary theology that vacillates between the two extremes of a fundamentalist and a Gnostic interpretation of the appearances. For Bernard Jesus has truly risen in his body but he cannot appear to us as he really is in his glorified, "divinized" state because we are still fleshly beings who can perceive and love only that which is proportionate to our sense experience. The purpose of these "accommodating appearances" is to provide an existential stimulus so that we can liberate ourselves from our clinging to this world and enable us to develop a spiritual love for the invisible, glorified Lord.

8. Process theology is attractive today because it presents creation, humankind in particular, as an active partner to God. God and humankind are mutually necessary for each other and humankind does contribute to God's evolving perfection. Bernard, on the other hand, makes it very clear that God does not need us, nor do we contribute anything to God's infinite perfection. Nevertheless, the final fruit of redemption is God's *Sponsa*: the bride, virgin and mother who, by sheer grace, is raised in some way to God's level and becomes a desirable, beautiful partner for God so that they make each other mutually happy.[168]

9. Today's feminist theology needs Bernard's perspective. The

---

[168] "Cum amat Deus, non aliud vult cum amari: quippe non ad aliud amat, nisi ut ametur, sciens ipso amore beatos, qui se amaverint" (83 SC 4: II, 301).

Word comes to us as a Bridegroom only in the sense that he is the initiator of the "love affair" and he is the source of the bride's life and love through the Holy Spirit. But the relationship between the Word Bridegroom and the soul Bride transcends any kind of sexual love. His transcendence is expressed by a complementary image to the Word Bridegroom in the Word Wisdom who is pictured as feminine.

In the light of the accusations which often label patristic theology as patriarchal and male chauvinist, it is somewhat ironic that Bernard's theology and the whole patristic and medieval tradition symbolize all of saved humankind, male and female, by a female image. Precisely to the extent that humankind comes to its own perfection as a free and highly desirable partner to God, it is called Bride, Virgin and Mother.

10. Bernard also provides a neglected perspective for liberation theology. One could hardly find anyone else who saw and criticized from the viewpoint of the Gospel ideal the "systemic" corruptions of the Church and the society of his age with more passion and theological clear-sightedness than Bernard. Nevertheless, he is convinced that the victory and dominion of the Christian over this world is possible even under the most corrupt ecclesial and political regime. It does not depend on overcoming structural sin and injustice in Church and society at large but on entering a religious community which models itself on the ideals of the primitive Church: the *vita apostolica*. Once we are conformed through humility and love to Christ in that community, all of creation conforms to us and recognizes our lordship over the world. For Bernard this means that both successes and failures, favors and persecutions, including the injustices of society, sickness and health, cooperate in serving the good of the Christian. These communities of truly free human beings, the "rulers of creation" will act as a leaven of justice and renewal for the whole Church, which has to assure that political leaders rule with justice. However, Bernard is more of a realist than to believe that in this world the Church and society will ever reach a utopian state of justice and holiness.

11. For our contemporary obsession with the well-being of

our bodies Bernard offers both the shock and comfort of what we may call an eschatological humanism: the role of the body in earthly life is to honor the soul, to help the soul to be reconciled to God and thus regain her own spiritual identity. If the body consumes itself in serving the salvation of the soul in her earthly life, then the body itself will be saved at the end. Just as the desire of the angels was fulfilled by the presence of the glorified body of Christ in heaven, so our desire for the body will be fulfilled at Christ's final coming which will effect the glorification of our bodies. The conformation of our bodies to the glorified body of Christ will be the final consummation of salvation history. While Bernard is single-mindedly dedicated to restoring (as much as is possible in this world) the freedom of the spirit over the desires of the body, he turns with almost tender affection towards the flesh, offering her the assurance that one day she will be the sole object of Christ's coming in glory and majesty:

> O, if you could only taste this sweetness and appreciate this glory! For I am going to talk about some marvelous realities which are nonetheless true and were never doubted by believers: the Lord of hosts himself, the Lord of power and the king of glory will come down in order to give a new shape to our bodies and conform them to his own body of glory. How great will that glory be, what an unspeakable joy, when the Creator of the universe, who had come beforehand humble and incognito in order to justify our souls, for your glorification, O wretched flesh, will come in a solemn and manifest way, not in weakness, but in his glory and majesty (7 Adv 5: IV, 194).

For the people of our age who are so concerned about the body's wellbeing in this life and so utterly pessimistic about its fate after death, Bernard's love for the body may serve as a reassuring perspective. His love for the body echoes the love of God who wants to unite even the lowest of his creatures with himself and thus imbue it with divine life and eternal value.

How To Use The Book
For Different Purposes

If you use *Jesus Christ* as a graduate text, the ideal framework would be two, semester-long three credit courses. Traditionally, schools divide the material into two courses, Christology in the strict sense, and Soteriology, whereas this work shows the inseparable connection between these two aspects of the mystery of Christ. Thus, my recommendation is to divide the two semesters between historical and systematic Christology (Christology in the broad sense of including both the person and the saving work of Christ). Under such optimal conditions you can fully utilize the footnotes, which conduct a condensed dialogue with other historians and contemporary systematic theologians. You can also study some of the recommended readings, treat some biblical themes, individual theologians or particular aspects of the mystery of Christ more in depth. If you must condense all the material into one semester, an intelligent selection process will be needed, unless the class is extremely bright and well prepared. You can drop most of the footnote texts, even some chapters of the historical Christology. For an undergraduate Christology course you could omit the entire historical part after Luther and Calvin.

If you were to use the book for an apologetics course, I recommend you to select chapters I, II, IV & V of Part I as well as chapter V of Part III, concentrating on the method of historiography, the death and resurrection of Jesus, the implicit Christology of the "historical Jesus" and his uniqueness in the history of religions. Of course, for theodicy and for showing the necessity and role of the Church in mediating faith, other works should also be used. In general, I found that the best apologetics is not an endless discussion with opponents (even though contemporary difficulties to Christian faith must be taken seriously) but rather a peaceful exposition of the full mystery of Christ. This should be done in such a way that the unique form of God's love manifested in Christ may become perceptible to those who are searching for pure love. The best apologetics is indeed the study of Christology in its integrity.

For personal enrichment, any part of the book can be read selectively; for spiritual reading I recommend most of the biblical part, the soteriology of the Fathers, St. Bernard, K. Barth, D. Bonhoeffer and most of the systematic part.

Following closely the structure of the work (parts & chapters), two items will be featured in the *Reader's Guide*:

1. Under the title, *Recommended Readings*, the reader will find a highly selective list of works that are essential for further orientation on the topic under discussion. The selected works present positions either close or opposed to varying degrees to my Christology. The order of recommended works will follow the topical sequence within a chapter and their perceived importance within the same topic.

2. A list of *Study Questions* for each chapter follows the *Recommended Readings* to pinpoint important issues, check understanding and help organize the reader's thoughts.

Part I

CHRISTOLOGY OF THE NEW TESTAMENT

Introduction

Recommended Readings

The following important works provide different approaches to Christology in general.

W. Kasper, *Jesus the Christ* (New York: Paulist, 1977). Although somewhat dated and poorly translated, Kasper's book remains a valuable synthesis. It integrates modern biblical scholarship and philosophy into the classic christological tradition. Its typically German perspective, however, creates difficulties for the average American reader. In order to locate the mystery of Christ in its Trinitarian context, the book should be complemented by parts of Kasper's most mature theological synthesis, *The God of Jesus Christ* (New York: Crossroad, 1984).

H.U. von Balthasar, *The Glory of the Lord: A Theological Aesthetics,* Vols. I-VII, *Theo-Drama,* Vols. I-IV (San Francisco: Ignatius Press, 1985-94; publication of *Theo-Logic,* Vols. I-III is in the process of being completed). This immense trilogy is a most impressive contemporary theological synthesis centered on Christ. It shows how the splendor of God's love manifested in Christ (theological aesthetics) is the one fully credible evidence of revelation. This love reveals its ultimate depth in the drama of salvation history played out between finite human and infinite divine freedoms. The theo-drama reaches its climax in the mystery of the cross. Finally, the implications of the truth of divine love are investigated in what is called "theo-logic." While rich in insights, this monumental work is often repetitious. Its greatest attraction for our contemporaries lies in its fundamental intuition: The unfolding mystery of Christ is God's response to the human yearning for pure, infinite love implicit in any genuine interpersonal relationship (cf. "Meeting God in Today's World," *Concilium,* Vol. 6).

Balthasar's interpretation of Jesus' descent to hell as a temporary suffering of hell (based not on patristic tradition but on Barthian theology and the mystic visions of Adrienne von Speyr), a descent that makes after-death conversions possible, seems to me the most questionable aspect of his Christology.

K. Rahner, *The Foundations of Christian Faith* (New York: Crossroad, 1978). While more comprehensive than a Christology, this provides a synthesis of Rahner's christological vision with references to his articles for a more detailed treatment of particular themes. I have profited much from his insights, especially regarding the openness of human nature toward God and the relationship between created and uncreated freedom.

However, we need to investigate further Rahner's understanding of the relationship between transcendental and historical Christology. Does he not try to deduce too much from the *a priori* conditions of God's absolute gift of self for the concrete shape of the Jesus event?

Moreover, it should also be researched to what extent Rahner's understanding of Trinitarian personhood as "mode of subsistence" (*Subsistenzweise*) jeopardizes the understanding of the personal, dialogical character of God's Trinitarian life. Does Rahner not end up with a divine-human partnership exemplified in Jesus Christ and participated in to varying degrees by other human beings, instead of seeing the goal of redemption as humankind's assumption into the eternal life of Trinitarian communion? Has Rahner's silence over God as personal communion of Three Divine Persons not led to the development of "Catholic" process theologies, a development that Rahner himself had rightly opposed?

G. O'Collins, *Christology: A Biblical, Historical, and Systematic Study of Jesus* (New York: Oxford University Press, 1995). O'Collins intends to remain faithful to the Catholic tradition while showing sensitivity to contemporary concerns. In general, he is balanced and helpful, but his treatment of biblical, patristic, and systematic soteriology remains incomplete.

J. Macquarrie, *Jesus Christ in Modern Thought* (Philadelphia: Trinity Press International, 1990). This treats not only modern Christologies, but provides an intelligent historical survey beginning with Christ in the New Testament. Its lucid summaries of modern Christologies, both Protestant and Catholic, are especially valuable. Yet, Macquarrie's own Christology, in spite of the author's intention, does not do justice to the essential claims of Christian faith. For instance, how can a Christian theologian provide two alternative endings to the story of Jesus: "the happy ending" that affirms resurrection and ascension, and the "austere ending" in which Jesus has not been raised from the dead?

R. Haight, *Jesus Symbol of God* (Maryknoll, NY: Orbis Books, 1999). Hailed as "a mind-clearing, landmark book" by some, it intends to provide a comprehensive Christology for the contemporary reader. It will be a challenging project to uncover the presuppositions or rather biases that govern Haight's hermeneutics of Scripture and to point out his misinterpretation of the hypostatic union. If Haight's understanding of what "classical Christology" calls hypostatic union is right, then we must indeed reject the hypostatic union with Haight in order to affirm Christ's concrete human existence. Haight seriously wants to position his Christology within the boundaries of Catholic faith, but he ends up with a Spirit Christology that is closer to that of Paul of Samosata or of the Ebionites than to that of Christian faith. Accordingly, his soteriology is also impoverished and unable to respond to the existential quest of the contemporary reader.

Study Questions

1. What is the one major presupposition for the shape and content of the book *Jesus Christ*?
2. What are the implications of this one major presupposition?
3. What is the role of the New Testament witness to Christ in relation to the Old Testament?
4. What is the role of the New Testament regarding future christological developments?
5. What is the role of the Magisterium regarding future christological developments?

6. On what grounds do we affirm that we can find valuable christological insights in the work of non-Catholic Christian theologians?
7. On what grounds do we affirm that we can find new perspectives for understanding the mystery of Christ in non-Christian religions?

Chapter I — The Method of Biblical Christology

Recommended Readings

Some of the most responsible works which are, to varying degrees, successful in reconstructing a "Jesus of History" are as follows:

B.F. Meyer, "Jesus Christ," *Anchor Bible Dictionary*, Vol. 3 (New York: Doubleday, 1992), pp. 773-796. It seems to me the best short summary of what a historian *as* historian can say about Jesus.

X. Léon-Dufour, *The Gospels and the Jesus of History* (New York: Desclée, 1967). Although somewhat dated, this is still a more plausible reconstruction than many more recent attempts.

J.H. Charlesworth, *Jesus within Judaism. New Light from Exciting Archaeological Discoveries* (New York: Doubleday, 1988). This locates Jesus within contemporary Judaism and provides a detailed bibliography on the "historical Jesus" research.

J.P. Meier, *A Marginal Jew: Rethinking the Historical Jesus*, Vols. I, II, & III (New York: Doubleday, 1991, 1994, 2001). These three volumes contain a treasury of vast knowledge and an impressive command of primary and secondary literature. Yet, in spite of the immense erudition, the conclusions at times come close to platitudes; the work does not sufficiently grasp what is unique in the Jesus phenomenon.

L.T. Johnson, *The Real Jesus. The Misguided Quest for the Historical Jesus and the Truth of the Traditional Gospels* (San Francisco: HarperSF, 1996). This is a brilliant critique of the latest phase in "the historical Jesus" research, but unduly restrictive about the scope of historical research in general.

Study Questions

1. What is the basic presupposition of the Liberal Quest for the historical Jesus?
2. What causes put an end to the Liberal Quest?
3. When and how did the New Quest begin? Why?
4. Explain the inadequacies of the New Quest.
5. What characterizes "The Third Quest" which emerged in the early 1990s? To what extent is it justifiable to say that the quest for the historical Jesus moves in cycles?
6. What can we learn for a biblical Christology from the study of Jesus by recent Jewish authors?
7. Define the basic presuppositions of the method of the biblical part of this book. In particular:

    a) Show how "facts" are the product of objective data and interpretation.

    b) Why must a historian, *pace* L.T. Johnson, go beyond facts?

    c) In order to understand the history of a person or persons, what else is needed beyond the knowledge of data and a rational analysis of the data? Why are the latter not sufficient?

    d) Why should a historian resist the rationalistic attempt at subsuming every new act and person under general categories?

    e) Why can every human person be understood only from the perspective of his death?

    f) Why and how does the question of meaning arise in the study of history?

    g) Why does the question of the meaning of history call for a philosophy or theology of history?

    h) In the light of what has been said above, how do the method of historiography and the question of meaning in history call for a theological history of Jesus?

    i) What can such a theological history of Jesus accomplish? What are its limitations?

8. What is assured by the inspiration of the biblical documents concerning Jesus?
9. What is not assured by inspiration?
   (For the answers to these last two questions see also the "Dogmatic Constitution on Revelation" *Dei Verbum,* 11 of the Second Vatican Council.
10. How is the historical uncertainty about some events and sayings of Jesus consistent with the reality of the incarnation?
11. How can you prove the general historicity of the New Testament records about Jesus?
12. Explain each criterion for an authentic Jesus tradition. Give examples for each.
13. What is the value of the construct, "historical Jesus," for apologetics? Besides this chapter consult also the sections "Credibility of the Resurrection" and "The Implicit Christology of Jesus," pp. 68-71; 136-147, for a full answer.

Chapter II — The Death and Resurrection of Jesus

Recommended Readings

S. Davis, D. Kendall, G. O'Collins, eds., *The Resurrection* (New York: Oxford University Press, 1997). The result of a well-coordinated symposium, this work treats the resurrection from a variety of perspectives. It is most informative of the current state of the question.

D. Kendall, G. O'Collins, "The Uniqueness of the Easter Appearances," *CBQ* 54 (1992), pp. 287-307. This thorough study concludes that the appearances of the risen Christ as reported in the New Testament are restricted with regard to time and persons. They belong to the foundational stage of the Church and therefore they were given only to a chosen group of witnesses. Their nature is different from later ecstatic experiences, verbal communications of Christ, and manifestations of the Holy Spirit that have continued in the history of the Church.

G. O'Collins, *Interpreting the Resurrection* (New York: Paulist, 1988). A balanced study, informative of contemporary opinions.

R. Brown, *The Virginal Conception and Bodily Resurrection of Jesus* (New York: Paulist, 1973). Even today, the part on the resurrection remains one of the best studies on the subject.

Study Questions

1. What are the advantages of starting biblical Christology with an analysis of the proclamation of Jesus' saving death and resurrection by his disciples?
2. How can you prove the historicity of Jesus' death on the cross?
3. Give an overview of the logical steps of the book's argument that concludes that it is reasonable to believe in the bodily resurrection of Jesus.
4. Give a detailed exegesis of 1 Cor 15:3-8. In particular, why is this text so important for our purpose? How old is the tradition embodied in 3b-5? Does Paul view the appearance of Jesus to himself as a historical event? If so, what special kind?
5. Interpret the appearance narratives of both the Gospels and Acts, as well as the empty tomb narratives.
6. What facts connected with the origin of resurrection faith can be established by the historian? In particular, how do you prove the historicity of the empty tomb?
7. Explain the theories that deny any form of resurrection.
8. Explain the various interpretations of the resurrection of Christ.
9. Interpret the epistemological status of the appearances of Jesus:
   a) What extreme interpretations should be excluded?
   b) What does it mean that the appearances were revelatory signs of the risen Christ?
   c) In order to recognize an appearance of the risen Christ, what else did the disciples need beside sense perception? Why was sense perception not sufficient to recognize the identity of the risen Lord?
   d) Were the appearances historical events? Explain.
   e) How are the appearances related to the sacraments?

f) How does the fact of the empty tomb contribute to our understanding of the reality of the risen Christ?

10. How can history, philosophy, and theology contribute to the credibility of the resurrection of Jesus?

Chapter III— The Beginning of the Gospel

Recommended Readings

W. Bauckham, "The Brothers and Sisters of Jesus: An Epiphanian Response to J.P. Meier," *CBQ* 56 (1994), pp. 686-700. See comments on pp. 78-79.

R. Brown, *The Birth of the Messiah: A Commentary on the Infancy Narratives in Matthew and Luke,* Revised ed. *Anchor Bible Reference Library* (Garden City: Doubleday, 1993). A wealth of information, but in theological depth and refinement the book is no match to R. Laurentin, *Structure et théologie de Luc I-II* (Paris: Gabalda, 1957); — *Jésus au Temple. Mystère de Pâques et foi de Marie en Luc 2,48-50* (Paris: Gabalda, 1966). Unfortunately, neither of these books has been translated into English.

Study Questions

1. Explain the analogy between the mystery of Jesus' virginal conception and the mystery of his resurrection.

2. How can you show that the tradition of the virginal conception of Jesus does not derive from Hellenistic religions?

3. How is the mystery of the virginal conception prepared in the Old Testament?

4. What is the theological meaning of Jesus' virginal conception? What is common to both Matthew and Luke? What is special to Matthew and what is special to Luke?

5. What can be shown historically about the fact of the virginal conception?

6. How is faith related to what is historically demonstrable? (Show the analogy between the fact of the empty tomb and the early pregnancy of Mary.)

7. What can and cannot be proved from the New Testament concerning the "brothers and sisters of Jesus"?

8. What arguments does Bauckham present in favor of the Epiphanian view regarding "the brothers and sisters of Jesus"?

9. How did Church tradition develop regarding the perpetual virginity of Mary?

10. How is the perpetual virginity of Mary connected with the mystery of her universal motherhood?

11. How is the mystery of Mary's perpetual virginity related to the mystery of the Church?

12. How does the mystery of the Holy Family shed light on the mystery of religious communities, ecclesial communities, and Christian marriage?

13. According to the New Testament, Jesus is the "Son of David." What historical evidence do we have for the Davidic descendance of Jesus? What is the theological meaning of this title?

14. Compare the story of the twelve-year-old Jesus in the Temple with the call of Samuel (1 S 2:19-26). What are the similarities and differences?

15. Comment on the theological meaning of Jesus' "private life" before his public ministry.

Chapter IV — Jesus and the Kingdom

From among an immense body of literature I selected two outstanding treatments of the theme "Kingdom of God":

B.F. Meyer, *The Aims of Jesus* (London: SCM Press, 1979), pp. 111-253.

W. Kasper, *Jesus the Christ*, pp. 72-88.

R. Latourelle, *The Miracles of Jesus and the Theology of Miracles* (New York: Paulist, 1988). This work is informative and helpful regarding the historicity of Jesus' miracles and their meaning.

I. de la Potterie, "The Multiplication of the Loaves in the Life of Jesus," *Communio* 16 (1989), pp. 499-516. This small article is a masterpiece that shows how to use and transcend the historical critical method in interpreting the fact and the meaning of the multiplication of the loaves.

Study Questions

1. How can you "prove" the historicity of the baptism of Jesus by John?
2. Explain the message of John.
3. How is Jesus' message opposed to that of John? How does John relate the good news of Jesus to the preaching of divine judgment?
4. Explain the meaning of Jesus' baptism by John as a prophetic sign action. How is this sign-action better understood in the light of the resurrection?
5. Explain the meaning of the words of the Father to Jesus at his baptism.
6. Show that the temptation accounts go back, in some form, to a genuine experience of Jesus.
7. How could Jesus be *really* tempted?
8. How does Jesus re-live the temptations of Israel according to Matthew?
9. How are the temptations of Jesus universal human temptations according to Luke?
10. How are the temptations of Jesus temptations for the Church in every age?
11. Give a probable outline of the public ministry of Jesus.
12. What is the meaning of the verb *euaggelizesthai*, "proclaim the good news," in the light of its Old Testament usage?
13. What does Jesus mean by the Kingdom of God? How is his understanding of the Kingdom different from that of his contemporaries?
14. Explain the meaning of the central image of the Kingdom.
15. Explain the meaning of *metanoia* in Jesus' preaching. How is it connected with the theme of the Kingdom?
16. Why do the poor, the lame, and the blind have a special advantage regarding the Kingdom?

17. What do the miracles of Jesus say about the Kingdom? What further light do they receive from the resurrection of Jesus?

18. What evidence do we have for the historicity of Jesus' miracles in general?

19. How is the multiplication of the loaves a turning point in the ministry of Jesus? Explain the evidence for its historicity and the meaning of this sign.

Chapter V — The Kingdom and the Death of Jesus

Recommended Readings

B.F. Meyer, "The Expiation Motif in the Eucharistic Words: A Key to the History of Jesus?" *One Loaf, One Cup. Ecumenical Studies of 1 Cor 11 and Other Eucharistic Texts* (Macon: Mercer, 1993), pp. 11-33. Perhaps the author wants to prove too much by the historical method, yet his fundamental insight on Jesus' intentions facing death is well established.

R. Brown, *The Death of the Messiah. From Gethsemane to the Grave. A Commentary on the Passion Narratives in the Four Gospels*, Vols. I-II, *The Anchor Bible Reference Library* (New York: Doubleday, 1994). Even if it is often too anxious to cling to a consensus on issues of historicity and is somewhat pedestrian in theological interpretation, no one can ignore the immense wealth of the well-digested information that this two-volume work provides.

I. de la Potterie, *The Hour of Jesus. The Passion and Resurrection of Jesus According to John* (Staten Island, NY: Alba House, 1997). A penetrating theological analysis of the Johannine accounts.

J. Jeremias, *The Prayers of Jesus* (Philadelphia: Fortress, 1978). In spite of some minor modifications by recent scholarship, this is still a respected classic on Jesus' relationship to the Father.

Study Questions

1. How can you show that Jesus saw his death as part of God's plan of salvation?

2. How do the words of Jesus at the Last Supper (Mk 14:22-

25) and his actions at this Supper shed light on Jesus' understanding of his own death?

3. Show that Jesus' death, as an expiating sacrifice, is not opposed to his initial announcement of freely offered forgiveness.

4. What indications do we have for the authenticity of Jesus' cry
on the cross, "My God, my God, why have you forsaken me?"

5. What indicates that Jesus predicted his resurrection? Yet, if
he did, how could he truly suffer anguish?

6. Do Mk 9:1, Mt 16:28, Mk 13:30 and Mt 24:34 necessarily
imply a chronologically imminent end of the world? Explain.

7. What is Jesus' position on the "day and hour" of the end?

8. How has the Kingdom become present in our world through
the death and resurrection of Jesus? What is still to be expected? Why do we pray every day for its coming?

9. Why could the earthly Jesus have only an implicit Christology?

10. Explain in detail the implicit Christology of Jesus.

Chapter VI — The Understanding of the Mystery of Christ in the Apostolic Church

Recommended Readings

C.H. Dodd, *According to the Scriptures. The Substructure of New
Testament Theology* (Collins, Fontana Books: 1965). Even today
this is an indispensable classic.

R.E. Brown, *An Introduction to New Testament Christology* (New
York: Paulist, 1994). One may not always agree with Brown's
position; yet no one can ignore this introduction to the present
state of biblical scholarship on New Testament Christology.

M. Hengel, *The Son of God. The Origin of Christology and the History of Jewish-Hellenistic Religion* (Philadelphia: Fortress, 1976).
This remains one of the best studies on the origins of New Testament Christology.

A. Feuillet, *The Priesthood of Christ and His Ministers* (Garden City: Doubleday, 1975). The author shows convincingly that, in spite of only one explicit treatment of Jesus' priesthood in the Letter to the Hebrews, the notion of sacrifice is central to a New Testament understanding of redemption.

O. Cullmann, *The Christology of the New Testament* (Philadelphia: Westminster, 1963). Even though the work is dated and the author sets up an arbitrary opposition between functional and ontological Christology, many of his exegetical insights remain unsurpassed.

Study Questions

1. How does 1 Peter 1:10-12 interpret christologically the whole of the Old Testament?

2. Show that the Suffering Servant passages, combined with the Son of Man texts, are the key to a christological interpretation of the Old Testament.

3. Interpret the four Suffering Servant songs in Deutero-Isaiah.

4. Explain:
   a) Jesus as the Son of Man
   b) Jesus as the New, Eschatological Israel
   c) Jesus as High Priest and Perfect Sacrifice
   d) Jesus as Messiah
   e) Jesus as Son of Adam and the Last Adam
   f) Jesus as the final and complete theophany of God (especially the absolute "I AM" statements in John).

5. What is irreducibly new in the New Testament in relation to the Old?

6. Explain the early Aramaic origin and the meaning of the most ancient confession of faith: "Jesus is Lord."

7. What is the relevance of Jesus' Lordship:
   a) in relationship to the Eucharist?
   b) as it regards the Christians' social status and relationships?
   c) as it affects their relationship to the emperor?

8. Explain the meaning of the affirmation: "Jesus is the Son of God." In particular,
   a) Does Jesus call himself "Son of God"?
   b) What are the sources for the Church's proclamation, "Jesus is the Son of God"?
   c) Explain the theology of the "Son of God" in Paul, Mark, and John.
9. Why was the Church so slow in attributing the title "God" to Jesus?
10. Show the central importance of the affirmation that Jesus is God in the Gospel of John.
11. Once the divinity of Jesus is clearly expressed conceptually, how does it shed new light on the work of our redemption?

Part II
HISTORICAL CHRISTOLOGY

Introduction To Patristic Christology

Recommended Readings

Evidently, the most important readings in the history of Christology are primary sources, possibly in the original language. Given the variety of sources and the many available translations, I entrust their selection to the instructor or reader.

H. de Lubac, "The Pagan Religions and the Fathers of the Church," *The Church: Paradox and Mystery* (Staten Island, NY: Alba House, 1969). The most penetrating survey of the Fathers' understanding of the relationship between Christianity and non-Christian religions and religious philosophies.

Study Questions

1. Explain the method of patristic theology.
2. Explain the relevance of patristic Christology and Soteriology for our age.
3. Why, according to the Fathers, can the word "religion" not be univocally applied to Christianity and to other religions?
4. What considerations ground the unique dignity of Christianity according to the Fathers?
5. Explain the two-way relationship between Christianity and other religions and religious philosophies, according to the Fathers.

Chapter I — The Soteriology of the Fathers

Recommended Readings

B. Studer, *Trinity and Incarnation: The Faith of the Early Church* (Collegeville: Liturgical Press, 1993). A precise, reliable work on Trinitarian theology, Christology and Soteriology.

H.E.W. Turner, *The Patristic Doctrine of Redemption* (London, Mowbray, 1952). In spite of its age, this is still a worthwhile reading.

R.J. Daly, *Christian Sacrifice. The Judeo-Christian Background before Origen* (Washington: CUA Press, 1978).

_____, *The Origins of the Christian Doctrine of Sacrifice* (Philadelphia: Fortress, 1978). These two works are the best available studies in English on this theme.

Study Questions

1. Why is patristic soteriology treated before patristic Christology in this book?
2. Explain the dimensions of sin according to the Fathers.
3. Explain the metaphysical foundation of patristic soteriology.
4. Explain the following soteriological themes:
   a) Christ as mediator,
   b) the descent and ascent of Christ,
   c) all the dimensions (metaphysical, existential and emotional) of the *admirabile commercium* (marvelous exchange),
   d) redemption as victory and deliverance.
5. Explain the doctrine of Augustine on sacrifice; show the connection between the following themes:
   a) the whole person being a sacrifice,
   b) the Old Testament sacrifices,
   c) the Eucharist,
   d) the sacrifice of Christ.
6. How does the doctrine of the Fathers on Christ as our teacher and example differ from the rationalist Christologies of liberal Protestantism?
7. Explain the christological implication of what Gregory the Great defined in these terms: *amor ipse notitia est* ("love itself is knowledge").
8. What are the results of sin on the material universe according to the Fathers?

9. Explain the role of Christ regarding the unity of the whole of creation according to Maximus Confessor.
10. Explain how all the above soteriological themes find a unifying center in the notion of communion.

Chapter II— The Christology of the Fathers

Recommended Readings

A. Grillmeier, *Christ in Christian Tradition*, Vols. I-II (Atlanta: John Knox, 1975, 1987). This is the best available in-depth history of patristic Christology.

W. Kasper, "'One of the Trinity'...: Re-establishing a Spiritual Christology in the Perspective of Trinitarian Theology," *Theology and Church* (New York: Crossroad, 1989), pp. 94-108. This important article shows that the intent of the Council Fathers at Chalcedon was not to present the whole mystery of Christ in their christological document but to provide a clarification of an article in the Nicene-Constantinopolitan Creed. Moreover, Kasper demonstrates that, according to Chalcedon, the ultimate subject of the incarnate Word is the Second Person of the Trinity.

J. Meyendorff, *Christ in Eastern Christian Thought* (Washington: Corpus Publications, 1969). This work is indispensable for learning the Orthodox perspective on the history of Christology.

Study Questions

1. Sketch out the stages of the development of patristic Christology up to the Third Council of Constantinople. (Remember the most important dates: 325, 431, 433, 451, 553, 680-681.)
2. How does St. Ignatius of Antioch react against Gnosticism?
3. How is Docetism part of the theological climate today?
4. Explain how the Fathers criticized and changed Gnosticism into an authentic Christian theology and spirituality.
5. Explain the Adoptionism of Paul of Samosata.

6. How does an adoptionist tendency manifest itself today in some Christologies?
7. Explain Arianism as a Hellenistic distortion of Christianity.
8. How does Gregory of Nazianzus argue against Apollinarianism?
9. Explain Gregory of Nazianzus's text, which anticipates so well the Chalcedonian definition (*Letter 101, I to Cledonius*, 4).
10. How does Tertullian's dialogical understanding of "persona" pave the way for a more precise formulation of the Trinitarian and christological mysteries?
11. Explain Augustine's doctrine on the person of Christ.
12. Explain the prevailing terminology as well as the strengths and weaknesses of Alexandrian Christology.
13. Explain the prevailing terminology of Antiochene Christology. (What is one and what is two in Christ, how is the union of the human and divine expressed?)
14. What is the Antiochene School unable to satisfactorily explain regarding the metaphysical constitution of Christ?
15. What are the strengths of Antiochene Christology?
16. Define the *communicatio idiomatum*. What are its basic rules?
17. Why did the Nestorians have problems with the *communicatio idiomatum*?
18. What are the logical consequences of the Nestorian position regarding the motherhood of Mary and our redemption?
19. Summarize the doctrine of the Council of Ephesus on Christ. What questions did the Council not answer?
20. Explain the progress made in the formula of union between John of Antioch and Cyril of Alexandria in 433.
21. Explain the Monophysite heresy.
22. Why is it important that the Chalcedonian decree on Christ is not a new Creed but a commentary on one of the articles of the Creed? What happened to Christology when this simple fact was forgotten?
23. What new meaning did the word "hypostasis" receive in the Chalcedonian decree?

24. What is new in the Chalcedonian decree in comparison to previous conciliar texts on Christ?
25. Show that Monophysitism is an uncritical acceptance of some Hellenistic philosophical principles.
26. What genuine christological truth did the Monophysites distort into a Hellenistic doctrine?
27. What is new regarding the teaching on Christ in the document of the Third Council of Constantinople? How is it rooted in the New Testament? How does the Council's teaching avoid "splitting Christ" into two subjects?

Chapter III — Medieval Christology

Recommended Readings

R. Kereszty, "Relationship between Anthropology and Christology. St. Bernard, a Teacher for Our Age." See Appendix of this book. This article shows the correlation between the stages in the mystery of Christ and our spiritual development.

Study Questions

1. Explain the correlation between man's spiritual journey and the stages of Christ's history in St. Bernard's thought.
2. Explain the notion of Wisdom in St. Bernard
3. What is man's sin according to Anselm?
4. Why, according to Anselm, can God not forgive us without requiring satisfaction?
5. Why does Anselm believe that the death of the God-man, Jesus Christ, is the only appropriate satisfaction for our sins?
6. Why, according to Anselm, can we not think of a greater and more just mercy than the death of the God-man?
7. What is time-conditioned and what is of lasting value in Anselm's theory?
8. How is the scholastic ideal of theologizing different from that of the Fathers and of monastic theology?
9. Is Christology located where it should be in the *Summa* of

St. Thomas (in the Third Part, after grace and morality)? Explain your reasons.
10. Explain the basic principle of St. Thomas's Christology. Show how everything else depends on this one principle.
11. Why, according to Thomas, is the suffering of Christ greater than any human suffering?
12. Explain the five ways by which, according to Thomas, the passion of Christ has been instrumental in our salvation (by way of merit, satisfaction, sacrifice, redemption and efficient causality).
13. Explain how the whole sacred history of the incarnate Word has caused our salvation according to Thomas.
14. Evaluate critically Thomas's Christology and soteriology.

Chapter IV — Christology of the Reformation

Recommended Readings

J. Dillenberger, C. Welch, *Protestant Christianity Interpreted through Its Development* (New York: Macmillan, 1988). This is a widely used history of Protestant thought.

P. Althaus, *The Theology of Martin Luther* (Philadelphia: Fortress, 1966). This remains a classic introduction to Luther's thought.

G. Aulén, *Christus Victor* (New York: Macmillan, 1931). This is still an influential Protestant interpretation of redemption.

Study Questions

1. How does Luther misunderstand the *communicatio idiomatum*?
2. Explain the existential starting point for Luther's theology.
3. How does Luther transform the *admirabile commercium* theme of the Fathers?
4. How does Luther transform the Anselmian notion of satisfaction?
5. What is the role of the humanity of Christ in our redemption according to Luther?

6. What are important new contributions to soteriology in Luther's thought?

7. Explain the difference between the Lutheran and Calvinist views on the relationship between the divine and human natures of Christ.

8. What is the role of Christ the human being in our redemption according to Calvin?

9. How does the mediation of Christ precede his coming in the flesh according to Calvin?

10. Explain the prophetic and kingly office of Christ according to Calvin.

11. Explain the priestly activity of Christ according to Calvin.

12. Explain the work of our sanctification according to Calvin.

13. How is the Eucharist truly a communion with the flesh and blood of Christ according to Calvin?

14. Explain those principles of the Enlightenment that distort liberal Protestant Christology.

15. How does Kant reduce the major mysteries of Christology (in particular, the pre-existent eternal Son, the incarnation and satisfaction) to presuppositions of the moral obligation?

16. How does Kant influence certain trends of contemporary christological thought?

17. How is Rahner's transcendental theological method influenced by Kant?

18. Explain Hegel's thought as opposed to, and yet dependent on, the Enlightenment.

19. How does Hegel explain the "immanent Trinity"?

20. Why are creation, incarnation, death and resurrection necessary moments of a process according to Hegel?

21. Compare the principles of Gnosticism with Hegel's philosophy.

22. What, according to Hegel, is the relationship between Christian religion and his philosophy?

23. What are the logical consequences of Hegel's system for theology?

24. What values can you see in Hegel's thought, that need to be transformed and integrated into Christian theology?
25. How does Schleiermacher defend Christianity against a rationalistic critique?
26. How, and on what basis, does Schleiermacher re-interpret all Christian teaching?
27. Did Schleiermacher make any lasting contributions to Christology? Explain.

Chapter V — Protestant Christologies in the Twentieth Century

Recommended Readings

P. Ricoeur, "Preface to Bultmann," *Essays on Biblical Interpretation*, tr. P. McCormick (Philadelphia: Fortress, 1980), pp. 49-72. Although too uncritical of Bultmann, this thought-provoking essay explains well the three interrelated reasons for demythologization in Bultmann's hermeneutics.

H.U. von Balthasar, *The Theology of Karl Barth: Exposition and Interpretation*, tr. E.T. Oakes (San Francisco: Ignatius, 1992). Barth himself acknowledged this work to be an authentic interpretation of his theology.

C. Marsh, *Reclaiming Dietrich Bonhoeffer. The Promise of His Theology* (New York: Oxford Univ. Press, 1994). Marsh intends to prove that the immanent Trinity is in Bonhoeffer's theology the necessary background to the understanding of his Christology and ecclesiology. Examine the cogency of Marsh's analysis.

For information on contemporary Christologies see

J. Macquarrie, *Jesus Christ in Modern Thought*, pp. 293-335;
W.M. Thompson, *The Jesus Debate. A Survey and Synthesis* (New York: Paulist, 1985).

Study Questions

1. What caused the collapse of liberal Protestant theology in the first decades of the 20th century?
2. Who were the chief representatives of "crisis theology"? Characterize the common traits in these theologians.
3. How does Bultmann define myth? What is the function of myth for primitive man?
4. How does the mythology of the New Testament differ from other mythologies according to Bultmann?
5. What does Bultmann mean by the demythologization of the New Testament? Why is it necessary? (Explain the three reasons he gives.)
6. Why does Bultmann still cling to the historical event of Jesus Christ? What does he retain from Christianity?
7. Give a critical evaluation of Bultmann.
8. In what different directions did Bultmann's disciples move?
9. Contrast the radical crisis theology of the early Barth with his later Christocentrism.
10. How does Barth interpret soteriologically and existentially the traditional doctrine of the two natures of Christ and the hypostatic union?
11. How does Barth justify universal salvation?
12. According to Bonhoeffer how does the history of theology continue the passion story of Christ?
13. How does Bonhoeffer interpret the humanity and divinity of Christ?
14. How does Bonhoeffer interpret God's transcendence?
15. How does Bonhoeffer's Christology lead to his involvement in the anti-Nazi conspiracy and how does his imprisonment lead to a new development in his Christology (his "wordly" interpretation of Christianity)?
16. Evaluate critically Bonhoeffer's Christology.

Part III
SYSTEMATIC CHRISTOLOGY

Introduction

Recommended Readings

W. Kasper, *The God of Jesus Christ* (New York: Crossroad, 1984).
B. de Margerie, *The Christian Trinity in History* (Still River: St.
Bede's Publications, 1982). These two books, which provide an
excellent historical and systematic treatise on the Trinity, are most
helpful for situating Christology in the right theological context.
K. Rahner, *Foundations of Christian Faith* (New York: Crossroad,
1978), pp. 138-175. The study of Rahner's view can stimulate a
discussion on the universality of the offer of salvation and its concrete historical manifestation in Christ.
E. Schillebeeckx, *Jesus: An Experiment in Christology* (New York:
Crossroad, 1981). On pp. 636-674 Schillebeeckx presents his
systematic Christology. Investigate to what extent this last part
is compatible with the author's reconstruction of the historical
Jesus.
H. Küng, *On Being a Christian* (Garden City: Doubleday, 1976), pp.
119-478. Evaluate whether or not his christological method corresponds to that of Catholic theology. Why is his use of the critical historical method in conflict with the nature of Christian
faith?

Study Questions

1. Discuss the criteria for a relatively successful christological
   synthesis.
2. Show by some examples how the existential questions of contemporary men and women need to be deepened and even
   transformed in order to receive an answer from the revelation
   of Christ.
3. Show how the mystery of the love of the Triune God provides coherence and intelligibility to the whole of Christology and soteriology.

Chapter I — Sin as a Threefold Alienation

Recommended Readings

T.S. Eliot, "The Wasteland," "The Family Reunion," *The Complete Poems and Plays 1909-1950* (New York: Harcourt, 1958). These works are more powerful expressions of contemporary alienation caused by sin than any abstract theological treatise.

Study Questions

1. Explain sin as a threefold alienation. Try especially to show how in every sin we distort ourselves into a false absolute that causes conflict with other human beings. Show also that even an atheist or agnostic who commits a sin sins against God the Father.
2. What is the role of the body and the structures of society regarding sin?
3. How does the threefold alienation of sin, expressed in and through the body, carry with itself its own punishment?
4. Why, left to his own resources, can the sinner not extricate himself from his sin?
5. Why is it appropriate that we have been redeemed through God's incarnate Son?

Chapter II — The Mystery of the Incarnation

Recommended Readings

W. Kasper, *Jesus the Christ*, pp. 230-252. How does Kasper formulate the mystery of the hypostatic union? What notion of person does he use in expressing the mystery?

_____, "Christology and Anthropology," *Theology and Church* (New York: Crossroad, 1989), pp. 73-93. How does Kasper see the relationship between Christology and anthropology?

E. Schillebeeckx, *Jesus*, pp. 636-674. How does Schillebeeckx formulate the hypostatic union? In what area(s) does his understanding deviate from that of the great christological Councils?

P. Schoonenberg, *The Christ. A Study of the God-Man Relationship in the Whole of Creation and in Jesus Christ* (New York: Herder & Herder, 1971).

_____, "Spirit Christology and Logos Christology," *Bijdragen* 38 (1977), pp. 350-375. Show the development of Schoonenberg's thought in these two studies. Why does he think it is necessary to reformulate the doctrine of the incarnation? What are the ultimate consequences of his position?

K. Rahner, "Dogmatic Reflections on the Knowledge and Self-Consciousness of Christ," *Theol. Invest.*, Vol. V, pp. 193-215. Compare Rahner's theory with that of Lonergan.

R. Kereszty, "Psychological Subject and Consciousness of Christ," *Communio* 11, (1984), pp. 258-277. This is a critical re-appropriation of Lonergan's theory on Jesus' consciousness.

E. Johnson, *She Who Is. The Mystery of God in Feminist Theological Discourse* (New York: Crossroad, 1992). This provides a leading feminist theologian's perspective on God-language and the doctrine of God in Christianity. Compare it with this book's position on the feminist critique of Christology.

F. Martin, "Feminist Hermeneutics: An Overview" (Part I & II), *Communio* 18 (1991), pp. 144-163, 398-424.

_____, "Feminist Theology: A Proposal," *Communio* 20 (1993), pp. 334-376. This is a reliable survey and critique of feminist theology as well as a proposal to move beyond its present *status quo*.

L. Bouyer, *The Seat of Wisdom* (Chicago: Regnery, 1965). Ahead of his times, Bouyer successfully re-appropriated the insights of the Bible and Christian tradition on the role of woman in the economy of salvation. It remains an indispensable classic.

Study Questions

1. Explain the process by which God enters into a growing solidarity with his people as reflected in the writings of the Old Testament.

2. How does the very "logic" of solidarity call for the hypostatic union?

3. What explains the contemporary tendency to define the pre-existence of the Logos in non-personal terms?

4. Why is the doctrine of the immanent Trinity a necessary condition for God's freedom regarding the incarnation?

5. How does the Old Testament reject a direct transfer of sexuality into divine existence? What is the meaning of masculine and feminine traits or images applied to God?

6. How does the Church's tradition express the transcendent character of divine fatherhood and sonship?

7. Provide some foundation for a theological anthropology of gender. (Starting point: Why do biological differences between man and woman have psychological and even metaphysical consequences?)

8. On what grounds does this book differentiate between (analogously) attributing masculine and feminine qualities to divine nature and (analogously) attributing masculine and feminine relationships to the Divine Persons as persons?

9. Regarding the ontological aspect of the hypostatic union, explain the following:

   a) How did the revelation of God's Trinitarian life and the incarnation revolutionize the understanding of "personhood" within Christianity?

   b) Define "person" in God.

   c) Explain the incarnation of the Second Divine Person in ontological terms.

   d) Why does the *anhypostasia* of Jesus' human nature (his humanity not subsisting as a human "person" in the ontological sense) not result in a diminution of his humanity?

   e) Show that the mystery of the hypostatic union does not necessarily imply a contradiction: a) either on the part of the Son, b) or on the part of human nature.

10. How can a modern understanding of person as consciousness and freedom lead to absurd consequences in Trinitarian theology and in Christology?

11. How should one understand person on the psychological level

in order to perceive the correspondence between the ontological and psychological aspects of the mystery of the incarnation?
12. Define consciousness and its characteristics.
13. Define psychological subject and distinguish it from consciousness.
14. Distinguish between consciousness and self-knowledge.
15. Describe the relationship between psychological and metaphysical subject: a) in general and b) regarding Christ.
16. How should consciousness and psychological subject be predicated about the Trinity and Christ according to Lonergan?
17. How does the role of empathy in loving personal relationships help us understand the mystery of the incarnation?
18. How can you show that the incarnation fulfills human nature on an unexpected level?
19. Explain the incarnation as a twofold existential process: a) the Word becoming a human being and b) the human being Jesus "becoming God."

Chapter III — The Humanity of the Son

Recommended Readings

K. Rahner, "Christology Within an Evolutionary View of the World," *Theol. Invest.,* Vol. V, pp. 157-192. Rahner integrates the Teilhardian vision of the cosmic Christ into his Christology.

Study Questions

1. What is human nature and what happens when the Son assumes it as his own? How does the incarnation change the concrete nature of every human being?
2. What does it mean that the Son has assumed a human nature (rather than the nature of an angel, animal or plant)?
3. What is the theological meaning of the *one* incarnation? Why

would it not be appropriate to have an incarnation of the same divine Word in every culture or age?

4. How was Jesus fully human without original and personal sin?
5. Explain the human knowledge of Jesus (his common human knowledge, his knowledge of the Father and the Father's will, based on self-awareness and the inspiration by the Holy Spirit).
6. How do Jesus' growing common human knowledge, his direct intuition of the Father, and his inspired knowledge cooperate in carrying out his mission?
7. Why is it important for soteriology that Jesus has a fully active human will?
8. Is the impeccability of Jesus' human will compatible with human freedom? Explain your answer.

Chapter IV — Redemption as Assumption of Humankind into Trinitarian Communion

Recommended Readings

J. Moltmann, *The Trinity and the Kingdom* (San Francisco: Harper, 1981). According to Moltmann, God becomes Trinity in Salvation History.

F. Varillon, *The Humility and Suffering of God* (Staten Island, NY: Alba House, 1983). How is Varillon's view different from the one adopted by Moltmann and from that of *Jesus Christ*?

The three most important perspectives on the origin of sacrifice in the history of religions are presented in these three studies:

W. Schmidt, *Der Ursprung der Gottesidee*. Vol. 5. *Endsynthese der Religionen der Urvölker Amerikas, Asiens, Australiens, Afrikas,* Münster, 1930-35;

M. Eliade, *The Sacred and Profane* (New York: Harcourt, Brace & World, 1959), pp. 99-104;

R. Schwager, *Must There Be Scapegoats? Violence and Redemption in the Bible* (San Francisco: Harper & Row, 1987). How could you reconcile the theories on the meaning of sacrifice in the works of Schmidt, Eliade, and Schwager with the phenomenological and theological approach of *Jesus Christ?*

"Instruction on Certain Aspects of the 'Theology of Liberation,'" Congregation for the Doctrine of the Faith, *Origins* 14 (1984), pp. 193-204.

"Instruction on Christian Freedom and Liberation," Congregation for the Doctrine of the Faith, *Origins* 15 (1986), pp. 713-728.

John Paul II, "Sollicitudo Rei Socialis," *Origins* 17 (1988), pp. 641-660. These three documents together form the response of the Magisterium to the challenge of liberation theology. They point out the errors and dangers of some forms of liberation theology while stressing the need and outlining the principles for an integral theology of liberation.

J. Sobrino, *Christology at Crossroads* (New York: Orbis, 1979).

_____, *Jesus in Latin America* (New York: Orbis, 1987).

_____, *Jesus the Liberator: A Historical Theological Reading of Jesus of Nazareth* (New York: Orbis, 1993).

J.L. Segundo, *The Historical Jesus of the Synoptics* (New York: Orbis, 1985). Evaluate the above works from the eschatological perspective of Christian revelation. Do they respect the transcendent nature of God's Kingdom as God's gratuitous gift and as a share in the eternal life and joy of the Trinity?

J.P. Meier, "The Bible As a Source for Theology," *Proceedings of the Forty-Third Annual Convention of the Catholic Theological Society of America* 43 (1988), pp. 1-14. Evaluate the criticism of Meier on the use of Scripture in the liberation theologies of Sobrino and Segundo.

Y. Congar, *I Believe in the Holy Spirit,* Vols. I-III. (New York: Seabury, 1983). This is a monumental storehouse of biblical and historical theology on the Holy Spirit both in its Western and Eastern form.

Study Questions

1. What is the logical connection between the hypostatic union and our redemption?

2. Regarding our redemption, under what aspect does God act as one, and under what aspect does each Divine Person have a different role?

3. What does it mean that the Father "gives" his Son? Compare it with a human father "giving his son."

4. Explain the Father's compassion for humankind and for his Son. Why does compassion not contradict God's transcendent perfection?

5. How is the Father both the origin and the final end of our redemption?

6. How does Jesus enter into the threefold alienation of the sinner without assuming the guilt of any sin?
   a) How does he carry "the weight of our sins" more than we ourselves can?
   b) How does this entering into the threefold alienation of the sinner culminate on the cross?

7. Why is it impossible for Jesus to "suffer hell"?

8. Through the analogy of human death (we experience the death of our body as our own death), explore the meaning of our belief that God the Son himself died for us in our human nature.

9. How does the self-giving of Jesus to God on the cross reverse our alienation?

10. Describe the notion of sacrifice.

11. Why can only a human being offer a sacrifice to God?

12. Why is Jesus' sacrifice the only perfect sacrifice?

13. Give some of the reasons why redemption as satisfaction (atonement) is much questioned today.

14. Explain the meaning of "satisfaction" or "atonement" among persons. What ultimately satisfies for an offense against a person?

15. How is satisfaction (atonement) similar to sacrifice even among humans?

16. On what conditions does the gravity of an offense against a human person depend?

17. How can sin "offend" God? Is this notion of personal offense

against God compatible with God's transcendence? Explain.

18. Show that, by demanding full satisfaction (atonement), God has treated us with respect as "adults" rather than acting out of vengeance.

19. Why are we, mere human beings, when left to our own resources, unable to offer a worthy satisfaction (atonement) to God for our sins?

20. Why is the most appropriate expression of this atoning love the death of Jesus?

21. How does the atoning sacrifice of Jesus restore the order of the universe?

22. Why does Jesus' satisfaction or atonement not work as a mere "balance of payments"?

23. How does the satisfaction or atonement of Jesus involve our cooperation?

24. Explain the role of the Holy Spirit: a) within the Holy Trinity, b) in the incarnation, c) in the earthly life and passion of Jesus, and d) in the resurrection.

25. How is the sending of the Holy Spirit related to the Body (personal and ecclesial) of Christ?

26. Explain some of the basic principles of a Catholic liberation theology:
   a) The role of the Spirit in transforming hearts and society;
   b) Respect for the autonomy of economic and political realities.

27. Where did the Constantinian symbiosis of Church and society lead in the past and where might it lead in the future?

28. Explain the three complementary perspectives of biblical and patristic theology on the final goal of redemption.

29. How can one interpret the return of Christ in glory? What interpretation of "return" must be excluded?

30. Explain the eschatological state of the *totus Christus*. What is the relationship of the *totus Christus* to the Father? What (or rather who) guarantees the exclusion of a pantheistic interpretation?

31. How does our eschatological growing into the full maturity of Christ the man and into that of the perfect woman correspond to the dimensions of human nature?
32. Show that only the eschatological totality of all the saved achieves the perfection of every individual as a human being.
33. What is the theological reason for the conclusion that there will be a renewed material universe in the eschatological state?
34. What ensures that this new material universe has a continuity with the present one?
35. What could "redemption" mean for matter?
36. Explain the eschatological state of the material universe by two analogies (role of the human body and of the sacraments).

Chapter V — The Universal Significance of Christ in the Context of Non-Christian Religions

Recommended Readings

J.A. Dinoia, *The Diversity of Religions. A Christian Perspective* (Washington: CUA, 1992). This book contains the most detailed bibliography on this issue (pp. 171-194). The theories on the relationship between Christ and non-Christian religions can be roughly divided into three categories: exclusive, inclusive and pluralist Christologies. The first is the position of fundamentalist Protestants: one can be saved only by an explicit faith in Christ. The second, in different varieties, has been well represented in the Catholic tradition. In our age, Rahner formulated this position most articulately: if we accept our full humanity (ordained toward eternal life with God) we accept Christ who is our salvation. Lately, the pluralist approach became fashionable even in some Catholic circles: every world religion is an equally valid road toward God. Jesus is the unique and unsurpassable mediator of salvation for Christians. But this does not exclude an analogous role of Muhammad for Muslims and of Siddharta Gautama for Buddhists. The most vocal representative of this trend is Paul Knitter.

Dinoia tries a fourth approach: he affirms the irreducible diversity of religions. To what extent is his approach valid? Compare these four approaches to that of *Jesus Christ*.

J. Dupuis, *Toward a Christian Theology of Religious Pluralism* (New York: Orbis, 1997). Comprehensive in its historical survey but ambiguous in its systematic conclusions, this work is an indispensable tool for anyone interested in the theological relationship between Christianity and other religions. Compare its major theses with the clarifications by the Congregation for the Doctrine of Faith, clarifications which Dupuis accepted ("Notification on the Book *Toward a Christian Theology of Religious Pluralism*," Congregation for the Doctrine of the Faith, January 24, 2001, and "Commentary on the Notification" by the same Congregation, March 12, 2001) and with the theology of missions in *Redemptoris Missio* by Pope John Paul II (December 7, 1990). All Vatican documents are easily downloadable from the website: www.vatican.va.

R. Gawronski, *Word and Silence. Hans Urs von Balthasar and the Spiritual Encounter between East and West* (Grand Rapids: Eerdmans, 1996). Compare Balthasar's approach to non-Christian religions with that of Rahner.

Study Questions

1. What can the history of religions conclude about Christianity's claim that Christ is God's final and complete self-revelation?
2. What can one know about this issue only through the light of grace?
3. What unique features can historically be established about Jesus?
4. What is historically unique in the suffering and death of Christ?
5. How does the mystery of the incarnation respond to human longing for a simultaneously transcendent and immanent God? How is the Christian doctrine of the incarnation different from the way other religions respond to the same problem?

6. What does the New Testament say about the uniqueness and finality of the Christ event?
7. What does the closing of the biblical canon in the 2nd century say about the Church's belief in the finality of the Christ event?
8. What truth of divine revelation postulates that God's self-communication (which has reached its historical culmination in Christ) must have been available in some way to all human beings in all ages?
9. Explain the two conflicting roles of non-Christian religions regarding the mediation of God's revelation to all humankind?
10. What can a Christian learn about Christ from non-Christian religions?

Chapter VI — Christ and Possible Other Universes and Extraterrestrial Intelligent Beings

Recommended Readings

T.F. O'Meara, "Christian Theology and Extraterrestrial Intelligent Life," *TS* 60 (1999), pp. 3-30. A most helpful survey and evaluation of existing literature on the subject.

C.S. Lewis, *Out of the Silent Planet, Perelandra, That Hideous Strength* (New York: Macmillan, 1965). This is a religious science fiction trilogy that assumes the universal importance of the Son's incarnation on our planet for other intelligent forms of life in the universe.

Study Questions

1. If there are other universes besides ours, what would their relationship be to the Father, the Son and the Holy Spirit?
2. What are the grounds (Scripture, Tradition, reasoning) for the book's conclusions regarding the response to the above question? To what extent are these conclusions conditionally certain (conditioned on the existence of "other universes")?
3. What is the range of theological possibilities for the relation-

    ship to the Father, Son and Holy Spirit of possible intelligent extraterrestrial beings?

4. From a theological perspective, can there be intelligent extraterrestrial beings who are totally "alien" to us? Explain.

5. Comment on the role and status of angels in God's one plan of salvation.

Conclusion

Study Question

1. How does the notion of communion (God entering through his Son into full communion with us, who are in the state of threefold alienation, so that we may enter into full communion in the Spirit through the Son with the Father) provide the unifying center for such diverse images and notions as the Kingdom of God, the "marvelous exchange," the hypostatic union, and sacrifice?

Index

ST PAULS

This book was produced by ST PAULS/Alba House, the Society of St. Paul, an international religious congregation of priests and brothers dedicated to serving the Church through the communications media.

For information regarding this and associated ministries of the Pauline Family of Congregations, write to the Vocation Director, Society of St. Paul, 2187 Victory Blvd., Staten Island, New York 10314-6603. Phone (718) 982-5709; or E-mail: vocation@stpauls.us or check our internet site, www.vocationoffice.org